THE MADHUR JAFFREY COOKBOOK

Madhur Jaffrey

TIGER BOOKS INTERNATIONAL
LONDON

Contents

Madhur Jaffrey

EASTERN VEGETARIAN COOKING

*To
the Hearty Eaters—
Sanford,
Zia, Meera, and Sakina
with
all my love*

Contents

Abbreviations

Measurements in this book are given in both imperial and metric, and in order to present these in the least cumbersome way the following abbreviations are used:

tsp	teaspoon	qt	quart
tbs	tablespoon	l	litre
oz	ounce	dl	decilitre
lb	pound	in	inch
g	gramme	cm	centimetre
kg	kilogramme	F	Fahrenheit
fl oz	fluid ounce	C	Centigrade
pt	pint		

Acknowledgments

I would like to acknowledge gratefully the help given to me by the following — Devi Mangaldas, Neela Patel, Mrs Patel, Pallavi Shah, Tatie Wawo-Runtu, Audrey Chan, Anne Loke, the management and staff of the Tawaraya Inn, Yien-koo King, the American departments of tourism for Korea, Hong Kong, Japan, Thailand, Philippines, and Singapore, Sudha Doshi, Snighda Mukerji, Vijay Bhatt, Terb Xoomsai, Taw Kritakara, Mrs Kalaya, the entire Roxas family, Glenda Barretto, Doreen Fernandez, Gary Jenanyan, Sandra Cahill, Mrs Chawdhry, Usha Ismail, Maribel Lin and Ahtong, Mrs Han, Jyothi Baswan, Jhab, Ismail, Zakiya Kurrien, Alun, Juji, Maya, Asha, K, Chub and Judith.

Introduction

Over the past decade, as my vegetarian friends and I have sat around nibbling on radishes smeared with sweet butter or dining more elegantly on asparagus soufflés, we have been elated at the thought of vegetarianism finally coming of age in the West. But with this elation, many vegetarian cooks have also expressed an awareness of the limitations of their repertoire.

I have lived in America for more than twenty years now. I grew up, however, in India where a majority of the population is vegetarian and where delicious vegetarian dishes are to be found under every proverbial bush. I found myself thinking back to the sweet-and-sour stuffed aubergines I had eaten in a royal Hyderabadi household, the crisp-soft split-pea and rice pancakes that are sold in every South Indian coffee shop, and the hot, spicy chick peas offered as a Sunday treat by our Punjabi neighbour.

My thoughts jumped beyond India to other Asian countries that I have explored over the years. In Bali, I have sat barefoot on the veranda of a seaside villa and dined on the most magnificent greens that had been cooked very simply with a mound of shallots and a touch of garlic. In Korea, I have climbed the seemingly endless steps of a Buddhist temple to partake of a vegetarian feast that included mung-bean noodles, stir-fried with julienned courgettes, mushrooms, carrots, and cabbage. When our children were quite little, we all shared a Kuwaiti breakfast at which we were served, among other things, pitta breads and freshly made yogurt cheese dressed with olive oil and paprika. And what about *falafel* — the chick pea patties we consumed in Israel?

I decided then that I would go again to many of the Asian countries that I already knew to ferret out as many treasures as possible. I would taste them on their home grounds, bring them back and then try to recreate them in my New York kitchen.

As I began collecting my recipes, I was amazed to find that in Asia the most ordinary vegetables can be cooked in hundreds of different ways. I love vegetables. This probably dates back to my very early childhood and a time when my father grew just about everything from potatoes to aubergines on several acres that stretched out on one side of our house. It was a yearly ritual — poring over the seed catalogues, waiting for the seeds to arrive from Calcutta, and then waiting for the first seedlings to show themselves. Until I was twelve, I had never eaten a store-bought vegetable. I plucked the tomatoes straight off the vines and ate them with salt and pepper that I carried around with me for the purpose; I helped dig up the tiny new potatoes that we would sauté with cumin seeds; I cut the upstanding white heads of cauliflower that would later be cooked with potatoes, fennel, and fenugreek seeds; and I pulled up the beetroot that would be stewed with tomatoes.

Over the years, my passion for vegetables has stayed with me. I can get quite excited in Hong Kong when I am served a dish of crisp asparagus that is tinged with sesame oil or in Japan over a dish of cabbage seasoned with *umeboshi* plums. The recipes for all these dishes are, of course, in this book.

If vegetables flesh out vegetarian meals and provide many of the minerals and vitamins, it is judicious combinations of dried beans, grains, and dairy products that provide much of the protein.

Nutritionists today are telling us that if we combine beans (such as soy or mung) with grains (such as wheat or rice) and a dairy product (such as yogurt) at the same meal, our protein needs for that meal are pretty much taken care of. Well, that is just what the vegetarians of India and China have been doing for over a thousand years. While an Indian might eat a cumin-flavoured mung-bean dish with whole-wheat griddle breads and wash them both down with buttermilk, a Chinese might be dining on bean curd spiced up with garlic, spring onions, and red pepper, some rice, and perhaps a Hot-and-Sour Soup which has egg in it. Indians make the most scrumptious pancakes out of bean batters, many of which they eat for breakfast so they may go to work well fortified. Another nourishing breakfast dish from South India is called Uppama. It is a kind of spicy pilaf, made out of semolina and filled with diced vegetables. It starts the day on a very perky note.

Spices and seasonings will do that. Perk things up, that is. They can also transform the same food so it tastes different from day to day. Potatoes taste one way when cooked with sesame seeds, another when stewed with soy sauce, and quite different when fried with mustard and cumin seeds.

Apart from giving variety to our foods, spices and seasonings in Asia have clearly defined (but not scientifically proven) attributes that are supposed to help the body in specific functions. Ginger, asafetida, and turmeric are all considered digestives and are therefore thrown into pots of beans or split peas to fight off their hard-to-digest stubbornness. Mint does the same thing. It also kills germs. Asafetida is also considered a nerve tonic. Cumin and green cardamom are cooling, so they are put into summer drinks. Clove and cinnamon are warming, so they are put into hot winter teas. Ginger teas are offered to those with a cold, while raw garlic is swallowed by thousands suffering from circulatory ailments and jangled nerves. Red chillies, in small doses, have an antiseptic action. Black pepper livens the appetite and acts as a tonic for new mothers . . . and so on. Asian herbalists have practised their art for thousands of years and a lot of what Asians eat has a firm basis in their ancient science.

I have given a lot of attention to condiments, dips, chutneys, relishes, and pickles, most of which may either be prepared in advance, or may be put together very quickly at the last minute. One of the exciting aspects of Asian food is that at every home-cooked meal, you get what amounts to a multiple-choice meal. Let us say that you are serving that exquisite Chinese bread with spring onions, Yow Bing. For one bite, you could dip it into my Chinese Dipping Sauce. For the next bite you might have it with Bean Curd with a Deliciously Spicy Sauce and a third bite might be with Hot-and-Sour Soup and the fourth with Ginger Quick-Pickled in Soy Sauce. Each bite will taste different, with the dips and relishes adding as much to the meal as the so-called main dishes. A dish of cauliflower may be sweetened, soured, or spiced, according to what relish we eat it with. Every meal becomes more of an adventure this way and every dish gets imbued with the possibilities of many added tastes.

How should meals be put together from this book? Should you try to stick to dishes from one country at a time or is it all right to 'mix and match'? Part of the fun of being a Western cook is that you may, indeed, put together anything that strikes your fancy. A Korean soup served with a Japanese bean-curd dish and a Chinese stir-fried vegetable sounds wonderful to me. The Indian casserole of aromatic *basmati* rice, nutty *chana dal* (a split pea), and fresh dill would, I think, be quite happy sitting beside a Greek salad that has lettuce, feta cheese, and tomatoes in it. A Persian *kookoo* (egg pie) could easily be eaten with an Indian rice dish and an American carrot salad.

Most foods from Lebanon, Armenia, Israel, and Syria are so lightly seasoned with herbs quite recognizable in the West that there should be no trouble at all in incorporating them into Western meals. Foods from the Philippines, especially their dried beans and vegetables, are so close to Spanish food that you could easily pick up, say, Green Beans with Onion, Garlic, and Tomato, and serve it with scrambled eggs and French bread.

Use your judgment and put together what *you* think goes together. At the end of the book, I have a whole lot of menus, some traditional ones, others pleasant international mixes that also happen to make nutritional sense. Use them as a guide if you feel the need.

No special utensils are absolutely necessary for Asian cooking. It helps to have a wok but, for most recipes, a heavy frying pan could be substituted. The grinding of spices, very important in Asia, is done on different types of grinding stones. These stones are heavy and unwieldy, particularly if you are not used to them. I find that an electric coffee grinder (or other spice grinder) works beautifully for dry ingredients, from sesame seeds to mustard seeds. For wet ingredients, a food processor or blender is essential. A great many Asian foods are steamed. Here again, you may buy cheap aluminium or bamboo steamers and set them up in a wok or on top of a large pot. Or else you can balance colanders on top of pots and improvise. Nonstick frying pans seem to be *made* for Persian egg *kookoos* and for Indian pancakes. I find that they are useful utensils to have around and take the worry out of cooking tricky dishes.

Whether you are a confirmed vegetarian or a partial one, I think you will find much here to tempt you. As well as exciting new dishes to serve at mealtimes, there are new ideas for snacks, treats for your children's lunchbox (or your own), cooling drinks, and cocktail nibbles. I hope this book will open up another world for you and that you will have as much fun with the recipes as I did.

1 Vegetables

Once, when I had just finished a lecture in Springfield, Illinois, I was approached by a lady whose daughter had become a vegetarian. 'What *do* vegetarians eat?' this lady asked me with a big, sad sigh; 'lots of boiled vegetables, I suppose.' Then she began listing 'frozen broccoli, frozen beans . . .' feeling sorrier and sorrier for her daughter as she went along.

This chapter is part of my answer to that worried mother. Nobody needs to be sorry for anyone eating *these* vegetables. Some of the vegetables here are stir-fried and seasoned with ginger and Chinese *shaohsing* wine (dry sherry makes a good substitute), others are smothered with a spicy yogurt sauce, and still others are dipped in a gram-flour batter and deep fried. All the vegetable dishes are different—and there are more than a hundred of them. The chapter starts with Stir-fried Asparagus, Flavoured with Sesame Oil, a dish from Hong Kong, and moves slowly (and alphabetically) towards Wakatake (Wakame Seaweed and Bamboo Shoots) and Water Chestnuts. After that follow recipes for mixed vegetables and batter-fried vegetables.

You will find some of the commonest vegetables here, cooked in uncommon ways: green beans, for example, are cooked with garlic and red pepper; cabbage is cooked with tomatoes in mustard oil; peas are cooked with fresh ginger; and potatoes are cooked with garlic and sesame seeds. There are a great many recipes for aubergine. From Japan, I have a recipe in which aubergine slices are smeared with fermented bean paste—*miso*—and then grilled. From a royal Indian household, I have sneaked out a recipe for tiny aubergines stuffed with a hot, sweet, and sour paste that includes sesame seeds and tamarind. And from Turkey I have a recipe for fried aubergine slices served with a garlic-flavoured yogurt sauce.

I have many recipes for potatoes as well. I love potatoes. If properly cooked, they can be so very good. From Nepal, I have a cold potato salad with a sesame seed, lemon, oil, and green chilli dressing. Then from western India I have a stew that combines potatoes, tomatoes, and fresh coconut. I can taste it even as I am writing about it. It is wonderful. In Bali, I was served one of the tastiest hot, sweet, and sour dishes of matchstick potatoes. You will find that in this chapter as well.

There are some recipes here where the main vegetable might be unfamiliar to you. For example, there are a few dishes using lotus roots, bitter gourd, kohlrabi, long beans, and a kind of cabbage

I

that is called *choy sum* in Cantonese. Unless you live in a large metropolitan area or in a town with Oriental grocery stores, you may not have access to these vegetables. On the other hand, you may be able to grow them at home. Lotus root tastes a bit like artichoke heart, only it is crunchier in its texture. Bitter gourd is a type of marrow. It *is* bitter. Asians like its taste and also believe that it helps cleanse the blood. Kohlrabi tastes like broccoli stems, and is excellent both raw and cooked. Long beans (sometimes called asparagus beans) are about a foot long. They taste like ordinary green beans, only their flavour is a bit more intense. *Choy sum* tastes like a cross between tender spring greens and cabbage. Once you discover this vegetable, you will not want to give it up.

There is a recipe for spring greens as well. It comes from Kashmir, India's most northern state. The greens are cooked very simply in mustard oil with a touch of asafetida. Even the liquid left at the bottom of the pot is irresistible. Kashmiris usually mop it up with their rice.

The use of different oils can make such a difference to a dish. In China and Korea, a dash of sesame oil is often dribbled over stir-fried vegetables. This enriches them, just as a dollop of butter might, and gives them a nutty flavour as well. In some parts of India, vegetables are cooked in mustard oil. This fiery, pungent oil turns sweet and docile when it is heated. It envelops vegetables in a gentle warmth.

Each Asian country has its own way of adding seasonings to vegetables. In China, one of the techniques used is to keep a mixture of soy sauce, wine, sugar, cornflour, and stock handy, and to pour it over the vegetables once they have been stir-fried. Then they are seasoned and a sauce is created, all in one step. In Indonesia, shallots, garlic, red peppers, and salt are first pounded into a paste. This paste is fried before vegetables are added. In India, hot oil is 'seasoned' first with whole spices, such as cumin seeds, fennel seeds, and mustard seeds. The oil, now perfumed with the smell of fried spices, proceeds to perfume any vegetables that are sautéed in it. Hundreds of such techniques are used throughout the length and breadth of Asia. You will find quite a few of them in this chapter.

It goes without saying that you should always use vegetables that are fresh, crisp, and in their prime. If the tomatoes you buy have no colour, leave them unrefrigerated until they turn red. I rarely use frozen vegetables. Peas and okra might well be the exceptions. But then, I do live in an area where good vegetables are constantly available. Buy whatever seems freshest in your grocery stores. Beetroot, carrots, broccoli, and beans can all be cooked in such interesting ways. Whenever you begin to wonder what new

thing you could do with some ordinary vegetable—such as cabbage—consult this chapter as well as the index to this book.

For information about ingredients and basic techniques that may be unfamiliar, see General
Information, pages 481-506.

STIR-FRIED ASPARAGUS
FLAVOURED WITH SESAME OIL
HONG KONG   *(serves 4–6)*

2½ lb/1125 g fresh green asparagus   *½ tsp salt*
3 tbs vegetable oil   *1½ tbs sesame oil*

Trim away the woody bottom section of the asparagus and wash it.
Peel the lower 2–3 in/5–8 cm of each spear with a potato peeler. Cut
each spear into 1-in/2½-cm lengths. Put the spears into a bowl of
cold water for half an hour. (This is not essential but it crisps up the
asparagus nicely.) Drain.

 Heat the vegetable oil in a 10–12-in/25–30-cm frying pan over a
medium-high flame. When hot, put in the drained asparagus. Stir
and fry for about 30 to 40 seconds. The asparagus should be coated
with oil. Add the salt and stir. Add 2 fl oz/½ dl water and bring to a
fast simmer. Cover, turn heat to medium-low, and cook gently for
2 to 4 minutes or until asparagus is cooked through but still crisp
and bright green. (This will vary according to the thickness of the
asparagus.) Remove lid. Turn heat to high and quickly boil away
any extra water, if there is any, stirring asparagus gently all the
time. Add the sesame oil. Mix gently and turn off heat. Serve at
once.

AUBERGINE SLICES WITH
WHITE MISO
JAPAN   *(serves 2–4)*

There is a slightly sweet, delicate white *miso* that is used in Kyoto
for this elegant and tasty aubergine recipe. If you cannot find it in a
Japanese shop, substitute the more readily available pale yellow
miso. Taste the *miso* for sweetness; add a teaspoon of honey to it if
you like.

¾–1 lb/340–450 g aubergine   *About 4 tbs sweet white or pale*
5–6 tbs vegetable oil   *yellow miso*
                                       ¼ tsp white poppy seeds

Wash the aubergine and wipe it dry. Trim away the stalk and sepal
area. Cut aubergine into about 8 ½-in/1½-cm-thick round slices.
Heat 5 tbs of oil in a large frying pan over a medium flame. When
hot, put in as many slices as the frying pan will hold easily in one
layer. Brown lightly, cooking slices 3 to 4 minutes on each side.

For information about ingredients and basic techniques that may be unfamiliar, see General
Information, pages 481-506.

When all the aubergine slices have been browned (you may need to add more oil to the frying pan), lay them out in a single layer on a grill pan.

Preheat grill.

Just as you would put jam on toast, smear the upper surface of each aubergine slice with about 1½ tsp of the white *miso*. Use the flat side of a wet knife to smooth out the *miso*. Use the cutting edge of a wet knife to make a pretty ½-in/1½-cm-wide diamond or grid pattern on the surface of the *miso*. Dust lightly with poppy seeds and place under the grill for about 2 minutes or until the *miso* gets some brown spots on it. Serve immediately.

SWEET-AND-SOUR AUBERGINE

INDIA   (*serves 6*)

Though normally served hot, this aubergine dish may also be served cold at a buffet or picnic.

2 lb/900 g aubergine	*2 tsp ground* amchoor *or lemon*
2 tsp salt	*juice*
1 medium-sized onion	*2½ tsp sugar*
Vegetable oil for shallow frying	*⅛–¼ tsp cayenne pepper*
1 tbs panchphoran	*1 tbs roasted and lightly crushed*
	sesame seeds

Cut off the stem ends of the aubergines and quarter them lengthwise. Cut the quarters crosswise into ½-in/1½-cm-thick slices and put in a sieve set over a bowl. Sprinkle with the salt and mix well. Set aside for 30 to 45 minutes. Pat dry.

Peel the onion, slice it in half lengthwise, then cut into ¼-in/¾-cm-slices.

Heat ⅓ in/1 cm oil in a 9-in/23-cm-wide frying pan over a medium-high flame. When hot, put in as many slices of the aubergine as the pan will hold in a single layer. Fry for about 3 minutes on each side or until aubergine slices turn a medium reddish-brown colour. Remove with a slotted spatula and set aside. Do all the aubergine this way.

Pour off all but 3 tbs of the oil in the frying pan and turn heat to medium. Put in the *panchphoran*. Within a second or two, the spices will begin to sizzle and pop. As soon as that happens, put in the sliced onion. Stir and fry until the onion just starts to turn brown at the edges. Now put in the fried aubergine, *amchoor*, sugar, cayenne, and sesame seeds. Stir gently and cook for 1 minute.

AUBERGINE 'FANS' IN BATTER
PHILIPPINES   *(serves 4)*

You can make this dish only with small aubergines that are about 4 in/10 cm in length. The aubergine skins are first charred – either over a flame or under the grill – and then they are peeled off. The flesh, now smelling slightly 'smoked' and still attached to stems and sepals, is fanned out and flattened, then dipped in beaten egg and fried. Filipinos eat the aubergines hot and crisp with a vinegar-based dipping sauce (see page 415).

4 small aubergines, with stems
   and sepals attached
Vegetable oil for shallow frying
1 large egg
¼ tsp salt

Prick the aubergines very lightly with a fork – about two jabs to a side – and place two each directly over the low flames of two gas burners. As one side gets charred, turn each aubergine a bit, using the stem end to do this. Char the entire surface of the aubergines this way, not forgetting their tips. If you have an electric cooker, preheat the grill. Arrange aubergines on a baking tray and place under the grill. As each side gets charred, turn the aubergines a bit. Char all the skins this way.

Peel the aubergines. Rinse them off quickly to rid them of little pieces of charred skin and then pat them dry. Flatten out the aubergine flesh, fanning it out as you do so; it must still stay attached to the stem and green sepals.

Heat ¼ in/¾ cm oil in an 8-in/20-cm frying pan over a medium-low flame to about 350–375° F/180–190° C.

Meanwhile, beat the egg in a shallow bowl, add about ⅛ tsp salt, and beat again to mix. Sprinkle about ⅛ tsp salt on both sides of each aubergine.

Dip the aubergines, one at a time, into the beaten egg and then place them gently in the frying pan. Fry 4 to 5 minutes on each side or until the aubergines are reddish-brown and crisp on the outside. Remove the aubergines from the frying pan with a slotted spatula and leave to drain briefly on kitchen paper.

For information about ingredients and basic techniques that may be unfamiliar, see General Information, pages 481–506.

CUBED AUBERGINE COOKED WITH ONIONS

INDIA   *(serves 6)*

Fennel and fenugreek seeds go particularly well with aubergine, as you will see in this simple North Indian recipe. It is usually served hot, but it is also fine at room temperature or cold.

*3 lb/1350 g aubergine (about 2
    largish aubergines)*
2 tsp salt
5 tbs vegetable oil
1 tsp whole fennel seeds
½ tsp whole fenugreek seeds
*2 medium-sized onions, peeled and
    very coarsely chopped*
1 tsp ground coriander
1 tsp ground cumin
*1 tsp ground amchoor or lemon
    juice*

¹⁄₁₆–⅛ tsp cayenne pepper

Peel aubergines and cut into 1-in/2½-cm cubes. Put cubes in a bowl. Sprinkle with salt. Rub well and set aside for 1 hour. Squeeze out as much liquid as possible from the aubergine cubes and pat them dry with kitchen paper. Set aside.

Heat oil in a large 12–14-in/30–35-cm heavy frying pan over a medium flame. When hot, put in the fennel and fenugreek seeds. As soon as they turn a few shades darker (this takes just a few seconds), put in the onions and aubergine cubes. Stir and fry the aubergines and onions for 20 minutes, lowering the heat a bit if necessary (the aubergine should not burn). Add the coriander, cumin, *amchoor*, and cayenne. Stir and fry another minute. Now add 8 fl oz/¼ l water, cover, lower heat, and simmer gently about 15 minutes or until aubergine is completely cooked. Stir a few times as the aubergine simmers. Check salt and *amchoor* (you may wish to add a bit more) and serve.

CREAMED AUBERGINE
INDIA   *(serves 6)*

2¾–3 lb/1230–1350 g aubergine (3   1½ tbs tomato purée mixed
   medium-sized aubergines)   thoroughly with 4½ tbs water
5 tbs vegetable oil   2 tsp finely grated fresh ginger
½ tsp whole fennel seeds   1 tsp salt
¼ tsp whole fenugreek seeds   ⅛ tsp cayenne pepper, or more
2 medium-sized onions, peeled and ½ tsp freshly ground black pepper
   chopped   ½ tsp ground roasted cumin seeds
8 cloves garlic, peeled and finely   3 tbs single cream
   chopped   2 tbs very finely chopped fresh
                                 green coriander (or parsley)

Preheat grill.

Prick the aubergines with a fork (about 2 to 3 jabs to a side) and lay them on a baking tray lined with aluminium foil. Put the tray under the grill. When the skin gets charred on one side, give the aubergines a quarter turn. Roast this side and turn a little bit again. Continue to do this until the entire aubergine skin is charred and the pulp of the vegetable is soft and mushy.

Peel away the charred skin under cold running water and chop up the softened aubergines. Heat the oil in an 8-in/20-cm frying pan over a medium flame. When hot, put in the fennel seeds and the fenugreek seeds. Five seconds later, put in the onions and garlic. Fry, stirring for 5 to 7 minutes, or until the onions are a golden brown. Now add the tomato purée mixture, a tablespoon at a time, and keep frying another 2 to 3 minutes. Put in the chopped aubergine, ginger, and salt. Turn heat to medium-low and sauté the aubergine for 10 to 15 minutes. Add cayenne, black pepper, cumin, cream, and fresh coriander. Cook for another minute to heat the cream.

Neela's
AUBERGINE AND POTATO
INDIA   *(serves 2–4)*

4 tbs vegetable oil   1 tsp ground cumin seeds
½ tsp whole black mustard seeds   ¼ tsp ground turmeric
5 oz/140 g peeled, diced potatoes   ⅛–¼ tsp cayenne pepper
   (½-in/1½-cm cubes)   ½ tsp salt
4 oz/115 g diced aubergine   1 tbs fresh green coriander
   (½-in/1½-cm cubes)   (optional)
1½ tsp ground coriander seeds

For information about ingredients and basic techniques that may be unfamiliar, see General Information, pages 481-506.

Heat the oil in an 8–10-in/20–25-cm frying pan over a medium-high flame. When hot, put in the mustard seeds. As soon as the mustard seeds begin to pop (this just takes a few seconds), put in the potatoes and aubergine. Stir once. Now put in the coriander, cumin, turmeric, cayenne, and salt. Stir and fry for a minute. Add 3 tbs water, cover immediately with a tight-fitting lid, turn heat to low and simmer gently 10 to 15 minutes or until potatoes are tender. Stir every now and then. If the vegetables seem to catch at the bottom of the frying pan, add another tbs of water.

You may garnish this dish with a tbs of finely chopped fresh green coriander.

AUBERGINE WITH TOMATOES
IRAN   *(serves 6)*

You could serve this dish with Rice with Fresh Herbs and Baby Broad Beans (see page 165) and a yogurt relish.

2 lb/900 g aubergine　　　　　　　*3 medium-sized tomatoes, peeled*
2½ tsp salt　　　　　　　　　　　　*and chopped*
Vegetable oil for shallow frying　　*½ oz/15 g chopped parsley*
6 spring onions　　　　　　　　　　*⅛ tsp freshly ground black pepper*

Cut off the stem ends of the aubergines and quarter them lengthwise. Cut the quarters crosswise into ½-in/1½-cm-thick slices and put them in a sieve set over a bowl. Sprinkle with 2 tsp of the salt and mix well. Set aside for 30–45 minutes. Pat dry.

Heat ⅓ in/1 cm oil in a 9-in/23-cm-wide frying pan over a medium-high flame. When hot, put in as many slices of aubergine as the pan will hold in a single layer. Fry for about 3 minutes on each side or until aubergine slices turn a medium reddish-brown colour. Remove with a slotted spoon and place in a colander to drain. Prepare all the aubergine this way.

Cut the spring onions into ⅓-in/1-cm rounds, using all of the green sections.

Pour off all the oil in the frying pan. Put the fried aubergine, the tomatoes, spring onions, parsley, pepper, and some of the remaining salt into the pan. (Put in only ¼ tsp salt first; add the rest if you need it.) Cover and bring to a simmer. Lower heat and simmer gently for 10 minutes.

Maya's
AUBERGINE COOKED WITH CRUSHED MUSTARD SEEDS AND YOGURT
INDIA   (serves 4)

This quick-cooking dish from eastern India uses three ingredients that are very typical of Bengali cooking – mustard oil, *panchphoran*, and crushed black mustard seeds.

1–1½ lb/450–675 g aubergine	*1½ tsp salt*
1½ tbs whole black mustard seeds	*8 fl oz/¼ l yogurt*
⅛ tsp cayenne pepper	*⅛ tsp freshly ground black pepper*
7 tbs mustard oil or vegetable oil	*⅛ tsp freshly ground cardamom*
1 tbs panchphoran	*seeds*

Discard the stem end of the aubergine and dice aubergine into 1-in/2½-cm cubes.

Grind the mustard seeds lightly in a coffee grinder (see page 497) and then empty into a bowl. Add the cayenne and 8 fl oz/¼ l water. Mix and set aside. Heat the oil in a 12-in/30-cm frying or sauté pan over a medium-high flame. When hot, put in the *panchphoran*. Stir the spices once. Immediately put in the mustard-seed mixture, the cubed aubergine, and 1 tsp salt. Keep stirring and cooking over a medium-high flame until most of the liquid is absorbed. Add another 8 fl oz/¼ l of water, cover, and turn heat to low. Simmer gently for about 15 minutes or until aubergine pieces are quite tender. Remove cover and turn up heat to boil off about half the liquid.

Just before serving, beat the yogurt and ½ tsp salt with a fork until it becomes a smooth paste and pour the yogurt over the aubergine. Heat through but do not bring to the boil. Sprinkle black pepper and ground cardamom over the aubergine, stir, and serve at once.

For information about ingredients and basic techniques that may be unfamiliar, see General Information, pages 481-506.

Sheila's
KHATTE BAIGAN
(Sour Aubergines)
INDIA   *(serves 4–5)*

Probably because Kashmir is tucked away in the upper reaches of India's northernmost Himalayan mountains, its inhabitants tend to use more dried, powdered ginger than any of the southern states. The other spices in the recipe are asafetida, powdered fennel seed, cumin, cayenne, and, for souring, tamarind. These seasonings, when mixed together, make up the very special 'Kashmiri taste' that I happen to love so much.

I use small aubergines for this dish. If you cannot get them, use larger aubergines, cut in half lengthwise and then cut crosswise into ¼-in/¾-cm-thick slices.

1 lb/450 g small aubergines	¼ tsp ground turmeric
Vegetable oil for shallow frying	⅛–¼ tsp cayenne pepper
2 tsp whole fennel seeds	A generous pinch of ground
¾ tsp dry, powdered ginger	asafetida
1 tsp ground cumin seeds	1 tbs tamarind paste (use lemon
¼ tsp whole black cumin seeds, or	juice as a substitute)
ordinary cumin seeds	½ tsp salt, or to taste

Cut off the sepals from the aubergines but keep the stems. Cut aubergines lengthwise into ¼-in/¾-cm-thick slices.

Heat ¼ in/¾ cm oil in a 9-in/23-cm frying pan over a medium-high flame. When hot, put in as many slices as the pan will hold in a single layer and fry them until they are a reddish-brown colour on both sides. On the pieces that have it, the skin side should be cooked very briefly as it tends to get tough. Remove the aubergine slices with a slotted spoon and keep on a plate lined with kitchen paper. Do all the aubergine slices this way. Turn off the heat. Remove most of the oil (save it for another dish). You will only need 3 tbs in the frying pan.

Put the fennel seeds in a coffee grinder reserved for spices and grind until you have a powder. Put this powder, as well as the ginger, ground cumin, whole black cumin, turmeric, and cayenne in a small cup.

Heat the 3 tbs of oil in the frying pan over a medium flame. When hot, put in the asafetida. A second later, add all the spices in the cup plus 2 tbs of water. Stir for 20 seconds and then put in another 2 fl oz/½ dl of water. Stir for another 10 seconds. Lower heat and add the tamarind, salt (you will probably need a bit more than ½ tsp), and another 8 fl oz/¼ l water. Mix. Put in the slices of aubergine and bring to a simmer. Spoon the sauce over the aubergine slices, cover, lower heat, and simmer gently for 5 minutes.

SPICY AUBERGINE WITH ONION
CHINA   (serves 4)

Here is one of those Chinese dishes that can be reheated and hence may be made ahead of time. Plain rice should be served to accompany it.

1 lb/450 g aubergine	8 fl oz/¼ l vegetable oil
1½–2 tsp chilli paste with soy bean and garlic	2 cloves garlic, peeled and finely chopped
5 tsp Chinese thin soy sauce	1 large onion, peeled and cut into
2 tsp sugar	¾-in/2-cm cubes

Cut the aubergine into 1½-in/4-cm cubes.

Mix the chilli paste, soy sauce, sugar, and 4 fl oz/1 dl water in a cup.

Heat 4 fl oz/1 dl of the oil in a wok over a medium flame. When hot, put in the aubergine. Stir and fry for about 4 to 5 minutes. The aubergine will absorb all the oil. Add the remaining 4 fl oz/1 dl of oil by pouring it around the edges of the wok and letting it slither down towards the vegetable. Stir and fry for another 5 minutes or until the aubergine has browned lightly and is tender enough to eat. Remove aubergine with a slotted spoon and place in a sieve set over a bowl.

Remove all but 2 fl oz/½ dl oil from the wok. Add the garlic. Stir and fry for 15 seconds. Put in the onion. Stir and fry until the pieces turn soft, about 3 to 4 minutes. Turn the heat down a bit if onion starts to brown. Separate the onion layers as you cook. Put the aubergine into the wok. Stir the mixture in the cup and pour it over the aubergine. Cook on medium heat, stirring as you do so, until all the liquid is absorbed. Remove aubergine with a slotted spoon, leaving all the oil behind in the wok.

For information about ingredients and basic techniques that may be unfamiliar, see General Information, pages 481-506.

Alun's
PATLICAN
(Fried Aubergine with a Yogurt Sauce)
TURKEY   *(serves 2–4)*

This is a delicate, melt-in-the-mouth dish that tastes best if eaten as soon as the aubergine is fried. Although it is not traditional, I have removed the aubergine skin at the suggestion of my husband because it tends to get quite tough when fried. I often serve 2 or 3 slices per person as an appetizer, each slice dotted with a dollop of the yogurt.

¾ lb/340 g aubergine	*Yogurt prepared as in the recipe*
1 tsp salt	*for Yogurt with Garlic in a*
1 tbs lemon juice	*Turkish style (see page 253)*
Olive oil for shallow frying	

Peel the aubergine and cut it into ½-in/1½-cm-thick slices. Lay the slices out flat on a board. Sprinkle with ½ tsp salt and 1½ tsp lemon juice. Rub this in. Turn the slices over and repeat with another ½ tsp salt and the remaining lemon juice. Put the salted slices in a bowl and leave for 30 minutes. Drain and pat dry.

Heat ¼ in/¾ cm olive oil in an 8–10-in/20–25-cm frying pan over a medium flame. When hot, put in as many slices as the pan will hold in a single layer. Fry about 2 to 3 minutes on each side or until aubergine turns a rich reddish-brown. Remove with a slotted spoon and arrange on a serving plate. Do all the slices this way. Serve the yogurt as a sauce.

PINAKBET
(Mixed Vegetable Stew with Aubergine and Long Beans)
PHILIPPINES   *(serves 6)*

This popular Filipino stew, eaten in the president's palace as well as in the poorest of homes, consists of aubergine, long beans (also called asparagus beans, the kind that are about a foot long and are found in Indian and Chinese grocery stores), okra, fresh broad beans, and bitter gourd, all stewed quickly with onions, garlic, and tomatoes. In the Philippines, a salty fish paste provides the final flavouring, but I have left that out and substituted a little soy sauce instead. The Filipinos use the slim, 6-in/15-cm-long, pinkish-purple aubergines that are found in many Oriental grocery stores. On the West Coast of America, I have heard them referred to as

'Japanese' aubergines. If you cannot find them, use slim, white aubergines, or small Italian aubergines. If none of the above can be found, use the familiar-sized oval aubergine cut into 1-in/2½-cm-thick and 2½-in/6½-cm-long 'fingers'. They may disintegrate a bit but the taste of the dish will not be greatly changed. You may easily substitute ordinary green beans for the long beans and frozen large broad beans for the fresh kind. If you cannot find bitter gourd, leave it out, though that would really be a pity. That slight bitterness gives *pinakbet* its special kick.

About ½ of a 6-oz/180-g bitter gourd
¾ lb/340 g slim aubergines
1¼–1½ tsp salt
8–10 whole okra
16 long beans or 5 oz/140 g green beans
2 fl oz/½ dl vegetable oil
4 five-pence-piece sized slices of fresh ginger

2 cloves garlic, peeled and cut into slivers
1 medium-sized onion, peeled and chopped
1¼ lb/560 g ripe tomatoes, chopped
4 tsp Japanese soy sauce
¾ lb/340 g fresh or frozen broad beans*

*If the broad beans are frozen, leave at room temperature until you can separate them.

Cut the half bitter gourd in half lengthwise, and remove all the seeds. Cut the halves into strips that are about 2 in/5 cm long and ½ in/1½ cm wide. Sprinkle the strips with ¼ tsp salt and then stand them up in a bowl for 20 to 30 minutes. Rinse the strips.

Trim away the stem end of the aubergines and cut them into 2–3-in/5–8-cm lengths. You should now have tube-like pieces. The Filipinos cut gashes at both ends of the tubes this way: hold the tube so it is standing on one end. Make a lengthwise cut down the centre but stop when you reach about halfway. Stand the tube on its other end. Give the tube a quarter turn and make another lengthwise cut down the centre again stopping about halfway. Your gashes should resemble a cross, with one side of the cross at one end of the tube and the other at the other end. The two gashes should never meet.

Trim away the okra caps and points. Cut gashes on it just as you did for the aubergine.

Trim away the ends of the long beans and cut them into 3-in/8-cm lengths.

Heat the oil in a 4-qt/4½-l pot over a medium-high flame. When hot, put in the ginger, garlic, and onion. Stir and fry for about 2 minutes. Add the tomatoes. Stir and cook for 4 to 5 minutes or until

For information about ingredients and basic techniques that may be unfamiliar, see General Information, pages 481–506.

tomatoes have softened. Turn the heat down a bit, if necessary. Add 16 fl oz/½ l water, the soy sauce, 1 tsp salt, the bitter gourd, aubergine, okra, long beans, and broad beans. Stir. Cook for 15 to 20 minutes on medium to medium-low heat. You should keep the pot at a vigorous simmer. Stir the vegetables gently throughout the cooking period (the Filipinos prefer to shake the pot and toss the vegetables every now and then). The liquid should reduce and become thick and all the vegetables should be tender. Check the salt. Add more if you need it. Remove the pieces of ginger.

Tatie Wawo-Runtu's
SAJUR LODEH
(Aubergine and Long Beans Stewed in Coconut Milk)
INDONESIA *(serves 6)*

Some of the best food in all of Bali is to be found at the Wawo-Runtus' home and at their charming Tanjung Sari restaurant, both located on fashionable Sanur Beach. This particular dish is traditionally cooked with tiny pieces of meat and is seasoned with pounded dried shrimp. One of the Wawo-Runtu daughters is a vegetarian and the version of *sajur lodeh* that I was served is one that the family has adapted for her.

The aubergines that Tatie used were ovals of a pale green colour, a variety that I have never seen in the United States or Britain. Use Italian aubergines or the slim, pinkish-purple aubergines sold in Chinese and Indian grocery stores.

¾ lb/340 g aubergines (see note above)
¾ lb/340 g long beans or fresh green beans
2 fresh hot red chillies
1 fresh hot green chilli
2 fl oz/½ dl vegetable oil
1 clove garlic, peeled and slivered
4 oz/115 g shallots, peeled and finely sliced

A piece of fresh galanga root, about 2 in/5 cm in diameter, lightly crushed, or ½ tsp dried, ground galanga root
6–7 dried daun salaam leaves
1¼ pt/¾ l fresh (or tinned, unsweetened) coconut milk
1½ tsp salt
1 tsp sugar

Trim away the stem end of the aubergines and cut them into 1-in/ 2½-cm, cube-like chunks. Trim away the ends of the long beans and cut them into 2-in/5-cm lengths.

Cut the chillies into strips, or just leave them whole if they are small.

Heat the vegetable oil in a 4-qt/4½-l pot over a medium-high flame. When hot, put in the red chillies, green chilli, garlic, shallots, and galanga. Stir and fry for about 3 minutes or until the mixture is lightly browned. Add the *daun salaam* and stir once or twice. Now put in the coconut milk and turn the heat down to medium. Slowly bring the milk to the boil, stirring all the time so that it does not curdle. Now add the aubergine, long beans, salt, and sugar. Continue to cook over a medium to medium-low heat, stirring gently so as not to break up the vegetables. The liquid should keep bubbling and the coconut milk should reduce a bit. Cook 8 to 12 minutes or until vegetables are just tender.

BAGHARA BAIGAN
(Aubergine Cooked in the Hyderabadi Style)
INDIA *(serves 6)*

When there were still maharajas and princes in India, Hyderabad, in the south, was the seat of successive, semi-independent Nizams, reputed to be among the richest men in the world. The Nizams, and the ruling aristocracy of Arab, Persian, and Central Asian ancestry, were Muslims but the people over whom they ruled were Hindus. The cuisine of the affluent reflected these divergent influences. The use of coconut, tamarind, jaggery, and mustard seeds was typical of the vegetarian Hindus. These seasonings are incorporated into this superb, festive dish in which small and tender aubergines are partially quartered, stuffed with a hot, sour, sweet, and salty mixture and then cooked slowly. A final *baghar*, or addition of hot oil flavoured with spices, finishes off the dish – and also gives it its name.

I use small, 3–4-in/8–10-cm, purple aubergines. On those occasions when I have been able to get small, white aubergines, I have preferred to use them, as their skin tends to be softer and they cook in barely 15 minutes. If you have a garden and are planning for a future season, keep these white aubergines in mind. (Whenever I have been able to buy them it has been from Chinese grocery stores.) If you want to serve this dish cold, use oil instead of *ghee* for the final garnish.

For information about ingredients and basic techniques that may be unfamiliar, see General Information, pages 481-506.

2 lb/900 g small, 3–4-in/8–10-cm-long aubergines (if unavailable, use the slightly larger 5–6-in/13–15-cm-long, slim aubergines)
2 tsp plus 1 tsp salt
2 tbs sesame seeds
2 tbs desiccated, unsweetened coconut
1 dried hot red pepper
1½ tbs ground coriander seeds
2 tsp whole cumin seeds
8 tbs vegetable oil

2 medium-sized onions, peeled and finely chopped
5 cloves garlic, peeled and finely chopped
¼ tsp ground turmeric
2–3 tbs tamarind paste
1 tbs shredded jaggery (gur) or soft brown sugar
2 tbs ghee or vegetable oil
1½ tbs black mustard seeds
½ fresh hot green chilli, seeded and cut into 1-in/2½-cm slivers

Wash the aubergines and wipe them. Do not remove any of the green portion (i.e., the stems and sepals). Quarter the aubergines lengthwise in such a way that the sections remain attached for at least ½ in/1½ cm at the stem end. Rub 2 tsp salt into all the cut sections and leave the aubergines, stems up, standing in a bowl for 45 minutes to an hour.

Meanwhile, heat a small cast-iron frying pan over a medium flame. Put in the sesame seeds, coconut, dried red pepper, coriander, and whole cumin seeds. Dry-roast, stirring constantly for 2 to 3 minutes, or until seasonings have turned a few shades darker and give out a delicious roasted aroma. Remove from heat and empty spices into a small bowl. When the spices have cooled a bit, put them into a coffee grinder reserved for spices. Grind and set aside.

Squeeze out as much moisture as possible from the aubergines and wipe them.

Heat the 8 tbs oil in a frying or sauté pan large enough to hold the aubergines in a single layer. Put in the finely chopped onions and garlic. Fry over a medium flame until reddish-brown at the edges. Take the frying pan off the heat and add the turmeric, the ground spices from the coffee grinder, the tamarind paste (put in 2 tbs first and add more later if you think you need it), the jaggery, and 1 tsp salt. Return to the fire, keeping the heat very low. Mix all the ingredients in the pan and cook, stirring, for 1 minute. Add just enough water to the spice mixture to make a thick but not dry paste (about 4 fl oz/1 dl). Keep stirring and cooking until jaggery has melted completely. This mixture will be the stuffing for the aubergines. Taste it for balance of sweet, sour, hot, and salty flavours. Make adjustments, if necessary. Turn off the heat.

Empty the stuffing into a small bowl. Spread a portion of the stuffing in between the cut sections of each aubergine and then lay the aubergines in a single layer in the same pan used earlier for cooking the stuffing. Leftover stuffing may be sprinkled on top.

Add 6 fl oz/1¾ dl water to the frying pan and bring to a simmer. Cover with a tight-fitting lid, turn heat to low, and cook gently for 40 to 60 minutes or until aubergines are quite tender. (Very young aubergines may cook faster.) Using tongs to pick up the aubergines by their stem ends, turn them over at least 4 to 5 times during this cooking period. Stir the sauce by sliding a spatula under the aubergines and spooning some of the sauce over them. If they seem to be catching at the bottom, add 1 tbs of hot water. Replace the lid every time you have stirred or turned the aubergines.

When the aubergines are tender, heat the *ghee* in a small frying pan or a very small pot over a medium flame. When hot, put in the mustard seeds and the green chilli. When the mustard seeds begin to pop — this just takes a few seconds — pour the *ghee* and spices over the cooked aubergines.

To serve, lay the aubergines out in a single layer, all stems pointing in the same direction, on a warmed platter. Spoon some of the thick sauce over them but leave behind all the fat.

Yien-koo's
GREEN BEANS WITH GARLIC AND RED PEPPER
CHINA   *(serves 6)*

Even though this recipe requires a lot of oil, most of it can be re-used later.

1½ lb/675 g fresh green beans
16 fl oz/½ l vegetable oil
10–12 cloves garlic, peeled and
  finely chopped

1 dried hot red pepper, coarsely
  crumbled
1 tbs Chinese thin soy sauce
¼ tsp salt
¼ tsp sugar

Trim the beans and cut them into 1½-in/4-cm lengths. Rub them with a tea towel to dry them out.

Heat the oil in a wok over a medium-high flame. When smoking hot, put in all the beans and turn the heat to high. Fry the beans, stirring now and then, for 1 to 2 minutes or until the skins just begin to crinkle but the beans are still crisp and bright green. Take out all the beans with a slotted spoon and put them in a colander that is resting in a large bowl. Turn off the heat under the wok.

For information about ingredients and basic techniques that may be unfamiliar, see General Information, pages 481-506.

Remove all but 4 tbs oil from the wok. Alternatively, you could use a fresh 10–12-in/25–30-cm frying pan and spoon 4 tbs of oil into it. Heat on a medium flame. When hot, put in the garlic and the red pepper. Stir and fry until the garlic turns a light to medium brown colour. Put in the beans and stir once. Now put in the soy sauce, salt, and sugar. Stir again to mix. Serve immediately.

GREEN BEANS WITH SESAME PASTE AND GARLIC
INDIA   (serves 6–8)

2½ lb/1125 g fresh green beans
1 tbs plus ½–¾ tsp salt
6 tbs vegetable oil
2 tsp black mustard seeds
8–9 medium-sized cloves of garlic,
   peeled and very finely chopped

A 1-in/2½-cm cube of fresh
   ginger, peeled and finely grated
3 tbs ground roasted sesame seeds
4 tbs well chopped fresh green
   coriander
⅛ tsp freshly ground black pepper
1/16 tsp cayenne pepper
1 tbs lemon juice

Trim the beans and cut them into 1-in/2½-cm pieces. Put about 3 qt/3½ l of water in a 5-qt/5½-l pot. Add 1 tbs salt and bring to a rolling boil. Put the beans in and boil over high heat 4 to 5 minutes or until they are tender but still crisp. Empty the beans into a colander and run cold water over them to fix the bright green colour. Drain.

Shortly before you sit down to eat, heat the oil in a 10–12-in/25–30-cm frying pan over a medium flame. When the oil is very hot, put in the mustard seeds. As soon as the mustard seeds begin to pop (this will take just a few seconds), add the garlic and stir. As soon as the garlic browns lightly, add the ginger and stir once. Now put in the drained beans, the ground roasted sesame seeds, fresh coriander, black pepper, cayenne pepper, lemon juice, and ½–¾ tsp salt. Turn heat to low and mix well. Taste for seasonings. When the beans are heated through, turn off the heat and serve.

Sandra's
GREEN BEANS WITH ONION, GARLIC, AND TOMATO
PHILIPPINES   (serves 6)

The Philippines have been influenced by the Chinese, the Portuguese, and the Spanish, to say nothing of the Americans. This simple but delicious recipe from that country hints at Mediterranean roots.

1½ lb/675 g fresh green beans
2 medium-sized onions, peeled
2 medium-sized cloves of garlic,
 peeled

1 lb/450 g red-ripe tomatoes (or
 7–8 tinned Italian plum
 tomatoes)
4 tbs vegetable oil
1½–2 tsp salt
Freshly ground black pepper

Trim the beans and cut them into 1-in/2½-cm pieces. Cut the onions in half, lengthwise, and then cut them crosswise into fine slices. Chop the garlic very fine. Drop the tomatoes into boiling water for 15 seconds. Remove with a slotted spoon, rinse in cold water, and peel. Chop tomatoes into ½-in/1½-cm dice. (If you are using tinned tomatoes, drain and chop them.)

Heat the oil in an 8–9-in/20–23-cm-wide pot over a medium-low flame. When hot, put in the chopped garlic and stir-fry for about 30 seconds. Add the onions. Stir-fry for another 2 to 3 minutes or until onions begin to turn translucent. (Do not let the onions take on any colour.) Now put in the tomatoes, beans, salt (start with 1½ tsp), some freshly ground black pepper, and 4 fl oz/1 dl water. Bring to the boil. Cover, lower heat and simmer gently 15 to 20 minutes or until beans are cooked. Remove lid. Turn up heat and reduce liquid in the pot by about three-quarters. Stir the beans gently a few times as you do so. Taste for salt.

GREEN BEANS WITH SOY SAUCE
JAPAN   *(serves 6)*

1½ lb/675 g fresh green beans
2 tbs Japanese soy sauce
2 tbs mirin
¼ tsp salt

¼ tsp sugar
1 tbs lemon juice
¹⁄₁₆ tsp 7-spice seasoning

Trim the beans and cut into 2-in/5-cm lengths. In a 5-qt/5½-l pot, bring about 3¾ qt/4 l water to the boil. Add the beans and bring back to the boil. Boil rapidly 4 to 5 minutes or until beans are just tender but still crunchy. Drain immediately in colander. Run cold water over the beans to fix their bright green colour. Drain well. Put beans in a bowl. Add the soy sauce, *mirin*, salt, sugar, lemon juice, and the 7-spice seasoning. Toss well.

For information about ingredients and basic techniques that may be unfamiliar, see General Information, pages 481-506.

GREEN BEANS WITH FRESH COCONUT AND SESAME SEEDS
INDIA   *(serves 4)*

*2 oz/60 g freshly grated coconut
   (about 8 tbs)*
*4 tbs finely chopped fresh green
   coriander, or parsley*
*A generous pinch of crushed
   asafetida (optional)*
*½–1 fresh hot green chilli, finely
   chopped*
½ tsp plus 1 tbs salt

*1 lb/450 g fresh green beans,
   trimmed and cut into 1-in/2½-
   cm lengths*
6 tbs ghee or vegetable oil
2 tbs sesame seeds
1 tbs whole black mustard seeds
⅛–¼ tsp cayenne pepper (optional)

Combine the coconut, fresh coriander, asafetida, green chilli, and
¼ tsp salt in a bowl. Rub mixture well with your hands. Set aside.

Add 1 tbs salt to 3½ pt/2 l of water and bring to the boil in a large
pot. Add the cut beans. Boil rapidly for 3 to 4 minutes or until beans
are tender but still bright green and crisp. Drain in a colander and
refresh by moving the colander under cold running water. Set
aside.

Heat *ghee* or oil in a 10–12-in/25–30-cm-wide sauté pan or heavy
pot over a medium flame. When hot, put in the sesame and
mustard seeds. As soon as the mustard seeds begin to pop (this
will happen within a few seconds), add the cayenne pepper.
Stir once and add the beans. Sauté the beans over medium-low
heat for 1 to 2 minutes or until they are heated through and well
coated with the seeds. Add ¼ tsp salt and stir. Now add the
coconut–coriander mixture, stir once, and remove from heat.
Serve immediately.

GREEN BEANS AND PEAS WITH GINGER
INDIA   *(serves 4)*

Here is a quick and delicious way to prepare a combination of
green beans and peas. You could substitute carrots, peeled and
diced into ¼-in/¾-cm cubes, for any one of the green vegetables. I
find it very interesting that this dish, cooked in the western region
of India, should be so similar to another dish, Peas with Ginger
(see page 61), cooked thousands of miles away in Japan. These
beans are also excellent cold and may be served as a 'salad' course
at a Western meal.

2 tbs vegetable oil
½ tsp salt

1 tsp sugar
*3 tbs finely chopped fresh green
   coriander*

1 lb/450 g fresh green beans,
trimmed and cut into ¼-in/¾-
cm rounds
8 oz/225 g shelled peas, fresh or
frozen

1 tbs peeled and finely grated fresh
ginger
½ fresh hot green chilli, finely
chopped (optional)

Put 8 fl oz/¼ l water, the oil, and salt in a 10-in/25-cm frying or sauté pan. Bring to the boil. Add the cut beans and peas (if using frozen peas, thaw first by running hot water over them). Bring to the boil again. Cover, and simmer on a medium-low flame for about 5 minutes or until vegetables are cooked. Arrange your heat so that there are 2–3 tbs of water left at the bottom of the frying pan at the end of this cooking period. Now add the sugar, the coriander, the ginger, and green chilli. Cook for about half a minute on a medium flame with the cover off, stirring as you do so. You should boil away the remaining water. Serve immediately.

It is best to make this dish just before you eat it, but if you do want to make it ahead of time, leave a tbs or so of water in the frying pan to enable you to reheat it. And do not cover it after the initial 5-minute cooking period or the vegetables will discolour. You could serve this dish with almost any Indian meal. Leftovers, once they have completely cooled, may be refrigerated in a closed plastic container.

Zakiya's
GREEN BEANS COOKED WITH MUSTARD SEEDS AND RED PEPPER
INDIA   *(serves 6)*

*1½ lb/675 g fresh green beans**
5 tbs vegetable oil
A pinch of ground asafetida
1 tsp whole black mustard seeds
1 tsp whole cumin seeds

2 tsp urad dal
1–2 whole dried hot red peppers
⅛–¼ tsp cayenne pepper
1¼–1½ tsp salt
1 oz/30 g freshly grated coconut

* Long beans found in Chinese and Indian grocery stores may be used instead.

Trim the beans and cut them into ¼-in/¾-cm rounds. Put them in a bowl, add 2½ pt/1½ l of water, and let the beans 'refresh' for 20 minutes. Drain.

Heat the oil in a 10-in/25-cm frying or sauté pan over a medium flame. When hot, put in first the asafetida, then, a second later, the

For information about ingredients and basic techniques that may be unfamiliar, see General Information, pages 481–506.

mustard seeds, cumin seeds, and *urad dal*. Stir once and put in the red peppers and cayenne pepper. Stir once again and put in the drained beans and salt. Turn heat down a bit and mix beans with the spices. Now cover, turn heat to low and simmer gently 6 to 7 minutes. Remove cover and turn heat up a bit. Stir and sauté beans 3 to 4 minutes or until *all* liquid has evaporated. The beans should have a *very* dry look. Add the coconut, stir, and turn off heat.

STEWED BEETROOT WITH TOMATOES
INDIA   *(serves 6)*

Because this is a 'wet' dish, it is best to serve it in small, individual bowls, such as Indian *katoris*.

1½ lb/675 g ripe tomatoes	1 tsp whole cumin seeds
2 lb/900 g raw beetroot	1 whole dried hot red pepper
3 tbs vegetable oil	1 tsp ground turmeric
⅟₁₆ tsp ground asafetida	1 tsp salt

Drop the tomatoes into boiling water for 15 seconds. Then peel, chop finely and put them in a bowl.

Peel the beetroot and cut them into ¾-in/2-cm dice.

Heat the oil in a 3½-qt/4-l stainless steel pot over a medium-high flame. When hot, put in the asafetida. Two seconds later, put in the cumin and the red pepper. Stir once and add the turmeric. Stir once again and put in the tomatoes. Cover the pot immediately and keep it covered until all the loud sizzling noises subside. Add the beetroot and the salt. Bring to a simmer. Cover, lower heat and simmer gently for 1 hour or until beetroot is tender.

STIR-FRIED BITTER GOURD
INDIA   *(serves 6)*

Bitter gourd is eaten all across southern and eastern Asia and is credited with preventing everything from cancer to cholesterol-related diseases. Bitter foods, Asians believe, cleanse the blood. Whether such theories would survive scientific scrutiny, I cannot say. I grew up with bitter gourds and love their taste. But I know that it is not easy for most Westerners to eat them. So I am providing just three simple recipes: this one from India and the one that follows from the Philippines, and Pinakbet (see page 13), also from the Philippines.

1¼ lb/560 g bitter gourd	3 medium-sized onions
2 tbs plus ¾ tsp salt	5 tbs vegetable oil

2½ tsp panchphoran
⅛–¼ tsp cayenne pepper

Trim away the two pointed ends of the bitter gourds and then cut them in half lengthwise. Remove the pale, seeded section with a grapefruit spoon and discard it. Now cut the outer shells crosswise, at a slight diagonal, into ¼-in/¾-cm-wide strips. Prepare a solution of 2 tbs salt and 1½ pt/8½ dl water in a bowl. Put in the bitter-gourd strips and soak for 2 hours. Drain. Rinse the strips under a tap. Drain and pat dry.

Peel the onions, cut in half lengthwise, then slice into fine half rings.

Heat the oil in a 9-in/23-cm frying pan over a medium flame. When hot, put in the *panchphoran*. Stir and cook for 10 seconds. Put in the onions. Stir and fry for 2 minutes. Add the bitter-gourd strips, the ¾ tsp salt, and the cayenne. Stir and fry for 10 to 12 minutes or until the bitter gourd is tender. If the onion pieces and parts of the bitter gourd turn a bit brown, that is all to the good.

Mrs Roxas's
BITTER GOURD WITH EGGS
PHILIPPINES   (serves 4–6)

Please read the opening remarks in the preceding recipe. For those unfamiliar with the taste of bitter gourd, this dish may well serve as the best introduction. The bitter taste of this unusual vegetable does not go away here − its aficionados would have a fit if it did − but it is modified somewhat by the tomatoes, onions, and eggs.

½ lb/225 g bitter gourd (1 large or 2 small)
1 tbs plus ⅛ tsp salt
1 spring onion
2 medium-sized onions
4 tbs vegetable oil

6 cloves of garlic, peeled and finely chopped
3 small tomatoes, peeled and chopped
3 large eggs, lightly beaten

Trim away the two pointed ends of the bitter gourds and cut them in half lengthwise. Remove the pale, seeded section with a grapefruit spoon and discard it. Cut the darker green outer shells crosswise, at a slight diagonal, into ¼-in/¾-cm-wide strips.

For information about ingredients and basic techniques that may be unfamiliar, see General Information, pages 481-506.

Prepare a solution of 16 fl oz/½ l water and 1 tbs salt in a bowl. Put the bitter-gourd strips into this bowl and set aside for 2 hours.

Drain the bitter gourd and rinse the strips under running water. Drain again and pat dry.

Cut the spring onion into 2-in/5-cm lengths and then cut each section lengthwise into thin strips. Peel the onions and cut them in half lengthwise; then slice them into fine half rings.

Heat the oil in a well-seasoned or nonstick 8-in/20-cm-wide frying pan over a medium flame. When hot, put in the garlic. Stir and fry until the garlic pieces start to brown. Add the onions. Stir and fry for about 2 minutes. Add the tomatoes. Stir and fry another 2 minutes. Now put in the bitter gourd. Turn down the heat. Stir occasionally and fry for about 10 minutes or until bitter gourd is tender. Stir in the beaten eggs and the ⅛ tsp salt. Stir and cook as you would scrambled eggs until the eggs have reached a consistency you like. Take off the heat, quickly fold in the spring onion strips, and serve.

BRUSSELS SPROUTS STIR-FRIED WITH DRIED CHINESE MUSHROOMS

CHINA *(serves 4)*

8 large Chinese dried black
  mushrooms
¾ lb/340 g Brussels sprouts,
  trimmed and washed
3 tbs groundnut oil

1 tsp finely chopped garlic
3 tbs shaohsing *wine or dry*
  sherry
½ tsp salt
¾ tsp sugar

Soak the mushrooms (if you have small ones, use more than 8) in 4 fl oz/1 dl water for 1 hour.

Remove mushrooms from their soaking liquid. (Do not discard this liquid. Save 3 tbs of it in such a way that you leave the grit behind. Put the 3 tbs in a small cup.) Cut off the coarse stems. Now cut the mushroom caps into quarters. (If the mushrooms are small, cut the caps in half.)

Quarter the Brussels sprouts lengthwise. Very small sprouts may be cut in half.

Heat the oil in a wok over medium-high heat. When hot, put in the chopped garlic. Stir and fry for 4 to 5 seconds or until garlic turns a light brown. Quickly add the mushrooms and Brussels sprouts. Stir-fry for about 20 seconds. Now add the wine, salt, and sugar and stir-fry another 20 seconds. Add the 3 reserved tbs of the mushroom-soaking liquid and cover the wok immediately. Turn heat to low and simmer 5 minutes or until sprouts are just cooked.

CABBAGE WITH CARROT AND SPRING ONIONS

CHINA *(serves 6)*

This dish is generally eaten hot; however, it is very good cold, too. If you want to have it that way, spread it out on a platter as soon as it is cooked and let it cool off. Then put it into a covered container and refrigerate.

*1¾ lb/800 g green cabbage
  (½ medium-sized head)*
1 carrot
3 spring onions
2 fl oz/½ dl vegetable oil

*2 five-pence-piece sized slices of
  fresh ginger, lightly mashed*
1¼ tsp salt
*2 tbs shaohsing wine or dry
  sherry*

Remove the coarse outer leaves of the cabbage as well as its hard core. Now cut the cabbage evenly into long, ⅛-in/½-cm-wide strips.

Peel the carrot and cut it crosswise, at a slight diagonal, into ⅛-in/½-cm-thick ovals. Cut the ovals, a few at a time, into ⅛-in/½-cm-wide julienne strips.

Cut the spring onions into 2½-in/6½-cm lengths. With a sharp pointed knife, cut these sections *lengthwise* into thin strips.

Heat the oil in a wok or large frying pan over a medium flame. When hot, put in the ginger. Stir and fry for about 20 seconds. Put in all the vegetables and the salt. Stir and fry for about 3 minutes. Add the wine, cover, and cook for about 4 minutes or until the cabbage is tender enough to eat but still retains some of its crispness. Uncover, turn heat to high. Stir and cook for 1 minute. Remove ginger before serving.

CABBAGE SEASONED WITH UMEBOSHI PLUMS

JAPAN *(serves 4)*

Umeboshi plums, small and exceedingly sour, come pickled in salt. The Japanese often eat them, one per person, for breakfast just as Westerners drink orange juice, which is the way I had them for the first time in Japan. But the same plums can also be used as a seasoning, and that is how I have used them in this recipe. They add a wonderful tartness to the dish. *Umeboshi* plums are available in health-food and Japanese stores.

For information about ingredients and basic techniques that may be unfamiliar, see General Information, pages 481-506.

½ medium-sized head of green
  cabbage (about 1½ lb/700g)
About 4 umeboshi plums (to
  make 2½ tsp pulp)
2½ tbs vegetable oil
¼–½ tsp salt
¼ tsp sugar

Core the cabbage and cut it into long, thin slivers. Remove the
stones from the plums. Pound the flesh in a Japanese *suribachi* or
mortar until you have a paste.

Heat the oil in a frying pan over a medium flame. Put in the
cabbage and salt. Stir and fry for 3 to 4 minutes or until the cabbage
has wilted and is just cooked. Add the sugar and plum paste. Stir
and mix.

SHREDDED CABBAGE
WITH MUSTARD SEEDS
AND FRESH COCONUT
INDIA   *(serves 6)*

In this quick-cooking recipe from Bengal, the cabbage stays green
and crunchy. It is flavoured very delicately with the mustard oil in
which it is cooked, and with mustard seeds, bay leaves, and
freshly grated coconut.

6 tbs mustard oil or other vegetable   ¾–1 tsp salt
  oil   ½ tsp sugar
1 tsp whole black mustard seeds   1 fresh hot green chilli, cut into
2 bay leaves   fine, long strips
3–3½ lb/1350–1500 g green   1½ oz/45 g freshly grated coconut
  cabbage, cored and finely
  shredded (1 medium-sized head)

Heat the oil in a heavy, wide, casserole-type pot over a medium-
high flame. When hot, put in the mustard seeds and bay leaves. As
soon as the bay leaves darken a bit and the mustard seeds begin to
pop (this just takes a few seconds), put in the shredded cabbage.
Turn heat to medium. Stir and cook for about 5 minutes. Add the
salt, sugar, and the green chilli strips. Stir and cook another 3 to 5
minutes. Cabbage should be bright green and slightly wilted,
though still crunchy. Turn off heat. Sprinkle with coconut, mix
well, and serve.

CABBAGE WITH YOGURT
INDIA   *(serves 4)*

Here, as in many South Indian foods, a dried split pea — *urad dal* —
is used as a seasoning. The dish is served warm, although I like it
cold as well.

1¾ lb/800 g green cabbage (½ medium-sized head)
2 fl oz/½ dl vegetable oil
3 tbs whole black mustard seeds
2 tsp urad dal, picked over
⅛–¼ tsp cayenne pepper
2 tsp ground coriander

1 medium-sized onion, peeled, cut in half lengthwise, then into ¼-in/¾-cm half rings
1½ tsp salt
1½–2 oz/45–60 g cup freshly grated coconut
8 fl oz/¼ l plain yogurt

Remove the coarse outer leaves of the cabbage as well as its hard
core. Now cut the cabbage evenly into ⅛-in/½-cm-wide strips.

Heat the oil in a wok or a large sauté pan over a medium flame.
When hot, put in the mustard seeds and *urad dal*. As soon as the
mustard seeds begin to pop — this just takes a few seconds — put in
the cayenne and the coriander. Stir once and quickly put in the
cabbage and onion. Stir for 1 minute. Add the salt. Stir to mix.
Cover, lower heat and cook about 5 to 8 minutes or until cabbage is
just tender. Add the coconut and mix. Keep warm.

Put the yogurt in the top of a double boiler and beat until creamy.
Heat. Stir continuously in one direction as it warms through. Do
not let it get hot.

Put the cabbage into a warmed serving bowl. Add the yogurt
and fold it in.

Sheila's
CABBAGE AND TOMATOES COOKED IN MUSTARD OIL
INDIA   *(serves 4–6)*

1 lb/450 g green cabbage (½ small head)
5 small Italian plum or 2 medium-sized tomatoes, peeled
6 tbs mustard oil or other vegetable oil

A generous pinch of ground asafetida (optional)
1 tsp ground cumin seeds
½ tsp whole black (or other) cumin seeds
1–1½ tsp salt
⅛–¼ tsp cayenne pepper

For information about ingredients and basic techniques that may be unfamiliar, see General Information, pages 481-506.

Core the cabbage and cut the leaves into 1-in/2½-cm squares.

Cut the tomatoes into ¼-in/¾-cm dice.

Heat the oil in a deep 9–10-in/23–25-cm frying pan or sauté pan over a medium-high flame. When hot, put in the asafetida. One second later, put in the tomatoes. Stir and fry for about 1 minute and then put in the ground cumin, black cumin, salt, and cayenne. Stir for another minute. Put in the cabbage and stir to mix. Cover, turn heat to low, and let the cabbage cook 12 to 15 minutes or until it is just done.

CABBAGE WITH MISO
JAPAN   *(serves 4–6)*

11 oz/310 g finely shredded green   *½ tsp salt*
  cabbage   *½ tsp sugar*
1½ tbs red miso   *⅛ tsp 7-spice seasoning*
1 tbs rice vinegar

Bring 3 qt/3½ l of water to the boil in a 4-qt/4½-l pot. Drop in the cabbage and boil for a minute. Drain in a colander, squeezing all the water out of the cabbage. Put cabbage in a bowl. Add the *miso*, vinegar, salt, and sugar. Mix well.

Either make small mounds and serve in individual Oriental dishes or make a large mound in the centre of a single large serving bowl. Dust with the 7-spice seasoning. Serve warm, either as a first course or as a salad.

CARROTS IN BATTER
KOREA   *(serves 2–4)*

This is a quick, wonderful way to cook carrot slices. It makes them delicately crunchy on the outside while keeping them sweet and tender inside. The dish should be eaten as soon as it is made. Have all the ingredients ready. The frying takes just a few minutes and can be done right at the end. The cooked carrots are usually eaten with a dipping sauce. Incidentally, you may cook sweet potatoes the same way.

2 medium-sized carrots
4 tbs plain white flour
1 large egg
⅛ tsp salt

Vegetable oil for shallow frying
Dipping sauce: any one of the five
    Korean Dipping Sauces on
    pages 415–17

Peel the carrots. Cut them crosswise at a slight diagonal so that you get ovals that are ⅓ in/1 cm thick. (If you are not frying the carrots immediately, put them into a plastic bag and refrigerate them.)

Spread the flour out on a plate.

Break the egg into a shallow bowl. Add the salt and beat the egg.

Put ¼ in/¾ cm oil in an 8-in/20-cm frying pan and heat over a medium-low flame until it reaches a temperature of 350–375° F/ 180–190° C.

Dip the carrot pieces in the flour so that they are well coated on all sides. Now, working fairly quickly, dip one carrot piece at a time into the beaten egg and then put it into the oil. Make sure that all the carrot pieces lie in a single layer in the frying pan. Fry until the slices turn golden brown on one side. Turn them over and fry the second side until it, too, is golden brown. Remove the carrot slices with a slotted spoon, drain briefly on kitchen paper, and serve immediately.

CARROTS WITH RAISINS AND DATES
IRAN   (serves 4)

5 medium-sized carrots
1 medium-sized onion, peeled
4 tbs unsalted butter
4 tbs raisins

4 tbs stoned dates, cut into
    ¼-in/¾-cm-thick slivers
⅓–½ tsp salt
¼ tsp sugar

Peel the carrots and slice, slightly diagonally, into ¼-in/¾-cm-thick ovals.

Cut the onion in half lengthwise, and then cut the halves crosswise into ¼-in/¾-cm-thick half rings.

Melt the butter in an 8-in/20-cm frying pan over a medium-low flame. Turn the heat to medium and put in the carrots, onion,

---

For information about ingredients and basic techniques that may be unfamiliar, see General Information, pages 481-506.

raisins, and dates. Stir and fry gently for 5 minutes. Add the salt and sugar. Stir and fry for another 4 to 5 minutes or until the carrots are just tender and onion is soft.

CARROTS COOKED IN DASHI
JAPAN   (serves 2–4)

2 medium-sized carrots   ½ tsp salt
4 fl oz/1 dl dashi (see page 339)   2 tsp sugar

Peel the carrots and cut them into ¼-in/¾-cm-thick slices. Put the carrots and *dashi* into a small pot and bring to a simmer. Cover, lower heat and simmer gently for 4 to 5 minutes or until the carrots are just tender. Remove cover, add salt and sugar, and turn the heat up a bit. Cook until almost all the liquid has been absorbed. (The little remaining liquid may be used to reheat the carrots, if necessary.)

CAULIFLOWER IN A CASHEW AND SESAME SEED SAUCE
INDIA   (serves 6)

2¾–3 lb/1250–1350 g cauliflower   1 fresh hot green chilli, sliced into
   (1 medium-sized head)   rounds, or ⅛–¼ tsp cayenne
2 oz/60 g freshly grated coconut   pepper
2 tbs sesame seeds   1 tsp whole black mustard seeds
5 tbs vegetable oil   1 tsp salt
2 oz/60 g raw cashew nuts   1 tsp sugar
                                          1 tbs lemon juice

Cut cauliflower flowerets in such a way that no piece is longer than 1½ in/4 cm and no wider at the head than ¾ in/2 cm. Longer stems, if tender, may be peeled and sliced into rounds.

Put the coconut into a small heated cast-iron frying pan over a medium flame. Dry-roast the coconut, stirring frequently until lightly browned, then empty into a bowl.

Put sesame seeds into the same pan and roast, shaking the pan frequently over a medium flame, until sesame seeds are lightly browned. Empty into bowl with coconut.

Heat 1 tbs oil in the same pan over a medium flame. Add the cashew nuts. Fry, stirring, until cashews turn a light brown. Remove with a slotted spoon and put them with the coconut and sesame seeds. Turn off heat.

Empty contents of bowl into the container of an electric blender or a food processor. Add ¼ pt/1½ dl water and the sliced green chilli. Blend until you have a smooth paste.

Heat 4 tbs of oil in a large, heavy frying pan over a medium-high flame. When very hot, add the mustard seeds. As soon as they begin to pop (this will happen almost immediately), put in the cauliflower. Stir the cauliflower around on medium heat for 3 to 4 minutes: some of the flowerets should pick up a few brown specks. Now add the paste from the blender, ½ pt/3 dl water, the salt, sugar, and lemon juice. Stir to mix. Bring to the boil. Cover. Lower heat and simmer gently about 10 to 15 minutes or until cauliflower is cooked through but still a bit crisp. Stir now and then during the cooking.

CAULIFLOWER WITH ALMONDS AND BROAD BEANS
CHINA   (serves 4)

1¾ lb/800 g cauliflower (1 smallish
   head)
6 oz/170 g shelled large broad
   beans, fresh or frozen
1½ tsp cornflour
1 tbs shaohsing wine or dry
   sherry
2 tsp sesame oil

2 fl oz/½ dl vegetable oil
2 oz/60 g whole blanched almonds
2 cloves garlic, peeled and mashed
   lightly
2 five-pence-piece sized slices of
   fresh ginger, lightly mashed
1¼ tsp salt

Cut the cauliflower into very slim flowerets that are about 2 in/ 5 cm long, 1 in/2½ cm wide at the head, and ¼ in/¾ cm thick. Leave them to soak in a bowl of cold water for half an hour. (This crisps them up nicely.) Bring 1½ pt/8½ dl of water in a pot to a rapid boil, then drop in the broad beans. Boil rapidly for about 5 minutes or until the beans are just barely tender. Drain.

Mix together the cornflour, wine, sesame oil, and 2 tbs water in a cup. Heat the oil in a wok or frying pan over medium heat. When it is hot, put in the almonds. Stir and fry until the almonds are golden brown. Remove them with a slotted spoon and leave to drain on kitchen paper. Put the garlic and ginger into the same oil. Stir and fry for about 10 seconds. Add the cauliflower, broad beans, and salt. Stir and fry for 2 minutes. Add 2 tbs water and cover immediately. Cook for about 2 minutes or until the cauliflower is crisply tender. Remove the cover. Turn the heat to medium-low, give the ingredients in the cup a stir, and add them to the wok. Stir and cook for about 30 seconds. Add the almonds and stir once. Empty into a warm serving dish and remove the garlic and ginger pieces.

For information about ingredients and basic techniques that may be unfamiliar, see General Information, pages 481-506.

CAULIFLOWER WITH COURGETTES

INDIAN STYLE   (serves 4)

1 lb/450 g cauliflower (½ smallish
  head)

2 medium-sized courgettes (about
  1 lb/450 g)

2½ tsp salt

4 tbs vegetable oil

1½ tsp peeled, finely chopped fresh
  ginger

3–5 medium-sized cloves of garlic,
  peeled and finely chopped

¼ tsp finely chopped fresh hot
  green chilli

1/16 tsp freshly ground black pepper

Cut up the cauliflower into flowerets as described for Cauliflower
and Potatoes . . . (see below).

Wash and trim the courgettes. Cut them in half lengthwise.
Remove the seeded area with the help of a sharp knife. Sprinkle
courgette shells with a little salt (less than ¼ tsp) and set aside for
half an hour. Drain and wipe well. Cut the shells crosswise into
¼-in/¾-cm-wide sections.

Bring 2½ qt/3 l of water to the boil in a 4–5-qt/4½–5½-l pot. Add
1½ tsp salt and the cauliflower. As soon as the water comes to the
boil again, turn off the heat. Drain the cauliflower in a colander.
(If not eating immediately, the cauliflower should be refreshed
under cold running water and set aside.)

Heat the oil in a large 10–12-in/25–30-cm, heavy frying pan over a
medium flame. When hot, put in the ginger, garlic, and green
chilli. Fry, stirring, until the garlic is lightly browned. Add the
courgette and cauliflower. Stir and fry on medium-low heat for 7 to
10 minutes or until vegetables are cooked through but still a bit
crunchy. Add about ½ tsp salt and the black pepper. Stir a few
times and serve.

CAULIFLOWER AND POTATOES
COOKED WITH FENUGREEK
AND FENNEL SEEDS

INDIA   (serves 6)

This North Indian dish, supplemented with stuffed Parathas and
Sour Lime Pickle (see pages 322 and 427), is put into small, brass
'tiffin-carriers' and taken as lunch by thousands of schoolchildren
and office workers. Rolled in the same parathas, it may be taken on
picnics or long car journeys.

2 lb/900 g cauliflower (1 smallish
  head)

2 medium-sized potatoes (about
  ¾ lb/340 g)

6 tbs vegetable oil
¼ tsp whole fenugreek seeds
1 tsp whole fennel seeds
1 tsp whole cumin seeds
1–2 whole dried hot red peppers

¾ tsp ground turmeric
1 tsp ground coriander seeds
1–1¼ tsp salt
⅛ tsp freshly ground black pepper
1 tsp garam masala

Discard leaves and coarse stem of cauliflower. Break head into 2-in/5-cm-long flowerets. Now cut each floweret lengthwise into very slim flowerets, with the heads never wider than ½ in/1½ cm. Soak in cold water for half an hour.

Peel the potatoes. Cut them into dice, about ½×½×⅓ in/1½×1½×1 cm. Soak in a bowl of cold water for half an hour.

Drain cauliflower and potatoes and dry them in a tea towel. Heat oil in a 12–14-in/30–35-cm frying pan over high heat. When the oil is smoking, scatter in the fenugreek seeds, the fennel seeds, the cumin seeds, and the red peppers. Stir once and quickly add the cauliflower and the potatoes. Stir again and turn the heat to medium. Sprinkle the turmeric, coriander, salt, and pepper over the vegetables and sauté them for about 8 to 10 minutes. Now add 2 fl oz/½ dl water and cover immediately. Turn heat to very low and steam vegetables gently about 7 to 10 minutes or until vegetables are tender. Sprinkle the *garam masala* over the vegetables, stir once, and serve.

CAULIFLOWER STEAMED WITH WHOLE SPICES
INDIA   (serves 6)

This Indian dish is both tasty and very easy to make.

3 lb/1350 g cauliflower (1 medium-sized head)
4–5 tbs vegetable oil
1 tsp whole cumin seeds
1 tsp whole coriander seeds
1 tsp kalonji
1 dried hot red pepper
1 medium-sized onion, peeled and finely chopped

7 to 8 cloves garlic, peeled and finely chopped
2 tsp ground coriander seeds
2 tsp ground cumin seeds
½ tsp ground turmeric
1 tsp salt
¼ tsp cayenne pepper (optional)

Break the cauliflower into small flowerets about 1 in/2½ cm long and ¾ in/2 cm wide at the flower.

For information about ingredients and basic techniques that may be unfamiliar, see General Information, pages 481-506.

Heat enough oil to line a 10–12-in/25–30-cm frying or sauté pan over a medium-high flame. When very hot, add the whole cumin and whole coriander seeds as well as the *kalonji*. As soon as the seeds begin to sizzle (this just takes a few seconds), put in the red pepper. It will brown immediately on one side. Quickly turn it over to brown on the other side. Lower heat to medium and put in the finely chopped onion and garlic. Stir and fry for about 5 minutes or until onion–garlic mixture is lightly browned.

Add the cauliflower, ground coriander, ground cumin, turmeric, salt, and cayenne pepper. Stir to mix. Now put in 2 fl oz/½ dl water and bring to a simmer. Cover with a tight-fitting lid and steam cauliflower on very low heat 10 to 15 minutes or until tender but still slightly crunchy. Stir every 3 to 4 minutes, replacing the lid each time. If any extra liquid is left, it should be boiled away so cauliflower has a 'dry' look.

Tatie Wawo-Runtu's
TUMIS SAWI
(Choy Sum with Shallots)
INDONESIA   *(serves 4–6)*

For a note on *choy sum*, a Chinese vegetable of the cabbage family, see General Information. Here is a simple and scrumptious way to cook it which requires a fair amount of shallots, a little garlic, and some fresh hot red pepper. If you cannot find these peppers, use slivers of fresh, sweet red pepper or bottled pimientos to give splashes of red to the greens and use hot green chillies to provide as much 'hotness' as you like. Mrs Wawo-Runtu makes this dish with a combination of *kang kung* (swamp cabbage) and *choy sum*, but since the former is less easily available, I have left it out. It is usually served with rice to sop up all the delicious juices.

1¼ lb/560 g choy sum
5 oz/140 g shallots, *peeled*
2 cloves garlic, *peeled*

1–2 *fresh hot red peppers*
2 fl oz/½ dl vegetable oil
1 tsp salt

Wash the *choy sum* thoroughly. Cut the leafy section crosswise into 2-in/5-cm-wide pieces and cut the stalks into 3-in/8-cm-long segments. Peel the coarser lower stems. Now cut all the stems lengthwise into ⅛–¼-in/½–¾-cm strips.

Cut the shallots into halves, lengthwise. Cut each half lengthwise into strips that are about ⅛ in/½ cm thick.

Cut the cloves of garlic into halves, lengthwise. Now cut each half lengthwise into strips that are about ⅛ in/½ cm thick.

Cut the red peppers crosswise into ⅛-in/½-cm-wide rings.

Heat the oil in a wok or heavy frying pan over a medium-high flame. When hot, put in the shallots and garlic. Stir and fry for 2 minutes. Add the red peppers and salt. Stir to mix. Add the cut greens. Stir again to mix. Add 4 fl oz/1 dl water. Cover and cook for 5 minutes.

Usha's
CORN WITH COCONUT MILK
INDIA   (*serves 6–8*)

This dish, from India's upper western coast, is a thick corn stew that is normally made with young maize cobs, each cut into 3 to 4 sections. As I cannot find maize in New York, I make the dish with sweet corn scraped off the cob. You may use frozen corn, if you wish. Defrost it quickly in boiling water and drain it well.

6 oz/170 g coconut, freshly grated
1½ lb/675 g uncooked corn, scraped
   from the cob
6 tbs vegetable oil
3 medium-sized onions, peeled, cut
   in half lengthwise, then cut into
   very fine half rings

2 cloves garlic, peeled and mashed
   to a pulp
1½ tsp ground cumin seeds
¼ tsp ground turmeric
⅛–¼ tsp cayenne pepper
1 tsp salt
1 tsp sugar

Make thick coconut milk (also called the first coconut milk) using 6 oz/170 g grated coconut and 8 fl oz/¼ l boiling water. See page 488 for directions. Set this milk aside. Now make a second coconut milk using the remaining coconut 'grounds' and another 8 fl oz/¼ l of boiling water, as directed on the same page. Keep this second milk separated from the first.

Combine the corn and the second coconut milk in a 2-qt/2¼-l flameproof casserole, bring to a boil, and cook for 1 minute on medium-high heat. Turn off the heat.

For information about ingredients and basic techniques that may be unfamiliar, see General Information, pages 481-506.

Heat the oil in a 7–8-in/18–20-cm frying pan over a medium-high flame. Put in the sliced onions. Stir and fry them for about 10 minutes or until they are a rich brown colour (do not burn them) and crisp. Remove with a slotted spoon and spread them out on kitchen paper. Turn the heat off under the frying pan and let the oil in it cool slightly.

Preheat oven to 350°F/180°C/Mark 4.

Combine the garlic, cumin, turmeric, cayenne, and 2 fl oz/½ dl water in a small cup. Mix it well. Heat the oil in the frying pan again, this time on medium heat. When hot, put in the spice paste. Stir and fry for about 1 minute or until the oil separates from the spices. Now stir and fry for another 30 seconds. Empty the contents of the frying pan into the pot with the corn. Add the first thick coconut milk, salt, fried onions and sugar. Stir, and bring to the boil. Cover well and place the pot in the oven. Bake for 45 minutes.

COURGETTES STUFFED WITH SMOKED AUBERGINE
INDIAN STYLE   (serves 4)

1 medium-sized aubergine (about
  1 lb/450 g)
4 medium-sized courgettes (about
  1½–2 lb/675–900 g)
About 1⅓ tsp salt
6 medium-sized cloves garlic
6 tbs vegetable oil
1 2 oz/60 g onion, peeled and
  finely chopped

½ tsp peeled, grated, fresh ginger
½–1 fresh hot green chilli, finely
  chopped
4 tinned plum tomatoes, chopped
  plus 2 tbs liquid from the tin
1/16 tsp freshly ground black pepper
½ tbs lemon juice
3 tbs Parmesan cheese, freshly
  grated (optional)

Line a gas burner with foil to protect it from aubergine juice. Turn flame to medium-low. Place aubergine directly over the flame and let it get charred on one side. Keep turning the aubergine until the entire skin looks burnt and the vegetable turns limp and soft. (If you have an electric cooker, prick the aubergine with a fork and place it under the grill. Turn it as its skin chars.) Peel away the charred skin under cold, running water. Chop the aubergine pulp.

Scrub courgettes and trim ends. Cut each courgette in half lengthwise. Using a grapefruit spoon, scrape away all the seeded area, leaving boat-shaped shells. Sprinkle shells with a little salt (about ⅓ tsp) and set aside for half an hour.

Peel the cloves of garlic. Chop 4 of them finely.

Heat 3 tbs oil in a frying pan over a medium flame. When hot, put in the chopped garlic and stir for about 10 seconds. Now put in the onion and sauté for about 5 minutes or until the onion looks translucent and just begins to brown at the edges. Add the aubergine pulp, the ginger, green chilli, the tomatoes and liquid, ¾ tsp salt, and the black pepper. Stir and sauté for 2 to 3 minutes. Add the lemon juice, stir and taste for salt. Cover, turn heat to low, and simmer gently for about 15 minutes, stirring occasionally.

Preheat grill.

Drain all the liquid from the courgettes and pat the shells dry. In one large 10–12-in/25–30-cm frying pan (you could use two smaller frying pans), heat 3 tbs oil over a medium flame. When hot, put in the 2 remaining whole cloves of garlic. Stir them around until they brown and then discard them. Put the courgettes, cut side down, into this garlic-flavoured oil. As soon as the cut edges turn a light brown, turn courgette boats over and let the green skin turn a light brown. Cover the pan. Turn heat to low and let the courgettes steam in their own juices for about 5 minutes or until tender but still slightly crunchy. Remove and place on a grill pan.

Divide the aubergine mixture into eight portions and fill the courgette boats with it. Sprinkle the Parmesan cheese on top and place under grill until lightly browned.

COURGETTES STIR-FRIED WITH GARLIC
CHINA   (serves 4–6)

1½ lb/675 g small (about 6 in/
   15 cm) courgettes
About 2¼ tsp salt
3 tbs vegetable oil

4 cloves garlic, peeled and finely
   chopped
¼ tsp sugar
1 tbs shaohsing wine or dry
   sherry

Trim away the courgette ends. Do not peel. Cut each courgette lengthwise into ¼-in/¾-cm-thick slices. Lay each slice down on a chopping board and, with a sharp pointed knife, cut it lengthwise into ¼-in/¾-cm-wide strips. These strips may now be cut so they are about 2½ in/6½ cm in length. Put the strips in a bowl. Add 2 tsp of the salt and mix well. Set aside for 15 minutes. Drain and pat as dry as possible in a tea towel.

Heat the oil in a wok or frying pan over medium-high heat. When hot, put in the garlic. Stir and fry for a few seconds until the garlic has browned lightly. Put in the courgettes. Stir and fry for about 3 minutes or until the courgettes have just cooked through but still retain some crispness. Add the sugar and stir quickly. Add

---

For information about ingredients and basic techniques that may be unfamiliar, see General Information, pages 481–506.

the *shaohsing* by pouring it around the edges of the wok and letting it slither down towards the courgettes. Stir again and serve immediately. Or if you wish to eat the courgettes cold, spread them out on a large plate as soon as they are cooked and let them cool off. Then put them in a covered container and refrigerate.

COURGETTES STUFFED WITH FRESH COCONUT AND CORIANDER
INDIA   (serves 6)

3 oz/85 g freshly grated coconut
8 tbs chopped fresh green coriander
1 fresh hot green chilli, finely
   chopped
1 tsp salt
⅛ tsp ground asafetida (optional)

6 medium-sized courgettes (about
   2½ lb/1125 g)
5 tbs vegetable oil
⅛ tsp freshly ground black pepper
2 tbs lemon juice
1 tsp sugar

Combine the coconut, fresh coriander, green chilli, ¾ tsp salt, and asafetida in a bowl. Rub the mixture well with your hands.

Wash and trim the courgettes. Cut each courgette into 4 1½-in/4-cm-long chunks. Sit the chunks on one of their cut ends and make two deep slits, like a cross, going 1 in/2½ cm down their lengths. The courgette chunks will seem quartered at the top but will remain whole at the bottom. Now gently prize apart the cut sections and stuff with the coconut mixture.

Pour the oil as well as 4 fl oz/1 dl water into a large, 12–14-in/30–35-cm frying pan. (Two smaller frying pans may be used.) Carefully place all the courgettes, stuffed side down, in the pan. If there is any stuffing left over, sprinkle that, as well as ¼ tsp salt, the black pepper, lemon juice, and sugar on top. Bring to a simmer, cover tightly, lower heat and simmer gently for about 5 to 6 minutes. Using two spoons, turn the courgette pieces over gently so their quartered, stuffed sections are on top. If cooking liquid has evaporated, add a little more hot water. Cover again and cook another 7 to 10 minutes. The courgettes should be cooked through but retain some of their crispness. There should be no liquid left in the frying pan. Serve immediately.

COURGETTES WITH ONIONS, TOMATO, AND CUMIN
INDIA   (serves 6)

This popular North Indian dish is normally made with the pale green, bowling-pin-shaped marrow available in Britain only in

Indian and Chinese grocery stores. If you can manage to find it, peel it first and then proceed with the recipe. Otherwise courgettes make a good substitute.

2 medium-sized onions
3 largish courgettes (about 2½ lb/ 1125 g)
4 tbs vegetable oil
1 tsp whole cumin seeds
1 large tomato (about ½ lb/225 g), peeled and chopped

About 1½ tsp salt
1/16 tsp freshly ground black pepper
1½ tbs lemon juice
1/16–1/8 tsp cayenne pepper (optional)
4 tbs finely chopped fresh green coriander, or parsley

Peel the onions, cut in half lengthwise, then slice into fine half rings.

Trim the ends off the courgettes, then quarter them lengthwise. Cut away the seeded section and then cut crosswise into ½–¾-in/ 1½–2-cm sections.

Heat the oil in a large frying pan over a medium flame. When hot, put in the whole cumin seeds. As soon as they turn a few shades darker (this takes just a few seconds) put in the onions. Turn heat to medium and sauté onions for about 2 minutes. Add the tomatoes and stir for a few seconds. Now cover, lower heat, and let onions and tomatoes cook for 10 minutes. Lift cover and gently mash down the tomato pieces. Add the courgettes and 1¼ tsp salt (add the other ¼ tsp salt towards the end if you think you need it). Stir and fry for another 2 minutes on medium heat.

Add 2 tbs water, cover immediately with a well-fitting lid, turn heat down and steam gently for 4 to 6 minutes or until the courgettes are tender but still retain some crispness. (Young courgettes will cook much faster.) Lift cover, and add black pepper, lemon juice, cayenne pepper, and chopped coriander. Mix and taste for salt–sour balance. Cover and steam for another minute. Serve either hot or cold on a bed of lettuce leaves as a salad.

For information about ingredients and basic techniques that may be unfamiliar, see General Information, pages 481-506.

COURGETTE 'MEATBALLS'

INDIA
(Makes 16 'meatballs' and serves 4–6 people)

An exquisitely elegant dish, it consists of tender 'meatballs' made out of grated courgette, bathed in a creamy, spicy sauce. In India, a long green marrow, shaped rather like a bowling pin, is used for this dish. If you can find such a marrow in a Chinese or Indian grocery store, do use it. It needs to be peeled and seeded before it is grated. If you cannot find it, courgettes make an excellent substitute.

FOR THE 'MEATBALLS'

3 medium-sized courgettes (about 1–1¼ lb/450–560 g)
½ tsp salt
About 1 fresh hot green chilli, finely chopped
3 tbs finely chopped onion
½ tsp peeled and very finely grated fresh ginger
2 tbs finely chopped fresh green coriander
1½ oz/45 g gram flour
Vegetable oil for deep frying

FOR THE SAUCE

5 tbs vegetable oil from deep frying
2 medium-sized onions, peeled and very finely chopped
¼ tsp ground turmeric
¹⁄₁₆ tsp cayenne pepper
1 tsp ground cumin seeds
2 tsp ground coriander seeds
½ lb/225 g tomatoes (about 2 tomatoes), peeled and finely chopped
8 fl oz/¼ l single cream
½ tsp garam masala
½ tsp ground roasted cumin seeds
¼–⅓ tsp salt

Wash, trim, and grate the courgettes. Put them into a bowl and sprinkle them with the ½ tsp salt. Set them aside for half an hour.

Squeeze as much liquid as possible out of the courgettes by pressing handfuls between your two palms. Save this courgette liquid for the sauce. Dry off the bowl and put the courgettes back in it. Add the chopped chilli (you may want to use more than 1 chilli, depending on your taste), the 3 tbs chopped onion, the grated ginger, and the fresh coriander. Sift the gram flour over this vegetable mixture. Mix well and form 16 neat balls.

In a frying pan, wok, or other utensil for deep frying, heat about 1½ in/4 cm of oil over a medium flame (a wok should have 1½ in/4 cm at its centre). When hot, put in 5 to 6 of the balls, or as many as the utensil will hold easily in one layer. Fry for about 1½ minutes, or until the balls turn a rich, reddish-brown colour. Turn the balls every now and then as they fry. Remove them with a slotted spoon when they are done and leave to drain on a plate lined with kitchen paper. Do all the 'meatballs' this way.

To make the sauce, remove 5 tbs of the oil used in deep frying and put this in a 10-in/25-cm frying or sauté pan. Heat the oil over a medium flame. When hot, put in the finely chopped onions. Stir and fry for 7 to 8 minutes or until the onions begin to turn brown at the edges. Take the pan off the fire for a couple of seconds and add the turmeric, cayenne, ground cumin, and ground coriander. Stir once and put the pan back on the fire. Stir for another 5 seconds and then add the chopped tomatoes. Stir and fry on medium heat for 5 minutes. Add the courgette juice. (You need 8 fl oz/¼ l; if you have less, add some water.) Bring to the boil. Cover, lower heat and let the sauce simmer gently for 15 minutes. (This much of the recipe may be prepared several hours ahead of time.) Add the cream, *garam masala*, ground roasted cumin, and the ¼ to ⅓ tsp salt. Mix well, bring to a simmer and cook for 1 minute. Now put in the 'meatballs'. Spoon the sauce over them. Cover, and simmer very gently for 6 to 7 minutes. Spoon the sauce over the 'meatballs' a few times during this cooking period.

These 'meatballs' turn very soft when cooked in the sauce, so handle them gently and serve immediately.

HIJIKI WITH SHIITAKE MUSHROOMS
JAPAN   (serves 4)

Hijiki is a black, twine-like, dried sea vegetable, rich in calcium, that is sold in health-food and Japanese stores. It is exceedingly tasty and combines well with a variety of vegetables. Because dried *hijiki* is fairly stiff, it is difficult to measure accurately. Just stuff it into a large breakfast cup and aim for an approximate amount. This dish may be eaten warm or at room temperature.

¼ cup hijiki	3 tbs vegetable oil
8 dried shiitake mushrooms*	5 tbs dashi (see page 339)
4 oz/115 g well-drained, julienned	½ tsp salt
bamboo shoots	2 tsp sugar
1 carrot, peeled and cut into	1 tbs mirin
julienne strips	1 tbs Japanese soy sauce

*Mushrooms used to make *dashi* may be re-used for this dish.

Rinse the *hijiki* quickly under cold running water. Put it to soak in 1½ pt/8½ dl of warm water for 30 minutes. Lift the *hijiki* out of the water, leaving all the grit behind, then rinse it again.

For information about ingredients and basic techniques that may be unfamiliar, see General Information, pages 481-506.

Rinse the mushrooms quickly and leave to soak in 1¼ pt/¾ l warm water for 30 minutes. Drain the mushrooms and remove the hard stems. Cut the mushroom caps into ⅛-in/½-cm-thick strips.

Heat the oil in a frying pan over a medium flame. When hot, put in the *hijiki*, mushrooms, bamboo shoots, and carrot. Sauté for 1 minute. Add the *dashi*, salt, sugar, *mirin*, and soy sauce. Bring to a simmer. Cover, lower heat and simmer gently for 10 minutes. Remove cover, turn up the flame a bit and boil off most of the liquid, stirring gently as you do so. This last step should take just a few seconds.

HIJIKI WITH SWEET POTATOES
JAPAN   (serves 4)

Read about *hijiki* in the introduction to the preceding recipe. Here, if you like, you can substitute seeded courgette strips or long cabbage shreds for the sweet potatoes. You would have to adjust the cooking times and seasonings slightly. This dish is good both warm and at room temperature. You might like to include it on a vegetable platter with Mangetouts Cooked in Dashi (see page 47), and Cabbage Cooked with Bean Curd (see page 200).

¼ breakfast cup hijiki (see   5 tbs dashi (see page 339)
   instructions in previous recipe,   ½ tsp salt
   page 42)   3–4 tsp sugar
1 medium-sized sweet potato   1 tbs mirin
   (about 10 oz/285 g)   1 tbs Japanese soy sauce
4 tbs vegetable oil   1 tbs roasted sesame seeds

Rinse the *hijiki* quickly under cold running water. Put it to soak in 1½ pt/8½ dl of warm water for 30 minutes. Lift the *hijiki* out of the water, leaving all the grit behind. Rinse it again.

Peel the sweet potato and cut it crosswise at a slight diagonal into ¼-in/¾-cm-thick slices. Now cut these slices into ¼-in/¾-cm-thick strips.

Heat the oil in a frying pan over medium heat. Add the sweet potatoes. Stir and fry for about 2 minutes. Add the *hijiki*. Stir and fry for another half minute. Add the *dashi*, salt, sugar, *mirin*, and soy sauce. Bring to a simmer. Cover, lower heat and simmer 4 minutes. Uncover, turn the heat up a bit and boil away most of the liquid, stirring gently as you do so. This last step should take you only a few seconds. Sprinkle the sesame seeds over the top.

KOHLRABI WITH CHINESE BLACK MUSHROOMS

CHINA   *(serves 4–6)*

Kohlrabi, a turnip-shaped vegetable of the cabbage family, is delicious eaten both raw and cooked. If you wish to eat it raw, just peel and slice it; then eat with a sprinkling of salt and pepper or put into salads. If you wish to eat it cooked, cut it into chunks and throw it into stews and soups. Here is a simple way to stir-fry it, Chinese style, with dried black mushrooms. If you cannot get kohlrabi, use broccoli stems. The taste is similar.

10 large Chinese dried black mushrooms
1½ lb/675 g kohlrabi (about 4 good-sized kohlrabi)
2 spring onions
1 tsp cornflour
1 tbs shaohsing wine or dry sherry

1 tsp sesame oil
¼ tsp salt
⅛ tsp freshly ground white pepper
¼ tsp sugar
3 tbs vegetable oil
2 five-pence-piece sized slices of fresh ginger, lightly mashed
1 tsp salt

Soak the mushrooms in 8 fl oz/¼ l boiling water for 30 minutes.

Take the mushrooms out of their soaking liquid. Strain the liquid. You will need 7 tbs of this strained liquid later in the recipe. Cut off and discard the hard mushroom stems. Cut the caps into ⅛-in/½-cm-thick strips.

For information about ingredients and basic techniques that may be unfamiliar, see General Information, pages 481-506.

Peel the kohlrabi, making sure you remove the tough, fibrous root ends of the vegetable. Slice into ⅛-in/½-cm-thick rounds and then cut the rounds into ⅛-in/½-cm-wide strips.

Cut the spring onions into 2-in/5-cm-long segments. Cut these segments, lengthwise, into fine strips.

Mix together in a cup the cornflour, wine, sesame oil, salt, pepper, and sugar with 3 tbs of mushroom water. Place near your cooking area. Have the remaining 4 tbs strained mushroom liquid at hand as well.

Heat the oil in a wok or heavy frying pan over a medium flame. Do not let the oil get too hot. Put in the ginger. Stir around for 10 seconds. Now put in the mushrooms, kohlrabi, and spring onions. Stir and cook for a minute. Add the 1 tsp salt and stir once. Add the remaining mushroom liquid, cover and cook for a minute. Uncover and turn heat to medium-low. Give the ingredients in the cup a stir and pour them over the vegetables. Cover and cook another minute. Lift cover and stir once. Turn off heat and serve immediately.

Sheila's
LOTUS ROOT AND TOMATOES COOKED WITH FENNEL AND DRIED GINGER
INDIA   (serves 6)

Have you ever wandered through a Chinese grocery store and stared with curiosity at lotus roots, which look like stiffened link sausages or brown sugar cane, and wondered what on earth you could do with them if you took them home? Lotus roots – they are a rhizome, really – are scrumptious in stews, mixed vegetable dishes, and, if they are young and tender, in soups and salads. First you have to scrape them as you would a new potato, or else peel them with a potato peeler and then slice them crosswise – often at a slight diagonal – into ⅛–1/16-in/½–¼-cm-thick slices. Lotus roots are harder than potatoes and full of the most prettily arranged holes. They take about as long to cook as raw beetroot – about 1–1½ hours – but you can do them in a pressure cooker in about 20 minutes. Very young lotus roots take less time to cook. When the roots are done, they do not become soft like a potato. Instead, they retain a nice crunchiness.

This dish is a Kashmiri 'stew' of sliced lotus roots and fresh tomatoes. It is not hot. It is not really spicy. It *is* very good. Kashmir's lakes are filled with lotus flowers – and therefore lotus roots. This dish is a fine example of that northern state's 'home-style' cooking.

2½ tsp whole fennel seeds
1¼ lb/560 g lotus roots
6 fl oz/1¾ dl mustard oil or other
  vegetable oil
½ tsp ground asafetida

1½ tsp whole cumin seeds
1¼ lb/560 g ripe tomatoes, peeled
  and cut into ½-in/1½-cm dice
2 tsp salt or to taste
½ tsp ground dried ginger

Grind the fennel seeds in a coffee grinder or other spice grinder.

Divide the lotus roots into links. Trim away the ends of each link. Now scrape the lotus-root skin. Cut the links, crosswise and at a slight diagonal, into ⅛–1/16-in/½–¼-cm-thick slices. Leave the slices in a bowl of water until you are ready to start cooking. Drain.

Use a pressure cooker, if you have one. Otherwise any 8-in/20-cm-wide, 3–4-qt/3½–4¼-l-capacity pot will do. Heat the oil in the pot over a medium-high flame. When it is hot, put in the asafetida and let sizzle for 5 seconds. Add the cumin seeds and, a few seconds later, the sliced lotus root. Stir and fry for 2 to 3 minutes. Now add the tomatoes, salt, fennel, and ginger. If you are using a pressure cooker, cover and bring it up to 15 lb/6½ kg pressure. Cook for 20 minutes. Relieve the pressure by putting the pot under cold running water. If you are using an ordinary pot, bring its contents to the boil, cover, lower heat, and simmer gently for 1½ hours or until lotus root is tender. Check the salt. Serve with rice to sop up the delicious sauce.

LOTUS ROOT WITH SOY-SAUCE DRESSING
KOREA/JAPAN/HONG KONG   (serves 2–4)

Lotus roots have the taste of artichoke hearts, a firm, crunchy texture, and make spectacularly pretty slices. Here is the salad-like version that I ate, with slight variations, in Korea, Hong Kong, and Japan, served warm or at room temperature or cold.

5 oz/140 g lotus roots
5 tsp Japanese soy sauce
1 tbs Japanese rice vinegar

1 tsp sugar
2 tsp sesame oil
2 tsp roasted sesame seeds

For information about ingredients and basic techniques that may be unfamiliar, see General Information, pages 481-506.

Separate the lotus-root links. Scrape off the skin with a knife or else peel it with a potato peeler. Cut into ⅛–1⁄16-in/½–¼-cm-thick slices. These slices could be rounds or, if you cut at a slight diagonal, ovals. Keep the slices in a bowl of water until you are ready to cook them.

Arrange a pot for steaming. You could have boiling water in a wok and then set a bamboo steamer just above the water, or you could place a perforated steaming trivet inside a large pot, making sure that the boiling water in the pot stays below the body of the trivet.

Drain the lotus-root slices and put them inside the perforated steaming utensil. (Some people like to line bamboo steamers with cheesecloth, lettuce leaves, or bamboo leaves first.) Cover and steam for about an hour. Remember that younger lotus roots will cook faster. Remove the lotus-root slices and place in a bowl. Mix all the remaining ingredients and pour over the lotus root. Stir to mix.

MANGETOUTS COOKED IN DASHI
JAPAN   (serves 4)

5½ oz/155 g mangetouts   1 tsp sugar
1 tsp salt   2 tsp Japanese soy sauce
2 fl oz/½ dl dashi (see page 339)

String the mangetouts by bending their little stems backwards and then dragging them along the spines of the pods. Put them in a bowl. Add ½ tsp salt and toss. Set aside for 10 minutes. Rinse the mangetouts.

Put the dashi, remaining ½ tsp salt, and sugar into a pot. Bring to a simmer. Add the mangetouts and simmer so the liquid is always bubbling, for 1 minute. Stir the mangetouts as you do this. Remove them with a slotted spoon and spread out on a plate to cool.

Add the soy sauce to the liquid in the pot. Stir and boil down for a few seconds. You should have about 2 tbs of liquid left. Let this liquid cool off. Then pour it over the mangetouts.

STUFFED MARROW
HONG KONG   (serves 4–6)

Here is a wonderful dish to make when you are entertaining. It consists of a dome made out of marrow shells, stuffed with a mixture of peas, bamboo shoots, carrots, mushrooms, and bean-curd skin. The dome sits in the centre of a platter topped with white fungus and surrounded by stir-fried broccoli.

There are several steps to the dish but since many of them can be done ahead of time, it is fairly easy to assemble quickly at the last minute. If you are going to eat the stuffed marrow in the evening, make the necessary vegetable stock (you need about 16 fl oz/½ l in all) a day in advance and refrigerate it. Do all the chopping of the vegetables and the soaking of the fungus on the morning of the same day. In the late afternoon, soak the bean-curd skin, steam the marrow and line a bowl with its outer shell. Stir-fry the stuffing and fill the marrow with it. Blanch the broccoli and rinse it under cold water. Mix the sauce that will go over the marrow. When you are ready to eat, steam the stuffed marrow to reheat it (10 minutes) and stir-fry the broccoli and white fungus (about 2 minutes).

¼ teacup white or silver ear fungus

8 sheets of dried bean-curd skin

2 small marrows (about 1¼ lb/560 g)

SAUCE FOR THE STUFFING

1 tbs cornflour

2 fl oz/½ dl Vegetable Stock (see page 340)

2 tsp Chinese thin soy sauce

1 tsp sesame oil

¼ tsp salt

⅛ tsp freshly ground white pepper

STUFFING

3 tbs vegetable oil

3 cloves garlic, peeled and finely chopped

2 five-pence-piece sized slices of fresh ginger, finely chopped

2 oz/60 g finely sliced spring onions

2 oz/60 g mushrooms, cut into ¼-in/¾-cm dice

5 oz/140 g fresh shelled or defrosted frozen peas

5 oz/140 g bamboo shoots cut into ¼-in/¾-cm dice

6 oz/180 g peeled carrots cut into ¼-in/¾-cm dice

2 fl oz/½ dl Vegetable Stock (see page 340)

6 oz/170 g broccoli flowerets, about ¾ in/2 cm at the head and 1½–2 in/4–5 cm long

SAUCE TO POUR OVER THE MARROW DOME

2 tsp cornflour

8 fl oz/¼ l Vegetable Stock (see page 340)

2 tsp Chinese thin soy sauce

1 tsp sesame oil

⅛ tsp freshly ground white pepper

¼ tsp salt

3 tbs vegetable oil

3 cloves garlic, peeled and finely chopped

¼ tsp salt

For information about ingredients and basic techniques that may be unfamiliar, see General Information, pages 481-506.

Soak the fungus in 1¼ pt/¾ l water for 15 minutes, then drain.

Rinse the dried bean curd under hot water, then soak it in hot water for 10 minutes and drain.

Meanwhile put the 2 whole marrows in a steamer and steam them for about 20 to 30 minutes or until they are tender but not mushy. Rinse them under cold water. Trim the ends of the marrows and cut them in half lengthwise.

1. Using a spoon, scoop out the seeded section in each half in such a way that it stays in one unbroken piece. Keep these seeded sections on a plate.

2. Lay the marrow shells skin side down in a single layer in a shallow, wide bowl so that they overlap very slightly. (You will eventually overturn these shells to form the dome, so neatness is important.) Press down on the shells very lightly near their ends so that they lie flat against the contours of the bowl. Rinse the soaked and drained white fungus. Feel with your fingers for the hard knots and cut them off.

Cut four of the rectangles of bean-curd skin into ½-in/¾-cm squares. Leave the other four as they are.

Mix together in a cup all the ingredients needed for the stuffing sauce and keep it beside you near the cooker.

Prepare the stuffing.

Heat 3 tbs of oil in a wok over a medium-high flame. When it is hot, put in the finely chopped garlic and ginger. Stir for about 5 seconds. Put in the spring onions and stir for about 10 seconds. Add the mushrooms. Stir-fry for about 30 seconds. Now put in the peas, bamboo shoots, carrots, and squares of bean-curd skin. Stir and fry the vegetables for about 4 minutes. Add the 2 fl oz/½ dl stock, cover and cook for 1 minute. Stir the reserved stuffing sauce and pour it over the vegetables. Stir and cook the vegetables for 30 seconds. Turn off the heat.

1   2

3. Spoon the vegetables into the marrow shell cavities. Spread them out evenly and pat them down lightly. Lay the strips of the seeded marrows in rows to cover the vegetables. Lay the rectangles of bean-curd skin in rows over the seeded marrow sections but at right angles to them. The marrow is now ready for a final steaming. Rinse the wok and dry it.

Bring 3¼ pt/2 l of water to the boil. Drop in the broccoli flowerets. Bring to the boil again. Boil rapidly for 30 seconds. Drain the broccoli in a colander and rinse it under cold running water. Leave the broccoli to drain.

About 15 minutes before you are to eat, put a round platter – about 10 in/25 cm in diameter – in a warming oven (just take the chill off).

Put the bowl with the stuffed marrows in a steamer and steam for 10 minutes or until the vegetables have heated through. (If you are not using a domed Chinese bamboo steamer, cover the vegetables lightly with a piece of foil before you steam them.) Lift the bowl out of the steamer and drain away any liquid that may have accumulated around the marrow.

3   4

For information about ingredients and basic techniques that may be unfamiliar, see General Information, pages 481-506.

4. Put the platter over the bowl.

5. Invert the bowl over the platter so the stuffed marrow looks like a dome sitting in the centre of the platter. Keep the platter in a warm place.

Mix together ingredients for the sauce that is to be poured over the marrow dome and keep it beside you near the cooker.

Heat 3 tbs of oil in the clean wok over a medium-high flame. When it is hot, put in the remaining finely chopped garlic. Stir it around for 10 seconds. Put in the broccoli and stir-fry it for about 30 seconds. Sprinkle ¼ tsp salt over the broccoli and stir to mix. Remove broccoli with a slotted spoon and quickly arrange it around the marrow dome. Put the fungus into the wok. Stir-fry it for about 30 seconds. Stir the sauce that you have near the cooker and pour it over the fungus. Stir the fungus around for 10 seconds in the sauce. Remove the fungus with a slotted spoon and put it on top of the marrow dome.

6. Pour the sauce in the wok over the dome so as not to disturb the fungus. Serve immediately.

5   6

MUSHROOMS COOKED IN ALUMINIUM FOIL
KOREA   *(serves 2–4)*

I was served these simply prepared mushrooms in many of Korea's older, traditional restaurants. The mushrooms, wrapped inside an aluminium foil packet, are cooked over direct heat— either a gas burner or live charcoal — so that all the aroma, flavour, and juices get trapped inside. The foil is then opened with notice-able flourish at the table. These mushrooms are not seasoned. They are either eaten plain as a contrast to other hot and garlicky Korean specialities, or with a dipping sauce.

6 oz/180 g mushrooms
Any one of the five Korean
*   Dipping Sauces on pages*
*   415–17.*

Wipe the mushrooms lightly with a damp cloth. Cut into ¼-in/¾-cm-thick slices that include the stem.

Cut a piece of aluminium foil, about 20 × 12 in/50 × 30 cm. Put the mushrooms in the centre of it. Cover first with the long ends and then with the short ends until you have a neat package.

You may now cook over a charcoal fire or over a gas burner. Set your grill about 4 in/10 cm above the charcoal. If you use gas, turn a burner on to low. Lay the package over the grill or the burner. As soon as steam begins to escape from the packet – a matter of 5 to 7 minutes – the mushrooms are done.

Eat the mushrooms as soon as they are done, dipping them in one of the above sauces.

Asha's
MUSHROOMS WITH ONION, GARLIC, AND GINGER
INDIA   *(serves 4)*

This is really my mother's recipe, which I have acquired via my sister-in-law. It is very simple – and good.

¾ lb/340 g medium-sized
*   mushrooms*
A 1-in/2½-cm cube of fresh
*   ginger, peeled and finely grated*
6 cloves garlic, peeled and mashed
*   to a pulp or grated*

4 tbs vegetable oil
1 medium-sized onion, peeled and
*   very finely chopped*
¼ tsp ground turmeric
⅛ tsp cayenne pepper, or more to
*   taste*
½–¾ tsp salt

Wipe the mushrooms with a damp cloth and then halve them.

Combine the ginger and garlic in a small cup with 3 tbs water.

Heat the oil in a 7-in/18-cm-wide pot over a medium-high flame.

For information about ingredients and basic techniques that may be unfamiliar, see General Information, pages 481-506.

When hot, put in the chopped onion and fry, stirring, for about 2 minutes or until onion is a golden-brown colour. Add the ginger–garlic paste. Keep stirring and frying for another 2 minutes. If the water evaporates, sprinkle a little more in (about 2 tsp). Now add the turmeric and cayenne. Stir for a second. Add the mushrooms, ½ tsp salt, and 4 fl oz/1 dl water. Stir, and bring to a simmer. Cover, lower heat, and simmer gently for 10 minutes. Check the salt. You may wish to add a bit more. Stir. Serve with an Indian bread or a rice dish.

MUSHROOMS IN A SAUCE, WITH SESAME SEEDS
INDIA   *(serves 6)*

This dish was, traditionally, made by North Indians with the seasonal and very delicate monsoon mushrooms that begin to sprout out of the damp earth around July and completely disappear by mid-September. Today, with common white-cap mushrooms available all year round, many well-heeled Delhi residents assuage their palates with the hardier, farm-grown variety.

30 medium-sized, well-formed
   mushrooms (1¼–1½ lb/
   560–675 g)
1 large or 2 small onions, peeled
   and coarsely chopped
4–6 cloves garlic, peeled and
   coarsely chopped
A ½-in/1½-cm cube of fresh
   ginger, peeled and coarsely
   chopped

5 tbs vegetable oil
2 tsp tomato purée mixed with
   2 tbs water
2 tsp ground coriander
1 tsp ground cumin
½ tsp salt
Freshly ground black pepper to
   taste
⅛ tsp cayenne pepper, or to taste
1 tbs lemon juice
1 tbs roasted sesame seeds

Cut off the mushroom stems so they are level with the caps. Reserve the stalks for making stock. Wipe mushrooms with a damp cloth.

Put the chopped onions, garlic, and ginger into the container of an electric blender or food processor along with 2 fl oz/½ dl water. Blend until you have a smooth paste.

Heat the oil in a 10-in/25-cm-wide pot, sauté pan, or deep frying pan over a medium flame. When hot, pour in the paste from the blender (keep face averted). Stir and fry for 8 to 10 minutes or until paste is a golden-brown colour. Lower the flame and add the tomato purée mixture, the coriander, cumin, salt, black pepper, and cayenne. Fry, stirring, for 1 minute. Now put in the mushroom caps, lemon juice, and ¼ pt/1½ dl water. Mix well and bring to the boil. Cover, lower heat, and simmer gently for 15 minutes. Stir every now and then during this cooking period.

Neatly arrange 5 mushrooms in the centre of each of 6 small, shallow bowls. Spoon a little sauce over each serving. Then sprinkle the roasted sesame seeds on top of the mushroom caps.

Audrey Chan's
THREE AUNTIES AND THREE GRANDMOTHERS
(Three Kinds of Mushrooms and Three Kinds of Vegetables)
SINGAPORE   *(serves 4–6)*

I love this dish. It is fairly easy to make, especially if you have access to the Chinese vegetable, *choy sum*, which I have seen only in Chinese grocery stores. Its stalks and leaves are a rich green colour and sometimes there are a few yellow flowers as well. If you cannot find it use broccoli as a substitute.

10 medium-sized Chinese dried
   black mushrooms
¾ lb/340 g choy sum
1 tsp cornflour
⅛–¼ tsp freshly ground white
   pepper
1 tsp salt
5 tbs vegetable oil
2 cloves garlic, peeled and finely
   chopped
2 shallots, peeled and finely
   chopped

1 tsp sesame oil
4 oz/115 g tinned button
   mushrooms, drained
4 oz/115 g tinned straw
   mushrooms, drained
6 tinned or cooked ears of baby
   corn, drained, cut in half
   lengthwise
3 fresh (or tinned) water
   chestnuts, peeled and sliced into
   ⅛-in/½-cm-thick rounds

For information about ingredients and basic techniques that may be unfamiliar, see General Information, pages 481-506.

Soak the dried mushrooms in 8 fl oz/¼ l hot water. Remove them after 1 hour, saving the liquid. Cut off and discard the coarse stems. Cut each cap in half and set aside. Strain the soaking liquid.

Trim away the coarse, woody section of the *choy sum* stems, if there are any. (Sometimes the lower stems can just be peeled.) Otherwise leave the stems attached, just as you bought them. Wash the *choy sum* and stack it neatly into a bundle so it looks very much like the bundle you bought, with all the stalks facing the same direction. (Broccoli may be cut into long, slim flowerets. Peel the coarser stalks.)

Combine the mushroom liquid, cornflour, white pepper, and salt. Mix thoroughly and set aside.

Heat 3 tbs oil in a large wok over a medium-high flame. When hot, put in half of the garlic and half of the shallots. Stir and fry for about 30 seconds. Then put in about 1 qt/11½ dl of water. Cover, and bring the water to the boil. Remove the cover and put in the bundle of greens, all stalks facing the same direction. The greens should be almost completely submerged; if they are not, add some more boiling water. The stalks must stay underwater as they need to cook more thoroughly. Boil the greens rapidly for about a minute, turning them over occasionally with tongs or chopsticks so that those on the top get a chance to go to the bottom. By this time, the stalks should be just tender. Turn off the heat. Lift the *choy sum* out of the water and put it, still in a bundle, on a cutting board. Cut it into 3-in/8-cm lengths. Put the *choy sum* on a long, warmed platter, re-forming the original bundle shape, with all the stalks on one side, the leaves on the other. Keep the platter in a warm place.

Work quickly now. Rinse the wok and dry it. Heat 2 tbs of vegetable oil and the 1 tsp of sesame oil in the wok over a medium-high flame. When hot, put in the remaining garlic and shallots. Stir them around for 10 seconds. Add the soaked, drained black mushrooms. Stir and fry them for about 30 seconds. Push them to one side and put in the button and straw mushrooms. Stir and fry them for about 30 seconds and push them to one side as well. Put in the baby corn and water chestnuts. Stir and fry them for a second. Mix up all the vegetables. Cover and cook for 1 minute. Uncover and turn the heat down to medium-low. Stir the cornflour mixture and add it to the vegetables. Stir to mix. Cover again for 30 seconds. Uncover and give a final stir.

Quickly spread the mushroom–chestnut–corn mixture over the *choy sum*. Pour the sauce in the wok evenly over all the vegetables. Serve immediately with plain rice.

SWEET AND SALTY DRIED SHIITAKE MUSHROOMS

JAPAN *(serves 4 at a Japanese meal)*

½ oz/15 g or about 6–7 medium-
  sized dried shiitake *mushrooms*
2 tbs *Japanese soy sauce*
2 tbs *sugar*

Rinse the mushrooms quickly under cold running water and then soak in 8 fl oz/¼ l boiling water for ½ hour.

Remove the mushrooms from their soaking liquid (save the liquid for soups) and cut away the coarse stems. Slice the mushroom caps into ⅛-in/½-cm-thick slices.

Put the mushroom caps, soy sauce, and sugar in a small pot and bring to a simmer. Cook on low heat for about 4 minutes. A little liquid should remain.

STIR-FRIED TREE EAR FUNGUS AND SUMMER OYSTER MUSHROOMS

HONG KONG *(serves 4–6)*

The Chinese believe very firmly in the curative powers of various varieties of fungi, with the expensive silver ear fungus often displayed in glass cases at Hong Kong restaurants as if it were priceless porcelain. Tree ear fungus is a cheaper variety, but still credited with preventing heart disease.

Because tinned vegetables can sometimes taste quite 'tinny', I boil them briefly in vegetable stock to rid them of this unpleasant flavour. (I have done so with the summer oyster mushrooms.)

¼ breakfast cup *tree ear fungus*
1 10-oz/285-g tin of summer
  oyster mushrooms
10 medium-sized fresh mushrooms
16 fl oz/½ l Delicious Stock . . . (see
  page 340) or any vegetable stock
1 tsp cornflour
1 tbs shaohsing wine or dry
  sherry

1 tsp sesame oil
1 tsp Chinese thin soy sauce
½ tsp sugar
2 fl oz/½ dl vegetable oil
1 clove garlic, peeled and finely
  chopped
½ tsp salt, or to taste
1 spring onion, cut into ⅛-in/½-
  cm-thick rounds

For information about ingredients and basic techniques that may be unfamiliar, see General Information, pages 481-506.

Rinse the tree ear fungus and soak in 16 fl oz/½ l boiling water for ½ hour. Remove from the soaking liquid and rinse. Feel for the hard 'eyes' and cut them out.

Drain the summer oyster mushrooms. The sizes of the pieces may vary, so make sure that none is longer than 1½ in/4 cm or wider than ½ in/1½ cm.

Wipe the fresh mushrooms and cut them into ¼-in/¾-cm-thick slices.

Combine the tree ear fungus and oyster mushrooms in a 1½-qt/1¾-l pot. Add the stock and bring to the boil. Cover, turn heat to low and simmer for 3 minutes. Uncover and allow to cool for at least 1 hour. Drain, reserving 3 tbs of the broth. (The rest of the broth may be saved for another dish.)

Combine the cornflour, wine, 3 tbs of broth, sesame oil, soy sauce, and sugar in a small cup. Mix until smooth and set aside.

Heat the oil in a wok or heavy frying pan over a medium-high flame. When hot, put in the garlic. Stir and fry for 15 seconds. Add the sliced fresh mushrooms. Stir and fry for 1 minute. Now put in the tree ear fungus, the summer oyster mushrooms, and the salt. Stir and fry for 2 minutes. Turn heat to medium-low. Stir the ingredients in the cup and pour them over the contents of the wok. Add the spring onion. Cover and cook for 1 minute. Remove cover and stir again. Serve immediately with plain rice.

MOREL MUSHROOMS WITH PEAS
INDIA   *(serves 4)*

Morels grow in the northern state of Kashmir. They are dried and shipped to the rest of the country. For more on the subject, see the introduction to Kashmir-Style Gucchi Pullao, page 171.

½ oz/15 g dried or 12 fresh morel
  mushrooms
A 1-in/2½-cm cube of fresh
  ginger, peeled

4 cloves garlic, peeled
3 tbs vegetable oil or ghee
1 tsp ground coriander seeds
2 tsp ground cumin seeds

¼ tsp ground turmeric
⅛ tsp cayenne pepper
6 oz/180 g tomatoes (1 large or 2
    small), peeled and finely
    chopped
12 oz/340 g fresh shelled or
    defrosted frozen peas
1½ tsp salt
¼ tsp garam masala

Rinse the dried morels quickly and then leave them to soak in
12 fl oz/3½ dl water for 20 to 30 minutes or until they are quite
tender; if you are using fresh, there is no need, of course, to soak
them. Lift out the mushrooms from the soaking liquid. Strain the
soaking liquid through a clean piece of cloth and set it aside. Cut
each mushroom in half lengthwise.

Put the ginger and garlic into the container of a food processor or
blender. Add 2 fl oz/½ dl water and blend until you have a smooth
paste. Heat the oil in a 2½–3-qt/3–3½-l pot over medium heat.
When hot, put in the paste from the food processor (keep face
averted). Stir and fry for 1 minute. Add the coriander, cumin,
turmeric, and cayenne. Stir and fry for another minute. Put in the
chopped tomato. Stir and fry for about 3 minutes, gently mashing
the pieces of tomato with the back of your stirring spoon. You
should end up with a relatively smooth paste. Now put in the
morels, their strained soaking liquid (or 12 fl oz/3½ dl water, if you
are using fresh morels), the peas, and the salt. Bring to a simmer.
Cover, lower heat and simmer gently for 10 minutes. Add the
garam masala. Stir to mix.

WHOLE OKRA
INDIA   *(serves 6)*

1½ lb/675 g fresh, tender okra   ½ tsp ground turmeric
6 tbs vegetable oil   1¼–1½ tsp salt
2 medium-sized onions, peeled and   ⅛ tsp freshly ground black pepper
    finely chopped   1/16–⅛ tsp cayenne pepper
6 cloves garlic, peeled and finely   (optional)
    chopped

---

*For information about ingredients and basic techniques that may be unfamiliar, see General
Information, pages 481-506.*

Wash okra and trim it. (To trim whole okra, cut off a small section at the tip. The stem end looks prettiest if trimmed in a conical shape.)

Heat oil in a 10–12-in/25–30-cm frying pan over a medium flame. Add the onions and garlic and fry, stirring frequently, for 5 minutes. Add okra and fry for another 5 minutes. Now put in the turmeric, salt, black pepper, cayenne, and 2 fl oz/½ dl water. Stir well to mix. Cover tightly, lower heat, and steam gently for about 15 to 20 minutes or until okra is tender. (Larger pods will take a bit longer to cook through.) Stir very gently every 5 minutes, replacing the lid each time. If any extra liquid remains in the frying pan, it should be boiled away so okra has a 'dry' look.

Usha's
SWEET-AND-SOUR OKRA WITH CHICK PEAS
INDIA   (serves 4–6)

This is a wonderful dish and a great family favourite. Not only is it fairly simple to make, but it can be made a day in advance. In fact, the flavour seems to improve if it sits overnight in the refrigerator. The original recipe called for only okra. You can make it that way, if you like – it is scrumptious. I added the chick peas to improve the food value of the dish and because I think that the combination of okra and chick peas, drenched in a sweet and sour tamarind sauce, is quite felicitous. This is an easy dish to prepare in advance. Remember that fresh okra should always be washed and wiped *before* it is cut.

¾ lb/340 g fresh okra
4 tbs vegetable oil
1 tsp whole black mustard seeds
6–7 fresh or 9–10 dried curry
   leaves (optional)
8 cloves garlic, peeled and finely
   chopped
1 tsp ground cumin seeds
2 tsp ground coriander seeds

½ tsp ground turmeric
⅛ tsp cayenne pepper, or more to
   taste
6 oz/180 g drained chick peas,
   tinned or home-cooked (see page
   103)
½ tsp salt
2 tbs tamarind paste
1 tbs sugar

Wash the okra and dry it off. Trim it at the ends. The top looks best if trimmed – almost peeled – in a cone shape. Now cut the okra crosswise into ½-in/1½-cm pieces.

Heat the oil in an 8–9-in/20–23-cm frying pan over a medium flame. When hot, put in the mustard seeds and the curry leaves. A few seconds later, put in the garlic. Stir and fry until the garlic pieces turn brown at the edges. Now put in the okra, cumin, coriander, turmeric, and cayenne. Stir and cook for 1 minute. Add 8 fl oz/¼ l water. Bring to a simmer, cover, turn heat to low, and cook gently for 10 minutes or until okra is almost done. Now add the chick peas, salt, tamarind paste, and sugar. Mix gently. Bring to a simmer again. Cover and cook on low heat another 5 minutes. Stir.

OKRA FRIED WITH ONION AND GREEN CHILLI

INDIA   (serves 2 as a vegetable, more as a
                                            topping for rice or in yogurt)

If you wish to double the recipe, double the okra, onion, green chilli, and salt. Use a 12-in/30-cm frying pan with a good ½-in/1½-cm of oil in it. The cooking time should remain about the same.

6 oz/180 g fresh okra   ½ fresh hot green chilli, finely
1 small onion   chopped
Vegetable oil for shallow frying   ⅛ tsp salt

Wash the okra and pat it as dry as possible. Trim the okra at both ends and cut into ⅛-in/½-cm rounds.

Peel the onion. Cut it in half lengthwise and then cut into very fine half circles. Heat ⅓ in/1 cm oil in an 8–9-in/20–23-cm frying pan over a medium flame. When the oil is very hot, put in the okra, onion, and green chilli. Turn heat to medium-high. Stir and fry for about 10 minutes or until okra is crisp and onion is a medium-brown colour and also crisp. Remove with a slotted spoon and put on a plate lined with kitchen paper. Sprinkle salt over okra, mix, and serve hot.

OKRA WITH TOMATOES

KUWAIT   (serves 6)

1½ lb/675 g fresh, tender okra   2 medium-sized tomatoes, peeled
6 tbs olive oil   and coarsely chopped
4 cloves garlic, peeled and finely   1 tsp ground coriander
   chopped   1½ tsp salt, or to taste
2 medium-sized onions, peeled and   ⅛ tsp freshly ground black pepper
   cut into ¾-in/2-cm dice   1 tbs lemon juice

For information about ingredients and basic techniques that may be unfamiliar, see General Information, pages 481-506.

Wash the okra and trim it. (To trim the okra, cut off a small section at the tip. The stem end looks prettiest if trimmed in a conical shape.)

Heat the oil in a 10–12-in/25–30-cm frying pan over a medium flame. Put in the garlic and onions. Stir and fry until onions turn translucent, turning the heat down if necessary. Put in the okra. Stir and fry for another minute. Now put in all the remaining ingredients plus 4 fl oz/1 dl water, stir, and bring to a simmer. Cover, turn heat to low, and cook gently for 15 to 20 minutes or until okra is tender. (Larger pods will take a bit longer to cook through.)

Serve either hot or cold.

PEAS WITH GINGER
JAPAN   (serves 4)

8 fl oz/¼ l dashi (see page 339)   10 oz/285 g shelled peas, fresh or
½ tsp sugar   frozen (if frozen defrost under
½ tsp mirin   running warm water)
1 tsp Japanese soy sauce   2 tsp finely grated fresh ginger
¼ tsp salt

Combine the *dashi*, sugar, *mirin*, soy sauce, and salt in a small (1½-qt/1¾-l) pot. Add the peas and bring to the boil. Cover, lower heat, and simmer about 5 minutes or until the peas are tender. Drain but do not discard the liquid.

Divide the peas into four portions, put each portion in the centre of a small bowl and add 1 tbs of the cooking liquid. Now arrange a small cone of grated ginger − ½ tsp to a serving − on top of each pile of peas. Before eating, each diner uses his chopsticks to mix the ginger with the peas.

PEAS WITH PARSLEY AND COCONUT
INDIA   (serves 6)

This Gujarati dish is normally made with fresh peas and fresh green coriander. Once, when those two ingredients were unavailable, I came up with this variation.

4 oz/115 g freshly grated coconut   3 tbs sesame seeds, dry roasted and
2 oz/55 g finely chopped parsley   coarsely ground
1 fresh hot green chilli, finely   ⅛ tsp freshly ground black pepper
   chopped   3 10-oz/285-g packets frozen peas
¾–1 tsp salt   4 tbs unsalted butter
2 tsp sugar

In a bowl, mix together the coconut, parsley, green chilli, salt, sugar, sesame seeds, and black pepper. Rub with your hands to mix thoroughly.

Bring 16 fl oz/½ l of water to the boil in a heavy saucepan. Add the peas. Bring to the boil again. Cover and cook 2 minutes. Empty the peas into a colander and drain away the water. Melt the butter in the same saucepan over a low flame. Add the peas and stir them around in the butter. Add the coconut–parsley mixture and mix gently. Cover the saucepan and steam the peas on very low heat for about 2 to 3 minutes. Stir once or twice as the peas steam.

GREEN PEPPERS COOKED WITH GRAM FLOUR
INDIA   *(serves 4–6)*

In this dish, tiny lumps of cooked gram flour cling to diced, sautéed green peppers just as bits of bread stuffing might cling to pieces of onion or celery. The use of gram flour makes the dish a bit more substantial and a bit more nutritious.

1½ oz/45 g gram flour	1 tsp whole black mustard seeds
3 large green peppers	1 tsp salt
5 tbs vegetable oil	1 tbs finely chopped fresh green
⅛ tsp ground asafetida	coriander
1/16–⅛ tsp cayenne pepper	1/16 tsp freshly ground black pepper

Sift the gram flour. Place the flour in a small, heavy, preferably cast-iron frying pan, and roast it on a medium flame, stirring constantly, until it turns a few shades darker. A good way to check if it is done is to taste a pinch of it. It should not taste raw. It will also have developed a 'roasted' aroma. Empty the gram flour in a bowl and set it aside.

Cut peppers in half, then core and seed them. Chop into ¼–⅓-in/ ¾–1-cm dice.

Heat the oil in an 8-in/20-cm (preferably nonstick) frying or sauté pan over a medium flame. When it is hot, put in first the asafetida and then, a second later, the cayenne pepper. Stir once. Add the mustard seeds. As soon as the mustard seeds begin to pop, put in the diced peppers. Stir and sauté them over a medium-high flame for about 5 minutes or until they are just cooked. Now turn heat to medium and put in the salt, the fresh coriander, the black pepper, and the roasted gram flour. Stir a few times. Gradually add 3 fl oz/

For information about ingredients and basic techniques that may be unfamiliar, see General Information, pages 481-506.

¾ dl water, stirring gently and scraping off all the gram flour that clings to the bottom of the pan. Cook for 2 minutes, stirring and scraping the bottom. Turn down the heat if the gram flour seems to be catching. Now turn off the heat. Let the pan sit for a minute. Stir and scrape the bottom once again.

Zakiya's
POTATOES AND ONIONS

INDIA
(serves 4–6 as a vegetable dish and will stuff 8 dosas)

This dish, while it can be eaten as part of any Indian meal, forms the traditional 'stuffing' for *dosas* (see page 310). The *dosa*, a kind of pancake or bread made with rice and *urad dal*, is put on a plate, some potato–onion mixture is placed on top of it, and the *dosa* folded over once. The stuffed *dosa* is called a *Masala Dosa* and serves the same function as a sandwich in the West.

4 medium-sized potatoes
   (1 lb/450 g)
A ¾-in/2-cm cube fresh ginger,
   peeled and cut into 3–4 pieces
1 fresh hot green chilli, or more to
   taste, cut into 2–3 pieces
2 fl oz/½ dl vegetable oil

A generous pinch of ground
   asafetida
1 tsp whole black mustard seeds
2 medium-sized onions, peeled and
   coarsely chopped
¼ tsp ground turmeric
1 tsp salt

Boil the potatoes until tender. Let them cool, then peel and cut them into ¾-in/2-cm dice.

Put the ginger and green chilli into the container of a food processor or blender along with 2 fl oz/½ dl of water and blend until you have a somewhat grainy paste. Set aside.

Heat the oil in an 8–9-in/20–30-cm frying pan over a medium flame. When hot, put in the asafetida first and then, a second later, the mustard seeds. As soon as the mustard seeds begin to pop (this takes just a few seconds), put in the onions. Turn the heat down slightly and sauté the onions for about 5 minutes or until they turn translucent. (Do not let them brown.) Now add the paste from the food processor as well as the turmeric. Stir and cook for 1 minute. Put in the potatoes, 8 fl oz/¼ l water, and the salt. Cover, and cook on medium-low heat for about 5 minutes. Lift cover and, using a slotted spoon, break the potato pieces into smaller ⅓–½-in/ 1–1½-cm cubes. Cover again and cook on very low heat for another 3 to 4 minutes. The 'sauce' for the potato dish should now be very thick. Serve either as it is or stuff *Masala Dosa* according to directions on page 312.

Usha's
POTATOES AND TOMATOES COOKED WITH FRESH COCONUT
INDIA   *(serves 6)*

I love this dish with an irrational passion. Irrational, because the basic ingredient, the very humble potato, does not go through some glamorous transformation. It does not, for example, turn into anything resembling the many-petalled Pommes Anna. Nor is it mashed and squeezed into soft, dainty patterns. No, here the humble potato stays the humble potato and is cooked, very simply, with rather prosaic ingredients − garlic, tomatoes, cumin, turmeric, and coconut. But the dish is utterly delicious, especially when eaten with Indian breads.

I am not sure what region of India is responsible for this tasty marvel. I got this recipe from a friend whose parents, from the western Kutch region, often cooked it. She suspects the dish is Kutchi, but is not sure. It is a kind of thick, earthy potato stew.

NOTE: Do not use an aluminium pot for this dish.

5 medium-sized potatoes (about 1¼ lb/560 g)	2 tsp ground cumin seeds
4 tbs vegetable oil	1¼ lb/560 g fresh, ripe tomatoes, peeled and diced into ½-in/
6 cloves garlic, peeled and finely chopped	1½-cm pieces, or a 16–20 oz/ 450–560 g tin of Italian
1 whole dried hot red pepper	tomatoes
1 tsp whole cumin seeds	2 tsp salt
5 oz/140 g freshly grated coconut	2 tsp sugar
½ tsp ground turmeric	1 tsp red wine vinegar

Peel the potatoes, then cut into ¾-in/2-cm dice and put into a bowl of cold water.

Heat the oil in a heavy, 3-qt/3½-l pot over a medium-high flame. When hot, put in the finely chopped garlic. Stir for about 5 seconds. Now put in the red pepper and the cumin seeds. Stir for another 3 seconds. The garlic should brown lightly, the red pepper should darken, and the cumin seeds should sizzle. Lower the heat to medium, put in the grated coconut and stir it around for 10 to 15 seconds.

Drain the potatoes. Add them as well as the turmeric, ground cumin, tomatoes (including any juice that may have accumulated or the juice in the tin), the salt, and 12 fl oz/3½ dl of water. Bring to

---

For information about ingredients and basic techniques that may be unfamiliar, see General Information, pages 481-506.

the boil. Cover, turn heat to low, and simmer for about 45 minutes or until potatoes are tender. Stir gently every 7 to 8 minutes during this cooking period.

Put in the sugar and vinegar. Stir again and cook, uncovered, for 1 minute.

POTATOES WITH CHICK PEAS

MIDDLE EAST   *(serves 6)*

6 tbs olive oil
3 cloves garlic, peeled and finely chopped
2 medium-sized onions, peeled and coarsely chopped
3 medium-sized tomatoes, peeled and chopped

4 medium-sized potatoes, freshly boiled, peeled, and cut into ¾-in/2-cm dice
8 oz/225 g drained, cooked chick peas (see page 103)
1½–2 tsp salt, or to taste
⅛ tsp freshly ground black pepper
1½ tbs lemon juice

Heat the oil in a 10-in/25-cm frying pan over a medium flame. When hot, put in the garlic and onions. Stir and fry until onions are translucent, turning the heat down if necessary. Add the chopped tomatoes. Stir and cook for 1 minute. Add all the remaining ingredients plus 8 fl oz/¼ l water. Bring to the boil. Cover. Lower heat and simmer gently for 20 minutes.

POTATO STEW

CHINA   *(serves 4–6)*

This is one of those Chinese vegetable dishes that is not stir-fried. There are many hearty stews cooked all over China, though such dishes are rarely served in Chinese restaurants in the West. Here is one such dish. The vegetables do not retain any of their crispness or their colour. They turn quite soft from the slower cooking and quite dark from the soy sauce. None the less, they are very tasty.

This dish may be cooked ahead of time and reheated. If you wish to do that, leave about 1 in/2½ cm of sauce at the bottom; this way you can do the boiling down and the reheating simultaneously.

2 fl oz/½ dl vegetable oil
2 cloves garlic, peeled and lightly
  crushed
2 five-pence-piece sized slices of
  fresh ginger, lightly crushed
¾ lb/340 g potatoes, peeled and cut
  roughly into 1½-in/4-cm cubes
½ lb/225 g green beans, trimmed
  and cut into 2-in/5-cm lengths

2 carrots, peeled and cut crosswise
  into 1½-in/4-cm-long segments
6 oz/180 g mushrooms (if possible,
  with approximately 1½-in/4-cm
  caps)
2 fl oz/½ dl Chinese dark soy sauce
4 tsp sugar
2 tbs shaohsing wine or dry
  sherry

Heat the oil in an 8-in/20-cm-wide, heavy-bottomed pot over a medium-high flame. When hot, put in the garlic and ginger. Stir and fry for 15 seconds. Add the potatoes, beans, and carrots. Stir and fry for 1 minute. Add the mushrooms. Stir and fry for another minute. Now put in 16 fl oz/½ l water, the soy sauce, sugar, and wine. Bring to the boil. Cover, lower heat, and simmer for about 20 minutes or until potatoes are just tender. Remove cover and turn heat to high. Boil away most of the liquid. You should have about ⅛ in/½ cm of sauce left at the bottom of the pot. Stir the vegetables gently as you boil the liquid down. Remove the ginger and garlic, if you like.

Pallavi's
ALOO ACHAAR
(Potato Salad)
NEPAL   (serves 4–6)

Eaten frequently as a snack, this potato salad comes from the kingdom of Nepal on India's northern frontier. Its dressing is made with ground sesame seeds, sesame oil, lemon juice, and hot green chillies. The chillies provide the 'hotness' and lots of vitamin C. If you do not like hot foods, green peppers can be substituted for the hot chilli. Asafetida is also used in this recipe, chiefly because

For information about ingredients and basic techniques that may be unfamiliar, see General Information, pages 481-506.

of its digestive powers. Even though *Aloo achaar* can be eaten an hour or two after it's made, it tastes best when the dressing has been allowed to be absorbed for 12 hours; it keeps well in the refrigerator for 3 to 4 days.

4 medium-sized waxy potatoes
  (about 1 lb)
4 tbs ground roasted sesame seeds
3 tbs or more lemon juice
1 tsp salt
1–4 fresh hot green chillies, very
  finely chopped, or 2 tbs finely
  chopped green pepper

4 tbs sesame oil
2 tsp vegetable oil
A pinch of ground asafetida
8–10 whole fenugreek seeds
3 tbs finely chopped fresh green
  coriander, or parsley

Put the potatoes to boil.

Combine the ground sesame seeds, lemon juice, salt, and green chillies in a stainless steel or non-metallic bowl. Add the 4 tbs of sesame oil a few drops at a time, and beat in with a thin wire whisk or a fork.

Heat the vegetable oil in a metal ladle (hold the ladle over the heat) or a small butter warmer. When very hot, put in the asafetida and the fenugreek seeds. As soon as the fenugreek seeds begin to darken (this takes just a few seconds), pour the oil and spices into the dressing. Mix well. Add the finely chopped coriander and mix again. Check seasonings.

When the potatoes are cooked, drain and peel them while they are still hot. If necessary, hold them with a fork to do so. Dice the hot potatoes into ¾-in/2-cm cubes. Put the diced potatoes into the bowl with the dressing and mix gently. Adjust seasonings, if necessary. Let cool, cover, and refrigerate if not eating within the next couple of hours. This salad may be eaten cold or at room temperature.

'DRY' POTATOES COOKED WITH MUSTARD SEEDS
INDIA   (serves 4)

Traditionally, this dish is made in a *karhai* (wok), but a frying pan will work very well also.

5–6 medium-sized potatoes, the
  waxier the better (1½ lb/675 g)
6 tbs vegetable oil
1/16 tsp ground asafetida

1 tbs whole black mustard seeds
¼ tsp ground turmeric
¾–1 tsp salt
1/16–1/8 tsp cayenne pepper

Peel the potatoes and dice them into ¾-in/2-cm pieces. Put the diced potatoes into a bowl of water and drain them just before you start to cook.

Heat the oil in a 10–12-in/25–30-cm frying pan over a medium-high flame. As soon as the oil is hot, put in the asafetida. A second after that, put in the mustard seeds. Half a second after that, put in the turmeric. Now quickly put in the drained potatoes. Stir and fry for ½ minute. Cover the potatoes and turn flame to low. Cook, covered, for about half an hour or until potatoes are cooked through but retain their shape. Stir gently every 5 to 7 minutes, replacing the cover each time. When the potatoes are done, sprinkle the salt and cayenne over them. Stir again to mix.

DUM ALOO
(Moghlai Potatoes in a Thick Brown Sauce)
INDIA   (serves 4–6)

When the Moghuls ruled India, not too many vegetables were eaten in their grand courts. They ate salads – raw cucumber, tomatoes, and radishes – as well as cooked spinach. And they ate potatoes. The potatoes were often cooked as if they were meat, in thick, dark sauces. A cooking technique that the formerly nomadic Moghuls had picked up during their sojourn in areas like modern Uzbekistan, Kazakhstan, Iran, and Afghanistan, was something they referred to as *dum*. It was a form of covered baking – of letting foods cook in their own steam – without using ovens of any kind. After a food had been browned, it was put into a heavy pot along with fried onions, spices, and herbs, and then covered with a heavy lid. A long, snake-like roll of dough was wrapped around the outer edges of the lid to seal the pot completely. The pot was placed over very low heat – often just smouldering ashes – and extra live coals were piled on top of the lid. The food, getting gentle heat from above and below, 'baked' slowly.

Even though what you see below is the classic recipe for *Dum Aloo*, I cook the dish entirely on top of the cooker, without any live coals on the lid!

12 smallish potatoes (about 1½ lb/ 675 g)
1 tbs plus about ¾ tsp salt
8–10 blanched almonds (½ oz/15 g)
2 tbs white poppy seeds

2 large black cardamom pods
2 tsp ground coriander seeds
1½ tsp whole cumin seeds
4 cloves garlic, peeled and chopped

For information about ingredients and basic techniques that may be unfamiliar, see General Information, pages 481-506.

A 1-in/2½-cm cube fresh ginger,
  peeled and chopped
8 tbs vegetable oil
1 medium-sized onion, peeled and
  finely chopped
5 whole cardamom pods, very
  lightly crushed
¼ tsp ground turmeric
⅛ tsp cayenne pepper
8 fl oz/¼ l plain yogurt
1 tsp garam masala

Peel the potatoes and prick them well with a fork. Soak them for 1 hour in a bowl with 1½ pt/8½ dl water and 1 tbs salt.

Meanwhile, put the almonds, white poppy seeds, black cardamom, ground coriander, and 1 tsp of the whole cumin seeds in a small cast-iron frying pan and dry-roast them, stirring frequently, until the almonds turn golden in spots. Put all the roasted ingredients into the container of a clean coffee grinder and grind as finely as possible. Leave in grinder container.

Put the garlic and ginger, along with 3 fl oz/1 dl water, into the container of an electric blender or food processor. Blend until you have a smooth paste. Leave in blender container.

When the potatoes have soaked for an hour, drain and wipe them well. Heat oil in a heavy, 10-in/25-cm-wide pot, sauté pan, or deep frying pan over a medium flame. Put in the potatoes and fry them, stirring, until they turn a golden brown on all sides. Remove with a slotted spoon and set aside on a plate.

Add the remaining ½ tsp whole cumin seeds to the oil in the pot and stir once. Now put in the finely chopped onion. Fry, stirring, until the onion turns a light brown. Add the crushed cardamom pods, the turmeric, and the cayenne. Fry and stir for a few seconds. Next, put in the garlic and ginger paste from the blender, the nut and spice mixture from the coffee grinder, and ¾ tsp salt. Stir and fry the mixture. Whenever it seems to dry up and begins to get ready to catch at the bottom, add a tbs of yogurt. Keep stirring and frying, adding yogurt whenever necessary, until all the yogurt is used up. (It is important that the yogurt fry and assimilate slowly with the sauce. This can only happen if a little yogurt is added at a time.)

Add *garam masala* and 4 fl oz/1 dl water. Mix well. Put in the browned potatoes and mix gently. Cover the pot tightly with aluminium foil, making sure you crimp and seal the edges, and then with its own lid. Turn heat to very low and cook gently for about 30 minutes or until potatoes are cooked through. Stir gently a few times while the potatoes are cooking, always replacing the foil and the lid. The potatoes should have a very thick sauce clinging to them when they are done.

DICED POTATOES WITH SPINACH
INDIA   *(serves 6)*

All over North India, potatoes are cooked with greens. Fenugreek greens are preferred, but spinach makes a good alternative.

5–6 medium-sized waxy potatoes (about 2 lb/900 g)
1 tbs plus 1 tsp salt
1 lb/450 g fresh or 1 packet frozen leaf spinach
6 tbs vegetable oil or ghee
½ tsp whole black mustard seeds

1 large onion (3–3½ oz/85–100 g), peeled and chopped
2 cloves garlic, peeled and finely chopped
1 tsp garam masala
¹⁄₁₆–⅛ tsp cayenne pepper (optional)

Bring 2½ pt/1½ l of water to the boil. Peel potatoes and dice into ¾-in/2-cm cubes, then add to boiling water with 1 tbs salt. Bring to the boil again. Cover, turn heat to low and cook potatoes until they are just tender – about 6 minutes. Do not overcook. Drain. Spread potatoes out and leave to cool.

If using fresh spinach, wash carefully and drop into large pan of boiling water to wilt. Drain. Squeeze out as much liquid as possible from spinach and chop fine. If using frozen leaf spinach, cook according to instructions. Drain, squeeze out liquid, and chop. Set aside.

Heat oil in a heavy, 12-in/30-cm, preferably nonstick frying pan over a medium-high flame. When very hot, put in the mustard seeds. As soon as the seeds begin to pop (this just takes a few seconds), add the onion and garlic. Turn heat to medium and fry for 3 to 4 minutes. Onions should turn very lightly brown at the edges. Now put in the chopped spinach and keep stirring and frying for another 10 minutes.

Add the cooked potatoes, 1 tsp salt, the *garam masala*, and the cayenne pepper. Stir and mix gently until potatoes are heated through.

For information about ingredients and basic techniques that may be unfamiliar, see General Information, pages 481–506.

POTATOES WITH WHOLE SPICES AND SESAME SEEDS
INDIA *(serves 6)*

Here is another scrumptious (and easy) dish in which the potatoes are first boiled, allowed to cool, diced, and then shallow-fried with cumin, fenugreek, and mustard seeds, as well as lots of sesame seeds. As the potatoes brown lightly, the spices form a delicious 'crust' around them.

8–9 smallish potatoes (2 lb/900 g)
2 tsp whole cumin seeds
¼ tsp whole fenugreek seeds
2 tsp whole black mustard seeds
6 tbs vegetable oil
⅛ tsp ground asafetida (optional)
1–3 dried hot red peppers

2 tbs sesame seeds
¼ tsp ground turmeric
2 tsp salt
Freshly ground black pepper to taste
2 tsp ground amchoor *(or lemon juice)*

Boil the potatoes in their jackets. Drain and allow them to cool for 3 to 4 hours. Peel the potatoes and then dice them into approximately ¾-in/2-cm cubes.

Combine the cumin, fenugreek, and mustard seeds in a small cup and arrange all the ingredients near the cooker in the order in which they go into the frying pan.

Heat the oil in a large 12–14-in/30–35-cm heavy frying pan over a medium flame. When very hot, put in the spices in this order: first put in the ground asafetida and let it sizzle for 3 seconds; then put in the combined cumin, fenugreek, and black mustard seeds and let them sizzle another 5 seconds; put in the red peppers and stir the spices around for 3 seconds; put in the sesame seeds and stir spices another 5 seconds; now add the turmeric, stir once, and put in the diced potatoes.

Turn heat up to medium-high. Stir and fry the potatoes for 5 minutes. Add the salt, pepper, and the *amchoor*. Stir and fry for another 5 minutes. The potatoes should get a few light-brown spots on them.

Tatie Wawo-Runtu's
SAMBAL GORENG KENTANG KERING
(Spicy 'Matchstick' Potatoes)
INDONESIA *(serves 4–6)*

It is hard enough for me to keep my hands off 'matchstick' potatoes when they are freshly made and seasoned very simply with salt and pepper. Indonesians go a step further and add a fried paste of

red chillies, shallots, and garlic to them as well. The result is quite
irresistible.

*4 oz/115 g shallots, peeled and
  coarsely chopped*
2 cloves garlic, peeled
*4 fresh or dried hot red chillies,
  seeded*
1 lb/450 g potatoes
Vegetable oil for deep frying
1 tsp salt

Put the shallots, garlic, and red chillies into the container of a food
processor or blender. Add 3 tbs water and blend until you have a
smooth paste.

Peel the potatoes and cut them into ⅛-in/½-cm thick slices. You
may use a mandolin, food processor, or knife to do this. Stack
about five slices together at a time and cut them into 'matchsticks',
about ⅛ in/½ cm thick. (You should either fry the potatoes as soon
as you have finished cutting them or leave them to soak in water
and then pat them dry whenever you are ready for the frying.)

Line a sieve with kitchen paper and place it over a bowl. Keep
another plate or bowl near by. Heat oil for deep frying, preferably
in a wok, over a medium flame. You should have about 2½ in/
6½ cm of oil in the centre of the wok and aim for a temperature of
about 350–375° F/180–190° C. When the oil is hot, put in just
enough of the potatoes to make a ⅓-in/1-cm-thick layer on top of
the oil. Stir and fry until the potatoes are golden and crisp, adjust-
ing the heat if necessary. Remove the potatoes with a slotted spoon
and leave them to drain in the sieve. Fry a second batch the same
way. Just before you remove this second batch from the wok, take
the first batch out of the sieve and put it on the plate near by.
Change the kitchen paper in the sieve. Now you are ready to take
the second batch out of the wok and let it drain in the empty sieve.
Do all the potatoes this way.

Turn off the heat under the wok and let the oil cool slightly.
Remove all but 2 fl oz/½ dl oil from the wok. Heat the oil again over
a medium-low flame. When hot, put in the paste from the food
processor. Stir and fry for 10 to 12 minutes or until the paste is fairly
dry. Add the potatoes and salt. Stir gently to mix.

---

*For information about ingredients and basic techniques that may be unfamiliar, see General
Information, pages 481-506.*

POTATOES COOKED WITH GARLIC AND SESAME SEEDS
INDIA   *(serves 4–6)*

For this Gujarati recipe, I prefer using potatoes that are no wider than 2 in/5 cm in diameter. The waxier the potato, the better this dish will taste and look.

2 lb/900 g medium-sized potatoes	½ tsp ground turmeric
5 tbs vegetable oil	⅛ tsp ground asafetida (optional)
1 tbs sesame seeds	1 tsp salt
3 good-sized cloves garlic, peeled and slivered	⅛ tsp cayenne pepper (optional)

Peel the potatoes and cut into fingers ('French fries'), ⅓–½ in/ 1–1½ cm thick. Put fingers into a bowl of cold water for half an hour or more. Drain and wipe dry.

Heat the oil in an 8–9-in/20–23-cm frying pan over a medium flame. When it is hot, put in the potatoes and cook them, turning once or twice, for 8 to 10 minutes. The potatoes should be partially cooked and not browned. Remove potatoes with a slotted spoon to a plate and set aside.

Put the sesame seeds into the same frying pan. Stir once. Now add the slivers of garlic, continuing to stir and fry over a medium flame. When the garlic begins to turn brown, put in the turmeric and asafetida. Stir once. Now quickly add the half-cooked potatoes, salt, and cayenne. Stir again. Cover. Turn heat to low and cook gently until potatoes are done. Stir frequently.

Mrs Chawdhry's FRIED POTATOES
PAKISTAN   *(serves 4)*

Mrs Chawdhry is a wonderful cook who has taught me a great deal about north-western Indian foods. She lives in Delhi now but her original home was in Multan which, since the Partition of 1947, has been part of Pakistan. As the north-western section of the Indo-Pakistan subcontinent is close to Afghanistan and Iran, it has always been the region most influenced by the cooking style of its northern neighbours. This potato recipe uses a Multani spice combination that has dried pomegranate seeds in it. The pomegranate, used with great frequency in Persian foods, as well as the very Indian dried green mango powder *(amchoor)*, add a tartness to this dish that is most pleasing. I love this potato dish so much that I can have it at almost any time of the day — with fried eggs and grilled tomato halves for breakfast, with a cup of steaming tea in the late afternoon, and with almost any Indian lunch or dinner.

8 small, waxy potatoes
  (¾–1 lb/340–450 g)
4 tbs vegetable oil
¼ tsp black (or other) cumin seeds
¼ tsp turmeric
¼ tsp or more salt

1/16 tsp cayenne pepper (optional)
¼ tsp Multani garam masala
¼ tsp ground amchoor
A generous pinch black salt
  (optional)

Boil the potatoes in their jackets. Either refrigerate overnight or allow the potatoes to cool for several hours, then peel and cut into quarters lengthwise.

Heat the oil in a heavy frying pan or wok over a medium flame. When smoking, put in the cumin seeds. They will begin to sizzle immediately. Quickly put in the turmeric, stir once, and add the potatoes. Gently stir and fry the potatoes until they are golden brown on all sides. Remove potatoes with a slotted spoon and place on a warm plate lined with kitchen paper. Mix the salt, cayenne, *garam masala*, *amchoor*, and black salt, making sure that there are no *amchoor* lumps. Arrange the potatoes on a warm serving dish in a single layer and sprinkle with the dry spice mixture. Serve immediately.

YELLOW PUMPKIN COOKED WITH SOY SAUCE
JAPAN   *(serves 4)*

This is an utterly delicious way of preparing autumn pumpkins. The vegetable cooks quickly and holds its shape. The Japanese use a green-skinned pumpkin for this recipe. They leave the cubes unpeeled, and often etch patterns, like the veins of leaves, on the skin. Many Japanese vegetable stores sell already cubed and 'etched' pumpkin pieces to grateful housewives — Japanese stores in Japan, that is.

At formal Japanese meals just one or two pumpkin cubes (without their liquid) are served to each person. The pumpkin generally shares a plate with other vegetables.

A 1 lb/450 g section of yellow
  pumpkin
3½ oz/100 g sugar

1 tbs soy sauce
½ tsp salt

For information about ingredients and basic techniques that may be unfamiliar, see General Information, pages 481–506.

Peel the pumpkin and cut into approximately ¾-in/2-cm cubes. Put 1½ pt/8½ dl water, the sugar, and the pumpkin cubes into a pot and bring to the boil. Cover, lower heat, and simmer about 5 minutes or until pumpkin is barely tender. Remove pumpkin with slotted spoon. Boil down the sweet cooking liquid until you have about 12 fl oz/3½ dl left. Add soy sauce and salt. Put the pumpkin back into the pot and simmer, uncovered, another minute. Let pumpkin cool in the liquid. Reheat before serving.

SARSON DA SAAG (MUSTARD GREENS) COOKED IN THE PUNJABI STYLE
INDIA   *(serves 4-6)*

Cold winter days in India's north-western state of Punjab are almost synonymous with soft, buttery *sarson da saag* (which can be bought here in Indian stores) eaten with flat cornmeal breads *(makki di roti).*

1 lb/450 g sarson da saag	*½ fresh hot green chilli*
(mustard greens)	*4½ oz/125 g unsalted butter*
½ lb/225 g spinach	*2½ tbs cornmeal*
A ½-in/1½-cm cube of fresh	*1 tsp salt*
ginger, peeled	

Trim and wash the greens. Chop them coarsely and place in a large pot. Add 8 fl oz/¼ l water and bring to the boil. Cover, turn heat to medium-low, and cook for about 15 minutes or until greens are tender.

Put the ginger and green chilli into the container of an electric blender or food processor and chop them very finely. (If your machine cannot manage this, chop the green chilli by hand and grate the ginger.) Remove the cooked greens with a slotted spoon and put them into the machine container with the ginger and chilli. Do not worry about squeezing out all the liquid from the greens; you will need the small amount that clings to them. Blend the greens with the ginger and green chilli until you have a smooth paste. Depending upon your machine, you may need to do this in two batches.

In a heavy 2½-qt/2¾-l pot, heat 3oz/85 g of the butter over a medium-low flame. Add the cornmeal and cook for about 2 minutes, stirring all the time. Do not allow it to turn brown. Turn the heat down, if necessary. Add 2 fl oz/½ dl water and keep stirring for another half a minute. Now put in the puréed greens and the salt. Cook on medium-low heat, stirring often, for about 10 minutes. Serve the greens in a warm dish topped with 1½ oz/40 g of butter, accompanied by any Indian bread.

FRESH SOY BEANS, STEAMED

CHINA   *(serves 4)*

Fresh soy beans, still green and in their pods, are available in America chiefly around the farmlands where they are grown. They are harder to find elsewhere, except in large cities with well-stocked Chinese grocery stores. And they are only available in season. But if you ever see a vegetable that resembles a hairy pea pod, ask if it is a soy bean and do buy it. Soy beans are excellent — and quite addictive — when steamed. The Chinese steam them for 15 to 20 minutes, often throwing a star anise into the steaming water for its special aroma, and then sit around with a bowlful between them, peeling the pods and eating the beans as a snack.

1 star anise (optional)
1 lb/450 g fresh green soy beans in
  their pods

Set up a steaming apparatus. You could place a bamboo steamer on top of a wok that has water in it or else place a steaming trivet inside a pot. Throw the star anise into the water and bring it to the boil. Remember that the water should stay just below the level of the perforated steamer. Once the water is boiling, put in the soy beans. Cover your bamboo steamer or pot and steam for 15 to 20 minutes or until beans are tender. Remove from heat.

Serve the beans in a bowl. Then just peel and eat them. They may be eaten hot, warm, or cold.

Sheila's
HAAK
(Spring Greens)

INDIA   *(serves 4–6)*

Kashmiris who come to the West yearn for one of their state's most popular dishes, *haak*. They suffer deep depression until an existing Kashmiri grapevine informs them that their beloved vegetable is, indeed, a close cousin of spring greens! In their own mountainous homeland, Kashmiris eat *haak* all through the year. In the summer and early autumn, they pluck the leaves right off the stalks and cook them very simply in mustard oil with a touch of asafetida. The asafetida has traditionally come from their neigh-

For information about ingredients and basic techniques that may be unfamiliar, see General Information, pages 481-506.

bour, Afghanistan. As the chill of winter sets in with a staying determination, *haak* is dried in plaited wreaths to preserve it for the long snowy winter months.

The very large, coarser leaves will not do for this dish. Kashmiris like to keep their leaves whole, stem and all, so only the younger, more tender greens should be used. If you have no access to the tender variety, use whatever greens you find, discard the very coarse leaves and then cut up the larger ones. This dish *is* hot — it is cooked with both red peppers and green chillies — and very delicious. You could, if you like, leave out the peppers and chillies. It will still be delicious. Kashmiris tend to put bicarbonate of soda in this dish to keep the leaves green. I have omitted it as I am told it kills the vitamins.

1¾ lb/800 g tender spring greens
4 fl oz/1 dl mustard oil or
*   groundnut oil*
¼ tsp ground asafetida
1¼ tsp salt or more to taste
1–5 whole dried hot red peppers
1–5 whole fresh hot green chillies

Trim away the coarse lower stems of the greens. Separate each leaf and wash it well. Keep the leaves whole.

Heat the oil in an 8–9-in/20–23-cm-wide, 4-qt/4½-l pot over a medium flame. When hot, put in the asafetida. Let it sizzle for 5 seconds. Put in the greens and cover the pot immediately. Uncover the pot after 10 seconds and stir the greens. Add the salt. Stir and sauté the greens for a minute. Now add the red peppers, the green chillies, and 1½ pt/8½ dl of water. Bring to the boil. Cover, lower heat and simmer gently for 1 hour or until greens are tender. There should be about 6 fl oz/1¾ dl liquid left at the bottom of the pot. If there is more, boil it away. Check the salt. Serve in a warm bowl with plain rice as an accompaniment.

OSHITASHI
(*Spinach with Roasted Sesame Seeds*)
JAPAN   (*serves 4*)

This simple spinach dish is also served in Korea, where it is called *sigumchi namul*.

10 oz–1 lb/285–450 g spinach, well   *1½ tbs* mirin
*   washed and trimmed*   *1 tbs sesame seeds, roasted and*
1½ tbs Japanese soy sauce   *   lightly crushed*

Fill a 4–5-qt/4½–5½-l pot three-quarters full of water and bring to a rolling boil. Drop the spinach into it. Push the spinach down, if necessary. Cook the spinach 2 to 3 minutes or until it has wilted completely. Drain spinach in a colander. Run some cold water over the spinach to cool it off and fix its bright-green colour. Squeeze all the water out of the spinach and put it into a bowl. Add the soy sauce, *mirin*, and crushed sesame seeds. Mix well. Divide into four portions. Make hillock-like piles of each portion. Place the hillocks in the centre of four small Japanese or Chinese dishes. Serve at room temperature.

Tatie Wawo-Runtu's
SPINACH WITH SHALLOTS
INDONESIA   *(serves 4)*

2 lb/900 g spinach, trimmed and washed
½–1 fresh hot red pepper or green chilli
2 fl oz/½ dl vegetable oil

4 oz/115 g shallots, peeled and slivered
About ¾ tsp salt, or to taste
1 tsp sugar

Cut the spinach crosswise into 2-in/5-cm-wide strips.

Cut the hot pepper crosswise into ⅛-in/½-cm-thick rings.

Heat the oil in a wok or a large, heavy frying pan over a medium-high flame. Add the shallots. Stir and fry for about 2 minutes. Put in the red pepper, salt, and sugar. Stir to mix. Add the spinach, stirring to mix. Add 4 fl oz/1 dl water, cover, and cook for 5 minutes on the medium-high flame. Remove cover. Stir and mix again.

Yien-Koo's
SPINACH WITH FERMENTED BEAN CURD
CHINA   *(serves 3–4)*

Fermented bean curd, best compared to a strong, ripe, soft cheese like Camembert, has quite a powerful taste and aroma. It gives its own very special flavour to foods that are cooked with it. As it is fairly salty, it seasons the foods at the same time. The bottled fermented bean curd that I have seen in New York comes in approximately ½-in/1½-cm cubes. My favourite is the winy Red Bean Curd.

For information about ingredients and basic techniques that may be unfamiliar, see General Information, pages 481-506.

1 tsp salt
1¼ tsp sugar
1 lb/450 g fresh spinach, trimmed
  and washed
3 cubes of fermented bean curd

½ tsp sesame oil
3 tbs vegetable oil
3 five-pence-piece sized slices of
  fresh ginger, very lightly
  mashed

Bring 4 qt/4½ l of water to the boil in a large pot. Add the salt, sugar, and the spinach. Bring the water to the boil again. Let the spinach boil for 1 minute or until it is tender. Drain and rinse under cold water. Press out as much liquid from the leaves as possible. Separate the leaves so they are not all entangled.

In a small bowl, mash the fermented bean curd. Slowly add 2 tsp of water so you have a thick paste. Add the sesame oil and mix it in.

Heat the vegetable oil in a wok over a medium-high flame. When hot, put in the ginger slices and stir them around for 15 to 20 seconds, pressing them against the sides of the wok. Remove the ginger with a slotted spoon and discard it. Put the spinach in the wok. Stir and fry it for about 1 minute. Pour the bean-curd mixture over the spinach. Stir to mix and serve at once.

SPINACH WITH SPRING ONIONS, COOKED IN THE MOGHLAI STYLE
INDIA   *(serves 6)*

3 lb/1350 g spinach, trimmed and
  washed
8 tbs ghee or vegetable oil
6 spring onions, trimmed, white
  and pale green sections finely
  chopped

2 tsp fresh ginger, peeled and
  finely grated
1 tsp finely chopped fresh hot
  green chilli
1½ tsp salt
½ tsp sugar
½ tsp garam masala

Fill a large 4–5-qt/4½–5½-l pot three-quarters full with water and bring to the boil. Put the spinach, a few handfuls at a time, into the water, just long enough to wilt it. Remove each batch with a pair of tongs and place in a colander. Do all the spinach this way.

Squeeze as much water as possible out of the spinach and chop it fine.

Heat *ghee* or oil in a wide, heavy pot over a medium flame. Put in the spring onions and sauté for 2 to 3 minutes. Spring onions should not brown but they should wilt slightly. Now add the ginger and green chilli. Sauté another minute or two. The spring onions should be quite translucent. If they start browning, turn down the heat. Add spinach, salt, and sugar. Sauté on low heat, stirring frequently, for 20 minutes. Sprinkle with *garam masala* and mix.

Mrs Sinha's
SPINACH COOKED IN A BIHARI STYLE
INDIA   *(serves 4–6)*

The Indian state of Bihar lies south of Nepal and just west of Bengal. Like their Bengali neighbours, Biharis cook many vegetables in mustard oil. This dish, traditionally made with mixed greens that include *chana* greens, mustard greens, and spinach, resembles an Italian *pesto*, though it is much thicker in consistency. In place of olive oil, mustard oil is used and, apart from the taste of the greens themselves, the other strong flavours include raw garlic, raw ginger, green chillies, and fresh green coriander. It is eaten for breakfast at room temperature, accompanied by *pooris* and hot tea.

For those who might recoil at the very thought of raw garlic so early in the morning, let me repeat here that Indians consider this seasoning to be much more than a mere culinary boon. They view it as medicinal manna, the cure-all for circulatory ailments. Hundreds of thousands in India swallow a crushed clove of garlic every morning in the same way that the Western world swallows vitamin and iron pills.

The mustard oil used in this dish is not cooked. Hence it has the lovely nose-tingling pungency characteristic of the raw oil (see General Information). You may, if you prefer, substitute olive oil.

1½ lb/675 g fresh spinach, washed
½ tsp finely grated fresh peeled
   ginger
½ tsp finely mashed peeled garlic
   (use a mortar, garlic press or
   grater)

½ tsp very finely chopped fresh hot
   green chilli
½ tsp salt
2 tbs very finely chopped fresh
   green coriander
2 tbs mustard oil

Bring 4 qt/4½ l of water to a rolling boil in a large pot. Put in the spinach and cook it on high heat for 1 to 2 minutes or until it is wilted. Drain it, rinse under running water, and then squeeze out as much liquid as you can easily.

Put the spinach in the container of a food processor or blender. Add 2 tbs of water and blend until spinach is smooth. You should have a fairly thick paste.

Take the spinach out and put it in a serving bowl.

Mix the ginger, garlic, green chilli, salt, fresh coriander, and oil in a cup just as you would a dressing. Pour the mixture over the spinach and mix it in thoroughly.

For information about ingredients and basic techniques that may be unfamiliar, see General Information, pages 481-506.

Sheila's
TOMATOES COOKED IN THE BENGALI STYLE
INDIA *(serves 4–6)*

This dish of what might be described as stewed tomatoes is very similar to the two dishes that follow – Tomatoes Cooked in the Gujarati Style and Tomatoes Cooked in the Delhi Style. I have included all three because they show how regional Indian foods can, at times, be inter-related and yet quite different in their final flavours. The Bengali tomatoes are accented with mustard oil – a Bengali favourite – and by the typically Bengali spice combination, *panchphoran* (see General Information), containing whole cumin, mustard, fennel, *kalonji*, and fenugreek seeds. The Gujaratis prefer using groundnut oil, and instead of the Bengali 5-spice combination, they use only cumin and mustard seeds as well as asafetida. They also add grated ginger when the dish is cooked to give a nice pungency. In Delhi, mustard seeds are rarely used for cooking; they *are* used for pickling, however. So the tomatoes there are cooked with cumin and asafetida as well as with sautéed onions. Sweetening, so frequently added to both Bengali and Gujarati foods, is entirely omitted in Delhi.

While fresh, ripe tomatoes are best for this recipe, tinned tomatoes, with some of the juice included, may be substituted. If too much juice is added, it will make the dish very watery. If the tinned tomatoes are large, cut them into ¾-in/2-cm pieces. Plum tomatoes should be halved.

2 lb/900 g ripe tomatoes
3 tbs mustard oil or groundnut oil
1½ tsp panchphoran
1 dried hot red pepper, or 1 fresh
    hot green chilli

1 tsp salt
¹⁄₁₆ tsp freshly ground black pepper
1½ tsp crumbled jaggery or dark
    brown sugar

Heat 4 qt/4½ l of water in a large pot. When it is boiling, drop in the tomatoes. Remove tomatoes after 15 seconds. Peel the tomatoes and dice them into ¾-in/2-cm pieces.

Heat the oil in a heavy stainless steel or porcelain-lined pot over a medium-high flame. When hot, put in the *panchphoran*. As soon as the mustard seeds pop (this takes just a few seconds), put in the red pepper or green chilli. Stir once. Now add the cut-up tomatoes and immediately cover the pot. (This keeps the aromatic fumes inside the pot.) Turn heat to medium. When tomatoes stop making noises from inside the pot, take off the lid and add the salt, black pepper, and jaggery or brown sugar. Cover again, turn heat to low, and simmer 7 to 10 minutes (less, if you prefer) or until tomatoes are just cooked through.

TOMATOES COOKED IN THE DELHI STYLE

INDIA *(serves 4–6)*

See introduction to Tomatoes Cooked in the Bengali Style, page 81.

2 lb/900 g ripe tomatoes
4 tbs vegetable oil
A pinch of crushed asafetida
1½ tsp whole cumin seeds
1 whole dried hot red pepper

1 medium-sized onion, peeled and
   coarsely chopped
1 tsp salt
1/16–1/8 tsp freshly ground black
   pepper

Heat 4 qt/4½ l of water in a large pot. When it is boiling, drop in the tomatoes. Remove the tomatoes after 15 minutes. Peel the tomatoes and dice them into ¾-in/2-cm pieces.

Heat the oil in a heavy stainless steel or porcelain-lined pot over a medium-high flame. When hot, put in the asafetida and, a few seconds later, the cumin seeds. As soon as the cumin seeds sizzle and turn a shade darker, put in the red pepper. It will swell and darken almost immediately. Now put in the onion and turn the heat to medium-low. Stir and sauté the onion until it turns translucent. Do not let it brown. Add the tomatoes, salt, and black pepper. Bring to the boil. Cover, turn heat to low, and simmer gently 7 to 10 minutes or until tomatoes are just cooked through.

TOMATOES COOKED IN THE GUJARATI STYLE

INDIA *(serves 4–6)*

This dish from western India should be made in the summer months when tomatoes are in season. During the rest of the year, tinned tomatoes (with juices) may be used, though they will not taste quite as good. (See introduction to Tomatoes Cooked in the Bengali Style, page 81.)

2 lb/900 g ripe tomatoes
3 tbs vegetable oil
A pinch of crushed asafetida
½ tsp whole cumin seeds
1 tsp whole black mustard seeds
1 whole dried hot red pepper

1 tsp salt
1/16 tsp freshly ground black pepper
1 tsp peeled, finely grated fresh
   ginger
1½ tsp chopped-up jaggery or
   brown sugar
1 tbs gram flour

For information about ingredients and basic techniques that may be unfamiliar, see General Information, pages 481-506.

In a large pot, heat about 4 qt/4½ l of water. When it is boiling, drop in the tomatoes. Remove the tomatoes after 15 seconds with a slotted spoon. Peel the tomatoes and dice them into ¾-in/2-cm pieces.

Heat the oil in a heavy stainless steel or porcelain-lined pot over a medium-high flame. When smoking hot, put in the asafetida. Two seconds later, put in the cumin and mustard seeds. As soon as the mustard seeds begin to pop (this takes just a few seconds), put in the red pepper. A few seconds later (the pepper should swell and darken), put in the cut-up tomatoes and immediately cover the pot (this keeps all the aromatic fumes inside the pot). Turn heat to medium. When the tomatoes stop making noises from inside the pot, take off the lid and add the salt, black pepper, ginger, and jaggery. Stir. Cover again, turn heat to low, and simmer gently 7 to 10 minutes or until tomatoes are just cooked through. Slowly mix gram flour with 2 tbs water to make a smooth paste. Add to the tomatoes, stirring, and let simmer for another minute.

TOMATOES STUFFED WITH POTATOES AND PEAS
INDIA   *(serves 6)*

My mother often made stuffed tomatoes for us. Generally, the tomatoes were stuffed with the same potato and pea combination that was used to make *samosas*. You could, if you like, stuff the tomatoes with Sprouted Mung Beans Cooked with Mustard Seeds (see page 121).

6 firm, flat-bottomed, medium- *Freshly ground black pepper*
  large tomatoes   *The potato-and-pea stuffing for*
¼ tsp salt   Samosas *(see page 380)*

Preheat oven to 400° F/200° C/Mark 6.

Wash and wipe the tomatoes. With a sharp, pointed knife, cut a cone-shaped cap at the stem end of the tomato, pull it out, and discard it. Keep this opening in the tomato as small as possible, allowing yourself just enough room to be able to go inside the tomato with a grapefruit spoon to scoop out all the pulp and the seeds. As you do this, be careful not to pierce or otherwise damage the shell of the tomato. Sprinkle the inside of the tomato shells with a little salt and pepper and drain the tomatoes by turning them upside down for 10 minutes. Then stuff them with the potato–pea mixture. (Do not overstuff or the tomatoes will crack open.) Let the stuffing protrude a little from the opening in the tomatoes and cover with small caps made out of aluminium foil. Place the tomatoes on a baking tray and bake in oven 10 to 15 minutes or until they are just cooked through. Remove foil caps and serve immediately.

TURNIPS COOKED IN DASHI

JAPAN   *(serves 4 at a Japanese meal)*

2 good-sized turnips (about ¾ lb/   1 tbs Japanese soy sauce
  340 g), peeled and quartered   1 tbs sugar
12 fl oz/3½ dl dashi (see page 339)   ⅛ tsp salt

Combine all ingredients in a small pot. Bring to the boil. Cover and simmer about 20 minutes on medium-low heat or until turnips are tender. Uncover and allow the turnips to cool in the liquid, turning the pieces around every now and then so that they colour evenly. Serve at room temperature or reheat in the same liquid.

WAKATAKE
(Wakame Seaweed and Bamboo Shoots)

JAPAN   *(serves 4)*

5 6-in/15-cm-long strips of dried   8 fl oz/¼ l dashi (see page 339)
  wakame *seaweed*   2 tsp Japanese soy sauce
4 oz/115 g bamboo shoots, sliced   1 tsp mirin
  into pieces 1½ in long × ½ in   1 tsp sugar
  wide × ¹⁄₁₆ in thick/4 cm ×
  1½ cm × ¼ cm

Soak the seaweed in 1½ pt/8½ dl water for 10 minutes, then drain. Cut away the coarse spines of the seaweed and then cut the leaves into 1½ × ½-in/4 × 1½-cm pieces.

Combine the seaweed, bamboo shoots, *dashi*, soy sauce, *mirin*, and sugar in a small pot. Bring to a simmer. Simmer uncovered, over a medium-low flame, for about 20 minutes. There should be some concentrated liquid left at the bottom of the pot.

WATER CHESTNUTS, PLAIN AND BOILED

Water chestnuts grow under water in the mud and there are several varieties that are eaten all over East, South-east, and South Asia. The Indian version is triangular. It has several hornlike protrusions and is a green or deep red colour. You will be lucky if you find an Indian shop selling it in Britain. But the dark, purplish-

---

For information about ingredients and basic techniques that may be unfamiliar, see General Information, pages 481–506.

black Chinese water chestnut *is* available in Chinese grocery stores and should be pounced upon whenever the opportunity presents itself.

I am referring, of course, to fresh water chestnuts. The tinned ones just do not compare. For me, fresh water chestnuts, raw or boiled, Indian or Chinese (the two varieties are fairly similar in taste), are a treat and once I start eating them, I find it impossible to stop. If you have never eaten fresh water chestnuts and if you find yourself in the neighbourhood of a Chinese grocery store that sells them, here is what I suggest you do.

Buy a dozen chestnuts. When you get home, rinse them under running water to wash off the mud. Peel one (just as you would a potato) with a paring knife. Rinse it again and eat it. The chestnut has the texture of a raw potato but is deliciously sweet. Now take about 4 of the chestnuts and put them in a small, 1½-qt/1¾-l pot. Put enough water in the pot so it is 1 in/2½ cm above the tops of the chestnuts. Bring the water to the boil. Cover, lower the heat, and simmer gently for 15 minutes. Peel with a paring knife (you can wait for them to cool), and eat them. See which you prefer, the raw chestnuts or the boiled ones. Eat the remaining chestnuts according to your preference.

In Asia, raw and boiled chestnuts are sold at outdoor festivals and sports events in the same manner as popcorn and hot dogs are sold. In India, water chestnuts are available only during the monsoon season. We buy 1–2 lb/450–900 g at a time. If they are tender and sweet, we just peel and eat them. If they have matured a bit, we boil them. Once boiled, the chestnuts are either eaten plain or sliced, along with boiled potatoes, bananas, and cucumber, and made into a hot, spicy, and sour 'salad', which is eaten as a snack. If bought in the bazaars of Delhi, this 'salad' is served on leaves and eaten with toothpicks.

AVIYAL
(Mixed Vegetables)
INDIA   (serves 4–6)

This mixed vegetable dish from south-western India is generally made with odd vegetables left over in the vegetable bin. The vegetables are cut or diced (never too small), cooked (by blanching, boiling, or steaming), and then folded in with what might be called a 'dressing' that includes fresh coconut, mustard seeds, green chillies, fresh coriander, and yogurt. I have used potatoes, green beans, carrots, and peas here but you could add broad beans, sliced white radishes, diced turnips, diced green pepper, and diced winter melon. (The last gives a wonderful flavour to the dish.)

1 medium-sized potato	1½ tbs vegetable oil
¾ lb/340 g green beans, trimmed and cut into 1-in/2½-cm lengths	A generous pinch of ground asafetida
2 carrots, peeled and cut into ½-in/1½-cm pieces (about ¼ lb/115 g)	1 tsp whole black mustard seeds 1 tsp whole cumin seeds
6 oz/180 g shelled fresh or defrosted frozen peas	2 tbs urad dal 12 fl oz/3½ dl plain yogurt 2 tsp salt, or to taste
1–2 fresh hot green chillies, finely chopped	2 tbs finely chopped fresh green coriander
3 oz/85 g grated fresh coconut	

Cover the potato with water in a small pot and bring the water to the boil. Cover pot, turn heat to low and allow potato to cook. Do not allow it to get mushy.

While potato boils, combine beans, carrots, and peas in another small pot. Add 8 fl oz/¼ l water and bring to the boil. Cover, lower heat, and cook for about 4 to 5 minutes or until vegetables are just tender (but still crunchy) and the water is almost all absorbed. You may have to adjust the heat to achieve this.

Drain the cooked potato. Peel and dice it into ⅔-in/1½-cm cubes. Combine all the vegetables in a wide, heavy 3–4-qt/3½–4½-l pot or sauté pan. Sprinkle the green chillies and coconut over the vegetables. Do not mix yet.

Heat the oil in a small, heavy frying pan or very small butter-warmer type pot over a medium flame. When hot, put in the asafetida and, a few seconds later, the mustard and cumin seeds. As soon as the mustard seeds begin to pop (this takes just a few seconds), put in the *urad dal*. Stir and fry until the *dal* turns a light reddish-brown. Empty contents of the small frying pan over the cooked vegetables.

Empty the yogurt into a bowl and mix with a fork or thin whisk until it is creamy. Add the salt to it and mix again. Pour this yogurt over the vegetables and mix gently. Heat the vegetable pot over a low flame, stirring gently, until its contents have just warmed through. Remove from heat before *aviyal* comes to the boil.

Serve warm, at room temperature, or even cold, sprinkled with the fresh coriander.

For information about ingredients and basic techniques that may be unfamiliar, see General Information, pages 481-506.

PECEL
(Vegetable Salad with a Spicy Peanut Sauce)
INDONESIA

Among Indonesia's salad-like dishes in which a combination of raw, blanched, boiled, and fried foods are served with different peanut sauces, *pecel* (pronounced 'pechel') is perhaps the easiest to make. This recipe, which comes from Betty's Restaurant in Denpasar, Bali, uses pounded shrimp in the sauce. I have substituted soy sauce for the shrimp. The sweetening in the sauce is provided by *gula Bali*, a palm sugar. You may find palm sugar in South-east Asian grocery stores, but if it isn't available, use light brown sugar.

The different items, neatly arranged on my plate in Denpasar, were bean curd, *tempeh*, potatoes, eggs, greens, cabbage, and mung-bean sprouts. Here is how you should prepare them, with the amounts being left to your discretion:

BEAN CURD — Sauté the bean curd according to the recipe on page 204. You may sprinkle the bean-curd pieces very lightly with salt before sautéing them.

TEMPEH — See recipe for Fried, Pre-seasoned Tempeh, page 128.

POTATOES — Use new or other waxy potatoes. Boil potatoes in their jackets. Let them cool without refrigerating them. Peel and cut into either ¼-in/¾-cm-thick slices or ½-in/1½-cm cubes.

EGGS — Hard-boil the eggs and let them cool. Peel and quarter lengthwise.

GREENS — Indonesians use swamp cabbage for this dish but you may use the more readily available spinach instead. Trim and wash fresh spinach, making sure all the leaves are separated. Drop the leaves into boiling water to which you have added a little salt and a little sugar. Bring the water back to the boil. Boil rapidly for 2 minutes. Drain and rinse under cold water. Squeeze out any extra moisture and loosen the wad of leaves.

CABBAGE — Shred the cabbage. You may use it raw or else drop it into lightly salted boiling water for 1 minute. Drain and rinse under cold water. Drain again.

MUNG-BEAN SPROUTS — Rinse them well. Break off their thread-like tails if you feel up to it. You may use them raw or else drop them into boiling water and boil rapidly for 15 seconds. Drain and rinse under cold water. Gently squeeze out all extra moisture and fluff up again.

To serve, arrange small amounts of each item on individual plates. Offer Spicy Peanut Sambal as an accompaniment (see page 421), about 2 tbs per person, either in small, shallow, individual bowls or saucers.

YUM TAVOY
(Salad of Cooked Mixed Vegetables)
THAILAND/BURMA   (serves 6)

This very aromatic dish could contain almost any combination of vegetables − carrots, cabbage, cauliflower, turnips, green peppers, aubergine, any of them may be used. As it happens, I use a firm, green marrow shaped rather like a fat baseball bat (called *hu lu* in Chinese grocery stores and *doodhi* in Indian ones), long beans, and that lovely green, *choy sum* (see General Information), all of which I buy at a Chinese grocer. You could, if you like, use aubergine instead of the marrow, ordinary green beans instead of the long beans, and throw in some cabbage or cauliflower if you cannot find *choy sum*. The vegetables are first cooked in coconut milk and then seasoned with a Thai curry paste, ground peanuts, and tamarind pulp. It is the curry paste that provides the aroma. It contains, among other things, lemon grass, galanga root, and the peel of the kaffir lime.

2–3 whole dried red peppers, seeded
2 tsp dried, sliced lemon grass
2 five-pence-piece sized rounds of dried galanga root
A 2-in/5-cm × 1-in/2½-cm (roughly) piece of dried kaffir lime peel
12–14 oz/340–400 g of aubergine or firm green marrow (see note above)
¼ lb/115 g long or ordinary green beans
¼ lb/115 g choy sum or cauliflower

1 pt/½ l fresh or tinned unsweetened coconut milk
1½ tsp salt
1 tsp sugar
2 tbs chopped, peeled shallots
2 cloves garlic, peeled
4 slim roots from fresh green coriander, washed
1½ tbs ground roasted or fried unsalted peanuts
3 tbs tamarind paste
1 tsp bright-red sweet paprika
2 tsp roasted sesame seeds

Put the red peppers, lemon grass, galanga root, and kaffir lime peel into the container of an electric coffee grinder or other spice grinder. Grind until you have a powder.

Cut the aubergine into 1½-in/4-cm cubes. If you are using the marrow, peel it with a potato peeler and cut it into 1½-in/4-cm chunks. Trim the beans and cut into 2-in/5-cm lengths. Cut the *choy sum* leaves crosswise into 2-in/5-cm strips. The *choy sum* stalks can be cut into 2-in/5-cm lengths. If you are using cauliflower, break it

---

For information about ingredients and basic techniques that may be unfamiliar, see General Information, pages 481-506.

into flowerets that are about 1½ in/4 cm across at the head.

Remove 4 fl oz/1 dl of the top coconut cream (see General Information) and set it aside.

Combine the cut vegetables, 16 fl oz/½ l of the remaining coconut milk, ½ tsp salt, and ½ tsp sugar in a 3½-qt/4-l pot and bring to the boil over a medium-high flame. Cover and cook on medium-high heat for about 10 minutes or until the vegetables are tender. Turn off heat and remove cover.

Put the shallots, garlic, and fresh coriander roots into the container of a food processor or blender. Add 2 fl oz/½ dl of liquid from the vegetable pot and blend until you have a smooth paste.

Put this paste, the 2 fl oz/½ dl coconut cream, and the spices you have just ground into a small, heavy pot. Bring to a simmer over medium heat. Keep stirring and cooking until all the liquid evaporates and the paste begins to fry a little in the oil released by the coconut cream. Turn the heat down a bit when this begins to happen. You should end up with a blob of paste.

Add this fried curry paste, the ground peanuts, tamarind paste, paprika, 1 tsp salt, and ½ tsp sugar to the cooked vegetables. Stir and bring to a simmer. Simmer for 1 minute. Sprinkle sesame seeds over the top.

TEMPURA
JAPAN *(serves 4)*

It is said that batter-fried foods like tempura were introduced into Japan in the sixteenth century by the Portuguese. Whatever the origin, the Japanese have done to this dish what they did to the Buddhist tea-drinking ceremony, which came from China, and floral designs for cotton prints, which came from India — they have made it totally Japanese.

The word 'tempura' translates as a woman in a gossamer-thin dress giving tantalizing glimpses of her barely hidden physical beauty. The actual dish contains beauties of another sort — fish, asparagus, aubergine slices, lotus-root slices, sweet pepper slices, green beans, onion slices, quails' eggs, etc. — that are dipped in a very light batter, deep fried, drained, and then served with a dipping sauce containing, among other things, soy sauce and grated white radish. In my own travels through Japan, I was never served bean-curd tempura in a tempura meal, but I usually include it in order to make the dish more nutritious. You may, if you like, smear the bean-curd pieces with a little *miso* — red, if you like a salty taste, white or yellow if you like a sweeter taste — before you dip them in the batter.

In Japan, there are 'bars', counters really, that specialize in serving just tempura. Diners sit on stools while the chef behind the counter dips foods in batter and deep fries them. The vegetables are not all fried at once. Very small batches go into the wok. One batch may consist of green beans, another of sweet potatoes, another of aubergine, and so on. As soon as the chef finishes cooking a batch, he hands it over to the diners, dividing it up among several plates. All batter-fried foods get soggy as they sit, so diners eat them as soon as they get them. This is very hard to manage in a home kitchen unless you, as chef, choose to stay by the cooker and feed your guests a batch at a time. There are ways around this. You could serve tempura only to small groups of people. You could also divide the frying duties with a friend, spouse, or child so that the eating and frying can go on continuously.

In a tempura, the fried vegetables remain light and crunchy. To achieve this, care has to be taken in several areas. Cut the vegetables evenly. All aubergine slices should be of the same thickness, as should all onion slices, and so on. You may put more than one kind of vegetable into the oil at the same time, but make sure — and here you have to use your judgment — that all the vegetables you put in require about the same cooking time.

The batter is also important. Recipes vary throughout Japan with some combining flour with a whole egg, others with just the yolk, and some with no egg at all. Tempura batter should not be well blended; it is left fairly lumpy and therein lies its success. I will give two recipes for the batter. Try both and see which you eventually prefer. Both are good. Many chefs sprinkle a little flour on the vegetables before dipping them in the batter, which makes the batter adhere a bit better. For this same reason, I like to wet hardboiled quails' eggs and *then* flour them lightly before dipping them in batter. Some tempura-makers specialize in building up the batter so it extends far beyond the extremities of the slice of vege-

For information about ingredients and basic techniques that may be unfamiliar, see General Information, pages 481-506.

table. This is done by dribbling extra batter along the length and width of the slice of vegetable while it is frying.

I use groundnut oil for frying but you may use salad oil or any mild vegetable oil. The temperature of the oil should be between 350 and 375° F/180 and 190° C. If the oil is smoking, it is too hot. As soon as the vegetables have fried, they should be drained. In Japan, this is done by removing them from the hot oil with a skimmer and then placing them on slightly elevated, coarse mesh trays. At some tempura bars, the 'plates' for tempura consist of baskets lined with kitchen paper or trays with an elevated napkin-lined mesh section to hold the fried food.

Clean the oil of all batter particles between each batch. Fine mesh skimmers are best, but a finely slotted spoon will do. In Japan these batter particles are not thrown away. After being rinsed quickly to remove extra oil, they are dropped into clear broths and make a good soup!

The dipping sauce for tempura varies. The base is generally soy sauce thinned out with Japanese Stock (see page 339). To this can be added finely grated white radish, finely grated horseradish, or finely grated ginger. At one tempura bar in Kyoto, I was offered plain salt and lemon juice as dips as well.

BATTER NUMBER I

1 egg yolk, from a large egg
8 fl oz/¼ l plus 1 tbs ice-cold water
4 oz/115 g plain flour, sifted

BATTER NUMBER II

1 large egg
8 fl oz/¼ l ice-cold water
4 oz/115 g plain flour, sifted with
½ tsp bicarbonate of soda

TEMPURA INGREDIENTS

½ lb/225 g medium or hard bean
curd, cut into 1½ × 2 × ½-in/
4 × 5 × 1½-cm pieces
8 even-sized green beans
8 asparagus spears
8 ¼-in/¾-cm-thick slices of peeled
onion
8 fresh or tinned quails' eggs (if
fresh, boil them for 5 minutes
and then peel)

Vegetable oil for deep frying
8 ¼-in/¾-cm-thick slices of peeled
sweet potato, cut crosswise
8 ½-in/1½-cm-wide slices of green
pepper, cut lengthwise
8 ¼-in/¾-cm-thick slices of small
aubergine, cut crosswise
About 2 extra tbs plain flour

Tilt a chopping board and lay some kitchen paper on it. Place the pieces of bean curd on the paper. Cover with another piece of paper and pat down lightly. Let the bean curd drain for 2 hours. Change the kitchen paper when it gets soaked.

Trim the green beans and cut them in half lengthwise. Lay 4 halves alongside each other and thread a toothpick through their centres. Do this with all the bean halves so you end up with four 'toothpicked' servings of beans.

Trim away the woody section of the asparagus. Peel the lower three-quarters of the remaining spear with a potato peeler.

Put a toothpick through each slice of onion to hold the rings together.

Put a toothpick crosswise through the middle of each egg.

Make a batter using one of the two suggested recipes. Put the egg or egg yolk in a bowl and beat until smooth. Slowly add the iced water, beating as you do so. Now put in all the flour (or flour and baking powder) all at once. Beat four or five times to mix. Do not overmix. The batter should be lumpy. Set the batter aside for 10 minutes while you heat the oil for deep frying. You may use a wok or a deep frying pan or an electric deep-frying pot. You need medium heat, about 350–375° F/180–190° C.

When the oil is hot, dip the beans in the batter to coat them lightly. Let any extra batter on the beans drip back into the bowl. Now put the beans into the oil and deep fry, turning once or twice, for 2 to 3 minutes or until the batter has turned golden and crisp. Remove the beans from the oil and drain on a wire mesh rack or on kitchen paper. Clear the oil of any batter drippings with a skimmer. Dip the sweet potato slices in the batter and cook them the same way as the beans. Follow these with the green peppers and the onion slices. Make sure you drain each batch thoroughly. Dust the aubergine slices very lightly with flour. Then dip them in the batter and fry. Drain. Do the same with the asparagus spears. Sprinkle a little water on the quails' eggs, dust lightly with flour, dip in the batter and fry. Drain. Give the bean-curd pieces a final pat with kitchen paper. (You may smear a little *miso* on them at this stage.) Dust lightly with flour, dip in batter and fry. Drain. Serve as soon after it is made as possible. With it, offer Tempura Dipping Sauce (see page 414), as well as tiny individual bowls of salt and lemon juice for those who might like a choice.

For information about ingredients and basic techniques that may be unfamiliar, see General Information, pages 481-506.

UKOY
(Vegetable Fritters)
PHILIPPINES   (makes 22–24 fritters)

This street snack is made with grated pumpkin (a special, small pumpkin is used), and bean sprouts, with a prawn embedded in the centre. I have removed the prawn and the result is still very good. *Ukoy* is eaten with a simple dipping sauce containing vinegar, garlic, and salt.

THE BATTER

4 oz/115 g plain flour
¼ tsp bicarbonate of soda
1½ tsp salt
½ tsp freshly ground black pepper
1 large egg
8 fl oz/¼ l cold Vegetable Stock (see page 340) or cold water
Vegetable oil for shallow frying

Peeled and coarsely grated pumpkin filled to the 15-fl oz/ 4½-dl level in a glass measuring jug
3 oz/85 g mung-bean sprouts, washed, drained thoroughly, patted as dry as possible
3 spring onions, cut into 2-in/ 5-cm pieces and then cut lengthwise into fine strips

Make the batter by sifting the flour, baking powder, salt, and pepper together in a large bowl. Beat the egg in a separate smaller bowl and slowly add the stock to it. Then slowly add the egg-stock mixture to the flour mixture, beating as you do so.

Heat ½ in/1–½ cm oil in a frying pan over a medium flame. The ideal temperature for frying the fritters is between 350 and 375° F/ 180 and 190° C.

Put the grated pumpkin, bean sprouts, and spring onions into the batter and mix. Remove heaped tablespoons of the fritter mixture and drop gently into the frying pan. Fry for about 3 minutes on each side or until fritters are a nice medium-brown colour. If the fritters begin to brown too fast, turn the heat down. Remove fritters with a slotted spoon and drain on kitchen paper or on a wire mesh rack. Do all fritters this way, putting only as many in the oil as the frying pan will hold easily.

Serve hot, with small, individual bowls of Filipino Dipping Sauce (see page 415).

VEGETABLE PAKORIS (BHAJJIAS)
(Vegetable Fritters)
INDIA   (serves 4–6)

This is the Indian version of Japan's tempura and Italy's *fritto misto*. Almost any vegetable, whole or sliced depending on its size, may be dipped in a gram-flour batter and fried until it is crisp on the outside. I like the batter to be quite thin, though some people prefer a more solid encasement. As no egg is used in the batter, these fritters would be particularly good for vegetarians who do not eat any animal products.

Almost any fresh vegetable may be used to make these *pakoris* — flowerets of cauliflower, slices of aubergine, slices of peeled potato or sweet potato, onion rings, green beans, slices of green pepper, and even fiery hot red peppers. Although *pakoris* may be eaten with just a sprinkling of salt, they are generally served with some sort of sour chutney which might be tamarind-based, mint-and-coriander-based, or it could even be tomato-based. It is nearly always sour and hot. These days, though, this 'chutney' could be tomato ketchup!

Pakoris should be eaten while they are hot and crisp or else they turn soggy. They are a snack food in India and are often served with tea, coffee, or soft drinks.

THE BATTER

5½ oz/155 g gram flour
¾ tsp salt
½ tsp bicarbonate of soda
¼ tsp ground turmeric
½ tsp ground cumin
¾ tsp ground coriander
¾ tsp whole ajwain seeds or whole cumin seeds
¼ tsp freshly ground black pepper
¼ tsp cayenne pepper

Vegetable oil for deep frying
1 medium-sized potato, peeled and cut into ⅛-in/½-cm-thick rounds

1 medium-sized onion, peeled and cut into ⅛-in/½-cm-thick rounds
½ medium-sized sweet potato, peeled and cut into ⅛-in/½-cm-thick rounds
16 cauliflower flowerets, about 2 in/5 cm long, 1–½ × ½ in/4 × 1–½ cm at the head
16 green beans, trimmed at the ends
4 hot Italian peppers (optional)

Sift the gram flour, salt, and bicarbonate of soda into a bowl. Add all the other spices for the batter. Very slowly and gradually pour in ½ pt/3 dl water, beating with a fork or a wooden spoon as you do so. You should have a smooth batter.

Heat the oil in a wok or other utensil for deep frying over a medium flame. The temperature of the oil should be between 350 and 375° F/180 and 190° C.

Put the potato slices into the batter. Lift out a handful with your

For information about ingredients and basic techniques that may be unfamiliar, see General Information, pages 481-506.

fingers and let any extra batter drip back into the bowl. Now put these slices into the hot oil, as many as the wok will hold in a single layer. Fry slowly, about 7 minutes on each side. When the outside is golden brown and crisp, remove fritters with a slotted spoon and leave to drain on a mesh rack or on kitchen paper.

Separate the onion rings, put them in the batter, and fry them the same way as the potatoes. Do all the vegetables this way, dipping them in the batter, frying them, and then draining them. The hot peppers may be left whole. Ideally, as each batch is fried it should be eaten. With the *pakoris*, you could serve one or all of these chutneys: Tamarind-Mint Chutney, Hot and Spicy Hyderabadi Tomato Chutney, and Fresh Coriander and Mint Chutney (see pages 421--3).

2   Beans and Dried Peas

Next to eggs, it is beans and peas, when combined with grains and a milk product at the same meal, that provide vegetarians with their best source of usable protein. Beans are also a cheap source of protein which the Asian world has depended upon for more than a thousand years, and it is only in Asia that the full range of bean dishes, from appetizers and snacks to desserts, has been fully explored.

In India, for example, I could have *dosas* for breakfast. These are crisp-soft bean-and-rice pancakes which are usually washed down in the mornings with coffee or glasses of buttermilk. For lunch, I might have Chana Dal with Cucumber and some whole-wheat griddle breads. *Dals* are split peas and India has dozens of varieties, each one with its own very distinct taste. At teatime, I might have *dhoklas*, savoury cakes made out of mung beans and quite encrusted with mustard and sesame seeds. After dinner, I might well munch on a fudge made with gram flour. In the course of this one day, no bean dish would have looked or tasted like another.

In eastern Asia, although many beans are eaten, it is the soy bean that wins out as being the most versatile, with mung beans coming a close second. Red beans are used chiefly for desserts. Soy beans may be boiled, fried, made into soy milk, bean curd, soy sauces, fermented cheeses, and thick pastes. Mung beans may be made into vermicelli, sprouted, or cooked in stews. If you are looking for a hearty bean stew that is also easy to make, try Mongo, a Filipino dish of whole mung beans, greens, tomatoes, onion, and garlic. Eaten with a squeeze of lime juice, this combination is most satisfying.

If some bean dishes are hearty, others have unsurpassable elegance. Take the Persian dish, Frozen Broad Beans, Braised with Swiss Chard and Dill. Persians are light-handed with their spices but most generous with fresh herbs. Here dill flecks the dish and flavours it most gently.

Beans seem to have changed miraculously over the years so that they no longer take hours to cook. It is quite a mystery to me why lentils cook in less than half an hour. This simple, quick-cooking legume may be puréed into soups, cooked with vegetables such as spinach, and made into Middle Eastern salads with the addition of lemon juice, olive oil, garlic, and parsley. Even the tougher beans, such as haricot or *azuki*, do not necessarily have to be soaked overnight. I much prefer the method whereby they are cooked for

2 minutes, left for 1 hour, and then cooked again until tender. Older beans will take longer to cook than those which have been recently harvested and dried.

All beans need to be picked over carefully and washed in several changes of water before they are cooked.

Broad Beans

Broad beans are similar to and a useful substitute for fava beans, which are large, meaty beans used in the cooking of both West and East Asia. In the Middle East, fava beans are often seasoned with herbs like dill and thyme and used to make cold salads and soothing main dishes; in China they can be stir-fried with vegetables or braised with seasonings to make hearty accompaniments for rice.

Fava beans are available in several forms. There are the fresh beans, hidden inside large green pods, that appear seasonally. To prepare these for cooking, you have first to open the pods and extract the beans. The beans themselves are also clothed in their own 'seed coats' or skins, which are hard and tasteless. Unless the beans are very young and tender, these skins need to be removed. Here is the best way to go about this: boil the beans for about 10 minutes in lightly salted water. By this time they should be quite tender inside their coats. The best way to check this is to bite into one. The coat will still be coarse but the bean inside should be tender. Drain and let them cool under running water. Now they are ready to be peeled. (Two pounds/900 g of pods yield about 1–1¼ lb/450–560 g of beans.) If I am not in too much of a hurry, I refrigerate the beans in a plastic container for a few hours before I peel them. This way the beans inside get a bit firmer and there are fewer breakages while peeling. Once the beans are peeled, their skins can be discarded and the beans folded into hot butter or oil, either alone or with other vegetables. Broad beans should be cooked in the same way, though for less time (5–6 minutes) if they are young.

Then there are dried fava beans which are available all year round at Chinese, Greek, Middle Eastern, and whole-food stores. They come without their pods, of course, but you can get them both with and without their skins. They taste somewhat like chestnuts after they have been cooked. I generally buy the beans with the seed coats on them because they are easier to find. I boil them for 2 minutes and then let them sit in the hot water for 1 hour. Then I boil them for another 30 to 45 minutes or until they are just tender. I cool them off under running water before I peel away the skins. The beans can then be put into salads or puréed and put into scrambled eggs. Half a pound/225 g of dried fava beans with skins yields about 1 lb/450 g of cooked, skinned beans. You can use dried broad beans in the same way; frozen broad beans are of course available in many supermarkets.

FRESH BROAD BEANS
WITH THYME
MIDDLE EAST　　　　　　　　　　　　　　　　　　　　*(serves 4–6)*

If you use frozen broad beans, cook them according to packet instructions and drain them. Then sauté them in the olive oil with the thyme.

1½ lb/675 g shelled fresh broad　　　*6 tbs olive oil*
　beans (see page 97)　　　　　　　*½ tsp dried thyme*
1 tsp salt

Put the beans, 16 fl oz/½ l water, and ½ tsp salt in a pot and bring to the boil. Cover, lower heat and simmer for 10 minutes or until beans are tender. Drain the beans and cool them under running water. Now peel away and discard their outer skins.

Heat the oil in an 8-in/20-cm frying pan over a medium flame. Put in the skinned beans, the thyme, and the remaining ½ tsp salt. Stir and sauté for 2 minutes.

FRESH BROAD BEANS WITH
STRAW MUSHROOMS
CHINA　　　　　　　　　　　　　　　　　　　　　　*(serves 4)*

Here the broad beans are served in their skins, but the skins are not to be eaten. The Chinese like to pinch them with the teeth (or their fingers) so the tender inner bean pops into the mouth.

½ lb/225 g shelled fresh broad　　　　*2 tbs vegetable oil*
　beans (see page 97)　　　　　　　*1 tbs sesame oil*
1 20-oz/560 g tin of straw　　　　　*½ tsp salt*
　mushrooms　　　　　　　　　　*1½ tsp sugar*
1 tbs Chinese shaohsing wine or　　　*1 star anise*
　dry sherry

For information about ingredients and basic techniques that may be unfamiliar, see General Information, pages 481-506.

Make a small cut in the outer shell of each bean with the point of a knife.

Combine the broad beans, the entire contents of the tin of mushrooms, wine, the two oils, salt, sugar, and the star anise in a pot and bring to the boil. Cover. Cook on medium heat for about 10 minutes or until beans are tender. There should be just 2–3 tbs liquid left at the bottom of the pot. If there is more, boil it away. Remove the star anise.

FROZEN BROAD BEANS BRAISED WITH SWISS CHARD AND DILL
IRAN (serves 4–6)

This is a delicate and delightfully simple dish. If you cannot find Swiss chard, you could substitute Cos lettuce or any other mild-flavoured, tender green.

1 10-oz/285-g packet frozen broad
   beans
1 head Swiss chard, cut
5 tbs unsalted butter

1 medium-sized onion, peeled and
   cut into ½-in/1½-cm dice
8 tbs fresh, chopped dill, or 1½ tsp
   dried
½ tsp salt

Defrost the broad beans under warm running water.

Separate the Swiss chard leaves and wash them well. Lay them side by side and cut them, crosswise, at ½-in/1½-cm intervals all the way from the leafy sections to the bottom of the stems.

Heat the butter in a heavy, wide, casserole-type pot over a medium flame. When the butter has melted and is frothing, put in the onion. Stir and sauté for 1 minute. Add the broad beans. Stir and sauté another minute. Put in the Swiss chard and the dill. Stir and sauté 2 to 3 minutes. Add the salt and 2 fl oz/½ dl water. Bring to a simmer. Cover tightly, lower heat and simmer gently for about 15 minutes or until chard is cooked.

DRIED BROAD BEAN (OR FAVA BEAN) AND GREEN PEPPER SALAD
MIDDLE EAST (serves 4–6)

½ lb/225 g dried broad or fava beans with skins (see page 97)
1 small green pepper
8 tbs finely chopped fresh parsley

THE DRESSING

5 tbs olive oil

4 tbs lemon juice

¾ tsp salt

⅛ tsp freshly ground black pepper

1 clove garlic, peeled and mashed
to a pulp

Combine the beans and 1 qt/11½ dl water in a pot. Bring to the boil. Cover, lower heat and simmer 2 minutes. Turn off the heat and let the pot sit, covered, for 1 hour. Bring the beans to the boil again. Cover, lower heat and simmer for 30 to 50 minutes or until beans are just tender. Drain and cool under running water. Peel the beans and discard their skins.

Remove the seeded section of the green pepper and cut into ¼-in/¾-cm dice. Put the peeled beans, green pepper, and parsley in a bowl. Beat all the ingredients for the dressing together and pour over the contents of the bowl. Stir gently to mix.

CANDIED BUTTER BEANS

JAPAN   (serves 4–6)

The Japanese candy various large, kidney-shaped beans and then serve them, sometimes in solitary splendour, arranged prettily on a plate that holds small servings of other foods as well. The sweet beans contrast beautifully with other salty and sour foods and, especially when there are just two or three of them, show off their exquisite shape as if Elsa Peretti had designed them for Tiffany.

Candied beans may be simmered in soy sauce, which gives them a dark brown colour, or, if they are white to begin with, they can be left with their natural colour.

Serve these in any well-matched combination of sweet and savoury dishes.

6 oz/180 g dried butter beans

4 tbs sugar

½ tsp salt

Pick over the beans, then wash and drain them. Put them with 1½ pt/8½ dl water in a heavy, 2½-qt/2¾-l pot and bring to the boil. Cover, lower heat and simmer gently for 2 minutes. Turn off the heat and let the pot sit, covered, for 1 hour. Uncover and bring to the boil again. Cover, lower heat and simmer gently for 30 to 40 minutes or until beans are tender but still retain their shape and some firmness. (Older beans might take longer to cook.) Drain the beans but save 2 fl oz/½ dl of their liquid. (The rest of the liquid may

For information about ingredients and basic techniques that may be unfamiliar, see General Information, pages 481-506.

be used for soups.) Now put the beans and the 2 fl oz/½ dl of liquid back into the pot and place the pot over a low flame. Add 2 tbs of the sugar as well as the salt. Simmer, stirring gently, for 5 minutes. Add the remaining 2 tbs of sugar and simmer, stirring gently again for another 3 to 4 minutes or until the sugar has melted completely.

Devi's
BUTTER BEANS WITH SULTANAS
INDIA   *(serves 3–4)*

This delicious dish is made by my friend, Devi Mangaldas of Ahmedabad. Gujarati food ranks among the best vegetarian food in the world and Devi's is cooked and presented with a special delicacy. Sometimes the food — like this dish — is very simple and easy to make. At other times, when she cooks the lightest rice-flour pancakes between two almond leaves, it tends to get fairly tricky — though not impossible — to master.

The chief spice in this dish is *ajwain* (see General Information), which looks like celery seed and tastes, as one of my students once said, like a cross between anise and black pepper. Sultanas complement the butter beans beautifully. It may seem like a very unusual combination, but it is a very tasty one.

It is best to use the medium-sized beans for this dish. You do have to soak them for 20 hours but they hold their shape and have a nice bite to them.

6 oz/180 g medium-sized dried butter beans	⅛ tsp cayenne pepper, or to taste
3 tbs vegetable oil	½ tsp salt, or to taste
1 tsp whole ajwain seeds	2–4 tbs sultanas
¼ tsp ground turmeric	2 tsp sugar, or to taste
	1 tbs lemon juice, or more to taste

Pick over the butter beans and wash them. Put them in a bowl and cover them with 1¼ pt/¾ l of water. Leave to soak for 20 hours. Drain.

Heat the oil in a heavy, 2–3-qt/2¼–3½-l pot over a medium-high flame. When hot, put in the *ajwain* seeds and stir at once. Now put in the drained butter beans and turn the heat to medium-low. Add the turmeric, cayenne to taste, salt, sultanas, sugar, and lemon juice. Stir to mix. Add 8 fl oz/2½ dl water and bring to a simmer. Cover tightly and simmer very gently for 45 minutes. Check the beans every 10 minutes. If the water evaporates, add a tablespoon of hot water whenever needed. There should be no liquid left when the butter beans have finished cooking. Adjust seasonings.

CHANA DAL WITH CUCUMBER
INDIA   (serves 4–6)

Chana dal has a warm, sweet taste which makes it good both when cooked alone and when combined with vegetables. In Bengal as well as in Delhi, *chana dal* is often cooked with a long, green marrow shaped somewhat like a long bowling pin. The marrow is peeled, seeded, cut into 1-in/2½-cm sections and added to the *dal* towards the end of the cooking time. I have found this marrow occasionally in Indian and Chinese grocery stores as well as in a few health-food stores. If you can find it, do use it. If not, cucumbers make a good substitute.

6½ oz/185 g chana dal	¾ tsp salt
½ tsp ground turmeric	½ tsp garam masala
2 cloves garlic, peeled	About ⅛ tsp cayenne pepper
2 five-pence-piece sized slices of	1 tbs vegetable oil
fresh ginger	½ tsp whole cumin seeds
A 6-inch long section of cucumber	2 tbs ghee or unsalted butter

Pick over the *dal* and wash it in several changes of water. Drain. Put it in a 2–3-qt/2¼–3½-l pot along with 1¾ pt/1 l of water. Bring to the boil. Remove the scum. Add the turmeric, garlic, and ginger and turn heat to very low. Cover the pot in such a way that the lid is just slightly ajar. (This prevents the *dal* from boiling over.) Cook gently for about 1½ hours or until *dal* is quite tender. Stir every 10 minutes during the last hour of cooking. If the *dal* sticks to the bottom, stir more frequently.

While the *dal* is cooking, peel the cucumber and cut it in half lengthwise. Scoop out all the seeds with a teaspoon or a grapefruit spoon. Now cut the two cucumber halves crosswise into 1-in/2½-cm-long segments.

For information about ingredients and basic techniques that may be unfamiliar, see General Information, pages 481-506.

When the *dal* is tender, add the cucumber, salt, *garam masala*, and cayenne pepper. Stir, and bring to a simmer. Cover and cook on very low heat for 5 to 10 minutes or until cucumber is tender but still a bit crisp. Turn off heat and uncover.

Heat the oil in a small frying pan or other very small butter-warmer-type pot over a medium flame. When hot, put in the cumin seeds. As soon as they sizzle and turn a shade darker (this takes just a few seconds), pour the hot oil with cumin seeds over the *chana dal* and cover the pot immediately. Reheat the *dal* before serving and mix in the *ghee* or butter.

On Cooking Dried Chick Peas

Pick over 8 oz/225 g of dried chick peas and wash them in several changes of water. Drain them. Put the chick peas and ⅛ tsp baking powder in 1 qt/11½ dl of water and soak for 12 hours. Now put the chick peas and their soaking liquid into a heavy pot and bring to the boil. Cover, lower heat, and let the chick peas simmer for 45 minutes. Add 1 tsp salt and simmer for at least another 15 minutes. Taste a chick pea. If it is still hard, continue the cooking. The cooking time generally varies with the freshness of the chick peas. Older and therefore harder peas take longer to cook. Sometimes my chick peas have been done in 1 hour; at other times I have cooked them for 3 hours. Another way of cooking the chick peas is by using a pressure cooker. After the chick peas have soaked, put them and their soaking liquid into a pressure cooker. Add 1 tsp salt. Cover and bring up the pressure to 15 lb/6¾ kg. Let the chick peas cook for 30 minutes and then let the pressure drop by itself.

Depending upon your recipe, the chick peas may now be drained. Save the liquid for soups. If any of your chick pea recipes call for water, you may substitute this liquid.

Half a pound/225 g of dried chick peas will yield about 1½ lb/ 675 g of cooked, drained chick peas.

You may, at times, substitute tinned chick peas for the home-cooked kind. A 15-oz/450-g tin of chick peas generally yields about 10 oz/285 g of drained chick peas.

CHICK PEA SALAD
INDIA   (serves 4–6)

Served as a snack throughout India, this is the simplest version of the Indian chick pea salad.

3 15-oz/450-g tins chick peas, or
10 oz/285 g dried chick peas,
cooked according to directions
(see p. 103) and their cooking
liquid
6 spring onions, trimmed and
finely sliced halfway up their
green sections
2 tbs lemon juice

¾–1 tsp salt
¼ tsp freshly ground black pepper
2 tbs finely chopped fresh green
coriander, or parsley
1 fresh hot green chilli, finely
chopped, or green pepper, finely
chopped
¼ tsp cayenne pepper

Pour contents of chick pea tins or home-cooked chick peas into a
saucepan. Bring to the boil. Drain, discarding liquid.

In a serving bowl, combine chick peas with all the other ingredients. Mix well and set aside, unrefrigerated, for 1 hour. Mix again.
Serve cold or at room temperature.

CHICK PEA AND GREEN BEAN SALAD
NORTH INDIAN STYLE   (serves 6)

This is a salad that I have made up. I find that the use of *garam
masala* and grated ginger in the dressing gives a very interesting
piquancy.

12 oz/340 g cooked chick peas (see
page 103) or 12 oz/340 g
drained, tinned chick peas

DRESSING FOR THE CHICK PEAS
4 fl oz/1 dl vegetable oil
2 fl oz/½ dl wine vinegar
¼–⅓ tsp salt
1 tsp garam masala
2 cloves garlic, peeled and crushed
to a pulp
1/16–⅛ tsp cayenne pepper

DRESSING FOR GREEN BEANS
2 fl oz/½ dl vegetable oil
2 tbs lemon juice
½ tsp salt
½ tsp garam masala
2 tbs finely chopped onions
1 tsp finely grated fresh ginger

½ lb/225 g fresh green beans
½ tsp salt

Heat the chick peas in their own liquid if they are home-cooked, or in ½ pt/¼ l water if they are tinned, and drain. Empty them into the bowl. Beat together all the ingredients for the chick pea dressing and pour it over them while they are still hot. Mix well and adjust seasonings. Cool, cover, and set aside.

Combine all the ingredients for the dressing to go on the green beans. Wash and trim the green beans and cut them into ¾-in/ 2-cm-long pieces. Bring 2½ pt/1½ l of water to the boil and add ½ tsp salt to it. When the water is boiling rapidly, put in the cut beans. Keep boiling on high heat for 3 to 4 minutes or until beans are just cooked through. Drain the beans thoroughly. Shake them about in the colander or sieve used for draining until they look very dry. Put beans in a bowl (not the same one as the chick peas). Pour their dressing over them and let them sit for 5 minutes. Combine the two salads and mix well. (I usually let the chick peas sit in their dressing for 2 to 5 hours before proceeding with the cooking of the green beans. This gives the chick peas time to absorb their dressing properly. However, if you are rushed, you may cook the green beans as soon as you have finished making the chick pea salad.) Serve at room temperature or cold in individual portions on small salad plates.

CHICK PEAS WITH GARLIC, TOMATOES, AND GREEN CHILLIES
INDIA   *(serves 8)*

This dish may be served with almost any Indian meal, accompanied by a green vegetable, a yogurt relish and a bread. When my daughters' friends drop in at odd hours, hungry of course, I often put out a bowl of these chick peas, some pitta bread, and a quick cucumber and yogurt combination.

18–24 cloves garlic, peeled
4 tbs vegetable oil
2 tsp whole cumin seeds
4 tbs tomato purée mixed with
    6 fl oz/1¾ dl water
4 15-oz/450-g tins of drained chick
    peas or 2¼ lb/1 kg boiled,
    drained chick peas (see page
    103)

6 medium-sized potatoes, boiled,
    peeled, and cut into ¾-in/2-cm
    cubes
1½–2 tsp salt
5 fresh hot green chillies
2 tsp ground cumin seeds
1 tsp ground amchoor or lemon
    juice
⅛ tsp cayenne pepper

Put the garlic into the container of a food processor or blender. Add 2 fl oz/½ dl water and blend until you have a smooth paste.

Heat the oil in a 10-in/25-cm-wide, heavy pot over a medium-high flame. When hot, put in the cumin seeds. A few seconds later, put in the garlic paste. Fry for about 2 minutes, stirring all the time. Add the tomato purée mixture. Keep stirring and cook for another minute. Add the drained chick peas, diced potatoes, 16 fl oz/½ l water, salt, green chillies, ground cumin, *amchoor*, and cayenne. Stir gently and bring to a simmer. Cover, turn heat to low, and simmer gently for 20 minutes.

CHICK PEA AND TOMATO STEW
MIDDLE EAST   *(serves 4–6)*

6 medium-sized tomatoes
4 fl oz/1 dl olive oil
2 medium-sized onions, peeled and
   chopped
4 cloves garlic, peeled and finely
   chopped
12–13 oz/340–370 g boiled, drained
   chick peas (see page 103) or
   drained tinned chick peas
4 tbs very finely chopped fresh
   parsley
½ tsp dried thyme
1 tsp salt, or to taste

Drop the tomatoes into boiling water for 15 seconds. Remove with a slotted spoon and peel. Chop the tomatoes finely.

Heat the oil in a 7–8-in/18–20-cm-wide pan over a medium flame. Put in the onions and garlic. Stir and fry for 3 to 4 minutes or until onions are soft. Put in the tomatoes. Stir and cook them for 3 to 4 minutes or until they are soft and paste-like. Add the chick peas, parsley, thyme, salt, and 8 fl oz/¼ l water. Bring to the boil. Cover, lower heat and simmer gently for 10 to 15 minutes.

VERY SPICY, DELICIOUS CHICK PEAS
INDIA   *(serves 4–6)*

This is my mother's recipe for chick peas. It is wonderfully tart and hot. My mother's family, still living in the narrow lanes of an Old Delhi built in the seventeenth century, tended to eat very spicy

For information about ingredients and basic techniques that may be unfamiliar, see General Information, pages 481-506.

foods. My father's side of the family, which had moved in the 1920s into a more Westernized section of town built outside the Old City walls, ate a calmer, less fiery cuisine. As a child, I loved both styles of food but because my father and his very 'proper' ways smacked of Establishment, I would often sneak off with my mother to eat spicy bazaar food served on leaves of dubious cleanliness in the narrow lanes of Old Delhi.

This chick pea dish is still sold in Delhi bazaars by hawking vendors. The chick peas used are the dried variety that have to be soaked overnight and then boiled until tender.

The paprika that I have used is a substitute for the Kashmiri red pepper, which gives a red colour − but no heat − to the dishes in which it is used.

These spicy chick peas can easily be made up to two days ahead of time. In fact, their flavour improves if they are left, refrigerated, for 24 hours.

5 tbs vegetable oil
2 medium-sized onions, peeled and finely chopped
8 cloves garlic, peeled and finely chopped
1 tbs ground coriander seeds
2 tsp ground cumin seeds
¼–½ tsp ground cayenne pepper
1 tsp ground turmeric
6 tbs finely chopped, skinned, fresh or tinned ripe tomatoes
2½ 15-oz/450-g tins chick peas, drained, or 1½ lb/675 g home-cooked, drained chick peas (see page 103)

2 tsp ground roasted cumin seeds
1 tbs ground amchoor
2 tsp sweet paprika
1 tsp garam masala
½–1 tsp salt (or to taste)
1 tbs or more lemon juice
1 fresh hot green chilli, finely chopped (use more or less as desired)
2 tsp very finely grated fresh ginger

Heat the oil in a wide pot over a medium flame. When hot, put in the finely chopped onions and garlic. Stir and fry until the mixture is a rich medium-brown shade. Turn heat to medium-low and add the coriander, cumin (not the roasted cumin), cayenne, and turmeric. Stir for a few seconds. Now put in the finely chopped tomatoes. Stir and fry until the tomatoes are well amalgamated with the spice mixture and brown lightly. Add the drained chick peas and 8 fl oz/¼ l water. Stir. Add the ground roasted cumin, amchoor, paprika, garam masala, salt, and lemon juice. Stir again. Cover, turn heat to low, and simmer for 10 minutes. Remove cover and add the chopped green chilli and grated ginger. Stir and cook, uncovered, for another 30 seconds.

FALAFEL
(Chick pea Patties)
MIDDLE EAST   *(makes about 18 patties)*

Falafel, made out of dried peas or beans, are a popular snack throughout the Middle East. Beans are soaked, ground, and seasoned with onions and parsley. They are then formed into balls or patties and deep fried.

6 oz/170 g dried chick peas, soaked
   in 1 qt/11½ dl water for 24
   hours
1 tsp bicarbonate of soda
1 tsp salt
1 small onion, very finely chopped
2 tbs very finely chopped parsley
1 tsp ground roasted cumin seeds

1 tsp ground coriander seeds
2 cloves garlic, peeled and mashed
   to a pulp
A little freshly ground black
   pepper
1 tbs lemon juice
⅛ tsp cayenne pepper
Oil for deep frying

Drain the chick peas and put them into the container of a food processor or blender. Add the bicarbonate of soda and salt. Turn the machine on and blend until you have the texture of coarse breadcrumbs or fine bulgar wheat. You should *not* have a paste.

Empty the chick peas into a bowl. Add the onion, parsley, cumin, coriander, garlic, black pepper, lemon juice, and cayenne. Mix gently with a fork. Do not pat down. This mixture should be loose and crumbly.

Put 2 in/5 cm of oil in a wok or other utensil for deep frying and set to heat on a medium-low flame. You need a temperature of 350–375° F/180–190° C. While the oil heats, form the first batch of patties. Using a very light touch, form patties that are about 2¼ in/5¾ cm in diameter, about ¾ in/2 cm thick in the centre and less so at the edges. Do not pat down or try to be too neat. The patties should just about hold together. Put as many patties into the hot oil as the utensil will hold in a single layer. Fry about 4 minutes or until the patties are reddish-brown on both sides. Turn at least once during the frying process. When the patties are done, remove them with a slotted spoon and drain on kitchen paper. Do all patties this way.

Serve hot, with Tahini Dipping Sauce. You may also tear open an edge of a pitta bread, stuff in two *falafel* and some shredded lettuce and sliced tomatoes, and then douse the stuffing with 2 tbs of Tahini Dipping Sauce to make a Middle Eastern sandwich.

For information about ingredients and basic techniques that may be unfamiliar, see General Information, pages 481–506.

Usha's Mother's
BESAN
(A Savoury Gram-Flour 'Quiche')
INDIA   *(serves 6–8)*

This dish resembles a quiche only in as much as it is like a set custard that can be cut and served in sections. There the similarity ends. If you have eaten a *socca* in Nice and can imagine something similar made out of gram flour but much thicker, then you have the Kutchi dish called *besan*.

To make it, a mixture of gram flour, spices, and water is cooked in a pot very much as you would *choux* pastry – with constant stirring. As the mixture thickens, it begins to leave the sides of the pot. It is then poured into a cake tin and allowed to set. Fresh coriander, finely chopped green chillies, and shredded fresh coconut are sprinkled over it as garnishes. Once it has cooled completely, it is cut into squares and served as a snack or with a meal.

9 oz/225 g gram flour, sifted
3–4 cloves of garlic, peeled and
   mashed to a pulp
½ tsp finely grated fresh ginger
1½ tsp ground cumin seeds
½ tsp ground turmeric
½–1 tsp cayenne pepper
1 medium-sized onion
5 tbs vegetable oil

5–6 dried or fresh curry leaves
2 tsp salt
1 tbs lemon juice
1 tbs finely chopped fresh green
   coriander
1–2 fresh hot green chillies, finely
   chopped
½ oz/15 g grated fresh coconut

Put the sifted gram flour in a bowl. Slowly add 1¾ pt/1 l water, a few tablespoons at a time. Stir as you do so, breaking up all lumps with the back of a wooden spoon. (If the batter still has lumps in it, put it through a strainer.)

Combine the garlic, ginger, cumin, turmeric, and cayenne, according to your taste, in a small cup. Add 2 fl oz/½ dl water and mix well. Set aside.

Peel and cut the onion in half lengthwise, then slice into fine half rings.

Heat the oil in a heavy, well-seasoned (or nonstick) 2–2½ qt/2¼–2¾ l pot over a medium flame. When hot, put in the curry leaves and then, a few seconds later, the sliced onions. Stir and fry the onions for 2 to 3 minutes. Do not let them brown. Add the spices in the small cup. Stir and fry them for about 1 minute. Now put in the gram-flour mixture and bring it to a boil, stirring all the time. Turn the heat to medium-low. Keep stirring vigorously with a wooden spoon until mixture seems to leave the sides of the pot. This should take about 20 minutes. Add the salt and lemon juice. Stir to mix. Taste the gram-flour mixture. It should have a cooked taste. (In other words, it should not taste raw.) Empty the mixture into a 9×9×1½-in/23×23×4-cm cake tin. Smooth over the top with a spatula. Sprinkle the fresh coriander, green chillies – as much as you like – and coconut over the top and allow to cool. Cut into 1½-in/4-cm squares.

You may have this dish as a snack at teatime or you may serve it as a part of an Indian meal.

LOBIO
(Red Kidney Bean Salad with a Walnut Dressing)
CAUCASUS   (serves 4)

When my husband and I were in the Soviet Union, we found that the food we liked the most came from areas that lie to the east and west of the Caspian Sea. We had *lobio* for the first time at the Aragvi restaurant in Moscow, where it is served as one of the appetizers, along with flat bread and pickled vegetables.

I use tinned red kidney beans for this recipe. If you wish to use the dried variety, here is how you go about it: pick over 6 oz/170 g of beans. Then wash and drain them. Put the beans in a pot along with 2½ pt/1½ l water and bring to the boil. Lower heat and simmer, uncovered, for 2 minutes. Turn the heat off and let the beans sit, uncovered, for 1 hour. Bring the beans to the boil again. Cover, and simmer on low heat for 40 minutes. Add 1½ tsp salt and simmer, covered, for another 15 minutes. Drain, but reserve some of the liquid for the dressing.

1 1-lb/450-g tin of red kidney beans	⅛ tsp salt
1 clove garlic, peeled	⅛ tsp freshly ground black pepper
3 oz/85 g shelled walnuts	⅟₁₆–⅛ tsp cayenne pepper
1 tbs plus 1 tsp red wine vinegar	1 tbs finely sliced spring onion
2 tbs vegetable or olive or walnut oil	2 tbs finely chopped fresh green coriander

Drain the beans and put them in a small bowl. *Save the liquid.*

You need a food processor or blender to make the dressing. (If you have neither, pound the garlic and walnuts in a mortar. Add the vinegar, salt, pepper, and cayenne. Mix. Slowly add the oil,

---

For information about ingredients and basic techniques that may be unfamiliar, see General Information, pages 481-506.

beating well with a fork.) Start your machine and put in the garlic. When it is finely chopped put in the walnuts. When they have turned crumb-like, add the vinegar. Slowly add 4 tbs of the reserved bean liquid. Blend until you have a paste. You may have to stop the machine and scrape down a few times. Now add the oil in a steady stream and then the salt, pepper, and cayenne. Blend until you have a smooth dressing.

Pour the dressing over the beans. Add half the spring onion and half the fresh coriander. Mix and taste for seasonings. You may cover and chill the salad until you are ready to eat; it improves if allowed to sit around for a few hours. Just before you are ready to eat, put the salad on a clean serving dish and sprinkle the remaining spring onion and fresh coriander over the top.

RED BEANS COOKED WITH GARLIC AND GINGER

INDIA   (serves 4–6)

6 oz/180 g small red azuki beans
2 whole cloves garlic, peeled
2 five-pence-piece sized slices of
  fresh ginger
1 whole dried hot red pepper
1 tbs lime or lemon juice
¾–1 tsp salt

⅓ tsp garam masala
4 fl oz/1 dl single cream
3 tbs ghee or vegetable oil
½ tsp very finely chopped garlic
½ tsp very finely chopped fresh
  ginger
¼ tsp cayenne pepper

Put the beans and 1 qt/11½ dl water into a heavy 2½-qt/2¾-l pot and bring to the boil. Turn heat to low and simmer for 2 minutes. Turn the heat off and let the beans sit, uncovered, for 1 hour. Add the whole garlic cloves, the slices of ginger, and the whole red pepper. Bring to the boil. Cover in such a way as to leave the lid very slightly ajar, lower heat and simmer gently for 1 hour. Mash the cloves of garlic against the sides of the pot. Remove and discard the ginger slices and the whole red pepper. Now take 12 fl oz/3½ dl of the beans and liquid as well as 4 fl oz of just the beans (removed with a slotted spoon) and put them into the container of a food processor or blender. Blend until smooth. Pour this paste back into the pot with the beans. Add the lime juice, salt, garam masala, and cream. Stir and taste. Leave the beans uncovered on a low flame.

Heat the ghee in a small frying pan or a very small pot over a medium flame. When hot, put in the finely chopped garlic and ginger. Stir for a few seconds. The garlic should brown slightly. Add the cayenne, stir once, and pour this ghee–spice mixture over the beans. Cover immediately and turn the heat off under the beans.

LENTILS WITH GARLIC AND TOMATOES
MIDDLE EAST   *(serves 4)*

4 tbs olive or other vegetable oil
5 cloves garlic, peeled and finely
  chopped
½ lb/225 g tomatoes (1 large or 2
  smaller ones), peeled and finely
  chopped

6½ oz/185 g dried whole green
  lentils, picked over, washed,
  and drained
¾–1 tsp salt
1 tbs lemon juice

Heat the oil in a heavy, wide, 2½-qt/2¾-l pot over a medium flame.
When hot, put in the garlic. Stir and fry until the garlic browns
lightly. Put in the tomatoes. Stir and cook about 5 minutes or until
tomatoes turn into a paste. Put in the lentils and 1 pt/5¾ dl water.
Bring to the boil. Cover, lower heat and simmer gently for one
hour. Add the salt and lemon juice. Stir to mix.

LENTIL SALAD
MIDDLE EAST   *(serves 8)*

This salad may be stored in the refrigerator for several days. It is
excellent to take on picnics.

1 lb/450 g dried whole green lentils
1 tsp ground cumin seeds
2½ tsp salt
4 spring onions
4–4½ tbs lemon juice
⅛–¼ tsp freshly ground black
  pepper
4 fl oz/1 dl olive oil
1 oz/30 g finely chopped parsley

In a 3–4-qt/3½–4½-l pot, combine the lentils with 2¼ pt/1¼ l of
water. Add the cumin, 1 tsp salt and bring to the boil. Cover, and

---

*For information about ingredients and basic techniques that may be unfamiliar, see General
Information, pages 481–506.*

simmer gently for 50 minutes or until tender. Remove cover and let the lentils cool a bit. Slice the spring onions in very fine rounds halfway up their green sections. When lukewarm, add the remaining salt, the lemon juice, the black pepper, oil, parsley, and spring onions.

Stir and cool. Serve at room temperature or cold.

LENTILS WITH SPINACH
MIDDLE EAST   (serves 6)

1¼ lb/560 g fresh or frozen leaf
  spinach
1 medium-sized onion, peeled
5 tbs vegetable oil
2 cloves garlic, peeled and finely
  chopped

7 oz/200 g dried whole green
  lentils, picked over, washed,
  and drained
1½–1¾ tsp salt
1 tsp ground cumin seeds
⅛ tsp freshly ground black pepper

Separate the fresh spinach leaves and wash well. Do not discard the pinkish roots. Wash them as well. (They will taste very good when cooked.) Bunch up a few leaves at a time and cut them crosswise into ½-in/1½-cm-wide strips. Cut each root into 2 to 3 pieces. If using frozen spinach, cook according to directions, drain and chop coarsely.

Cut the onion in half lengthwise, and then cut the halves into fine half rings.

Heat the oil in a heavy, wide, casserole-type pot over a medium flame. When hot, put in the onion and garlic. Stir and sauté for 2 minutes. Now put in the lentils and 1¼ pt/¾ l of water. Bring to the boil. Cover, lower heat and simmer about 50 minutes or until lentils are just tender. Add the spinach leaves and roots, salt, and cumin. Stir to mix and bring to a simmer. Cover and simmer another 10 to 15 minutes or until spinach is tender and well mixed into the lentils. Stir gently a few times during this period. Put in the black pepper and mix again. This dish may easily be made ahead of time and reheated.

MUNG OR MASOOR DAL
INDIA   (serves 4–6)

These two basic split peas are North Indian staples and are cooked in pretty much the same way. The cooking time and amount of water can vary slightly according to the age of the dal. Masoor dal is salmon-coloured when uncooked and is sold as red split lentils or Egyptian lentils in supermarkets.

There are many variations of the final flavouring that is provided in this recipe by the asafetida, cumin, and red peppers. You might like to try them at some time or other. Into the 2 tbs of hot oil, you may put: (1) 2 tsp whole black mustard seeds, 1 bay leaf, ½ tsp finely grated fresh ginger, and 3 fresh hot green chillies; (2) 1 tsp *kalonji*, 1 bay leaf, ½ tsp finely grated fresh ginger, and 3 fresh hot green chillies; (3) 1 tsp ground cumin, 1 tsp ground coriander, ½ tsp finely grated fresh ginger, and ⅛–¼ tsp cayenne pepper; or (4) 1 tbs finely chopped onion, ½ tsp finely chopped garlic. Let them fry a bit and then add 1 tsp ground cumin, and ⅛–¼ tsp cayenne pepper.

6½ oz/185 g mung or masoor dal
1 five-pence-piece sized slice of
   fresh ginger
¾ tsp ground turmeric
1 tsp salt

2 tbs vegetable oil or ghee
A pinch of ground asafetida
1 tsp whole cumin seeds
2 whole, hot dried red peppers

Pick over the *dal* and wash in several changes of water. Drain, then put with 1½ pt/8½ dl of water into a heavy, 2½-qt/2¾-l pot. Bring to the boil and skim away all the surface scum. Add the ginger and turmeric. Turn the heat to low and cover in such a way as to leave the lid just very slightly ajar (or else the *dal* will boil over). Cook for 1 to 1½ hours or until *dal* is no longer grainy. When done, a thick purée settles at the bottom and a thin *dal* 'water' rises to the top. You should stir the *dal* a few times during the last 15 minutes of the cooking time and turn the heat to very low if necessary in order to avoid sticking. Add the salt and mix it in. Keep the *dal* covered and hot.

Heat the oil in a small frying pan or a very small pot over a medium flame. When hot, put in first the asafetida, then, a second later, the cumin and, when the seeds start to sizzle, the red peppers. Turn the red peppers over so all sides turn dark and crisp. This entire step should take about 10 seconds. Quickly pour the oil and all the spices into the hot *dal*. Cover the *dal* immediately and let it absorb the flavourings for at least 1 minute before serving.

Maya's
ROASTED MUNG DAL
INDIA

Here the *dal* is cooked almost exactly as in the preceding recipe, with this one difference — it is roasted lightly before it is cooked in

---

For information about ingredients and basic techniques that may be unfamiliar, see General Information, pages 481-506.

water. To do this, pick over the *dal* but do not wash it. Rub it in a dishcloth to get rid of loose dust. Then put it into a 6–7-in/15–18-cm frying pan or heavy wok over a medium-low flame. Stir and roast the *dal* until it turns light brown in spots. Remove it from the fire. *Now* wash it in several changes of water and proceed with the recipe.

Finish off the *dal* with either the first or second suggestion in the introduction on page 114.

MONGO
(Mung Beans with Spinach and Tomatoes)
PHILIPPINES   *(serves 4–6)*

This earthy dish consists of cooked mung beans added to a medley of sautéed vegetables — garlic, onion, and tomatoes. Then, during the final minutes of cooking, the very nutritious *malunggay* leaves, rich in vitamin A, or bitter-gourd leaves are thrown into the pot. Just before eating, the dish is further perked up with the juice of the *kalamansi* lime and a little olive oil. I have substituted spinach for the Filipino greens. Instead of the *kalamansi* lime, ordinary lime or lemon may be used.

6 oz/180 g whole mung beans
5 tbs vegetable oil
7 cloves garlic, peeled and lightly
   mashed
2 medium-sized onions, peeled and
   chopped
¾ lb/340 g ripe tomatoes, peeled
   and chopped

½ lb/225 g tender spinach leaves,
   well washed and separated
1 tsp salt
1 tbs lime juice
1 lime, cut into wedges
2 fl oz/½ dl fruity olive oil
   (optional)

Clean and pick over the beans. Wash in several changes of water. Drain. Put the beans and 1 qt/11½ dl water into a 2-qt/2¼-l pot and bring to the boil. Cover, lower heat and simmer for 2 minutes. Turn off the heat and let the pot sit, covered, for 1 hour. Bring the beans to the boil again. Turn heat to low and simmer gently for 1½ hours or until the beans are tender and slightly mushy. Stir gently during the last half hour of cooking to prevent sticking.

Heat 5 tbs vegetable oil in an 8-in/20-cm-wide sauté pan over a medium flame. When hot, put in the garlic. Stir and fry until the garlic turns a pale brown colour. Add the onions. Stir and sauté them until they turn translucent. Add the tomatoes. Stir and fry for 5 to 6 minutes or until tomatoes just start to catch. Add the cooked mung beans and bring to a simmer. Simmer, stirring now and then, for 5 minutes. Now put in the spinach leaves, salt, and the

1 tbs lime juice. Stir and bring to a simmer. Simmer, stirring occasionally, for about 5 minutes or until spinach is cooked.

Pass the lime wedges and olive oil separately, and serve with rice.

'DRY' MUNG DAL

INDIA *(serves 4)*

As opposed to the more 'soupy' *dal* dishes, here each grain stands, plump and firm, all by itself. To achieve this, the split peas are first soaked for 3 hours and then cooked, simply and quickly, in a small quantity of water. The cooking time is only about 15 minutes. For a quick lunch, I often stuff whole-wheat pitta halves with this *dal* along with some sliced ripe tomatoes and lettuce.

6½ oz/185 g mung dal
3 tbs vegetable oil
A generous pinch of crushed
  asafetida
1½ tsp whole cumin seeds

½ tsp ground turmeric
⅛ tsp cayenne pepper
½ tsp salt
3 tbs ghee or unsalted butter

Pick over the *dal* and wash it in several changes of water. Drain. Put *dal* in a bowl. Add 16 fl oz/½ l water and soak *dal* for 3 to 4 hours. Drain.

Heat the oil in a heavy, 2–3-qt/2¼–3½-l pot over a medium-high flame. When hot, put in the asafetida and, 2 seconds later, the whole cumin seeds. As soon as the cumin seeds turn a shade darker (this takes just a few seconds), put in the *dal*, turmeric, cayenne, and salt. Turn heat to medium-low and stir to mix. Now put in 8 fl oz/¼ l water and bring to a simmer. Cover tightly, turn heat to very, very low and cook gently for about 15 minutes. The *dal* should be tender enough to eat but each grain should be quite separate. Put in the *ghee* or butter, stir, and serve at once.

HOW TO SPROUT YOUR OWN MUNG BEANS FOR CHINESE, JAPANESE, AND OTHER FAR EASTERN AND SOUTH-EAST ASIAN DISHES

Wherever there are Chinese grocery stores, you should be able to buy fresh mung-bean sprouts by the pound. The sprouts, which look like 3-in/8-cm tails attached to small whitish heads, are not only used in rice, noodle, and vegetable dishes, but are excellent to

---

For information about ingredients and basic techniques that may be unfamiliar, see General Information, pages 481-506.

put in salads along with more mundane things like raw mushrooms, lettuce, and cucumber. If you cannot buy any fresh sprouts in your neighbourhood, make them at home. They are not difficult to make, though they do take 3 to 4 days to reach the correct length.

In Britain most people are familiar only with the Oriental type of bean sprout which is more tail than bean. Just to avoid any confusion, there is another mung-bean sprout that I will be referring to in this book and that is the Indian version. In India, we let the mung bean sprout, but just barely. Only the tiniest shoots are allowed to emerge before the beans are gobbled up. I will describe these sprouts later, in the recipes that require them.

Health-food stores today sell dry mung beans and, very often, an array of gadgets in which you can do your sprouting. If you happen to have such a gadget, by all means use it. But there is no need at all to go and buy one, because the equipment that you already have in your home can be made to work just as well.

(makes about ¾ lb/340 g)

3 oz/85 g whole mung beans

Pick over the mung beans and discard any broken ones. Rinse in lukewarm water. Put the beans in a bowl and pour 1¼ pt/¾ l of lukewarm water over them. Cover the bowl and let the beans soak for 8 hours. Drain.

Rinse the beans in lukewarm water again and put them in a plastic bag that has been punched all over with holes (you can do this with a fork). Put the bag in a colander or sieve. Leave the mouth of the bag open. Cover this opening with a doubled or tripled well-dampened tea towel. Now put the sieve or colander in a large bowl (if it is a sieve, it should be balanced on a bowl) and then place the bowl in a dark and, if possible, humid place with the ideal temperature ranging between 70° and 75° F/21 and 24° C. Some people use the area under their sinks. Every 4 hours, take out the bowl. Put the sieve or colander under a tap and let lukewarm water pour through the tea towel, over the beans, out through the holes in the plastic bag, and, finally, out through the sieve or colander. Place the sieve or colander back in the bowl (some dripping will continue) and put the bowl back in the selected dark place for another 4 hours. Never disturb the beans. Continue to do this for 3 to 4 days or until the sprouts are 2–3 in/5–8 cm long. (This is the ideal method for sprouting. However, since I do not believe in losing sleep over bean sprouts, I give the beans a good soaking before I retire and another when I get up in the morning. As a result, not all my sprouts are perfect. Some actually look a bit stunted. That does not bother me. My sprouts are still crunchier and less waterlogged than 90 per cent of the sprouts than can be bought in grocery stores.)

Now put the sprouts in a very large bowl or basin and fill it with water. 'Rinse' the sprouts by rubbing them gently with your hands. This should make the green skin of the bean slip off. Tilt the basin to get rid of the skins. Those that do not float away should be picked off. Drain the sprouts. Put the sprouts in a container, fill the container with water, and refrigerate until needed. Do not cover the sprouts. If you change the water in this container every day, the sprouts should stay looking healthy for at least 3 days.

For information about ingredients and basic techniques that may be unfamiliar, see General Information, pages 481-506.

SOY-BEAN SPROUTS

There are many ways to make these sprouts. You could follow the method used for mung-bean sprouts and continue the sprouting process for about 6 days until you have sprouts of the right size. You must remember to water and drain the soy beans at least 3 to 4 times a day or they will go bad, which can happen easily if you are at all negligent. The easier method is to buy a dark sprouting jar with a mesh lid that is available in most health-food and even some gardening stores. Here is the jar method.

(makes about ½ lb/225 g)

3 oz/85 g dried soy beans

Pick over the beans and remove any cracked or broken ones. Rinse the beans in several changes of water. Drain. Soak the beans in 1 qt/l of water for 12 hours. Drain. Rinse gently and drain again. Put the beans in the jar and put on its mesh lid. Place the jar on its side in a warm, draught-free, dark place. I use my empty oven *without* the pilot light turned on. Now for the next 6 days or so, remove the jar from its warm place at least 4 times a day. Without tilting it about unduly, fill it with water and then pour *all* the water out. Put the jar back in its warm place. Keep doing this until the sprouts are about 3 in/8 cm long. Empty the contents of the sprouting jar into a bowl of water. The soy-bean skins will float to the top. Pour them out. Put the sprouts in a bowl of water and refrigerate until you need them. They should last at least 4 to 5 days. Change the water every day.

STIR-FRIED MUNG-BEAN SPROUTS, CARROTS, AND CABBAGE
CHINA

(serves 4)

3 spring onions
½ lb/225 g cabbage (¼ small to medium-sized head)
2 carrots
12 oz/340 g mung-bean sprouts
1–2 fresh hot green chillies
4 tbs vegetable oil
2 cloves garlic, peeled and very lightly mashed

3 five-pence-piece sized slices of fresh ginger
1 tbs Chinese shaohsing wine or dry sherry
½ tsp salt, or to taste
½ tsp sugar
1 tbs sesame oil

Prepare the vegetables: cut the spring onions into 3-in/8-cm-long sections and then cut lengthwise into thin strips. Remove the core from the cabbage, then shred the leaves into fine, long strips. Peel the carrots, trim them, and cut into fine julienne strips. Rinse the bean sprouts, drain and pat dry. Cut the chillies into fine, long shreds.

Heat the vegetable oil in a large wok over a high flame. When hot, put in the garlic and ginger. Stir them around for about 15 seconds, pressing the pieces against the sides of the wok. Put in the spring onions and stir once. Now put in the cabbage, carrots, mung-bean sprouts, and green chillies. Stir and fry for about 1½ minutes. Add the wine by pouring it around the sides of the wok. Stir once. Add the salt, sugar, and sesame oil. Stir for 3 to 4 seconds. Remove the ginger slices and serve at once.

Yien-Koo's
SALAD OF MUNG-BEAN SPROUTS AND EGG STRANDS
CHINA   *(serves 4)*

3 large eggs	1 lb/450 g mung-bean sprouts,
1 tbs Chinese shaohsing *wine or*	rinsed and drained
dry sherry	1 tbs distilled white cider vinegar
⅛ plus ¼ tsp salt	1 tbs Chinese thin soy sauce
4 tsp vegetable oil	1 tbs sesame oil
	½ tsp sugar

Beat the eggs well (but not to a froth) in a large bowl. Add the *shaohsing* wine, 2 tbs water, and ⅛ tsp salt. Beat lightly to mix.

Brush a 7–8-in/18–20-cm nonstick frying pan with 1 tsp oil and let it heat on a low flame. Pour in a quarter of the beaten eggs — just enough to barely cover the bottom of the frying pan. You will have to tilt the pan around in order to let the egg mixture flow evenly to the edges. Let the mixture set until firm. This may take 6 to 7 minutes. Ease a plastic spatula under the egg crêpe and remove it. Put it on a plate and let it cool. Make four crêpes this way, letting each cool on separate plates. Roll up each crêpe and then cut it crosswise into fine, ¼-in/¾-cm-wide strands.

Heat 1½ pt/8½ dl of water in a large pot. When boiling furiously, drop in the bean sprouts. Bring to the boil again. Turn off the heat immediately and drain the sprouts. Rinse the sprouts under cold water and leave to drain for 15 minutes. Pat dry.

Put the egg strands and sprouts in a serving bowl. Add the vinegar, soy sauce, ¼ tsp salt, sesame oil, and sugar. Toss to mix and taste for seasonings.

For information about ingredients and basic techniques that may be unfamiliar, see General Information, pages 481-506.

Devi's
SPROUTED MUNG BEANS COOKED WITH MUSTARD SEEDS
INDIA   *(serves 6)*

Indians eat sprouted mung beans, too, but these are sprouted quite differently from the ones in East and South-east Asia. We barely allow our sprouts to emerge from the beans before we eat them. The result of this is that even though Indian mung-bean sprouts are easy to digest, they are much more substantial.

In the Indian state of Gujarat, these beans are often served for breakfast, along with Soft Yogurt Cheese with Fresh Coriander and Spring Onions Gujarati Style (see page 273), a fresh mint chutney, and kakra, which resembles Scandinavian crispbread.

12 oz/340 g whole mung beans, picked over and washed
4 tbs vegetable oil
2 tsp whole black mustard seeds
5–6 medium-sized cloves of garlic, peeled and finely chopped
½ tsp ground turmeric
About ⅛–¼ tsp ground cayenne pepper
1¾–2 tsp salt
⅛–¼ tsp freshly ground black pepper
2–3 tbs lemon juice

Soak beans in 2¾ pt/1½ l of water. Cover and leave for 12 hours. Drain. Line a bowl with a wet tea towel in such a way as to leave enough of the towel on one side to cover the beans. Put the beans inside the towel-lined bowl. Cover them with the overhanging towel section. Now cover the bowl loosely with any lid that will not press down on the beans. Leave in a dark place (like an oven) for another 12 hours. The beans will just begin to sprout.

Heat the oil in a heavy saucepan over a medium-high flame. When very hot, put in the mustard seeds and turn the heat down to medium. As the mustard seeds pop (this will happen almost immediately), put in the finely chopped garlic and stir until garlic browns lightly. Now add the turmeric, cayenne, and, a few seconds later, the sprouted beans. Stir. Add the salt and 3 fl oz/¾ dl water. Bring to the boil. Cover tightly. Turn heat to low and cook gently for 15 to 20 minutes or until beans are tender. Stir a few times during the cooking. If the water evaporates. add a tablespoon of hot water.

Add the black pepper and lemon juice. Mix well. Taste for balance of hot, sour, and salty seasonings. This dish may be made ahead of time and reheated.

SPROUTED MUNG BEANS WITH SPINACH
INDIA   *(serves 8)*

Here is another Indian dish using barely sprouted mung beans. This time they are combined with spinach and fresh coriander. While this dish may be served hot at breakfast, lunch, or dinner, it is wonderful when served cold at picnics and buffet-style parties.

1 lb/450 g fresh spinach, trimmed and well washed, (or 1 packet frozen chopped spinach, cooked and drained)
5 tbs vegetable oil
1 tbs whole black mustard seeds
1 tbs whole cumin seeds
2 tsp coarsely grated fresh ginger
9–10 medium-sized cloves garlic, peeled and finely chopped
1 fresh hot green chilli, or more to taste, finely chopped

12 oz/340 g whole mung beans, semi-sprouted (according to directions in preceding recipe)
4 tbs finely chopped fresh green coriander
2 tsp salt
2 tsp ground cumin seeds
2 tsp ground coriander seeds
1 tsp garam masala
2 tbs lemon juice, or more to taste

In a large pot, bring about 3½ qt/4 l of water to a boil. Drop in the spinach and let it cook 2 to 3 minutes or until it is completely wilted. Drain, squeeze out as much liquid as you can, and then chop the spinach finely. Set aside.

Heat the oil in a wide, 3½–4-qt/4–4½-l pot over a medium flame. When very hot, put in the black mustard seeds and the whole cumin seeds. As soon as the seeds begin to pop and sizzle (this takes just a few seconds), put in the ginger, garlic, and green chilli. Stir and fry for about 1 minute or until garlic pieces turn a light brown. Now add the sprouted beans, the chopped spinach, the fresh coriander, the salt, and 8 fl oz/¼ l of water. Bring to the boil. Cover tightly and simmer gently for 10 minutes.

Remove the cover and add the ground cumin seeds, the ground coriander seeds, the *garam masala*, and the lemon juice. Stir to mix. Cover and simmer another 5 minutes.

Devi's
SALAD OF SPROUTED MUNG BEANS
INDIA   *(serves 6–8)*

This cool, green and white, lemony salad is a Gujarati favourite. Celery, considered foreign and therefore exotic in India, is not one

---

For information about ingredients and basic techniques that may be unfamiliar, see General Information, pages 481-506.

of its normal ingredients. However, my friend Devi Mangaldas does grow it in her Ahmedabad home and often adds it, most imaginatively, to a host of Indian foods — like this salad. The salad also contains onions, green peppers, and fresh coriander, all chopped very small so the pieces are of the same size as the beans themselves.

For this recipe, the whole mung beans are sprouted somewhat differently from the method used in the two preceding recipes.

The beans soak for 48 hours and are then left to sprout for 12 to 16 hours. These sprouts are meant to be eaten raw.

Here is how you make Indian-style bean sprouts for raw salads: soak 6½ oz/185 g mung beans in 2½ pt/1½ l of water. Cover and leave for 48 hours, making sure to change the water every 12 hours. Drain. Line a bowl with a wet tea towel in such a way as to leave enough of the towel on one side to cover the beans. Put the beans inside the towel-lined bowl. Cover with the overhanging towel section. Now cover the bowl loosely with any lid that will not press down on the beans. Leave in a dark place (like a cool oven) for 12 to 16 hours. The beans should just begin to sprout. 6½ oz/185 g of mung beans will make about 1 lb/450 g of Indian-style sprouts. If you are not going to eat the sprouts immediately, rinse them and put them in an uncovered bowl filled with water. Refrigerate for up to 36 hours.

1 lb/450 g Indian-style (see above) mung-bean sprouts, washed and drained
2 sticks celery, very finely chopped
1 medium-sized green pepper, seeded and very finely chopped
1 medium-sized onion, peeled and very finely chopped

1 oz/30 g washed, dried, and finely chopped fresh green coriander, or parsley
3 cloves garlic, peeled and very finely chopped
1 fresh hot green chilli, very finely chopped
1½ tsp salt
¼ tsp finely ground black pepper
3½ tbs (or more) lemon juice

Combine all the ingredients. Toss well and check the seasonings. Serve at room temperature or cold.

SOY-BEAN AND MUNG-BEAN SPROUTS SEASONED WITH SESAME OIL
KOREA   *(serves 4–6)*

This simple, refreshing dish may be served in place of a salad.

1 lb/450 g soy-bean sprouts   *1 lb/450 g mung-bean sprouts*

2 fl oz/½ dl Japanese soy sauce
2 tbs sesame oil
1 tbs sugar

¼ tsp salt
2 tsp roasted and lightly crushed
    sesame seeds

Bring 2½ qt/2¾ l of water to the boil in a 4-qt/4½-l pot. Put in the soy-bean sprouts and boil rapidly for 10 minutes. Add the mung-bean sprouts and boil another 2 minutes. Drain thoroughly, squeezing out as much of the water as possible.

Put the sprouts in a bowl. Add all the other ingredients and mix well. Taste for seasonings.

HARICOT BEAN SALAD
MIDDLE EAST   (serves 4–6)

6½ oz/185 g dried haricot beans,
    picked over, washed, and
    drained
5 tbs olive oil
3 tbs lemon juice

¾ tsp salt
8 tbs finely chopped fresh parsley
2 spring onions cut into fine
    rounds including green
⅛ tsp freshly ground black pepper

Put the beans and 1½ pt/8½ dl water in a heavy 2½-qt/2¾-l pot. Bring to the boil. Cover, lower heat and simmer 2 minutes. Turn off the heat and let the pot sit, covered, for 1 hour. Uncover, and bring to the boil again. Cover, lower heat, and simmer gently for 40 minutes or until beans are tender but still retain their shape. (Older beans will take longer to cook.) Beat the oil, lemon juice, and salt together, then add to the beans while they are still hot. Add all the other ingredients and mix well. Adjust seasonings, if necessary.

Tatie Wawo-Runtu's
KACANG ASIN
(Salted Peanuts with Garlic)
INDONESIA   (makes ¼ lb/115 g)

These peanuts may be added to Sambal Goreng Tempeh Kering (see page 129). If you wish to do that, double all the ingredients for the spicy paste in that recipe and then fold in the peanuts when you put in the tempeh. You may, of course, just serve these peanuts as a nice, crisp snack.

5 oz/140 g raw, shelled, and
    skinned peanuts
2 tsp salt

6 tbs vegetable oil
8 cloves garlic, peeled and cut into
    slivers

For information about ingredients and basic techniques that may be unfamiliar, see General Information, pages 481-506.

Soak the peanuts in 1¼ pt/¾ l water for 8 hours or overnight. Drain. Combine the salt and 8 fl oz/¼ l water in a bowl. Put the peanuts into it and let them soak for 1 hour. Drain and pat dry.

Heat the oil in an 8-in/20-cm frying pan over a medium flame. Put in the peanuts. Stir and fry for 3 to 4 minutes or until peanuts just begin to lose their white colour. Put in the garlic. Stir and fry another minute or until peanuts are golden. Remove with a slotted spoon and drain on kitchen paper.

Mrs Bannerji's
SPINACH WITH RAW PEANUTS
INDIA *(serves 3–4)*

Raw peanuts are used in many regions of India to make a host of delicious foods, not the least of which is this simple and tasty dish from Bengal in which peanuts (the Bengalis call them *cheena badaam* or the 'almonds of China') are cooked with spinach. As you may already know, raw peanuts, once cooked, do not taste like peanuts at all (rather, not like roasted peanuts) but more like peas and beans – they are a legume, after all – and like a heavenly cross between chestnuts and water chestnuts.

Peanuts are a concentrated food. Pound for pound, they have more proteins, minerals, and vitamins than beef liver. They do tend to be high in fat, but this is vegetable fat which the body needs. Peanut dishes make an excellent substitute for meat dishes. For vegans who do not eat dairy products, peanut and soy-bean dishes are well worth exploring.

It is best to get raw, shelled peanuts for the recipe that follows. They are available in health-food, Chinese, and Indian grocery stores. If you can get raw peanuts that are skinned, so much the better. Otherwise the reddish skins have to be removed after the soaking period. This dish was prepared with ½-in/1½-cm-long nuts. Peanuts come in various sizes and you may prefer to use another size.

5 oz/140 g raw, shelled peanuts
3 tbs vegetable oil
⅛ tsp whole fenugreek seeds
¾ lb/340 g fresh spinach, trimmed, washed, and finely chopped
1 tbs finely chopped jaggery or dark molasses or dark brown sugar

½–1 fresh hot green chilli, finely chopped
¼ tsp salt
1 oz/30 g plus 2 tbs freshly grated coconut

Put the peanuts in a bowl. Add 16 fl oz/½ l of water and soak for 3 to 4 hours. Drain and remove the reddish skins if the peanuts are of the unskinned variety.

Heat the oil in a wide, heavy, 3–4-qt/3½–4½-l pot over a medium flame. When hot, put in the fenugreek seeds. As soon as the seeds begin to sizzle and turn a shade darker (this takes just a few seconds), add the spinach (with the water from washing still clinging to the leaves), the drained peanuts, jaggery, green chilli, and salt. Stir for about 30 seconds. Cover, turn heat to low, and simmer gently for 20 minutes. Remove cover. Turn heat to medium and dry off excess liquid if there is any. The dish should have a fairly dry look. Just before serving, add 1 oz/30 g grated coconut and stir once. Remove from heat. Spoon spinach and peanuts into a warm serving dish. Sprinkle with the remaining 2 tbs of grated coconut.

Anne Lokes's
PEANUTS WITH LONG GREEN BEANS
SINGAPORE CHINESE   *(serves 4)*

Long green beans, the kind that are slim and about a foot long, are available in Indian, Chinese, and other Oriental grocery stores. If you cannot find them, ordinary green beans may be substituted. Another ingredient normally used in this dish is Chinese preserved radish. Instead, I substitute any one of the following Japanese pickles: White Radish Preserve (see page 439); Cabbage Tsukemono (see page 434); Quick-Salted White Radish Pickle (see page 435); or Shoyu Daikon (see page 436). Each gives a slightly different flavour to the dish and all are good.

½ lb/225 g long green beans   5 oz/140 g fried, unsalted peanuts
6 shallots, peeled   (see page 373)
Preserves or pickles (see note   1 tsp salt
  above), about 1½ oz/45 g   ⅟₁₆–⅛ tsp freshly ground white
3 tbs vegetable oil   pepper

Trim the ends of the beans and cut them crosswise at ¼-in/¾-cm intervals.

Cut the shallots into slim slivers.

Cut the pickles or preserves into pieces that are the same size as the cut beans.

For information about ingredients and basic techniques that may be unfamiliar, see General Information, pages 481-506.

Heat the oil in a wok or a heavy frying pan over a medium flame. Put in the shallots. Stir and fry for 1 minute. Put in the beans. Stir and fry for 2 minutes. Put in the peanuts, salt, and pepper. Stir and fry for another 2 to 3 minutes. Add 2 tbs of water and cover immediately for 30 seconds. Remove cover and add the pickles or preserves. Stir and fry for about 10 seconds.

TEMPEH

I was first introduced to *tempeh* a few years ago on a trip to Indonesia. My hostess had cooked Sambal Goreng Tempeh Kering for me. I found myself biting into deliciously spicy 'matchsticks' without having any idea what they were made from. All I could identify was a nutty, almost meat-like taste.

Tempeh, I found out, is an ancient Indonesian product (now also found in Singapore and Malaysia) which has almost as much usable protein as chicken. A 4 oz/115 g serving has about 230 calories. It has no saturated fats and is one of the few vegetable products that contains vitamin B12. *Tempeh* is also rich in roughage and is easy to digest. It almost seems to be a perfect food.

While the *tempeh* available in macrobiotic and Chinese shops at the moment is made from the nutritious soy bean, in Indonesia it is sometimes made from seeds, grains, and other beans as well. Soybean *tempeh* is not hard to make, though it does require a warm 85–95° F/29–35° C temperature.

The soy beans are first hulled and split. Then they are boiled for 1 hour, after which they are drained and dried off a bit. At this stage a culture is introduced and the beans are packed into lightly perforated plastic bags. The bags need to be flattened out so thinnish, even cakes can form. This takes about a day. A cotton-candy-like film miraculously covers the beans and binds them together. This is *tempeh*. It can now be sliced and fried, or cut into cubes and put into stews for about 10 minutes. As *tempeh* is now fairly easily available, I am not providing a recipe.

FRIED TEMPEH
INDONESIA   *(serves 2–6)*

Fried *tempeh* may be eaten with just a sprinkling of salt. After frying, *tempeh* turns nicely crisp, rather like French fries, and may be served with a dipping sauce. This sauce could be a hot Indonesian *sambal*, a spicy Indian chutney, a Japanese or Korean dipping sauce, or even tomato ketchup.

8 oz/225 g tempeh
8 fl oz/¼ l vegetable oil
½ tsp salt

Cut the *tempeh* into pieces that are approximately 1×½×¼ in/ 2½×1½×¾ cm.

Heat the oil in an 8-in/20-cm frying pan over a medium flame. When hot, drop in half the *tempeh* pieces. Stir and fry for 5 to 6 minutes or until the *tempeh* turns golden brown — the same colour as French fries. Remove them with a slotted spoon and drain on kitchen paper. Sprinkle this batch with ¼ tsp salt. Fry a second batch exactly the same way. Drain on kitchen paper and sprinkle with the remaining ¼ tsp salt.

Tatie Wawo-Runtu's
FRIED, PRE-SEASONED TEMPEH
INDONESIA   *(serves 2–6)*

Uncooked *tempeh* absorbs seasonings like a sponge. So what the Indonesians frequently do is to dip *tempeh* pieces in what could be called a marinade — the marinating period is usually less than a minute — before they proceed with the frying.

8 oz/225 g tempeh   *1½ tsp ground coriander seeds*
1 tsp salt   *8 fl oz/¼ l vegetable oil*
2–3 cloves garlic, peeled and
*   mashed to a pulp*

Cut the *tempeh* into 'sticks' that are about 2½×½×¼ in/6½×1½× ¾ cm.

In a bowl, mix together the salt, garlic, coriander, and 4 fl oz/1 dl water.

Set the oil to heat in an 8-in/20-cm frying pan over a medium flame. Meanwhile, put half the *tempeh* sticks into the bowl with the seasonings and stir them about to coat them. Remove the *tempeh*

For information about ingredients and basic techniques that may be unfamiliar, see General Information, pages 481-506.

from the bowl, shaking off excess moisture as you do so, and put them into the heated oil. Stir and fry for 5 to 6 minutes or until *tempeh* is golden to reddish-brown and crisp. Remove with a slotted spoon and drain on kitchen paper. Do a second batch exactly the same way.

Tatie Wawo-Runtu's
SAMBAL GORENG TEMPEH KERING
(Sweet and Sour Tempeh)
INDONESIA   (serves 4–6)

This may well be my favourite *tempeh* recipe. The first time I cooked it, my husband made off with the entire bowlful, muttering something about how well it would go with beer. Here *tempeh* 'matchsticks' are fried until crisp, just as they are in the first *tempeh* recipe, then folded into a thick paste that is hot, sour, sweet, and salty at the same time. This *tempeh* may be eaten as a snack or used as a topping for rice. Sometimes fried, seasoned peanuts (see Kacang Asin, page 124) are added to the *tempeh* 'matchsticks' before they are enveloped in their spicy paste, making the dish even more nutritious.

4 oz/115 g shallots, peeled and coarsely chopped

2 cloves garlic, peeled

4 dried red hot chillies, seeded

1 five-pence-piece sized slice of dry galanga root, shredded by hand

8 oz/225 g tempeh *(see page 127)*

8 fl oz/¼ l vegetable oil

3 daun salaam leaves, if available

4 tsp tamarind paste

1 tsp salt

2 tsp light brown sugar

Put the shallots, garlic, red chillies, and galanga root into the container of a food processor or blender together with 3 tbs of water. Blend until smooth.

Cut the *tempeh* into 'matchsticks' that are 1½×¼×¼ in/4×¾× ¾ cm.

Heat the oil in an 8-in/20-cm frying pan over a medium flame. When hot, put in half the *tempeh* pieces. Stir and fry for 5 to 6 minutes or until the *tempeh* turns a golden to reddish-brown and is crisp. Remove *tempeh* with a slotted spoon and drain on kitchen paper. Fry a second batch exactly the same way.

Remove all but 2 fl oz/½ dl of oil from the frying pan. Put in the *salaam* leaves and stir for a second. Put in the paste from the food processor as well as the tamarind paste. Stir and fry on medium heat for 7 to 8 minutes or until the paste has a dryish look. Add the salt and sugar. Stir to mix. Add the fried *tempeh*. Stir gently to mix. Remove the *salaam* leaves. Serve immediately.

TEMPEH COOKED IN COCONUT MILK
INDONESIA   *(serves 4)*

6 oz/180 g tempeh *(see page 127)*
3 tbs vegetable oil
4 oz/115 g slivered, peeled shallots
1 clove garlic, finely chopped
1 fresh hot green chilli, seeded and
   cut into thin diagonal rings
2 daun salaam *leaves*
1 five-pence-piece sized slice of
   dried galanga root
12 fl oz/3½ dl coconut milk
¾ tsp salt

Cut the *tempeh* into ½-in/1½-cm cubes.

Heat the oil in an 8-in/20-cm frying pan over a medium flame.
Put in the shallots, garlic, and green chilli. Stir and fry for 2
minutes. Put in the *salaam* leaves and galanga root. Stir for another
minute. Now put in the coconut milk, salt, and *tempeh* pieces.
Bring to a simmer. Cover, lower heat and simmer gently for 10
minutes. Remove *salaam* leaves and galanga root and serve with
plain rice.

OILY TOOVAR DAL WITH CLOVES
INDIA   *(serves 4–6)*

Oily *toovar dal* (*dal* rubbed with oil to preserve it from infestation) is
used with great frequency in Gujarat and needs to be washed very
well before it is cooked. It has a dark, earthy taste and cloves help
bring a spicy sparkle to it.

6½ oz/185 g oily toovar dal   2 tbs vegetable oil
½ tsp ground turmeric   8 whole cloves
¾ tsp salt   A 2-in/5-cm stick of cinnamon
½ tsp sugar   3 tbs ghee or unsalted butter
⅛ tsp cayenne pepper, more or less
   to taste

Pick over the *dal* and wash it in several changes of water. Put *dal* in
a heavy 2–3-qt/2½–3½-l pot with 1 qt/11½ dl of water. Bring to the
boil. Remove scum and add the turmeric. Turn heat to very low
and cover in such a way as to leave the lid very slightly ajar. (This

---

*For information about ingredients and basic techniques that may be unfamiliar, see General
Information, pages 481-506.*

prevents the *dal* from boiling over.) Cook for 1½ hours or until *dal* is very tender. Stir every 10 minutes during the last half hour of cooking. The *dal* should be like a thick soup. Add the salt, sugar, and cayenne. Stir, and turn off heat.

Heat oil in a small frying pan or a very small butter-warmer type pot over a medium flame. When hot, put in the whole cloves and cinnamon. When the cloves swell (this takes just a few seconds), pour the oil with spices into the pot with the *dal*. Cover pot immediately.

Reheat the *dal* before serving and stir in the *ghee* or butter. This *dal* is usually served with plain rice.

OILY TOOVAR DAL WITH GREEN BEANS AND TOMATOES
INDIA   *(serves 6)*

Oily *toovar dal* (see preceding recipe) may be cooked with almost any vegetable, making a thick 'stew' that can then be eaten with rice or bread.

10 oz/280 g oily toovar dal,
  picked over, washed, and
  drained
½ tsp ground turmeric
2 five-pence-piece sized slices of
  fresh ginger
3 tbs chopped fresh green coriander
½ lb/225 g green beans, trimmed
  and cut in half
7 cherry or other small tomatoes,
  peeled

1¼ tsp salt
1 tsp jaggery or brown sugar
⅛–¼ tsp cayenne pepper
2 tbs lemon juice
3 tbs vegetable oil
⅛ tsp whole fenugreek seeds
2 tsp whole black mustard seeds
½ tsp whole cumin seeds
2 whole hot dried red peppers
2 tbs unsalted butter or ghee

In a heavy 3-qt/3½-l pot, combine the *dal*, turmeric, ginger, fresh coriander, and 1½ pt/8½ dl of water. Bring to the boil. Cover partially (just leave the lid slightly ajar) and simmer on a low flame for about 45 minutes. Stir a few times during the last 10 minutes. Add the green beans, cherry tomatoes, salt, brown sugar, cayenne pepper, lemon juice, and another 8 fl oz/¼ l of water. Stir well and bring to the boil. Cover, lower heat, and simmer for 15 to 20 minutes or until the green beans are tender. Turn off the heat and leave *dal* covered.

Heat the oil in a small frying pan or a small pot over a medium flame. When hot, put in the fenugreek seeds, mustard seeds, cumin seeds, and red peppers. The spices will begin to sizzle and pop in seconds. When they do, lift the cover of the pot with the *dal* and empty the contents of the frying pan – oil and spices – into it. Replace cover immediately.

Just before serving, heat the *dal* and ladle into a warm serving dish. Cut the butter into 4 to 6 pats and place on top of the hot *dal*. If using *ghee*, spoon it over the hot *dal*.

Neela's
SAMBAR
(South Indian Dal with Vegetables)
INDIA   *(serves 4–6)*

This South Indian *dal* may be cooked in combination with almost any vegetable. Carrots, long beans (found in Chinese and Indian grocery stores), ordinary green beans, aubergine, marrow, and cauliflower should be sliced or diced and then lightly steamed before being added to the cooked *dal*. Vegetables like okra, onions, radish (white or red), and kohlrabi should be sliced and lightly sautéed in oil or *ghee* before being mixed in with the cooked *dal*.

Some South Indians like to boil their vegetables quickly in water to which they have added salt and some tamarind paste. This water is then mixed in with the *dal*, along with the vegetables.

Traditionally, *sambar* is made very, very hot with fistfuls of dried hot red peppers. I have used ground cayenne pepper, which you can adjust to your own taste. Also, in South India, this *dal* is cooked with enough water to make it thin and soup-like. It is served in individual bowls and eaten with boiled or steamed rice.

Since most Westerners are not used to eating soup-like dishes with their hands, I often serve *sambar* in a Western manner. I take warmed soup plates (the shallow, old-fashioned kind) and place a healthy scoop of rice or an *idli* in its centre. I then pour the *sambar* carefully around the scoop of rice, letting the top of the scoop rise like an island in the centre. As cutlery, I offer a soup spoon. I serve *papadum* (see page 499) as an accompaniment and have buttermilk, Indian style (see page 405), as a beverage.

4½ oz/125 g toovar (arhar) dal
2½ tbs ghee *or vegetable oil*
A generous pinch of ground
  asafetida
1 tbs whole coriander seeds
1½ tsp whole cumin seeds

1 tsp whole fenugreek seeds
2 whole cloves
10–12 black peppercorns
A ¾-in/2-cm piece of stick
  cinnamon
¼–½ tsp cayenne pepper

For information about ingredients and basic techniques that may be unfamiliar, see General Information, pages 481-506.

2–3 tbs freshly grated coconut,
  roasted
½ tsp whole black mustard seeds
1 medium-sized onion, halved and
  thickly sliced
6 radishes, trimmed and thickly
  sliced
1 medium-sized tomato, peeled
  and diced

½ tsp ground turmeric
1–2 tbs tamarind paste
¾–1 tsp salt
¼ tsp sugar
1 fresh hot green chilli, finely
  chopped
1 tsp finely grated fresh ginger
2 tbs finely chopped fresh green
  coriander

Clean and wash the *dal*. Drain. Add 1½ pt/8½ dl water and bring to the boil. Turn heat to low, cover in such a way as to leave the lid slightly ajar, and simmer gently until the *dal* is quite tender, about 1½ hours. Stir every now and then during the last 10 minutes of the cooking.

Heat 1 tbs of the *ghee* in a small, heavy frying pan or a very small pot over a medium flame. When hot, put in the asafetida and, a few seconds later, the coriander seeds, cumin, fenugreek, cloves, peppercorns, and cinnamon. As soon as the spices turn a few shades darker (this takes just a few seconds), put in the cayenne pepper. Stir once and remove from heat.

Put contents of small frying pan immediately into the container of an electric blender. Add the roasted, grated coconut and 2 fl oz/ ½ dl water. Blend until you have a smooth paste. Set aside.

In a 2–3-qt/2½–3½-l pot, heat the remaining 1½ tbs of *ghee* over a medium flame. When hot, put in the mustard seeds. As soon as the seeds begin to pop (this just takes a few seconds), lower the heat and put in the sliced onion and sliced radishes. Sauté for 3 to 4 minutes. Do not allow any browning. Now add the paste from the blender and stir for a few seconds. Put in the cooked *dal*, the diced tomato, turmeric, the tamarind paste (put in 1 tbs of the paste first, adding more later if you think you want it), salt, and sugar. Add more water, if necessary, to get a thin, soup-like consistency. Stir well, check for seasoning, and bring to the boil. Cover partially, lower heat, and simmer gently for about 10 minutes.

Add the green chilli, ginger, and fresh coriander. Simmer, uncovered, for another 2 minutes.

3 Rice and Other Grains

Rice originated in Asia. Emotionally and nutritionally, Asians have depended upon it ever since for their sustenance. For many Asians, a meal without rice is quite inconceivable, and an invitation to dinner often translates as an invitation to 'eat rice'.

There is something about this soothing, ingratiating grain that is quite addictive. While it has character, fragrance, and texture, it does not obtrude. It seduces without ever having to exert itself.

But it has to be cooked well first. That is the reason I have devoted quite a few pages to basic methods of cooking long-grain rice, Japanese rice, glutinous rice, brown rice, and Persian-style rice.

It is not hard to cook rice. First, see that you have a heavy iron or aluminium pot with an even distribution of heat and a good, tight-fitting lid. If you do not have a tight-fitting lid, put a sheet of aluminium foil, well crimped at the edges, between the top of the pot and the lid. The reason for this is that if you are going to cook in a minimum amount of water – as you should – very little steam should be allowed to escape. A tight lid will hold it in, and the rice will actually cook in steam.

What is the correct proportion of rice to water? Disregard the directions on top of rice packets. They suggest far more water than rice ever needs. Instead, follow the recipes in this chapter carefully, as the amount of water will vary depending upon the type of rice and whether it has been washed and soaked. I like to measure my rice in a clear measuring jug. For long-grain rice, you certainly do not need more than 1½ parts of liquid for every 1 part of rice. If the rice has been soaked, you can even use 1⅓ parts of liquid. Brown rice is an exception. For that you should use 2 parts of water for every 1 of rice. The texture of brown rice improves considerably if you soak it first. Japanese rice requires the least amount of water – 1¼ parts of water for every 1 part of rice.

Rice is such an amenable grain. It can be elevated to an almost hallowed position when it is served in lacquer bowls – plain, unadorned, and in the shape of oval rolls – at the start of the very formal Japanese meals that precede a tea ceremony. It seems equally comfortable combined with millet by a Korean peasant, or brightened with saffron and orange rind for a Persian banquet, or stir-fried with eggs and spring onions for a Chinese snack. You can season it with any herb or spice, cook it with any vegetable or bean, eat it as a gruel, make Japanese-style sandwiches – or *sushi* – with it, and even use it to make a variety of meal-in-a-pot dishes.

Rice with Fresh Herbs and Baby Broad Beans is one such meal-in-a-pot dish. Here long-grain rice is cooked in a Persian style with lots of butter, a heap of fresh green coriander, parsley, dill, spring onion tops, and the conveniently frozen baby broad beans. You could serve this dish all by itself — just as you would pasta — with perhaps a cooling glass of buttermilk to wash it down.

There is another kind of meal-in-itself rice dish which, although not prepared in a single pot, is served as if it had been and actually consists of separately cooked foods arranged prettily over rice. My favourite among such dishes is the Korean Bibimbab. A fried egg sits triumphantly over a mound of rice. Radiating down from it are different stir-fried vegetables such as courgettes, bean sprouts, and spinach. A generous dollop of very hot bean sauce is put in a lettuce-leaf cup and also set on the rice. All that is needed then are a pair of chopsticks and an icy cold bottle of beer!

There are other grains besides rice in this chapter — bulgar wheat, which may be cooked in ways very similar to rice; millet and barley, which may be added to rice; and semolina, which is used in South India to make a kind of vegetarian pilaf called Uppama.

SOME GENERAL NOTES ON RICE

Plain, milled rice may be cooked with great ease in an electric rice-cooker. These cookers are now used all over Japan, even in some of the most traditional inns. When all my cooker burners are in use, I, too, use the electric rice cooker for plain rice. On the whole, you can follow the directions suggested by the manufacturer. But do not put in the amount of water recommended. Follow my general guidelines and consult specific recipes for different types of plain rice.

Should you wash rice? Asians always do, mainly to get rid of dust and to wash off extra starch left from the milling process. Washing and soaking prevent rice grains from splitting and from sticking to each other. Packaged rices sold in Britain are generally enriched with vitamins after milling. These vitamins are mixed with a little starch and then added to the rice. When you wash rice, you get rid of this unnecessary starch — and also the vitamins. If you feel you need the vitamins, do not wash packaged rices. But rices from Eastern countries *must* be picked over and washed in several changes of water.

HOW TO SERVE RICE

When long-grain rice has finished cooking, it tends to sit in the pot as one large lump. To serve it, place a warmed platter near by. Now ease a slotted metal spoon gently into the rice. Put whatever your spoon collects on to the platter. Break up this 'lump' by pressing gently with the back of the same slotted spoon.

GARNISHES FOR RICE

Rice may be served the way it comes out of the pot or it may be garnished. Asian garnishes are not just decorative. They contribute new flavours and textures as well as nutritional value to the rice. Here is a list of some of these garnishes: 1. roasted sesame seeds (see General Information); 2. toasted *nori* (see page 377), cut into shreds, plus roasted sesame seeds; 3. crushed, fried, or roasted peanuts; 4. washed and drained bean sprouts; sliced shallots, fried until brown and crisp; sprigs of mint and fresh green coriander; 5. sliced spring onions and egg strands (see page 241); 6. crisply fried onions (see page 418); 7. chopped parsley and pats of butter; 8. finely chopped dill and sliced spring onions.

LEFTOVERS

We always make extra plain rice in our house. Whatever is left can be refrigerated and then fried the next day with spring onions and egg. If you wish to heat leftover rice, break up all lumps gently and put the rice in a frying pan. Sprinkle some water over the top, cover, and heat slowly over a low flame.

PLAIN BOILED RICE

(serves 4–6)

This is the simplest method of cooking rice. If the rice being used is American or Australian packaged rice, it requires no picking over and no washing. And it requires no soaking. The use of butter and salt is optional. If you are cooking a Chinese meal, for example, both should be omitted. This rice may also be made in an electric rice-cooker; put in all the ingredients, cover, and switch on. Depending upon the type of cooker used, the rice should be ready about 10 to 15 minutes after its red light switches off.

Long-grain rice measured to the   1 tbs unsalted butter (optional)
15-fl oz/4¼-dl level in a glass   1 tsp salt (optional)
measuring jug

Combine the rice, butter, salt, and 1¼ pt/¾ l water in a heavy-bottomed, 1½–2½-qt/1¾–2¾-l pot that has a tight-fitting lid. Bring to the boil. Cover, turn the flame as low as it will go and cook for 25 minutes. (If you are using an electric cooker, set a second burner on 'simmer'. Once the rice comes to the boil, cover it and shift it to the second burner. Let the rice cook for 5 minutes and then switch this second burner to 'warm'. Cook another 20 minutes.) Let the rice rest, covered and undisturbed, for another 5 to 10 minutes.

To serve, ease a slotted spoon gently into the rice. Lift some of it out and put it on a warmed platter or bowl. Gently press down on this rice with the back of the slotted spoon to separate the grains. Remove as much rice from the pot as needed, breaking up all 'lumps' the same way.

PLAIN BAKED RICE I

(serves 4–6)

This is a fairly foolproof method of making light, fluffy rice. Rice is first thrown into plenty of boiling water and cooked rather like pasta. It is not cooked completely, though, but left *al dente*, with a slim, hard core still running down its centre. Then the rice is drained and put in a slow oven to dry off and finish cooking.

Long-grain rice measured to the   1 tbs salt (optional)
15-fl oz/4¼-dl level in a glass   3–4 tbs unsalted butter (optional)
measuring jug

Preheat oven to 325° F/170° C/Mark 3.

Put about 5 pt/3 l water and the salt into a 4-qt/4½-l pot and bring to the boil. Meanwhile wash the rice in several changes of water and drain it.

When the water is at a rolling boil, put in the rice. Keep stirring until the water comes to the boil for a second time. Boil rapidly for about 6 minutes. The rice grains should be almost done but should retain a slim, hard core down their centre. The way to check this is to remove a grain and press it between the first finger and the thumb. You should be able to both see and feel the hard core. Now drain the rice and quickly empty it into a 2–3-qt/2¼–3½-l ovenproof pot that has a tight-fitting lid. Add the optional butter, cover, and place in the oven for 25 minutes.

Before serving, mix the butter, if you have used it, evenly into the rice with a slotted spoon.

PLAIN BAKED RICE II

(serves 4–6)

This method of cooking rice, used with slight variations in China, North India, and the Middle East, does not leave the rice light and fluffy. Instead, each grain stays whole, firm, and unsplit. For many North Indian and Middle Eastern meals, the soaked, drained rice is sautéed in 3–4 tbs of oil or butter before the final liquid is added.

Long-grain rice measured to the   1 tsp salt (optional)
  15-fl oz/4¼-dl level in a glass
  measuring jug

Wash the rice in several changes of water and drain. Put it in a bowl, add 1 qt/11½dl of water and let the rice soak for 30 minutes. Drain thoroughly and let it sit in a strainer set over a bowl for 10 minutes.

Preheat oven to 325° F/170° C/Mark 3.

Put the drained rice, 1 pt/5¾ dl water, and the salt in a heavy, 1½–2½-qt/1¾–2¾-l pot that is both flameproof and ovenproof and has a tight-fitting lid. Bring to the boil. Turn heat to medium and cook, stirring gently, until all the liquid has evaporated. You may have to turn the heat down slightly towards the end of this period. Cover the pot tightly and place in the oven for 25 minutes.

This rice may be eaten with almost any kind of meal. Japanese rice is perhaps better suited to Japanese and Korean foods.

PLAIN BASMATI RICE
INDIA
(serves 4–6)

Basmati rice is more aromatic and much more delicate than ordinary long-grain rice and requires less water. The texture and aroma

---

For information about ingredients and basic techniques that may be unfamiliar, see General Information, pages 481-506.

of *basmati* rice make it somewhat inappropriate for South Indian meals and for foods from South-east and East Asia, but it may be eaten with almost all Western, Middle Eastern, and North Indian meals. You may omit the sautéing step, if you so prefer. Just combine the soaked, drained rice, salt, and 1 pt/5¾ dl of water in a pot and cook as in the recipe for Plain Boiled Rice (see page 137).

basmati *rice, picked over and measured to the 15-fl oz/4¼-dl level in a glass measuring jug*

2 tbs unsalted butter (optional)
¾ tsp salt (optional)

Wash the rice in several changes of water and drain it. Put it in a bowl, add 1 qt/11½ dl of water and let it soak for 30 minutes. Drain thoroughly and let it sit in a strainer set over a bowl for 10 minutes.

Melt the butter in a heavy, 2–3-qt/2¼–3½-l pot that has a tight-fitting lid. Add the drained rice. Stir and cook over medium heat, making sure you are gentle and do not break up the grains of rice. Once all the grains are properly coated with butter – this will take about a minute or so – add a scant 1 pt/5¾ dl of water and the salt. Bring to the boil. Cover, turn heat to very low and cook for 20 minutes. Turn off the flame. Led the pot sit, covered and in a warm place, for another 10 minutes.

KATEH
(Plain Boiled Rice with a Crust)
IRAN   (serves 4–6)

It is the pride of Persian housewives, rich and poor, to provide rice that has crusted at the bottom and sides of the pot so that it can be inverted on to a plate like an upside-down cake. Pieces of the crisp crust are always offered to honoured guests first. Making the crust is both easy and infuriatingly confounding at the same time. The method, in theory, is simplicity itself – just follow the basic directions for making Plain Boiled Rice (see page 137) and then turn up the heat slightly and let the rice cook for another half hour or so. But to get an evenly golden crust and to get it to come off the sides of the pot require some experimenting with different pots and different temperatures. Here are some hints that will help you to get a perfect *tahdig* or crust the very first time you try it.

Use a heavy pot that has an even distribution of heat. Tin-lined copper and heavy cast-aluminium pots both work very well.

Tight-fitting lids are a great help.

Do not use a very large pot for a small amount of rice. I cook this dish, which requires about 12 oz/340 g of rice, in a 1½-qt/1¾-l pot.

For the last half hour or so of cooking, find a temperature that is just slightly higher than 'low'. I call that 'medium-low'. It is the temperature at which water would keep up a very active simmer. You will have to work this out on your own cooker.

Long-grain rice measured to the 15-fl oz/4¼-dl level in a glass measuring jug	1 tsp salt 2 tbs melted unsalted butter (optional)

Put the rice, salt, and 1¼ pt/¾ l water in a heavy, 1½–2-qt/1¾–2¼-l pot that has a tight-fitting lid and bring to the boil. Cover, turn heat to very low and cook for 25 minutes. Now turn the heat up to medium-low and continue to cook for 35 minutes.

While the rice is cooking, fill the sink or a large bowl with enough water to come three-quarters of the way up the sides of the rice pot. When the rice has finished cooking, lift the pot off the cooker and immediately put it in the water for 3 minutes. If the water warms up before the 3 minutes are over, change it. Remove the lid and dribble in the butter. Now turn the pot upside down over a warm plate. The 'cake' of rice should just slip out. If not, try tapping the back of the pot or try to ease the rice out with a narrow spatula.

If you have a perfect 'cake', it can be cut in wedges. If you just have a bottom crust that you have to prize out separately, lay it neatly over the rice. Serve each person some of the soft rice and at least one piece of the crust.

PLAIN BROWN LONG-GRAIN RICE

(serves 4)

Brown rice is generally not eaten in Asia except by a few who follow the macrobiotic diet in Japan. However, it is more nutritious than milled and polished rices and should, therefore, be included in all our diets — at least some of the time.

That is all very well. But what if you like the taste of cooked brown rice but cannot abide its mushy texture? I am afraid I had

For information about ingredients and basic techniques that may be unfamiliar, see General Information, pages 481-506.

that problem for a while. Of course, I was either eating it in restaurants or following recipes worked out by people who were basically not rice-eaters. One day I brought a large bag of brown rice home and decided to keep cooking it until I came up with a texture that pleased me. Well, here is the result. I prefer the taste of long-grain brown rice, but you could use the short-grain variety as well. Once you have followed this basic method, you could easily substitute brown rice for the milled, polished rices in this chapter.

Long-grain brown rice measured
 to the 13-fl oz/3¾-dl level in a
 glass measuring jug

¾ tsp salt (optional)
2 tbs unsalted butter (optional)

Wash the rice in several changes of water. Drain thoroughly. Put in a bowl, add 1¼ pt/¾ l water and leave to soak for 1 hour.

Put the rice and its soaking liquid in a heavy, 2-qt/2¼-l pot that has a tight-fitting lid. Add the salt and bring to the boil. Cover, turn heat to very low and cook for 35 minutes. Turn the heat off and let the rice sit, covered and undisturbed, for 10 minutes. Put in the butter and mix gently with a fork.

BROWN RICE WITH SPINACH
NORTH INDIAN STYLE   (serves 6)

Long-grain brown rice measured
 to the 13-fl oz/3¾-dl level in a
 glass measuring jug
1½ lb/675 g fresh spinach*
4 tbs vegetable oil

1 medium-sized onion, peeled and
 chopped
1 tsp ground cumin seeds
1 tsp ground coriander seeds
½ tsp ground mace
1 tsp salt

*Frozen spinach may be used as an alternative; cook it according to instructions, squeeze out all the liquid and then chop it.

Put the rice in the bowl and wash in several changes of water. Drain. Soak the rice in 1¼ pt/¾ l water for 1 hour.

While the rice is soaking, separate the spinach leaves and wash them. Do not discard the roots. They taste very good when they are cooked.

Bring 3 qt/3½ l of water to a rolling boil in a 4-qt/4½-l pot. Drop in the spinach. Bring to the boil again and let the spinach cook on high heat for 2 minutes. Drain. Rinse spinach under running water to cool off. Squeeze out all the moisture from the spinach and then chop it, roots and all.

Heat the oil in a heavy, 2¾-qt/3-l pot over a medium flame. When hot, put in the onion. Stir and fry until onion pieces turn slightly brown at the edges. Put in the spinach. Stir and fry the spinach for

20 minutes, turning the heat down a bit as the moisture in the spinach reduces. Add the rice and its soaking liquid, the cumin, coriander, mace, and salt. Bring to the boil. Cover with a tight-fitting lid, turn heat to very, very low and cook for 35 minutes. Turn off heat. Remove the lid and immediately cover the pot of rice with a tea towel. Place the lid over the towel. Let the pot sit this way for 15 to 20 minutes in a warm place so that the extra moisture may be absorbed.

GLUTINOUS RICE

Also known as 'sweet' rice and 'sticky' rice, this short-grain, opaque variety of rice is very popular in East and South-east Asia. It is put into soups, used in stuffings, topped with coconut cream to accompany fresh fruit, and made into all manner of snacks and desserts. In some parts of Asia, like northern Thailand, it is prefer-red to other types of rice and is eaten, plain and ungarnished, just as long-grain rice might be. Once glutinous rice is cooked, it turns shiny and translucent. It is somewhat sticky but that is the very quality which endears it to its enthusiasts.

As with other types of rice, there are several methods of cooking glutinous rice. These methods include cooking it in a double boiler and steaming it. I love glutinous rice. If you have never eaten it, make a point of buying some and cooking it.

PLAIN GLUTINOUS RICE
COOKED IN A DOUBLE BOILER

(serves 4)

This is an excellent rice to take on picnics, as it does not harden the way all other rices do. It is also considered to be the ideal rice to eat with sweet, luscious tropical fruit such as mangoes (see page 448 for recipe).

Glutinous rice measured to the
13-fl oz/3¾-dl level in a glass
measuring jug

Put the rice in a bowl and wash it well in several changes of water. Drain. Cover the rice with 2½ pt/1½ l of water and leave to soak for 6 to 8 hours. (Alternatively, you may soak the rice in hot water for 1 to 2 hours.) Drain the rice and wash it again in fresh water. Drain again.

Get your double boiler ready by putting a sufficient quantity of water in the lower portion and bringing it to the boil. Put the rice in the top portion of the double boiler. Add enough water to it so it comes to ½ in/1½ cm above the top of the rice. Set the top of the double boiler over the lower portion. When the water with the rice begins to simmer, cover the pot and cook the rice on medium heat for 25 minutes.

AZUKI MESHI
(Glutinous Rice Cooked with Azuki Beans)
JAPAN   (serves 4–6)

If you are one of those people who, like me, has a partiality for glutinous rice, you will love this simple dish. If you do not like glutinous rice, substitute plain Japanese rice or a long-grain rice. You could also make this dish with brown rice. Soak it for just 1 hour in water (hot water is not needed) and use 12 fl oz/3½ dl of the bean liquid instead of the 8 fl oz/¼ l plus 2 tbs. Cook for 35 minutes.

Azuki meshi consists of rice and beans, perked up with a little salt, some *sake*, and roasted sesame seeds. I can make a meal of just this, some Japanese pickles, and green tea. You could, and I have done this, serve *azuki meshi* with a Greek salad containing lettuce, tomatoes, olives, and broken-up pieces of feta cheese in an olive oil and lemon dressing.

Glutinous rice measured to the 6-fl oz/1¾-dl level in a glass measuring jug	¾ tsp salt
	1 tbs sake
	2 tbs roasted sesame seeds
Azuki beans measured to the 6-fl oz/1¾-dl level in a glass measuring jug	

Wash the glutinous rice in several changes of water. Drain. Now soak the rice in 16 fl oz/½ l of hot water for 2 hours. Drain.

Pick over the beans. Put them in a heavy pot and add 1½ pt/8½ dl of water. Bring to the boil. Lower heat and simmer, uncovered, for 2 minutes. Turn off the heat and let the pot sit, uncovered, for 1 hour. Bring the beans to the boil again. Cover, lower heat and simmer gently for 30 minutes. Add ½ tsp salt and simmer, covered, for another 30 minutes. Drain the beans but *save the liquid*.

Put the drained rice in a heavy, 2½-qt/2¾-l pot. Add the salt, 8 fl oz/¼ l plus 2 tbs of the bean liquid, as well as the drained beans. Bring to the boil. Cover with a tight-fitting lid and cook on very, very low heat for 20 minutes. Dribble the *sake* over the rice and beans, cover, and continue cooking for another 5 minutes.

Sprinkle sesame seeds over the top before serving.

PLAIN JAPANESE RICE

*(makes enough cooked rice to fill a 2½-pt/1½-l
measuring jug and serves about 6)*

If you are preparing a Japanese meal, you could, of course, eat plain long-grain rice with it. But you would be losing the real texture of Japanese food. The plump, short-grain, slightly sticky rice that the Japanese eat is an essential component of their cuisine. Rice — Japanese rice — is so interwoven with the tastes and aesthetics of all Japanese food that it might be jarring to replace it, especially in an all-Japanese meal, with fluffy, long-grain rice or, for that matter, with heavy brown rice.

But since the purpose of this book is not to be dogmatic, rather to open up a reservoir of good vegetarian food, perhaps it is best if you decide for yourself which rice you wish to have. If you get yourself familiar with cooking and eating Japanese rice, you will, at least, be making a considered choice.

Japanese rice is sold in Japanese grocery stores. If you do not have such a store in your area, check the mail-order sources at the end of this book. There are several brands available. The most popular in Britain is Japan Rose. The rice comes in large sacks and then is usually put into 5-lb/2¼-kg bags by the grocery stores.

Traditionally, Japanese rice was always cooked in iron cauldrons that had curved bottoms and heavy, wooden lids. Grains that got caught at the bottom and were slightly burned were either formed into balls and eaten with pickles and soy sauce, or they were put into a bowl, boiling water was poured over them, and diners were served this burned rice 'tea' at the conclusion of their repast. Today, most homes use electric rice-cookers that perform beautifully. Even very old and traditional establishments like the three-hundred-year-old Tawaraya Inn in Kyoto has shifted to a cauldron-sized electric rice-cooker. But once the rice is cooked, tradition reasserts itself here. The shiny, slightly sticky grains are removed with a dampened wooden paddle (dampened so the rice will not stick to it) and stored in a large, lidded, wooden tub. The wood, being a poor conductor of heat, does not allow the warmth to escape; so the rice stays hot for several hours. Whenever any rice is needed, it is put into smaller wooden containers and then carried up to the private rooms of the inn's guests.

The Japanese rice-cooker almost duplicates the Japanese method of cooking rice. (It must be remembered that rice-cookers will cook any plain rice very well.)

For information about ingredients and basic techniques that may be unfamiliar, see General Information, pages 481-506.

Japanese rice measured to the
16-fl oz/4½-dl level in a glass
measuring jug

Put the rice in a bowl and wash it in several changes of water, rubing the rice gently as you do so. Keep washing until the water is no longer milky. Drain the rice in a sieve. Put the sieve over an empty bowl and let the rice drain for 1 hour.

Put the rice in a heavy, 2½-qt/2¾-l pot that has a well-fitting lid. Add 1 pt/5¾ dl water, cover, and bring the water to the boil over a medium flame. When steam begins to escape from under the lid, turn the heat to *very* low and cook for 20 minutes. Turn the heat to high for 3 seconds and then turn it off. Let the pot sit, covered and undisturbed, for another 15 minutes. Do not lift the lid at any stage.

Use a dampened wooden paddle, if you have one, to serve as much of the rice as needed in individual bowls or in a covered wooden or lacquer container.

Leftover rice should be allowed to cool. Then separate the grains with a chopstick, put in a closed container, and store in the refrigerator. The rice can then be reheated with a little water — about 1 tbs per ¼ lb/115 g.

SUSHI RICE
JAPAN   *(serves about 6)*

Sushi rice is freshly cooked Japanese rice, seasoned or 'pickled' with a mixture of vinegar, sugar, and salt and then cooled off quickly to room temperature with a fan. This rice is used to make different types of *sushi*: there is *nigiri-zushi*, small rice ovals that for vegetarians may be topped with wheels of *datemake* (rolled omelette); there is *norimake-zushi*, in which the seasoned rice, together with ingredients like strips of cucumber or pickles are rolled inside paper-thin, crisp black laver (*nori*) to make what may be called closed sandwiches; there is *chirashi-zushi* in which the rice is piled into a bowl and topped with all manner of edibles that could include shredded eggs, blanched peas, pickles, fried bean curd, blanched and seasoned spinach, and seasoned mushrooms; and there is *inari-zushi* or *sushi* rice stuffed into fried bean-curd bags. You will find recipes for *norimake-zushi* and *chirashi-zushi* directly following; *nigiri-zushi* may be found in the chapter on eggs (see page 236), and *inari-zushi* in the bean-curd chapter (see page 209). Nearly all *sushi* dishes are served with pickled and sliced ginger, *amazu shoga*, available in Japanese grocery stores.

4 tbs rice wine vinegar
4 tbs sugar
½ tsp salt

Freshly cooked Plain Japanese Rice
(see page 144) measured to the
2½-pt/1½-l level in a glass
measuring jug

Mix the rice, wine vinegar, sugar, and salt together thoroughly in a cup.

As soon as the rice has completed its cooking, including its resting period, empty it out on to a large platter or baking tray.
1. Pour the seasonings in the cup over it.
2. Now fan the rice with one hand (you could use a magazine for this) while you mix it with a dampened wooden paddle or spoon. Continue to do this until the rice has reached room temperature. Put the rice in a covered pot or bowl to prevent it from drying out. Do not refrigerate. The rice will hold for a few hours, though the fresher the rice the better.

NORIMAKE-ZUSHI
(Sushi Rice Rolled in Dark Laver)
JAPAN   (serves 4–6)

The dark laver (*asakusa nori*) used to make this comes in thin, crisp sheets that are usually about 7×8 in/18×20 cm in size. Sometimes they are packed in cellophane, at other times in elegant tins. *Nori*

For information about ingredients and basic techniques that may be unfamiliar, see General Information, pages 481–506.

sheets need to be toasted before being used. The sheets may be used whole to make thickish rolls or they may be cut in half to make more slender rolls. The rolling is best done with the help of a special mat called a *sudare*, though a tea towel may be used as a substitute. Embedded in the rice down the centre of the roll could be anything from cucumber lengths to seasoned spinach and simmered mushrooms. The roll is then sliced crosswise into wheels and served with pickled ginger (*amazu shoga*) and soy sauce for dipping.

4 medium-sized dried shiitake
   mushrooms
3 tbs Japanese soy sauce
2 tbs plus ½ tsp sugar
1 tbs mirin
1 large egg
Salt
½ tsp vegetable oil
1 ridge cucumber, or 6-in/15-cm
   section of an ordinary
   cucumber, unpeeled

3 sheets of asakusa nori
Sushi Rice (see page 145)
   measured to the 1¼-pt/7-dl level
   in a glass measuring jug
2 tsp roasted sesame seeds
About ¼ tsp wasabi (see page
   417)
½ tsp paste from stoned and
   mashed umeboshi plums
6 tbs finely sliced amazu shoga

Soak the mushrooms in 12 fl oz/3½ dl hot water for ½ hour. Lift them out of the water and cut off the hard stems. (Save the water for soups.) Cut the caps crosswise into ¼-in/¾-cm-thick strips. Put the strips as well as the soy sauce, 2 tbs sugar, and *mirin* into a small pot. Bring to a simmer. Turn heat down and simmer for about 5 minutes. You should have a little syrupy liquid left. Set aside.

Put the egg, ½ tsp sugar, and a pinch of salt in a bowl. Beat well but not to a froth. Brush a 7-in/18-cm nonstick frying pan with the oil and heat over a medium flame. Pour in the egg mixture. Tilt the frying pan around in order to spread it to the edges. Cook until set. Ease a spatula under the pancake and turn it over. Cook until the second side is set. Remove to a plate and let it cool. Roll up as soon as it has reached room temperature and cut crosswise at ½-in/1½-cm intervals. Cover loosely and set aside.

Cut whichever type of cucumber you are using into 3-in/8-cm-long by ¼-in/¾-cm-wide by ¼-in/¾-cm-thick strips.

1. Toast the *nori*: hold a sheet between your fingers or with a pair of tongs and wave it systematically, going from one end to the other, directly over a medium-low flame. As each area gets done, it will turn somewhat lighter in colour. The *nori* should be about 1 in/2½ cm away from the flame. Cut each roasted sheet in half so you have two pieces, each about 7×4 in/18×10 cm.

2. Lay the *sudare* mat in front of you. (Use a clean tea towel as a substitute.) Place a piece of *nori* on it so its long side is parallel to

1

2

3

4

5

6

but about ½ in/1½ cm away from the end of the mat nearest you. Dip your hand in water and remove some rice − about ⅙ of the total amount − and spread it on the *nori*, leaving ½-in/1½-cm borders on the near end and the far end. The rice layer should be about ½ in/1½ cm thick.

3. Now make a long, horizontal indentation, rather like a shallow trench, running along the centre of the rice. Remove half the mushroom slices from their syrupy liquid and lay them in the trench.

4. Now begin rolling the *sudare* mat tightly away from you, keeping the mushrooms in place with your index fingers, if necessary. Your first roll should take you just past the mushrooms. When the edge of the *sudare* touches the rice, press down slightly to firm up the roll.

5. Keep rolling, this time making sure that the mat stays on top of the roll and does not get rolled *into* it. When the roll is finished, put it on a cutting board and,

6. Using a very sharp, slightly dampened knife, cut it crosswise into six equal parts. Make a second roll with the remaining mushrooms.

Make two more rolls with the eggs in exactly the same way. Just sprinkle 1 tsp of the sesame seeds over the eggs before rolling.

For the cucumber rolls, spread half of the *wasabi* and half of the *umeboshi* plum paste in each trench before laying the cucumber pieces down. Put about 6 strips of cucumber in each roll and dot each lot with ½ tsp sesame seeds. Roll and cut them in the same way as the others.

Serve the *sushi* pieces cut side up with small servings of soy sauce and *amazu shoga*.

CHIRASHI-ZUSHI
(Sushi Rice with Vegetable Topping)
JAPAN   (serves 5–6)

This dish is really a meal in itself.

Freshly made Sushi Rice (see page 145), measured to the 1¼-pt/ 7-dl level in a glass measuring jug
2 tbs finely sliced amazu shoga
Peas with Ginger (see page 61, but do not add the ginger)
Egg Strands (see page 241)

Cabbage with Miso (see page 29)
Lotus Root with Soy Sauce Dressing (see page 46)
Sweet and Salty Dried Shiitake Mushrooms (see page 56)
Carrots cooked in Dashi (see page 31)
1 tbs roasted sesame seeds

Using a dampened wooden paddle or spoon, empty the Sushi Rice into a large bowl. Add the *amazu shoga* and the peas and mix gently. Put this rice on a large serving platter or in individual bowls. Scatter the egg strands over the rice. Drain all the vegetables of extra liquid and arrange them prettily over the top. You could either make neat piles of the vegetables or scatter the cabbage over the eggs, arrange the mushroom caps in the centre and ring them with the lotus-root slices and carrots. Sprinkle the sesame seeds over the top.

PERSIAN-STYLE STEAMED RICE
IRAN   *(serves 6)*

Kateh (see page 139) is the rice Persians might eat with their every-day meals. For special occasions, they steam their rice in such a way that each grain comes out looking elegant and refined. First they soak their rice in salty water overnight. They then parboil it in more salty water to which a little vinegar has been added. These steps, they say, preserve the strength, whiteness, and separate-ness of each grain. The rice is then left to steam slowly in butter, with a cloth covering the underside of the lid so that it may catch the steam as it condenses and not allow it to fall back on the rice. This last step is done on top of the cooker in Iran. The heat is adjusted to allow the very prized crust to form at the bottom. If you do not want the crust, the steaming can be done in the oven. Here is a recipe for the oven method — Persian-style steamed rice with-out the crust.

Long-grain rice (use Persian   5 tbs salt
    Domsiah rice if possible,   1 tbs any white vinegar
    otherwise Indian or Pakistani   6 tbs melted unsalted butter
    basmati *rice can be used),*
    measured to the 15-fl oz/4¼-dl
    level in a glass measuring jug

Pick over the rice and wash it in several changes of water. Drain. Put rice in a bowl. Add 1 qt/11½ dl of water and 2½ tbs of salt. Stir and leave to soak overnight or for at least 8 hours. Drain rice in a sieve. Place sieve under running water and wash rice again. Drain thoroughly.
    Preheat oven to 325° F/170° C/Mark 3.
    Bring 3 qt/3½ l of water to the boil in a large pot. Add 2½ tbs salt as well as the vinegar. Pour the drained rice into the boiling water in a steady stream. Stir the rice and let it boil rapidly for exactly 6 minutes after the water comes to the boil again. Turn off heat and

drain the rice by emptying it into a sieve. Wash the rice again, this time under running lukewarm water. Drain.

Pour 4 tbs of the melted butter plus a tbs of water into a 9-in/ 23-cm-wide, heavy, casserole-type pot and place the pot on a low flame. Put the rice on top of the melted butter. Pour the remaining 2 tbs of melted butter over the rice. Now cover the pot with a doubled piece of kitchen paper, just slightly larger than the circumference of the pot. Put a piece of aluminium foil, larger than the paper towel, over the paper towel. Attach the paper towel to the foil with 4 straight pins. Crimp the edges of the foil to seal the pot. Now cover the pot with its own lid and place in the oven for 30 minutes.

Mix the rice gently and offer it with almost any Western, Middle Eastern, or North Indian meal.

STEAMED RICE WITH LENTILS
IRAN   *(serves 6)*

To make this dish, follow the directions in the preceding recipe. After the rice has finished soaking overnight and the oven has been lit, drop 3 oz/85 g whole green lentils into rapidly boiling, salted water (about 1½ tsp salt in 3 pt/1¾ l of water) and boil for 7 to 8 minutes or until lentils are somewhat soft but not fully cooked. Drain. Proceed to parboil the rice. Drain the rice and wash it. Mix it with the drained lentils and then proceed with the recipe.

This dish would be good with Okra with Tomatoes (see page 60) and Yogurt with Fresh Mint, Sultanas, and Walnuts (see page 254).

RICE PORRIDGE OR CONGEE

Rice porridges, eaten from Japan to Iran as breakfasts, snacks, and lunches, are considered warming and soothing, as well as a stabilizing influence on the stomach and digestive tract. The English word 'congee' is derived from the Indian *'kanji'* (meaning 'boilings'), a Tamil word for the water in which rice is boiled. ('They gave him to drink the water squeezed out of rice with pepper and cumin,' a marvelling Portuguese wrote in India in 1563.) In India today, *kanji* refers both to this 'rice water' that is drained off when rice is cooked like pasta (see Plain Baked Rice I, page 137) and to the thick gruel made by boiling a little rice with a lot of water.

This thick gruel, or rice porridge, is made in pretty much the same way all over Asia with minor local variations. In China, the congee may be made out of ordinary raw rice (short-grain rice is considered good enough for gruel), or with burned rice (the rice that 'catches' and sticks to the bottom of the pot), or with a combination of short-grain and glutinous rice. Vegetables like *bok choy* or *choy sum* may be cut up and thrown in to add extra flavour. The unsalted congee is then served with a choice of flavourings. When I had this porridge in Hong Kong, it was called *chuk* − the 'u' pronounced as in 'put' − and the seasonings in the centre of the table included finely sliced spring onions, finely shredded ginger, fresh green coriander, sesame oil, hot sauces (commercial red and green chilli sauces), thin soy sauce, vinegar, boiled salted eggs, thousand-year eggs, pickled turnips, and fermented bean curd. Each person put in a favoured combination.

In the Philippines, the same rice porridge took on quite a different form. It was flavoured with hot chocolate − something that the early Spaniards had brought over from the New World − and called *chumpurado*.

In India, the flavourings added to porridge range from salt, *ghee*, black pepper, and cumin to more elaborate hot and salty pickles. In Gujarat, *ghains* is made by combining rice porridge with beaten yogurt and a little fresh ginger. It is served hot and is considered a good standby for days when one is feeling a little under the weather. Another gruel from India includes both rice and split peas. It is called *khichri* (the English turned this word into 'kedg-eree') and has been known since ancient times as a nourishing meal-in-a-bowl. It is always served seasoned with *ghee*, salt, and pepper, although other spices and vegetables may be added to the basic dish. My mother always added greens and sliced onions and then called the porridge *saag vali khichri*. It might be noted here that there are actually two types of *khichri* in India − the porridge or wet *khichri* and a dry, puffy, grainy form sometimes known as *khili hui khichri* or the 'khichri that has bloomed'.

If you want to eat congee in the Indian style, salt it first. Then add lots of freshly ground pepper and *ghee* or butter. If you like, this *ghee* can be heated, some whole cumin seeds can be popped in it, and the *ghee*–cumin poured over the congee and mixed in. You can also serve Indian-style vegetables, sauced and unsauced, as an accompaniment.

Feel free to make your own congee combinations. If you want it sweet, try adding unsalted butter, cream, and brown sugar.

NOTE: Rice gruels should be made in heavy pots with an even distribution of heat.

For information about ingredients and basic techniques that may be unfamiliar, see General Information, pages 481-506.

PLAIN UNSEASONED CONGEE

(serves 4–6)

Long-grain or short-grain rice,
   measured to the 4-fl oz/1-dl
   level in a glass measuring jug
   or an equal mixture of short-
grain and glutinous rice if you
are going to use Chinese
seasonings

If the rice is 'enriched', do not wash it. Otherwise, wash and drain the rice. Put the rice and 2¾ pt/1½ l of water into a heavy, 3½–4-qt/ 4–4½-l pot and slowly bring to the boil. Stir now and then as the water comes to the boil. Turn heat to medium and let the rice cook for 10 minutes. Stir once or twice during this period. Now cover, leaving the lid very slightly ajar, and cook on very low heat for 1¼ hours.

Congee may be made ahead of time and reheated. It tends to get thick and gummy as it sits. Thin it out with a little boiling water and then reheat, stirring frequently, over a low flame. For serving suggestions, see preceding note as well as the recipes that follow.

CONGEE WITH CHINESE
CABBAGE AND SPRING ONIONS
CHINA

(serves 6–8)

This congee is deliberately undersalted so you can season it as you wish later. As seasonings, you might offer finely grated ginger, finely sliced spring onions, fresh green coriander, thin Chinese soy sauce, white vinegar, sesame oil (use just a little), fermented bean curd, pickles (both salty and sour varieties bought from Chinese grocery stores), commercial hot chilli sauces, boiled and salted ducks' eggs, salt, and white pepper. People can sprinkle whatever and however much they wish. I often reheat leftover stir-fried Chinese vegetables from the day before and stir them into the congee.

Long-grain or short-grain rice,
   measured to the 4-fl oz/1-dl
   level in a glass measuring jug,
   or half-and-half combination of
   short-grain and glutinous rice
1 tsp salt
¾ lb/340 g Chinese cabbage or bok
   choy, washed and cut into
   ¼-in/¾-cm-wide strips,
   including leaves
3 spring onions, finely sliced,
   including green

If the rice is 'enriched', do not wash it. Otherwise, wash and drain it. Combine rice with 2¾ pt/1½ l water and slowly bring to the boil in a 3½-qt/4-l pot. Stir occasionally as rice comes to the boil, making sure that no grains are sticking to the bottom. Turn heat to medium and cook for 10 minutes, stirring once or twice during this period. Add the cabbage, spring onions, and salt. Stir and bring to a simmer. Cover, lower heat, and cook very gently for 1¼ hours.

Devi's
GHAINS
(Congee with Yogurt)
INDIA   (serves 2–3)

8 fl oz/2¼ dl plain yogurt
2 tsp vegetable oil or ghee
⅓ tsp whole cumin seeds
¼ tsp salt, or to taste
¹⁄₁₆ tsp freshly ground black
  pepper, or to taste
¼ tsp finely grated fresh ginger

⅛–¼ tsp very finely chopped fresh
  hot green chillies
Plain Unseasoned Congee (see
  page 153), measured to the
  8-fl oz/2¼-dl level in a glass
  measuring jug

Put the yogurt in a small bowl. Beat gently with a fork or a whisk until the yogurt is creamy and smooth.

Heat the oil in a small 1½-qt/1¾-l pot over a medium flame. When the oil is hot, put in the cumin seeds and remove the pot from the flame. Pour oil and cumin seeds over the yogurt and stir it in immediately. Now put the yogurt in the same pot in which you heated the oil. Add the salt, pepper, ginger, green chillies, and prepared congee. Heat slowly over a medium flame, stirring constantly in one direction. *Do not bring to the boil.* As soon as the *ghains* is heated through, turn off the heat.

Put the *ghains* in small bowls and serve hot for breakfast or as a light lunch. You may also serve this dish cold, with some finely diced cucumber thrown into it at the last minute. You may have to adjust the salt if you add the cucumber. Eat the *ghains* with a spoon.

GEELI KHICHRI
('Wet' Khichri)
INDIA   (makes about 1 qt/11½ dl and serves 6–8)

See note on Rice Porridge or Congee, page 151. You could also make the *khichri* with other *dals*, or with yellow split peas that are available in many supermarkets. Because *khichri* is wet, serve it in

---

For information about ingredients and basic techniques that may be unfamiliar, see General-Information, pages 481-506.

small individual bowls and spoon accompanying vegetables, pickles, and chutney over as you eat it.

3 oz/85 g mung dal, *picked over,*
washed, and drained

Long-grain or short-grain rice,
measured to the 4-fl oz/1-dl
level in a glass measuring jug,
then washed and drained

2 *five-pence-piece sized slices of*
fresh ginger

1¼ *tsp salt, or to taste*

¹⁄₁₆–¹⁄₈ *tsp freshly ground black*
pepper

3 *tbs* ghee *or vegetable oil*

½ *tsp whole cumin seeds*

Put the *dal*, rice, ginger slices, and 2¾ pt/1½ l water in a heavy 2½–3-qt/2¾–3½-l pot over medium heat and bring to the boil. Stir once, cover, turn heat to low and cook for about 1½ hours or until you have a porridge-like consistency. Stir every 6 to 7 minutes during the last 40 minutes of the cooking to make sure that the *khichri* is not sticking to the bottom of the pot. Remove and discard the ginger slices. Add the salt and pepper. Stir to mix.

Khichri may be made up to this stage several hours ahead of time. Whenever you are getting ready to serve, reheat it over a flame, stirring all the time, or reheat it in a double boiler. Sometimes adding a little water and thinning it out slightly helps in the reheating process. Put the *ghee* in a small frying pan or in a small pot and heat it over a medium flame. When hot, put in the cumin seeds and let them sizzle for a few seconds. Now pour the hot *ghee* and cumin seeds over the *khichri* and cover the *khichri* pot immediately. One minute later, uncover, and mix.

SAAG VALI KHICHRI
(Porridge of Rice, Mung Beans, and Spinach)
INDIA   (serves 6–8)

I have never had this dish in any house but ours. Perhaps it was my mother's invention. On the other hand, it could be thousands of years old, as most *khichris* date back to antiquity. In India, one is never too sure about these things.

3 oz/85 g *whole mung beans,*
picked over, washed, and
drained

Long-grain rice, white or brown,
measured to the 4-fl oz/1-dl
level in a glass measuring jug,
then washed and drained

1 *five-pence-piece sized slice of*
fresh ginger

1 lb/450 g *fresh spinach, well*
washed, with the leaves
separated

1½ *tsp salt, or to taste*

4 *tbs vegetable oil or ghee*

¹⁄₁₆ *tsp ground asafetida*
(optional)

1 tsp whole cumin seeds
1 small onion, peeled, cut in half
 lengthwise, then sliced into fine
 half rounds
1 tsp ground cumin seeds
2 tsp ground coriander seeds
1/16 tsp cayenne pepper

Freshly ground black pepper to
 taste
(Extra optional seasonings: lemon
 juice, to taste; a pat of butter
 per serving; 1 tsp finely chopped
 fresh green coriander per
 serving)

Put the mung beans in a heavy 3½-qt/4-l pot. Add 2½ pt/1½ l water and bring to the boil over a medium-high flame. Cover, lower heat, and simmer 2 minutes. Turn off the heat and let the pot sit, covered, for 1 hour. Bring the water to the boil again. Add the rice and the ginger and bring to a simmer. Cover, turn heat to low, and cook gently for 1 hour. Stir occasionally during this period. Now add the spinach and salt. Bring to a simmer. Cover and cook gently for ½ hour, stirring now and then to avoid sticking. Add a little hot water if the porridge seems too thick.

Heat the oil in a 6–7-in/15–18-cm frying pan over a medium flame. When hot, put in the asafetida. Two seconds later, put in the whole cumin seeds. Five seconds later put in the onion. Stir and fry until the onion begins to turn brown at the edges. Add the ground cumin, coriander, and cayenne. Stir and fry for 1 minute. Empty the contents of the frying pan into the rice and bean pot. Stir. Cover and cook for 5 more minutes. Discard the piece of ginger. Sprinkle with freshly ground black pepper. Serve in individual bowls with some or all of the optional seasonings.

GUINATAAN WITH RICE AND MUNG BEANS
(Rice Porridge with Mung Beans)
PHILIPPINES   (serves 6)

Here is a Filipino version of the Asian rice porridge, this time flavoured with mung beans – not the ordinary whole or split beans, but beans that have been roasted slightly and crushed. The roasting gives the porridge a nutty, smoky taste; the crushing allows the beans to cook much faster than they would ordinarily. Instead of the porridge being cooked in water, it is cooked in coconut milk. In the Philippines it is always sweetened and served with a dollop of coconut cream on the top. It is eaten hot or cold, generally at snack-time. You could eat it unsweetened, seasoning it as

For information about ingredients and basic techniques that may be unfamiliar, see General Information, pages 481-506.

you might a Chinese congee or an Indian *khichri* (see pages 151–2).

8 oz/225 g freshly grated coconut
2 tbs whole mung beans
Glutinous rice, measured to the
  4-fl oz/1-dl level in a glass
  measuring jug

3½ tbs brown sugar, or to taste, or
  honey
¼ tsp salt, or to taste

Put the grated coconut into the container of a blender or food processor and start the machine. Slowly add 1½ pt/8½ dl of hot water. (If your machine will not hold so much, you could do this in two batches.) Run the machine for 1 minute. Turn it off. Balance a sieve in a bowl and line it with a triple layer of cheesecloth or a man's handkerchief. Pour the contents of the blender or food processor into the lined sieve. Draw up the four corners of the straining cloth and squeeze out as much coconut milk as you can. Pour the milk into a clear glass measuring cup or jug and let it sit for 1 hour. The coconut cream will rise to the top. You will be able to see it through the clear glass. Spoon off 4 fl oz/1 dl of this cream and set it aside. You should have 1½ pt/8½ dl of coconut milk left. If you do not, add enough water to make up the quantity.

Pick over the mung beans and put them in a small cast-iron frying pan over a medium flame. Keep shaking the pan and dry-roast the beans until they turn a brown colour and give off a nutty, roasted smell. Take the beans off the fire and put them between two sheets of waxed paper. Now crush them lightly with a pestle or a rolling pin. Each bean should break up into 2 to 4 pieces. The skins will come off the beans and may be just blown away.

Wash the rice in several changes of water and drain. Combine the crushed mung beans, rice, and 1½ pt/8½ dl coconut milk in a heavy 1½-qt/1¾-l pot. Place over a medium flame and bring to the boil. Cover, turn heat to low, and simmer gently for 1¼ hours. Stir now and then during this period, making sure that the rice does not stick to the bottom of the pot.

Add the salt and as much sugar as suits your taste. Mix well.

This dish may be eaten hot or cold, with some coconut cream spooned over the top.

KONGNAMUL BAB
(Rice with Soy-Bean Sprouts)
KOREA   (serves 4–6)

I like this dish very much — the rice gets soft and shiny while the soy sprouts retain a nice crunch. Serve it with Simple Korean Sauce, page 416.

Japanese rice, measured to the   *½ lb/225 g soy-bean sprouts, with*
  16-fl oz/4½-dl level in a glass   *the thread-like ends of their tails*
  measuring jug   *picked off*

Put the rice in the bowl and wash in several changes of water. Drain. Add 2½ pt/1½ l water and leave to soak for ½ hour. Drain.
    Bring 3¼ pt/2½ l of water to the boil in a 3½-qt/4-l pot. Add the soy-bean sprouts and boil rapidly for 2 minutes. Drain thoroughly.
    Put the rice at the bottom of a heavy 2½-qt/2¾-l pot. Lay the drained soy-bean sprouts over the rice. Add 1 pt/5¾ dl water and cover with a tight-fitting lid. Bring to the boil over a medium-high flame. When the steam begins to escape from under the lid, turn the heat down to very, very low and cook for 20 minutes. Turn the flame up to medium for 10 seconds. Now turn it off. Let the pot sit, covered and undisturbed, for 15 minutes.

HONSIK BAB
(Rice with Barley)
KOREA   (serves 4–6)

The Koreans cook their rice with all kinds of grains and beans in order to make it more nutritious. Here it is combined with pressed barley, a skinned, quick-cooking variety, that takes just as long to get tender as the rice does.

Japanese rice, measured to the   *2 oz/55 g pressed barley*
  16-fl oz/4½-dl level in a glass
  measuring jug

Combine the rice and barley in a bowl. Wash in several changes of water. Drain. Add 2½ pt/1½ l of water and let the mixture soak for ½ hour. Drain well.
    Put the drained grains and 1 pt/5¾ dl water in a heavy 1¾-qt/2-l pot. Cover with a tight-fitting lid and bring to the boil over a medium-high flame. When steam begins to escape from under the

---

For information about ingredients and basic techniques that may be unfamiliar, see General Information, pages 481-506.

lid, turn heat down to very, very low and cook, undisturbed, for 20 minutes. Turn the heat up to medium for 10 seconds and then turn it off. Let the pot sit, covered, for 10 minutes.

RICE WITH BEAN SPROUTS, SPINACH, AND LAVER
KOREA   *(serves 4–6)*

I had this dish for the first time at the Jang Won restaurant in Seoul. As I sat across from my host at a low lacquered table, almost twenty dishes drifted in. This was not a vegetarian restaurant but there was enough here to please the palate of the most finicky vegetarian: raw peeled autumn chestnuts (how sweet and wonderful they are in this crunchy form); tender bean curd in a hot-water bath, to be eaten with a spicy dipping sauce; fried carrot slices, all encased in an egg and flour batter; cabbage, radish, and garlic pickles; sweetened walnuts and pine nuts; crisp, lacy seaweed; mountain mushrooms, wrapped in foil and grilled; a 'salad' of fresh ginseng, green peppers, cucumbers, and tomatoes; and this delicious rice dish — all followed by fresh fruit and quince tea.
NOTE: This rice dish is not salted and is generally eaten with a spicy sauce, such as Spicy Korean Sauce, page 417.

Japanese rice, measured to the
16-fl oz/4½-dl level in a glass
measuring jug
½ lb/225 g soy-bean or mung-bean
sprouts
½ lb/225 g spinach, well washed
1½ sheets nori (approximately
7 × 8 in/18 × 20 cm)

1 carrot
3 tbs Japanese soy sauce
2 tsp sesame oil
2 spring onions, cut into fine
rounds including green
1 clove garlic, finely chopped
2 tsp roasted sesame seeds
½ tsp sugar

Wash the rice in several changes of water. Drain it. Put the rice in a bowl, add 2½ pt/1½ l water and let the rice soak for ½ hour. Empty the rice into a sieve and let it drain for 15 minutes.

While the rice is soaking, prepare all the other ingredients. Break off the wispy, thread-like ends of the sprouts (if you feel up to it). Wash them well and drain them. Cut the spinach crosswise into ¼-in/¾-cm-wide strips. Cut up the roots, too; they taste very good.

Heat a large pot of water. When it comes to a rolling boil, drop in the sprouts and the spinach. Bring to the boil again and boil rapidly for 1 minute. Drain, squeezing out as much liquid as you can.

With a pair of scissors, cut the *nori* into thin strips, about 3 in/ 8 cm long and ¼ in/¾ cm wide.

Peel the carrot, cut it first into three sections and then into julienne strips.

Combine the bean sprouts, spinach, *nori*, and carrot in a bowl. Add the soy sauce, sesame oil, spring onions, garlic, sesame seeds, and sugar. Mix and set aside for 15 minutes.

Put the drained rice and seasoned vegetables in a heavy 3-qt/3½-l pot. Mix gently. Add 1 pt/5¾ dl water, cover with a tight-fitting lid and bring to the boil over a medium flame. When steam escapes from under the lid, turn the heat to very, very low. Cook for 20 minutes. Turn the heat off and let the pot sit for 10 minutes in a warm place. Do not uncover the pot during this period.

RICE WITH MILLET
KOREA   *(serves 4–6)*

Both plain and glutinous millet are often cooked in conjunction with rice in Korea. This gives the rice added nutritional value as well as an extra texture. Serve with Simple Korean Sauce (see page 416) and other vegetables.

Japanese rice, measured to the   *3 oz/85 g hulled plain or glutinous*
  16-fl oz/4½-dl level in a glass   *millet*
  measuring jug

Put the rice and millet in a bowl. Wash in several changes of water. Drain. Add 2½ pt/1½ l of water and leave to soak for ½ hour. Drain thoroughly.

Combine the drained grains and 1 pt/5¾ dl water in a heavy 2-qt/2¼-l pot. Cover with a tight-fitting lid and bring to the boil over a medium-high flame. When steam begins to escape from under the lid, turn the flame down to very, very low and cook for 20 minutes. Turn the flame up to medium for 10 seconds and then turn it off. Let the rice sit, covered and undisturbed, for 15 minutes.

RICE WITH SPINACH
AFGHANISTAN   *(serves 4–6)*

This rice dish, some beans, yogurt, and a chutney or relish would make a nice, simple meal.

Long-grain rice, measured to the   *1½ lb/675 g fresh spinach, washed*
  15-fl oz/4¼-dl level in a glass   *and trimmed, or 2 packets*
  measuring jug   *frozen*
1 tbs salt   *6 tbs vegetable oil*
                                               2 medium-sized onions, peeled and
                                                 chopped

For information about ingredients and basic techniques that may be unfamiliar, see General Information, pages 481–506.

Wash the rice in several changes of water and drain it. Put in a bowl, add 1 qt/11½ dl of water and leave to soak for 30 minutes. Drain again.

Put about 4 qt/4½ l of water in a 5-qt/5½-l pot. Add 2 tsp salt and bring to the boil. Put a little fresh spinach at a time into the boiling water. As soon as it wilts, lift it out with a slotted spoon and place it in a colander to drain. Do all the spinach this way. Rinse under cold running water and then squeeze out as much moisture as possible. Chop the spinach finely. If using frozen spinach, cook according to packet instructions, drain, and squeeze out moisture.

Heat the oil in a wide, heavy 3-qt/3½-l pot that has a well-fitting lid. Put in the onions. Stir and sauté over medium heat until they turn soft. Put in the spinach. Stir and sauté for about 25 minutes, turning the heat down if necessary. The spinach should turn dark and rather dry. Add the rice and the remaining 1 tsp salt. Continue sautéing for another 5 to 7 minutes, being careful not to break the grains of rice. Add 1 pt/5¾ dl water and bring to the boil. Cover, turn heat to very low and cook for 25 minutes. Take the pot off the flame. Remove the lid and quickly cover the pot with a clean tea towel. Put the lid on, over the tea towel. Let the rice sit, undisturbed and in a warm place, for 10 to 15 minutes.

BIBIMBAB
(Korean Rice with Egg and Vegetable Topping)
KOREA   (serves 6)

This is Korea's answer to Japan's Chirashi-Zushi — lots of good things arranged neatly on top of rice, this time with a fried egg in the centre and some spicy, *kochu chang*-based sauce just beside (or at times under) the egg. I have used the Chinese dish Courgettes Stir-Fried with Garlic as one of the toppings as it is quite similar to a Korean dish. This is really a meal-in-a-bowl and makes a fine lunch or dinner.

Freshly cooked Plain Japanese Rice (see page 144), measured to the 2½-pt/1½-l level in a glass measuring jug
6 fried eggs
Oshitashi (see page 77)
Soy-Bean and Mung-Bean Sprouts Seasoned with Sesame Oil (see page 123), drained
Korean-Style Cucumber Salad (see page 368), drained

Courgettes Stir-Fried with Garlic (see page 38), drained
6 crisp, smaller inner leaves lettuce
4 tbs kochu chang
2 tsp sugar
2 tsp sesame oil
1 tsp lightly crushed, roasted sesame seeds

Divide up the rice among six bowls that are about 8 in/20 cm in diameter at the top and about 2½ in/5 cm in height, heaping it in the centre in the shape of a mound. (Old-fashioned soup plates may be used.) Put a fried egg on top of each mound of rice. Radiating down from it, in somewhat triangular segments, arrange the Oshitashi, Soy-Bean and Mung-Bean Sprouts Seasoned with Sesame Oil, Korean-Style Cucumber Salad, and the Courgette Stir-Fried with Garlic. Leave a little room for the lettuce leaf 'cups'. Mix the *kochu chang*, sugar, sesame oil, and sesame seeds and put a dollop in each 'cup'.

RICE WITH GARLIC
PHILIPPINES

(serves 4–6)

Long-grain rice, measured to the
 15-fl oz/4¼-dl level in a glass
 measuring jug
5 tbs vegetable oil
6 cloves garlic, lightly mashed and
 peeled
1 tsp salt

Wash the rice in several changes of water. Drain. Soak rice in 2½ pt/1½ l water for ½ hour. Drain thoroughly.

Heat the oil in a heavy 2-qt/2¼-l pot over a medium flame. When hot, put in the pieces of garlic. Stir and fry until the garlic pieces turn a medium-brown colour. Add the rice and the salt. Stir and fry another minute. Add 1 pt/5¾ dl water and bring to the boil. Cover tightly, turn heat to very, very low and cook gently for 25 minutes.

For information about ingredients and basic techniques that may be unfamiliar, see General Information, pages 481-506.

RICE WITH TOMATOES
PHILIPPINES   (serves 4–6)

Spain ruled the Philippines for three hundred years, right until the end of the last century. During this period, hundreds of Spanish recipes were absorbed into the Filipino repertoire, some with slight Asian amendments, others almost in their pure European forms. This recipe seems to have altered little in its new tropical habitat.

Long-grain rice, measured to the 15-fl oz/4¼-dl level in a glass measuring jug
5 tbs vegetable oil (you may use olive oil)
8 cloves garlic, peeled and finely chopped
1 medium-sized onion, peeled and chopped
2 medium-sized tomatoes, peeled and chopped
1 tsp salt

Wash the rice in several changes of water. Drain. Soak rice in 2½ pt/1½ l of water for ½ hour. Drain.

Heat the oil in a heavy 2-qt/2¼-l pot over a medium flame. When hot, put in the garlic. Stir and fry until the garlic turns a medium brown. Put in the onion. Stir and fry until onion turns translucent. Add the tomatoes. Stir and fry until tomatoes begin to brown lightly. Add the rice. Stir and sauté for a minute. Add the salt and 1 pt/5¾ dl water. Bring to the boil. Cover tightly, turn heat to very, very low and cook gently for 25 minutes.

RICE WITH SAUTÉED ONIONS AND MUSHROOMS
INDIA   (serves 4–6)

Long-grain rice, measured to the 15-fl oz/4¼-dl level in a glass measuring jug
4 tbs vegetable oil
½ tsp cumin seeds
1 medium-sized onion, peeled and finely chopped
4 medium-sized mushrooms, wiped and finely chopped
1 tsp salt

Wash the rice in several changes of water and leave to drain.

Heat the oil in a heavy 2–3-qt/2¼–3½-l pot that has a tight-fitting lid, over a medium flame. When hot, put in the cumin seeds. Stir and fry for a few seconds. Put in the onion and sauté for a few minutes or until the onion turns soft. Add the mushrooms and sauté for another 2 to 3 minutes. Put in the drained rice and salt. Keep sautéing gently for another 3 to 4 minutes. Add 1 pt/5¾ dl water and bring to the boil. Cover, turn heat to very low and cook for 25 minutes.

RICE WITH COCONUT MILK
ALL SOUTH AND SOUTH-EAST ASIA *(serves 4–6)*

There are versions of this dish throughout coastal and southern India, Sri Lanka and eastwards, all the way to the Philippines. For the simplest version, follow directions for Plain Boiled Rice (see page 137), leave out the butter, include the salt, and substitute coconut milk (see General Information) for the water. If you want a Thai-Malaysian-Indonesian flavour, you could add the lower third of a bruised stalk of lemon grass to the rice. If fresh lemon grass is unavailable, 2 tsp of sliced and dried lemon grass tied up in a cheesecloth bundle would work just as well. Remove the lemon grass before you serve the rice.

Mrs Wawo-Runtu's
NASI KUNING
(Yellow Turmeric Rice Cooked with Coconut Milk)
INDONESIA *(serves 6)*

This is one of those delicately flavoured, decidedly festive Indonesian dishes that is served exquisitely garnished with red peppers, green peppers, cucumber slices, as well as sundry *sambals* and side dishes, some of which are first ensconced in banana-leaf cups and then embedded in the rice. Apart from its good taste, this dish can be quite a visual delight as well.

In Indonesia, it is fresh turmeric that is used to tint the rice yellow. Fresh turmeric looks a bit like fresh ginger only it is more slender and bright yellow inside. It is not easily available, but if you can find some, use a piece that is 1 in/2½ cm long and about ½ in/1½ cm thick. You will need to peel and then grate it to a fine pulp. Put it in a strainer and then pour the coconut milk through it.

This rice dish is basically cooked in the upper half of a steamer. I set a small-holed colander over a pot of boiling water and then cover the colander with a lid. You could also use a large sieve set over boiling water or else use the more conventional aluminium or bamboo steamer. If your steamer has very large holes, cover them with a layer of cheesecloth.

Long-grain rice, measured to the 15-fl oz/4¼-dl level in a glass measuring jug

16 fl oz/½ l coconut milk, fresh or tinned
2 daun salaam *leaves*

For information about ingredients and basic techniques that may be unfamiliar, see General Information, pages 481–506.

5 in/13 cm fresh lemon grass,	*¾ tsp ground turmeric powder*
lightly crushed, or 2 tsp dried,	*1 tsp salt*
tied up in a cheesecloth bundle	

For garnishes, you could use:

4–5 in/10–13 cm of unwaxed cucumber − score the skin with a fork, creating ridges that run lengthwise, and then cut the cucumber crosswise into thin slices

5 fresh hot green or green and red chillies − slice the chillies lengthwise at ⅛-in/½-cm intervals, starting ½ in/1½ cm below the stem and going straight down all the way to near the tip area; seed and leave in iced water for 1 hour

A few sprigs of mint

Wash the rice in several changes of water and drain. Put in a bowl, add 1 qt/11½ dl water and leave to soak overnight. Drain again.

Set up your steaming apparatus and bring the water in the lower container to the boil. (The water should never touch the rice.) Put the rice in the upper container. Make a few vertical 'steam holes' with a chopstick. Now cover the upper container and steam the rice for 10 minutes.

While the rice is steaming, put the coconut milk in a 2-qt/2¼-l pot and add the *salaam* leaves, lemon grass, turmeric, and salt. Stir and bring to the boil. Turn heat to low and simmer 2 to 3 minutes.

Empty the rice into the hot coconut milk. Stir it gently and bring to the boil. Cover, turn the heat off and let the rice sit, undisturbed, for 15 minutes. By this time all the liquid will have been absorbed. Mix gently.

Put the rice back in the steamer. Make fresh 'steam holes' with a chopstick and cover. Steam over medium heat for 30 minutes.

Remove the *salaam* leaves and the lemon grass. Put the rice on a platter and arrange garnishes around it.

RICE WITH FRESH HERBS AND BABY BROAD BEANS
IRAN   *(serves 4–6)*

This is a scrumptious, meal-in-itself rice dish, fragrant with the aroma of fresh herbs. I first had it at the Tavooz Restaurant in New York City and have eaten many variations of it since then. You could make it with fresh broad beans, black-eyed beans, lentils, peas, and vary the herbs to suit your taste. You can eat this dish as a main course, just like a pasta dish.

*Long-grain rice, measured to the
15-fl oz/4¼-dl level in a glass
measuring jug*
5 tbs plus ¼ tsp salt
*1 10-oz/285-g packet frozen baby
broad beans*
6 tbs melted unsalted butter

*8 tbs finely chopped fresh green
coriander*
8 tbs finely chopped fresh parsley
8 tbs finely chopped fresh dill
*1 oz/30 g very finely sliced spring
onion tops (green only)*

Pick over the rice and wash it in several changes of water. Drain.
Put the rice in a bowl. Add 1 qt/11½ dl of water and 2½ tbs of salt.
Stir and leave to soak overnight or for at least 8 hours.

Cook baby broad beans according to packet instructions but
undercook them so they are still firm. (My packet suggested a
cooking time of 15 minutes, so I cooked the broad beans for 8
minutes only. Also, I added ¼ tsp salt to the cooking liquid, even
though the beans were 'lightly salted' already.) Drain the broad
beans and set them aside.

Preheat the oven to 325° F/170° C/Mark 3. Drain the rice in a
sieve. Place the sieve under running water and wash the rice.
Drain.

Bring 3 qt/3½ l of water to the boil in a large pot. Add 2½ tbs salt.
Pour the drained rice into the boiling water in a steady stream. Stir
the rice and let the water come to the boil again. Boil rice rapidly for
exactly 5 minutes. Turn off heat and drain the rice by pouring it
into a sieve. Wash the rice again, this time under running
lukewarm water. Drain.

Pour 4 tbs of the melted butter plus a tbs of water into a 9-in/23-
cm-wide, heavy, casserole-type pot and place the pot on a low
flame. Put half the rice over the butter, spreading it out over the
bottom of the pot. Spread the broad beans over the rice. Spread the
herbs and spring onion tops, mixed together, over the broad
beans. Spread the remaining rice over the herbs. Pour the remaining 2 tbs of melted butter over the rice. Now cover the pot with a
doubled piece of kitchen paper, just slightly larger than the circumference of the pot. Put a piece of aluminium foil, larger than the
kitchen paper, over the kitchen paper. Attach the kitchen paper to
the foil with 4 straight pins. Crimp the edges of the foil to seal the
pot. Now cover the pot with its own lid and place in the oven for 30
minutes. Take the pot out of the oven and uncover. Stir the rice
gently to mix all the ingredients. Put all the covers back on and put
rice back in the oven for another 20 to 30 minutes or until rice is
cooked through.

*For information about ingredients and basic techniques that may be unfamiliar, see General
Information, pages 481-506.*

RICE WITH PANEER AND PEAS
INDIA   (serves 6)

Long-grain rice, measured to the
   15-fl oz/4¼-dl level in a glass
   measuring jug
Paneer made according to the
   recipe on page 277
1¼ tsp salt
6 tbs vegetable oil
3 bay leaves
A 1-in/2½-cm stick of cinnamon

5 whole cardamom pods
6 oz/180 g shelled fresh peas
   (frozen, defrosted peas may be
   substituted)
1 tsp sugar
1 fresh hot green chilli, sliced into
   fine half rings
1 tsp ground cumin seeds

Wash the rice in several changes of water and drain. Put in a bowl, add 2 pt/11½ dl water and leave to soak for 30 minutes. Drain again.

Cut the *paneer* into ½-in/1½-cm cubes and sprinkle ¼ tsp salt over them. Mix gently.

Heat the oil in a seasoned cast-iron or nonstick frying pan over a medium flame. When hot, put in the *paneer* cubes and fry until golden on two sides. This will happen rather quickly. Remove with a slotted spoon and set aside on a plate.

Pour the oil from the frying pan into a heavy, wide, 2½–3-qt/ 2¾–3½-l pot that has a tight-fitting lid. Heat it again over a medium flame. When hot, put in the bay leaves, cinnamon, and cardamom. Stir once. Now put in the drained rice, peas, 1 tsp salt, sugar, green chilli, and cumin seeds. Stir and fry for 5 minutes, turning the heat down a bit if the rice begins to stick. Add 1 pt/5¾ dl water and bring to the boil. Cover, turn heat to very low and cook for 25 minutes. Take off the lid and quickly put in the *paneer* pieces. Cook for another 2 to 3 minutes. Turn off the heat and let the pot sit, covered and undisturbed, for 10 minutes.

The bay leaves, cinnamon, and cardamom are not to be eaten – you might remove them from the serving platter. Mix the rice gently so that the *paneer* and peas are evenly distributed. With this rice, you could have almost any Indian, Persian, or Indonesian dishes.

BASMATI RICE COOKED WITH CHANA DAL AND DILL
(Khili Hui Khichri)
INDIA   (serves 6)

I have used the Indian long-grain *basmati* rice for this recipe but you could use any long-grain rice. Again, I have used the Indian *chana dal*, but you could substitute yellow split peas. The rice, bean, dill, and stock combination makes this an extremely nourishing dish.

2 oz/55 g chana dal, *picked over*
  and washed
Basmati *rice, measured to the*
  15-fl oz/4¼-dl level in a glass
  measuring jug, then picked over
  and washed

3 tbs vegetable oil
½ tsp garam masala
1 tsp salt
4 tbs fresh chopped dill
1¼ pt/¾ l Delicious Stock . . . (see
  page 340) or water

Soak the *dal* in ¾ pt/4¼ dl hot water for 3 hours.
  Soak the rice in 1 qt/11½ dl of water for 1 hour.
  Drain the *dal* and the rice.
  Heat the oil in a heavy pot (with a tight-fitting lid) over a medium flame. When hot, add the drained *dal* and rice. Stir and fry for 2 to 3 minutes or until all grains are coated with oil. Add the *garam masala*, salt, and dill. Stir and fry for another minute or so. Now put in the stock and bring to the boil. Cover tightly, turn heat to very, very low, and cook gently for 25 minutes. Turn off the heat and let the pot sit in a warm place, covered, for 15 minutes.

Mrs Patel's
EK HANDI NA DAL CHAVAL
(Rice and Dal, Cooked in One Pot)
INDIA   *(serves 4 as a main dish,*
                                     6–8 as part of a larger meal)

Here is one of those 'casserole' dishes from Gujarat that is a complete meal in itself. It contains rice, *toovar dal*, potatoes, onions, as well as the delicate spicing provided by *garam masala*. The name of the dish translates as 'rice and beans [and therefore a meal] cooked in one pot'.
  There are several stages to making this dish. The *dal*, rice, and potatoes have to be partially cooked first, then layered and baked.

6½ oz/185 g toovar dal, *oily or*
  plain
¼ tsp ground turmeric
2 tbs salt
1 *five-pence-piece sized slice of*
  fresh ginger
4 fl oz/1 dl vegetable oil
2 *medium-sized boiling potatoes*
  (about ½ lb/225 g), peeled and
  cut into ¾-in/2-cm dice

A 1½-in/4-cm stick of cinnamon
5 whole cardamom pods
3 bay leaves
3 *medium-sized onions, peeled,*
  cut in half lengthwise, then
  sliced into very fine half rings
1 tsp garam masala
Long-grain rice, *measured to the*
  15-fl oz/4¼-dl level in a glass
  measuring jug

For information about ingredients and basic techniques that may be unfamiliar, see General Information, pages 481-506.

Garnish: hard-boiled eggs
  (optional)

Pick over the *toovar dal*, wash and drain it, and then soak it in 1¼ pt/
¾ l water for 1 hour. Drain. Put the *toovar dal* in a 1½-qt/1¾-l pot
along with 16 fl oz/½ l water, the turmeric, 1 tsp salt, and the slice of
ginger. Bring to the boil. Cover, lower heat and simmer for 10
minutes. Drain (the liquid may be saved for soup) and set aside.

Heat the oil in a 9-in/23-cm-wide, heavy, casserole-type pot over
a medium flame. When hot, put in the potatoes. Fry them, stirring,
about 8 to 10 minutes, or until they turn golden on all sides.
Remove with a slotted spoon and put on a plate. (Do not turn off
heat under pot.) Sprinkle potatoes with ¼ tsp salt and set aside.

Put the cinnamon, cardamom, and bay leaves into the remaining
oil in the casserole dish. Stir them once and immediately put in the
sliced onions. Turn the heat up slightly. Fry the onions, stirring,
until medium brown. Add ¼ tsp salt and the *garam masala*. Stir once
and turn off the heat.

Preheat oven to 325° F/170° C/Mark 3.

Bring 3 qt/3½ l of water to the boil in a large pot. Add 1½ tbs of salt
to it. When the water is at a rolling boil, pour in the rice in a steady
stream. Stir. Let the water come to the boil again and then boil
vigorously for 6 minutes. Turn off the heat and drain the rice.

Put a thin layer of rice over the fried onions at the bottom of the
casserole. Now put in all the potatoes, in one layer. Add another
thin layer of rice. Follow that with a layer of *toovar dal*, using up all
the *dal*. End with a final thin layer of rice. Cover the pot with
aluminium foil, crimping the edges to seal the pot. Now cover the
pot with its own lid. Bake in the oven for 35 to 40 minutes.

To serve, stir the contents of the casserole dish gently and turn
out on to a large, warmed platter. Garnish, if you like, with quartered hard-boiled eggs.

VANGI BHAT
(Rice and Aubergine Cooked in the Maharashtrian Style)
INDIA   *(serves 6)*

Even though this dish belongs to the vegetarian Maharashtrians of
western India, it can be found, with slight variations, in many
regions of South India as well. The rice and aubergine are cooked
separately first. They are then combined and seasoned, very much
as a rice salad might be. *Vangi bhat* is tangy, spicy, and smells
enticingly of roasted coconut.

Long-grain rice, measured to the
   15-fl oz/4¼-dl level in a glass
   measuring jug
2½ tsp salt
1 medium-sized aubergine (about
   1 lb/450 g)
1 tsp plus 7 tbs vegetable oil
2 tbs whole coriander seeds
2 tsp chana dal

A generous pinch of ground
   asafetida
½ whole hot dried red pepper
A ¾-in/2-cm stick of cinnamon
3 tbs desiccated, unsweetened
   coconut
2 tbs lemon juice
¼ tsp turmeric

Put the rice, 1¼ pt/¾ l water, and 1 tsp salt in a 1½-qt/1¾-l pot with a tight-fitting lid. Bring to the boil. Cover, turn heat to very, very low, and cook gently for 25 minutes. Turn off heat and let rice sit, covered, for another 10 to 15 minutes. (You may make your rice in an electric rice-cooker instead. Use the same proportions of rice, water, and salt.)

Peel aubergine and dice into ½–¾-in/1½–2-cm cubes. Place in a bowl and sprinkle with 1 tsp salt. Mix well and set aside for half an hour.

Heat 1 tbs oil in a small cast-iron frying pan over a medium flame. When hot, put in the coriander seeds, *chana dal*, asafetida, red pepper, and cinnamon. Keep stirring. When spices darken by a few shades, remove them with a slotted spoon and place them on a plate lined with kitchen paper.

Put the desiccated coconut in the same frying pan. Fry, stirring all the time (there will be hardly any oil in the pan, but that is all right), until the coconut turns a fairly uniform golden-brown colour. Remove coconut and place on the kitchen paper, next to the spices.

Heat 5 tbs of oil in a 9–10-in/23–25-cm frying pan over a medium flame. When hot, add the aubergine. Stir and fry for 5 to 8 minutes or until aubergine is cooked through. Remove with a slotted spoon and keep warm.

Put spices and coconut into an electric coffee grinder and grind as finely as possible. Leave in coffee grinder.

Combine the lemon juice, about ½ tsp salt (you may use a bit less), the turmeric, and 2 tbs water in a very small pot (you could use a butter warmer). Bring to the boil. Turn heat to very low and simmer very gently for 3 minutes. Turn off heat.

Spread the freshly cooked rice out on a warmed serving platter. Dribble 2 tbs of oil on the rice and mix well, breaking up all lumps as you do so. When the rice is no longer steaming (it should still be

---

For information about ingredients and basic techniques that may be unfamiliar, see General Information, pages 481-506.

warm to the touch), add the aubergine, the coconut–spice mixture, and the lemon–turmeric mixture. Mix well and serve warm or at room temperature. If it is to be served a few hours later, it should be cooled quickly (you may fan it), and then stored, *un*refrigerated, in a tightly closed container (a plastic bag will do).

KASHMIRI-STYLE GUCCHI PULLAO
(Pilaf with Morel Mushrooms)
INDIA   *(serves 4–6)*

When I was growing up in India, we had this *pullao* about once every three weeks and always for a Sunday lunch. Dried morels came all the way from the northern state of Kashmir and were, as my mother often told us, worth their weight in gold. Naturally, there were never too many of them in a *pullao*. I hid my morels under a mound of rice or under a lettuce leaf. When the meal was almost over, I would suddenly 'discover' my treasure with great glee. I ate the morels very, very slowly, savouring each bite for as long as possible.

If you are lucky enough to have access to fresh morels — they generally make their appearance in the spring — use them instead of the dried ones in this recipe. You will not have a 'soaking liquid', but water or any of the stocks listed in this book could be used instead.

Basmati *rice, measured to the*
  15-fl oz/4¼-dl level in a glass
  measuring jug
½ oz/15 g *dried morels (10–12*
  mushrooms)

3 tbs *unsalted butter*
1 small *onion, peeled, cut in half*
  lengthwise, then sliced into fine
  half rounds
1 tsp *salt*

Pick over the rice and wash it in several changes of water. Drain. Put in a bowl. Add 2½ pt/1½ l fresh water and leave to soak for half an hour. Drain.

Rinse the morels and soak them in ½ pt/3 dl of boiling water for 15 to 20 minutes or until they are soft. Remove mushrooms from their soaking liquid (reserve this liquid) and rinse them again. Now cut each mushroom in half lengthwise.

Strain the soaking liquid through a clean handkerchief. Add enough water to it to make 1 pt/5¾ dl.

Heat the butter in a heavy 2-qt/2¼-l pot over a medium flame. When hot, put in the onion. Sauté until it turns translucent. Add the morels and sauté them for 1 minute. Add the rice and the salt. Stir and sauté the rice for a couple of minutes. Lower the heat a bit if the rice starts to stick. Now add the morel soaking liquid and bring to the boil. Cover tightly, turn heat to very, very low, and cook, undisturbed, for 25 minutes.

VEGETABLE PULLAO
INDIA

6½ oz/185 g whole mung beans, picked over and washed
Long-grain rice, measured to the 15-fl oz/4¼-dl level in a glass measuring jug
4½ tbs vegetable oil
1 tsp whole black mustard seeds
1 medium-sized onion, peeled and finely chopped
4 medium-sized cloves garlic, peeled and finely chopped
1 tsp peeled, finely chopped fresh ginger

⅓ lb/140 g string beans, trimmed and cut into ¼-in/¾-cm-long pieces
¼ lb/115 g medium-sized mushrooms, diced into ¼-in/ ¾-cm pieces
2 tsp garam masala
1½ tsp ground coriander
2½ tsp salt
2 tbs finely chopped fresh green coriander, or parsley

Put mung beans in a bowl with 1¼ pt/¾ l of water. Cover lightly and set aside for 12 hours. Drain beans and wrap in a very damp tea towel. Put the wrapped bundle in a bowl. Put this bowl in a dark place (like an unused oven) for 24 hours.

Wash rice well and soak in 1½ pt/8½ dl of water for half an hour. Drain well.

Preheat oven to 325° F/170° C/Mark 3.

Heat oil in a wide, heavy, 4–5-qt/4½–5½-l ovenproof pot over a medium-high flame. When hot, put in the mustard seeds. As soon as the mustard seeds begin to pop (this takes just a few seconds), put in the onion. Stir and fry for about 5 minutes or until onion turns brown at the edges. Add the garlic and ginger. Fry, stirring, for about 1 minute. Turn heat to medium-low and add the mung beans, rice, string beans, mushrooms, *garam masala*, ground coriander, and salt. Stir and sauté for about 10 minutes or until rice turns translucent and vegetables are well coated with oil. Add 1½ pt/8½ dl hot water and the chopped parsley. Turn heat to a medium-high flame and cook, stirring, for about 5 minutes or until most of the water is absorbed. (There will be 1 in/2½ cm or so of water at the bottom.) Cover the pot first with aluminium foil, crimping and sealing the edges, and then with its own lid. Place in heated oven for half an hour. Fluff up with a fork and serve.

For information about ingredients and basic techniques that may be unfamiliar, see General Information, pages 481-506.

SPICED RICE WITH CASHEW NUTS

INDIA   *(serves 6)*

This dish can be found, with interesting local variations, all over India. It is not hot, just lightly, fragrantly spiced.

Long-grain rice or Indian basmati
  rice, measured to the 15-fl oz/
  4¼-dl level in a glass measuring
  jug
4 tbs vegetable oil
2 tbs raw cashew nuts, split in
  half lengthwise
1 medium-sized onion, peeled, cut
  in half lengthwise, then sliced
  into paper-thin half rings

1 clove garlic, peeled and finely
  chopped
1 tsp peeled, grated fresh ginger
½ tsp finely chopped fresh hot
  green chilli or ⅛ tsp cayenne
  pepper
¾ tsp garam masala
1 tsp salt
1¼ pt/¾ l hot Vegetable Stock (see
  page 340) or water

Place rice in a bowl. Add water to cover. Rub the rice grains with your hands. Drain the water. Add more water and repeat the process four or five times until the rice is well washed (the water should not be milky). Cover the rice with 1¾ pt/1 l of fresh water and leave to soak for half an hour. Drain, and leave rice in a strainer.

Preheat oven to 325° F/170° C/Mark 3.

This rice dish cooks on top of the stove and in the oven, so it is more convenient to use a heavy, flame- and ovenproof, 2-qt/2¼-l sauté pan. Heat the oil over medium heat. Put in the split cashew nuts. Fry for a few seconds, stirring all the time, until they turn a golden brown. Remove with slotted spoon and leave on kitchen paper to drain.

Put the onion slices into the same oil. Fry them for 2 to 3 minutes or until they turn brown at the edges. Add the drained rice, the garlic, ginger, green chilli, *garam masala*, and salt. Turn the heat to medium-low. Stir and fry the rice for 7 to 8 minutes or until the rice is translucent and well coated with the oil.

Add the heated stock. Keep stirring and cooking on a medium-low flame for another 5 to 6 minutes. When the top of the rice begins to look dry (there will still be a little liquid left at the bottom of the pot), cover with a well-fitting lid (or aluminium foil plus a looser-fitting lid) and place in the oven 20 to 25 minutes or until rice is cooked through. Remove rice pan from the oven and leave, covered, in a warm place for 10 minutes. (If kept covered and in a warm place, this rice will retain its heat for a good half hour.)

Remove rice gently with a slotted spoon, and place on warmed serving platter. Break up all lumps with the back of the slotted spoon. Garnish with the cashew nuts and serve immediately.

SPICED RICE
WITH NUTS AND SULTANAS
INDIA   *(serves 8)*

This is a superb North Indian rice dish for parties. If you can find the fine-grain *basmati* rice, use it here. If not, a long-grain rice will do almost as well. You may garnish this dish with any nuts and dried fruit that you like. I have chosen almonds and sultanas because they are traditional; peanuts, cashew nuts, and sesame seeds because they are so nutritious.

Long-grain rice, measured to the 1-pt/5¾-dl level in a glass measuring jug
10 tbs vegetable oil
1½ tbs blanched, slivered almonds
2 tbs raw shelled peanuts
2 tbs raw cashew nuts, split in half lengthwise
1–2 oz/30–60 g sultanas
1 onion, peeled, cut in half lengthwise, then sliced into very fine half rings

1 clove garlic, peeled and finely chopped
A ¾-in/2-cm piece of fresh ginger, peeled and finely grated
½–1 fresh hot green chilli, finely chopped
1 tsp garam masala
1½ tsp salt
2 tbs roasted sesame seeds

Wash the rice well and leave to soak in a bowl filled with 1 qt/11½ dl of water for half an hour. Drain and leave rice in a strainer.

Preheat oven to 325° F/170° C/Mark 3.

Line a plate with kitchen paper and keep beside the cooker.

Heat oil over medium heat in a wide, heavy, ovenproof pot. (I use a 10-in/25-cm-wide, flame- and ovenproof sauté pan.) When hot, put in the almonds. Stir and fry until almonds turn golden. Remove with a slotted spoon and place on a kitchen-paper-lined plate. Put the peanuts into the same oil, stirring and frying them until they are golden. Remove them with a slotted spoon and place them beside the almonds. Now fry the cashew nuts in the same way. When they are golden, spread them out near the peanuts. Finally, put in the sultanas. Within a second, they will puff up. Remove them immediately and spread them out beside the cashews.

Remove all but 5 tbs of the oil from the pot (you can re-use it for some other dish). Put the onion slices into the oil and fry them for 2 or 3 minutes or until they turn brown in spots. Add the drained rice, the garlic, ginger, green chilli, *garam masala*, and salt. Turn the

For information about ingredients and basic techniques that may be unfamiliar, see General Information, pages 481-506.

heat to medium-low and fry the rice, stirring constantly, for 7 to 8 minutes or until all the grains are well coated with oil.

Add 1½ pt/8½ dl of water and bring to the boil. Turn heat to medium-low, stirring and cooking the rice for about 5 minutes or until most of the liquid has evaporated. (There will be a little liquid left at the bottom of the pot.) Now cover the rice first with aluminium foil, crimping the edges to seal the pot, and then with its own lid. Place pot in the centre of the oven for 20 to 25 minutes or until rice is cooked through.

This dish will stay hot if left covered in a warm spot for at least half an hour. Just before you eat, spoon the rice out on to a warm platter with a fork or the side edge of a slotted spoon. Break up any lumps and garnish rice with the nuts, sultanas and roasted sesame seeds.

FRIED RICE WITH EGG AND VEGETABLES
CHINA   (serves 6)

6 tbs vegetable oil
4 medium-sized mushrooms, cut
    into ¹⁄₁₆-in/¼-cm slices
4 oz/115 g very finely sliced
    Chinese cabbage or bok choy
1⅛ tsp salt
Cooked, unsalted, long-grain rice,
    crumbled so it is free of lumps,
    measured to the 2½-pt/1½-l
    level in a glass measuring jug*

1 large egg
8 oz/225 g mung-bean sprouts,
    washed and drained (see page
    116)
2 oz/60 g very finely sliced spring
    onions (including green)
2 tbs Chinese chives cut into 1-in/
    2½-cm lengths

* Use cooked rice that has been steamed, boiled, or baked and cooled 4 to 5 hours or, better, refrigerated overnight.

Heat 2 tbs oil in a wok over a medium-high flame. When hot, put in the mushrooms. Stir and fry them for about 30 seconds. Remove mushrooms with a slotted spoon and place on a plate.

Put the Chinese cabbage into the same oil. Stir and fry it for 1 minute. Remove and put on plate with the mushrooms. Sprinkle mushrooms and cabbage with ⅛ tsp salt.

Put 4 tbs of oil into the wok and heat it on the same medium flame. When hot, put in the rice and stir it once. Make a hole in the centre of the rice and break an egg into the hole. Stir the egg, first in its hole and then, when it sets a bit, mix it up with the rice. Stir and fry the rice for another minute. Now add the bean sprouts. Stir and fry for another 5 minutes. Add the spring onions, chives, the mushrooms, and cabbage. Stir once and sprinkle in 1 tsp salt. Stir and fry for another minute.

THAI FRIED RICE

THAILAND *(serves 6)*

It is not so much the ingredients in this dish that make it different from Chinese fried rice as the sauce it is eaten with. The main ingredient in this sauce is fermented bean curd, strong cheesy cubes that are available bottled in most Chinese grocery stores, which sell many types of fermented bean curd. The type used here consists of cubes that are doused in a red, winy liquid and are bottled as Red Bean Curd or Nam Yee. At Thai grocery stores, ask for red *tao hoo yee*.

FOR THE RICE
5 tbs vegetable oil
4–5 cloves garlic, peeled and finely chopped
6 oz/180 g peeled and finely slivered shallots
4 five-pence-piece sized slices of fresh ginger, cut into fine slivers
1 fresh hot green chilli, seeded and cut into fine slivers
Cooked, unsalted, cold Plain Boiled Rice (see page 137), measured to the 2½-pt/1½-l level in a glass measuring jug
3 oz/85 g mung-bean sprouts, washed and drained
1 large egg
1½ tsp salt, or to taste
2 tbs finely chopped fresh green coriander

FOR THE SAUCE
Enough mashed Red Bean Curd to make 6 tbs
1 tbs peeled, very finely grated fresh ginger
2 tbs very finely chopped fresh hot green chillies
2 tbs very finely chopped peeled shallots
4 fl oz/1 dl fresh lime or lemon juice

OPTIONAL GARNISHES
6 sprigs fresh mint
12 cucumber sticks, 3 in/8 cm long, ⅓ in/1 cm thick and ⅓ in/1 cm wide

For information about ingredients and basic techniques that may be unfamiliar, see General Information, pages 481-506.

Put the oil in a wok or a heavy frying pan and heat over a medium flame. When hot, put in the garlic. Stir and cook for 1 minute. Add the shallots. Stir and fry for another 2 minutes. Add the ginger and the chilli. Stir and fry another minute. Put in the cooked rice and mung-bean sprouts. Stir and fry for 2 minutes. Make a hole in the centre of the rice and break the egg into it. Stir the egg, first in its hole and then, when it sets a bit, mix it up with the rice. Add the salt. Stir and fry the rice for 10 minutes or until it has heated through properly. Stir in the chopped fresh coriander.

Mix all the ingredients for the sauce and put them in a bowl.

To serve, make a mound of the rice on a large platter. Garnish with the mint and cucumber. Pass the sauce separately.

SWEET RICE WITH ORANGE RIND
IRAN   (serves 8)

Here is a simplified, vegetarian version of the Persian Shirin Polo or Sweet Pilaf. It would be perfect for festive days — Christmas, New Year, or a wedding. It is sweet but not cloyingly so and goes very well with savoury foods.

Long-grain rice, measured to the
  15-fl oz/4¼-dl level in a glass
  measuring jug
2 medium-sized carrots
4 tbs unsalted butter
The peel from 1 orange
7 oz/200 g sugar

2 oz/60 g slivered, blanched
  almonds
½ tsp leaf saffron or ¼ tsp yellow
  liquid food colouring
1–2 tbs sultanas
¾ tsp salt

Wash the rice in several changes of water and drain. Put in a bowl, add 1 qt/11½ dl water and leave to soak for 1 hour. Drain and set aside in a sieve set over a bowl.

Meanwhile, peel the carrots and cut them into ⅛-in/½-cm-thick diagonal slices. Cut the slices lengthwise into ⅛-in/½-cm-thick julienne strips.

Melt the butter in a wide, flame- and ovenproof, 3-qt/3½-l pot with a tight-fitting lid over a medium flame. Put in the carrots. Stir and fry for about 5 minutes or until carrots are lightly browned. Turn off the heat. Remove the carrots with a slotted spoon and set aside. Leave the remaining butter in the pot and set that aside as well.

Cut the orange peel into 2-in/5-cm-long by ⅛-in/½-cm-wide julienne strips. Put them in a pot with 1½ pt/8½ dl water and bring to a rolling boil. Immediately invert the pot into a colander set in the sink. Rinse the peel under cold water. Now put the peel and 1½ pt/8½ dl fresh water back into the same pot and repeat the entire blanching process, rinsing the peel for a second time at the end of it.

In a heavy saucepan, combine the orange peel, sugar, almonds, saffron or food colouring, and ¼ pt/1½ dl water. Bring to the boil. Turn heat down and simmer gently for about 30 minutes, stirring frequently. Add the carrots and sultanas. Simmer another 5 minutes or so. The peel mixture should be thick and syrupy, rather like melted jam; be careful not to let it burn. Leave this mixture in a warm place.

Preheat oven to 325° F/170° C/Mark 3.

Put the pot with the butter back on the cooker and heat it over a medium flame. Put in the drained rice. Stir and fry it for 4 to 5 minutes, turning the heat down slightly if it begins to catch. Add 1 pt/5¾ dl water and the salt. Stir gently and cook until almost all the water has evaporated. Quickly spread the peel mixture over the rice, cover tightly and place in the oven for 25 minutes.

Stir the rice gently to mix it before spooning it out on to a warm serving platter.

ZARDA PULLAO
(Sweet Saffron Rice)
INDIA/IRAN   (serves 4)

Not very far from the house where I grew up in Delhi is a large seventeenth-century mosque, Jama Masjid, that was built by the same bejewelled potentate, Shah Jahan, who built the Taj Mahal to entomb his beloved wife. The mosque is built on a natural hill, a fact somehow hidden by the rows of steps that lead down from it on three sides. Near these steps and in the shadows of a graciously proportioned dome and minarets are rows of somewhat shabby stalls that pass as restaurants. They may be shabby and of dubious cleanliness but, as all Delhiwalas know, they serve some of the best Muslim food in town. Among the dishes that are openly displayed here are platters of yellow, glistening sweet saffron rice. The price of saffron being what it is, yellow food colouring is now often substituted. But the sweet festive rice still tastes wonderful, eaten either plain or as a foil for hot, spicy foods.

I do use some saffron in my rice to give it the rich aroma. But I, too, have started using some yellow colouring to provide the right, traditional colour. You may leave it out, if you so wish.

For information about ingredients and basic techniques that may be unfamiliar, see General Information, pages 481-506.

½ tsp leaf saffron, roasted (see
  page 501)
1 tbs warm milk
Long-grain rice, measured to the
  8-fl oz/2¼-dl level in a glass
  measuring jug
4 tbs ghee or unsalted butter
2 tbs unsalted, shelled pistachios

4 whole cardamom pods
A 1-in/2½-cm stick of cinnamon
¼ tsp liquid yellow food colouring
⅓ tsp salt
5–7 tbs sugar, depending on
  sweetness desired
1 tbs sultanas (optional)

Crumble the saffron into the warm milk and set aside for 2 hours.

Wash the rice in several changes of water and drain. Put the rice in a bowl, add 1½ pt/8½ dl water, and leave to soak for 30 minutes. Drain thoroughly.

Preheat oven to 325° F/170° C/Mark 3.

Heat the *ghee* in a wide, heavy, flame- and ovenproof pot with a tight-fitting lid over a medium flame. When hot, put in the pistachios. Stir and fry for about 5 seconds or until the pistachios have picked up a faintly brownish tint. Remove the pistachios with a slotted spoon and set aside. Put the cardamom and cinnamon into the same *ghee*. Stir and fry for half a minute. Now put in the drained rice. Stir and fry gently for about 3 minutes, turning the heat down a bit if the rice begins to catch. Add 11 fl oz/3 dl water, the yellow food colouring, and salt. Turn the heat back to medium. Gently stir and cook until all the water is absorbed. Put in the saffron milk, sugar, and sultanas. Stir to mix, cover very tightly and place in the oven for 25 minutes.

To serve, turn the rice into a warmed bowl, removing the cardamom and cinnamon, then sprinkle the pistachios over the rice.

BULGAR WHEAT
(also called Cracked Wheat, Bulghur or Burghul)

This is wheat that has been cooked, dried, and cracked. It is used in the Caucasus region of Asian Russia and in parts of the Middle East to make soups, salads, stuffings, and pilafs. To make pilaf, it is cooked very much like rice, though it does require much less water than rice does. To make soup, bulgar can be thrown into the broth, again, very much like rice. Allowance must be made for it to expand and absorb liquid. For salads, it does not need to be cooked at all. A soaking — ½ to 1½ hours — is all that is required. After that the grains of cracked wheat are squeezed to discard excess liquid and then mixed with a traditional Middle Eastern dressing that includes olive oil and lemon juice.

Bulgar wheat may be bought in different-sized grains. The finer grains which require no cooking are used for salads. The medium-sized and coarse grains are used for pilafs and stuffings. The taste and texture of the grains do not vary with the size. Cracked wheat is always nutty in taste and firmer than rice in its texture.

BULGAR WHEAT WITH SPRING ONIONS AND MUSHROOMS

MIDDLE EAST   *(serves 6)*

4 tbs vegetable oil
2 spring onions, trimmed and
  sliced in fine half rings
  (including green)
6 medium-sized mushrooms,
  wiped with a damp cloth and
  sliced

Medium- or coarse-grained bulgar
  wheat, measured to the 15-fl oz/
  4¼-dl level in a glass
  measuring jug
  (about 11 oz/310 g)
1¼ tsp salt

Heat the oil in a heavy 1½–2-qt/1¾–2¼-l pot over a medium flame. Put in the spring onions and sauté them for 30 seconds. Now add the mushrooms and sauté for another minute. Add the bulgar wheat and the salt. Stir and sauté for another minute or until the grains of wheat are coated with oil. Now add 1 pt/5¾ dl water and bring to the boil. Cover, turn heat to very low and simmer gently for 25 minutes. Turn off heat. Put a tea towel between the lid and the pot, covering quickly so as not to dissipate the heat. Leave in a warm place for another 20 minutes. The wheat will puff up and not turn soggy.

PILAF OF BULGAR WHEAT AND RED LENTILS

MIDDLE EAST   *(serves 4–6)*

Red split lentils, *masoor dal* (that is what they are called in Indian stores), and Egyptian lentils are one and the same thing – a salmon-coloured, hulled and split legume that turns a yellowish

---

For information about ingredients and basic techniques that may be unfamiliar, see General Information, pages 481-506.

colour when cooked. We often have this pilaf for brunch with some goat's cheese, sliced ripe tomatoes dressed with olive oil and lemon juice, and some olives.

3 oz/85 g masoor dal (red split lentils)
4 tbs olive oil or any vegetable oil
1 medium-sized onion, peeled and finely chopped
2 cloves garlic, peeled and finely chopped

Medium- or coarse-grained bulgar wheat, measured to the 8-fl oz/ 2¼-dl level in a glass measuring jug (about 5½ oz/155 g)
2 tbs finely chopped fresh parsley
1 tsp salt
Freshly ground black pepper

Pick over the lentils and wash in several changes of water. Put in a bowl, add 16 fl oz/½ l water, and leave to soak for 6 hours. Drain.

Heat the oil in a heavy 2–3-qt/2¼–3½-l pot with a tight-fitting lid over a medium flame. Put in the onion and garlic. Stir and fry for about 2 minutes or until onion is soft. Add the bulgar wheat and lentils. Stir and cook another 3 minutes or until wheat is lightly browned. Add the parsley, salt, and 12 fl oz/3½ dl water. Bring to a simmer. Cover, turn heat to very low and cook for 35 minutes. Turn off the heat. Let the pot sit, covered and undisturbed, for 20 minutes. Add the black pepper and mix.

BULGAR WHEAT WITH CHICK PEAS AND TOMATOES
SYRIA   (serves 4–6)

This is a very tasty way to cook cracked wheat and makes a dish that is almost a complete meal in itself.

4 tbs vegetable oil
1 medium-sized onion, peeled and finely chopped
2 medium-sized tomatoes, peeled and finely chopped
6 oz/180 g cooked, drained chick peas, tinned or homemade (see page 103)

½ tsp plus ¾ tsp salt
2 tbs finely chopped fresh parsley
Medium- or coarse-grained bulgar wheat, measured to the 8-fl oz/ 2¼-dl level in a glass measuring jug (about 5½ oz/115 g)
Freshly ground black pepper

Heat the oil in a heavy 2–3-qt/2¼–3½-l pot with a tight-fitting lid over a medium flame. Put in the onion. Stir and sauté for 2 minutes or until onion is soft. Add the tomatoes. Stir and cook for 3 to 4 minutes or until tomatoes are paste-like. Add the chick peas, ½ tsp salt, and parsley. Cook for about 10 minutes on lowish heat, stirring gently as you do so. Now put in the bulgar wheat, 8 fl oz/¼ l water, and the ¾ tsp salt. Stir and bring to a simmer. Cover, turn heat to very low and cook for 35 minutes. Turn off the flame. Remove the lid and quickly cover the pot with a tea towel. Put the lid back on over the tea towel. Let the pot sit in a warm place for 20 minutes. Put in the black pepper and stir the wheat gently.

Amal's
TABOULEH
(Bulgar Wheat and Parsley Salad)
LEBANON   (serves 6)

When I first arrived in America, I took a job as a guide at the United Nations in order to support myself. This 'support' turned out to be more than just financial. Every evening, we guides found ourselves gathering at each other's homes to have heated, informative discussions on international affairs, and to eat superb food. It was Amal, a Palestinian refugee from Beirut, who introduced me to *tabouleh*. I saw a mound of it on her dining table and could not even begin to guess what it was. It looked speckled — brown, green, and red — was meant to be eaten with scoops of lettuce, and was a sort of salad but not quite. I fell in love with its grainy texture and tart taste then and have continued to make it ever since.

Fine-grained bulgar wheat,
    measured to the 6-fl oz/1¾-dl
    level in a glass measuring jug
    (about 4 oz/115 g)
2 medium-sized tomatoes, peeled
4 tbs very finely chopped onions
2 oz/55 g very finely chopped
    parsley

3 tbs lemon juice
1 tsp salt
2 tbs olive oil
Crisp inner leaves from a head of
    Cos lettuce

Soak the bulgar wheat in 1½ pt/8½ dl of water for 45 minutes.

Cut the tomatoes in half crosswise. Cup one half at a time in your hand, cut side down, and gently squeeze out and discard the seeds. Core the tomato halves and cut them into ¼-in/¾-cm dice. Put them in a bowl and set aside for 45 minutes.

Line a colander with a clean tea towel. When the bulgar wheat has finished soaking, empty it, with its soaking liquid, into the towel-lined colander. Draw the tea towel together so it closes over the bulgar. Now squeeze out as much liquid as you can. Empty the bulgar into a bowl.

For information about ingredients and basic techniques that may be unfamiliar, see General Information, pages 481-506.

Water will have collected in the bowl of tomatoes. Drain the diced tomatoes, squeezing them very gently.

Now add the tomatoes, onion, parsley, lemon juice, salt, and oil to the bulgar and mix well. Taste and adjust seasonings if you need to.

To serve, heap *tabouleh* neatly in the centre of a large platter, patting it down into a clean mound. Cut or break the lettuce leaves into 2½–3-in/6½–8-cm lengths and arrange them around the *tabouleh* to be used as scoops.

HOW TO COOK WHOLE, HULLED MILLET
(serves 6)

Millet has been cooked in Asia since antiquity. When properly prepared, it has a nutty flavour and a firm, grainy but fluffy texture. If it tastes like Russian kasha, it is with good reason. One of the grains that kasha is made from is millet. It is a good replacement for rice at almost any kind of meal.

Whole, hulled millet, measured to the 12-fl oz/3½-dl level in a glass measuring jug (about 9 oz/255 g)	*¾ tsp salt* *2 tbs butter (optional)*

Heat a 7-in/18-cm cast-iron frying pan over a medium flame. Put in the millet and stir to toast it. The millet is done when it emits a roasted aroma and when some of the seeds begin to turn a light-brown colour. A few of the seeds might actually burst open like popcorn.

Put the millet into a heavy, 1½–2-qt/1¾–2¼-l pot. Add 22 fl oz/6 dl water and the salt. Bring to the boil. Cover tightly, turn heat to very, very low and cook for 30 minutes. Have some boiling water ready. Add 2 fl oz/½ dl hot water to the millet, stir quickly with a fork, cover, and keep cooking on very, very low heat for another 10 minutes. Turn off the flame and let the pot sit, covered and undisturbed, for 15 minutes. Add the butter, mix gently and serve.

WHOLE, HULLED MILLET COOKED WITH CARROTS AND ONION

(serves 6)

I often make a large Greek salad with lettuce, radishes, cucumbers, tomatoes, pickled hot peppers, and feta cheese and then, instead of bread, serve this millet with it. Again, serve this as you might serve a rice dish.

Whole, hulled millet, measured to the 12-fl oz/3½-dl level in a glass measuring jug (about 9 oz/ 255 g)
3 tbs unsalted butter or vegetable oil
1 carrot, peeled and julienned in 1½-in/4-cm strips

1 medium-sized onion, peeled, cut in half lengthwise, and sliced into fine half rings
A 2-in/5-cm stick of cinnamon
5 whole cloves
2 tbs raisins
¾ tsp salt

Roast millet as suggested in preceding recipe and set aside.

In a heavy 1¾–2-qt/2–2¼-l pot, melt the butter over a medium flame. Add the carrot, onion, cinnamon, and cloves. Stir and sauté for about 5 minutes or until the onion is translucent. Add the raisins. Stir and sauté another 5 minutes or until onion just begins to turn brown at the edges. Add the roasted millet, salt, and 22 fl oz/6 dl water. Bring to the boil. Cover tightly, turn heat to very, very low and cook for 30 minutes.

Have some boiling water ready. Pour in 2 fl oz/½ dl boiling water over the millet, stir quickly with a fork, cover again and continue to cook on the same low heat for another 10 minutes. Turn the heat off and let the pot sit, covered and undisturbed, for another 15 minutes.

Remove the cinnamon stick and the cloves before serving.

WHOLE, HULLED MILLET COOKED WITH YELLOW SPLIT PEAS

NORTH INDIAN STYLE   *(serves 4)*

3 oz/85 g yellow split peas
Whole, hulled millet, measured to the 8-fl oz/2¼-dl level in a glass measuring jug (about 6 oz/ 170 g)
3 tbs vegetable oil

½ tsp whole cumin seeds
1 small onion, peeled, cut in half lengthwise, and sliced into very fine half rings
1 clove garlic, peeled and finely chopped

For information about ingredients and basic techniques that may be unfamiliar, see General Information, pages 481-506.

½ tsp ground turmeric

½ tsp ground cumin seeds

1 tsp ground coriander seeds

⅛ tsp cayenne pepper

¾ tsp salt

Soak the split peas in ¾ pt/½ l water for 5 hours. Drain.

Roast millet as suggested on page 183 and set aside.

Heat the oil in a heavy 1¾-2-qt/2-2¼-l pot over a medium-high flame. When hot, put in the whole cumin seeds. Five seconds later, put in the onion and garlic. Stir and fry for a few minutes until the edges of the onion begin to turn brown. Put in the millet, split peas, turmeric, ground cumin, coriander, cayenne, and salt. Turn the heat to medium. Stir and sauté for about 2 minutes. Add ¾ pt/½ l water and bring to the boil. Cover, turn heat to very, very low and cook for 30 minutes.

Have some boiling water ready. Pour in about 2 tbs of this water over the millet, stir quickly with a fork, cover, and cook for another 10 minutes. Turn the heat off and let the pot sit, covered and undisturbed, for 15 minutes.

Zakiya's
UPPAMA
(Savoury South Indian Cereal)
INDIA   (serves 4)

Uppama is made out of semolina and resembles a very fine-grained bulgar wheat pilaf that has been highly spiced and loaded with vegetables. It is generally served at breakfast with a coconut chutney, but it could easily be served at lunch or dinner as well. Although it is not traditional, you could use uppama to stuff vegetables like tomatoes, aubergines, green peppers, and even okra.

6 tbs vegetable oil

A generous pinch of ground
  asafetida (optional)

½ tsp whole black mustard seeds

1 whole dried hot red pepper

1 tsp chana dal

2 tsp urad dal

½ medium-sized onion, peeled and
  finely chopped

3 oz/85 g finely shredded cabbage

1 small potato (about 2 oz/60 g),
  peeled and cut into ¼-in/¾-cm
  dice

2 tbs shelled fresh or defrosted
  frozen peas

1 fresh hot green chilli, finely
  chopped

½ tsp finely grated fresh ginger

¾ tsp salt

Semolina, measured to the 8-fl oz/
  2¼-dl level in a glass measuring
  jug (about 6 oz/170 g)

1 tbs finely chopped fresh green
  coriander

Put some water to boil. You will need approximately ½ pt/3 dl in about 10 minutes from the time you start the cooking.

Heat the oil in an 8–10-in/20–25-cm frying pan over a medium flame. When hot, put in, in quick succession, first the asafetida, then the mustard seeds, then the red pepper, *chana dal*, and *urad dal*. When the *dals* turn a reddish colour, put in the onion, cabbage, potato, peas, green chilli, and ginger. Stir and fry on medium-high heat for about 2 minutes. Cover, turn heat to low, and let the vegetables cook through. This should take about 5 to 6 minutes. Check to see if the potatoes are done. Add the salt and mix. Turn heat to medium and put in the semolina. Stir and fry for about 5 minutes but do not let it brown. Turn heat to low.

Slowly add boiling water, about 2 tbs at a time, to the semolina, stirring until it is absorbed before adding any more. Add all the ½ pt/3 dl boiling water this way, taking at least 5 minutes to do so. (You may make your *uppama* a little wetter by adding a few more tablespoons of water. I like mine fairly dry.)

Keep stirring and cooking on low heat for another 10 minutes. Each grain should have puffed up by now and should have shed its dry, whitish look. Serve, garnished with the fresh coriander.

For information about ingredients and basic techniques that may be unfamiliar, see General Information, pages 481-506.

4 Soy Milk, Bean Curd, and Wheat Gluten

BEAN CURD AND SOY MILK

What an amazing product bean curd really is. It is high in protein — 9–10 oz/250–285 g provide most average people with about a third of their daily protein requirements — very low in saturated fats, easy to digest, low in calories, and cheap! It lends itself to being cooked with almost all other foods. If you are in a rush, you could make a quick sauce with finely chopped fresh green coriander and toss it over cubes of bean curd; you could crumble and add bean curd to lightly sautéed cabbage; or you could cook it along with dainty broccoli spears. It accepts hot-and-sour sauces, sweet-and-sour sauces, and peanut-filled sauces with equal equanimity. It even allows itself to be puréed and become a salad dressing.

These dishes are, of course, made with the plain white bean curd that has become a fairly common sight in health-food stores and even in some grocery stores. But there are, as well, several other products, all closely related to the white bean curd, that are eaten throughout East Asia.

First of all, there is soy milk. Once soy beans have been soaked, puréed and strained, they produce a thick, cream-coloured liquid. This is soy milk, which must be boiled before it is drunk. It may be sweetened, or else seasoned with drops of soy sauce, sesame oil, and spring onions. It is a very common sight in East Asian markets to see whole families drinking this seasoned soy milk from soup bowls in the early hours of the morning. I have sat on wooden benches in Singapore, Bangkok, Hong Kong, and Seoul and done it myself. Soy milk is served steaming hot and is an excellent breakfast food.

When soy milk cooks at a very low temperature, a skin forms on top of it. If this is done systematically in shallow, rectangular trays, then neat, rectangular sheets form, one after another, and are lifted out and then hung up to dry. Chinese grocery stores call this bean-curd skin or dried bean curd. In Japanese stores, it is called *yuba*. The difference in taste between bean curd and bean-curd skin would be about the same as between milk and cream. Bean-curd skin is richer and creamier. Because it is available here only in its dried form, it needs to be reconstituted by being soaked in water.

Soy milk may be converted into bean curd with the help of a coagulant. In Japan's best bean-curd shops, natural *nigari* is put into hot soy milk, which makes it curdle. The soft, satiny curds are quickly scooped up and emptied into rectangular wooden boxes that are riddled with holes. A weight is placed on top to help firm up and shape the curds. What soon emerges is a quivering block of bean curd which is then quickly cut into smaller blocks. These are lowered into cold water to await sale. (The whey from the curds is not wasted. It is used, rather like soapy water, to clean utensils and mop up the floor.)

Some of the bean curd is cut into thick slices and left to drain on cheesecloth-covered slats. After a few hours, it is fried to make what the Japanese call *age* — fried bean curd, and *aburage* — fried bean-curd pillow cases meant for stuffing. Fried bean curd holds its shape very well when cooked with other foods, It also has a firmer, meat-like texture. *Aburage* is used to make one of Japan's most amusing (and delicious) foods — *inari-zushi* — little pouches filled with pickled rice and tied with ribbons of dehydrated gourd.

It is not hard to make good, sweet-tasting bean curd at home. But it is hard to make excellent bean curd at home unless one invests in proper equipment and then buys the freshest, best quality soy beans, preferably in bulk. Many health-food stores stock all the equipment in a kit form. My own suggestion would be that you go out and buy bean curd, if you have access to it. This way you will be guaranteed excellent quality at a low price.

However, if you cannot get bean curd or suspect its freshness, use my recipe which requires no special containers other than a colander and a round steaming trivet that can fit snugly somewhere down the colander. Of course, the shape of my bean curd is somewhat untraditional — round instead of rectangular — but it has a fresh, sweet taste and a medium-firm texture. You may use this bean curd for all my recipes, even those calling for soft bean curd.

If you are buying bean curd, you will notice that it is sold as 'soft', 'medium' (or 'regular'), and 'hard'. Get whatever the recipe calls for.

There are some types of bean curd mentioned in this book that are fairly hard to make at home. These should be purchased from Oriental stores. Among them are the cheese-like, fermented bean-curd cubes, the hard, brownish, pressed bean curd and the fried bean-curd pillow cases or *aburage*. For more on all three of them and on where they can be purchased, consult General Information at the back of the book.

WHEAT GLUTEN

Meat-like in its chewy texture and very rich in protein, wheat gluten is used primarily in China and Japan to add nutritional value to all manner of dishes. In this country, too, it is not entirely unknown. But it is more disguised and appears in tinned versions of mock vegetarian fish and meat dishes.

Once you start making wheat gluten at home, I am sure you will get as excited about it as I am. It lends itself to the cooking of every nationality. You will find some traditional gluten recipes here, such as Fried Wheat Gluten with Broccoli, Carrot, and Mushrooms from China, and Japan's delectable Stew of Baked Wheat Gluten, Potato, Turnip, Carrot, and Cabbage Rolls. But I have gone a step further and concocted some really delicious Indian-style dishes, such as Shredded Wheat Gluten and Cabbage with Fennel Seeds, just to show you how inventive we can all be with this new food.

Most wheat flour has some gluten in it. To extract it and get more concentrated protein, the flour has to be made into a dough and then washed repeatedly to get rid of all the starch. Naturally, it helps to start with a flour that has a high content of gluten to begin with, so it is best to buy plain strong flour.

Once the gluten has been extracted − it sits in a big, spongy lump − it needs to be pre-cooked before being used in a dish. It is usually broken up into pieces and then fried, boiled, or steamed. I have discovered that it can also be baked with excellent results. Gluten, already spongy before pre-cooking, expands and turns even spongier and lighter as it cooks. This helps it to absorb the flavours of other foods it is eventually combined with, a very important factor for a protein that has little taste of its own. Because frying and baking allow gluten to expand to its maximum and also give it a nice crust, I really prefer these methods of pre-cooking to boiling and steaming.

Pre-cooked wheat-gluten balls may be cut into any shape you like − they may be minced, cut into strips, and cut into halves − and then added to whatever you happen to be making, provided the dish has at least some moisture for the gluten to absorb. Wheat gluten cooks well in soups, braised dishes, and stews. If, for example, you like to braise celery in stock and butter, try braising it with the addition of quartered gluten balls. You will be 'inventing' a wonderful dish. If you wish to use gluten in a stir-fried dish, it is a good idea to cook it for 15 minutes in stock or lightly seasoned water first.

It is also a good idea to 'wash' the fried gluten balls in a little boiling water to rid them of extra oil.

Once you make the balls, you can keep whatever you do not use in the refrigerator, where they will last for several days, and freeze the rest. Gluten balls freeze beautifully. They may be defrosted very fast by simply throwing them into stock or lightly seasoned boiling water and boiling for a few minutes.

For information about ingredients and basic techniques that may be unfamiliar, see General Information, pages 481-506.

SOY MILK

(makes about 1½ pt/8½ dl)

Soy milk 'soups', generally savoury but sometimes sweet, are drunk throughout many parts of East and South-east Asia for breakfast. Early in the morning, vendors can be seen busily ladling out steaming portions of this nutritious meal-in-a-bowl. The version I liked best consisted of thick milk, seasoned with some soy sauce and spring onions and containing large rounds of a doughnut-like bread. Sometimes this soy milk had been set, just barely, so it was like a delicate custard. At other times it had been sweetened with dark sugar. All versions were very good.

6 oz/170 g dried soy beans

Pick over the beans and wash them in several changes of water. Drain. Soak the beans in 1½ pt/8½ dl of water for 10 hours.

Drain the beans and wash them again in several changes of water. Drain. Measure the beans in volume. You probably have enough to fill a 1-pt/5¾-dl jug. Put the beans in a blender. Add an equal amount — that is 1 pt/5¾ dl — of warm water and blend for several minutes until you have a very smooth purée.

Line a colander with an open 16×16-in/40×40-cm muslin bag or an open pillow case (old and clean). Set colander in a large bowl.

Bring 8 fl oz/¼ l of water to the boil in a heavy, 4-qt/4½-l pot. As soon as it is boiling, pour in the purée from the blender. Bring to the boil again and immediately turn off the heat. Pour the liquid into the open bag in the colander. Close the bag. Using the bottom of a jar or a potato masher, press out as much milk as you can. As the liquid cools a bit, it will become easier to handle. Squeeze out whatever milk is left in the grounds. Open up the bag and let the grounds cool off some more for a couple of minutes. Pour 6 fl oz/1¾ dl warm water over them and squeeze out some more milk. You do not need the grounds any more.

Wash out the pot and pour the soy milk into it. Bring to the boil. As soon as the milk begins to rise, turn the heat to low and simmer gently for 10 minutes or until the raw bean taste has disappeared.

You may serve this milk plain, lightly sweetened with sugar, brown or white, or you could pour it into soup bowls and offer sliced spring onions, vinegar and Chinese soy sauce as seasonings. Only a few drops of the vinegar and soy sauce should be used.

MAKING YOUR OWN BEAN CURD

(makes about 1 lb 6 oz/630 g of 'medium-hard' bean curd)

1¾ lb/800 g dried soy beans   *About 2½ tsp natural nigari flakes*

Pick over the soy beans and then wash them in several changes of water. Drain. Soak the soy beans in 2½ pt/1½ l of water for 10 hours. Drain and wash them in several changes of water again. Drain.

You should end up with enough soy beans to fill a 1¾ pt/1 l jar and you need to purée them with 1¾ pt/1 l of warm water. This is best done in two batches in an electric blender or food processor. 1. Blend half the beans at a time with half the warm water, for several minutes or until you have a smooth purée. You should end up with about 3½ pt/2 l of purée. 2. Line a colander with an open 16×16-in/40×40-cm muslin bag or an open pillow case (use an old, clean one). Place the colander in a large bowl. Bring 3½ pt/2 l of water to the boil in a large pot. Immediately pour in all the soy-bean purée and stir. Now pour this liquid into the open muslin

1   2   3

bag. Close the muslin bag over the liquid and, 3. using the bottom of a jar, press out as much soy milk as you can. As the liquid cools off a bit, it will become easier to handle. Squeeze out whatever milk is left in the grounds.

Clean out your large pot and pour the strained soy milk into it. (The grounds are not needed any more.) Bring this milk to the boil but watch it closely. As soon as it begins to rise, turn down the heat and simmer 10 minutes.

For information about ingredients and basic techniques that may be unfamiliar, see General Information, pages 481-506.

While the milk simmers, take 1½ tsp of the *nigari* and dissolve it in 5 tbs of warm water.

Set the colander in your sink. Inside it, place a trivet used for steaming. It should have small holes, be round, and fit somewhere in your colander. My trivet is about 6½ in/16 cm in diameter and fits about two-thirds of the way down my colander. Spread a 16×16-in/40×40-cm piece of doubled cheesecloth over the trivet and let it hang over the edges of the colander.

When the soy milk has simmered for 10 minutes, take it off the flame. Stir the *nigari* solution once and, 4. using a circular arm motion, pour it into the soy milk. Stir very gently and cover the pot for 10 minutes. Curds should have formed and separated from a thin, greenish, watery whey. Sometimes this does not happen or does not happen completely. A few curds form and the whey remains milky. If that happens, repeat the process. Bring the milk to the boil again, remove from the flame and pour in a solution of 1 tsp *nigari* and 2 tbs water. Stir gently and cover. Wait another 10 minutes. The curds should have formed.

5. Pour the curds and whey into the colander in the sink.

6. Cover the curds with the overhanging cheesecloth and put a 1–1½-lb/450–675-g weight that is about the same circumference as the top of the bean curd on top of it. I happen to have a pot with just the right weight and circumference that fits snugly over the top of the bean curd. You could cut out a piece of wood, lay it over the

4   5

bean curd, and then put the required weight on the centre of it. Let the weight sit for 15 minutes.

Fill a large bowl or pot with 5 in/13 cm of water. 7. Lift up the cake of bean curd gently from the colander, cheesecloth and all, and slide it into the water. Remove the cheesecloth, gently and carefully, while the bean-curd cake is submerged.

You may now eat the bean curd immediately, using it up in one of the many recipes in this book, or you could refrigerate it in its water bath for about four days. Change the water every day.

To make the bean curd 'hard', instead of pressing it for 15 minutes, press it for 2 hours and increase the weight to 3 lb/1350 g.

UDOFU
(Simmering Bean Curd with Seasonings)
JAPAN   (serves 6)

Sometimes spelled *yudofu* (and pronounced 'you-doe-foo'), this simple, elegant, and light dish tastes just as good as the bean curd used to make it. Use the freshest bean curd possible, whether

---

For information about ingredients and basic techniques that may be unfamiliar, see General Information, pages 481-506.

homemade or shop-bought. Ideally, the bean curd should be soft, though you could, at a pinch, use medium bean curd as well. In Japan, where the best foods are seasonal, this dish is served during the cold winter months in a spectacular wood and bamboo container that holds the bean curd in a hot broth, some dipping sauce, and some charcoal to keep the dish piping hot, all in separate compartments. Because bean-curd cubes retain heat for a long time, *udofu* is even served out of doors on the most chilling of days.

4 *spring onions*
8 *oz/225 g white radish*
1 *sheet of* nori, *approximately*
   7×8 in/18×20 cm
8 *fl oz/¼ l Japanese soy sauce*
7 *tbs* mirin
A piece of kombu, *about 5 in/*
   13 cm square, wiped lightly
   with a damp cloth and cut into
   two sections

6 *dried* shiitake *mushrooms,*
   soaked in 8 fl oz/¼ l hot water
   for 20 minutes
6 *fresh, soft or medium bean-curd*
   cakes, about 4 oz/115 g each, cut
   into 1-in/2½-cm cubes
Sprinklings of 7-spice seasoning

Cut the spring onions into very, very fine rounds halfway up their green sections. Soak them in iced water for half an hour. Drain and pat dry.

Peel the radish and grate it over the smallest holes of your grater. The radish should be closer to pulp than shreds.

Toast the *nori* by holding the sheet over a medium-low flame and moving it back and forth for a few seconds. Now crumble the *nori*, not into powder but into small, roughly ⅛–¼-in/½–¾-cm squares.

Combine the soy sauce and *mirin* in a small pot and bring to the boil. Turn off the heat immediately and keep warm.

In a large pot, bring 3 qt/3½ l of water to the boil. Throw in the two pieces of *kombu*. Cut off the mushroom stems and put the mushroom caps as well as the mushroom soaking liquid (strain it if it is gritty) into the pot. Boil for 1 minute. Add the bean-curd cubes and bring to the boil again. Turn heat to low and simmer for 5 minutes.

To serve, transfer the bean curd and liquid to one or two chafing dishes placed in the centre of your dining table. If you do not have chafing dishes, use an electric frying pan turned to 'warm' or a flat-bottomed serving dish set on a hot tray. Place a pretty slotted spoon or small Japanese skimmer near the dish of bean curd. Pour the heated sauce into warmed toy teapots or into small warmed bowls. Provide spoons to go with the bowls. Give each person small dishes containing crumbled *nori*, sliced spring onions and mounds of grated radish with the 7-spice seasoning sprinkled on top.

Each person should have a bowl to eat from and chopsticks to eat with. Once the bean curd is lifted out of the broth with the skimmer, it should first be seasoned with the heated sauce and then with a combination of the other seasonings. Diners should do this in their own individual bowls. The liquid in the serving dish as well as the pieces of *kombu* are not for consumption.

BEAN CURD WITH WATERCRESS
SINGAPORE CHINESE   *(serves 2–4)*

In this dish, the watercress is finely chopped and used as a kind of dressing for the bean curd. As both red and green hot chillies are added to the dressing, the sauce is as pretty as it is fiery. If fresh hot red chillies are hard to find substitute fresh sweet red pepper. If you do not want to make this dish hot, use a few slices of green pepper instead of the hot green chilli.

*1 large bunch (about 5 oz/140 g)
   watercress
½–1 fresh hot green chilli
4 ⅛-in/½-cm thick slices fresh red
   chilli
½ tsp salt
½ lb/225 g medium bean curd
½ pt/3 dl Delicious Stock . . . (see
   page 340), any vegetable stock
   or water
½ tsp cornflour*

*2 tsp Chinese thin soy sauce
1 tsp sesame oil
¼ tsp sugar
2 tbs vegetable oil
2 cloves garlic, peeled and very
   lightly mashed
2 five-pence-piece sized slices of
   fresh ginger, peeled and very
   lightly mashed
1 tsp roasted sesame seeds*

Chop the watercress finely, stalks and all, and put in a bowl. Chop the green chilli finely, removing seeds if you so desire. Chop the slices of red pepper somewhat more coarsely than the watercress and the green chilli. Sprinkle ½ tsp salt over the vegetables. Mix well and set aside for 20 to 30 minutes.

Put the bean curd in a small pot. Pour 8 fl oz/¼ l of the stock over it. Bring to a gentle simmer over a lowish flame. Now turn the heat to very low and let the bean curd sit in this barely simmering broth for 10 minutes. Turn off the flame and let the pot sit in a warm place.

Put the cornflour in a small cup. Slowly add 2 fl oz/½ dl stock and mix. Add the soy sauce, sesame oil, and sugar. Mix again.

For information about ingredients and basic techniques that may be unfamiliar, see General Information, pages 481-506.

Heat the vegetable oil in a wok over a medium flame. When hot, add the garlic and ginger. Stir and fry the garlic, pressing down upon it with the back of a slotted spoon every now and then. When it turns dark, remove with the slotted spoon and discard. Put the watercress mixture into the wok. Stir and fry for about 1 minute or until the watercress has wilted. Turn the heat to low. Give the cornflour mixture a quick stir and pour it over the vegetables. Stir and cook for another 30 seconds or until the sauce has thickened slightly. Turn off the heat.

Carefully lift the bean curd out of the liquid and put on a serving dish. (You do not need the liquid any more.) Cut into ¾–1-in/2–2½-cm cubes. Pour the vegetable dressing over the bean curd. Sprinkle the sesame seeds over the top and serve.

Hsu Hung Ying's
BEAN CURD WITH FRESH CORIANDER
TAIWAN   (serves 2–4)

This refreshing and simple dish is served frequently by the Chinese family that a daughter of mine is staying with in Taipei. It calls for fresh hot red chillies, just as the preceding recipe does. Again, I have substituted strips of fresh sweet red pepper for the colour and used green chillies for the actual fire. The heat of this dish will depend upon the hotness of the chillies. If you prefer the bean curd to be less hot, use just one hot chilli and increase the sweet red pepper.

2 green chillies	½ lb/225 g medium bean curd, cut
½ smallish sweet red pepper	into ¾-in/2-cm cubes
1 tsp cornflour	1 tbs Chinese thin soy sauce
2 tbs vegetable oil	4 tbs finely chopped fresh green
¼ tsp salt	coriander

Cut the hot and sweet peppers into very thin, 1½-in/4-cm-long strips.

Mix the cornflour with 2 fl oz/½ dl water in a small cup.

Heat the oil in a wok over a medium flame. When hot, put in the pepper strips and the salt. Stir and fry for 30 seconds. Put in the cubes of bean curd. Stir gently to mix. Turn heat to low. Dribble the soy sauce over the bean curd. Give the cornflour mixture a quick stir and pour it over the bean curd. Scatter the coriander over the top. Turn the heat up very slightly and cook until the sauce thickens slightly. Stir very gently during this time. Serve hot.

KOREAN-STYLE BEAN CURD IN A HOT-WATER BATH
KOREA   (serves 4–6)

Heated bean curd is so very warming when the cold winds of autumn and winter start to blow. In Korea, it is served with a spicy sauce.

3 cakes soft or medium bean curd
  (about 4 oz/115 g each)

In a wide pan, bring about 4¾ pt/2½ l of water to the boil. Turn the heat down to medium. Add the bean-curd cakes in a single layer and bring to a simmer. Lower heat and simmer gently for 5 minutes. Now remove the cakes with a spatula and place them in a serving dish deep enough so the cakes can be almost submerged in water. Pour in enough of the heating water so it comes about three-quarters of the way up the sides of the cakes.

Serve immediately with Spicy Korean Sauce (see page 417). (For 6 people, you should double the sauce recipe. You could, if you like, divide the sauce up in small, individual saucers.) The purpose of the hot water is to keep the bean curd hot. It should not be drunk. Break off pieces of the bean curd with your chopsticks and dip it into your sauce before eating it.

HIYA-YAKKO
(Chilled Bean Curd)
JAPAN   (serves 4)

Japanese cuisine, perhaps more than any other in the world, emphasizes the seasons. Just as udofu (see recipe, page 194) is served in the chilly winter months, hiya-yakko is served during the sultry summer. The dish itself is simple enough — cold bean curd surrounded by tiny dishes containing soy sauce, grated ginger (or grated white radish), and sliced spring onions. For this dish to be good at all, the bean curd has to be absolutely fresh and soft. Once you have that, and you chill the bean curd appropriately, the dish is glorious.

4 cakes fresh, soft or medium bean   4 tsp peeled and finely grated fresh
  curd (about 16 oz/450 g in all)   ginger
3 spring onions   4 fl oz/1 dl Japanese soy sauce

For information about ingredients and basic techniques that may be unfamiliar, see General Information, pages 481-506.

Cut the bean curd into 1-in/2½-cm cubes. Put the bean curd gently into a large bowl, cover with iced water. You may even put some ice cubes in the bowl. Chill in the refrigerator for an hour or longer.

Cut the spring onions into very, very fine rounds, halfway up their green sections. Soak the sliced spring onions in 8 fl oz/¼ l of iced water for half an hour. Drain and pat dry.

Just before serving, put 4 or 5 ice cubes in four individual bowls. Drain the bean-curd cubes and divide them up among the bowls, laying them on top of or beside the ice cubes.

Each diner needs three small, shallow, saucer-like dishes, one containing a quarter of the sliced spring onions, another 1 tsp of the ginger made into a tiny mound, and the third, 2 tbs of soy sauce.

To serve, each diner has a bowl of bean curd in front of him and the three small dishes with the seasonings arranged on one side. Everyone can now mix a dipping sauce as he or she pleases, adding as much of the ginger and spring onions to the soy sauce as desired. Or the seasonings can be kept unmixed, and a little ginger and spring onions picked up when wanted. The bean-curd cube is picked up with chopsticks, dipped into the soy sauce − seasoned with the ginger and spring onions or unseasoned − and then eaten.

BEAN CURD WITH BROCCOLI
HONG KONG   *(serves 4)*

You will need about ½ lb/225 g of broccoli for this dish. Cut the broccoli into small, slim flowerets, peeling the stem wherever it looks too coarse. Each piece should be no more than 1½-in/4-cm long. Sometimes I soak the broccoli in cold water for half an hour before cooking it in order to make it extra crisp. If you use some of the thicker parts of the stem too, just peel them and cut into somewhat coarse julienne strips.

1½ tsp cornflour
6 fl oz/1¾ dl Delicious
  Stock . . . (see page 340), any
  vegetable stock or water
1 tbs shaohsing wine or dry
  sherry
2 tsp Chinese thin soy sauce
1 tbs sesame oil
1 spring onion
4 tbs vegetable oil

2 five-pence-piece sized slices of
  fresh ginger, peeled and cut into
  strips
2 cloves garlic, peeled and cut into
  thin strips
½ lb/225 g broccoli flowerets and
  stems (see page 199)
½ tsp salt
½ lb/225 g medium bean curd, cut
  into 1×½-in/2½×1½-cm pieces

Put the cornflour in a cup. Slowly add 2 fl oz/½ dl stock and mix. Add the wine, soy sauce, and sesame oil. Mix again.

Cut the spring onion into 1½-in/4-cm lengths and then cut each piece lengthwise into strips.

Heat the vegetable oil in a wok over medium heat. When hot, put in the ginger and garlic. Stir and fry for 10 seconds. Put in the broccoli and spring onion. Stir and fry for a minute. Add 4 fl oz/1 dl stock and the salt. Bring to a simmer. Cover and cook on medium-low heat for a minute or until broccoli is tender-crisp. Remove the broccoli with a slotted spoon and keep in a bowl. Turn heat to low and put in the bean curd. Let it heat through in the small amount of remaining liquid. Give the cornflour mixture a quick stir and pour it over the bean curd. Mix very gently. Put the broccoli back into the wok. Stir gently to mix. Serve as soon as the sauce is thick and everything is heated through.

CABBAGE COOKED WITH BEAN CURD
JAPAN   (serves 3–4)

One very cold winter day, when I was scouring Kyoto for vegetarian dishes, I walked into a tiny macrobiotics shop on the outskirts of the city. There I was offered warming tea and, as we talked, told of many simple dishes that are not a part of Japan's haute cuisine but are, none the less, very tasty and nourishing. This is one of those dishes.

3 large dried shiitake mushrooms
2 cakes medium or hard bean curd
  (about 8 oz/225 g)

1 lb/450 g cabbage — ½ small-sized
  cabbage
3 tbs vegetable oil

For information about ingredients and basic techniques that may be unfamiliar, see General Information, pages 481-506.

½ tsp salt   1 tsp mirin
2 tsp Japanese soy sauce

Soak mushrooms in ¼ pt/1½ dl hot water for ½ hour.

Put the bean curd on a tilted, kitchen-paper-lined board and leave to drain for 20 minutes.

Cut the cabbage half in two, lengthwise. Remove core. Slice cabbage into long shreds, ¼ in/¾ cm wide.

Remove mushrooms from their soaking liquid. (Save soaking liquid to make *dashi* or other soup.) Cut off and discard coarse stems. Slice the caps into ¼-in/¾-cm-wide strips.

Heat the oil in an 8-in/20-cm frying pan over a medium-high flame. When hot, put in the cabbage and mushrooms. Stir and fry for about 1 minute or until cabbage wilts. Now turn heat down to medium. Crumble the bean curd and add it to the frying pan. Add the salt, soy sauce, and *mirin* as well. Stir and fry for another 4–5 minutes.

BEAN CURD WITH A DELICIOUSLY SPICY SAUCE

CHINA   *(serves 4)*

If I was *forced* to pick my favourite bean-curd recipe − *forced*, mind you, since I do not normally make such commitments − I might pick this dish. From start to finish, it takes me about 10 minutes to prepare, as I always have vegetable stock sitting in my refrigerator or freezer.

You may make this dish with any fresh bean curd − soft, medium, or hard. Each will give its own very different texture to the dish.

THE SAUCE

2 tsp cornflour

4 fl oz/1 dl Vegetable Stock (see page 340), any vegetable stock or water

1 tsp chilli paste with soy bean

2 tbs Chinese thin soy sauce

1 tbs sesame oil

½ tsp salt

½ tsp sugar

2 tbs vegetable oil

3 cloves garlic, peeled and finely chopped

1 tsp very finely chopped fresh ginger

3 spring onions, very finely sliced into rounds, including three-quarters of the green

1 lb/450 g bean curd, cut into 1-in/ 2½-cm cubes

Prepare the sauce. Put the cornflour in a small bowl. Slowly add the vegetable stock, mixing as you do so. Now add the chilli paste, soy sauce, sesame oil, salt, and sugar. Mix again. Set the sauce aside.

Heat the vegetable oil in a wok over a medium-high flame. When hot, put in the garlic and ginger. Stir and fry for 10 seconds. Add the spring onions. Stir and fry for 5 seconds. Put in the bean curd. Stir and fry for 1 minute. Turn heat to low. Stir the sauce and pour it over the bean curd. Mix gently and bring to a simmer. Let the sauce thicken, stirring gently every now and then as it does so.

CARROTS AND BEANS WITH A BEAN-CURD DRESSING
JAPAN   *(serves 6–8)*

For this dish, you can use soft, medium, or hard bean curd.

2 bean-curd cakes (8 oz/225 g)	*1 tbs mirin*
¾ lb/340 g green beans	*1 tsp salt*
¾ lb/340 g (about 4) carrots	*1 tsp soy sauce*
4 tbs roasted and ground sesame seeds	*2 tbs dashi (see page 339) or water*
1 tbs sugar	

Put the bean-curd cakes into a small pot and cover with water (about 1¼ pt/¾ l). Bring to the boil. Lower heat and simmer very gently for 10 minutes. Drain.

Meanwhile, prepare the vegetables: trim and slice the beans into 2-in/5-cm-long diagonal strips. Trim, peel, and cut carrots into very fine, 2-in/5-cm-long julienne strips.

Put the drained bean curd, the roasted and ground sesame seeds, sugar, *mirin*, salt, soy sauce, and *dashi* into the container of a food processor or blender. Blend until you have a paste. Set aside.

Bring two pots, each containing about 3 qt/3½ l of water, to the boil. When boiling, drop the sliced beans into one pot and the julienned carrots into the other. Drain the carrots after 2 to 3 minutes. They should be cooked through but still crunchy. Drain the beans after about 4 minutes. They should be cooked through but still have a bite to them.

Put the carrots and beans in a bowl. Add the dressing and mix well. Serve hot, warm, or at room temperature.

For information about ingredients and basic techniques that may be unfamiliar, see General Information, pages 481-506.

BEAN CURD, MUSHROOMS, AND PEANUTS IN HOISIN SAUCE
CHINESE STYLE   *(serves 4–6)*

Stir the hoisin sauce before pouring it out for this recipe.

4 fl oz/1 dl hoisin sauce
1 tbs Chinese thin soy sauce
1 tbs shaohsing wine or dry sherry
1 tsp sesame oil
Salt
Freshly ground black pepper
½ lb/225 g medium bean curd
¼ lb/115 g fresh mushrooms

1 clove garlic, peeled
2 five-pence-piece sized slices of fresh ginger, peeled
4 tbs vegetable oil
6 oz/180 g bamboo shoots, cut into ¾-in/2-cm dice
3 tbs roasted or fried, unsalted peanuts
2 tbs finely sliced spring onions

Mix together the hoisin sauce, soy sauce, wine, sesame oil, ½ tsp salt, black pepper, and 4 fl oz/1 dl water in a bowl.

Cut the bean curd into ¾-in/2-cm dice.

Wipe the mushrooms and, depending upon their size, halve or quarter them so that they are about the same size as the bean curd.

Cut the clove of garlic into fine slivers.

Cut the slices of ginger into slivers.

Heat a wok over a medium flame. Put in 2 tbs of oil and half of the garlic and ginger. Stir for 5 seconds. Put in the mushrooms. Stir-fry for 30 seconds. Sprinkle about ⅛ tsp salt over the mushrooms. Stir once and then remove them and keep in a bowl. Wipe out the wok.

Add 2 more tbs of oil to the wok. Put in the remaining garlic and ginger. Stir for 5 seconds. Put in the bamboo shoots and stir-fry for 30 seconds. Put in the hoisin sauce mixture and bring to a simmer. Put in the bean curd and bring to a simmer again. Turn down the heat and simmer very gently for 5 minutes, stirring now and then. Put back the mushrooms and add the peanuts as well. Stir. Heat through and empty into serving dish. Garnish with the spring onions.

SAUTÉED BEAN CURD

KOREA   *(serves 6)*

4 4-oz/115-g cakes of medium bean   3 tbs vegetable oil
   curd

Cut the bean curd into rectangles that are roughly 1½×¾×¾ in/
4×2×2 cm. Pat dry.

Heat the oil in a 9-in/23-cm nonstick or other well-seasoned
frying pan over a medium-high flame. When hot, put in half the
bean curd. Cook for about 3 minutes on one side, or until that side
turns a golden colour. Turn over and cook the opposite side for
about 3 minutes or less or until it, too, is golden. Remove with a
slotted spatula and keep on a warmed platter. Do a second batch
just as you did the first.

Serve hot, with Korean Dipping Sauce Number 2 (see page 415).

TOFU DENGAKU
(Toasted Bean Curd with a Miso Topping)

JAPAN   *(serves 4)*

Among the very popular winter dishes in Japan is bean curd that is
toasted directly over a charcoal fire and then smeared with what
looks like a *miso* jam. The toasting is done by the same method
used for marshmallows. Small rectangles of bean curd are pierced
with skewers and then held up over the fire. The skewers have to
be very light and supportive — the Japanese use dainty, double-
pronged bamboo skewers — or else the bean curd would fall off
them. Also, the bean curd itself has to be made fairly firm by
pressing it under a weight before it can be expected to hold its
shape.

If you can find forked *dengaku* skewers, toast the bean curd on
both sides over a direct flame, either charcoal or gas. If you cannot
find the skewers, follow my method of cooking the bean curd on a
hot cast-iron griddle or in a frying pan.

12 oz/340 g medium or hard bean   *2 tbs mirin*
   curd   *1 tbs sugar*
6–7 spinach leaves   *2 fl oz/½ dl dashi (see page 339) or*
6 tbs white miso   *water*
2 tbs sake   *1 tsp roasted sesame seeds*

---

*For information about ingredients and basic techniques that may be unfamiliar, see General
Information, pages 481-506.*

Wrap the bean-curd cakes in a tea towel and put a ½-lb/225-g weight – such as a plate or a baking tray with a small jar – on top. Let the bean curd sit this way for 1 to 1½ hours, depending upon whether it is hard or medium to begin with. Change the tea towel whenever it gets soaking wet.

Drop the spinach leaves into 1 qt/11½ dl of boiling water and boil rapidly for a minute. Drain and rinse under cold water. Chop finely.

Combine the *miso, sake, mirin*, sugar, and *dashi*. Mix to form a smooth paste. Pour this paste into a small, heavy pot or a small, heavy frying pan (I use a well-seasoned, 5-in/13-cm, cast-iron frying pan) and set over a medium-low flame. When the mixture begins to bubble, turn the flame to low. Stir and cook the mixture until it is as thick as a béchamel. Remove from the fire and cool. Add the spinach and the sesame seeds. Mix.

Cut the bean curd into rectangles that are no bigger than 2½×1×¾ in/6½×2½×2 cm.

Heat a cast-iron frying pan or griddle over a medium flame until it is very hot. Lay the bean-curd pieces in it. Cook each side 2 to 3 minutes or until lightly browned, turning the pieces over carefully with a spatula.

Now smear one side of each piece generously with the *miso* paste. Serve this way or place under a grill, *miso* side up, until a few dark spots develop. Serve hot.

FRIED BEAN-CURD CUBES
MOST OF EAST ASIA

Fried bean curd develops a nice chewy crust and is used in many meatless dishes throughout East Asia. This recipe will make cubes of fried bean curd. It will not make *aburage*, the fried bean-curd pillow cases used for Japanese stuffed bean-curd recipes.

Cakes of medium bean curd
Vegetable oil for deep frying

Spread out a tea towel or kitchen paper on a slightly tilted board. Lay one or more cakes of bean curd on it in a single layer. Fold the towel or paper over the bean curd. Now put a weight – about ½ lb/ 225 g – on top of the cakes. (If you are frying more than one cake, you could put a baking tray over the towel or paper and then put a small jar on the tray.) Press the bean curd this way for about 1½ hours, changing the towel or paper whenever it gets soaking wet.

Heat oil for deep drying in a wok over a medium flame. Cut the bean curd into 1-in/2½-cm cubes. When the oil is hot, put in as many bean-curd cubes as the wok will hold in a single layer. Fry, stirring now and then, until cubes are a golden colour – about 7 minutes. Remove with a slotted spoon and drain on kitchen paper.

NOTE: To remove some of the grease from fried bean curd and in order to soften their crusts somewhat, the cubes are often dunked in boiling water. This also makes them more porous and more capable of absorbing other flavours.

Yien-Koo's
SOY-BEAN SPROUTS SAUTÉED WITH FRIED BEAN CURD
CHINA   *(serves 4–6)*

½ lb/225 g fried bean-curd cubes (see preceding recipe) or ½ lb/ 225 g shop-bought fried bean- curd cubes
4 tbs vegetable oil
2–3 five-pence-piece sized slices of fresh ginger

1¼ lb/560 g soy-bean sprouts, thread-like ends removed, washed, and drained
3 tbs preserved snow cabbage
¼ tsp salt
¼ tsp sugar
1 tbs Chinese thin soy sauce

Pour 3 pt/1¾ l of boiling water over the bean-curd cubes. Dunk them a few times in the water to remove extra oil. Take the cubes out of the water and squeeze them gently to remove extra water. Quarter each cube diagonally to form small triangles.

Heat the oil in a wok over a medium-high flame. When hot, put in the ginger slices. Stir them around for 5 to 6 seconds, pressing them occasionally against the sides of the wok. Turn heat to medium and put in the soy-bean sprouts. Stir the sprouts for 2 to 3 minutes. Now put in the fried bean curd and the preserved snow cabbage. Stir-fry another 2 minutes. Add the salt, sugar, and soy sauce. Stir to mix.

For information about ingredients and basic techniques that may be unfamiliar, see General Information, pages 481-506.

Remove the ginger slices and serve hot or cold. I find that this dish makes an excellent lunch if taken to work in a plastic container.

FRIED BEAN CURD WITH A SWEET-AND-SOUR SAUCE

CHINA   *(serves 4–6)*

THE SAUCE

1½ tsp cornflour

3 tbs plus 6 fl oz/1¾ dl Delicious
  Stock . . . (see page 340),
  vegetable stock or water

3 tbs distilled white vinegar

3 tbs sugar

1 tbs tomato ketchup

2 tbs Chinese thin soy sauce

½ tsp salt

⅛–¼ tsp cayenne pepper

Freshly ground black pepper

1 tbs vegetable oil

1 clove garlic, peeled

1 five-pence-piece sized slice of
  fresh ginger

1 carrot

½ small sweet red pepper

½ medium-sized green pepper

2 spring onions

¾ lb/340 g bean curd, cut into
  1-in/2½-cm cubes and fried (see
  page 205)

2½ tsp salt

2 tbs vegetable oil

Mix the cornflour with 3 tbs of the stock in a small cup.

Combine the 6 fl oz/1¾ dl stock, vinegar, sugar, ketchup, soy sauce, ½ tsp salt, cayenne pepper, and black pepper in the bowl.

Heat the 1 tbs oil in a small pot over a medium flame. When hot, put in the garlic and ginger. Stir. As soon as the garlic browns, take the pot off the flame and pour the vinegar mixture from the bowl into it. Put the pot back on the fire and bring to the boil. Turn heat to low and simmer very gently for 4 minutes. Give the cornflour mixture a quick stir and add that to the pot. Stir and cook gently until the sauce thickens. Check seasonings and add more salt if you think you need it. Remove the garlic and ginger.

Peel the carrot and cut into ¹⁄₁₆-in/¼-cm-thick diagonal slices. Cut a few slices at a time into very thin strips.

Cut the red and green pepper into very thin strips.

Cut the spring onions into 1½-in/4-cm lengths. Cut each section lengthwise into very thin strips.

Put the cubes of fried bean curd in a bowl. In a pot add 2 tsp salt to 2½ pt/1½ l of water and bring to the boil. Pour this boiling water over the bean curd. Dunk the bean-curd cubes a few times and then leave them in the water.

Heat the 2 tbs of oil in a wok over a medium-high flame. Put in ½ tsp salt and the carrot, red and green pepper, and spring onions.

Stir-fry for 30 seconds. Turn off the heat.

Heat the prepared sauce over a low flame. Take the bean curd out of the hot water. Squeeze gently to get rid of extra moisture and put the cubes on a serving platter. Spread the vegetables over the bean curd. Pour the sauce over the vegetables.

Ichehara Takao's
FRIED BEAN-CURD CAKES WITH A MUSTARD SURPRISE
JAPAN   *(serves 4)*

This dish is quite scrumptious – and very easy to make. You need whole cakes of bean curd for it. The size does not really matter as long as they are not much larger than 3 × 3 × 1½ in/8 × 8 × 4 cm. If you are using homemade bean curd, cut it to form such cakes.

4 medium bean-curd cakes	1 tsp dry mustard
4 spring onions	4 cut pieces of nori, each about
2 tbs plus 2 tsp Japanese soy sauce	1½ in/4 cm square
2 tbs plus 2 tsp mirin	Vegetable oil for deep frying
2 fl oz/½ dl dashi (see page 339)	

Lay two of the bean-curd cakes side by side on a tea towel, towards one end of it. Cover with the longer remaining portion of tea towel. Lay the two other cakes of bean curd on top of the first two pieces. The towel will, of course, be between the two layers. Fold the towel again over this second layer. Now place a baking tray over the top of the towel and put a ½-lb/225-g weight in the tray. Press the bean curd this way for 2 hours, changing the towel and moving the top layer to the bottom every time the tea towel gets soaked.

Cut the spring onions into very fine rounds. Put the rounds into iced water and refrigerate for 1 hour or longer. Drain and pat dry.

Mix the soy sauce, *mirin*, and *dashi*.

Mix the mustard with 1 tsp hot water so you have a paste.

Scoop out a hole, about ¾ in/2 cm in diameter and of about the same depth, in the centre of one of the larger sides in each cake of bean curd. If possible, remove the scooped-out section in one single conical piece. Now put a quarter of the mustard in the centre of each piece of *nori*. Turn up the corners of the *nori* to cup the mustard and stuff these cups into the holes in the bean curd. Cover these holes with the conical pieces of bean curd that you scooped out. A little protruding *nori* is to be expected.

For information about ingredients and basic techniques that may be unfamiliar, see General Information, pages 481-506.

Heat oil for deep frying in a wok over a medium flame. When hot, put in as many cakes, mustard side up, as the wok will hold in a single layer. Fry for about 5 to 7 minutes or until a nice golden-red colour. Every now and then, push the cakes into the oil or else baste them with the hot oil. Remove the cakes with a slotted spoon and drain on kitchen paper.

Divide the soy-sauce mixture among four saucer-shaped shallow bowls. Put the fried bean-curd cakes in the centre of each bowl, right on top of the sauce. Top each cake with a mound of spring onions. Serve hot, warm, or even at room temperature. As each mouthful of bean curd is eaten, it should be dipped in the sauce.

INARI-ZUSHI
('Bags' of Fried Bean Curd, Stuffed with Sushi Rice)

JAPAN   (makes 6 bags)

It is easiest to make this dish with shop-bought fried, thin bean curd, sold in Japanese and Korean shops as *aburage* or *abura-age*. If you can buy the fresh 'pillow cases' that are about 6 × 3 in/ 15 × 8 cm and fairly flat, do use them. Your second choice should be the 'dry pack' *aburage* that is unseasoned and comes in a tin. Your third choice should be the seasoned, prepared *aburage* that is also tinned and comes all ready to be stuffed.

Once it is stuffed, *inari-zushi* resembles old-fashioned money pouches. These pouches are, visually, at their most charming when tied with a 'ribbon' made out of *kampyo*, or dried gourd strips. The entire pouch is, of course, edible and is a most popular picnic food. The Japanese often carry their picnic foods in wooden boxes, but for us, box-shaped plastic containers that could hold the bags in a single layer would work equally well. As with all Sushi Rice dishes, these stuffed bean-curd bags should not be refrigerated. They will keep well enough if left in a cool spot for a day. *Inari-zushi* makes for a very amusing − and tasty − appetizer. Pickled ginger slices, *amazu shoga*, available in Japanese shops, should be served with it.

3 aburage *pieces (about 6 × 3 in/
15 × 8 cm, or 6 pieces 3 in/8 cm
square)*
8 fl oz/¼ l dashi *(see page 339) or
water*
2 fl oz/½ dl *plus 1 tsp Japanese soy
sauce*
2 tbs *mirin*

3 tbs *plus 1 tsp sugar*
36 in/90 cm of *kampyo*
Freshly made Sushi Rice *(page
145), measured to the 12-fl oz/
3½-dl level in a glass measuring
jug*
1 tbs *roasted sesame seeds, lightly
crushed*

If you have the larger *aburage* pieces, cut them into halves so you
end up with six squares. If you have the smaller pieces, cut a thin
strip off one end of each square so the 'bags' can open. Put the
aburage in a bowl and pour about 1 qt/11½ dl of boiling water over it.
This will remove some of the oil. Drain and squeeze gently to
remove extra moisture.

Combine the *dashi*, soy sauce, *mirin*, and sugar in a small pot. Stir
and bring to a simmer. Put in the *aburage* pieces and the *kampyo*.
Cover partially and simmer for about 8 minutes, spooning the
liquid over the bean curd every now and then. Uncover and let the
bean curd and *kampyo* cool in the liquid.

Mix the Sushi Rice and the sesame seeds. Using dampened
hands, divide the rice into six parts and form into balls. Gently
prise open the bean-curd bags one at a time and stuff each with a
ball of rice. Cut the *kampyo* into six 6-in/15-cm lengths and tie each
bag just above the area where the rice is. Arrange the bags in a
single layer in a plastic bag or box and close. Leave in a cool place
until ready to serve.

*For information about ingredients and basic techniques that may be unfamiliar, see General
Information, pages 481–506.*

PRESSED BEAN CURD WITH CABBAGE

CHINA   *(serves 4)*

*1 cake (about 3 oz/85 g) pressed,
    seasoned bean curd*
*½ lb/225 g cabbage (about ½ a
    medium-sized head)*
*1–2 fresh hot green chillies
    (optional)*
*4 dried black Chinese mushrooms,
    soaked in hot water for ½ hour*
3 spring onions
4 tbs vegetable oil

*3 five-pence-piece sized slices fresh
    ginger, lightly mashed*
*3 cloves garlic, peeled and finely
    chopped*
2 tbs Chinese shaohsing *wine or
    dry sherry*
1 tbs Chinese thin soy sauce
⅓–½ tsp salt
½ tsp sugar
2 tsp sesame oil

Cut the pressed bean curd into fine julienne strips.

Core the cabbage and cut into fine, long shreds.

Cut the green chillies into fine, long strips.

Drain the mushrooms (save the liquid for soups), remove the coarse stems, and then cut the caps into ⅛-in/½-cm-thick slices.

Cut the spring onions into 3 pieces each. Now cut each piece lengthwise into thin strips.

Heat 1 tbs oil in a wok over medium-high heat. Put in the pressed bean curd. Stir and fry for about 10 seconds. Remove with a slotted spoon and place in a bowl.

Add the remaining 3 tbs oil to the wok. Put in the ginger slices. Stir and fry them for about 20 seconds, pressing them against the sides of the wok. Add the garlic, stirring and frying for another 15 seconds until the garlic turns a bit brown. Now put in the green chillies, mushrooms, and spring onions. Stir and fry for about 30 seconds. Put in the cabbage. Stir and fry for 1 minute. Add the wine by pouring it around the side of the wok, then stir. Add the soy sauce, salt, sugar, and sesame oil. Stir and fry for another minute or until the cabbage has just wilted. Add the bean curd. Stir again. Remove ginger pieces.

Yien-Koo's

SALAD OF PRESSED BEAN CURD, MUNG-BEAN SPROUTS, AND AGAR-AGAR

CHINA   *(serves 4)*

This is a simple, easy-to-make, and very tasty salad. A word about the agar-agar. It is available in several forms in Oriental shops — powdered, in small cakes, as well as in vermicelli-like strands. It is the strands that you require for this dish. Nothing else will do. As all Chinese and Japanese grocery shops stock this type of agar-agar, it should not be hard to find.

You need about a ⅓ oz/10 g of agar-agar. Some Japanese shops sell packets that have ⅓ oz/10 g in them. That amount is just right for this dish. Packets weighing 2 oz/60 g are sold in Chinese grocery shops. Use one-sixth of such a Chinese packet.

Uncooked soaked agar-agar is a very interesting salad ingredient. It is unflavoured, clear, and bouncy. While it picks up the taste of the seasonings, it contributes its own hard jelly-like texture to the salads in which it is used.

All the ingredients for this dish can be assembled ahead of time, covered, and then refrigerated. The seasonings, though, should be added only at the last minute or the salad ends up becoming too watery.

⅓ oz/10 g agar-agar strands	*1 tbs distilled white vinegar*
1 cake (about 3 oz/85 g) pressed,	*1 tbs Chinese thin soy sauce*
* seasoned bean curd*	*1 tbs sesame oil*
1 lb/455 g mung-bean sprouts,	*¾ tsp salt*
* rinsed and drained*	*1¼ tsp sugar*

Cut the agar-agar strands into 3-in/8-cm pieces with a pair of scissors, then soak them in ¾ pt/½ l of cold tap water for half an hour. Drain and pat dry.

Cut the pressed bean curd into fine, julienne strips.

Bring 1½ pt/8½ dl of water to the boil in a large pot. When boiling furiously, drop in the mung-bean sprouts. Bring to the boil again. Turn the heat off immediately and drain the sprouts. Rinse the sprouts under cold water and leave to drain for 15 minutes.

Combine the drained agar-agar, the julienned pressed bean curd, and the drained sprouts in a serving bowl. Cover and refrigerate until ready to eat. You may do this a couple of hours

---

For information about ingredients and basic techniques that may be unfamiliar, see General Information, pages 481-506.

ahead of time. Just before serving, add the vinegar, soy sauce, sesame oil, salt, and sugar. Toss to mix. Taste for seasonings.

HOW TO MAKE FRIED AND BAKED WHEAT-GLUTEN BALLS

(makes 14 fried balls or 28 smaller baked ones)

1 lb/450 g strong flour
Vegetable oil for deep frying and/
  or greasing baking dish

Put the flour in a large bowl. Slowly add about 9½–10 fl oz/2¾ dl (or a bit more) water and bring the flour together to make an unsticky ball of medium firmness. 1. Knead for 10 to 12 minutes until the dough is smooth. Leave the dough in a bowl, covered with some aluminium foil, for 1 hour. Knead the dough briefly again. Form a ball and put the dough back in the bowl. Now cover the ball of dough with cold water from the tap and leave overnight.

2. Begin to wash the dough: treat the dough like a piece of sponge and squeeze it under the water. Keep doing this until the water turns exceedingly milky from the starch. Throw this starchy water away and cover the dough with fresh cold water. You will be throwing away several batches of water as each turns milky until you are left with just gluten, at which point the water remains almost clear. Place this ball of gluten on a tilted board and let it drain for 15 minutes.

FOR FRYING THE BALLS Set up a platter lined with kitchen paper. Pour oil into a wok for deep frying and heat over a lowish flame. You should aim for a temperature around 325°F/170°C.

3. Break the dough into 1-in/2½-cm balls, working each in your hand so it is as round as possible.

2

3

4. Drop four balls into the wok at a slight distance from each other. Baste the balls gently but constantly with the hot oil as you fry them. The frying should take at least 4 minutes. The balls should expand to at least twice their size and turn a reddish colour on the outside. If they brown too fast, they will not expand properly. Adjust the heat if that happens.

5. Remove the balls with slotted spoon and leave to drain on the platter. The balls will collapse as they cool.

4

5

FOR BAKING THE BALLS Preheat oven to 375°F/170°C/Mark 3.

Grease a baking sheet lightly with oil. Break the dough into ½-in/ 1½-cm balls and lay as many as will fit on the baking sheet, about 2½ in/6½ cm apart. Bake for 15 to 20 minutes or until they are quite puffed up and lightly browned.

When fried or baked gluten balls have cooled, they should be packed in plastic bags or plastic containers and either refrigerated or frozen. They should last in the refrigerator for at least 3 days. To defreeze frozen balls, just throw them into boiling water or boiling stock and cook for a few minutes.

Baked balls are particularly suited to light stews and soups. Fried balls are better in heartier stews and in stir-fried dishes.

STEW OF BAKED WHEAT GLUTEN, POTATO, TURNIP, CARROT, AND CABBAGE ROLLS
JAPAN   (serves 2–4)

This is one of the many one-pot Japanese dishes that is cooked and served in the same casserole-type utensil. This utensil is sometimes an iron kettle, quaint and old-fashioned; at other times it is a ceramic masterpiece, made out of hard clay. You may use a humbler and less quaint piece of cooker-to-table ware, or else use a nice porcelained pot to bring to the table. Such stews are very popular in the wintertime.

4 baked wheat-gluten balls (see
  pages 213–15)
1 medium-sized potato
1 medium-sized turnip
1¼ pt/¾ l Delicious Stock…(see
  page 340) or any vegetable
  stock

1½ medium-sized carrots
Salt
3 large, unbroken outer leaves
  from a Chinese cabbage
15 fresh spinach leaves
Japanese soy sauce
2 tsp dry mustard

Cut each ball of wheat gluten into 2 pieces. Peel the potato and turnip and dice each into about 6 pieces. Put the gluten, potato, turnip, and stock into a casserole-type pot that is wider than its height. Bring to the boil. Cover, turn heat to low and simmer gently for 20 minutes.

Meanwhile, peel the carrots and cut them into ¾-in/2-cm-long chunks. Bring about 2½ pts/1½ l of water to a rolling boil in a large pot. Put about 2 tsp salt into it. Now put in the cabbage leaves and bring to the boil again. Cook for a couple of minutes or until the leaves wilt. Throw in the spinach leaves and let them wilt, too. Drain the leaves and rinse under cold running water. Gently squeeze some of the moisture out of the leaves. You do not have to be too thorough. 1. Lay one cabbage leaf in front of you with its root end to your left. Lay another cabbage leaf directly over it but with its root end to your right. Lay the third cabbage leaf over the second, with its root end to your left. 2. Lay the spinach leaves lengthwise along the centre of the top cabbage leaf. 3. Roll the cabbage leaves lengthwise away from you. Make a tight roll. The spinach will be in the centre. 4. Squeeze each of the rolls gently to firm up the shape and get rid of extra water. 5. Cut the roll crosswise at 1-in/2½-cm intervals.

Once the stew has cooked for 20 minutes, season it very lightly with about ⅛ tsp salt or less, leaving it slightly undersalted. 6. Carefully place the cabbage rolls, cut side up, inside the pot, all bunched together in a single layer in one area. Make room for the carrots somewhere near the cabbage rolls and keep the pieces near each other. Bring to a simmer. Cover and simmer on low heat for another 5 to 10 minutes or until carrots are just tender.

For information about ingredients and basic techniques that may be unfamiliar, see General Information, pages 481-506.

Serve hot, with shallow bowls containing extra soy sauce, salt, and a mustard paste made by mixing the 2 tsp dry mustard with 2 tsp hot water. The stew should be seasoned at the table to taste.

FRIED WHEAT GLUTEN WITH BROCCOLI, CARROT, AND MUSHROOMS

CHINA *(serves 4–6)*

FOR THE GLUTEN BALLS
4 *fried wheat-gluten balls (see*
  pages 213–15)
¾ *tsp salt*
1 *tsp Chinese thin soy sauce*
1 *tsp sugar*

FOR THE SAUCE
2 *fl oz/½ dl Delicious Stock...(see*
  page 340) or gluten cooking
  water, or vegetable stock or
  water
1 *tsp cornflour*
1 *tsp sesame oil*

1 *tbs Chinese thin soy sauce*
½ *tsp sugar*

About ½ *lb/225 g broccoli*
1 *carrot*
4 *medium-sized mushrooms*
2 *tbs vegetable oil*
¾ *tsp salt*
2 *cloves garlic, peeled and very*
  lightly crushed
2 *fl oz/½ dl Delicious Stock...(see*
  page 340) or water from boiling
  the gluten, or vegetable stock or
  water

Combine all the ingredients listed under gluten balls with 1 qt/ 11½ dl water and bring to the boil. Cover, turn heat to low, and simmer for 15 minutes. Remove the balls with a slotted spoon and cool slightly. Reserve 4 fl oz/1 dl cooking water, if using it. Cut the balls into ⅓-in/1-cm-wide strips.

Add the 2 fl oz/½ dl stock or gluten cooking water gradually to the cornflour and make a paste in a small cup. Add all the other ingredients for the sauce and mix.

Cut the broccoli into very slim flowerets that are about 2 in/5 cm long. Peel the carrot and cut at a slight diagonal into ⅛-in/½-cm-thick slices. Wipe the mushrooms with a damp cloth and cut them into ⅛-in/½-cm-thick slices, including the stem.

Heat the oil in a wok over a medium flame. When hot, put in the salt and garlic. Stir and fry until the garlic browns lightly. Now put in all the vegetables and the strips of wheat gluten. Stir-fry for about 2 minutes. Pour in the 2 fl oz/½ dl stock, cover immediately and cook for 30 seconds. Remove the cover and turn the flame to low. Give the cornflour mixture a quick stir and pour it over the vegetables. Turn the heat to medium-low and cook, stirring, until the sauce thickens and reduces slightly. Serve at once.

FRIED WHEAT GLUTEN AND POTATO STEW

INDIAN STYLE   *(serves 4)*

A ¾-in/2-cm cube of fresh ginger,
 peeled
3–4 cloves garlic, peeled
4 fried wheat-gluten balls (see
 pages 213–15)
3 medium-sized boiling potatoes
2 tbs vegetable oil
1 tsp whole cumin seeds

¼ tsp ground turmeric
⅛ tsp cayenne pepper
4 fl oz/1 dl Tomato Sauce,
 homemade (see page 419) or
 2 tbs tomato purée mixed with
 6 tbs water
¾ tsp salt

Put the ginger and garlic into the container of an electric blender or
food processor. Add 2 fl oz/½ dl water and blend.

Put the fried wheat-gluten balls in a bowl. Pour about
1½–2 pt/¾–1 l boiling water over them. Squeeze them a few times
with a pair of spoons to get rid of the extra oil. Now take them
out of the hot water and cut into halves.

Peel the potatoes and cut roughly into ¾–1-in/2–2½-cm cubes.

Heat the oil in a 2½–3-qt/2¾–3½-l pot over a medium flame.
When hot, put in the cumin seeds. Stir once. Put in the turmeric
and cayenne. Give another stir and pour in the ginger–garlic mixture, making sure you get all of it out of the blender container. Stir
for a few seconds until the paste thickens. Put in the potato pieces
and stir a few times. Now put in ¾ pt/4 dl water, the tomato sauce,
salt, and wheat gluten. Stir to mix and bring to the boil. Cover,
lower heat, and simmer for half an hour or until potatoes are
tender. Check the salt.

SHREDDED WHEAT GLUTEN AND CABBAGE WITH FENNEL SEEDS

INDIAN STYLE   *(serves 6)*

About ¾ lb/340 g cabbage (½ a
 small-sized head)
4 fried wheat-gluten balls (see
 pages 213–15)
3 tbs vegetable oil
1 tsp whole fennel seeds

1 tsp whole cumin seeds
1 tsp whole black mustard seeds
¼ tsp ground turmeric
⅛ tsp cayenne pepper
¾ tsp salt

Core the cabbage and cut it into very thin, long shreds.

Put the wheat-gluten balls in a bowl. Pour 1½–2 pt/¾–1 l boiling
water over them. Squeeze them a few times with a pair of spoons to

---

*For information about ingredients and basic techniques that may be unfamiliar, see General
Information, pages 481-506.*

rid them of extra oil. Take them out of the water and cut them into
⅛-in/½-cm-thick strips.

Heat the oil in a wok over a medium flame. When hot, put in the
fennel, cumin, and mustard seeds. As soon as the mustard seeds
begin to pop, put in the cabbage and the wheat gluten. Stir for 10
seconds. Sprinkle the turmeric, cayenne, and salt over the top. Stir
to mix. Add 2 fl oz/½ dl water, turn heat to low and partially cover.
Simmer gently for 15 to 20 minutes or until cabbage and gluten are
tender. Stir several times during this cooking period.

Ahtong's
BUDDHA'S DELIGHT
(A Mixed Chinese Stew)
HONG KONG   (serves 6)

It is customary for many people in Hong Kong, especially those of
Buddhist ancestry, to eat vegetarian food on the first day day of the
Chinese New Year. Large white radishes are hung in doorways for
good luck — banging into them is considered auspicious — peach
blossom branches and potted mandarin orange plants, all loaded
with fruit, are decoratively scattered about the house. Fried melon
seeds are nibbled on and, when it comes to sitting down and
eating, many homes serve Buddha's Delight and rice.

In fact, just before New Year's Day, the grocery stores are filled
with clear plastic packets containing all the dry ingredients needed
to make this dish. The ingredients are many: dried black mushrooms; a dried seaweed that resembles crinkly hair; mung-bean
cellophane noodles; dried bean-curd skin; tree ear fungus, both
black and silver; ginkgo nuts; and red Chinese jujubes. To these
dry ingredients are added fresh vegetables. The vegetables can
vary. One may put in carrots and mangetouts. Or one may add
baby corn, straw mushrooms, and Chinese cabbage.

There is a certain amount of preparation that has to be done in
advance — a lot of soaking, the first ingredient requiring 6 to 8
hours. But the dish cooks quickly and easily.

10 dried jujubes (red Chinese
    dates)
10 ginkgo nuts, shelled (or tinned
    ginkgo nuts, shelled and peeled)
6 Chinese dried black mushrooms
Salt
5 tbs plus 1 tsp vegetable oil

2 oz/60 g mung-bean 'cellophane'
    noodles or threads
¼ breakfast cup dried hair
    seaweed, firmly packed
4 fl oz/1 dl shaohsing wine or dry
    sherry
2 tbs tree ear fungus

2 tbs silver ear fungus (or white fungus)

4 rectangles dried bean-curd skin (about 5 × 1½ in/13 × 4 cm each)

5 1½-in/4-cm cubes fried bean curd, each cut diagonally into two pieces

3 fried wheat-gluten balls, each cut into 4 pieces

2 five-pence-piece sized slices of fresh ginger

2 spring onions, one cut into 2-in/5-cm lengths, the other into very fine slices

2 oz/60 g coarsely julienned carrot

10 mangetouts, trimmed with strings removed

12 fl oz/3½ dl Delicious Stock . . . (see page 340) or vegetable stock

1 tbs Chinese thin soy sauce

2 tsp sesame oil

1 tbs finely chopped fresh green coriander

Soak the dried jujubes in 3 fl oz/¾ dl water for 6 to 8 hours. Drain them and remove the seeds, if you wish.

Soak the ginkgo nuts, if you are using fresh ones, in 3 fl oz/¾ dl water for 2 hours. Then drain and peel them.

Rinse the Chinese mushrooms and soak them in 8 fl oz/¼ l hot water for half an hour. Then simmer them, covered, in the same water with ¼ tsp salt and 1 tsp of the vegetable oil for 15 minutes. Cut off the coarse stems and discard. Slice the caps in half. Reserve the mushroom liquid in case you need it.

Soak the mung-bean noodles in 2½ pt/1½ l cold water for half an hour. Drain and put them in a bowl.

Soak the hair seaweed in a mixture of 4 fl oz/1 dl hot water and 4 fl oz/1 dl shaohsing wine or dry sherry for half an hour. Then swish the seaweed in its soaking liquid, rinsing it and separating the strands. Drain and put it in a saucer, separating the strands again.

Soak the tree ear fungus in 8 fl oz/¼ l water for half an hour and the silver ear fungus in a separate cup of water the same amount of time. Drain both and rinse under running water. Feel with your fingers and snip off any hard, coarse sections or knots. Put them together in a bowl

Cut each bean-curd skin, crosswise, into three pieces and rinse in hot water.

Put the fried bean curd and the wheat gluten in a sieve and pour about 2½ pt/1½ l boiling water over them. Gently squeeze the water out of them and put them together in a bowl.

Arrange all your ingredients near the cooker. Now heat the 5 tbs oil in a wok or a wide saucepan over a medium flame. When hot, put in the ginger and the 2-in/5-cm lengths of spring onion. Stir and fry until they turn brown. Remove the ginger and spring onion pieces with a slotted spoon and discard them. Put in the tree ear and silver ear fungus. Stir once. Add the fried bean curd, wheat gluten, carrot, mangetouts, ginkgo nuts, jujubes, and mushrooms. Stir and fry for 1 minute. Add the cellophane noodles, hair seaweed (make sure that the strands are separated), bean-curd skin, stock, salt, and soy sauce. Bring to the boil. Cover, lower heat and simmer gently for 5 minutes. There should be some liquid at the bottom of the wok. If there is not, add some of the mushroom liquid. Add the sesame oil and stir. Turn off the heat.

Sprinkle with sliced spring onions and chopped fresh coriander just before serving. (This dish can be made ahead of time and reheated.)

5 Eggs

Eggs have more usable protein than almost any other food on earth and, as a double blessing for us, there are such wonderful ways of cooking them. Nothing seems more perfect for a cold winter day than a cup of *chawanmushi*, that amazing cross between a soup and a savoury custard. As you ease your spoon into the smooth, barely set, trembling mass, you might come across a crisp piece of water chestnut, a slice of mushroom, or even a noodle.

Chawanmushi is a Japanese dish. Asians have their own approach to eggs which makes them taste quite different from their Western counterparts. I once watched a Chinese mother in Singapore prepare a soft-boiled egg for her four-year-old daughter. After the egg had boiled in the usual way, it was removed from its shell and put in a bowl. Then, instead of seasoning it with salt and pepper, the mother dribbled a few drops of soy sauce and a few drops of sesame oil over it, stirred it up, and handed it to her daughter. The daughter kindly allowed me a taste. Just those tiny amounts of seasoning made the egg taste entirely different — and very good. You might also try eating hard-boiled eggs with salt and pepper, Chinese-style and fried eggs with salt and pepper, Indian-style.

Among the brunch dishes that I have added to my repertoire is the Persian *kookoo*. It is an egg pie, not entirely unlike a *frittata*, that is cooked with generous handfuls of fresh herbs, or with cauliflower, or courgettes, or what you will. It is an ideal food to serve to guests in the country and to take out cold on picnics.

Instead of making the more common type of European omelette, you could, instead, have Omelette with Bean Curd. Cut into squares and served with a dipping sauce, it may be eaten with plain rice and a crisp green salad. Or you could have the Indian Omelette with a Spicy Tomato Stuffing. It will perk up your appetite and make you hunger for more. I love to have it with toast and hot cups of tea.

A very charming dish from Korea consists of cooked egg strips, tied into bundles with blanched spring onions. The bundles look very pretty and may be served at a buffet or as a first course.

If you are looking for a filling main course for dinner, try the Hard-Boiled Eggs in a Spicy Almond Sauce. It is rich, hot, nutty, and quite excellent when served with an Indian or Persian pilaf.

For information about ingredients and basic techniques that may be unfamiliar, see General Information, pages 481-506.

CHAWANMUSHI
(Steamed Savoury Custards)
JAPAN

I do not know why savoury custards are not eaten more here. They are so delicate and delicious that they should be added to every cook's repertoire of fine foods. Instead of milk, in a *chawanmushi* the Japanese use a delicate stock and then they add bits of vegetables and herbs for colour and flavour, such as spinach, spring onions, mushrooms, and ginger.

These custards are generally cooked and served in individual, lidded *chawanmushi* cups which resemble handleless teacups, only they are a bit taller. The custards are steamed. This is done by first filling the cups with the egg mixture, covering them, and then immersing them in simmering water in such a way that the water comes about three-quarters of the way up the sides of the cups. The steaming utensil is covered and the custards allowed to steam for about 13 minutes. In order to get the correct texture − the custards should just set, be free of bubbles, and they should not separate − several things should be watched for. 1. Do not let the steaming water bubble vigorously. This causes bubbles in the custard. The heat should be adjusted so the water simmers very, very gently. 2. Begin counting your 13 minutes from the moment you put your custard cups into the water and cover the steaming utensil. Then, if the custard is not set in the required time, give it another minute or so. Overcooking will cause the custards to separate. To check if the custards have set, insert the tip of a pointed knife into one of them. 3. It is best not to let the custard cups rest on the bottom of the steaming utensil. Improvise a rack − this could be a steaming tray or a flat plate − that sits on a bowl or a set of bowls. Now you can pour in just the correct amount of water so the *chawanmushi* cups will be partially submerged.

What should you use for a steaming utensil and what if you have no *chawanmushi* cups? Any wide pot with a lid will do for a steaming utensil. Whether you need one such pot or two will depend on the width of your cups, which should not be too crowded inside or they'll be hard to remove. You may use small custard cups, ramekins, small bowls — anything with the approximate capacity of 8 fl oz/¼ l. If the containers have lids, well and good. If not, cover each with aluminium foil, crimping the edges to seal as thoroughly as possible.

Once the custards are cooked, the cups have to be lifted out of the very hot water. In Asia, there are all kinds of gadgets that are specially engineered for this purpose. I have in my kitchen a three-pronged (it looks three-legged) piece of Chinese wizardry that can lift plates or cups out of hot water or steam. Then I have an Indian gadget that looks like a set of pliers. The end that grips is angled, rather like a beak on a parrot's head. So *it* gets the brunt of the steam or hot water and not your hands. If you cannot get such gadgets in your local Oriental shop, the best solution is to ladle out some of the hot water so it is nowhere near the upper portions of the cups. Then, wearing an oven mitten, lift out the cups one by one. This has to be done rather quickly, as the custards should not go on cooking.

Chawanmushi should be served as soon as it is made. If there are lids, serve the custard covered. If you are using aluminium foil as a cover, take it off in the kitchen. Even though the custard has to be cooked just before it is eaten, the ingredients may be prepared well in advance. The stock may be prepared ahead of time, cooled, and mixed in with the eggs. This mixture may be refrigerated. It should be stirred and strained before being poured into the custard cups. The vegetables that are required may be cut and sliced beforehand, too.

In Japan, *chawanmushi* is often served like a soup course. You may serve it that way or have it as a light lunch, followed by a green salad and fruit.

I have given two recipes for *chawanmushi*, one with dried mushrooms and water chestnuts and the other with bean curd, fresh mushrooms, and spinach. You can be as creative as you like with this dish, and add leftover vegetables like carrots, peas, and beans to it at will. The Japanese often put cooked noodles into a *chawanmushi* base and call this dish *odamakimushi*. That recipe follows the two recipes for *chawanmushi*.

For information about ingredients and basic techniques that may be unfamiliar, see General Information, pages 481-506.

CHAWANMUSHI WITH SHIITAKE MUSHROOMS, WATER CHESTNUTS, AND MANGETOUTS

JAPAN   *(serves 4)*

Read general notes on *chawanmushi*, pages 223–4.

22 fl oz/6¼ dl freshly made
   Japanese Stock (see page 339)
2 tsp Japanese soy sauce
1 tsp mirin
4 mushrooms reserved from stock
4 large eggs
⅛–¼ tsp salt, or to taste
1 fresh or tinned water chestnut,
   peeled and quartered
1 tbs very finely sliced spring
   onion, including green

2 mangetouts, cut in half at a
   slight diagonal

Let the stock cool completely. Add the extra soy sauce and *mirin* to it.

Remove the coarse mushroom stems and slice each mushroom cap into ⅛-in/½-cm-wide slices.

Get your steaming utensil ready. See pages 223–4 for details.

Beat the eggs lightly. Try not to create froth. Add the salt and the stock, mixing gently as you do so. Taste for salt. You may want to add a bit more.

Divide the sliced mushrooms and quartered water chestnut among four 8-oz/225-g *chawanmushi* cups. Pour about 6 fl oz/ 1¾ dl of the egg-stock mixture through a strainer into each of the four cups. (Just divide the liquid evenly.) Now sprinkle the spring onion over the liquid and then float a mangetout half prettily on the top. Cover each cup with its lid or with a piece of aluminium foil. If using the foil, crinkle the edges to seal the cup.

Put the covered cups into barely simmering water, making sure that the water comes about three-quarters of the way up the sides of the cups. Cover the steaming utensil. Steam for about 13 minutes or until custard is just set. Turn off heat and immediately remove custard cups from the hot water. Serve at once. Diners should remove the lids of their cups and then eat the custard with a Chinese (or Japanese – they are the same, really) soup spoon. *Chawanmushi* seems to retain its heat for a long time, so let the first few portions in your spoon cool off slightly before you put them in your mouth.

CHAWANMUSHI WITH BEAN CURD, FRESH MUSHROOMS, AND SPINACH
JAPAN   *(serves 4)*

Read general notes on *chawanmushi*, on pages 223–4.

1 4 oz/115-g cake medium or
   slightly hard bean curd
2 tbs Japanese soy sauce
1 tbs mirin
2 tsp sesame oil
1 tsp sugar
3 medium-sized mushrooms
22 fl oz/16¼ dl Japanese Stock (see
   page 339), at room temperature,
   or any vegetable stock

4 large eggs
⅛ tsp salt, or to taste
½ tsp very finely grated ginger
4 tender spinach leaves, cut
   crosswise into ¼-in/¾-cm-wide
   strips
4 very, very thin lemon slices
1 tbs very finely sliced spring
   onion

You need 8 ¾-in/2-cm cubes of bean curd for this dish (save the remaining curd for a soup or a dressing). In a small bowl, mix 4 tsp soy sauce, 2 tsp *mirin*, 1 tsp sesame oil, and ½ tsp sugar. Add the bean-curd cubes and turn them around gently. Let them sit in this marinade for half an hour, turning them every 5 minutes or so.

Remove stems from mushrooms (reserve for another use) and wipe the mushroom caps with a damp cloth, then cut into ⅟₁₆-in/¼-cm slices.

Put 2 tsp soy sauce, 1 tsp *mirin*, 1 tsp sesame oil, ½ tsp sugar, 2 fl oz/½ dl of the stock, and the sliced mushrooms into a small pot. Bring to a simmer. Cover and simmer for 30 seconds. Turn off heat and uncover. Let the mushrooms cool in this liquid.

Get your steaming utensils ready. See pages 223–4 for details.

Beat the eggs gently in a bowl. Try not to create froth. Add the salt and the ginger. Slowly add the remaining stock, mixing gently as you do so.

Put 2 bean-curd cubes at the bottom of each of four 8-oz/225-g-capacity *chawanmushi* cups. Lift the mushrooms out with a slotted spoon and divide them up among the four cups. (Save the mushroom liquid.) Stir the egg–stock mixture and pour it through a strainer into the four cups, dividing it up equally. Float the shredded spinach on top of the liquid in each cup. Put a thin slice of lemon on top of the spinach. Spoon 2 tsp of the mushroom liquid over each piece of lemon and then top the lemon with some spring

For information about ingredients and basic techniques that may be unfamiliar, see General Information, pages 481-506.

onion slices. Now cover the *chawanmushi* cups and steam according to directions in preceding recipe. Serve immediately.

ODAMAKIMUSHI
(Savoury Custard with Noodles)
JAPAN   *(serves 4)*

Read general notes on *chawanmushi*, pages 223–4.

Cooked udon *noodles, measured to the 15-fl oz/4¼-dl level in a glass measuring jug, rinsed and drained*
2 tbs Japanese soy sauce
1 tbs mirin
1 tsp sugar
1 tsp sesame oil
4 large eggs

22 fl oz/6¼ dl Delicious Stock . . . (see page 340; or other vegetable stock), at room temperature or cold
¼ tsp salt
4 squares of nori, 2½ × ½ in/6½ × 1½ cm
1 spring onion, sliced very fine, including green
4 smallish mushrooms

Put the noodles in a bowl. Mix the soy sauce, *mirin*, sugar, and sesame oil together and pour over the noodles. Toss to mix and set aside for 15 minutes.

Beat the eggs well but not to a froth. Add the stock and the salt. Beat gently to mix. Strain.

Divide the noodles among four 12-oz/340-g bowls. Stir the egg mixture and divide it evenly among the four bowls. Float a square of *nori* in the centre of each bowl. Sprinkle the spring onion slices over the *nori*. Cut each mushroom into 4 slices and float the slices just outside the *nori*. Cover each bowl with a lid or with a piece of aluminium foil. If using foil, crinkle the edges to seal the bowl.

Put the covered bowls in barely simmering water, making sure that the water comes three-quarters of the way up the sides of the bowls. Cover the steaming utensil. Steam for about 13 minutes or until custards are just set. Turn off the heat and immediately remove the custard bowls from the hot water. Serve right away.

SCRAMBLED EGGS WITH CABBAGE
JAPAN   *(serves 2)*

I make all my scrambled eggs in nonstick frying pans. You can, of course, use a heavy, well-seasoned frying pan instead.

3 medium-sized dried shiitake
  mushrooms
2 large eggs
¼ tsp plus ⅛ tsp salt
1 tbs dashi (see page 339) or other
  vegetable stock

½ tsp sugar
¾ tsp Japanese soy sauce
¾ tsp mirin
2 tbs vegetable oil
4 oz/115 g cabbage leaves cut into
  ½-in/1½-cm squares

Soak the *shiitake* mushrooms in 8 fl oz/¼ l hot water for half an hour; you may use mushrooms left from making *dashi*.

Beat the eggs lightly. Add the ¼ tsp salt, *dashi*, sugar, soy sauce, and *mirin*.

Drain the mushrooms (save the soaking liquid for stock). Cut off and discard their coarse stems and then quarter the mushroom caps.

Heat the oil in a 7–8-in/18–20-cm nonstick frying pan over a medium flame. When hot, put in the mushrooms and sauté them for about 30 seconds. Add the cabbage and sauté it for about 2 minutes or until it is wilted but still slightly crunchy. Sprinkle with ⅛ tsp salt and stir.

Strain the eggs into the frying pan and stir them around, 'scrambling' them to the consistency you like. Try and keep them on the soft side. Remove from frying pan as soon as eggs are done.

Yien-koo's
SCRAMBLED EGGS WITH CHINESE CHIVES
CHINA
(serves 2)

3 tbs groundnut oil
⅛ tsp salt, or to taste

About 2 tbs Chinese chives, cut
  into 1½-in/4-cm lengths
4 large eggs, beaten

Heat the oil in an 8–10-in/20–25-cm, well-seasoned or nonstick frying pan over a medium-high flame. Add the salt to the pan and stir it around. Put in the chives and stir-fry them for 3 to 4 seconds. Now put in the eggs. Stir them gently 3 to 4 times in the next 5 to 10 seconds. The eggs should be very softly scrambled. Empty eggs immediately on to warm plates and serve with plain rice, Chinese style, or with toast.

For information about ingredients and basic techniques that may be unfamiliar, see General Information, pages 481-506.

SCRAMBLED EGGS
WITH SPICY TOMATOES
INDIA   *(serves 4)*

I like to make this dish very hot (chilli hot) but you could leave out
the green chillies and still have a very tasty dish. Also, if you have
no access to good tomatoes, use tinned ones. Just drain them well
before chopping them. You should end up with enough drained,
chopped tomatoes to fill a 1¼ pt/8 dl jar.

The spicy tomato sauce used to make these scrambled eggs is
very interesting in its own right. You can serve it under or over
fried eggs to have an Indian version of the Mexican *huevos
rancheros*. You could make a Persian-style *kookoo* with it (see page
236), or you could use it to stuff an omelette (see page 230).

The thick sauce is nice to have around in the refrigerator or
freezer. It serves as an excellent relish and turns into a superb
sauce for pasta.

THE SPICY TOMATO SAUCE

1 lb/450 g ripe tomatoes, peeled
3 tbs vegetable oil
1½ tsp whole black mustard seeds
2 oz/60 g very finely sliced spring
   onions (about 4 whole spring
   onions, including green)
2 large cloves garlic, peeled and
   finely chopped (about 1 tbs)
½ tsp finely grated fresh ginger

3 tbs finely chopped fresh green
   coriander
1 fresh hot green chilli (or to
   taste), finely chopped
½–¾ tsp salt
1⁄16 tsp freshly ground black pepper

7 large eggs
Salt to taste

Chop the tomatoes very fine.

Heat the oil in an 8-in/20-cm, very well-seasoned or nonstick
frying pan over a medium-low flame. When hot, put in the mustard seeds. As soon as the mustard seeds begin to pop (this takes
just a few seconds), put in the sliced spring onions and garlic. Stir
and fry for about 3 minutes or until the spring onion whites are
almost translucent but not browned at all. Now add the tomato
pulp, the ginger, fresh coriander, and the green chilli. Stir and fry
over medium heat for 6 to 8 minutes. The tomatoes should not
remain watery. Add ½ tsp salt and the black pepper. Mix, and
correct seasonings. Turn off heat.

Beat the eggs lightly with a fork or a whisk. Add less than ¼ tsp
salt to the eggs and mix.

Bring the sauce in the frying pan to a simmer. Turn heat to low.
Add the eggs to the pan. Stir gently but continuously to scramble
the eggs. Remove from the fire when the right degree of doneness
has been achieved. Serve immediately.

OMELETTE WITH A
SPICY TOMATO STUFFING

INDIA   *(serves 2)*

6 large eggs   *Spicy Tomato Sauce (see preceding*
About ⅛ tsp salt, or to taste   *recipe), heated*
2 tbs unsalted butter

Put the eggs in a bowl. Add 2 tbs water and the salt. Beat
thoroughly until eggs are light and bubbly.

Heat 1 tbs butter in a 7–8-in/18–20-cm, very well-seasoned or
nonstick frying pan over a medium flame. When the butter has
melted and is foaming, pour in half the beaten eggs. Keep stirring
the eggs with the flat bottom of a fork or with a narrow plastic
spatula until the eggs begin to set. (Those who like their omelettes
fairly firm should cover the frying pan for a minute and turn the
heat to low.) Spread half the tomato sauce over the half of the
omelette that is nearest you. Now slide your spatula under the half
of the omelette that is farthest from you and fold it over the tomato
mixture. Slide the folded omelette on to a warm plate.

Make a second omelette the same way.

OMELETTE WITH BEAN CURD

JAPAN   *(serves 4 as a main course,*
                                          up to 24 as an appetizer)

This is a thick Japanese omelette that is cut into squares and served
with a dipping sauce. It is delicious and very nourishing at the
same time. Unlike French omelettes, it can be served several hours
after it is made and at room temperature. It seems to be equally
popular as an appetizer and as a main course.

Like most of my egg dishes, I make this omelette in a nonstick
frying pan. A heavy, well-seasoned frying pan would also work
well. For this dish you could use bean curd that has been sitting
around in the refrigerator for a few days.

6 oz/180 g hard bean curd (about   *½ tsp salt*
1½ cakes)   *½ tsp sugar*
3 medium-sized dried shiitake   *2 tbs shelled fresh or defrosted*
mushrooms   *frozen peas*

---

*For information about ingredients and basic techniques that may be unfamiliar, see General
Information, pages 481–506.*

2 large eggs
1 tsp mirin
1 tbs Japanese soy sauce

½ tsp plain white flour
A dash of 7-spice seasoning
1 tbs vegetable oil

Put a piece of kitchen paper on a slightly tilted board and let the bean curd sit on it for an hour. Soak the mushrooms in 8 fl oz/¼ l hot water for half an hour. Put the bean curd on a plate and mash it up with a fork. Now put the bean curd in the centre of a tea towel. Bring the ends of the towel together and squeeze out as much liquid as you can. Set the bean curd aside.

Bring 8 fl oz/¼ l of water to the boil in a small pot. Add ¼ tsp of the salt, ¼ tsp of the sugar, and the peas. Boil gently for about 3 minutes or until peas are just cooked through. Drain through a strainer. Put the strainer under cold running water and cool off the peas. Set the peas aside.

Drain the mushrooms (save the liquid for stock). Cut off the coarse stems and slice the caps into ¹⁄₁₆-in/¼-cm-wide strips. Set aside.

Beat the eggs lightly. Add ¼ tsp salt, ¼ tsp sugar, *mirin*, soy sauce, flour, and the 7-spice seasoning. Mix well. Now add the bean curd, peas, and mushrooms. Mix again.

Heat the oil in a 7–8-in/18–20-cm-wide, nonstick frying pan over a lowish flame. When hot, pour the egg–bean-curd mixture in the centre of the frying pan. Using a plastic spatula, spread the mixture so it forms a square cake, about 6½×6½ in/16½×16½ cm and flat on the top. Tidy up the edges by pushing inwards with the spatula. Make neat corners, if possible. Cover, and let the omelette cook for about 10 minutes or until it is quite set. It will get lightly browned on the bottom.

Remove omelette and place, brown side down, on a flat plate large enough to hold it. Cut into roughly 1-in/2½-cm squares. (Smaller squares — ½ in/1½ cm in length and width — may be cut if serving this omelette with drinks.) Serve omelette hot, warm, or at room temperature. Once it has cooled off, it should be covered to prevent it from drying out. With it, pass Japanese Dipping Sauce (see page 415).

INDONESIAN OMELETTE: Without too much trouble, this very Japanese dish can be transformed into an Indonesian one! Just put the omelette cubes on a bed of lightly sautéed and lightly salted mung-bean sprouts. Sprinkle some chopped-up fresh green coriander as well as some Crisply Fried Onions over the top and serve with Spicy Peanut Sambal.

EGG FU YUNG
AMERICAN CHINESE   *(serves 2–4)*

When I first went to New York and was scouting around for cheap places to eat, I was taken to a Chinese restaurant on Eighth Avenue in the Times Square area and advised to order a speciality called 'egg foo yong'. It consisted of a thick, round omelette, filled with bean sprouts and spring onions and doused with a tasty brownish sauce. I loved it. Now my sophisticated Chinese friends tell me that the dish I ate was not authentically Chinese. Well, all that I can say to them is that it is too late. I have acquired a taste for it and refuse to give it up. Here is my vegetarian version of it, which is best eaten with rice. I make rather a lot of sauce because I like to spoon it over the rice.

FOR THE SAUCE
3 oz/85 g fresh or frozen peas
½ pt/3 dl Delicious Stock . . . (see
    page 340) or any vegetable stock
2½ tsp cornflour
¾ tsp Marmite
1 tbs shaohsing *wine or dry*
    sherry
¼ tsp salt
Freshly ground black pepper
1½ tbs vegetable oil
5 medium-sized mushrooms, sliced

FOR THE OMELETTE
4 *large eggs*
2 *spring onions, sliced fine,*
    including green
3 oz/85 g *mung-bean sprouts,*
    washed and drained
⅛ tsp salt
Freshly ground black pepper
4 tbs vegetable oil

Drop the peas in ¾ pt/½ l rapidly boiling water for 2 to 5 minutes or until they are just cooked through. Drain and rinse immediately under running water to set their bright-green colour. These peas will now be added to the sauce just before serving.

Slowly add 2 fl oz/½ dl stock to the cornflour, mixing it well as you do so. Also add the Marmite, *shaohsing* wine, the ¼ tsp salt, and some black pepper. Mix until Marmite is dissolved. Add the remaining stock and mix.

Over a medium flame, heat the 1½ tbs of oil in a small saucepan. When hot, put in the mushrooms. Stir and fry for 1 minute. Give the stock mixture a stir and pour it in. Bring to a simmer. Turn heat to low and simmer for 2 minutes. Keep the sauce warm.

Beat the eggs but not to a froth. Add the spring onions, bean sprouts, ⅛ tsp salt, and some black pepper. Mix.

For information about ingredients and basic techniques that may be unfamiliar, see General Information, pages 481-506.

Heat the 4 tbs oil in a nonstick or well-seasoned 8-in/20-cm frying pan over a medium flame. When hot, pour in the egg mixture. Now, working quickly with a spatula, collect the solids in the centre. As the liquid flows to the outer edges and sets slightly, fold it over the centre. Keep doing this on all sides until you have a 6-in/15-cm, cake-like omelette. Turn the heat down and cover. The omelette may turn slightly brown at the bottom. It should definitely set properly and not be runny in the middle. This will take about 2 minutes. Using one large or two smaller spatulas, turn the cake over and cook the second side on low heat for a couple of minutes.

Put the omelette cake into the centre of a warm serving platter. Add the peas to the warm sauce and spoon about half the sauce over the omelette. The rest of the sauce may be served separately.

DATÉMAKI
(Japanese Rolled Omelette)
JAPAN   (serves 4–6 as an appetizer)

Datémaki is a very delicate Japanese omelette that is made up of several rolled layers. It looks initially like a log and, in the shops in Japan that specialize in the product, it is sold in various sizes. The logs are then sliced into 'wheels' and served as appetizers, first courses, or on top of rice for lunch. A dipping sauce is often served with them.

This omelette is traditionally made in rectangular frying pans. I have one that might be considered small − about 5 in/13 cm wide, 7½ in/20 cm long, and 1 in/2½ cm in height. If you cannot obtain a rectangular frying pan, use a 6-in/15-cm circular nonstick frying pan. Increase the number of eggs in the recipe to four, and trim the omelettes to the correct shape.

3 large eggs   ¼ tsp Japanese soy sauce
2 fl oz/½ dl dashi (see page 339) or   ¼ tsp sugar
  any vegetable stock   About 2 tbs vegetable oil
⅛–¼ tsp salt, or to taste

Beat the eggs lightly in a bowl. Add the dashi, salt, soy sauce, and sugar. Mix.

1. Brush a 5×7½-in/13×20-cm datémaki frying pan with oil and let it heat on a lowish flame.

2. When hot, pour in about 3 tbs of batter. Tilt the frying pan to

spread it around evenly. It should cover the entire bottom of the pan. Let the batter set.

3. Now roll it towards you in as tight a roll as you can manage. You may use chopsticks or a spatula to do this. Brush the frying pan again with oil.

4. Push the roll away from you so it rests at the far end of the frying pan. Brush the end near you with oil.

5. Pour in another 3 tbs of batter and spread it around, lifting the roll a little so the batter can flow under it. Let this second layer set. Now roll towards you again, this time incorporating the new layer. The first roll will now be inside the second one. Push the roll towards the far end of the frying pan. Keep repeating this process until all the batter is used up. Remove the hot roll from the frying pan and place it at one end of a bamboo *sudare* mat. Roll the mat tightly around the *datémaki* and set aside to cool. The omelette will pick up the ridges obligingly provided by the bamboo strips. To serve, remove the mat and slice the omelette, crosswise, into ⅓-in/ 1-cm thick wheels. Offer Japanese Dipping Sauce (see page 415) as an accompaniment.

1   2

NIGIRI-ZUSHI
(Sushi Rice with Datémaki)
JAPAN

To make *nigiri-zushi*, make small ovals of Sushi Rice (see page 145), using about 1½ tbs of rice for each oval. Wet your hands to help you form the ovals more easily. Dab a little *wasabi* (see page 417) on top of each oval. Balance a slice of *datémaki* over the *wasabi* and serve with a little soy sauce and some pickled ginger, *amazu shoga* (available in Japanese shops).

KOOKOOS

These are thick Persian versions of the omelette which sometimes border on being soufflés. Several eggs are beaten and then combined with herbs and/or vegetables. The mixture is cooked slowly in a frying pan on top of the cooker (this is the more traditional method) until it acquires a slightly crusty bottom. Then it is turned over to cook on the second side. The pie-like omelette is cut into wedges and served hot, warm, or even cold. It is considered excellent picnic fare and is usually accompanied by yogurt. *Kookoos* can also be made in the oven.

Like omelettes, *kookoos* may be cooked with all manner of vegetables and herbs. I have given recipes here for *kookoos* with smoked aubergine, with fresh herbs, with cauliflower, with courgette, and with tomatoes and spring onions. You can make your own combinations using asparagus, green peas (purée them), mushrooms, and green peppers.

Well-seasoned omelette pans or nonstick frying pans are the ideal utensils for cooking *kookoos* on top of the cooker. When I bake the soufflé-like *kookoos* in the oven, I use a nonstick cake tin.

KOOKOO WITH CAULIFLOWER AND PARSLEY
IRAN
(serves 6)

This *kookoo* is a great favourite with my family. We often have it for Sunday lunches, accompanied by a green salad, French bread, and lots of tea. Leftovers, if any, are covered and refrigerated. Then a hungry child coming in later, saying, 'What is there to eat in the house?' can be led directly to a wedge of cauliflower *kookoo*.

I make the *kookoo* in a nonstick frying pan that measures 7½ in/ 20 cm in diameter at the bottom and 10 in/2½ cm across the top. So my *kookoo* ends up being a little over 1 in/2½ cm high at its centre and it takes 25 easy minutes of cooking time. If your frying pan has a different set of measurements, you may have to adjust your cooking time and your heat. Remember that the *kookoo* should turn a brown colour on the bottom, it should be somewhat crisp at the edges, and the top should end up with brown specks on it. And, of course, it should cook through. *Kookoos* are not runny in the centre. Instead, they are slightly spongy.

You will need only half a medium-sized head of cauliflower to make this dish. A 2-lb/900-g head may be considered a medium-sized head, I suppose. At any rate, use a 1-lb/450-g section of cauliflower.

1lb/450 g cauliflower (see note
   above)
1 tbs plus ¾ tsp salt
2 tbs vegetable oil
3 cloves garlic, peeled and finely
   chopped

2 finely sliced spring onions,
   including green
Freshly ground black pepper
7 large eggs
¾ tsp bicarbonate of soda
2 tbs finely chopped parsley
1 tbs unsalted butter

Break the cauliflower up into flowerets, about 1½ in/4 cm at the top and 1½–2 in/4–5 cm long.

Bring 3 qt/3½ l of water to the boil in a 4½-qt/5-l pot. Add 1 tbs salt to it. When the water is at a rolling boil, drop in the flowerets of cauliflower. Boil rapidly for about 2 minutes. The cauliflower should be cooked through but still crunchy. Drain the cauliflower, run it quickly under cold water while still in the sieve or colander, let it drain thoroughly again, and then chop it.

Heat oil in an 8-in/20-cm frying pan over medium heat. When hot, put in the chopped garlic. Stir garlic around for about 20 seconds. Now put in the spring onions. Stir and cook for another 30 seconds. Add the chopped cauliflower, ½ tsp salt, and a generous amount of freshly ground black pepper. Stir and cook for about 2 to 3 minutes. Turn off the heat and let the cauliflower cool slightly.

Beat the eggs well in a large bowl. Add ¼ tsp salt, some black pepper, and the bicarbonate of soda. Mix thoroughly. Add the cauliflower and the parsley. Mix again.

Heat the butter in a nonstick frying pan that is about 7½ in/20 cm wide at the bottom (see note above) over a low flame. When hot, pour in the egg–cauliflower mixture. Cover, and let the *kookoo* cook for 20 minutes. It should now be brown on the bottom and slightly crisp at the edges. Turn the *kookoo* over. I just slide a plastic spatula under the *kookoo*, lift it up 1 in/2½ cm, tilt the frying pan, and turn the *kookoo* over, using the side of the pan as an aid. If you are unsure about turning over such a large, thick 'pie', you can put a plate over your frying pan and then flip the pan over the plate so that the *kookoo* lands on the plate with its bottom side up. You can then slide the *kookoo* back into the frying pan.

Cook the *kookoo* on the second side, uncovered, also on low heat, for about 5 minutes, or until it develops brown spots.

Put the pie-like *kookoo* on a plate, brown side down, and serve hot, warm or cold, cut into wedges.

KOOKOO WITH COURGETTE, DILL, AND SULTANAS
IRAN   *(serves 6)*

I make this *kookoo* in a nonstick frying pan that measures 7½ in/ 20 cm in diameter at the bottom and 10 in/25 cm across at the top, so my *kookoo* ends up being about 1 in/2½ cm high in the centre and takes about 20 minutes of cooking time. If your frying pan has a different set of measurements, you may have to adjust your cooking time and your heat. Remember that your *kookoo* should turn a brownish colour on the bottom, it should be somewhat crisp at the edges, and the top should end up with brown specks on it. And, of course, it should cook through. *Kookoos* are not runny in the centre. Instead, they are slightly spongy.

2 tbs sultanas	½ tsp bicarbonate of soda
2 medium-sized courgettes	5 tbs finely chopped fresh dill
(¾ lb/340 g in all), trimmed	2 finely sliced spring onions,
and grated	including green
1 tsp salt	1 tbs unsalted butter
7 large eggs	

For information about ingredients and basic techniques that may be unfamiliar, see General Information, pages 481-506.

Soak the sultanas in 8 fl oz/¼ l hot water for 1 hour. Put the grated courgette and ¾ tsp salt into a bowl. Mix well and set aside for half an hour.

After half an hour, take small amounts of the grated courgette between your two palms and squeeze out as much moisture as possible. Do all the courgette this way and set aside.

Beat the eggs well in a large bowl. Add ¼ tsp salt, the bicarbonate of soda, drained sultanas, dill, and spring onions. Mix. Now add the courgette and mix it in, making sure that it has not bunched up anywhere but is well distributed.

Heat the butter in a 7½-in/20-cm-wide (measured at the bottom), nonstick frying pan over a low flame. When hot, pour in the egg–courgette mixture. Cover, and let the *kookoo* cook for 15 minutes. It should now be brown at the bottom and slightly crisp at the edges. Now turn the *kookoo* over. I just slide a plastic spatula under the *kookoo*, lift it up 1 in/2½ cm, tilt the frying pan, and turn the *kookoo* over, using the side of the pan as an aid. If you are unsure about turning over such a large, thick pie, you can put a plate over your frying pan and then flip the pan over the plate so that the *kookoo* lands on the plate with its bottom side up. You can then slide the *kookoo* back into the frying pan.

Cook the *kookoo* on the second side, uncovered, also on low heat, for about 5 minutes, or until it develops brown spots. Put the pie-like *kookoo* on a plate, with its brown side down. Now cut it, just like a pie, into wedges. Serve hot, warm, or cool.

KOOKOO WITH POTATOES

IRAN   (serves 6)

2 medium-sized potatoes
Salt
Freshly ground black pepper
3 tbs vegetable oil
8 eggs

½ tsp bicarbonate of soda
2 tbs finely chopped fresh parsley
2 spring onions, cut into fine
    slices halfway up their green
    sections

Peel the potatoes and slice them crosswise very, very thin, just as you would for potato crisps. I use a mandolin to do this slicing. Starting from the outside and going around in rings of overlapping slices, line the bottom of a 7–8-in/18–20-cm nonstick frying pan with the cut potatoes. Not only should the slices overlap as you build each ring, but the rings should overlap slightly as well. Sprinkle about ⅛ tsp salt and some black pepper over the potatoes. Dribble the oil over them. Set the frying pan over a low flame, cover and cook for 10 minutes.

Meanwhile, beat the eggs well. Add the bicarbonate of soda, parsley, spring onions, as well as ½ tsp salt and some black pepper. Mix. Pour this egg mixture over the potatoes. Cover tightly and continue to cook over low heat for 20 minutes.

Slide the *kookoo* on to a round serving platter. Cut into wedges and serve hot, at room temperature, or cold.

KOOKOO MADE WITH SPICY, INDIAN-STYLE TOMATOES

(serves 6)

Spicy Tomato Sauce (see page 229)　½ tsp bicarbonate of soda
7 large eggs　1 tbs unsalted butter
⅛–¼ tsp salt, or to taste　1 tbs lightly roasted sesame seeds

Let the tomato sauce cool and come to room temperature.

Beat the eggs well with a fork or a whisk in a large bowl. Add the salt (I usually need a little less than ¼ tsp), bicarbonate of soda and the tomato sauce. Mix well.

Heat the butter in a nonstick, 7–8-in/18–20-cm frying pan over a low flame. Pour in the egg–tomato combination. Cover, and proceed to make the *kookoo* as in the recipe for Kookoo with Courgette, Dill, and Sultanas (see page 238) *but with this difference*: after the *kookoo* has cooked for 6 minutes, lift the lid, quickly sprinkle the sesame seeds over the top, and cover again. Follow all the other steps in the recipe, including the turning over of the *kookoo*, in exactly the same way.

Like all *kookoos*, this may be served hot, warm, or cold. Put the pie-like *kookoo* on a plate with its brown side down and cut it, just like a pie, into wedges.

KOOKOO WITH ROASTED AUBERGINE
IRAN　*(serves 4–6)*

Aubergines roasted over flames have their own very special smoky taste. In my New York apartment, I do this roasting over a gas burner fitted with an aluminium-foil liner. You could also do the roasting under a grill. As the aubergine can burst, it is a good idea to prick it all over with a fork first.

For information about ingredients and basic techniques that may be unfamiliar, see General Information, pages 481-506.

1 medium-sized aubergine (about
   ¾ lb/340 g)
2–3 tsp lemon juice
½ tsp salt
2 tbs very finely chopped parsley

2 tbs very finely sliced spring
   onions
2 tsp melted unsalted butter or
   vegetable oil
6 large eggs at room temperature
Freshly ground black pepper

Prick the aubergine in 5 to 6 places with a fork. Now lay the aubergine directly over or under a flame. If you are roasting on top of the cooker, keep the heat on low. If you are roasting under the grill, keep the aubergine a little distance from the heat. As one side gets charred, turn the aubergine over slightly, using a pair of tongs to do so. Do the entire aubergine this way. It should get very limp by the time it finishes roasting, which may take about 25 minutes.

Peel the aubergine under cold, running water and leave to drain in a colander for 5 minutes. Chop the aubergine and put it in a large bowl. Add the lemon juice and about ¼ tsp salt. Adjust the salt and lemon juice according to your taste. Now add the parsley and spring onion. Mix and set aside.

Preheat oven to 350° F/180° C/Mark 4. Brush a nonstick round cake tin, 9 × 1½ in/23 × 4 cm, with the butter or oil.

Separate the eggs. Beat the yolks well. Add ¼ tsp salt and pepper to them. Mix. Fold the beaten egg yolks into the aubergine.

Beat the egg whites until they stand in stiff peaks (just as you would for a soufflé). Empty the egg whites on top of the aubergine–egg yolk mixture. Using a rubber spatula, fold the egg whites gently into the aubergine–egg yolk mixture, taking care not to deflate them. When well mixed, pour the contents of the large bowl into the cake tin. Put the cake tin in the oven and bake for 45 minutes.

This particular kookoo does rise like a soufflé and is a delicate treat if eaten the second it comes out of the oven. However, it is still very good a few (or several) hours later, eaten warm or cold. Plain yogurt or yogurt relishes are always served with kookoos.

EGG STRANDS
ALL OF EAST AND SOUTH-EAST ASIA   (makes about 1 large cupful)

These strands, used mainly for garnishing and salads, may be seasoned before being cooked with sugar and salt, or they may be left unseasoned, depending upon how they are to be used. I use a nonstick frying pan to make the initial pancakes but you could also try a very well-seasoned cast-iron frying pan.

3 large eggs
1½ tsp sugar

About ⅛ tsp salt
About 2 tsp vegetable oil

Combine the eggs, sugar, salt, and 3 tsp water and beat well but not to a froth.

Brush a 7–8-in/18–20-cm nonstick frying pan lightly with about ½ tsp oil and heat on a medium flame. When hot, but not smoking, 1. pour in a quarter of the egg mixture, just enough barely to cover the bottom of the frying pan. You will have to tilt the pan around quickly in order to let the egg mixture flow evenly to the edges. Let the mixture set, which it will do quite quickly. 2. Now turn the pancake over carefully. I loosen the edges first with a flexible spatula, then ease the spatula to the middle of the pancake before flipping it over. Cook for a few seconds on the other side, just until it is firm. Remove the pancake and put it on a plate. Cover loosely with waxed paper or aluminium foil and leave to cool. Make 4 pancakes this way, putting each on its own plate for faster cooling.

1   2

3. Roll up each pancake and 4. cut it crosswise at ⅛-in/½-cm intervals. Put the egg strands in a closed container. They may now be used to garnish rice and noodle dishes, soups, vegetables, and salads.

For information about ingredients and basic techniques that may be unfamiliar, see General Information, pages 481-506.

3   4

EGG BUNDLES
KOREA   *(serves 4–6)*

Here rectangular egg 'pancakes' are cut into neat strips and the strips tied into bundles with blanched spring onions. This dish, served with a dipping sauce, is as pretty as it is tasty and makes an excellent first course for almost any kind of dinner. The bundles are made in the rectangular frying pans which are widely used in Korea and Japan to make a vast variety of dishes. You are unlikely to be able to buy a rectangular frying pan in this country, so use a 6-in/15-cm crêpe pan or a 6-in/15-cm nonstick frying pan. Increase the number of eggs to 5 and be prepared for some waste. After the two egg 'pancakes' are made, trim the edges so you have a neat square.

4 large eggs   *12 spring onions, trimmed and*
2 tsp vegetable oil   *washed*
2 tsp salt

Beat the eggs but not to a froth. Put 1 tsp of oil into the frying pan. Spread it around and heat it over a medium-low flame. When hot, pour in half the beaten eggs. Turn heat to low and cover loosely (with aluminium foil, if necessary). Cook for 5 to 6 minutes or until the bottom of the 'pancake' is no longer soft. Ease a spatula under the 'pancake' and turn it over. Cook the other side for 2 to 3 minutes or until it, too, is firm. Remove the 'pancake'. Add another tsp of oil to the frying pan and make the second 'pancake' the same way. Allow both 'pancakes' to cool. Then cut them into strips that are about 2½ in/6½ cm long and ¼ in/¾ cm wide.

Bring 2 qt/2¼ l of water to a rolling boil in a 4-qt/4½-l pot. Add the salt. Put the spring onions, bulbs first, into the water. Like spaghetti, the upper ends of the spring onions will have to be eased into the water as they soften. Boil rapidly for 2 minutes. You may have to hold the spring onions down with a spoon so they stay submerged. Drain the spring onions in a colander and rinse immediately under cold running water. Pat the spring onions dry. Split each spring onion lengthwise into two or more strands by first cutting the bulb with a knife and then tearing upwards.

Now put four egg strips together to form a neat bundle. Place the bulb end of a spring onion strip on the centre of the bundle and then wrap round and round over it. Tuck the end of the strand underneath the binding. It will hold. Make as many bundles as you can this way.

Arrange bundles prettily on a round or rectangular platter. If not to be eaten immediately, cover dish with cling film and refrigerate for a few hours. Korean Dipping Sauce Number 2 (see page 415) should be served as an accompaniment.

Jhab's
PARSI-STYLE EGGS WITH OKRA
(Bhinda par Inda)
INDIA   (serves 6)

The Parsis of western India are ancient immigrants from Persia and, like modern Iranis, love eggs in all forms. They often break eggs over cooked okra and then bake them until they are done. The eggs are sometimes beaten before being put over the okra, and at other times they are left whole with their yolks intact. This egg dish can also be cooked on top of the cooker and that is how I have chosen to do it.

Make the okra according to the recipe for Whole Okra (see page 58) *but with this difference*: after trimming the okra, cut it into ⅓-in/1-cm rounds. Now proceed with the recipe. Keep the okra warm in an 8-in/20-cm frying pan.

6 large eggs   ¹⁄₁₆ tsp freshly ground black pepper
⅛ tsp salt   Okra cooked as described above

For information about ingredients and basic techniques that may be unfamiliar, see General Information, pages 481-506.

Separate the eggs. Put the whites into a large bowl and beat with a whisk until soft peaks form. Put the yolks into another large bowl and beat until smooth. Add the salt and pepper to the yolks and beat once more. Empty the egg whites over the yolks. Fold the egg whites gently into the yolks with a rubber spatula.

Pour the eggs over the okra. Cover and cook on low heat until the eggs have set to the desired consistency. Serve the portions straight from the frying pan.

SOY-SAUCE EGGS
THAILAND/CHINA   *(makes 4 eggs)*

These eggs may be eaten for breakfast with rice or congee or as snacks. They may also be taken on picnics.

4 large hard-boiled eggs, peeled
2 tbs vegetable oil
3–4 cloves garlic, peeled and
  mashed to a pulp

2 fl oz/½ dl Chinese dark soy sauce
2 tbs dark brown sugar

Using a very sharp, pointed knife, score the eggs lengthwise in such a way that the scored lines are at ¼-in/¾-cm intervals at the widest part of the egg. Do not let the lines meet anywhere. Instead, stop before you reach the top or bottom of the egg.

Put the oil in a small, 1½-qt/1¾-l pot and heat over a medium flame. Put in the garlic. Stir and fry until it browns lightly. Now add the soy sauce and sugar. Bring to a simmer and mix. Turn heat to low. Add the eggs and continue to simmer and cook over low heat. As you do this, turn the eggs around again and again and spoon some sauce over them as well. Make sure that they pick up the soy-sauce colour evenly. Keep doing this until the soy sauce is reduced to a thick syrup. Remove the eggs from the syrup. The eggs should either be eaten as soon as they are made or put in a tightly covered container so that they do not harden.

HARD-BOILED EGGS WITH
STRAW MUSHROOMS
THAILAND/INDONESIA   *(serves 4 with other dishes)*

1 whole hot dried red pepper, or
  more to taste
1 tsp sliced, dried lemon grass
4 tbs vegetable oil
2 oz/55 g finely chopped, peeled
  shallots

2 cloves garlic, peeled and finely
  chopped
A ¾-in/2-cm cube of peeled fresh
  ginger, finely chopped

8 fl oz/¼ l *Spicy Tomato Sauce,*
  homemade (see page 229) or
  4 tbs tomato purée mixed with
  6 fl oz/1¾ dl water
4 oz/115 g *drained, tinned straw*
  mushrooms

1 tbs *lime or lemon juice*
8 fl oz/¼ l *coconut milk, fresh or*
  tinned
1¼ tsp *salt, or to taste*
2 tsp *sugar*
4 *large hard-boiled eggs, peeled*

Put the red pepper and lemon grass into the container of a clean coffee grinder and grind until fairly fine.

Over a medium flame, heat the oil in a 7–8-in/18–20-cm sauté pan or frying pan. Put in the shallots, garlic, and ginger, as well as the red pepper–lemon grass mixture. Stir and fry for 4 to 5 minutes or until shallots are very lightly browned. Now put in the tomato sauce, straw mushrooms, lime juice, coconut milk, salt, and sugar. Stir and bring to a simmer. Turn heat to low and simmer gently for 7 to 8 minutes.

Meanwhile, using a sharp, pointed knife, score the eggs lengthwise in such a way that the scored lines are at ¼-in/¾-cm intervals at the widest part of the egg. Do not let the lines meet. Instead, stop ¼ in/¾ cm before you reach the top or bottom of the egg.

Put the eggs into the sauté pan and spoon some of the sauce over them. Simmer gently for 5 minutes, spooning the sauce over the eggs again and again.

EGGS, POTATOES, AND CAULIFLOWER
INDIA   *(serves 4–6)*

This dish can be made ahead of time and reheated. I love it with Uppama and Yogurt with Chick Peas and Tomatoes (see pages 185 and 258).

1 lb/450 g *cauliflower (½ small*
  head)
4 oz/115 g *freshly grated coconut*
2½ tsp *salt*
2 *smallish tomatoes (¼ lb/115 g),*
  peeled
A 1-in/2½-cm *cube of fresh*
  ginger, peeled and cut into 3 or
  4 pieces
6–7 *cloves garlic, peeled*
4 tbs *vegetable oil*
½ tsp *whole fenugreek seeds*
A 1-in/2½-cm *stick of cinnamon*

1 *medium-sized onion, peeled and*
  finely chopped
1–2 *fresh hot green chillies, finely*
  chopped
½ tsp *ground turmeric*
5–6 *fresh curry leaves, if available,*
  or 10 dried ones
2 *medium-sized potatoes, boiled,*
  cooled, peeled, and cut into
  ¾-in/2-cm dice
4 *hard-boiled eggs, peeled and cut*
  in half crosswise
2 tbs *lemon juice*
½ tsp garam masala

Break the cauliflower into flowerets 1½ in/4 cm long and ¾ in/2 cm at the top.

Put the coconut into the container of a food processor or blender and turn the machine on. Slowly add 8 fl oz/¼ l hot water. Let the machine run for 1 minute. Strain this mixture through a double thickness of cheesecloth, squeezing out as much liquid as you can. This is the first coconut milk. Set it aside.

Put the coconut that remains in the cheesecloth back into the processor or blender and repeat the process with another 8 fl oz/¼ l of hot water. After this coconut milk has been strained, set it aside separately from the first. This is the second coconut milk.

Bring about 4 qt/4½ l of water to a rolling boil in a large pot. Add 1 tsp salt to the water. Drop in the cauliflower. Let the water return to the boil and then boil rapidly for 30 seconds. Drain the cauliflower and rinse it immediately under cold running water.

Dice the tomatoes into ¼-in/¾-cm pieces.

Put the ginger, garlic, and 2 fl oz/½ dl water into the container of a blender or food processor and blend until you have a paste.

Heat the oil in a 9–10-in/23–25-cm sauté or frying pan over a medium flame. When hot, first put in the fenugreek seeds and, a couple of seconds later, the cinnamon stick. Now put in the onion. Stir and fry on medium heat for about 2 minutes. Add the ginger–garlic paste and the finely chopped chilli. Stir and fry for another minute. Add the tomatoes, turmeric, and curry leaves. Keep stirring and frying for 2 minutes. Now add half of the second coconut milk, cover, turn heat to low and simmer for 10 minutes.

Uncover, add the potatoes, cauliflower, 1½ tsp salt, and the remaining half of the second coconut milk. Stir gently to mix and bring to a simmer. Cover, and simmer on low heat for 5 minutes, stirring once or twice during this period. Uncover again and put in the halved eggs, cut side up, the first coconut milk, and the lemon juice. Mix very gently, spooning the sauce over the eggs. Cover and simmer another 5 minutes. Sprinkle in the *garam masala*. Mix gently.

Jyothi's
EGGS PULUSU
INDIA   *(serves 4 with other dishes)*

Here is a simple, exceedingly pleasant dish from South India that may be eaten with rice, or, as one of my daughters seems to prefer, on slices of toasted bread.

1 tsp ground cumin seeds
1 tsp ground coriander seeds
½ tsp ground turmeric
¼ tsp cayenne pepper
3 tbs vegetable oil

1 medium-sized onion, peeled and
  finely chopped
2 tbs tamarind paste
1 tsp salt
4 large hard-boiled eggs, peeled
  and cut in half crosswise

Mix together the cumin, coriander, turmeric and cayenne in a small cup.

Over a medium-low flame, heat the oil in a sauté or frying pan that is about 7–8 in/18–20 cm wide. Put in the onion. Sauté, stirring, for about 5 minutes. Put in the spice mixture and sauté for another minute. Now put in the tamarind paste, 8 fl oz/¼ l water, and the salt. Cover and simmer on low heat for 2 to 3 minutes. Put in the eggs, cut side up, and spoon some of the sauce over them. Cook the eggs gently for 3 to 4 minutes, spooning the sauce over them again and again.

HARD-BOILED EGGS IN A SPICY ALMOND SAUCE
INDIA
(serves 4)

You may eat this dish with rice or with any bread. I often have it for lunch or dinner with thick slices of French bread and a green salad.

1 oz/30 g blanched, slivered
  almonds
2 tsp whole cumin seeds
2 tbs white poppy seeds
1 tsp ground coriander seeds
1 whole dried hot red pepper
5 tbs vegetable oil
3 whole cardamom pods
1 medium-sized onion, peeled and
  finely chopped
4 cloves garlic, peeled and finely
  chopped

A ¾-in cube of fresh ginger, peeled
  and finely chopped
2 fl oz/½ dl plain yogurt
2 fl oz/½ dl Spicy Tomato Sauce,
  (see page 229) or 1 tbs tomato
  purée mixed with 3 tbs water
1 tsp salt, or to taste
4 fl oz/1 dl single cream
1 tbs lemon juice
½ tsp garam masala
4 hard-boiled eggs, peeled and cut
  in half crosswise

Put the almonds in a small, heavy frying pan (cast iron would be best) and stir them around over medium-low heat until they are lightly browned. Then put them into the container of a clean coffee grinder and pulverize them. Remove from coffee grinder.

For information about ingredients and basic techniques that may be unfamiliar, see General Information, pages 481–506.

Put 1 tsp of the cumin seeds, the poppy seeds, coriander seeds, and red pepper into the same frying pan. Stir and dry-roast over medium-low heat until the poppy seeds are a few shades darker (they turn greyish) and a pleasant 'roasted' aroma arises from the frying pan. This takes just a few minutes. Put these spices in the coffee grinder and pulverize. Leave in coffee grinder.

Heat the oil in a 7–8-in/18–20-cm sauté or frying pan over a medium flame. When hot put in the remaining 1 tsp cumin seeds and the whole cardamom pods. Stir and fry for a few seconds until the cardamoms turn a darker shade. Put in the finely chopped onion, garlic, and ginger. Stir and fry for about 5 minutes or until the onion mixture is lightly browned. Now put in 1 tbs of the yogurt. Stir and cook for about 30 seconds or until the yogurt is incorporated into the onion mixture. Add the remaining yogurt 1 tbs at a time in exactly the same way. Now put in the tomato sauce, also 1 tbs at a time, incorporating it into the sauce each time just as you did the yogurt. Put in the ground spices sitting in the coffee grinder and stir for 10 seconds. Put in the ground almonds and stir for another 10 seconds. Add 8 fl oz/¼ l water and the salt. Bring to a simmer. Cover, turn heat to very low and simmer gently for 5 minutes.

Add the cream, lemon juice and *garam masala*. Stir to mix. Simmer, uncovered, on very low heat for 4 to 5 minutes. Put the eggs into the sauce, cut side up, laying them out in a single layer. Spoon some sauce over them. Simmer the eggs very gently for 7 to 8 minutes, spooning the sauce over them frequently as you do so. Spoon off any oil that rises to the top.

6 *Milk Products*

Just as products of the soy bean, such as soy milk and bean curd, help sustain vegetarians in East Asia, products made out of milk give nutritional balances to most vegetarian meals in South Asia. And these products are as varied as those derived from the soy bean.

It would be quite conceivable for an Indian to eat, say, a soft yogurt cheese flavoured with fresh green coriander for breakfast, have a cumin-flavoured glass of buttermilk as a mid-morning snack, have *paneer* (milk-cheese cubes) and peas for lunch, and have a steamed yogurt custard with dinner. Oh yes, I forgot tea-time. For tea, the entire family might go out to the bazaar and eat *dahi-baras* out of disposable leaf-plates. *Dahi-baras* are fried, split-pea patties that are dunked in beaten yogurt, showered with ground spices, and then served with a generous swirl of a brown, hot, sweet, and sour tamarind-mint chutney.

Yogurt itself is eaten in so many different ways. When sweetened and flavoured with saffron, it becomes the West Indian *shrikhand;* when beaten together with grated cucumber and mint, it becomes a North Indian *raita;* when added to sautéed courgette, it becomes a South Indian accompaniment for rice; and when mixed with gram flour, it becomes the all-Indian *karhi. Karhis* are a very interesting food. They may be thick or thin but are always soup-like. They may well have originated with the desire to have a heated yogurt dish. Yogurt, of course, curdles when it is heated, disintegrating into the most inedible particles. The way to avoid this is to blend it with some flour before it is cooked. In India, this flour is invariably gram flour, as it has so much flavour of its own. After the basic *karhi* is made, it is enriched with spices, vegetables, and sometimes even dumplings. Today, nothing evokes my childhood more than the sight of two big bowls, one containing steaming hot *karhi*, and the other, steaming hot *basmati* rice.

There are many dishes made with heated yogurt in the Middle East as well. The grandest of them all, I think, is Stuffed Courgettes in a Hot Yogurt Sauce. A whole courgette is stuffed with an absolutely delicious mixture of bulgar wheat, red lentils, tomatoes, and parsley. It is steamed lightly, cut into thick rounds, and then served with a hot yogurt sauce that is stabilized, not with gram flour, but with a small amount of corn flour.

YOGURT
For those of us who have grown up with it, yogurt is a protein-rich,

easy-to-digest, tasty, versatile food that may be eaten plain or used in the making of soups, cold drinks, breads, sauces, relishes, and all manner of main dishes. But while all of us in West, Central, and South Asia — the regions where yogurt has always been abundantly eaten — believe that yogurt, especially when combined with milled rice, has a very settling effect on queasy stomachs, we have not endowed it with any greater powers. Nor do we fuss and fret when we make it — an activity that is carried on in our homes on a daily basis. We take it for granted that on some days the yogurt will turn out excellently and that on other days it will not be quite as good. On hot days it will set quickly and sour easily, while on cold days we may almost have to pray to get it to set and its taste might remain colourlessly bland. At least once a month my brother in India turns to his wife at the dining table, just as I remember my father and grandfather doing, and makes a bit of a face. 'So,' he says, 'your yogurt didn't turn out too well?' She, just as my mother and grandmother before her, grunts as if to say, how little you understand, and goes on eating. Of course there are no thermometers for yogurt in Asia but then neither are there great pangs of anxiety. In my family, yogurt has always been made as the last thing at night. After that everyone goes to sleep and just *expects* to have yogurt for lunch the following day.

Here are some things to keep in mind when making yogurt:

Use a good starter. This starter consists of a few tablespoons of yogurt, commercial or homemade. The quality of your own yogurt will depend on the taste, freshness, and sourness of your starter. Pick a starter from a yogurt you like. In Asia, good starters are often 'borrowed' from neighbours.

You may make your yogurt from whole milk, skimmed milk, or reconstituted dried milk.

Yogurt sets best at a temperature of 85–100° F/29–38° C. If you do not have an electric yogurtmaker, see how you can approximate this temperature. You could use the oven of your cooker with the pilot light turned on, you could wrap your yogurt bowl loosely in an electric blanket, or you could find a warm spot in your attic or basement.

MAKING YOUR OWN YOGURT

(makes 1½ pt/8½ dl)

1½ pt/8½ dl milk
2 tbs plain yogurt

Put the milk in a heavy pot and bring to the boil. As soon as the milk begins to rise, turn the heat to very low and simmer for a minute. Turn the heat off and let the milk cool to anywhere between 100–110°F/38–43°C. It should feel slightly warm to the touch. A skin will probably form on top of the milk. You may either remove it or just stir it in.

While the milk cools, put the yogurt into a non-metallic bowl. Beat it with a whisk until it is smooth and creamy. When the milk has reached the required temperature, add a tablespoon of it at a time to the yogurt and whisk it in. After you have added 2 fl oz/ ½ dl, the rest may be poured in a bit faster. Keep beating gently as you pour. Now cover the bowl with cling film and then wrap a large, heavy towel all around it in such a way that you do not tilt the bowl in one direction or another. Place the wrapped bowl in an unused oven or other undraughty place for about 8 hours or until set. If you have a pilot light going in the oven, the yogurt is apt to set more quickly — about 6 to 7 hours. Once set, the yogurt should be refrigerated.

The yogurt should be good for at least 4 days. A second batch may be prepared by using 2 tbs of this first batch.

NOTE: You may prepare half this amount of yogurt by halving the ingredients.

YOGURT WITH DILL
IRAN   *(serves 2–4)*

8 fl oz/2¼ dl plain yogurt
⅓–½ tsp salt
2 tbs finely chopped fresh dill

Put the yogurt and salt in a bowl. Beat with a fork or whisk until smooth and creamy. Add the dill and mix. Serve cold.

For information about ingredients and basic techniques that may be unfamiliar, see General Information, pages 481-506.

Alun's
YOGURT WITH GARLIC
TURKEY   *(serves 1–4)*

This yogurt dish may be served as a relish or it may be used as a sauce over cooked vegetables. Of course, it also tastes quite wonderful if eaten plain, with a spoon. Some finely chopped fresh mint may be added to it, if you like.

8 fl oz/2¼ dl plain yogurt   *¹⁄₁₆ tsp freshly ground black pepper*
¼ tsp salt, or to taste   *2 tsp fruity olive oil*
1 clove garlic, mashed to a pulp in
a mortar

Put the yogurt in a bowl. Beat gently with a fork or whisk until smooth and creamy. Now add all the other ingredients. Beat to mix. Cover and chill until needed.

YOGURT WITH CUCUMBER.
SULTANAS, AND ALMONDS
IRAN   *(serves 4–6)*

When almonds are left to soak for some time, they become rather like green almonds – white, tender, crunchy, and quite unlike their more 'nutty' selves. They can be eaten just as they are (I love them that way) or they can be combined with other foods. They taste very nice in this yogurt dish, where they are combined with sultanas and cucumbers. Serve as a snack or as part of a Persian or Indian meal.

15 fl oz/4¼ dl plain yogurt   *1 oz/30 g sultanas, soaked in*
1 tsp salt   *8 fl oz/¼ l hot water for 1 hour*
⅛–¼ tsp freshly ground black   *and then drained*
pepper   *2 tbs halved, blanched almonds,*
A 6-in/15-cm section of cucumber   *soaked in 8 fl oz/¼ l hot water 6*
                                       hours (or overnight) and then
                                       drained

Put the yogurt in a bowl and add the salt and pepper. Beat the yogurt lightly with a fork or whisk until smooth and creamy.
Peel the cucumber and cut it in half lengthwise. Remove the seeds if they are large. Now cut the cucumber into ¼-in/¾-cm dice. Put the diced cucumber as well as the sultanas and almonds into the yogurt. Mix well. Serve chilled.

YOGURT WITH FRESH MINT, SULTANAS, AND WALNUTS

IRAN   *(serves 4–6)*

Have this yogurt as a relish with any Persian or Indian meal. Or serve it in small bowls as a first course.

15 fl oz/4¼ dl plain yogurt
¾ tsp salt
⅛–¼ tsp freshly ground black
* pepper*
4 tbs finely chopped fresh mint
* leaves*

1 oz/30 g sultanas, soaked in
* 8 fl oz/¼ l hot water 1 hour and*
* drained*
2 tbs chopped walnuts

Put the yogurt in a bowl. Add the salt and pepper. Beat the yogurt with a fork or whisk until smooth and creamy. Add all the other ingredients and mix.

YOGURT WITH CUCUMBER AND CRUSHED MUSTARD SEEDS

INDIA   *(serves 4)*

This relish goes well with almost all Indian meals.

8 fl oz/¼ l plain yogurt
½ tsp salt
¹⁄₁₆ tsp freshly ground black pepper
⅛ tsp cayenne pepper, or to taste
2 tbs finely chopped fresh green
* coriander*

1 tsp lightly ground black mustard
* seeds*
A 6-in/15-cm section of cucumber,
* peeled and coarsely grated*

Put the yogurt in a bowl. Beat gently with a thin whisk until creamy. Add all the other ingredients. Mix well and chill.

YOGURT WITH CUCUMBER AND MINT

INDIA   *(serves 6)*

15 fl oz/4¼ dl plain yogurt
A 6-in/15-cm section of cucumber,
* peeled and cut into*
* ¾-in/2-cm dice*
2 tbs finely chopped fresh mint
¾ tsp salt

¾ tsp ground roasted cumin seeds
¼ tsp cayenne pepper (optional)
Freshly ground black pepper
Garnish: 1 small sprig mint

For information about ingredients and basic techniques that may be unfamiliar, see General Information, pages 481-506.

Put the yogurt in a bowl. Beat lightly with a fork or whisk until smooth and creamy. Add the cucumber, mint, salt, ½ tsp of the cumin, ⅛ tsp cayenne, and a little black pepper. Mix. Empty into a serving bowl. Sprinkle the remaining ¼ tsp cumin, ⅛ tsp cayenne, and some black pepper over the top. Plant the mint sprig in the centre.

YOGURT WITH ROASTED AUBERGINE
MIDDLE EAST   (serves 6)

2 spring onions
1 medium-sized aubergine (about
   ¾ lb/340 g)
15 fl oz/4¼ dl plain yogurt
1 clove garlic, peeled and mashed
   to a pulp

3 tbs finely chopped fresh mint
¾–1 tsp salt
2 tbs olive oil
Freshly ground black pepper

Cut the spring onions into paper-thin rounds three-quarters of the way up their green sections. Put in a bowl. Pour 1½ pt/8½ dl of iced water over them. Cover and refrigerate for an hour.

Prick the aubergine in five to six places with a fork. Now lay it directly over or under a flame. If you are roasting it on top of the cooker, keep the heat on low. If you are roasting it under the grill, keep the aubergine a little distance from the heat. As one side gets charred, turn the aubergine over slightly, using a pair of tongs to do so. Roast the entire aubergine this way. It should turn very limp by the time it is done.

Peel the aubergine under cold running water and leave it to drain in a colander for 5 minutes. Then finely chop the flesh.

Put the yogurt in a bowl and beat lightly with a fork or a whisk until smooth and creamy. Add the aubergine, garlic, mint, salt, olive oil, and black pepper. Drain the spring onions and pat dry. Add them to the yogurt and mix.

Serve at room temperature or chilled.

CELERIAC WITH YOGURT
                                                     (serves 4)

I was trying to work out a low-calorie version of celeriac *rémoulade* using yogurt instead of mayonnaise and I came up with this deliciously refreshing recipe. Serve it chilled as a first course or as a salad.

1 celeriac root, about ½ lb/225 g in weight
1 tsp salt
1 tsp lemon juice

8 tbs plain yogurt (low-fat, if preferred)
1 tbs finely chopped parsley
Freshly ground black pepper

Peel the celeriac. Cut it in half, lengthwise. Cut each half into very fine slices and cut the slices into fine, matchstick, julienne strips. Put the strips into a stainless steel or non-metallic bowl. Add ¾ tsp salt and the lemon juice. Toss well and leave for half an hour.

Drain the celeriac strips. Add the yogurt, parsley, ¼ tsp salt, and some freshly ground pepper to them. Mix well, cover, and refrigerate for a couple of hours or overnight, if you so desire.

YOGURT WITH SPINACH AND PARSLEY
MIDDLE EAST   (serves 6)

5 tbs olive oil
1 medium-sized onion, peeled and finely chopped
2 cloves garlic, peeled and mashed to a pulp
4 tbs finely chopped fresh parsley
2 tsp salt

1 tsp sugar
10–16 oz/285–450 g fresh spinach, trimmed and washed or frozen spinach, cooked, drained, squeezed, then finely chopped
15 fl oz/4¼ dl plain yogurt
Freshly ground black pepper

Heat the oil in a 7–8-in/18–20-cm frying pan over a medium flame. Put in the onion. Stir and fry, turning the heat down when necessary, until the onion is soft. If the onion picks up a few specks of brown colour, it will not hurt. Put in the garlic. Stir and sauté for 15 seconds. Put in the parsley and sauté for another 15 seconds. Turn off the heat and allow this mixture to cool in the frying pan.

Bring 3 qt/3½ l of water to a rolling boil in a large pot. Add 1 tsp salt, 1 tsp sugar, and the spinach. Boil rapidly for 2 to 3 minutes. Drain and rinse under cold running water. Squeeze out as much liquid as you can from the spinach and then finely chop it.

Put the yogurt into a bowl and beat it lightly with a fork or a whisk until it is smooth and creamy. Add all the ingredients in the frying pan, the spinach, the remaining 1 tsp salt, and some freshly ground pepper. Mix.

Serve dish chilled or at room temperature.

For information about ingredients and basic techniques that may be unfamiliar, see General Information, pages 481-506.

YOGURT WITH BANANA IN THE GUJARATI STYLE
INDIA   (serves 4)

8 fl oz/2¼ dl plain yogurt
  (preferably whole-milk)
⅓–½ tsp salt
1/16 tsp freshly ground black pepper
½–1 fresh hot green chilli, or to
  taste, very finely chopped
  (optional)

1 tsp sugar
1 firm but ripe medium-sized
  banana, sliced into ¼-in/¾-cm-
  thick rounds

Put the yogurt in a bowl. Beat gently with a whisk until creamy. Add the other ingredients and mix.

Refrigerate until you are ready to eat.

As a slight variation, you might like to add 1 tsp lightly ground black mustard seeds to the yogurt as well. This makes the dish a bit more pungent.

Another possible variation is to substitute for the banana 8 oz/225 g ripe mango that has been peeled and diced into ½-in/1½-cm cubes. If you like, you may add 1 tsp of lightly ground black mustard seeds to this relish as well.

CAULIFLOWER AND PEAS WITH YOGURT
INDIA   (serves 4–6)

This is a lovely, salad-like dish that can almost be eaten by itself as a very light lunch. It can be made several hours ahead of time and refrigerated.

1 lb/450 g cauliflower (half a head)
2¾ tsp salt
2 oz/60 g shelled fresh (or defrosted
  frozen) peas
15 fl oz/4¼ dl plain yogurt

½ tsp ground roasted cumin seeds
1/16 tsp freshly ground black
  pepper, or more to taste
1/16–⅛ tsp cayenne pepper
  (optional)

Break the cauliflower into flowerets that are about 1½ in/4 cm long and 1 in/2½ cm wide at the top.

Bring 1¼ pt/¾ l of water to the boil in a large pot. Add 2 tsp salt. When the water is at a rolling boil, drop in the cauliflower and peas. Boil vigorously for about 2 minutes or until cauliflower is just cooked but still slightly crunchy. Drain vegetables in a sieve and run under cold water to cool off. Leave in the sieve to drain some more.

Put the yogurt in a bowl. Beat it lightly with a fork or whisk until smooth and creamy. Add the remaining ¾ tsp salt, cumin, black pepper, and cayenne. Mix. Fold in the cauliflower and peas. Cover, and refrigerate until ready to eat.

YOGURT WITH POTATOES AND CHICK PEAS IN THE DELHI STYLE
INDIA   *(serves 4–6)*

In Delhi, this combination is generally eaten as a snack but you could serve it as a spicy salad.

1 medium-sized potato (about
  ¼ lb/115 g)
6 oz/180 g homemade (see page
  103) or tinned, drained chick
  peas
15 fl oz/4¼ dl plain yogurt
1–1½ tsp salt

¼ tsp freshly ground black pepper
1 tsp ground roasted cumin seeds
⅛–¼ tsp cayenne pepper ·
½ fresh hot green chilli, finely
  chopped
1 tbs finely chopped fresh green
  coriander

Boil the potato until tender, then peel and cut into ½-in/1½-cm dice.

Put the chick peas in a sieve and wash them well if they are tinned.

Put the yogurt in a bowl. Beat with a fork or whisk until creamy. Now put in the chick peas as well as all the other ingredients. Mix. Check seasonings. You can make this dish as hot as you like. Refrigerate until ready to eat.

If you like, 2 fl oz/½ dl of Tamarind-Mint Chutney for Snack Foods (see page 422) may be swirled over the chick peas before they are served.

YOGURT WITH CHICK PEAS AND TOMATOES
INDIA   *(serves 4–6)*

While tinned chick peas are very convenient to use, saving all the time and labour of soaking and boiling, I cannot say that I like their taste too much for dishes that require no cooking and that are not heavily spiced. However, there is a way to get rid of their tinny taste. I drain the chick peas and wash them thoroughly in cold water. Then I simmer them in water that has been flavoured with spices for a bare 5 minutes, letting them cool in the liquid. If you are in a rush, this extra step may be eliminated.

6 oz/180 g drained, tinned chick
  peas
A 1-in/2½-cm-long stick of
  cinnamon
8 whole cloves
1 tsp whole black peppercorns
1 bay leaf
1 tsp whole cumin seeds
1 tsp whole fennel seeds
1 tsp salt

12 fl oz/3½ dl plain yogurt
2 smallish tomatoes (about ¼ lb/
  115 g), peeled, and cut into
  ¼-in/¾-cm dice
½ tsp ground roasted cumin seeds
⅛ tsp freshly ground black pepper
⅛–¼ tsp cayenne pepper (optional)
1 tbs finely chopped fresh green
  coriander (optional)

Put the chick peas in a strainer under running water and wash them well. Leave to drain in the strainer.

Tie the cinnamon, cloves, peppercorns, bay leaf, cumin, and fennel seeds in a cheesecloth bundle. Bring 1¼ pt/¾ l of water to the boil. Put in the cheesecloth bundle as well as ½ tsp of the salt. Cover, lower heat, and simmer 15 minutes.

Put the chick peas into the simmering liquid and bring to the boil. Cover, lower heat, and simmer for 5 minutes. Uncover and let the chick peas cool in the liquid. Drain.

In a bowl, combine the yogurt, chick peas, tomatoes, the remaining ½ tsp salt, the cumin, black pepper, cayenne, and fresh coriander. Mix. Cover and refrigerate until ready to eat.

YOGURT WITH FRIED OKRA
INDIA   (serves 4)

For this very tasty dish, the yogurt may be prepared, covered, and refrigerated ahead of time. The okra, onions, and green chilli may be sliced ahead of time also. But you do need to fry the vegetables as you do in the recipe for Okra Fried with Onion and Green Chilli just before you eat or else they get too soggy. The frying takes only about 10 minutes.

12 fl oz/3½ dl plain yogurt
½ tsp salt
1/16 tsp freshly ground black pepper

Okra cooked according to recipe for
  Okra Fried with Onion and
  Green Chilli (see page 60)

Put the yogurt in a bowl. Add the salt and black pepper. Beat gently with a fork or whisk until smooth and creamy. Fold in the okra mixture and serve at once.

YOGURT WITH WHITE RADISH
INDIA *(serves 6)*

White radishes are available in most Oriental markets. Sometimes incorrectly labelled 'horse radish', they can be sweet or sharp like their cousins, the red radishes. The taste of this dish will vary according to the pungency of the vegetable. The two radishes used in this recipe were about 1½ in/4 cm in diameter and weighed about 1½ lb/675 g. White radishes of any size will do. This is a South Indian dish.

2 tbs vegetable oil	1 fresh hot green chilli, sliced
1½ tsp whole black mustard seeds	1½ tsp salt
1½ lb/675 g white radish,	3 tbs chopped fresh green coriander
trimmed, peeled, and cut into	15 fl oz/4¼ dl plain yogurt
½-in/1½-cm dice	¹⁄₁₆ tsp freshly ground black pepper

Heat the oil in a saucepan on a medium-high flame. When very hot, put in the mustard seeds. As soon as the seeds begin to pop (this will happen almost immediately), put in the diced radish, green chilli, ½ tsp salt, and 2 tbs water. Stir and bring to a bubble. Cover. Turn heat to very low and steam gently for about 10 minutes or until radish is tender but still somewhat crisp. Add the fresh coriander, stir, and leave uncovered. Let cool slightly.

Put yogurt in a serving bowl. Add 1 tsp salt and the black pepper. Beat with a fork or a whisk until smooth and creamy. Now empty the contents of the saucepan into the bowl. Mix well.

This yogurt dish goes well with most Indian food. It can be served at room temperature or cold.

YOGURT WITH COURGETTES
INDIA *(serves 4–6)*

This is an absolutely wonderful dish that may be served warm or cold. I find that I can eat it by the spoonful, all by itself. I often do!

2 medium-sized courgettes (about	3 tbs vegetable oil
12–14 oz/340–400 g)	1 tsp whole black mustard seeds
¾ tsp salt	¹⁄₁₆ tsp freshly ground black pepper
1 medium-sized onion	¹⁄₁₆ tsp cayenne pepper (use as
12 fl oz/3½ dl plain yogurt	much as you like)

Trim the courgettes and grate them coarsely. Put them in a bowl and sprinkle with ½ tsp salt. Toss to mix and set aside for half an

---

For information about ingredients and basic techniques that may be unfamiliar, see General Information, pages 481-506.

hour. Drain the courgette and press out as much liquid as you can. Separate the shreds so you do not have lumps.

Peel the onion, cut it in half lengthwise, and then cut into fine, half-moon-shaped slices.

Put the yogurt in a bowl. Beat it lightly with a fork or whisk until it is smooth and creamy.

Heat the oil in an 8-in/20-cm frying pan over a medium flame. When hot, put in the mustard seeds. As soon as the mustard seeds begin to pop (this takes just a few seconds), put in the onion. Stir and fry it for about 2 minutes or until the slices are translucent. Add the courgette. Stir and fry for another 3 minutes. Turn off the heat and let the courgette cool slightly. When cooled, fold it into the yogurt. Add the remaining ¼ tsp salt, pepper, and cayenne. If you wish to eat the dish cold, cover and refrigerate it. If you wish to eat it warm, put the yogurt–courgette combination in a double boiler over a low flame. Then heat, stirring in one direction, until warm. *Do not let it boil.*

DAHI-BARAS
(Dal Patties in Yogurt)
INDIA   (makes 12 patties)

In this dish, yogurt, nicely seasoned with salt, pepper, and cumin, is poured over flat patties that look rather like potato cakes. These patties are made out of *urad dal*, a split pea that has been soaked overnight and then ground. In India, this grinding is done on a heavy grinding stone, after which the paste has to be beaten in order to make it somewhat airier. In British kitchens, these two steps can be combined in a food processor or blender.

FOR THE PATTIES
6 oz/170 g urad dal, *picked over, washed, and drained*
¾ tsp salt
⅛ tsp bicarbonate of soda
⅛ tsp cayenne pepper
½ fresh hot green chilli, *coarsely chopped*
Vegetable oil for deep frying

FOR THE YOGURT
1¼ pt/7 dl plain yogurt
1 tsp salt
1 tsp ground roasted cumin seeds

¼ tsp cayenne pepper
Freshly ground black pepper

FOR THE GARNISHING
2 fl oz/1½ dl Tamarind-Mint Chutney for Snack Foods (see page 422), optional
⅛ tsp cayenne pepper
⅛ tsp salt
⅛ tsp ground roasted cumin seeds
Freshly ground black pepper
1 tbs finely chopped fresh green coriander (optional)

Soak the *dal* in 1 qt/11½ dl of water for 13 to 14 hours. Drain. Put in a food processor or blender, add 2 fl oz/½ dl water, the ¾ tsp salt, bicarbonate of soda, ⅛ tsp cayenne, and the green chilli. Blend, pushing down with a rubber spatula, if necessary, until you have a smooth paste. Now let the machine run for another 5 minutes so the mixture gets lighter and airier. Spread out a wet, smooth tea towel (one without ridges) or a wet 16-in/40-cm square torn out from an old, clean sheet, somewhere near the cooker. Put a bowl of water near the cooker as well. Now, working with wet hands, form twelve equal-sized balls and put them down at some distance from each other on the wet cloth. Using wet fingers, press down on the balls to form patties that are about 2½ in/6½ cm in diameter and a little less than ¼ in/¾ cm thick.

Set a large bowl of hot water on or near the cooker.

Put 2 in/5 cm of oil in a wok or frying pan and heat over a medium-low flame. When it is hot, carefully ease one of the patties off the cloth and slip it into the oil. It helps if you lift the cloth under the patty slightly as you do this. Working quickly, put as many patties into the oil as the wok can hold in a single layer. Fry them for 5 to 6 minutes, turning them halfway through, until they are a reddish-golden colour. Remove the patties with a slotted spoon and put them in the hot water. Make all the patties this way. Let them sit in the hot water for 15 to 20 minutes. Then lift out one patty at a time, put it on the palm of one hand and squeeze down gently with the other to expel some of the water. Do the same to all

For information about ingredients and basic techniques that may be unfamiliar, see General Information, pages 481-506.

the patties. Lay the patties out in a single layer on a large serving platter. (You may cover the patties with cling film and refrigerate for several hours.)

Put the yogurt in a bowl and beat lightly with a fork or whisk until smooth and creamy. Add all the other ingredients listed under 'For the yogurt'. Mix. Pour this yogurt over the patties, making sure that some goes under them as well.

If you are using the Tamarind-Mint Chutney, swirl it over the patties in such a way that both the white colour of the yogurt and the brown of the chutney are clearly visible. Sprinkle all the other garnishing ingredients evenly over the top.

This dish is served either at room temperature or cold.

YOGURT WITH GREEN BEANS AND HARICOT BEANS
MIDDLE EAST   (serves 4)

This yogurt dish is served hot, not warm or cold. Heating yogurt can sometimes be problematic, as it curdles easily. But there is an easy solution to this problem, one that is used widely in West and South Asia. Adding a small amount of flour, almost any flour, holds yogurt together, even when it boils.

I have used dried haricot beans for this dish. You could, if you like, use the cooked, tinned variety. Just drain and rinse them.

1½ oz/45 g dried haricot beans, picked over, washed, and drained
2¾ tsp salt
1 tbs olive oil

6 oz/180 g fresh green beans, cut into ¾-in/2-cm-long segments
1¼ tsp cornflour
12 fl oz/3½ dl plain yogurt

1–2 *cloves garlic, peeled and*   *Freshly ground black pepper*
   mashed to a pulp

Put the haricot beans and 1¼ pt/¾ l water in a small pot and bring to
the boil. Cover, lower heat and simmer for 2 minutes. Turn off the
flame and let the pot sit, covered, for 1 hour. Bring the beans to the
boil again. Turn heat to low and simmer, covered, for 45 minutes or
until beans are tender but still retain their shape. Drain. (You could
save the liquid for soup.) Put the beans in the bowl. Add ¼ tsp salt
and the olive oil. Mix.

Bring 2 qt/2¼ l of water to a rapid boil. Add 2 tsp salt and the
green beans. Boil rapidly for 3 to 4 minutes or until beans are just
tender. Drain and rinse under cold running water. Set aside in a
colander.

Put the cornflour in a bowl. Add 1 tbs water and mix. Add the
yogurt. Beat lightly with a fork or whisk until smooth and creamy.

Put the yogurt mixture in a 1½-qt/1¾-l pot and set it over a
medium-low flame. Heat slowly, stirring in one direction as you do
so. When the yogurt starts to bubble, turn heat to low and cook,
still stirring in the same direction, for another 5 minutes. Add the
garlic, ½ tsp salt, some black pepper, the green beans, and the
haricot beans. Stir gently to mix. Cook over a low flame until the
beans are heated through.

SPICED, HEATED YOGURT
INDIA   *(serves 3–4)*

This very tasty dish is traditionally served warm but it may be
served cold. It is normally offered in individual bowls and is eaten
with Indian rice dishes and Indian breads. I sometimes serve it in
quite another way. I use it as a sauce for cooked vegetables. You
could blanch vegetables like cauliflower, green beans, peas, carrots, shredded cabbage, and courgettes in salted water, drain and
then fold them into this yogurt. You could also pour the yogurt
over boiled, diced potatoes and over slices of fried aubergines.

12 fl oz/3½ dl plain yogurt   ½–1 fresh hot green chilli, finely
½ tsp very finely grated ginger   chopped
2 cloves garlic, peeled and mashed   ¼ tsp ground turmeric
   to a pulp   1 tsp ground coriander

---

*For information about ingredients and basic techniques that may be unfamiliar, see General
Information, pages 481-506.*

⅛ tsp cayenne pepper (optional)
3 tbs vegetable oil
¼ tsp whole cumin seeds

1 medium-sized onion, peeled and
   very finely chopped
½ tsp salt
1/16 tsp freshly ground black pepper

Put the yogurt in a bowl. Beat it lightly with a fork or whisk until smooth and creamy.

Put the ginger, garlic, chilli, turmeric, coriander, and cayenne pepper, if you want to use it, in a small bowl with 1 tbs water and mix well.

Heat the oil in a 7–8-in/18–20-cm frying pan over a medium flame. When hot, put in the cumin seeds. A few seconds later, put in the onion. Stir and fry for about 3 minutes. Do not let the onion brown. Now put in all the spices that are in the small cup. Stir and fry for 1 minute. Turn off the heat and let the spice mixture cool. Empty the spices and the frying oil into the bowl with the yogurt. Add the salt and pepper. Mix well. The yogurt may now be heated in a double boiler or it may be put in the frying pan used for cooking the spices and then heated over a low flame. Stir gently *all the time* and *do not let the yogurt come to the boil*. Just heat until the yogurt is warm.

STUFFED COURGETTES IN A
HOT YOGURT SAUCE
MIDDLE EAST   (serves 4)

This is an exceedingly elegant main dish. Bright green courgette halves stuffed with a really delicious mixture of bulgar wheat, red split lentils (called *masoor dal* in Indian stores and Egyptian lentils in some Middle Eastern stores), tomatoes, and parsley are served with a garlicky yogurt sauce.

I use medium-sized courgettes for this, each about ½ lb/225 g in weight, about 7½ in/20 cm long, and about 1½–2 in/4–5 cm in diameter at the centre. If your courgettes are of a different size, you may have to adjust the amount of stuffing and the steaming time. It is useful to know that the courgettes may easily be stuffed ahead of time and refrigerated. All the ingredients for the sauce can also be mixed ahead of time. The final cooking, both of the courgettes and the sauce, may be done simultaneously, about 15 minutes before you sit down to eat.

4 medium-sized courgettes (about   Salt
   2 lb/900 g; see note above)

FOR THE STUFFING
1½ oz/45 g masoor dal
3 oz/85 g fine-grained bulgar
  wheat
3 tbs olive oil
1 medium-sized onion, peeled and
  finely chopped
½ good-sized tomato, peeled and
  finely chopped
1 clove garlic, peeled and mashed
  to a pulp
1 tsp salt

4 tsp lemon juice
2 tbs finely chopped fresh parsley
Freshly ground black pepper

FOR THE YOGURT SAUCE
2 tsp cornflour
1 pt/5¾ dl plain yogurt
1¼ tsp salt, or to taste
1 clove garlic, peeled and mashed
  to a pulp
Freshly ground black pepper

Wash the courgettes well but do not trim the ends. Cut each courgette in half, crosswise. Now, using a grapefruit spoon or something similar, work your way into each courgette half from the cut section and take out all the seeded portion. You should be left with eight hollow shells. Sprinkle about ⅟16 tsp salt into each shell, spreading it about inside. Stand the shells, cut side up, in a bowl. Rub the outsides of the shells with another ¼ tsp salt. Set aside for 1 to 1½ hours.

Meanwhile, pick over the dal, wash and then drain. Put it in a small pot. Add ¾ pt/½ l water and bring to a simmer. Lower heat and simmer gently for 2 minutes. Turn off the heat and let the dal sit, covered, for 45 minutes.

Put the bulgar wheat in a bowl. Cover with 1¼ pt/¾ l water and set aside for 1 hour.

When the dal has finished sitting for 45 minutes, bring it to a simmer again. Turn heat to low and simmer for 10 to 12 minutes or until dal is tender. Drain and put in a bowl. (The liquid may be saved for soup.)

Drain the bulgar wheat and squeeze out as much liquid as you can easily. Put the wheat into the same bowl as the dal.

Heat the olive oil in a 7–8-in/18–20-cm frying pan over a medium flame. Put in the onion and sauté for about 2 minutes. Add the tomato and sauté for another 2 minutes. Put all the contents of the frying pan into the bowl with the lentils and the wheat. Add all the other ingredients for the stuffing as well and mix.

Arrange an apparatus for steaming. I use a large pot to hold a few inches of water and set a colander on top of it. The water should not touch the bottom of the colander. Bring the water in the pot to the boil.

For information about ingredients and basic techniques that may be unfamiliar, see General Information, pages 481-506.

As you wait for this, turn the courgette halves upside down to rid them of any accumulated liquid and then stuff them with the wheat-dal mixture. Once the water is boiling rapidly, stand the courgette halves in the colander, cut side up. Put a cover over the colander and steam for 10 to 15 minutes or until courgette shells are just tender.

While the courgettes steam, make the sauce. Put the cornflour in a bowl. Add 1 tbs water and mix. Add the yogurt. Beat with a fork or whisk until smooth and creamy.

Put the yogurt into a heavy saucepan and set over medium-low heat. Bring to a simmer, stirring constantly in one direction as you do so. When the yogurt begins to bubble, turn heat to low and cook 5 minutes, stirring gently in the same direction. Add all the other ingredients for the yogurt sauce and mix.

Put the courgettes on a serving dish or in individual plates. Spoon some sauce over them.

KARHIS

Karhis are soup-like dishes from India made out of yogurt or buttermilk and gram flour. The gram flour holds the yogurt or buttermilk together and prevents it from curdling as it heats, giving a very special flavour — and nutritional value — to the dish. I adored *karhis* as a child and continue to love them today. Give me a bowl of rice topped with some *karhi* and I begin to purr.

There are different types of *karhis* in India. In western states like Gujarat, *karhis* cook in 10 minutes, are very thin, and generally combine both sweet and tart flavours. Northern *karhis* cook slowly and long, are much thicker — they use more gram flour — and do not have even a hint of sweetness. All *karhis* may be made plain, or with the addition of vegetables and dumplings.

AALAN KA SAAG
(Karhi with Spinach)
INDIA   (serves 8)

I have only had this exceedingly tasty and nutritious dish in my family. It is like a thick soup and is either eaten with Indian breads or with plain rice. It calls for sour yogurt which you can provide either by leaving freshly made yogurt unrefrigerated for 24 hours or by using old, and therefore already soured, yogurt. If you cannot get fresh spinach, frozen leaf spinach, cooked according to instructions and then drained, may be substituted.

3 oz/85 g gram flour
½ tsp turmeric
8 fl oz/2¼ dl sour yogurt
2 tbs mung dal, *picked over,*
    washed and drained (optional)
1½ lb/675 g fresh spinach, *washed,*
    drained, and chopped
2½ tsp salt, *or to taste*

2 tbs lemon juice
⅛ tsp cayenne pepper
Freshly ground black pepper
2 tbs vegetable oil
A generous pinch of ground
    asafetida (optional)
1 tsp whole cumin seeds
2 whole dried hot peppers

Sift the gram flour and turmeric into a bowl. Add 4 fl oz/1 dl water, a little bit at a time, and keep stirring until you have a smooth paste.

Put the yogurt into a second bowl and beat it lightly with a whisk until it is smooth and creamy. Add 1 qt/11½ dl of water to the yogurt, beating lightly.

Add the yogurt mixture slowly to the gram-flour mixture, beating gently as you mix the two. Now empty this combination into a heavy 4-qt/4½-l pot and bring to a simmer over a medium heat. Add the *mung dal,* spinach, salt, lemon juice, and cayenne. Bring to a simmer again. Cover, turn heat to low and simmer very gently for 1½ hours. Stir every 10 minutes or so. If the *aalan ka saag* gets too thick, thin it out with a little hot water. It should have the consistency of a pea soup. Check the salt and add some freshly ground black pepper. Turn off the heat but leave the pot covered.

Heat the oil in a small frying pan or a very small pot over a medium flame. When very hot, add the asafetida, then, a second later, the cumin seeds, and 2 seconds later, the red peppers. As soon as the peppers turn dark on one side, turn them over. As soon as the second side darkens, pour the oil and all the spices in it over the *aalan ka saag.* Cover the *aalan ka saag* immediately and let it stay covered until the sizzling noises stop. You may now stir the contents of the pot.

PLAIN GUJARATI KARHI
INDIA   *(serves 4)*

If you want a very simple lunch or dinner, put some plain rice in a bowl, pour the *karhi* on top, and eat with a spoon. You might serve the Gujarati Carrot Salad (see page 370) with it.

For information about ingredients and basic techniques that may be unfamiliar, see General Information, pages 481–506.

2 tbs gram flour, sifted

15 fl oz/4¼ dl sour yogurt (see introduction to preceding recipe)

1 tsp whole cumin seeds

½ tsp whole fenugreek seeds

½–¾ tsp salt

1½ tsp sugar

½–1 fresh hot green chilli, chopped (optional)

1 tbs vegetable oil

A generous pinch of ground asafetida

A ¾-in/2-cm stick of cinnamon

5 whole cloves

1 dried hot red pepper

6 dried or preferably fresh curry leaves

½ tsp finely grated fresh ginger

2 finely chopped fresh green coriander

Put the gram flour in a 1¾-pt/1-l bowl. Slowly add 2 tbs of water so you have a smooth paste. Put the yogurt in another 1¾-pt/1-l bowl. Beat it with a narrow whisk or fork until it becomes smooth and paste-like. Slowly add 8 fl oz/5¾ dl of water to the yogurt, beating as you do so. Now pour the yogurt mixture into the gram-flour mixture little by little, beating all the time.

Pour the contents of the full bowl into a heavy 2-qt/2¼-l pot. Add ½ tsp of the whole cumin seeds and ¼ tsp of the whole fenugreek seeds. Bring to the boil. Cover, but leave the lid very slightly ajar. Turn heat to low and simmer very gently for 7 to 8 minutes. Add the salt, sugar, and chopped green chilli. Cover and cook another 2 minutes. Turn off heat and leave *karhi* covered.

Heat the oil in a very small frying pan or small pot over a medium flame. When hot, put in the following spices very quickly and in this order: first the asafetida; then, all together, the cinnamon, cloves, ½ tsp whole cumin seeds, and ¼ tsp whole fenugreek seeds; then the red pepper and curry leaves. Shake the spices once and immediately empty oil and spices from frying pan into the pot with the *karhi*. Cover *karhi* again as soon as this is done. Let the *karhi* rest for 5 minutes. Now put in the grated ginger and fresh coriander and serve hot.

GUJARATI KARHI WITH OKRA
INDIA   (serves 4)

Follow the preceding recipe through the first paragraph. Pour the contents of the full bowl into a heavy 2-qt/2¼-l pot. Add the ½ tsp whole cumin seeds, ¼ tsp whole fenugreek seeds, *and* 3 oz/85 g (buy ¼ lb/115 g) okra, trimmed at the ends, and sliced into ⅛-in/ ½-cm rounds. Now follow the rest of the recipe. You might add all the ¾ tsp salt.

SPICED BUTTERMILK TO EAT WITH INDIAN RICE DISHES
INDIA   *(serves 2)*

In South India, meals often end with plain rice, buttermilk, and pickles. The buttermilk can be unseasoned, or it can be spiced, as in this recipe. It is generally served in small individual bowls and is then poured over the rice on one's plate — or banana leaf! South Indians manage to pick up this wet, soup-like combination very deftly with their fingers. For those who are not South Indian, the feat is somewhat difficult. When serving Western guests, I find it more convenient to put small mounds of rice in the centre of individual plates and then pass the buttermilk around in a gravy boat. And I supply soup spoons. It may also be served as part of an Indian meal, with *dals* and vegetables.

8 fl oz/¼ l buttermilk
2 tsp vegetable oil
¼ tsp whole black mustard seeds
¼ tsp whole cumin seeds
⅛ tsp finely grated ginger

⅓ fresh hot chilli, finely sliced
  (optional)
⅛ tsp salt
Freshly ground black pepper

Put the buttermilk into a serving gravy bowl.

Heat the oil in a small heavy frying pan or other small pot over a medium flame. When hot, put in the mustard seeds and cumin seeds. As soon as the mustard seeds begin to pop (this takes just a few seconds), turn off the heat and allow the oil to cool a little. Now pour it over the buttermilk. Add the ginger, green chilli, salt, and pepper. Mix well.

SPICED BUTTERMILK WITH TOMATO
INDIA   *(serves 2)*

This soupy South Indian dish, like the one just before it, is meant to be eaten with rice. Here chopped-up tomatoes and garlic are added to the buttermilk to give it a slightly different flavour.

1 tbs vegetable oil
4 cloves garlic, peeled
⅓–½ fresh hot green chilli, cut
  into fine slices (optional)
¼ tsp whole cumin seeds
⅛ tsp ground turmeric

1 medium-sized, ripe tomato,
  peeled and seeded, and finely
  chopped
¼ tsp salt, or to taste
8 fl oz/¼ l buttermilk
Freshly ground black pepper

For information about ingredients and basic techniques that may be unfamiliar, see General Information, pages 481-506.

Heat the oil in a small pot over a medium flame. When hot, put in the garlic and green chilli. Stir and fry until the garlic turns a light-brown colour. Add the whole cumin seeds and stir for 2 seconds. Put in the turmeric and the tomato. Stir once. Now add 6 fl oz/ 1¾ dl water and the salt. Bring to a simmer. Cover, turn heat to low, and simmer for 10 to 15 minutes or until tomatoes are quite tender. Uncover and allow to cool off slightly. Add the buttermilk and black pepper. Stir to mix. Taste for seasonings. Serve at room temperature.

SPICED BUTTERMILK WITH COCONUT AND SHALLOTS
INDIA   *(serves 2)*

Here is another South Indian buttermilk dish that is meant to be eaten with rice. For details, see page 270. The buttermilk for this should be quite sour. You could, if you like, add a little lemon juice to achieve this. Or else you could try leaving the buttermilk un-refrigerated for 12 to 24 hours before seasoning it.

2 tbs vegetable oil
¼ tsp urad dal
½ tsp whole black mustard seeds
8 dried or fresh curry leaves (optional)
1 dried hot red pepper
2–3 good-sized shallots, peeled and cut into slivers
1 five-pence-piece sized slice of fresh ginger, peeled and cut into thin slivers

5 fenugreek seeds
2 oz/60 g grated fresh coconut
¼ tsp cayenne, or to taste
⅛ tsp ground turmeric
¼ tsp ground cumin seeds
8 fl oz/¼ l buttermilk
¼ tsp salt
Freshly ground black pepper

Put the oil in a saucepan that is about 6 in/15 cm in diameter and heat it over a medium flame. When hot, put in the *urad dal* and the mustard seeds. As soon as the mustard seeds begin to pop, add the curry leaves and the red pepper. Stir for a few seconds until the red pepper swells and turns dark. Put in the shallots and the ginger. Stir and fry until the shallots are very lightly browned. Now put in the fenugreek seeds, coconut, cayenne, turmeric, and cumin. Stir and fry for 1 minute. Empty into a small serving bowl. Pour the buttermilk over the coconut mixture. Add the salt and the pepper. Mix and taste for seasonings.

SOFT YOGURT CHEESES

While cheeses like *paneer* (see page 276) may be made by curdling milk, tying the curds in cheesecloth, and letting the whey drip overnight, another kind of soft cheese very popular in the Middle East and India is made with yogurt. Yogurt is tied up in cheese-cloth and left to drip from 3 to 8 hours — the 3 hours making for a very soft, creamy cheese and the 8 a slightly firmer but still creamy variety.

Some people prefer to salt the yogurt before they hang it up. I generally leave my salting and spicing to last-minute moods, preferring to do it when the yogurt has turned to cheese. This spicing can take any form that one fancies. In Iran, where tarragon, parsley, fresh coriander, dill, mint, and chives are loved so much that they are munched by themselves, fresh herbs are often chopped and mixed in with the cheese. In Kuwait, on a burning summer morning, our family once had a wonderful — and simple — breakfast consisting of pitta-like breads, olives, and cool yogurt cheese over which some olive oil had been floated. In parts of the Middle East little balls of yogurt cheese are first rolled in paprika, then some olive oil is dribbled over them and the dish eaten at breakfast. In Gujarat, India, I was once served a yogurt cheese that had chopped spring onions and fresh coriander in it; Gujarat has also developed a strained, saffron-enriched, and slightly sweetened yogurt cheese which is served in small individual bowls as part of the main meal, especially at banquets and weddings.

Yogurt cheeses are lighter and less calorific than cream cheeses. They are ideal to serve at breakfast and to put out at parties as dips and spreads.

HOW TO MAKE
SOFT YOGURT CHEESE
(makes enough to fill an 8-fl oz/2¼-dl cup)

Whole-milk yogurt makes a creamier cheese. You may, if you prefer, substitute skimmed-milk yogurt. I have not put any salt in this recipe. If you wish to add salt — and you should if you are going to eat it plain — sprinkle ¼ tsp over the yogurt before you hang it up.

16 oz/450 g whole-milk yogurt

For information about ingredients and basic techniques that may be unfamiliar, see General Information, pages 481-506.

Balance a strainer over a bowl. Line the strainer with a tripled thickness of cheesecloth, about 14 in/35 cm square. Put the yogurt in the middle of the cheesecloth. Bring the four corners of the cheesecloth together. Now tie the yogurt so as to make a loose bundle. You can do this by using one of the four corners of the cheesecloth or by using a piece of string. Alternatively, you could sew a cheesecloth bag, put the yogurt inside the bag, and then tie the bag. Suspend the bundle or bag of yogurt where it can drip. I tie mine to the tap of the kitchen sink. Let it drip for 3 to 8 hours, as your recipe requires. Remove cheesecloth. Refrigerate until needed in a closed plastic container. If adding herbs or spices, do this before you refrigerate it.

SOFT YOGURT CHEESE WITH DILL
IRAN   *(makes enough to fill an 8-fl oz/2¼-dl cup)*

Again, this cheese is wonderful for breakfast, along with crisp-breads, apples, pears, grapes, pomegranates, and figs.

It is good, too, for lunch, again with a Scandinavian crispbread and a slice of melon. And it is quite excellent as a spread for crispbreads at parties.

16 oz/450 g whole-milk yogurt   *2 oz/55 g finely chopped dill*
¼ tsp salt

Follow directions for making soft yogurt cheese above, using 16 oz/ 450 g of whole-milk yogurt. Let the yogurt drip for 8 hours.

Combine yogurt cheese with the salt and the dill in a stainless steel or non-metallic bowl. Mix well. Cover and refrigerate for at least 1 hour. If some liquid accumulates, just discard it before you serve.

SOFT YOGURT CHEESE WITH
FRESH CORIANDER AND
SPRING ONIONS, GUJARATI STYLE
INDIA   *(makes enough to fill an 8-fl oz/2¼-dl cup)*

This Gujarati dish is generally served at breakfast and eaten with *khakra*, a fine crispbread, any sprouted mung-bean dish, and a fresh green chutney, like Fresh Coriander and Mint Chutney (see page 422). Because *khakra* is a fairly complicated bread to master I have not included a recipe, but you could substitute Scandinavian crispbreads as they are similar to *khakras*. I often put this cheese out in a ½-pt/3-dl ceramic bowl, filling it all the way to the top and then either smoothing the top or making a design in it with the flat side of a knife, as one would with rough icing. This cheese may be served as a spread with biscuits and crispbreads.

Make sure that the fresh coriander is thoroughly dry before you chop it.

16 oz/450 g whole-milk yogurt
2 tbs finely chopped fresh green
  coriander

1 tsp finely chopped white part of
  spring onion
¼ tsp salt
½ tsp sugar

Follow directions for making soft yogurt cheese on page 272, using 16 oz/450 g of whole-milk yogurt. Let the yogurt drip for 4 to 5 hours.

Combine the yogurt cheese with all the other ingredients in a stainless steel or non-metallic bowl. Mix well. Cover and refrigerate for at least 1 hour. If some liquid accumulates, just discard it before you serve.

SOFT YOGURT CHEESE
WITH CRUSHED BLACK PEPPER

INDIA   *(makes enough to fill an 8-fl oz/2¼-dl cup)*

You could substitute crushed green peppercorns in this recipe, if you like.

16 oz/450 g whole-milk yogurt
¼ tsp salt

¼–½ tsp crushed, or very coarsely
  ground black peppercorns

Follow directions for making soft yogurt cheese on page 272, using 16 oz/450 g of whole-milk yogurt. Let yogurt drip for 4 to 5 hours.

Combine yogurt cheese with the other ingredients in a stainless steel or non-metallic bowl. Mix well. Cover and refrigerate for at least 1 hour. If some liquid accumulates, just discard it before you serve.

For information about ingredients and basic techniques that may be unfamiliar, see General Information, pages 481-506.

SOFT YOGURT CHEESE
WITH CHIVES AND PARSLEY

IRAN   *(makes enough to fill an 8-fl oz/2¼-dl cup)*

Be sure that the chives and parsley are thoroughly dry before chopping them.

16 oz/450 g whole-milk yogurt   *1 tbs very finely sliced chives*
¼ tsp salt   *1 tbs finely chopped parsley*

Follow directions for making soft yogurt cheese on page 272, using 16 oz/450 g of whole-milk yogurt. Let the cheese drip for 8 hours.

Combine yogurt cheese with all the other ingredients in a stainless steel or non-metallic bowl. Mix well. Cover and refrigerate for at least 1 hour. If some liquid accumulates, just discard it before you serve.

SOFT YOGURT CHEESE
WITH PAPRIKA AND OLIVE OIL

MIDDLE EAST   *(makes enough to fill an 8-fl oz/2¼-dl cup)*

16 oz/450 g whole-milk yogurt   *¼–⅓ tsp sweet paprika*
¼ tsp salt   *1 tbs fruity olive oil*

Follow directions for making soft yogurt cheese on page 272, using 16 oz/450 g of whole-milk yogurt. Let the cheese drip for 8 hours.

Put the cheese and salt in a stainless steel or non-metallic bowl. Mix well. Cover and refrigerate until ready to serve.

Spread the cheese out in a shallow, saucer-like bowl and sprinkle the paprika over it. Dribble the oil over the cheese and serve with whole-wheat pitta bread and olives (Middle Eastern olives, black or dark green, in oil).

SOFT YOGURT CHEESE
WITH FRESH TARRAGON

IRAN   *(makes enough to fill an 8-fl oz/2¼-dl cup)*

16 oz/450 g whole-milk yogurt   *⅛ tsp freshly ground black pepper*
¼ tsp salt   *1 tbs finely chopped fresh tarragon*

Follow directions for making soft yogurt cheese on page 272, using 16 oz/450 g of whole-milk yogurt. Let the yogurt drip for 8 hours.

Combine yogurt cheese with all the other ingredients in a stainless steel or non-metallic bowl. Mix well. Cover and refrigerate for at least 1 hour. If some liquid accumulates, just discard it before you serve.

SHRIKHAND
(Sweet Soft Yogurt Cheese with Saffron)
INDIA   *(makes enough to fill an 8-fl oz/2¼-dl cup and serves 2)*

This Gujarati cheese, made by hanging yogurt up for just 3 hours, has the consistency of a very, very thick cream. The use of saffron and pistachios makes it somewhat expensive, hence it is generally reserved for weddings and banquets.

You may serve this cheese with a meal or after it. If you serve it as dessert, you may wish to make it even sweeter.

This recipe may be doubled easily by doubling all the ingredients. The time for hanging up the yogurt will, of course, remain the same.

16 oz/450 g plain yogurt, preferably made from whole milk
¼ tsp leaf saffron
2 tsp warm milk

2 oz/60 g caster sugar, or less, according to taste
⅛ tsp cardamom seeds
1 tsp shelled, unsalted pistachio nuts, cut into slivers

Follow the directions for making soft yogurt cheese on page 272. Hang the yogurt up for just 3 hours.

Meanwhile, soak the saffron in the milk for about 1 hour.

Combine the yogurt cheese, saffron milk, and sugar in a bowl. Mix well with a fork or whisk until creamy. Push this mixture through a very fine sieve to make sure that there are no lumps left. Crush the cardamom seeds to a powder in a mortar and add them to the yogurt. Spoon this mixture neatly into two small bowls. Sprinkle the pistachios over the top. Cover tautly with cling film and chill until ready to eat.

PANEER (MILK CHEESE)

In order to get a balanced intake of protein, most Indians tend to eat quite a few milk products at each meal, ranging from glasses of plain cold buttermilk to complicated milk-based sweets. Because of the generally high temperatures in the sub-continent, cheeses, as

For information about ingredients and basic techniques that may be unfamiliar, see General Information, pages 481-506.

understood in the West, have never been made in India. But the life of milk has to be stretched in every possible way that the climate allows, and various fresh cheeses — all with the short life of 24 to 48 hours — have been concocted since earliest times with great success.

Paneer is one such cheese and it is made with curdled milk. Actually, paneer simply means cheese in most North Indian languages but because this particular cheese is popular and well known, it seems to have appropriated the name for itself. Whenever a North Indian says that he has cooked a dish of paneer, it is probably this paneer that he is referring to. As fresh paneer is readily available in Indian bazaars and grocery stores (just as bean curd is in China and Japan), it is seldom made at home. However, making it is not too complicated, though it does require an overnight wait.

PANEER
(Fresh Cheese)
INDIA

(This amount, when mixed with vegetables, will serve 6)

1 qt/11½ dl whole milk
2½ tbs lemon juice

Bring the milk to the boil. As soon as it begins to bubble, put in the lemon juice, stir once, and take the pot off the heat. Leave it for 15 minutes. The milk will curdle and the curds will separate from the whey.

Strain the curds through 3 layers of cheesecloth. Squeeze out as much whey as you can easily. (Do not discard this whey. Refrigerate it and use it in cooking instead of water.) Tie up the curds in the cheesecloth, using twine to make a small, round bundle. Use sufficient twine, as you now need to hang up this bundle somewhere to drip overnight. (I just hang it on the tap in the sink.)

Next morning, remove the hanging bundle and untie it. Gently flatten it out to make a 4-in/10-cm patty, keeping the cheese loosely wrapped in the cheesecloth. Put the cheesecloth-wrapped cheese patty on a sturdy plate and place a very heavy object (5–6 lb/2¼–2¾ kg) on top of it. I use one of my very heavy, porcelain-covered cast-iron pots filled with water. If the pot seems in danger of tipping over to one side, I balance it by standing appropriately sized jars under its two handles. Leave the weight on the cheese for 4 to 5 hours. After the cheese has been pressed, it should be ½–¾-in/1½–2-cm thick.

Remove the cheese from the cheesecloth and, with a sharp knife, cut it into cubes, diamond shapes, or rectangles. If your cheese has pressed down to ½ in/1½ cm, diamonds or rectangles no longer than 1 in/2½ cm are best. If the cheese is about ¾-in/2-cm thick, it can be cubed.

NOTE: Some people like to add a little freshly ground pepper and some finely chopped fresh green coriander − 1 tbs − to the curds just after the whey has been strained, before it is tied and hung up.

Paneer, once made, is quite crumbly and breakable. Because of this, it is generally fried and lightly browned before it is cooked. It is a good idea to do this frying in a well-seasoned cast-iron or Teflon-lined frying pan, as the cheese tends to stick a bit. There are some dishes in which the cheese is not fried at all.

Rather like bean curd, fresh *paneer* has very little taste of its own. It does have texture − and lots of protein. The taste comes from the flavours of the foods with which it is cooked. In a very traditional dish from the Punjab, *paneer* is combined with peas and tomatoes. It is frequently cooked with puréed spinach. It can also be crumbled and added to various grated vegetables (like marrow and courgettes) to form 'meatballs'. It can be crumbled, layered with partially cooked rice, and baked.

MATAR PANEER
(Peas with Paneer)
INDIA   (serves 6)

This Punjabi dish, with some variation in the spices, is eaten over all of North India. Indian restaurants, whether in India or outside it, almost always serve it on their *thali*, or vegetarian platter. (As an interesting variation, you could substitute a diced 6-oz/180-g cake of regular bean curd for the *paneer*.)

For information about ingredients and basic techniques that may be unfamiliar, see General Information, pages 481–506.

1 medium-sized onion, peeled and
  chopped
About a 1-in/2½-cm cube fresh
  ginger, peeled and chopped
6 tbs vegetable oil
Paneer, see page 277 (plus
  16 fl oz/½ l of the whey)
1 whole dried hot red pepper

1 tbs ground coriander seeds
¼ tsp ground turmeric
3 medium-sized tomatoes, peeled
  and finely chopped
1 tsp salt
⅛ tsp freshly ground black pepper
1¼ lb/570 g shelled fresh or 2
  packets defrosted frozen peas

Put the chopped onion and ginger into the container of an electric
blender or food processor along with 3 fl oz/¾ dl water and blend
until you have a smooth paste. Leave paste in the blender
container.

Heat the oil in a heavy, 10-in/25-cm-wide pot (preferably Teflon-
lined) over a medium flame. When hot, put in the pieces of *paneer*
in a single layer and fry them until they are a golden brown on all
sides. This happens pretty fast. With a slotted spoon remove fried
paneer to a plate. Put the dried red pepper into the same oil. Within
2 seconds, turn the pepper over so that it browns on both sides.
Now put in the contents of the blender (keep your face averted as
the paste might splatter). Fry, stirring constantly, for about 10 to 12
minutes, or until paste turns a light-brown colour.

Add the coriander and turmeric and fry, stirring, for another
minute. Put in the chopped tomatoes. Stir and fry for another 3 to 4
minutes or until tomatoes turn a dark, reddish-brown shade. Now
pour in 16 fl oz/½ l of the whey. Add the salt and the black pepper.
Mix well and bring to the boil. Cover, lower heat, and simmer
gently for 10 minutes. Lift cover and put in the *paneer* pieces and
the peas. Cover and simmer for 10 minutes or until peas are
cooked.

SAAG PANEER
(Spinach with Paneer)
INDIA   (serves 4–6)

Saag paneer, a combination of greens and *paneer*, is eaten all over
North India with slight variations in the spices. The greens change
with the seasons and local preferences: fenugreek greens, spring
greens, beetroot greens, escarole, *sarson da saag* — all can be used.
In India, the spinach, which turns into a sauce for the *paneer*, is
sometimes creamed. At other times it is left in its chopped state,
thus allowing it to stand in equal partnership with the *paneer*. I like
the latter method because this way the spinach retains its texture.

I use a 12-in/30-cm-wide, 4-in/10-cm-high, nonstick sauté pan to make this dish. If you do not have such a pan, fry the *paneer* separately, in a Teflon or a well-seasoned cast-iron frying pan. Then transfer the oil to a pot large enough to hold the raw spinach, and continue the cooking.

For this recipe, I have used fresh spinach because I prefer its taste. You could use two packets of frozen, chopped spinach if you like. Cook spinach according to packet directions, drain well, and proceed with the recipe. Do not salt the spinach twice and remember to cook it very briefly with the ginger–garlic mixture.

For a quick lunch, heat up leftover *Saag Paneer* and stuff it into whole-wheat pitta-bread halves with thin slices of raw onion and tomato.

A 1-in/2½-cm cube of fresh ginger, peeled and coarsely chopped	¼ tsp garam masala
	⅛ tsp cayenne pepper (optional)
3–6 cloves garlic, peeled	6 tbs vegetable oil
½–1 fresh hot green chilli, sliced roughly	1½ lb/675 g spinach, washed, trimmed, and very finely chopped
Paneer (see page 277)	3 tbs single cream
Salt	

Put the ginger, garlic, and green chilli into the container of an electric blender or food processor along with 2 fl oz/½ dl water. Blend until you have a smooth paste. You may need to push down with a rubber spatula once.

Heat the oil in a large, wide, preferably nonstick sauté pan over a medium flame. Put in all the pieces of *paneer* and fry them, turning them over gently with a slotted spatula, until they are golden brown on all sides. (This happens fairly quickly.) Remove *paneer* with a slotted spoon and place on a plate in a single layer. Sprinkle *paneer* quickly with the ⅛ tsp salt, the *garam masala*, and the cayenne pepper. Set aside.

Put the paste from the blender into the hot oil in your pan (keep face averted) and fry it, stirring constantly, for about 30 seconds. Now put in the spinach and ½ tsp salt. Stir the spinach around for 1 minute. Cover the pan, lower the heat, and let the spinach cook gently with the ginger–garlic paste for 15 minutes. There should be enough water clinging to the spinach leaves to cook them. If all the water evaporates, add 1–2 tbs and continue cooking.

Now put in the *paneer* and cream, stir gently, and bring to a simmer. Cover, and continue cooking on low heat for another 10 minutes. Stir once or twice during this period.

For information about ingredients and basic techniques that may be unfamiliar, see General Information, pages 481-506.

BHAPA DOI
(Steamed Yogurt, Bengali Style)
INDIA   *(serves 4–6)*

Bhapa doi may be described as a sweet Bengali custard made with boiled-down (and thus thickened) milk and yogurt. Traditionally it is served with meals, though it could easily be served as a dessert or a snack. The Bengalis often use raw palm sugar as the sweetening agent. Jaggery (available only in Indian stores) or brown sugar may be substituted. I tend to go very light on the sugar. If you feel that the custard is not sweet enough for your taste (the time to taste it is just before the steaming), add more sugar.

Bengalis often add saffron to this custard. You may, if you like, throw ¼ tsp leaf saffron into the milk while it is cooking down.

(To my amazement, I found that a kind of yogurt known as *ryazhenka*, which is found in Soviet cities like Moscow and Leningrad today, closely resembles the Bengalis' *bhapa doi*. Yogurt was, supposedly, introduced to the Russians by the Mongols. As the Mongols began raiding India as early as the thirteenth century and finally managed to conquer it in the sixteenth century, the connection between the two yogurt dishes may be more than coincidental.)

1 qt/11½ dl milk	*6 fl oz/1¾ dl plain yogurt*
2 tbs sugar	*(preferably whole-milk)*
	1 tbs shelled pistachios, slivered

Put the milk in a heavy pot. Bring to the boil, being careful not to let it bubble over. Turn heat to low and simmer, stirring, until reduced to 1 pt/5¾ dl. Stir in the sugar and allow to cool. Strain.

Beat yogurt lightly until it is smooth and creamy. (Avoid making bubbles.) Pour in the cooled milk, a little at a time, mixing it in as you do so. Pour the yogurt–milk mixture into a serving dish capable of being steamed (I often use a soufflé or custard dish). Cover tightly with aluminium foil or a lid.

In a larger pan that can hold the serving dish, place a trivet to hold the custard 1 in/2½ cm above the bottom. Now pour in 1 in/2½ cm of water and bring it to the boil. Place the covered serving dish with the yogurt–milk mixture on the trivet. Cover the steaming pan. Lower heat and simmer very, very gently until yogurt sets, about 15 minutes.

Lift custard container out carefully, without tilting. Uncover and allow to cool.

Garnish with slivered pistachios, cover and refrigerate.

7 Noodles, Pancakes, and Breads

NOODLES

Asian noodles, made from both grain flours and bean flours, can be thick and starchy as well as thread-like, transparent, and slippery. And, rather like Italian pasta, they may be tossed with cold sauces, hot sauces, and sautéed vegetables.

If you are looking for pleasant first courses to serve during the hot summer months, I cannot imagine anything nicer than Cold Noodles with a Peanut Sauce or Cold Noodles with Sesame Sauce, both of Chinese origin. Or you might serve your noodles the Japanese way, on a bed of ice, with cooling dipping sauces and crisp relishes on the side.

For heartier winter fare, you might try Noodles with Spinach and Mung-Bean Sprouts. I had this extraordinary dish on Cheju Island in South Korea. A mound of freshly cooked noodles was piled in a bowl, standing like a rising island in a sea of steaming broth. The noodles were topped with blanched, seasoned spinach and the spinach topped with blanched, seasoned bean sprouts. The entire hillock had been sprinkled with roasted sesame seeds and crushed red pepper. All we had to do was mix the noodles at the table and eat it with healthy bites of fiery *kimchee* pickles.

Among the more soothing noodle dishes, and one which my children invariably ask for when they return home for holidays, is Crisp-Soft Noodles with a Broccoli, Mushroom, and Courgette Topping. It looks quite grand. Cooked noodles are fried into a cake, which turns brownish and crisp on the outside but stays quite soft inside. The cake is then smothered with sauced, stir-fried vegetables.

Even though Oriental noodles are used for most of the dishes here, you may use any other pasta of your choice. Spaghetti, spaghettini, and vermicelli make perfectly fine substitutes.

PANCAKES

Pancakes in Asia are made from a variety of beans and grains, the method of cooking depending upon the type of batter. Hoppers from Sri Lanka, for example, are made with a leavened white flour and rice-flour batter. They are cooked, covered, in a wok, and end up with lots of crumpet-like holes. I like to eat them with butter and jam, though the more traditional way would be to dip them into mouth-burning *sambals*.

282

The Filipino Lumpia is no more than a very thin skin made with cornflour, eggs, and water. It, too, is cooked traditionally in a wok, though I find it more convenient to use a nonstick frying pan. The skins are used to enclose a stuffing that can vary from lettuce and fresh heart of palm (when one says *fresh* heart of palm in the Philippines, it usually means that the palm has been felled that morning) to lettuce and sautéed vegetables. The pancakes are wrapped or 'packaged' most amusingly to resemble vases, with the greens all popping out enthusiastically from one side.

It is not always easy to separate breads and pancakes in Asia as they are often eaten in the same way. This is certainly true of many pancakes from India.

Indian pancakes, made out of bean flour, soaked bean, or soaked rice and bean batters, are among India's favourite breakfast and snack foods. Generally speaking, Indian pancakes are made without eggs, white flour, or leavening agents, though in some cases the batter is allowed to stand long enough to ferment naturally. Sometimes the batter is seasoned just with salt. At other times, especially when the pancake is not going to be stuffed, finely chopped ginger, fresh green coriander, and green chillies are mixed in.

Cooking these India-style pancakes – and here I include the Korean Bindaetuk, made from mung beans, because it is very similar – is quite an art but one which is not at all difficult to master. In India, the pancakes are always cooked on seasoned, cast-iron griddles. As the batters have a tendency to stick to the griddles, Indian cooks use various methods to make their griddles as 'nonstick' as possible. One South Indian housewife I know always grates her coconut on to her griddle, using it as a platter. The natural oil released by the coconut keeps her griddle permanently seasoned. She does not, of course, ever wash it. Another South Indian chef rubs heated griddles with cut onion halves. This simple procedure, he says, makes his griddles 'nonstick'. My own feeling on the matter is that since one can now buy real nonstick griddles and frying pans, why work so hard on cast-iron ones?

The general method for making Indian pancakes is the same: a batter is made, most frequently with beans, or rice and beans that have been soaked and ground. In India, this grinding is done on heavy grinding stones. In Britain it can be done with the greatest of ease in blenders and food processors. This part of the pancake-making process is simplicity itself. The moment of truth comes in spreading out the batter.

Unlike white-flour and egg batters, bean batters do not flow. You cannot tilt your frying pan around expertly and have the batter flow to the edges as it would for a crêpe. Instead, the batter will sit obstinately like a lump in the centre of your frying pan. It has to be coaxed to move. This is best done with a round soup spoon.

The first step should be to grease the nonstick frying pan very lightly and heat it. Then, drop a blob of batter in the centre. Next, put the rounded bottom of the soup spoon *very lightly* on the centre of this blob of batter and, using a slow, gentle, but continuous spiral motion, spread the batter outwards with the back of the spoon. You can make the pancakes as thin as you like. You may not be able to manage a 'continuous spiral' motion the first time. Do not worry about that. As long as you get the batter to spread, basically using circular motions, that is good enough. Because nonstick frying pans have no grip, if you push too hard with the spoon, the entire batter may begin to move. If you have that problem, use a lighter touch and try *not* greasing the frying pan before you put in the pancake.

Many of the batters for Indian pancakes can be made ahead of time and refrigerated. So if you want to eat the pancakes for breakfast, you can easily make the batter the night before. Sometimes the pancakes themselves can be made ahead of time and wrapped in aluminium foil. They can then be reheated by being placed in a medium-hot oven for about 15 minutes, still covered in foil.

BREADS

Oven breads, griddle breads, frying-pan breads, steamed breads, and deep-fried breads, Asia has them all.

When ovens are used, they tend to be made out of clay, stones, or bricks. Sometimes they are even built inside pits. Yeast dough is rolled or patted into round or leaf shapes and then slapped on to the walls or floor of the oven to make breads such as pittas and *naans*. Similar oven breads can be found all over the Caucasus–Caspian Sea region and down through Iran, Afghanistan, and Pakistan into northern India.

Griddle and frying-pan breads include the *rotis* and *parathas* of India and the Chinese *yow bing*. No yeast is added to the flour. *Rotis* are made with just whole-wheat flour and water and are similar to tortillas except that they puff up like balloons and are much more delicate. Some people serve their *rotis* plain, others smear them with *ghee* as soon as they are made. *Parathas* and *yow bing* are somewhat grander frying-pan breads. During the process of rolling them out and folding them, several layers of oil are incorporated inside. As they cook, they turn all flaky. *Yow bing* is stuffed with lots of spring onions to make it entirely irresistible.

I think Asians do much more steaming than we do here and a great many cakes, buns, breads, and muffins are cooked by this method. *Putu*, for example, is a Filipino muffin made with rice flour and baking powder. Originally, it was steamed in banana-leaf cups but now even the Filipinos have begun to use muffin tins. Chinese buns are made out of white flour and yeast. They puff up into spongy balls as they steam. India has all manner of steamed, savoury cakes. *Idlis*, which emerge from the steamer looking like small, harmless flying saucers, are made here from a well-spiced mixture of yogurt and semolina. Served with coffee or buttermilk, they are as common a breakfast food in South India as croissants and coffee are in France.

And then there are the deep-fried breads, such as the Indian *pooris* which puff up into balls in seconds and are quite marvellous when torn and eaten with vegetables.

I have noticed that when making flat Indian breads, it is best to use *ata* or 'chapati flour', which is available in Indian grocery stores. It is usually made from hard wheat which is low in gluten. Failing that, you could mix wheatmeal with plain flour in equal proportions to get a less elastic dough.

COLD NOODLES WITH SESAME SAUCE

CHINA   *(serves 4 if eaten with other dishes)*

This is a lovely dish to have in the summer. It is best to use fresh (or frozen) Chinese egg noodles, the kind used to make *lo mein*, but if you have no access to them, dry spaghettini, vermicelli or thin Japanese buckwheat noodles — *ki soba* — may be substituted; be sure to cook them *al dente*. The noodles are served topped with the ground sesame-seed dressing which, in turn, is topped with very finely sliced cucumbers and roasted sesame seeds.

You may, if you like, serve these noodles as a hot dish, in which case do not rinse the noodles after draining them; toss them, while still very hot, first with the 1 tbs sesame oil and then with the sesame sauce.

A 6-in/15-cm length of cucumber
½ lb/225 g fresh thin Chinese egg noodles (or see above suggestions)
1 tbs plus 1 tsp sesame oil
4 tbs roasted sesame seeds (3 of them ground)
1 tbs Chinese thin soy sauce
1 tbs Chinese dark soy sauce

2 tsp Chinese black vinegar
1½ tsp sugar
⅛ tsp cayenne pepper
½ tsp salt
⅛ tsp freshly ground white pepper
1 tbs vegetable oil
1 tbs Vegetable Stock (see page 340), mushroom soaking liquid, or water

Peel the cucumber, cut it in half lengthwise, and remove all the seeds. Cut into fine julienne strips. Put in a plastic bag and refrigerate.

Bring 2 qt/2¼ l of water to the boil in a large pot. Separate the strands of noodles and, when the water is at a rolling boil, drop them in. Let the water come to the boil again. Pour in 8 fl oz/¼ l of cold water from the tap. The boiling will subside. Let the water come to the boil a third time. Pour in another 8 fl oz/¼ l of cold water. Let the water come to the boil a fourth time. Drain the noodles in a colander, then run cold water over the noodles and rinse them off. Let them drain for 5 minutes. Put the noodles in a serving bowl. Add the 1 tbs sesame oil to them and toss. You can, if you like, cover and refrigerate the noodles at this stage for a couple of hours.

Combine the 1 tsp sesame oil, the *ground* sesame seeds, thin soy sauce, dark soy sauce, vinegar, sugar, cayenne, salt, white pepper, vegetable oil, and stock in a small bowl. Mix well and beat with a

---

For information about ingredients and basic techniques that may be unfamiliar, see General Information, pages 481-506.

fork until you have a smooth paste (you may do this in a food processor or blender).

When ready to serve, pour the sauce over the noodles. Put the julienned cucumber in a little heap on top of the mound of noodles, and top the cucumbers with the remaining roasted whole sesame seeds. Take the noodle bowl to the table this way. The noodles should be tossed — with chopsticks preferably — at the table.

COLD NOODLES WITH A PEANUT SAUCE
CHINA   *(serves 4 if eaten with other dishes)*

Cold noodle dishes are lovely to serve in the summer months. As in the preceding recipe, you need fresh thin Chinese egg noodles, the kind that are used in *lo mein*. If you have no access to them, use the thinnest noodles you can find, cooked *al dente*. The noodles are tossed with a ground peanut dressing and served topped with sliced spring onion shreds and some crushed peanuts.

This dish may also be served hot. Do not rinse the noodles after draining them and toss, while still very hot, first with the 1 tbs sesame oil and then with the peanut sauce.

½ lb/225 g fresh thin Chinese egg
  noodles (or see above)
2 tbs sesame oil
1 oz/30 g plus 1 tbs shelled, salted
  roasted peanuts
1 clove garlic, peeled
1 tbs groundnut oil

1 tbs Chinese thin soy sauce
2 tsp Chinese black vinegar
1 tsp sugar
⅛ tsp cayenne pepper
A 2½-in/6½-cm piece spring onion
  bottom, cut lengthwise into
  very, very fine strips

Bring 2 qt/2¼ l of water to the boil in a large pot. Separate the strands of noodles and, when the water is at a rolling boil, drop them in. Let the water come to the boil again. Pour in 8 fl oz/¼ l of cold water from the tap. The boiling will subside. Let the water come to the boil a third time. Pour in another 8 fl oz/¼ l of cold water. Let the water come to the boil again. Drain the noodles in a colander, run cold water over them and rinse. Let them drain for 5 minutes. Put the noodles in a serving bowl. Add 1 tbs of the sesame oil to them and toss. You can, if you like, cover, and refrigerate the noodles at this stage for a couple of hours.

Combine the 1 oz/30 g peanuts, 1 tbs sesame oil, garlic, groundnut oil, soy sauce, vinegar, sugar, cayenne, and 2 fl oz/½ dl water in a food processor or blender. Blend until you have a smooth sauce.

Crush the remaining 1 tbs peanuts to a coarse crumb texture in a spice grinder, mortar, or food processor.

When you are ready to eat, pour the sauce over the noodles and toss. Garnish by putting the strips of spring onions in a heap on top of the mound of noodles and top with the peanut crumbs. Serve this way and toss the noodles at the table, preferably with chopsticks.

HOT OR COLD NOODLES WITH A SOY-SAUCE DRESSING
CHINA   (serves 4)

½ lb/225 g fresh thin Chinese egg
  noodles (for substitute, see page
  286)
2 tbs sesame oil
3 tbs Chinese thin soy sauce
1 tbs distilled white vinegar
1 clove garlic, peeled and mashed
  to a pulp

½ tsp sugar
4 oz/115 g fresh, crisp mung-bean
  sprouts
4 crisp inner Cos leaves, cut
  crosswise into ¼-in/¾-cm-wide
  shreds

Bring 2 qt/2¼ l of water to the boil in a large pot. Separate the strands of noodles and, when the water is at a rolling boil, drop them in. Let the water come to the boil again. Pour in 8 fl oz/¼ l of cold water from the tap. The boiling will subside. Let the water come to the boil a third time. Pour in another 8 fl oz/¼ l of cold water. Let the water come to the boil again. Drain the noodles in a colander. Run cold water over the noodles and rinse them off. Put the noodles in a serving bowl. Add 1 tbs of the sesame oil and toss. You can, if you like, cover and refrigerate the noodles at this stage for a couple of hours.

Combine the remaining 1 tbs sesame oil, the soy sauce, vinegar, garlic, and sugar in a small bowl. Set aside.

Wash the mung-bean sprouts thoroughly, drain, and pat dry.

Just before you get ready to eat, distribute the lettuce and bean sprouts over the noodles. Stir the dressing, pour it over the noodles and vegetables, and toss.

COLD, SUMMER NOODLES
JAPAN   (serves 4)

This is very much a summer dish. I know of a restaurant in Kyoto, set right on the river, where thin *somen* noodles, awash in iced water, float by the customers in a man-made stream that runs along the dining tables. Diners are provided with sauces, season-

---

For information about ingredients and basic techniques that may be unfamiliar, see General Information, pages 481-506.

ings, cold barley tea — and chopsticks with which to fish out the moving noodles.

If you cannot find the very thin *somen* noodles, use spaghettini. Just cook it *al dente*, drain and rinse it out well in cold running water. The 1-lb/450-g *somen* packets I get in my area are divided into five portions with ribbons. I cook three portions — about 9 oz/250 g — for four people.

Japanese cucumbers are singularly free of large seeds. The closest thing in Britain is the pickling cucumber. I used two in this recipe. You may use ordinary cucumbers. Scrape out any large seeds first.

9 oz/250 g somen

FOR THE DIPPING SAUCE
2 spring onions
8 fl oz/¼ l Delicious Stock . . . (see
    page 340) or dashi (see page
    339)
6 tbs mirin
6 tbs Japanese soy sauce
⅛ tsp 7-spice seasoning
1 tsp peeled and very finely grated
    fresh ginger

FOR THE CUCUMBER RELISH

5¼ oz/150 g peeled cucumber, cut   *4 tsp Japanese soy sauce*
    into julienne strips   *1 tsp roasted and lightly crushed*
1 tbs Japanese rice vinegar   *sesame seeds*
1 tbs sugar

About 16 ice cubes

Bring 1¼ pt/¾ l of water to a rolling boil. Put in a third of the noodles. Stir quickly to separate them. Put in another third of the noodles. Stir briskly again. Put in the remaining noodles and stir briskly. When the noodle water comes to the boil again, pour in 8 fl oz/¼ l of cold tap water. When the noodle water boils a third time, empty the contents of the pot into a colander set in the sink. Rinse the noodles well in running water. Put the noodles in a bowl, cover with water, and refrigerate for at least 1 hour.

Cut the spring onions into fine rings. Put in a bowl of water and refrigerate for at least 1 hour.

Combine the stock, *mirin*, soy sauce, and 7-spice seasoning in a bowl. Put the grated ginger in a small sieve and lower it partially into the stock mixture. Stir the ginger around to release its juice. Lift up the sieve. Press the ginger with the back of a spoon to release more of the juice. Refrigerate the stock.

Put the cucumber in a small plastic container, cover tightly, and refrigerate. Combine all the seasonings except sesame seeds for the cucumber relish in a small bowl. Mix well until the sugar is dissolved. Refrigerate separately.

To assemble the dish, crack each ice cube into two to three pieces. Put some ice at the bottom of four chilled bowls. Drain the noodles and divide them up among the bowls. Tuck some ice all around them and even lay some over. Pour the dipping sauce into four smaller bowls. Remove the spring onions from their water and scatter them over the dipping sauce. Pour the seasoning sauce for the cucumber relish over the julienned cucumbers and toss. Divide this relish among four small bowls. Sprinkle the sesame seeds over the cucumbers. To eat, pick up some noodles with chopsticks (or a fork), dunk in the dipping sauce, and suck them in. Refresh yourself now and then with some of the cucumber.

NOODLES WITH A HOT-AND-SOUR BEAN SAUCE
CHINA   *(serves 4–6)*

8 Chinese black dried mushrooms
2 tsp cornflour
4 fl oz/1 dl bean sauce
1 tbs Chinese thin soy sauce
3 tbs white distilled vinegar
3½ tbs sugar
2 tbs chilli paste with soy beans
   and garlic
1 tbs sesame oil
2 tbs vegetable oil
3 cloves garlic, peeled and finely
   chopped

3 five-pence-piece sized slices of
   fresh ginger, peeled and finely
   chopped
3 spring onions, cut into fine
   rings, including green
1 tbs roasted and very lightly
   crushed sesame seeds
12 oz/340 g fresh Chinese lo mein
   egg noodles (or spaghettini
   cooked al dente)

Soak the mushrooms in 12 fl oz/3½ dl hot water for half an hour. Lift out of the soaking liquid. Remove the hard stems and cut the caps into ⅛-in/½-cm-wide strips.

For information about ingredients and basic techniques that may be unfamiliar, see General Information, pages 481–506.

Put the cornflour into a bowl. Slowly mix in 12 fl oz/3½ dl water. Add the bean sauce, soy sauce, vinegar, sugar, chilli paste, and sesame oil. Stir to mix.

Heat the vegetable oil in a wok or pot over a medium flame. When hot, put in the garlic and ginger. Stir briskly and fry for 5 seconds. Add the mushrooms and spring onions. Stir and fry for another minute. Turn heat to low. Give the cornflour mixture a quick stir and pour it into the wok. Turn heat up to medium-low and cook for a minute or two or until the sauce thickens. Add the sesame seeds and mix. (This sauce may be made ahead of time and reheated.)

Bring 5 pt/2¾ l of water to a rolling boil. Separate the strands of noodles gently and drop into the water. When the water boils a second time, pour in 8 fl oz/¼ l of cold tap water. When the water comes to the boil for a third time, pour in another 8 fl oz/¼ l of cold tap water. When the water comes to the boil for the fourth time, empty the contents of the pot into a colander set in the sink. Put the noodles in a bowl. Spoon as much of the sauce as you think you need over the noodles. Toss and serve.

THICK NOODLES IN A WINTER STEW
JAPAN   (serves 4)

This is a one-pot, Hokkaido-style dish that may be cooked at the table in a hot pot or in a not-very-large electric frying pan. It may also be cooked in a pretty, casserole-type pot in the kitchen and then brought to the table in the same pot.

Udon, the thick, dried noodles that are used in this stew, may be made out of white or whole-wheat flour and you can find them in Japanese and some health-food stores. If you cannot find *udon*, use spaghetti. Time it so that it is ready just when the vegetables have finished cooking, then drain and add directly to the stew.

If you cannot find fresh water chestnuts in your area, just leave them out.

8 dried shiitake *mushrooms*
⅓ lb/140 g udon
2 spring onions
1 carrot
4 Chinese cabbage leaves or 5 of the softer leaves from an ordinary cabbage
4 fresh water chestnuts
About 4–6 oz/115–180 g medium bean curd

1½ pt/8½ dl Delicious Stock . . . (see page 340)
¼ tsp salt
1 tsp Japanese soy sauce
1 tsp mirin
8 pieces peeled white radish, about ½ in/1½ cm thick and 1 in/2½ cm across

FOR THE DIPPING SAUCE

4 fl oz/1 dl Japanese soy sauce   *4 fl oz/1 dl lemon juice*

Soak the mushrooms in 8 fl oz/¼ dl hot water for half an hour. Lift them out of the hot water and cut off the hard stems. Cut each cap in half.

Cook *udon* according to packet instructions. Drain immediately and rinse under cold running water. Put in a bowl and cover with cold water.

Cut the spring onions into 2-in/5-cm lengths.

Peel the carrot and cut into ½-in/1½-cm thick rounds.

Lay the cabbage leaves one on top of the other and cut, crosswise, at 1-in/2½-cm intervals.

Peel the water chestnuts and cut into halves.

Cut the bean curd into ½–¾-in/1½–2-cm cubes.

Combine the stock, salt, 1 tsp soy sauce, and *mirin* in a bowl.

Mix the ingredients for the dipping sauce and divide among four small, shallow bowls (or as many bowls as there are people). Set these bowls on the table. Also arrange chopsticks, soup spoons, and eating bowls at each setting. Drain the noodles. You may now proceed to cook at the table or in the kitchen.

Heat the stock. When it is simmering, put in the spring onions and radish pieces. Simmer for a minute. Put in the carrot. Simmer another minute. Put in the water chestnuts. Simmer a minute. Put in the cabbage and mushrooms. Cook for 6 minutes more or until all vegetables are just tender. Put in the noodles and the bean curd and cook until they are just heated through. (If you are 'cooking' at the table, the noodles and the bean curd will be dipped by each diner, one mouthful amount at a time, in the barely simmering broth and heated through.) Either pick choice ingredients out of the common pot, dip in the sauce and eat, or serve yourselves in the bowls.

NOODLES WITH TEMPURA VEGETABLES
JAPAN   *(serves 4)*

The Japanese seem to love everything about tempura, or batter-fried foods. Even the tiny pieces of batter that float free of the vegetables are scooped up to be used later in soups as dumplings.

For information about ingredients and basic techniques that may be unfamiliar, see General Information, pages 481-506.

Leftover vegetables have another use. They are mounted over hot noodles (or rice), the combination moistened with some broth, and then quickly slurped up for thousands of quick lunches and quick dinners throughout the country.

1½ pt/8 ½ dl Delicious Stock . . . (see page 340)	16–20 pieces Tempura (see page 89)
2 tsp Japanese soy sauce	2 spring onions, cut into fine rounds
2 tsp mirin	
½ lb/225 g soba noodles	About ¼ tsp 7-spice seasoning
	Additional soy sauce

Combine the stock, 2 tsp soy sauce, and *mirin* and bring to a simmer. Leave on a very low flame.

Cook the noodles according to the instructions on the packet. Drain them and divide among four bowls. Put 4 to 5 pieces of tempura over each mound of noodles. Pour the hot broth over the tempura and noodles. Scatter the spring onions over the top and sprinkle some 7-spice seasoning into each bowl. Cover the bowls immediately and leave for 3 to 4 minutes.

Serve extra soy sauce as required.

CRISP-SOFT NOODLES WITH A BROCCOLI, MUSHROOM, AND COURGETTE TOPPING
CHINA   (serves 4)

Here is another dish that our family eats with great relish. I learned how to make it from a Jamaican-Chinese immigrant who owned a tiny restaurant near an Off-Broadway theatre where I worked many years ago. I had hardly any money then and this dish was cheap. The Jamaican lady put in any scraps of vegetables that she happened to have lying around − I remember that there were always more onions than I cared for − and, because she had grown quite fond of me during the course of a long run, a good bit of cayenne pepper to please my Indian palate. This dish is somewhat more elegant − there is no cayenne in it, though you could add that, if you like, and it has positively *no* onions.

My Jamaican friend used a wok to fry her noodles. I find it much easier to use a nonstick frying pan.

You do need a large, preferably round plate to serve the noodles, at least as large as the bottom circumference of your frying pan and with some depth so it can hold the vegetables and sauce.

½ lb/450 g fresh Chinese lo mein
  egg noodles
1 medium-sized courgette
1 tsp salt
About ½ lb/225 g broccoli
8 medium-sized mushrooms
2 tsp cornflour
6 fl oz/1¾ dl Delicious
  Stock . . . (see page 340) or any
  vegetable stock

2 tbs bean sauce
2 tsp sugar
1 tbs sesame oil
7 tbs vegetable oil
2 cloves garlic, peeled and finely
  chopped
1 five-pence-piece sized slice of
  fresh ginger, finely chopped
1 tbs shaohsing wine or dry
  sherry

Bring 2½ qt/2¾ l water to a rolling boil. Gently separate the noodle strands and drop them into the water. When the water comes to the boil again, pour in 8 fl oz/¼ l of cold tap water. When the water boils a third time, pour in another 8 fl oz/¼ l of cold tap water. When the water boils a fourth time, empty the contents of the pot into a colander set in the sink. Rinse the noodles under running water, washing off a lot of the starch. Leave to drain for at least half an hour.

Trim the courgette ends and then cut it in half, lengthwise. Cut the halves crosswise at ¼-in/¾-cm intervals. Put the courgette in a bowl. Sprinkle ¼ tsp salt over it and mix. Set aside for half an hour. Drain and pat dry.

Cut the broccoli into slim flowerets, not more than 2 in/5 cm long. You can use some of the stems, too. Just peel and cut them into ¼-in/¾-cm thick strips.

Wipe off the mushrooms and then cut them, stem and all, into ¼-in/¾-cm thick slices.

Put the cornflour in a small bowl. Slowly add the stock, mixing as you do so. Add the bean sauce, sugar, and sesame oil. Mix well.

Heat 3 tbs of the vegetable oil in a 7–8-in/18–20-cm, nonstick frying pan over a medium flame. When the oil is hot, put in the noodles, spreading them out evenly over the entire bottom of the frying pan. Fry without stirring for about 4 minutes or until the bottom of the noodle patty is a reddish-golden colour and is crisp. Now slip one spatula under the noodles and hold the top of the patty with another spatula. Turn the patty over. Dribble another tbs of vegetable oil along the edges of the frying pan, allowing it to slither downwards. Cook the second side until until it, too, has turned a reddish-golden colour. Carefully lift up the patty and put it on a warm plate.

Heat 3 tbs of vegetable oil in a wok or frying pan over a medium

---

For information about ingredients and basic techniques that may be unfamiliar, see General Information, pages 481-506.

flame. When hot, put in the garlic and ginger. Stir a couple of times. Put in the mushrooms, broccoli, and ¾ tsp salt. Stir and fry, turning the vegetables around briskly. Put in the courgette. Stir and fry for another 30 seconds. Now add the wine, cover immediately and turn heat to low. Cook for 1 minute. Uncover, give the cornflour mixture a quick stir and pour it over the vegetables. Turn heat up a bit and cook, stirring gently, until the sauce thickens. Spoon the vegetables and sauce over the noodles and serve immediately.

NOODLES WITH SPINACH AND MUNG-BEAN SPROUTS
KOREA   (serves 4)

This dish should be served surrounded by several small bowls of seasonings and relishes. Of these, perhaps the most essential are finely crushed dried hot red peppers, soy sauce, and Cabbage Kimchee. The ideal eating implements would be chopsticks and a soup spoon for each person. Of course, you can use whatever you feel comfortable with.

I have used the fresh *lo mein* egg noodles for this dish but you could use spaghetti or vermicelli, cooked according to instructions, then rinsed under cold running water.

5 Chinese dried black mushrooms
½ lb/225 g fresh Chinese lo mein
  egg noodles
1 lb/450 g fresh spinach
2 tsp salt
1 tbs sugar
4 oz/115 g fresh mung-bean
  sprouts, washed and drained
3 tbs Japanese soy sauce
1 tbs sesame oil
16 fl oz/½ l Delicious Stock . . . (see
  page 340)
1 tbs fresh Chinese chives or
  spring onion tops, cut into
  ½-in/1½-cm lengths

1 tbs roasted and lightly crushed
  sesame seeds
⅛ tsp finely crushed dried hot red
  pepper or cayenne pepper

TO SERVE AS AN ACCOMPANIMENT
A very small bowl with finely
  crushed dried hot red pepper or
  cayenne pepper
A very small bowl with Japanese
  soy sauce in it
A bowl of Cabbage Kimchee,
  homemade (see page 440) or
  bought

Soak the mushrooms in 8 fl oz/5¾ dl hot water for half an hour. Lift them out of the water and cut off the hard stems. Cut the caps into ⅛-in/½-cm-wide strips. Bring 3 qt/3½ l of water to a rolling boil. Gently separate the noodle strands and drop them into the water.

When the water comes to the boil again, pour in 8 fl oz/5¾ dl of cold tap water. When the water boils a third time, pour in another 8 fl oz/5¾ dl of cold tap water. When the water boils a fourth time, empty the contents of the pot into a colander set in the sink. Wash the noodles in cold running water and leave to drain.

Wash the spinach and separate the leaves. Do not discard the pinkish roots, if there are any. Just peel and then quarter them lengthwise.

Bring 1¼ pt/¾ l of water with the salt and 1 tsp of the sugar to a rolling boil. Put the bean sprouts into a small sieve and lower the sieve into the water. After the water comes to the boil again, cook the sprouts for about 20 seconds. Drain and rinse under running water. Set the sieve on a bowl and leave to drain.

Drop the spinach into the same water and boil for about 2 minutes or until it has wilted completely. Drain in a large sieve or colander and rinse under running water. Leave to drain.

Mix together 2 tbs soy sauce, 2 tsp sugar, and the 1 tbs sesame oil in a small cup.

Just before you sit down to eat, add 1 tbs soy sauce to the stock and heat it. Drop the noodles into the stock. As soon as the noodles have heated through, remove them with a slotted spoon or a pair of tongs and pile them in the centre of a serving bowl. Keep warm. Put the spinach and mushrooms into the stock. When they have heated through, lift them out with a slotted spoon and put them in a work bowl. Put the sprouts into the same stock. When they have heated through, lift them out also with a slotted spoon and put them in another work bowl. Quickly season the spinach and mushrooms with 2 tbs of the soy mixture and the sprouts with the remaining soy mixture. Heap the spinach over the noodles and the sprouts over the spinach. Pour the remaining stock around the mound of noodles and vegetables. Scatter the chives on top of the mound. Sprinkle the sesame seeds and the ⅛ tsp cayenne pepper over the entire dish. Serve at once, with the suggested seasonings and *kimchee*.

VEGETARIAN MEE KROB
(Crisp Noodles with Pressed Bean Curd and Eggs)
THAILAND   (serves 4–6)

A very fine rice vermicelli, called *mee* in Thailand, is used to make this dish. The vermicelli is first fried until it is crisp and then tossed

---

For information about ingredients and basic techniques that may be unfamiliar, see General Information, pages 481-506.

with a hot, sweet, salty, and sour combination of pork, shrimp, pressed bean curd, and eggs. (I have eliminated the pork and shrimp.) This combination has to be cooked until it is quite dry, or the vermicelli turns soggy.

Mee may be bought from Thai grocery shops. Get the thinnest variety available. Fine Chinese rice sticks may be used instead.

6 oz/180 g mee (see above)
Vegetable oil for deep frying,
    about 16 fl oz/½ l
4 oz/115 g very finely chopped,
    peeled shallots
1 tbs peeled and finely chopped
    garlic
1–2 fresh hot green chillies, finely
    chopped
1 cake pressed bean curd, cut into
    julienne strips
5 large eggs
1½ tsp salt
2 tbs Japanese soy sauce
2 fl oz/½ dl distilled white vinegar

2 tbs sugar
2 tbs tomato ketchup
¼–½ tsp cayenne pepper
Freshly ground black pepper
Peel from ½ lemon, cut into very
    thin, 1-in/2½-cm-long strips
3 tbs fresh Chinese (or other)
    chives, cut into ½-in/1½-cm
    lengths
3 tbs fresh green coriander leaves
4 oz/115 g fresh mung-bean
    sprouts, washed, drained, and
    patted dry
Garnish: additional green
    coriander sprigs

Soak the *mee* in hot, not boiling, water for a minute or until they soften. Drain immediately.

Line two large platters with kitchen paper and keep near by.

Heat the oil over a high flame. When very hot, throw in a small handful of *mee*. Fry for about 30 to 40 seconds, then turn over what will look like a thin pancake of vermicelli. Fry for 30 to 40 seconds on the second side. The *mee* should turn a lovely reddish-golden colour and be quite crisp. Remove it with a slotted spoon and leave to drain on the kitchen paper. Fry all the *mee* this way.

Take the wok off the flame and remove all but 2 fl oz/½ dl of the oil. Heat this over a medium flame. Put in the shallots, garlic, and green chilli. Stir and fry until the shallots are lightly browned. Put in the bean curd and stir for a minute. Now break all the eggs into the wok. Stir for a minute, breaking up the yolks. Add the salt, soy sauce, vinegar, sugar, ketchup, cayenne, and lots of black pepper. Stir and fry until the eggs have solidified completely. Turn the heat to medium-low. Continue stirring and frying another 15 to 20 minutes or until the mixture is completely dry, lowering heat if necessary.

Just before you are ready to eat, toss the *mee* with the egg mixture, the lemon peel, chives, and fresh coriander leaves. Arrange on a platter. Scatter the bean sprouts over the top and garnish with the additional coriander sprigs.

NOODLES WITH QUAILS' EGGS, MUSHROOMS, SPINACH, AND YUBA
JAPAN (serves 4)

This dish tastes best with freshly boiled quails' eggs. If you cannot find them, use 2 small chickens' eggs, hard-boiled, peeled, and cut into halves.

Yuba is the Japanese name for the skin that forms on top of cooling soy-bean milk. When fresh, this skin is creamy and quite heavenly. It can only be purchased in its dried form here and therefore needs to be reconstituted by a soaking in water. The trouble is that there are so many forms of dried soy-milk skin in Oriental markets, each requiring a different soaking time, and each with a different shape and thickness. Japanese stores sell very fine, flaky *yuba* rolls, all tied with a *konbu* 'thread'. These would be ideal for this dish. They require about 15 minutes' soaking. Chinese stores sell packets of what is called 'Dried Bean Curd, Slice Type'. These slices need to be soaked for 45 minutes and then cut into 1-in/2½-cm squares.

8 small yuba rolls or 8 1-in/
   2½-cm squares of bean-curd
   skin
4 dried shiitake mushrooms
½ lb/225 g udon or soba
   (Japanese noodles)
4 quails' eggs
¼ lb/115 g fresh spinach leaves

1½ pt/8½ dl Delicious
   Stock . . . (see page 340)
¼ tsp salt
1 tbs plus extra Japanese soy sauce
1 tbs mirin
2 tsp peeled and very finely grated
   fresh ginger

Soak the *yuba* in 16 fl oz/½ l water until it is creamy in colour and soft (see note above).

Soak the mushrooms in 12 fl oz/3½ dl hot water for half an hour. Lift out of the water. Cut off the hard stems and cut each cap into ⅛-in/½-cm-thick strips.

Cook the noodles according to packet instructions. Drain and rinse under cold running water.

Cook the quails' eggs 5 minutes in barely simmering water. Cool in cold water and peel.

Bring 1¼ pt/¾ l of water to a rolling boil. Throw in the spinach leaves and cook rapidly for 2 minutes. Drain and rinse under cold water. Leave to drain.

Bring the stock to the boil. Add the salt, 1 tbs soy sauce, and

---

For information about ingredients and basic techniques that may be unfamiliar, see General Information, pages 481-506.

mirin. Put in the noodles and heat through. Remove the noodles with tongs and divide among four bowls. Put the spinach and mushrooms into the stock. When they have heated through, lift them out with a slotted spoon and lay them on top of the noodles. Drop in the *yuba* and eggs. Simmer for 30 seconds. Lift out of the liquid and place somewhere near the vegetables. Pour some of the broth into each bowl. Divide the ginger into four neat heaps and place each in a tiny saucer. Offer extra soy sauce that may be mixed with the ginger and used for added seasoning.

VEGETABLE LO MEIN
CHINA   (serves 4–6)

½ lb/225 g fresh Chinese lo mein
   egg noodles
5 medium-sized Chinese dried
   black mushrooms
6 stalks (about 10–12 oz/
   285–340 g) choy sum
About 6 oz/180 g cabbage (¼
   small-sized head)
1 fresh hot green chilli
2 spring onions
2 cloves garlic, peeled
4 oz/115 g mung-bean sprouts

2 fl oz/½ dl Chinese dark soy sauce
1 tbs sesame oil
2¾ tsp sugar
⅛ tsp cayenne pepper
Freshly ground black pepper
6 tbs vegetable oil
Salt
4 fl oz/1 dl Delicious Stock . . . (see
   page 340)
1 oz/30 g fresh Chinese (or other)
   chives, cut into 1½-in/4-cm
   lengths

Bring 2½ qt/2¾ l of water to a rolling boil. Gently separate the noodle strands and drop them into the water. When the water comes to the boil again, pour in 8 fl oz/¼ l of cold tap water. When the water boils a third time, pour in another 8 fl oz/¼ l of cold tap water. When the water boils a fourth time, empty the contents of the pot into a colander set in the sink. Rinse the noodles thoroughly in cold running water, washing away any extra starch. Leave the noodles in the colander to drain for half an hour.

Soak the mushrooms in 8 fl oz/¼ l hot water for half an hour. Lift them out of the water and cut off their hard stems. Cut the mushroom caps into ⅛-in/½-cm-wide strips.

Cut the leaves of the *choy sum* crosswise into ⅛-in/½-cm-wide strips. Cut the stems lengthwise into thin, 2–3-in/5–8-cm-long strips, peeling them wherever the skin seems too coarse.

Core the cabbage and cut it into long, ⅛-in/½-cm-wide strips.

Cut the green chilli into ⅛-in/½-cm-thick strips. Seed it if you do not want the dish to be somewhat hot.

Cut the spring onions into 2½-in/6½-cm-long sections and then cut these sections lengthwise into very thin strips.

Cut the garlic into very thin strips.

Wash the bean sprouts well and leave to drain.

In a cup, mix together the soy sauce, sesame oil, 2 tsp sugar, cayenne pepper, and black pepper.

Heat 3 tbs of vegetable oil in a large wok over a medium flame. Put in the garlic and give it a few stirs. Put in the green chilli and give another few stirs. Put in the mushrooms. Stir for 5 seconds. Now add the *choy sum*, cabbage, spring onions, ¾ tsp salt, and ¾ tsp sugar. Stir-fry for about 3 minutes or until the vegetables wilt. Remove the vegetables and put them in a bowl.

Add another 3 tbs of vegetable oil to the wok. When it is hot, put in the drained noodles. Let the noodles just sit for a few seconds. Then stir-fry them for another few seconds. Put in the stock and turn the heat up slightly. Stir gently and cook until all the liquid seems absorbed. Put in the soy-sauce mixture and stir to mix. Put back the cooked vegetables. Stir gently to mix. Put in the bean sprouts and chives. Stir-fry another 2 minutes.

CHAPCHAE
('Cellophane' Noodles with Vegetables)
KOREA   (serves 4)

2 oz/60 g 'cellophane' mung-bean noodles	4 spring onions
6 Chinese dried black mushrooms	4 tbs vegetable oil
5 oz/140 g tender spinach leaves	1 tbs sesame oil
1 carrot	3 cloves garlic, peeled and finely chopped
1 small courgette	1 tbs Japanese soy sauce
3 medium-sized mushrooms	1 tsp sugar
2 Chinese cabbage leaves	½ tsp salt

Soak the noodles in 2½ pt/1½ l of water for half an hour. Drain.

Soak the Chinese mushrooms in 8 fl oz/¼ l hot water for 20 minutes. When they have softened, cut off the hard stems and slice the caps finely.

Drop the spinach into 2 qt/2¼ l of boiling water. Boil rapidly for 2

For information about ingredients and basic techniques that may be unfamiliar, see General Information, pages 481-506.

minutes. Drain. Run under cold water. Squeeze out as much moisture as possible.

Peel the carrot, cut into 3 sections and then into fine julienne strips.

Trim the courgette ends and cut into fine julienne strips.

Wipe off the fresh mushrooms and break off their stems. Cut the caps into very fine slices. Cut the non-woody part of the stems into matchstick pieces.

Cut away and discard the curly, tender part of the cabbage leaves. Save only the V-shaped core of the leaves. Cut this into julienne strips.

Cut the spring onions into 2½-in/6½-cm sections. Quarter the sections with the bulbs lengthwise.

Combine the Chinese mushrooms, spinach, carrot, courgette, mushrooms, cabbage, and spring onions in a bowl. Mix well, separating all the spinach leaves.

Heat the vegetable oil and the sesame oil in a wok or a 10-in/25-cm sauté pan over a medium-high flame. When hot, put in the garlic. Stir and fry for 10 seconds. Add all the vegetables in the bowl. Stir and fry for 3 to 4 minutes or until the vegetables are tender-crisp. Turn the heat to low. Add the drained noodles, soy sauce, sugar, and salt. Stir well, distributing the noodles evenly, and cook 2 to 3 minutes. Taste for seasonings.

BIBINGKA
(Sweet Rice Pancake)
PHILIPPINES   (serves 6)

Everywhere the colonial Portuguese went, they taught the locals to make sweetmeats out of eggs. On India's west coast they taught the Goans to make a cake of stacked pancakes that used forty eggs;

Thais were taught how to make glazed egg yolks and sweet egg-yolk vermicelli; and in the Philippines, *bibingka* soon became dominant among snack-time favourites. In its simplest form the *bibingka* is made from fermented ground rice, eggs, sugar, and either coconut milk or water. These days the natural fermentation process is replaced by the faster-working baking powder. More elaborate *bibingkas* are studded with pieces of carabao cheese and salted, boiled ducks' eggs. When the *bibingka* is served, it is smeared with butter and then dusted with icing sugar as well as freshly grated coconut.

Traditionally, *bibingkas* are cooked in banana-leaf-lined clay baking trays placed over live charcoal. These individual baking trays are covered with a second tray that holds more live charcoal. I have made my *bibingka* quite a bit larger and cooked it in an oven. Instead of ground rice, I have used rice powder.

In the Philippines, these pancakes are often served with hot Salabat (ginger tea).

2 large eggs
2½ oz/70 g sugar
5 oz/140 g rice powder (rice flour)
2 tsp baking powder
About 2 tbs unsalted butter
1 tbs or more icing sugar
*1 oz/30 g or more freshly grated
  coconut*

Preheat oven to 400° F/200° C/Mark 6.

Beat the eggs and sugar together until light and creamy. In a blender or food processor, combine the rice powder, baking powder, and 4 fl oz/1 dl water. Let the machine run for 3 to 4 minutes or until the batter is smooth and satiny. If some rice flour clings to the sides of the container, release it with a rubber spatula. Pour the rice-flour mixture into the egg mixture and fold it in. It should be thoroughly blended.

Grease an 8-in/20-cm cake tin generously with butter and pour the batter into it. Bake about 15 to 20 minutes or until batter has just set and a toothpick inserted inside the pancake comes out clean. Remove the pancake from the baking tin and put it on a plate. Smear with butter — as much butter as pleases you — and then dust first with the icing sugar and then the coconut. Serve hot, cut into wedges.

For information about ingredients and basic techniques that may be unfamiliar, see General Information, pages 481-506.

Mrs Roxas's
LUMPIA
(Vegetables Wrapped in Pancakes)
PHILIPPINES   *(makes 8 stuffed pancakes)*

You could stuff these pancakes yourself for your family and friends or, better still, you could teach them to do it themselves. It is great fun and keeps everyone gainfully employed. Each pancake contains a crisp leaf of lettuce, which sticks out merrily like a plume at the top, as well as some stir-fried vegetables which stay discreetly inside. Lumpia is considered 'finger-food' and is generally not eaten with cutlery.

Lumpia pancakes may be made several hours in advance and kept covered between sheets of waxed paper.

FOR THE PANCAKES
2 oz/60 g cornflour
2 large eggs, separated
About 2 tsp vegetable oil

FOR THE STUFFING
4 tbs vegetable oil
2 tsp peeled and finely chopped
    garlic
1 small onion, peeled and sliced
    into fine half rings
11 oz/310 g finely shredded
    cabbage
2 oz/60 g carrot, peeled and cut
    into ¼-in/¾-cm dice
4 tbs celery, cut into ¼-in/¾-cm
    dice

3 oz/85 g fresh green beans, cut
    crosswise at ⅛-in/½-cm
    intervals
¾ tsp salt, or to taste
Freshly ground black pepper
8 crisp Cos leaves

FOR THE SAUCE
1 tbs cornflour
4 fl oz/1 dl Delicious Stock . . . (see
    page 340) or any vegetable stock
3½ oz/100 g dark brown sugar
1½ tbs Japanese soy sauce
1 tbs lightly crushed, fried, or
    roasted peanuts (optional)
A few drops of Tabasco sauce
    (optional)

Make the pancakes first. Mix the cornflour slowly with 8 fl oz/¼ l water. In a separate bowl, beat the whites of the eggs until frothy. Fold in the yolks, beating lightly to mix. Give the cornflour mixture a stir and pour it into the bowl with the eggs. Strain the batter.

Heat an 8-in/20-cm nonstick frying pan over a low flame. When hot, pour in ¼ tsp oil and spread it with a piece of kitchen paper or brush. Stir the batter and pour 2 fl oz/½ dl into the frying pan. Quickly tilt the pan in a circular motion so the batter covers the entire bottom surface. Cook on low heat for about 1½ minutes or until the batter has set. Peel off the thin pancake (I find it easier to use my fingers) and put the pancake on a large plate. Cover with a sheet of waxed paper. Make all the pancakes this way, stirring the batter each time. Stack the pancakes on top of each other, with a layer of waxed paper in between. Cover the pancakes with an inverted plate.

Make the stuffing next. Heat the oil in a wok or frying pan over a medium flame. Put in the garlic. Stir for a few seconds or until the garlic browns lightly. Put in the onion and stir-fry for 30 seconds. Put in the cabbage and stir-fry for about 1 minute or until the cabbage wilts. Put in the carrot, celery, green beans, and salt. Turn heat to low. Stir and cook another 6 to 8 minutes or until all vegetables are cooked but still crisp. Add some freshly ground black pepper and mix. Leave until the mixture reaches room temperature.

Wash the lettuce leaves and pat them with a tea towel until they are completely dry. If not used immediately, refrigerate in a plastic bag.

Make the sauce. Mix together the cornflour and 4 fl oz/1 dl water until smooth. Add the stock, sugar, and soy sauce. Heat in a small pot over a lowish flame, stirring as you do so. When the sauce thickens, turn off the flame. Add the peanuts and Tabasco, if you want to. The sauce may be served lukewarm or at room temperature.

Assemble the *lumpia* as illustrated. 1. Lay a pancake in front of you. Put a lettuce leaf down in the centre, its pointed end away from you and protruding a little outside the pancake. Divide the vegetable stuffing into eight parts. Lay one part along the length of the lettuce leaf that is inside the pancake. 2. Fold the left side of the pancake tightly over the vegetable stuffing.

1   2

3   4

3. Fold the bottom of the pancake — that is, the end nearest you — over the stuffing. Now fold the right side of the pancake over the stuffing to form a roll. 4. Dribble some sauce inside the roll from its open end and start eating.

Neela's
CHAURA NA POORA
(Black-Eyed Bean Pancakes)
INDIA   (makes 12–14 pancakes)

This scrumptious savoury pancake, given here with its Gujarati name, is eaten in western and southern India. It is spicy, light, but quite satisfying, and exceedingly nourishing. It can be eaten at any time of the day, but is ideal for breakfasts and snacks. To make it, black-eyed beans have to be soaked overnight in water. Next morning, their skins are rubbed off and the beans are ground in a food processor or blender into a batter. Ginger, garlic, green chillies, fresh green coriander, salt, and turmeric are added to the batter and then the pancakes are cooked on a nonstick griddle or frying pan. Please read the section on Indian Pancakes, page 283, especially the part that deals with cooking the pancakes, before you make *chaura na poora*. Also, remember that the batter can be made up to 24 hours in advance and then covered and refrigerated. Stir it well before you begin cooking.

8 oz/225 g dried black-eyed beans,   A ¾-in/2-cm cube of fresh ginger,
*   picked over, rinsed, and drained   peeled, and cut into 4 pieces*

5 cloves garlic, peeled
1–2 fresh hot green chillies, cut
   into quarters
1 tsp salt

¼ tsp ground turmeric
1 tbs finely chopped fresh green
   coriander
About 6 fl oz/1¾ dl vegetable oil

Soak the beans for 12 to 16 hours in a bowl filled with 1½ pt/8½ dl of water. Then peel the beans by dipping your hands into the bowl of beans and water and rubbing them between your two palms. Drain and spread the beans out on a large platter and pick off the skins that have been loosened. (Do not worry if not all the skins have come loose.)

Start your food processor with the metal blade in place. Through the funnel, drop in the ginger pieces first, followed by the garlic cloves and the green chilli (or chillies). When they are finely chopped, stop the machine and put in all the drained black-eyed beans. Start the machine again and let it run until the beans turn paste-like. Now stop the machine and add ½ pt/3 dl water, the salt, turmeric, and fresh coriander. Run the machine for another minute to make a thickish batter. Empty batter into a bowl. (This batter can also be made in an electric blender.)

See that you have everything you need for *poora*-making. Not far from your nonstick frying pan should be your oil (put it in a cup) and a teaspoon, a rounded soup spoon for spreading out the batter, your bowl of batter, a small measuring cup, and a plastic spatula. Also have a plate beside you on which you can put the *pooras* as they are cooked.

Pour 1 tsp of oil into an 8-in/20-cm nonstick frying pan. Spread the oil around by tilting the pan. Now put the pan to heat over a medium-low flame. When the oil is hot, stir the batter well, scoop up 3 fl oz/¾ dl, and flop this down in the centre of your heated frying pan. Let it just sit there for 3 to 4 seconds. Now place the rounded bottom of your soup spoon very lightly on the centre of your blob of batter. Using a slow, gentle, and continuous spiral motion, spread the batter outwards with the back of the soup spoon. You should now have a pancake about 6–7 in/15–18 cm in diameter. Dribble ½ tsp of oil over the pancake and another ½ tsp just outside its edges. Using your plastic spatula, spread the oil on top of the pancake and also smooth out any lumps or ridges. Let the pancake cook for about 2 minutes on the first side or until it turns a nice reddish colour. Flip the pancake over with the plastic spatula and cook the other side for about 2 minutes or until it develops small red spots. Remove the pancake and put it on a

For information about ingredients and basic techniques that may be unfamiliar, see General Information, pages 481–506.

plate. Make all the pancakes this way, *making sure you stir the batter before you make each pancake.* (If you do not do this, you will be left with a very watery batter towards the end.) Stack the pancakes one on top of the other. If not eating immediately, wrap the whole stack of pancakes in aluminium foil. This way, they can be eaten a couple of hours later at room temperature or reheated, still wrapped in foil, in a 450° F/230° C/Mark 8 oven for 15 minutes.

These pancakes are always served with their first side up (the first side that was cooked, that is) and eaten with relishes, pickles, chutney, or cooked vegetables.

Mrs Patel's
MUNG DAL NA POORA
(Savoury Mung-Dal Pancakes with Onions)
INDIA   *(makes about 9 pancakes)*

Like the *poora* made out of black-eyed beans, this pancake, too, is light, spicy, and very nourishing — ideal food for breakfasts and snacks. Because *mung dal* is hulled and split, it needs only 4 to 5 hours of soaking. Finely chopped onions are added to the batter to give it an edge (you may use very finely sliced spring onions instead of onions). This *poora* is slightly thicker than the black-eyed bean *poora* mainly because it has onions in it. Without the onions, you could spread it out much thinner. Though the use of bicarbonate of soda is not traditional to Indian pancakes, Mrs Patel, a very talented cook (and doctor) from Bombay, does add a little bit to her batter to give extra lightness to her pancakes. Please read the section on Indian pancakes (page 283), especially the part that deals with cooking the pancakes, before you make these *pooras*. If you wish to eat them for breakfast, remember that the batter can be made a day ahead and refrigerated. Add the onions and baking powder just before you get ready to do the cooking and stir the batter well before you make each pancake. Served with yogurt relishes and sweet chutney, these pancakes take the place of bread.

6½ oz/185 g mung dal, *picked over, washed, and drained*
A ¾-in/2-cm cube of fresh ginger, *peeled, and cut into 3–4 pieces*
3 cloves of garlic, *peeled*
1–2 fresh hot green chillies, *cut into 3 pieces each*
1 tsp salt
¼ tsp bicarbonate of soda
¼ tsp ground turmeric
2 tbs finely chopped fresh green coriander
1 smallish onion, *peeled, and finely chopped*
About 4 fl oz/1 dl vegetable oil

Put the *dal* in a bowl. Add 1½ pt/8½ dl of water and soak for 5 hours. Drain.

Start your food processor with the metal blade in place. (You could also use an electric blender to make this batter.) Through the funnel, drop in the ginger pieces first, then the garlic, and finally the green chilli (or chillies). When they are finely chopped, stop the machine and put in the drained *mung dal*. Start the machine and let it run until the *dal* turns paste-like. Now stop the machine and add 4 fl oz/1 dl water, the salt, bicarbonate of soda, and turmeric. Run the machine for another 2 minutes to make a thick batter. Empty the batter into a bowl and mix in the fresh coriander and onion thoroughly.

See that you have everything you need for *poora*-making. Not far from your nonstick frying pan should be your oil and a teaspoon, a rounded soup spoon for spreading out the batter, your bowl of batter, a small measuring cup, and a plastic spatula. Also a plate for the cooked *pooras*.

Pour 1 tsp of oil into an 8-in/20-cm nonstick frying pan. Spread the oil around by tilting the pan. Now put the pan to heat over a medium-low flame. When the oil is hot, stir the batter well and remove 3 fl oz/¾ dl of it from the bowl. Plop this batter down in the centre of your heated frying pan. Let it just sit there for 3 to 4 seconds. Now place the rounded bottom of your soup spoon very lightly on the centre of your blob of batter. Using a slow, gentle, and continuous spiral motion, spread the batter outwards with the back of the soup spoon. Make a pancake that is about 5½ in/14 cm

For information about ingredients and basic techniques that may be unfamiliar, see General Information, pages 481-506.

in diameter. Dribble ½ tsp of oil over the pancake and another ½ tsp just outside its edges. Using the plastic spatula, spread out the oil on top of the pancake and also smooth out any lumps or ridges. Cover the frying pan and let the pancake cook for about 2 minutes or until its underside turns a nice reddish colour. Uncover and turn the pancake over. Let the second side cook, uncovered, for about 1½ minutes or until it develops small red spots. Remove the pancake and put it on a plate. Make all the pancakes this way, *making sure you stir the batter before you make each pancake*. Stack the pancakes one on top of the other. If not eating immediately, wrap the whole stack of pancakes in aluminium foil. This way, they can be eaten a couple of hours later at room temperature or reheated, still wrapped in foil, in a 450° F/230° C/Mark 8 oven for 15 minutes.

These *pooras* are served either with yogurt relishes or with sweet chutneys (like Apricot Chutney with Sultanas and Currants, page 425).

GRAM-FLOUR PANCAKES
INDIA   *(makes 4 large pancakes)*

This is the Indian pancake that most resembles the *socca* of Nice. I happen to think that the Indian version, which gets crispy on the bottom while retaining a silkiness on the top, is much more delicate. The ideal utensil for cooking this is a nonstick frying pan. I use one that is 7½ in/19 cm in diameter at the bottom. If yours is larger or smaller, you will have to adjust the amount of batter you pour in. Unlike other Indian pancakes, the batter here is thin and can be spread around by tilting the frying pan in different directions, just as you would for a crêpe. In fact, this pancake ends up by being about as thin as a crêpe, though for some reason it starts off looking a bit thicker when first poured into the frying pan. The gram-flour batter tends to 'set' quickly, just as egg batters do, so you have to move your wrist with a certain degree of urgency.

4 oz/115 g gram flour   ⅛–¼ *tsp cayenne pepper*
½ tsp salt   *About 2 fl oz/½ dl vegetable oil*
½ tsp ground turmeric

Sift the gram flour into a bowl. Slowly add 8 fl oz/¼ l water, 2 tbs at a time. After each addition stir well with a wooden spoon, breaking up all lumps. Now add another 4 fl oz/1 dl water, the salt, turmeric, and cayenne. Stir to mix.

Put a small cup with the oil, as well as a pastry brush, a teaspoon, and a small measuring cup somewhere near your frying pan. Have plates ready so you can serve the pancakes as soon as they are made. Each pancake takes about 7 to 8 minutes to cook. If you have two similar frying pans, you can have them both going at the same time.

Brush a 7–8-in/18–20-cm, nonstick frying pan with about 1 tsp of oil. Let the oil heat on a lowish flame. When it is hot, stir the batter well and remove 4 fl oz/1 dl from the bowl. Pour this into the frying pan. Now tilt the pan around to spread the batter to the very edges. Keep doing this until all the batter in the frying pan is evenly distributed and is set. Dribble 1 tsp of oil around the edges of the pancake and another tsp over the pancake. Cover the frying pan and let the pancake cook for 7 to 8 minutes. It should be slightly crisp at the edges and on the bottom. Carefully ease a plastic spatula around the edges of the pancake. Now ease the spatula under the pancake. Lift it up and put it on a plate. It is best if eaten at once. Otherwise, cover the plate with another inverted plate. Do all pancakes this way.

Serve with any chutney, sambal, or dipping sauce of your choice.

SOUTH INDIAN DOSAS
(Rice and Urad-Dal Pancakes)
INDIA   (makes 8 pancakes)

Dosas, plain or stuffed, may be served at breakfast, brunch, lunch, or as a snack. In South India, they are often accompanied by glasses of buttermilk or cups of steaming hot, sweet, milky coffee. Dosas may also be served as any Indian bread might be, with an assortment of vegetables and relishes.

Please read the section on Indian pancakes (page 283), especially the part that deals with cooking the pancakes, before making these dosas. Since the dal and rice must be soaked 8 hours and the paste must ferment almost a day, plan ahead.

3 oz/85 g urad dal   ¾ tsp ground cumin seeds
7 oz/200 g long-grain rice   About 4 fl oz/1 dl vegetable oil
¾ tsp salt

For information about ingredients and basic techniques that may be unfamiliar, see General Information, pages 481-506.

Pick over the *urad dal*, wash well, drain, and then soak in 16 fl oz/½ l water for 8 hours.

Wash the rice well, drain, and then soak in 1¼ pt/¾ l water for 8 hours.

Drain the *dal*. Put it into the container of a food processor (with the metal blade in place) or a blender. Run the machine for 2 minutes, pushing down the *dal* with a rubber spatula every now and then. Now add 2 tbs of water and let the machine run another minute. Add another 2 tbs of water and let the machine run another minute. Keep doing this until you have added 6 fl oz/1¾ dl water. The *dal* should be very well ground, light, and fluffy. Put this paste into a bowl.

Drain the rice. Put it into the container of the food processor or blender. Run the machine for 2 minutes, pushing down the rice with a rubber spatula every now and then. Now add 2 tbs of water and run the machine for 1 minute. Add another 2 tbs of water and run the machine for another minute. Keep doing this until you have added 6 fl oz/1¾ dl water and the rice is reduced to *very* fine, semolina-like grains. Pour this rice paste over the *dal* paste. Mix. Cover, and leave to ferment in a warm place for 16 to 20 hours.

See that you have everything ready for *dosa*-making. Not far from your 8-in/20-cm nonstick frying pan should be your oil (take it out in a cup), a teaspoon, a rounded soup spoon, your bowl of batter, a small measuring cup, and a plastic spatula. Also have a plate beside you on which you can put the *dosas* as they cook. If you like, this plate may be kept in a warming oven.

The batter should by now have a frothy, fermented look. Add the salt and cumin to it and stir. Heat 1½ tsp of oil in the nonstick frying pan over a medium-low flame. Remove 4 fl oz/1 dl of the batter and pour it into the middle of the frying pan. Let it sit there for 3 to 4 seconds. Place the rounded bottom of the soup spoon very lightly in the centre of the batter. Using a slow, gentle, and continuous spiral motion, spread the batter outwards with the back of the soup spoon until you have a pancake that is about 7-in/18-cm in diameter. Dribble ½ tsp oil over the pancake and another ½ tsp just around its edges. Using a plastic spatula, spread out the oil on top of the pancake and also smooth out any lumps or ridges. Cover the frying pan. Cook for about 1½ to 2 minutes on the first side or until the *dosa* turns a nice, reddish-brown colour. Lower your heat, if necessary. Turn the *dosa* over and cook, uncovered, for another minute, or until the second side develops reddish spots. Put the cooked *dosa* on a warm plate. Stir the batter and make another *dosa*, just as you made the first. Make all *dosas* this way. Serve with the first side cooked up, accompanied by South Indian Coconut Chutney.

TO MAKE STUFFED DOSAS OR MASALA DOSAS

Make a recipe of Potatoes and Onions (see page 63) first. This dish may even be made a day ahead of time and then reheated. Now make the *dosas*. Lay out each *dosa* on an individual plate, with its 'good' side – the side that was cooked first – down. Spread 3–4 tbs of the heated potato stuffing over half the *dosa*. Fold the *dosa* over to form a capital D. Once the *dosa* is stuffed, it should be served immediately.

RICE-FLOUR DOSAS WITH MUSTARD SEEDS AND BLACK PEPPER

INDIA *(makes 8 pancake-breads)*

The batter for these pancakes may be made almost entirely in a food processor or blender. It may also be made several hours in advance. Please read general notes on Indian pancakes (page 283).

4 oz/115 g plain white flour
5 oz/140 g rice flour (also called rice powder)
⅛–¼ tsp cayenne pepper
4 oz/115 g peeled and chopped onion
1 oz/30 g freshly grated coconut
1¼ tsp salt

8 fl oz/2¼ dl plain yogurt (the sourer the better)
About 7 tbs vegetable oil
1 tsp whole black mustard seeds
¾–1 tsp coarsely crushed or very coarsely ground black peppercorns

Put the white flour, rice flour, cayenne, onion, coconut, salt, yogurt, and 6 fl oz/1¾ dl water into the container of a food processor or blender. Blend until smooth and pour into a bowl.

Heat 1 tbs oil in a small frying pan or pot over a medium flame. When hot, put in the mustard seeds. As soon as the mustard seeds begin to pop (almost immediately), pour the seeds and oil over the batter. Add the black pepper and mix thoroughly.

See that you have everything you need for making the pancakes: a 7–8-in/18–20-cm, nonstick frying pan, a cup containing oil, a teaspoon, a rounded soup spoon for spreading out the batter, and a small measuring cup. You also need a plate to hold the pancakes and a second plate that you can invert over the first to keep the pancakes warm and moist.

For information about ingredients and basic techniques that may be unfamiliar, see General Information, pages 481-506.

Set the frying pan over medium-low heat. Dribble ½ tsp oil into it. When the frying pan is hot, pick up 3 fl oz/1 dl of batter and plop it right in the centre of the frying pan. Immediately put the rounded bottom of a soup spoon very lightly on the blob of batter and, using a gentle but continuous spiral motion, spread the batter outwards. You should end up with a pancake 6–7-in/15–18-cm in diameter (the thinner, the better). Dribble ½ tsp of oil over the pancake and another tsp just outside its edges. Cover and cook for 3½ to 5 minutes or until the pancake has turned a reddish-gold colour on the bottom and is slightly crisp along the edges. It may not colour uniformly. Remove the cover and turn the pancake over. Cook the second side uncovered until it, too, has developed reddish-gold spots, about 4 minutes. Remove with a spatula and keep on the nearby plate. Cover with the second inverted plate. Make all the pancakes this way, stacking them all on the same plate.

If you wish to reheat these pancakes cover them well in aluminium foil, and place in a 400° F/200° C/Mark 6 oven for about 15 minutes.

Serve with South Indian Coconut Chutney or any vegetables of your choice.

SEMOLINA DOSAS WITH CUMIN SEEDS
INDIA   *(makes 8 pancake-breads)*

The batter for these pancakes may be made several hours in advance.

11 oz/310 g fine-grained semolina   *1 tsp salt*
1 tbs plain white flour   *About 7 tbs vegetable oil*
½–1 fresh hot green chilli   *1 tsp whole cumin seeds*
8 fl oz/2¼ dl plain yogurt

Put the semolina, white flour, chilli, yogurt, salt, and 8 fl oz/¼ l water into the container of a food processor or blender. Blend until smooth. Empty the batter into a bowl.

Heat 1 tbs oil in a small frying pan or pot over a medium flame. When hot, put in the cumin seeds. Stir for a few seconds. Now pour the seeds and oil over the batter. Stir to mix. Cover and set aside for half an hour.

Now make the pancakes following the directions given in the preceding recipe, Rice-Flour Dosas with Mustard Seeds and Black Pepper.

Serve with South Indian Coconut Chutney and/or any vegetables of your choice.

BINDAETUK
(Mung-Bean Pancakes)
KOREA   (makes about 8 pancakes)

It is surprising how similar these pancakes are to the mung-bean pancakes made miles away in India. When I first saw them in Seoul and asked what they were, I was told that they were 'Korean pizzas'. They are a popular street snack but they are also made in homes on festive occasions like birthdays, weddings, and New Year's Day. The street version is usually a fairly thick, 7-in/18-cm round. In homes and in restaurants, the pancakes can be much smaller. The batter contains not only soaked and ground mung beans but a little glutinous rice, mung-bean sprouts, onions, and green peppers. *Bindaetuk* are eaten with a soy-based dipping sauce.

The method for making these pancakes is very similar to that for making Mung Dal Na Poora (see page 307) — read the general notes on Indian pancakes (page 283) before making *bindaetuk*. I have used whole mung beans for this recipe because that is what the Koreans use. You could, if you like, use mung *dal* instead, which would allow you to reduce the soaking time to 5 hours and do away with the problem of rubbing away the green skin.

2 tbs glutinous rice
6½ oz/185 g whole mung beans
3 oz/85 g mung-bean sprouts
2 spring onions, cut into thin
    rounds, including green
2 oz/60 g green pepper, cut into
    ¼-in/¾-cm dice
2 oz/60 g finely chopped onion

¼ tsp bicarbonate of soda
2 tsp sesame oil
1 tbs roasted and lightly crushed
    sesame seeds
2 tsp Japanese soy sauce
1 tsp salt
About 6 fl oz/1¾ dl vegetable oil

Wash the rice and drain.

Pick over the mung beans and wash them. Drain. Put the rice and beans in a bowl. Add 1 qt/11½ dl water and set aside for 10 hours. Now dip your two hands into the soaking water and rub the beans between your palms to loosen the skins. Pour off the water. A lot of

---

For information about ingredients and basic techniques that may be unfamiliar, see General Information, pages 481-506.

the skins will float away with the water. Add more water to the bowl. Rub the beans again. Pour this water off, too. Keep doing this until nearly all the skins have been removed. Drain the rice and bean mixture thoroughly and put it into the container of a food processor. Turn the machine on and blend until you have a thick paste, stopping the machine and pushing down the batter with a rubber spatula, if necessary. Slowly add 6 fl oz/1¾ dl water to the running machine and blend again.

Empty the batter into a bowl.

Bring 1½ qt/1¾ l of water to the boil and drop in the mung sprouts. Boil rapidly for 2 minutes and drain. Squeeze out as much moisture as possible. Separate the sprouts and add them to the batter. Also add the spring onions, green pepper, onion, bicarbonate of soda, sesame oil, sesame seeds, soy sauce, and salt. Mix well.

Brush a 7-in/18-cm nonstick frying pan with about 1 tsp oil and heat over a medium-low flame. When the oil is hot, pour 3 fl oz/ ¾ dl of the batter into the centre of the skillet. Place the rounded bottom of a soup spoon very lightly on the centre of the blob of batter. Using a gentle but continuous spiral motion, spread the batter outwards with the back of the spoon until you have a 5-in/13-cm pancake. Dribble 1 tsp of oil on top of the pancake and another tsp around it. Cover the frying pan. Adjust the heat so the bottom of the pancake turns a nice reddish-brown colour in 2½ to 3 minutes. Turn the pancake over, dribble another tsp of oil around the outside of the pancake and cook, uncovered, for another 2½ to 3 minutes. Do all the pancakes this way, adding oil to the frying pan each time.

Serve *bindaetuk* hot, with Korean Dipping Sauce Number 3 (see page 416).

HOPPERS
(Yeast Pancakes)
SRI LANKA   *(makes 8 hoppers)*

If a French crêpe were to marry an English crumpet, the couple would probably become the proud parents of a Sri Lankan hopper. The hopper has the softness, delicacy, and pliability of the crêpe teamed with the airy, hole-filled, puffy, and browned-on-the-outside quality of the crumpet. What is more, it is quite easy to make, especially if your freezer already has grated fresh coconut sitting expectantly in a plastic container.

The hopper is not baked. Nor is it made in a crêpe pan. Instead, it is cooked, covered, in a wok which allows it to be thicker, whiter, and softer in the centre and crisp around its delicate browned edges. The batter is a simple one containing white flour, rice flour, and yeast. (The traditional leavening agent used to be palm toddy. Many people use yeast as a substitute now.) The batter, once made, needs to ferment overnight. In the morning it is thinned out with coconut milk.

The word 'hopper' is, of course, European, and a distortion of the Tamil word *appam* (which comes from the Tamil word *apu*, 'to clap with the hands' and thus form flat breads). Sixteenth-century Europeans who travelled through South India, where this dish probably originated, were quite taken with the bread and began to pronounce its name fairly accurately. By the early eighteenth century they were calling it 'oppers' and in the nineteenth century, when it was quite the preferred 'morning's repast' of British residents in Sri Lanka, the name had become 'hoppers'.

Traditionally, Sri Lankan hoppers are eaten for breakfast or as snacks, accompanied by a fiery hot *sambal* or sauce that has ground, dried Maldive fish in it. I have worked out an equally fiery vegetarian *sambal* for those who wish to eat their hoppers that way (see Spicy Peanut Sambal, page 421). Hoppers can also be eaten with syrups or honey. I find that I have a weakness for eating hot hoppers smeared with butter and raspberry jam! You could also eat hoppers as a bread with an Indian meal. They are good any way you eat them.

To make hoppers more quickly, you can have two small woks going at the same time.

1 tsp active dry yeast	2½ oz/70 g rice flour (also called
1 tbs sugar	rice powder), sifted
1 tsp salt	8 fl oz/¼ l coconut milk, at room
6 oz/180 g plain white flour, sifted	temperature
	About 3 tbs vegetable oil

Put the yeast in a large bowl. Slowly add 8 fl oz/¼ l lukewarm water, stirring all the time. Add the sugar and salt and mix.

Slowly add the white flour and the rice flour, mixing with a wooden spoon as you do so. You should end up with a very thick, pasty, dough-like batter. Cover the bowl with a lightly dampened tea towel (do not let the towel touch the batter) and leave it in a dark, warm spot for 10 hours. (I leave mine on an oven shelf.)

For information about ingredients and basic techniques that may be unfamiliar, see General Information, pages 481-506.

The batter should now have risen and become filled with air bubbles. Slowly add the coconut milk, mixing thoroughly as you do so. The batter will deflate; let it sit for 10 minutes as you get yourself organized for making hoppers.

Set up your wok or *karhai*, with its lid handy. Have near you: the oil in a cup, with a pastry brush alongside; two 6–7-in/15–18-cm plates to hold the hoppers as they are cooked; the batter; a small measuring cup; and a spatula, curved if possible.

Turn the flame under your wok on low and brush the centre of the wok — a diameter of about 7 in/18 cm — with approximately 1 tsp oil. Let the wok heat. Now pour in 3 fl oz/¾ dl of the batter. Quickly pick the wok up by its two handles (if it has one handle wear an oven mitt and put your second hand where the second handle would be). Swish the batter around by moving your arms in a circular motion so the batter covers ¾ in/2 cm more than its original radius (see drawing). Cover the wok and let the hopper cook on low heat for about 11 to 12 minutes or until the centre resembles a thin crumpet, the outer edges turn light brown and crisp, and the bottom is a nice reddish-golden colour. Remember that the time taken for the hopper to cook will depend upon the size and shape of your wok or *karhai*.

Lift the hopper up with the spatula and put it on a plate. Cover the plate with another plate, the second inverted over the first.

Make all the hoppers this way.

Hoppers are best eaten soon after they are made. If you wish to reheat them, divide the eight hoppers into two stacks, wrap each stack in aluminium foil, and heat in an oven preheated to 400° F/ 200° C/Mark 6 for 10 minutes.

EGG HOPPERS
(Yeast Pancakes with Eggs)
SRI LANKA   (makes 8 egg hoppers)

Egg hoppers are hoppers with whole eggs embedded in them. To make them, you need all the ingredients for hoppers (see preceding recipe) plus 8 large eggs. These pancakes may be served as a light lunch, accompanied by a green salad.

Make the batter for hoppers exactly as in the preceding recipe, letting it ferment for 10 hours and mixing it afterwards with coconut milk.

As you get ready to cook the hoppers, have the 8 eggs near by as well and a cup to break them into.

Break open an egg and put it carefully into the cup reserved for the purpose without breaking the yolk.

Pour the batter into the oiled wok as in the preceding recipe, swishing it around in a circular motion. Cover, and let the batter set for 20 to 30 seconds. Remove cover. Make a space in the centre of the batter with a spoon — do not go all the way to the bottom — and carefully slide the egg into this space. The yolk should nestle in the hole you created while the white should spread around part of the hopper. Now cover and cook the hopper as in the preceding recipe. Keep each egg hopper, covered, on a separate plate. It is really best to eat these as soon as they are made, though you can keep them covered in a warming oven.

Make all egg hoppers as you made the first one.

For information about ingredients and basic techniques that may be unfamiliar, see General Information, pages 481-506.

STEAMED BUNS
CHINA   (makes 12 buns)

These white, spongy buns may be eaten with almost any food in a
sauce. I love them with Hard-Boiled Eggs in a Spicy Almond Sauce
or Stewed Beetroot with Tomatoes and Potato Stew. As with my
other leavened breads, I have used a strong flour which is high in
both protein and gluten.

1 tsp active dry yeast   14 oz/395 g strong white flour
1 tsp plus 3 tbs sugar

Combine the yeast, 1 tsp sugar, and 2 fl oz/½ dl lukewarm water in
a cup. Set aside for 5 to 6 minutes.

Put the flour into a warm bowl. Add the 3 tbs sugar and mix
gently. Make a depression in the centre of the flour and pour in the
yeast mixture and 8 fl oz/¼ l lukewarm water. Gather the dough
together to form a ball, adding more warm water as you need it.
You will probably need to add another 2 fl oz/½ dl water. Knead the
dough for 10 to 12 minutes or until smooth. Form a ball and put it in
a large bowl. Cover the bowl with a damp cloth and set it aside in a
warm place for about 2 hours or until the dough has doubled in
bulk.

Punch down the dough and knead again for 2 to 3 minutes.
Working on a lightly floured surface, make a 12-in/30-cm roll out of
the dough. Cut the roll into twelve equal parts. Form a ball out of
each part. Dust a baking sheet lightly with flour and lay the balls on
it, at least 2 in/5 cm apart. Cover with a dry cloth and let them rise
for 45 minutes.

Set up your steaming equipment. I use a wok filled with water
over which I set up several tiers of bamboo steamers. The water in
the wok should never touch the buns. Line the bamboo steamers

with wet cheesecloth. Place as many buns in a tier as you can, making sure that they are at least 2 in/5 cm apart. Cover and steam over high heat for 15 minutes. If the water in the wok starts to boil away, be sure to replenish it with more boiling water. After the 15 minutes of steaming, turn off the heat. Let the buns sit, covered and undisturbed, for another 10 minutes. If not eating immediately allow the buns to cool. You may now pack them in plastic bags and either refrigerate them or freeze them. To reheat, steam again until heated through.

ROTI
(Flat Whole-Wheat Bread)
INDIA   (makes 12 rotis)

8 oz/225 g chapati *flour or 4 oz/*   *Additional flour for dusting*
   115 g wheatmeal flour mixed
   with 4 oz/115 g plain flour

Put the flour in a bowl. Slowly add enough water so that you will be able to gather the flour together and make a soft dough. You may need about 2½ tbs less than 8 fl oz/¼ dl water. Knead the dough for 7 to 8 minutes or until it is smooth. Make a ball and put it inside a bowl. Cover the bowl with a damp cloth and set it aside for half an hour.

If the dough looks very runny, flour your hands and knead for another few minutes. Form twelve equal balls and dust each with a little flour. Keep them covered.

Set a cast-iron griddle or frying pan to heat over a medium-low flame. Allow at least 5 minutes for that. Keep about a cup of dusting flour near you. Remove a ball of dough and flatten it between the palms of your hands. Dust it on both sides with flour. Roll it out, as thinly and evenly as you can, aiming for a 5½-in/14-cm round. When the griddle is hot, slap the *roti* on to its heated surface. Cook for about a minute or until soft bubbles begin to form. Turn the *roti* over. (Most Indians use their hands to do this.) Cook for half a minute on the second side. If you have a gas cooker, light a second burner on a medium flame and put the *roti* directly on it. Using tongs with rounded ends, rotate the *roti* so that all areas are exposed to the shooting flames. Take 5 seconds to do this. Turn the *roti* over and repeat for about 3 seconds. The *roti* should

---

For information about ingredients and basic techniques that may be unfamiliar, see General Information, pages 481-506.

puff up. Put the *roti* on a plate and cover with a clean tea towel. Make all *roti* this way. If you have an electric stove, place the griddle and *roti* under a grill for a few seconds, until the *roti* puffs up. Serve hot.

PARATHA
(Whole-Wheat Griddle Bread)
INDIA   *(makes 6 big parathas)*

4 oz/115 g wheatmeal flour plus   Additional flour for dusting
  4 oz/115 g plain flour or 8 oz/   ½ tsp salt
  225 g chapati flour   About 9 tbs vegetable oil

Put the flour and salt into a bowl. Dribble 2 tbs of oil over the flour and rub it in with your fingertips. Slowly add about 6 fl oz/1¾ dl plus 1 tbs water, gathering the dough together into a ball as you do so. You should end up with a soft dough. Knead the dough for 10 minutes and then make a ball. Put the ball in a bowl and cover the bowl with a damp cloth. Set the dough aside for half an hour.

Knead the dough again and divide it into six parts. Keep five parts covered with a damp cloth as you work with the sixth. Make a round patty out of it and then roll it out on a floured surface until you have a 6-in/15-cm round. Dust with extra flour whenever necessary. Spread about 1½ tsp oil on the top of this round. Gather the edges of the round together, forming pleats as you go. Soon you will have a closed pouch. Give the top of the pleats a small twist to close the pouch. Dust the pouch lightly with flour and put it, pleated side down, on a floured surface. Roll it out until it is about 7 in/18 cm in diameter. Heat a cast-iron griddle or frying pan over a medium-low flame. When hot, spread a tsp of oil on it and slap the *paratha* on to its heated surface. Cook for about 2 minutes.

The top of the *paratha* should now have turned fairly pale. Spread a tsp of oil over it with the back of a spoon. Cook another minute or so, turning the heat down a bit if necessary. The first side should have developed some pale, reddish-brown spots. Turn the *paratha* over and cook the second side for about 3 to 3½ minutes or until it, too, develops pale, reddish-brown spots. Take the *paratha* off the fire and wrap in aluminium foil. Make all the *parathas* this way, stacking them in the same aluminium-foil bundle. (*Parathas* may be reheated in the foil; place in a 350° F/180° C/Mark 4 oven for about 15 minutes.)

STUFFED PARATHAS
(Stuffed Whole-Wheat Griddle Breads)
INDIA   (makes 8 parathas)

8 oz/225 g chapati *flour or*
   4 oz/115 g wheatmeal flour plus
   4 oz/115 g plain flour
Additional flour for dusting
½ tsp salt plus some more for
   sprinkling
2 tbs unsalted butter, cut into 6
   pats
6 tbs peeled, finely grated, and
   well-squeezed white radish

¼ tsp garam masala
½ tsp ground cumin seeds
½–1 finely chopped fresh hot green
   chilli
¼ tsp ground dried ginger
1 tbs finely chopped fresh green
   coriander
¼ tsp ajwain seeds
6 tbs ghee *or vegetable oil*

Put the flour, ½ tsp salt, and butter into the container of a food processor with the metal blade in place. Turn on the machine for 30 seconds. Now pour in 4 fl oz/1 dl plus 3 tbs water for the *chapati* flour and about 2 tbs more for the wheatmeal mixture. Let the machine run until you have a ball of dough. Take the ball out and knead it for 10 minutes. You should have a soft but workable dough. If you do not have a processor, put the flour, salt, and slightly softened butter into a bowl. Rub with your fingers until you have the consistency of fine bread crumbs. Add the same amount of water as above and gather into a ball. Knead for 10 minutes. Form a ball with the dough and put inside a bowl. Cover the bowl with a damp cloth and set aside for ½ to 1 hour.

Combine the white radish, *garam masala*, cumin seeds, green chilli, ginger, and fresh coriander. Crush the *ajwain* seeds lightly in a mortar and add them to this mixture as well. This is the stuffing.

For information about ingredients and basic techniques that may be unfamiliar, see General Information, pages 481-506.

Heat a cast-iron griddle or a cast-iron frying pan (about 8 in/ 20 cm in diameter) over medium-low heat for about 10 minutes.

As the griddle heats, divide the dough into eight balls. Keep seven of them covered with cling film. Roll the eighth ball out on a floured board until it is 3½ in/9 cm in diameter. Place a heaped teaspoon of stuffing in its centre. Sprinkle the stuffing with a little salt. 1. Now gather the edges of the dough round and bring towards the centre, 2. twisting them slightly to form a closed ball. Flatten the ball. Sprinkle it lightly with flour and roll out on a floured board until you have a 6-in/15-cm round.

Place the *paratha* on the heated griddle. Let it cook slowly until its underside develops light-brown spots. Turn and cook the same way on the other side. Now dribble 1 tsp of *ghee* along the edges of the *paratha* so it goes under it, and 1 tsp on top. Turn the *paratha* over again and cook for about a minute. Turn a fourth time and cook, slowly, another minute. In all, the *paratha* should cook about 5 minutes and not remain raw inside. It should also not burn, so adjust your heat accordingly. Wrap the *paratha* first in kitchen paper and then in a large piece of aluminium foil. Do all *parathas* this way, stacking them one on top of the other in the same piece of foil.

Shalimar's
WONDERFUL FLAKY PARATHAS
(Flat Griddle Breads)
INDIA   *(makes 6 large parathas)*

Shalimar, one of the older Indian restaurants in New York City, makes some of the best *parathas* to the west of the Atlantic. These are not the simple, everyday *parathas* that I have described and given a recipe for in my first cookbook, *An Invitation to Indian Cooking*, nor does their distinction come from being stuffed or cooked in a *tandoor* (clay oven). They are 'plain' *parathas*, but so crisp and flaky that they are an absolute joy to eat.

The best utensil for cooking these *parathas* is a cast-iron griddle or cast-iron frying pan. The *parathas* are fairly large − about 9 in/23 cm in diameter − so you should use a griddle or frying pan that can accommodate them easily.

12 oz/340 g plain white flour, plus some extra flour for dusting
2 oz/60 g finely ground wheat-meal flour

½ tsp salt
About 12 fl oz/3½ dl melted ghee *or melted margarine*

Sift the white flour, whole-wheat flour, and salt into a bowl. Add 5 tbs of melted *ghee* and rub it into the flour until the mixture resembles coarse bread crumbs. Very slowly add 8 fl oz/¼ l plus 1 tbs water or just enough to make a very soft, pliable dough. Work the water into the flour. Gather the dough into a ball. Knead the ball for 10 minutes or until the dough is smooth and elastic. Roll the dough into a ball. Rub the ball with a little melted *ghee* and put it in a plastic bag. Set aside for half an hour.

Knead the dough again and divide it into six equal parts. Keep all the parts that you are not working with covered with cling film. Take one part and roll it into a ball. Flatten the ball. Sprinkle some flour over the area where you will make the *paratha*. Using a rolling pin, roll out the ball until it is a round, about 9 in/23 cm in diameter. If it seems to stick, sprinkle a little flour both on the rolling surface and on the *paratha*. Brush the round with melted *ghee*. Now, starting at the edge farthest away from you and using both hands, begin rolling up the *paratha* tightly towards you. Once you have completed the process, you should have a 9-in/23-cm-long 'rope' in front of you. Brush the top of this 'rope' with more melted *ghee*.

For information about ingredients and basic techniques that may be unfamiliar, see General Information, pages 481-506.

1. Coil the rope so as to form a tight cone. Flatten the cone into a patty. Press down on the patty a bit to make sure that it will not open up. Now put the patty on a plate and cover it with cling film. Take the other five remaining parts of dough and work them, one at a time, into similar patties. Put all the patties on to the same plate in a single layer. Make sure they are well covered and then refrigerate them for 1 to 2 hours. (You may even refrigerate them overnight.)

Heat a large cast-iron griddle or frying pan over a medium-low flame for 10 minutes. Turn the heat down a bit to low (not *very* low). Flour your rolling surface. 2. Take one patty and roll it out with a rolling pin until it is about 9 in/23 cm in diameter, dusting with flour whenever necessary. Brush the griddle lightly with melted *ghee*. Put the *paratha* on the hot griddle and let it cook for about 3 minutes. The top of the *paratha* should now have turned whitish. Brush the top of the *paratha* with melted *ghee* and let the bread cook, on the same side, for another 3 minutes. The first side, which should now have cooked 6 minutes, should have nice brown specks on it. If it is too dark, your heat is too high. Adjust it. Turn the *paratha* over and cook the second side for 5 to 6 minutes. It, too, should get nice medium-brown specks on it. The *paratha* should be crisp and flaky outside, soft and pliable (but not uncooked) inside.

Take the *paratha* off the griddle, cut it into quarters, and eat it immediately. If such hasty consumption is impractical, wrap the *paratha* in aluminium foil and put it in a warming oven. Do all *parathas* this way. As they are cooked, stack the *parathas* on top of each other and keep them covered.

Juji's
NAAN
(Leavened Flat Breads)
SOVIET CENTRAL ASIA, AFGHANISTAN, *(makes 9 breads)*
PAKISTAN, AND INDIA

Some version of the *naan* is made all the way from the southern part of the Soviet Union to North India, often in clay, brick, and stone ovens. The version here, simplified for home kitchens, is cooked on top of the cooker and under the grill.

1 lb/450 g plain white flour   *About 15 fl oz/4¼ dl plain yogurt*
1 tsp baking powder   *Soft, unsalted butter (optional)*
¼ tsp salt

Sift the flour, baking powder, and salt into a bowl. Slowly add as much yogurt as you need to gather the flour together and make a soft, resilient dough. Knead for about 10 minutes and form a ball. Put the ball in a bowl and cover the bowl with a damp cloth. Set aside in a warm place for 1½ to 2 hours. Knead the dough again and divide into nine equal parts. Keep them covered.

Heat a cast-iron frying pan or griddle over a lowish flame.

Preheat the grill.

Take one of the parts of dough and make a ball out of it. Flatten it and then roll it out on a lightly floured surface until you have a round that is about ⅛ in/¼ cm thick. When the frying pan is very hot, pick up the *naan* and slap it on to the heated surface. Let it cook slowly for about 4 to 5 minutes. It will puff up either completely or partially. Now put the whole frying pan under the grill for 1 to 1½ minutes or until the puffing-up process completes itself and there are a few reddish spots on the *naan*. Remove the *naan* with a spatula and brush with butter if you like. Make all the *naans* this way, keeping them stacked and covered with a clean cloth. Serve hot.

If you wish to have the *naans* later, wrap them in a plastic bag when they have cooled. Before you eat, wrap as many as you need in aluminium foil and heat in a 400°F/200°C/Mark 6 oven for 15 minutes.

PITTA BREAD
(Pocket Breads)
MIDDLE EAST   *(makes 12 breads)*

These oval, all-purpose breads are now available throughout this country. If you wish to make them at home — and it is certainly cheaper to do so — here is a recipe. I have used a strong flour which is high in both protein and gluten. You could substitute plain white flour or 14 oz/400 g plain white flour and 2 oz/50 g whole-wheat flour.

If you have a gas oven, the baking is best done on the floor of the oven. If you have an electric oven, do the cooking in the middle of the oven.

1 lb/450 g strong white flour, plus some extra for dusting	¼ oz/8 g active dry yeast
1 tsp salt	1 tsp sugar
	1 tbs olive oil

For information about ingredients and basic techniques that may be unfamiliar, see General Information, pages 481-506.

Sift the flour and salt into a large, warmed bowl. Leave in a warm place.

Combine the yeast, sugar, and 2 fl oz/½ dl lukewarm water in a small cup. Mix and set aside for 5 to 6 minutes.

Make a depression in the centre of the flour. Pour in the yeast mixture, 8 fl oz/¼ l lukewarm water, and the olive oil. Gently gather the dough to form a ball, adding more lukewarm water as you need it. You will probably need another 4–5 tbs. Once you have a ball, knead it for 10 minutes or until it is smooth. Put the ball in a large bowl and cover the bowl with a damp cloth. Set aside for 1½ to 2 hours in a warm, draught-free place until it has doubled in bulk.

Punch the dough down again and knead until smooth. Working on a surface dusted lightly with flour, make a long (12 in/30 cm or so) roll and then cut it into twelve equal parts. Roll each into ¼-in/¾-cm-thick rounds and lay these rounds on baking sheets that have been lightly dusted with flour. (I use two large baking sheets.) Cover first with a dry cloth, lightly dusted with flour, and then with a damp cloth. You may also cover with a thick plastic sheet that has been dusted with flour. Set aside in a warm, draught-free place for 45 minutes.

Sometime during this second rising, preheat your oven to its highest temperature. Put a large cast-iron frying pan or griddle on the floor of your oven if it is gas and in the middle of your oven if it is electric. Allow it to heat. Put one or two pitta breads in the hot frying pan (this will depend upon the size of your pan — my 14-in/ 35-cm pan holds two) and immediately return it to its place in the oven. Cook for 2½ to 3 minutes. The breads will puff up. You may take the breads off the frying pan the way they are, or else put them under a grill for a minute if you want the tops to brown lightly. As the breads get done, wrap them in a damp tea towel to cool them off (this gives them their leathery look) and then put them in plastic bags. You may freeze the pitta bread, if you like.

To reheat pittas, put them under a grill for a couple of minutes.

Glenda Barretto's
PUTU
(Ground Rice Muffins)
PHILIPPINES   *(makes 12 small muffins)*

Traditionally, these muffins are made out of rice that has been soaked overnight and then ground to a thick, satiny paste. Since I have been unable to find a machine here that can grind out such a paste, I have resorted to using rice powder (also called rice flour). It is best to use a rice powder of Chinese or Filipino origin.

In the Philippines, these muffins are steamed in banana-leaf cups. Other than the subtle flavour the leaves provide, muffin or large-size plain bun tins work just as well. If your steaming apparatus is similar to mine — here I use a bamboo steamer set over a wok that is half filled with water — it might be easier to steam in two batches, using six-muffin tins. A single twelve-muffin tin would just be too large.

In the Philippines, *putu* is eaten with morning chocolate and with thick stews.

9 oz/255 g rice powder *1½ tsp baking powder*
¼ tsp salt *3½ oz/100 g sugar*

Put the rice powder into the container of a food processor or blender. Add 8 fl oz/¼ l water and blend until well mixed. Stop the machine and release any flour sticking to the sides of the container with a spatula, if necessary. Let the machine run for 3 to 4 minutes or until the mixture appears smooth and satiny. Add the salt, baking powder, and sugar. Blend to mix. Pour this batter into two six-hole plain-bun tins filling each mould only half full. Steam one tin at a time, covered, over rapidly boiling water, for about 15 minutes or until a toothpick inserted inside a muffin comes out clean. As soon as you remove a bun tin, put it in a shallow pan of cold water. This loosens the muffins from the moulds.

SEMOLINA IDLIS
(Savoury Cakes)
INDIA *(makes 12 small cakes)*

Idlis are a breakfast and snack food all over South India. They are round, slightly tart cakes, about 2½–3 in/6½–8 cm in diameter and about ¾ in/2 cm thick in the centre. Rather like Madeleines, they taper off towards the edges. The most common *idlis* are made of a fermented batter of ground rice and *dal*. But there are other much simpler, quick-cooking variations. This is one of them. It is made from the supermarket variety of semolina and may be served in its traditional way with *sambar*, chutneys, and relishes or it may be served as the grain in any combination of foods that you like.

For information about ingredients and basic techniques that may be unfamiliar, see General Information, pages 481-506.

Idlis need to be steamed over rapidly boiling water. The special steaming moulds used in South India are now available in Indian grocery stores. They consist of a central trunk on which several discs may be fitted at spaced intervals. Each disc is filled with tiny steam holes. It also has round depressions in it which act as moulds for the *idlis*. The entire 'tree' is placed over boiling water, covered and steamed.

If you cannot find the *idli* moulds, it is not hard to improvise. Use a steaming trivet, about 6 in/15 cm in diameter, and put it inside a colander. It will probably come to rest somewhere above the bottom of a rounded colander. Line the trivet and the sides of the colander with a double layer of wet cheesecloth. Pour a ½-in/1½-cm thickness of batter into the cheesecloth, cover the colander, and then fold the overhanging edges of cheesecloth over the lid so they do not burn. The colander should be set over a pot of boiling water in such a way that the water stays below the level of the *idlis*. Instead of ending up with lots of small *idlis*, you will have large cakes which you can cut up into diamonds, squares, or wedges.

Whatever method of steaming you use, have plenty of extra boiling water at hand to replenish the water in your steamer.

2 tbs vegetable oil plus a little
    more for greasing the moulds
1 tsp whole black mustard seeds
6 oz/170 g semolina
3 tbs freshly grated coconut

¾ tsp salt
1–2 fresh hot green chillies, finely
    chopped
12 fl oz/3½ dl plain yogurt (the
    sourer the better)

Heat the 2 tbs oil in a frying pan over a medium flame. When the oil is hot, put in the mustard seeds. As soon as the mustard seeds begin to pop, turn the heat to medium-low and put in the semolina. Sauté for 2 to 3 minutes. The semolina should not brown. Remove the frying pan from the fire. Add the coconut, salt, and green chillies. Mix and allow to cool somewhat. Add the yogurt and mix. You should have a thick batter.

Prepare your steaming apparatus and get the water to a rolling boil. (See note at the top of the recipe.) Oil the *idli* moulds and fill each with the batter. Cover and steam for 20 minutes. Ease each *idli* out with the help of a knife and serve hot with its smoother underside up.

Sudha Doshi's
MUNG DAL DHOKLA
(*Savoury Cakes Made with Mung Dal*)
INDIA   (*makes 25–30 cubes*)

Dhoklas are served at room temperature and may be eaten at a meal or as a snack with a drink of tea, coffee, lemonade, *lassi*, or *thandai*.

6½ oz/185 g mung dal, *picked over, washed, and drained*

A ¾-in/2-cm cube of fresh ginger, *peeled and coarsely chopped*

2 fresh hot green chillies, *coarsely chopped*

2 tbs plain yogurt

1 tbs lemon juice

1 tsp salt

¼ tsp ground turmeric

1 tbs plus 2 fl oz/½ dl vegetable oil

1 tbs Eno's sparkling antacid

¹⁄₁₆ tsp ground asafetida

1 tbs whole black mustard seeds

2 tbs sesame seeds

2 tbs finely chopped fresh green coriander

1 oz/30 g grated fresh coconut

Pick over the *dal*, then wash, and drain. Soak in 1¼ pt/7 dl of water for 3 hours. Drain.

In the container of an electric blender or food processor, combine the ginger, green chillies, yogurt, lemon juice, and 8 fl oz/¼ l water. Blend thoroughly. Now add the drained *dal*, salt, and turmeric. Blend again until you have a fairly smooth batter. Let the batter rest, unrefrigerated, for 2 to 3 hours.

Arrange a utensil for steaming. (I use a bamboo steamer with a domed lid which I place inside a wok. If you decide to put a trivet inside a large pot, make sure that the pot is wide enough to hold an 8-in/20-cm cake tin easily. Also, line the lid of your pot with a tea towel so droplets of water will not fall on to the steaming *dhokla*.) Rub the inside of an 8-in/20-cm round cake tin with 1½ tsp of the oil. Pour enough water into the steaming utensil so it stays just

---

For information about ingredients and basic techniques that may be unfamiliar, see General Information, pages 481-506.

below the cake tin. (If using a wok, pour in enough water so it stays just below the bottom of the bamboo steamer. If using a trivet inside a pot, the water should stay ¼ in/¾ cm below the top of the trivet.) Bring the water to the boil. Keep an extra kettle of boiling water handy in case you begin to run low on the steaming water.

Stir the batter and pour half of it (about 12 fl oz/3½ dl) into a clean bowl. Stir it again. Now sprinkle 1½ tsp of the Eno's antacid over the batter and immediately begin to stir *gently* and in *one direction*. Keep stirring slowly, even as the batter froths and foams, until it is well mixed. Pour this batter into the cake tin and place the cake tin in the steamer. Cover and steam for 10 minutes or until a toothpick inserted into the *dhokla* comes out clean. Remove the cake tin from the steamer and let it sit for 10 minutes. Meanwhile prepare a second batch for steaming just as you did the first, using a fresh cake tin. Put it to steam, removing it after 10 minutes also.

Cut the first *dhokla* into 1½-in/4-cm squares. When the second *dhokla* has rested for 10 minutes, cut it into similar squares. If not eating immediately, let the squares cool completely in the tins and then cover with aluminium foil or cling film. They can stay this way, unrefrigerated, for 4 to 5 hours.

Just before serving, take squares carefully out of the cake tins and arrange neatly in a single layer on one or two serving platters. (I arrange them in the same circular shape as the cake tin.) Heat the 2 fl oz/½ dl oil in a small frying pan or small pot over a medium flame. When hot, put in the asafetida, mustard and sesame seeds, immediately covering the frying pan with a mesh splatter shield, if you have one. Keep shaking the frying pan. When the sesame seeds have browned lightly (this happens very quickly), turn off heat and remove splatter shield. Quickly spoon the oil and seeds evenly over the *dhoklas*. Garnish the *dhoklas* with sprinklings of fresh coriander and fresh coconut.

Hsu Hung Ying's
YOW BING
(Fried Bread with Spring Onions)
TAIWAN   *(makes 4 very large breads)*

This bread may be eaten with Chinese Dipping Sauce (see page 414).

About 8–12 oz/225–340 g plain
   white flour
4 tsp vegetable oil
1¼ tsp salt

3 oz/85 g very finely sliced spring
   onions
vegetable oil for shallow frying

Put 6 oz/180 g flour in a bowl. Pour 6 fl oz/1¾ dl very hot (but not boiling) water over it. Stir quickly with a pair of chopsticks or with a wooden spoon. Begin to add flour, a little at a time, and try to gather the flour into a ball. You will need at least 2½ oz/75 g of flour, or more. The dough should remain soft. Take the dough out of the bowl and knead for 10 minutes, adding more flour if it is too sticky. Form a ball and put it in a bowl. Cover the bowl with a damp cloth and set aside for an hour.

Flour your work surface and knead the dough again. Roll the dough out into an oval shape that is about ¼–⅛ in/¾–¼ cm thick. As you do this, keep lifting up the dough and dusting its underside as well as the top with flour. Spread 4 tsp of oil over the surface of the dough. Then sprinkle the salt over it evenly. Scatter the spring onions evenly over the salt. Using both hands, roll the dough tightly away from you. You should now have a long stuffed roll. (If the dough sticks at all to the work surface, use a knife to release it.) Now cut the roll into four equal sections. Dust each lightly with flour. Pick up one section at a time with two hands and give it a few twists along its length. Now bring the ends of the section together to form a patty. Flatten the patty somewhat and dust it lightly with flour. Make four patties this way, dusting each with flour and setting them down on a floured surface at some distance from each other so they do not stick together.

On a floured surface, roll out one patty until you have an ⅛-in/¼-cm-thick round. You may need to dust it with flour several times during this rolling.

Cover a 10–12-in/25–30-cm heavy frying pan with a thick coating of oil and heat over a medium-low flame. When it is hot, put in the bread. Cook it for about 2 minutes, pressing down now and then so all parts touch the bottom of the frying pan. Turn the bread over and cook the second side the same way for 2 minutes. Now turn back to the first side. Keep doing this until both sides develop reddish-gold spots and the bread is cooked through. Remove with a slotted spatula and place on a plate lined with kitchen paper. Make all the breads this way, stacking one on top of the other, between layers of kitchen paper. Replenish the oil, whenever necessary. Serve hot, each bread cut in quarters.

For information about ingredients and basic techniques that may be unfamiliar, see General Information, pages 481-506.

POORIS
(Deep-Fried Breads)
INDIA   *(makes 8 large pooris)*

Pooris may be made out of all kinds of flours. Here is a flour combination that makes wonderfully soft, pliable *pooris*.

1 oz/30 g whole-wheat flour	*¼ tsp salt*
2 oz/60 g plain white flour plus	*1 tbs vegetable oil*
some extra for dusting	*Vegetable oil for deep frying*
2 oz/60 g fine-grained semolina	

Put the whole-wheat flour, the 2 oz/60 g white flour and semolina into a bowl. Add the salt. Dribble 1 tbs oil over the flours and rub it in with your fingertips. Add water, a little bit at a time, and gather the dough together to make a ball. As you need a fairly soft dough, the amount of water may well be around 4 fl oz/1 dl plus 1 tbs. Knead the dough for 10 minutes or until it is smooth. Put dough in a bowl and cover with a damp cloth. Set aside for half an hour.

Put the oil for deep frying in a wok and set it to heat on a flame that is slightly lower than medium. Knead the dough again and divide it into twelve equal parts. Keep the parts you are not working with covered with the damp cloth. Make a round ball out of one of the parts and then flatten it with your palm to form a patty. Sprinkle a little flour on it. Flour your work surface and roll out the patty into a 5½-in/14-cm round.

When the oil in the wok is very hot (it should not be smoking, though), pick up the rolled-out *poori* and take it as close as possible to the oil. Lay it over the oil, making sure that it does not double over. (If the *poori* sinks quietly to the bottom of the wok, the oil is not hot enough.) The *poori* will start sizzling. Using quick but very gentle taps with the back of a slotted spoon, keep pushing the *poori* slightly under the oil. Within seconds it should balloon. Turn it over and cook the second side for a few seconds. Remove with a slotted spoon and place in a bowl lined with kitchen paper. Cover the bowl with a plate or lid. Make all the *pooris* this way. (Keep an eye on the oil as you are rolling out the *pooris*. If it starts to overheat, remove it from the flame for a while.)

Ideally, *pooris* should be eaten as soon as they are made. If you keep them tightly covered, you may eat them somewhat later at room temperature. They will have deflated but will still taste good.

BANANA POORIS
INDIA   *(makes 8 pooris)*

These *pooris* are flavoured with freshly mashed bananas and may be eaten with an Indian meal or may be sprinkled with icing sugar and eaten at tea-time. They are excellent either way. Care must be taken to roll these *pooris* out as thinly as possible or the inside will not cook properly. As with the potato *pooris* which follow, you should start off with a fairly stiff dough. The dough will soften as it 'rests'.

About 1 ripe banana, or less
5 oz/140 g plain white flour
Vegetable oil for deep frying

4 tsp icing sugar (optional)
About 1½ tbs vegetable oil

Mash the banana thoroughly. You may do this in a food processor or blender. You will need 4 tbs of banana paste.

Sift the flour into a bowl. Add 1 tbs oil. Rub the oil into the flour until the mixture resembles coarse bread crumbs. Add the 4 tbs banana paste and rub that into the flour as well, making sure to distribute it as thoroughly as possible. Now add about 1 tbs of water and gather the dough into a ball. Knead for about 10 minutes. You should have a fairly stiff dough. Make a ball out of the dough and rub the ball with a little oil. Put the ball in a plastic bag and set it aside for 1 hour.

The dough ball should be softer now. Knead it again for a couple of minutes. Divide the dough into eight equal parts. Keep all the parts covered with cling film.

Heat the oil for deep frying in a wok or *karhai* over a medium flame. You should have a good 2½ in/6½ cm in the centre of the wok. Wait for the oil to get very hot.

As the oil heats, lightly flour your work surface. Take out one part of the dough and make a ball out of it in your palms. Flatten the ball and flour it lightly. Now roll it out evenly with a rolling pin, sprinkling the surface and the *poori* with flour whenever you need to, until you have a round about 4½–5 in/12–13 cm in diameter.

Fry the *poori* in the hot oil as in the directions given on page 333. Put the cooked *poori* on a platter lined with kitchen paper. Do all the *pooris* this way. If the *pooris* are to be eaten sweet, they should be eaten as soon as they are made, each sprinkled with about ½ tsp of icing sugar. If the *pooris* are to be eaten up to half an hour later with a meal, they may be put into a bowl or deep plate lined with kitchen paper and then covered with an inverted plate.

For information about ingredients and basic techniques that may be unfamiliar, see General Information, pages 481-506.

POTATO POORIS
INDIA   *(makes 8 pooris)*

The dough for these *pooris* has both white flour and mashed potatoes in it, making for a very interesting taste. I have seasoned my dough with just salt, cumin, and *garam masala*, though you could add cayenne and very finely chopped fresh green coriander as well. I love the smell of these *pooris*: if one could bottle the smell of a traditional Delhi or Uttar Pradesh kitchen at a time when a banquet was being prepared, one would probably come up with the delicate aroma of these fried potato breads.

1 medium-sized potato, freshly boiled in its jacket	½ tsp ground cumin seeds
5 oz/140 g plain white flour	½ tsp garam masala
½ tsp salt	About 1½ tbs vegetable oil
	Vegetable oil for deep frying

Peel the potato while it is still hot and mash it well. (I put the hot potato through a ricer.) Let it cool off a bit.

Sift the flour, salt, cumin, and *garam masala* into a bowl. Add the potato and rub it into the flours, distributing it as thoroughly as you can. Add 4 tsp oil and rub that in as well. Collect the dough and try to form a ball. You may need to add a tbs of water. The ball will be hard but this is as it should be. Knead the dough for 10 minutes. Form a ball again. Rub the ball lightly with a little oil and put it in a plastic bag. Set it aside for 15 minutes.

Knead the dough again for a couple of minutes. Divide the dough into eight equal parts. Keep the parts covered with cling film.

Heat oil for deep frying in a wok or *karhai* over a medium flame. You should have a good 2½ in/6½ cm in the centre of the wok. Wait for the oil to get very hot.

As the oil heats, lightly flour your work surface. Take one part of the dough and make a ball out of it in your hands. Flatten the ball and flour it lightly. Now roll it out evenly with a rolling pin, sprinkling the surface and the *poori* with flour whenever you need to, until you have a round about 5½–6 in/14–15 cm in diameter.

Fry the *poori* in the hot oil as in the directions given on page 333. Put the cooked *poori* on a platter lined with kitchen paper and continue with the rest. If the *pooris* are not going to be eaten within 10 to 15 minutes, they should be kept covered. Put them on a deep plate or a bowl lined with kitchen paper and cover with an inverted plate. You can keep them this way for half an hour in a warm spot.

BHATURAS
(Deep-Fried Leavened Breads)
INDIA   *(makes 24 breads)*

1 lb/450 g plain white flour
½ tsp salt
1 tsp bicarbonate of soda
2 tsp sugar
4 fl oz/1 dl plain, slightly warmed
  yogurt

2 large eggs, at room temperature
2 tsp vegetable oil
Vegetable oil for deep frying
Additional flour for kneading and
  rolling

Sift the flour, salt, and bicarbonate of soda into a warm bowl. Add sugar, yogurt, and eggs. Mix well. Now add lukewarm water, a little at a time, until the dough holds together in a ball. (You will need a little less than 4 fl oz/1 dl.) Knead well for 10 to 15 minutes or until the dough is smooth and elastic but soft. Form the dough into a ball. Rub the ball with about 2 tsp of oil and place in a clean bowl. Cover the bowl with cling film or a wet towel and leave in a warm, draught-free area to rise for 5 hours (or overnight in a 68–75°F/ 20–24°C kitchen).

Knead dough again. Divide it into twenty-four equal balls and keep them covered. Line a platter with kitchen paper and keep near stove. Heat about 2 in/5 cm of oil in a deep frying pan over a medium flame. (A wok could be used instead.) Let it get very hot. Meanwhile roll out each ball until it is about 5½ in/14 cm in dia-meter, dusting with flour if it sticks. As soon as it is rolled out, drop into the hot fat. It will first sink to the bottom and then, in a few seconds, rise and sizzle. Press down on it gently, again and again, with the back of a slotted spoon, using quick, light strokes. The bread should puff up and turn golden on its under-side. Turn it over and let the other side turn light brown. The entire process should take less than 1 minute. Put the *bhatura* on the lined platter and cover with a lined plate or inverted bowl. Do all *bhaturas* this way and keep covered.

For information about ingredients and basic techniques that may be unfamiliar, see General Information, pages 481-506.

8 Soups

Perhaps the hardest thing for vegetarians to arrive at is a good, sound stock. I remember once when I was shepherding an out-of-town vegetarian friend through New York's eateries, he was willing to go to most places — but not Chinese restaurants. 'It's the stock,' he said. 'Even when you order stir-fried greens, you just know that they will put a little meat stock in it.' Which is probably true. A good stock enriches the simplest of dishes very quickly. For light, brothy soups, it is absolutely essential. You can, of course, use the water left over from boiling beans and vegetables. But some soups demand that the broth have more taste and character.

The classical Japanese vegetarian stock — *dashi* — uses *kombu* (dried kelp) and dried *shiitake* mushrooms, plus seasonings such as soy sauce and *mirin* (sweet *sake*). It is light and delicate, with its quality depending upon the grade of *kombu*. The Chinese use the water left over from boiling soy beans or just plain water seasoned with soy sauce and monosodium glutamate. Even though msg is used from Korea down to Bali, I never cook with it. It is unnecessary. I have devised quite a wonderful stock of my own that uses soy-bean sprouts and dried mushrooms — Chinese or Japanese — as a base. I add some spring onions, a carrot, lettuce leaves, soy sauce, sesame oil, and a little sugar for extra flavour. That sugar is important as it balances the soy sauce and brings out the flavour of the stock. I've called this stock Delicious Stock Made with Soy-Bean Sprouts and you will find it on page 340. There are a few other stocks, too, for you to experiment with. See what you like and add extra seasonings as you see fit.

A good stock is essential for soups such as Clear Soup with Soft Bean Curd and Chinese Leaves, Hot-and-Sour Soup, and Thai Noodle Soup. My favourite cold soup, Naeng Myon, would taste quite insipid without it. I am just waiting for the day when *naeng myon* is served in every vegetarian restaurant. It consists of a mound of thin noodles in cold broth. The noodles are covered with sliced hard-boiled eggs, sliced cucumber, sliced white radish pickle, and slices of crisp Korean pear-apple (hard pears may be substituted). This is topped with sliced hot chillies, spring onions, and roasted sesame seeds. The soup is served with an array of additional sauces. It is spectacular in every way.

Needless to say, not all soups require stock. The very pleasant cold yogurt soups from Iran and the Caucasus region require only soothing vegetables such as cucumber or else varying combinations of nuts, dried fruit, fresh herbs, grains, and beans. Some vegetable soups, such as those made with tomatoes and potatoes, require no assistance either. And then there is the whole world of thick and thin bean and split-pea soups that tend to create their own broth.

Asia has several types of bean and split-pea soups. Those in Japan are made out of fermented bean and grain pastes known as *miso*. *Miso* comes in various hues according to the bean and grain used, ranging from dark brown, red, ochre, and yellow to white. The degree of saltiness and sweetness varies in each one of them. *Miso* is now available in Britain not just in Japanese stores, but in many health-food stores as well. I have identified the pastes by colour as that is how they are sometimes sold. The two *miso* soups here, one with bean curd and the other with carrot and mushrooms, should give you a good idea of how these soups are put together. You can improvise your own *miso* soups after that, putting anything into them that you fancy.

When split peas are cooked − and in many Indian homes they are cooked for every single meal − a thin liquid rises to the top while the heavier split peas sink to the bottom. In South India, this thin liquid is removed to make *rasam*, a tart, tamarind-flavoured, soupy dish that is either drunk at the start of a meal or eaten with rice. The thicker split peas − or *dal* − are used to make *sambar*. This way the same *dals* end up doing double duty most efficiently.

The Middle East has many thick, hearty bean soups, such as Chick Pea Soup and Haricot Bean and Celeriac Soup, that are almost a meal in themselves. All that you need to serve with them is some pitta bread, a yogurt cheese, and a crisp salad.

For information about ingredients and basic techniques that may be unfamiliar, see General Information, pages 481-506.

DASHI
(Kombu and Shiitake Mushroom Stock)
JAPAN   (makes 1¼ pt/¾ l)

This is the basic, classical Japanese stock used for cooking vegetables and for making vegetarian soups. It requires *kombu*, a
long, leaf-like kelp, filled with vitamins, calcium and flavour.
Dashi may be refrigerated and will keep for 3 to 4 days.

1 piece of kombu, about 4 × 7 in/   1 tsp Japanese soy sauce
   10 × 18 cm   ½ tsp mirin
5 medium-sized dried shiitake (or
   Chinese black) mushrooms

Wipe the *kombu* lightly with a damp cloth and put it into a 2–3-qt/
2¼–3½-l pot. Add 1¼ pt/ ¾ l water and bring to the boil. When the
water begins to boil rapidly, remove the *kombu* with a pair of tongs
(save it for Kombu Relish or for making a second stock) and turn off
the heat. Rinse the mushrooms quickly and throw them into the
hot liquid. Let them soak for 30 minutes. Remove the mushrooms
(they can be used in soups and other dishes). Add the soy sauce
and *mirin*. Strain the stock through three layers of cheesecloth if
the mushrooms have left any grit at the bottom of your pot.

JAPANESE STOCK
JAPAN   (makes about 1 pt/5¾ dl)

This is a richer and somewhat less austere stock than the preceding
Dashi. It may also be used for cooking vegetables and for making
Japanese soups.

8 medium-sized dried shiitake (or   ½ tsp salt
   Chinese black) mushrooms   1 4-in/10-cm square of kombu
6 spring onions, each cut into 3   2 tsp Japanese soy sauce
   sections   ¼ tsp sugar
2 carrots, trimmed, peeled, and   1 tsp mirin
   each cut into 3 sections   ½ tsp sesame oil

Rinse the mushrooms quickly. In a small pot, combine the mushrooms, spring onions, carrots, 1¼ pt/¾ l water, and ¼ tsp of the
salt. Cover and simmer gently on a low flame for 30 minutes. Wipe
the *kombu* lightly with a damp cloth and put into the pot. Simmer
for 1 minute. Turn off the heat and strain the stock immediately
through three layers of cheesecloth. (The *kombu* may be saved to
make Kombu Relish.) Add the remaining ¼ tsp salt, soy sauce,
sugar, *mirin*, and sesame oil to the stock. Stir to mix.

DELICIOUS STOCK MADE WITH SOY-BEAN SPROUTS

(makes 1 qt/11½ dl)

This tasty stock may be used for any Asian soup.

6 oz/170 g soy-bean sprouts
16 medium-sized dried shiitake
   (or Chinese black) mushrooms
1 carrot, peeled
6 outer lettuce leaves

5 spring onions
1 tsp salt
2 tsp Japanese soy sauce
1 tsp sesame oil
½ tsp sugar

Wash the sprouts well and drain them. Rinse the mushrooms quickly. In a large pot, combine the sprouts, mushrooms, carrot, lettuce, spring onions, salt, and 3¼ pt/1¾ l water. Bring to the boil. Cover, turn heat to low and simmer for 1 hour. Strain the stock through three layers of cheesecloth. Add the soy sauce, sesame oil, and sugar. Mix. Bring the stock to the boil again and reduce it until you have 1 qt/11½ dl.

This stock may be refrigerated for 2 to 3 days or else frozen.

VEGETABLE STOCK
(For Chinese Dishes and Soups)

(makes 1½ pt/8½ dl)

Vegetable stocks do not taste like meat stocks. They have their own delicate taste which can vary with the vegetables that you happen to have around in your refrigerator. You could add pea pods, celery, parsnips, courgette tips, fresh mushroom stems, asparagus bottoms, watercress stems, green peppers, and parsley.

16 medium-sized dried shiitake
   (or Chinese black) mushrooms
4 carrots, washed and scrubbed
8 whole spring onions
6 outer lettuce leaves

1 tsp salt
1 tsp Chinese thin soy sauce
2 tsp sesame oil
¼ tsp sugar

Rinse the mushrooms quickly in cold water. Wash and scrub the carrots, leaving 4 in/10 cm of their tops on, if possible.

Combine the mushrooms, carrots, spring onions, lettuce, salt, and 1 qt/11½ dl water in a 4-qt/4½-l pot and bring to the boil. Cover, lower heat and simmer for half an hour. Strain the stock through

---

For information about ingredients and basic techniques that may be unfamiliar, see General Information, pages 481-506.

three layers of cheesecloth. (Discard all the vegetables except the mushrooms. Save the mushrooms for other dishes — you can slice and put them in scrambled eggs, you can put them in soups, you can put them in fried rice, and you can stir-fry them with various greens.) Boil down the stock to 1½ pt/8½ dl. Add the soy sauce, sesame oil, and sugar. Mix and check seasonings.

Alun's
CACIK
(Cold Yogurt Soup in a Turkish Style)
TURKEY   (serves 4–6)

This is an excellent soup to have on hot summer days.

A 6-in/15-cm length of cucumber
¾ tsp salt, or to taste
15 fl oz/4¼ dl plain yogurt
4 fl oz/1 dl milk

1 clove garlic, peeled and mashed
   to a pulp in a mortar
1 tbs fruity olive oil

Peel the cucumber. Cut it in half lengthwise and scrape out all the seeds with a grapefruit spoon. Now cut the cucumber into ¼-in/¾-cm dice. Sprinkle with ¼ tsp salt and set aside for half an hour. Squeeze out as much moisture as you can.

Put the yogurt in a bowl. Beat with a fork or whisk until it is smooth and creamy. Slowly add the milk, beating gently as you do so.

Add the cucumber to the yogurt, along with the remaining ½ tsp salt, garlic, and olive oil. Mix well and chill until ready to serve.

PERSIAN-STYLE COLD YOGURT SOUP
IRAN   (serves 4–6)

2 tbs sultanas
A 6-in/15-cm length of cucumber
15 fl oz/4¼ dl plain yogurt
¾ tsp salt
⅛ tsp freshly ground black pepper

8 fl oz/¼ l single cream
2 tbs very finely sliced tender
   green of spring onions
3 tbs coarsely chopped walnuts
1 tbs finely chopped fresh dill

Soak the sultanas in 8 fl oz/¼ l hot water for 1 hour, then drain.

Peel the cucumber. Remove seeds if they are very large, then grate the cucumber.

Put yogurt, salt, and pepper into a bowl. Beat yogurt with a fork or whisk until it is creamy. Slowly add 8 fl oz/¼ l iced water and then the cream, beating as you do so. Now add all the other ingredients. Mix well.

If the soup is not to be drunk immediately, it should be refrigerated. It is best served on hot days.

NAENG MYON
(Cold Noodle Soup)
KOREA   *(serves 4)*

This is easily one of the greatest cold soups on this earth. I often had it for lunch in Korea. As it is almost a meal in itself, not much else needs to be served with it except, of course, some *kimchee*. And even though it has many parts to it, these various components as well as the sauces may be made in advance and refrigerated.

In the dining room of Seoul's King Sejong Hotel, a separate buffet table is set aside, loaded with all the prepared components of the more common, non-vegetarian version of this soup. Diners come with empty soup bowls and put the soup together themselves. Cold, cooked noodles are first piled in the centre of the bowl. Cold broth is then ladled over the noodles. Various fruits and vegetables, all sliced thin, are laid over the noodles like the rays of the sun. The central 'sun' consists of slices of hard-boiled egg. The soup is then seasoned to taste with various sauces which include prepared English mustard, a soy-vinegar sauce, and the cool liquid from Dong Chimi, the white radish water *kimchee*. Additional seasonings, such as sliced chillies, sliced spring onions, sliced Chinese chives, and roasted sesame seeds are sprinkled over the top.

I developed such a passion for this soup that I found myself hunting for it in every Korean city. In Pusan, I discovered a very interesting variation. The vegetables and fruit had been cut into very fine julienne strips. The hard-boiled eggs had been replaced by very fine Egg Strands (see page 241). All of these had been piled on top of the noodles in a big mound.

½ lb/225 g thin Japanese or Korean buckwheat noodles*
1 qt/11½ dl Delicious Stock . . . (see page 340), refrigerated at least 3 hours, or any flavourful vegetable stock
1 tsp sesame oil
A 6-in/15-cm length of cucumber
2 cold hard-boiled eggs
8 rectangles Dong Chimi (pickled white radish, see page 443)
½ pear-apple, if available, or a whole, very hard and crunchy pear

*If you can't get the buckwheat noodles, substitute vermicelli, spaghettini, or fresh Chinese noodles.

SAUCES FOR NAENG MYON
Mustard Sauce: put 4 tsp of dry English mustard in a small cup, add 4 tsp water and mix.
Korean Dipping Sauce Number 3 (see page 416)
8 fl oz/¼ l cold liquid from the Korean water pickle, Dong Chimi (see page 443): stir before pouring the liquid out

ADDITIONAL OPTIONAL SEASONINGS
1–2 fresh hot green chillies, sliced into very, very fine rounds
A ¾-in/2-cm cube of peeled fresh ginger, cut into very fine shreds
1½ tbs roasted and lightly crushed sesame seeds
2 tbs very finely sliced spring onions or Chinese chives

Cook the noodles according to the instructions on the packet. (Directions for cooking Chinese noodles are given on page 286.) Drain the noodles in a colander and rinse thoroughly under cold running water. Put the noodles in a bowl. Toss with 4 fl oz/1 dl of the stock and the sesame oil. Cover and set aside.

Do not peel the cucumber. Scrub it under running water and cut into 2–2½-in/5–6½-cm chunks. Trim away the ends. Now cut lengthwise into ⅛-in/½-cm-thick slices. Cut these slices, lengthwise, in half. Ideally, you should end up with rectangles that are 2 in/5 cm long, ¾ in/2 cm wide, and ⅛ in/½ cm thick. The ends that are almost all skin may be discarded.

Peel the eggs and cut them crosswise into ¼-in/¾-cm-thick slices.

Cut the rectangles of pickled white radish lengthwise into slices that are about 1½ in/4 cm long, ½ in/1½ cm wide, and ⅛ in/½ cm thick.

Peel the pear-apple or pear and core it. Cut it into ⅛-in/½-cm-thick slices. The pear should be cut at the last minute so it does not discolour.

To serve, divide the noodles among four bowls. Pour one quarter of the stock over each pile of noodles. Put a few neatly overlapping egg slices right on top of the noodles in the centre. Arrange a few slices each of the vegetables and fruit all around like slightly overlapping rays of the sun. Put the mustard sauce in a very small bowl and the dipping sauce and pickle water in 'slightly larger bowls. Put the optional seasoning in shallow bowls or saucers. The sauces and seasonings should be passed around to each diner. Diners should put in whatever they want and as much as they like. Offer chopsticks and soup spoons as eating implements. Serve Cabbage Kimchee (see page 440) as an accompaniment.

COLD YOGURT SOUP WITH BARLEY
CAUCASUS   (serves 4)

1½ oz/45 g hulled barley, washed
    and drained
3 tbs unsalted butter or vegetable
    oil
3 tbs finely chopped fresh mint

1 small onion, peeled and finely
    chopped
15 fl oz/4¼ dl yogurt
8 fl oz/2¼ dl milk
¾ tsp salt
Freshly ground black pepper

Put the barley and 16 fl oz/½ l water in a small pot and bring to the boil. Cover, turn heat to low and simmer for 50 to 60 minutes or until barley is tender. Pour the contents of the pot into a sieve to drain. Hold the sieve under running water and rinse the barley. Set the sieve over a bowl and leave to drain.

Heat the butter or oil in a frying pan over a low flame. Put in the mint and onion. Stir and sauté gently for 5 to 6 minutes or until onion is quite tender but not at all brown. Turn the heat off under the frying pan and let the mixture cool slightly.

Put the yogurt in a bowl. Beat lightly with a fork or whisk until smooth and creamy. Add the milk. Beat again to mix. Now add the barley, salt, black pepper, and the mixture in the frying pan. Stir to mix. Refrigerate until ready to eat.

Gary Jenanyan's
TAN ABOUR
(Cold Yogurt Soup with Chick Peas and Wheat)
TURKEY/ARMENIA   *(serves 4)*

Gary lives in California and it was his maternal grandfather, still hale and hearty in his nineties, who brought this simple recipe out with him when he fled Turkey during the massacre of the Armenians by the Turks. It is a dish that is eaten in their house almost every day.

I often double this recipe and leave whatever is uneaten in the refrigerator. It keeps beautifully for days and may be served as a soup course or for breakfast or lunch. The drained chick pea broth may be used as stock.

2 oz/60 g whole-wheat berries,   *Salt*
   picked over, washed, and   *15 fl oz/4¼ dl plain yogurt*
   drained   *2 tbs finely chopped fresh mint*
3 oz/85 g dried chick peas, picked
   over, washed, and drained

Soak the wheat in 12 fl oz/3½ dl water for 12 hours.

Soak the chick peas in 1¼ pt/¾ l water for 12 hours.

Drain and rinse the wheat. Put it in a small pot along with 1¼ pt/¾ l water and bring to the boil. Cover partially, turn heat to low and simmer for 45 minutes. Add ½ tsp salt and simmer another 30 minutes. Drain and rinse.

While the wheat is cooking, drain and rinse the chick peas and put them in another pot with 1½ pt/8½ dl water. Bring to the boil. Cover partially, turn heat to low and simmer for 1½ hours. Add 1 tsp salt and simmer for 30 minutes or until chick peas are tender. Drain and put in a bowl. Cover with cold water. Rub the chick peas gently with your hands to loosen the skins. Pour off the water and the loosened skins. Cover the chick peas again with water. Rub to remove more skins. Keep doing this until most of the skins have been taken off. Drain. (The removal of the skins is not essential to this soup. I just think that it improves both the taste and appearance somewhat.)

Put the yogurt in a bowl. Beat lightly with a fork or whisk until smooth and creamy. Add the mint, wheat, and chick peas. Stir to mix. While it is not common to add salt at this stage, you may do so if you wish.

CLEAR SOUP WITH MUSHROOMS, BEAN-CURD SKINS, AND SPINACH

JAPAN   *(serves 4)*

1 sheet dried bean-curd skin, about
   5 × 1½ × ⅟₃₂ in/13 × 4 × ⅛ cm
1½ pt/8½ dl Japanese Stock (see
   page 339) or any light vegetable
   stock

5 medium-sized mushrooms, sliced
12 spinach leaves, well washed
1 tsp lemon juice
8 slivers of lemon peel, each about
   1 in/2½ cm long

Rinse the bean-curd skin in hot water, then soak in hot water for 10 minutes. Drain and cut it crosswise into ⅟₁₆-in/¼-cm-wide strips.

Bring the Japanese Stock to the boil in a 2-qt/2¼-l pot. Add the bean-curd-skin strips, mushrooms, and spinach leaves. Simmer the soup on medium heat until the spinach leaves have wilted, about 1 minute. Add the lemon juice, stir, and taste for seasonings. I usually do not need any more salt than is in the broth but you might want a bit more.

Divide the soup among four soup bowls. Garnish each bowl with 2 slivers of lemon peel and serve immediately. The Japanese like to drink their soup directly from the soup bowls. Solids are picked up with chopsticks.

CLEAR SOUP WITH SOFT BEAN CURD AND CHINESE LEAVES

CHINA   *(serves 6)*

This is a light, very pleasant soup.

1¾ pt/1 l Vegetable Stock (see page
   340) or any stock of your choice
¼ tsp salt
½ lb/225 g Chinese leaves, cut into
   1¼-in/3¼-cm-wide strips

1 lb/450 g soft or medium bean
   curd, cut into approximately
   1-in/2½-cm cubes

Heat the stock in a wide pot or a casserole-type dish that can be taken to the table, over a medium-high flame. When it is simmering, put in the salt and the Chinese leaves. Cover, lower flame, and simmer gently for about 3 minutes or until the Chinese leaves are just tender. Uncover, and put in the bean-curd cubes. Cook, uncovered, for another minute to allow the bean curd to heat

---

For information about ingredients and basic techniques that may be unfamiliar, see General Information, pages 481-506.

through. Serve immediately in a large, warmed soup tureen or in the casserole dish in which it was cooked.

SWEET CORN AND EGG SOUP
CHINA   (serves 4)

1½ pt/8½ dl Vegetable Stock (see page 340) or any stock of your choice
2 tsp cornflour
2 tsp sesame oil
2 small or 1½ large eggs

5 oz/140 g tinned sweet-corn kernels (or frozen), drained and coarsely chopped
⅓–½ tsp salt
⅛ tsp freshly ground white pepper
¾ tsp Chinese thin soy sauce
2 tsp very finely sliced spring onions

Remove 2 fl oz/½ dl of cool stock and slowly mix it with the cornflour to make a smooth paste. Add 1 tsp sesame oil and set this mixture aside. Beat the eggs lightly (they should not froth) and add the remaining 1 tsp sesame oil to it. Mix well and set aside.

Heat the remaining stock in a 2–3-qt/2¼–3½-l pot over a medium-high flame. When hot, add the corn, salt, pepper, and soy sauce. Bring to a simmer and turn heat to low. Stir the cornflour mixture and pour it into the hot stock. Stir and cook on low heat until the mixture thickens slightly. Turn off the heat. Immediately pour in the egg mixture in a slow, steady stream, covering the entire surface of the soup with it. Stir gently.

Pour the soup into individual bowls and sprinkle each bowl with some of the sliced spring onions.

WHITE RADISH SOUP
KOREA   (serves 4–6)

This was one of my favourite breakfast soups in Korea. It is very soothing and warming, especially on cold, blustery days.

2½ pt/1½ l Delicious Stock . . . (see page 340) or any vegetable stock
16 Chinese mushrooms (from the above stock)*
1 lb/450 g white radish, peeled and cut into ¾-in/2-cm dice

10 oz/285 g mung-bean sprouts, washed and drained
½–1 tsp Japanese soy sauce
½ tsp sugar

*If you haven't saved the mushrooms from the stock, soak 16 Chinese dried black mushrooms in 12 fl oz/3½ dl hot water for ½ hour.

Put the stock to boil in a 3½-qt/4-l pot. Meanwhile, cut off the hard mushroom stems and then cut the caps into fine slices.

Put the mushrooms and diced radish into the boiling stock. Cover, turn down heat, and simmer gently for about 10 minutes or until the radish pieces are tender. Add the sprouts and bring to the boil again. Cover, turn heat down and simmer 3 to 4 minutes. Taste the soup. Add the soy sauce according to the saltiness you think you need. Add the sugar and mix gently.

CLEAR SOUP WITH CUCUMBER, COOKED WITH THAI SEASONINGS

(serves 4)

This is quite a wonderful soup, especially for those who like Thai seasonings like lemon grass and kaffir lime leaves. You will not find this soup in Thailand. It is my own vegetarian adaptation of a popular shrimp soup. The main 'solid' in this clear soup consists of julienned cucumbers, which I barely cook, so they stay very crisp. I prefer to use pickling cucumbers, which I can get almost all year round in New York City. They have small, tender seeds which are ideal if one wishes to cut the entire cucumber into julienne strips. If you cannot find pickling cucumbers, use an ordinary cucumber. Peel it, cut it in half lengthwise, and then cut it into julienne strips.

1½ pt/8½ dl Vegetable Stock (see page 340) or Delicious Stock . . . (see page 340) or any vegetable stock of you choice
12–16 whole stalks of fresh green coriander
8 dried kaffir lime leaves
1 tbs dried, sliced lemon grass
About ½ tsp salt
4 tsp lime or lemon juice

4 oz/115 g peeled, julienned cucumber (see note above)
Freshly ground black pepper to taste
1 tbs chopped fresh green coriander
1 tbs finely sliced spring onions
About 1 tsp very, very finely chopped fresh hot green chillies (optional)

Combine the stock, fresh coriander stalks, kaffir lime leaves, and lemon grass in a 2–3-qt/2¼–3½-l pot and bring to the boil. Cover, lower heat, and simmer gently for 20 minutes. Strain. Add the salt, lime or lemon juice, and cucumber. Stir and bring to the boil again. Turn heat to low and simmer, uncovered, for 15 seconds. Turn the heat off. Add the black pepper.

For information about ingredients and basic techniques that may be unfamiliar, see General Information, pages 481-506.

Pour soup into individual bowls and garnish with the chopped fresh coriander, spring onions, and green chillies.

CHINESE-STYLE NOODLE SOUP

HONG KONG *(serves 4–6)*

The noodle 'soups' of Eastern Asia are much more substantial than their Western counterparts. Each soup bowl does, of course, have some clear broth in it but it is also quite filled with a generous quantity of noodles and vegetables – enough to make a very satisfying lunch or snack. In Hong Kong's noodle restaurants – sometimes they are just little sheds – the kitchens have huge cauldrons of simmering stock. As orders come in, fresh noodles are put into a sieve and the sieve is lowered into the simmering stock. Chopsticks are used to separate the strands. As soon as the noodles are cooked, and this takes almost no time at all, they are put into individual bowls which sit ready with some sliced spring onions and droplets of soy sauce in them. Then vegetables – it could be *bok choy, choy sum*, Chinese leaves, spinach, or bean sprouts – are put into a sieve and lowered into the broth. These are emptied on top of the noodles. A little broth is ladled in, some chopped fresh coriander is sprinkled on the top, and the bowls are ready to be carried to the table. Diners are offered a variety of sauces to season their soups further – hot chilli sauces (the red and green commercial kind), hot oil, soy sauce, and vinegar are always on the table.

¼ lb/115 g thin, fresh Chinese lo mein *egg noodles, or* ¼ lb/115 g *freshly cooked spaghettini*

1¾ pt/1 l Vegetable Stock (see page 340) or Delicious Stock . . . (see page 340) or any stock of your choice

1 medium-sized carrot, peeled, and cut at a slight diagonal into ¹⁄₁₆-in/¼-cm-thick slices

½ lb/225 g Chinese leaves, cut crosswise into 1-in/2½-cm-wide strips

20 tender leaves of either choy sum *or* spinach

2 spring onions cut into very fine rounds, including ¾ of one green

About ¼ tsp salt

2 tbs chopped fresh green coriander

Bring 3 pt/1¾ l of water to the boil in a large pot. Separate the noodles and when the water is at a rolling boil, drop them in. Let the water come to the boil again. Put in 8 fl oz/¼ l of cold tap water. The boiling will subside. Bring the water to the boil a third time. Pour in another 8 fl oz/¼ l of cold water. Let the water boil again. Turn off the heat and drain the noodles in a colander. Run cold water over the noodles and rinse them. Leave to drain. (If you are using freshly cooked spaghettini, drain and rinse it as well.)

Heat the Vegetable Stock in a 3-qt/3½-l pot. Add the carrot, Chinese leaves, *choy sum*, and spring onions. Simmer, uncovered, on medium heat for a minute or until vegetables are just done. Add the noodles and bring to a simmer again. Let the noodles heat through. Add the salt, stir, then taste and correct seasoning, if necessary.

Divide the soup evenly among all the soup bowls. Sprinkle the fresh coriander over the top. These soups are generally eaten with both chopsticks and soup spoons. Extra sauces (see note above) should be offered at the table.

THAI NOODLE SOUP

THAILAND   *(serves 6)*

In Thailand, this soup is made with chicken stock and seasoned with fish sauce. I have taken the liberty of changing the dish somewhat. Instead of the chicken stock, I use a vegetable stock; for the fish sauce, I have substituted soy sauce. You may use mushroom soy, if you prefer.

Noodles are Thailand's favourite lunch and snack food. Any visitor to Bangkok will find the city dotted with noodle shops, as well as with basket-toting noodle vendors who squat on the pavements, hoping to catch the hungry and the greedy as they rush by.

Thai noodle shops generally offer several kinds of noodles. I have a preference for the fresh Chinese *lo mein* noodles but you could use Japanese whole-wheat or buckwheat *soba* or *udon* or *somen* or you could use vermicelli or spaghettini. In a seasoning combination typical of many Thai foods, this soup has hot, sweet, sour, and salty flavourings. Apart from being exceedingly tasty, it is also quite nourishing, as it is always topped with fresh bean sprouts, green beans, fresh coriander, and crushed peanuts.

½ lb/225 g fresh Chinese lo mein *egg noodles (for substitutes, see above)*

2 tbs finely sliced fresh hot green chillies

4 tbs Japanese rice vinegar

4 fl oz/1 dl Chinese or Japanese soy sauce

3 oz/85 g roasted or fried unsalted peanuts (see page 373)

7 oz/200 g washed and drained mung-bean sprouts

Granulated sugar to pass around

3½ pt/2 l Vegetable Stock (see page 340) or Delicious Stock . . . (see page 340) or any stock of your choice

4–5 oz/115–140 g fresh green beans cut into ¾-in/2-cm pieces

For information about ingredients and basic techniques that may be unfamiliar, see General Information, pages 481-506.

Bring 4 qt/4½ l of water to the boil in a large pot. Separate the noodles and when the water is at a rolling boil, drop them in. Let the water come to the boil again. Put in 8 fl oz/¼ l of cold tap water. The boiling will subside. Bring the water to the boil a third time. Pour in another 8 fl oz/¼ l of cold water. Let the water boil again. Turn off the heat and drain the noodles in a colander. Run cold water over the noodles and rinse them. Leave to drain. (If you are using dried noodles, cook them according to packet instructions, then drain and rinse them.)

Set up the seasonings and extras that go on top of the noodles. You will need four bowls for this. Combine the green chillies and the vinegar and put the mixture in one small bowl; the soy sauce should be poured into another small bowl; crush the peanuts or grind them coarsely in a clean coffee grinder and put them in the third bowl; put the bean sprouts in a larger bowl. Arrange these four bowls as well as the sugar bowl neatly in the centre of the dining table.

Bring the stock to the boil. Throw in the green beans and let them boil for a minute. Now add the noodles and let them heat through.

Divide the soup among individual bowls. Diners should put bean sprouts over their soup and then season it, to taste, with the chilli–vinegar mixture, soy sauce, peanuts, and sugar. (I rarely use more than a half teaspoon of sugar.)

HOT-AND-SOUR SOUP
CHINA   (serves 4)

1 tbs tree ear fungus
6 Chinese dried black mushrooms
24 dried day-lily buds
1½ pt/8½ dl Vegetable Stock (see page 340)
2 tsp cornflour
2 tsp sesame oil
1 large egg
2 oz/60 g finely julienned bamboo-shoot strips

4 oz/115 g medium bean curd, cut into julienne strips
⅓–½ tsp salt
2 tbs distilled white vinegar
¼–½ tsp freshly ground white pepper
2 tsp Chinese thin soy sauce
2 tsp very finely sliced spring onions

Soak the tree ear fungus and Chinese mushrooms in 8 fl oz/¼ l water each for half an hour, and the day-lily buds in 12 fl oz/3½ dl water for half an hour.

Drain the tree ear fungus and rinse it. Feel for any hard knots with your fingers. Cut off and discard them. Now cut the fungus into long strips, about ¼ in/¾ cm wide.

Remove the mushrooms from their soaking liquid. (Save the liquid for stock or for cooking vegetables.) Cut off and discard the coarse stems and then cut the caps into ¼-in/¾-cm-wide strips.

Remove the day-lily buds from their soaking liquid. Cut off and discard the hard knots that can sometimes be found at one end.

Remove 2 fl oz/½ dl of the stock and set the remainder to heat in a 3-qt/3½-l pot over a medium-high flame.

Put the cornflour into a small bowl. Slowly add the 2 fl oz/½ dl cold stock and 1 tsp sesame oil. Set aside.

Beat the egg very lightly. (Do not let it froth.) Mix in 1 tsp sesame oil and set aside.

The stock should now be boiling. Add the tree ear fungus, mushrooms, day-lily buds, bamboo-shoot strips, bean-curd strips, and salt to it. Bring to a simmer. Turn heat to low and simmer, uncovered, for 5 minutes. Now add the vinegar, white pepper, and soy sauce. Bring to a simmer. Stir the cornflour and stock mixture and add it to the pot. Stir and cook until the soup thickens slightly. Turn off the heat. Immediately pour in the beaten egg mixture in a steady stream, covering the surface of the soup with it. Stir gently.

Pour soup into individual bowls. Sprinkle with the sliced spring onions and serve hot.

QUAILS' EGG SOUP
CHINA   (serves 4–6)

Apart from being a very tasty soup, this is also a very pretty soup – the kind that elicits exclamatory gasps when it first appears on the table. In order to get full dramatic mileage out of your efforts, bring the soup to the table in a single Chinese serving bowl. If you do not have a Chinese serving bowl, use a light-coloured or white ceramic or porcelain bowl of roughly a 2½–3-pt/1½-l capacity. (There is actually only 1¾ pt/1 l of broth). Let me describe to you what the soup looks like when it first appears on the table. The bowl is lined with the bright-green stalks and leaves of the

---

For information about ingredients and basic techniques that may be unfamiliar, see General Information, pages 481–506.

Chinese vegetable, *choy sum,* to form a kind of nest. The quails'
eggs, steamed in small dishes so they form tiny flying-saucer-
shaped discs, are placed on top of the green nest. Steaming hot
broth seems to hold this nest and its contents in suspension. It is
quite a sight.

Choy sum is the best vegetable for this soup. However, if you live
in an area quite devoid of Chinese grocery stores, substitute 1½ lb/
675 g of fresh spinach. If you do have access to *choy sum,* buy about
1½ lb/675 g. You actually need ¾–1 lb/340–450 g of trimmed *choy
sum.* As it is hard to calculate exactly how much will need to be
trimmed away, it is best to buy a little extra. If some *choy sum* is left,
you can always steam it the following day. It is such a tasty
vegetable.

Fresh quails' eggs are available in specialist grocers. If you just
cannot get quails' eggs, use the smallest hens' eggs that you can
find, one per person, and steam them in the saucers of demi-tasse
coffee cups. For steaming the quails' eggs, you need the tiny,
shallow, bowl-like dishes that Chinese restaurants use for serving
soy sauce, duck sauce, and mustard. I have a collection of such
dishes and the ones that I like best measure about 2⅔ in/7 cm in
diameter (inside) and about ¾ in/2 cm in depth (inside). You need
to steam 12 eggs but they may be done in several batches, re-using
the dishes.

About 3 tsp sesame oil
12 fresh quails' eggs
12 single, unblemished leaves of
   fresh green coriander
Choy sum (see note above for
   quantity)
2 tsp salt
3 tbs vegetable oil
2 cloves garlic, peeled and finely
   chopped
2 spring onions, trimmed and cut
   into fine rings, including three-
   quarters of the green
1 tbs Chinese thin soy sauce
1¾ pt/1 l Vegetable Stock
   (see page 340) or Delicious
   Stock . . . (see page 340), or any
   stock of your choice, steaming
   hot

Get your steaming equipment ready. If you are using a Chinese
bamboo steamer set inside a wok, make sure that you put just

enough water inside the wok so it stays below the slats on the 'floor' of the steamer. Do not put the steamer over the water yet. Bring the water to the boil first. (If you do not have a bamboo steamer, set a trivet inside a large pot. Set a plate over the trivet. Pour just enough water into the pot so it stays below the plate. Bring the water to the boil. The egg dishes can then be put on the plate and the pot covered for steaming.)

Use 1½ tsp sesame oil to grease the small soy-sauce dishes generously (see note above). Crack open a quail's egg near its middle and empty the whole egg into the soy-sauce dish. Do not let the yolk break. Do all eggs this way. Place a single unblemished coriander leaf on the centre of each egg yolk. Put the dishes in the steamer in a single layer (you may need to do more than one batch) set over the boiling water, cover, and steam for 2½ to 4 minutes or until the whites of the eggs are set and the yolks are semi-hard. Remove from the hot water, uncover, and set aside.

Trim the *choy sum* by cutting off and discarding the tough lower sections. Pull off the larger leaves on the lusher stalks to thin them out. Arrange these leaves as well as the remaining *choy sum* so that all the stalks and stems face one direction and the leaves the opposite direction. You will have to keep this 'bundle' shape throughout the cooking.

Bring 3 pt/1¾ l of water with 2 tsp salt to a rolling boil. Heat 3 tbs of vegetable oil in a wok over high heat. When hot, put in the garlic. Stir the garlic around until it has browned. Pour in the boiling water (keep your face averted). Put in the *choy sum*, still preserving its 'bundle' form. Make sure that the stem ends are completely submerged. Cover and boil vigorously for 2 minutes or until the *choy sum* is just tender. Drain the *choy sum* by pouring the water out of the wok. Lift the whole *choy sum* bundle up with a pair of tongs and place it on a chopping board. Cut the *choy sum* into 3–4-in/8–10-cm lengths. Work quickly now.

Put the spring onions, soy sauce, and 1½ tsp sesame oil in the centre of a warmed soup bowl. Arrange the *choy sum* pieces around the seasonings in such a way that they seem to radiate from the spring onions and go up the sides of the bowl. Slide the quails' eggs out of their dishes and place them, coriander leaf up, over the green nest. Pour the steaming broth over the eggs and serve at once.

Take the serving bowl to the table and then ladle out portions into individual soup bowls.

For information about ingredients and basic techniques that may be unfamiliar, see General Information, pages 481-506.

BEETROOT AND TOMATO SOUP
INDIA   *(makes about 1 pt/5¾ dl and serves 2–3)*

This simple dish was probably concocted by English families in India who were quite taken with Indian spices but yearned to have elegant European soups on their tables. In the nineteenth century, the soup was probably thickened with flour. I prefer it unthickened. The use of cream is entirely up to you. Without it, the soup is light and broth-like; you could serve thin slices of oven-crisped bread with it. Actually, I often drink it like broth when I am working late into the night. When thickened with cream, the soup becomes slightly richer and needs no accompaniment.

½ lb/225 g raw beetroot (about 3, medium-sized)
1 tsp ghee or vegetable oil
½ tsp whole cumin seeds
1 tsp whole black peppercorns
4 whole cloves

A ¾-in/2-cm piece of stick cinnamon
3 medium-sized tomatoes, peeled and then chopped (or equivalent amount of tinned tomatoes)
½ or more tsp salt
2 fl oz/½ dl single cream (optional)

Peel the beetroot and cut it into large dice. Put it into the container of a food processor or blender together with 12 fl oz/3½ dl water. Blend for 1 minute. Strain the juice through a fine sieve, getting out as much of the liquid as possible.

Heat the *ghee* in a 1½–2-qt/1¾–2¼-l pot over a medium flame. As soon as it is hot, put in the cumin seeds, black peppercorns, cloves, and cinnamon. Stir for a second and then put in the chopped tomatoes. Stir for another 3 to 4 seconds and add the beetroot juice, salt, as well as another 4 fl oz/1 dl of water. Bring to the boil, cover, turn heat to low and simmer 10 minutes. Strain. Add cream if you desire and reheat.

MY CREAM OF TOMATO SOUP
INDIA   *(serves 4–6)*

Cream of tomato soup has been adopted by India with a passion. The same small coffee houses that offer the most traditional *dosas* and vegetable *pakoris* also have, to the surprise of many tourists, tomato soup on their menus. When cooking tomato soup in their homes, most Indians cannot resist putting in a few spices or herbs. My sister-in-law, for example, puts in fresh curry leaves from the tree that grows just outside her kitchen door. The soup immediately becomes very aromatic. In New York, I put in dried curry leaves, more for the aroma I remember than for the limited flavour provided by the dried leaves, as well as ginger, ground roasted cumin, and a few other things besides. Here is my tomato soup, which can be had hot or cold.

1½ lb/675 g ripe tomatoes, chopped
1 tbs dried, sliced lemon grass
1 tbs dried or fresh curry leaves
1 five-pence-piece sized slice fresh
  ginger
1¼ tsp salt
4 tbs unsalted butter
2 tbs plain white flour
4 fl oz/1 dl single cream

1 pt/5¾ dl milk
½ tsp ground roasted cumin seeds
¹⁄₁₆–⅛ tsp freshly ground black
  pepper
⅛ tsp cayenne pepper
2 tsp lime or lemon juice
1 tbs fresh finely chopped green
  coriander

Combine the tomatoes, lemon grass, curry leaves, ginger, ½ tsp salt, and 4 fl oz/1 dl water in a 2½-qt/2¾-l pot and bring to the boil. Cover, lower heat, and simmer gently for 15 minutes. Uncover, turn heat to medium, and simmer a little more aggressively for another 15 minutes. Put the tomatoes through a sieve. You should have about 16 fl oz/½ l of thick tomato juice. Bring this juice to a simmer and keep on a very low flame.

Melt the butter in a heavy saucepan. Add the flour. Stir and cook the flour on low heat for 2 to 3 minutes. Do not let it brown. Now pour in the hot tomato juice, stirring all the time. Add the cream and the remaining ¾ tsp salt. Stir to mix and bring to a simmer. Add all the other ingredients except the fresh coriander. Stir to mix. Heat over a medium flame. As soon as the soup is about to come to the boil, turn off the heat. Ladle the soup into warmed soup bowls and serve garnished with a little chopped fresh coriander. If you wish to serve the soup cold, stir it occasionally as it cools so it does not form a thick film. Then cover and refrigerate.

For information about ingredients and basic techniques that may be unfamiliar, see General Information, pages 481-506.

CALDO VERDE
(Green Soup)
INDIA   (serves 6)

This hearty soup is served in the former Portuguese colony of Goa on the west coast of India. It is not unlike a basic leek and potato soup, only it is flavoured with *couve* — kale, garlic, and olive oil.

4 *medium-sized potatoes, peeled and chopped into ¾-in/2-cm dice*
1 *medium-sized onion, peeled and coarsely chopped*

3 *oz/85 g coarsely chopped kale leaves*
12 *cloves garlic, peeled*
1¼ *tsp salt*
1 *tbs fruity olive oil*
Freshly ground black pepper

In a large pot, combine the potatoes, onion, kale, garlic, and salt. Add 2½ pt/1½ l water and bring to the boil. Cover, lower heat, and simmer very gently for 1 hour and 15 minutes or until kale is quite tender.

In as many batches as necessary, pour the soup into the container of an electric blender and blend until you have a smooth texture. Pour soup back into soup pot and taste for seasonings. Add more water if the soup seems too thick. Just before serving, add the olive oil and black pepper.

MISO SOUP WITH BEAN CURD
JAPAN   (serves 4–5)

1 *strip* kombu, *about 11 × 3 in/ 28 × 8 cm*
4 *tbs dark yellow* miso
A 4 *oz/115 g cake fresh bean curd, cut into ½-in/1½-cm cubes*

2 *spring onions, trimmed and sliced into very fine rounds, including half their green*

Bring 1½ pt/8½ dl water to the boil in a 2½-qt/2¾-l pot. Wipe the *kombu* with a damp cloth, then drop into the water, making sure that it is well submerged. Turn off the heat. Leave *kombu* in the water 2 to 3 minutes. Remove the *kombu*. (Do not discard it. It can be re-used to flavour a second broth or to make Kombu Relish).

Partially submerge a small sieve in the *kombu* broth. Put the *miso* into the sieve and push it through with a wooden spoon. If any little pieces are left in the sieve, they may be discarded. Add the bean curd and bring to the boil. As soon as the first bubbles form, turn off the heat. Stir in the spring onions and serve immediately in covered Japanese lacquer bowls or in ceramic bowls.

MISO SOUP WITH CARROTS AND MUSHROOMS

JAPAN   (serves 4)

1 strip kombu, about 7×4 in/
   18×10 cm
1 carrot, peeled, and cut into very
   fine julienne matchsticks
½ medium-sized onion, peeled,
   and sliced into very fine half
   rings
4 medium-sized mushrooms,
   wiped, and cut into very thin
   slices

A piece of lemon peel, 1 in/2½ cm
   long and ⅓ in/1 cm wide, cut
   lengthwise into very fine, long
   slivers
4 tbs red (its actual colour is a rich
   brown) miso
⅛ tsp 7-spice seasoning

Bring 1½ pt/8½ dl of water to the boil in a 2½-qt/2¾-l pot. Wipe the
kombu lightly with a damp cloth, then drop into the water, making
sure that it is well submerged. Turn off the heat. Leave kombu in the
water 2 to 3 minutes. Remove the kombu. (This kombu may be
re-used to make Kombu Relish.)

Add the carrot, onion, mushrooms, and lemon peel to the kombu
broth. Bring to the boil again, cover, and simmer on low heat for 5
minutes. Turn off the heat. Put miso in a small sieve. Partially
submerge the sieve in the soup and press out the miso with a
wooden spoon. Bring to the boil again. Just as the first bubbles
form, turn off the heat. Stir the soup and ladle it into soup bowls
(lidded Japanese bowls are best). Sprinkle each bowlful with some
of the 7-spice seasoning and serve immediately.

For information about ingredients and basic techniques that may be unfamiliar, see General
Information, pages 481-506.

Jyothi Baswan's
RASAM
(A Tomato, Tamarind, and Dal Broth)
INDIA *(serves 4–6)*

Rasam is a thin South Indian broth that is served in clear glasses, cups, or small bowls and then either sipped as an appetizer or else eaten with rice. I love to serve it in cups as a soup and find that it makes a light, spicy, and very refreshing first course.

When *dals* (split peas) are boiled in water, the heavy grains sink to the bottom and a thin broth separates itself and rises to the top. South Indians, who cook *dals* for almost every meal, manage very cleverly to make two dishes out of the contents of the same pot. The thin broth is removed to make *rasam* while the thicker *dal* is used to make dishes like *sambar*.

There are many types of *rasam*. The most common kind combines tomatoes, tamarind, and thin *dal* water to produce a broth that has herbs, seeds, and bits of tomato floating around in it. I find it much more convenient to strain the broth before serving it.

Another thing: *rasam* has a kind of sediment — a quite tasty sediment, I might add — that sinks to the bottom of the pot. South Indian housewives feel obliged by custom to serve honoured guests the lighter top broth and to eat the leftover sediment themselves. I prefer to divide the broth and sediment more equally. So I just give the broth a good stir before ladling it out into cups. As diners sip the broth, the thicker particles begin collecting at the bottom of their cups. A spoon may be used to finish them off.

3½ oz/100 g toovar dal *(also*
   called arhar dal), *picked over,*
   washed, and drained
2 *five-pence-piece sized slices of*
   fresh ginger
½ tsp ground turmeric
1 lb/450 g ripe tomatoes (about 2
   large ones), chopped
4 tsp tamarind paste, or to taste
2½ tsp salt, or to taste
7 cloves garlic, peeled and lightly
   crushed
1 whole, dried hot red pepper, or
   more to taste

1½ tbs dried curry leaves
10–15 fresh green coriander stalks
A generous pinch of ground
   asafetida
¾ tsp ground cumin seeds
¾ tsp ground coriander seeds
2 tsp vegetable oil
¾ tsp whole black mustard seeds
¾ tsp whole cumin seeds
½ tsp urad dal
2 tsp finely chopped fresh green
   coriander leaves

Put the *toovar dal*, 1½ pt/8½ dl water, ginger, and ¼ tsp turmeric in a small pot and bring to the boil. Cover, leaving the lid slightly ajar, turn heat to low and simmer for 1½ hours. Stir 3 to 4 times in the last half hour, mashing the *dal* slightly as you do so. Turn the heat off and let the *dal* sit, covered, for 10 minutes.

Meanwhile, combine the tomatoes, tamarind paste, ¼ tsp turmeric, salt, 5 of the garlic cloves, red pepper, 1 tbs of the curry leaves, fresh coriander stalks, asafetida, ground cumin, ground coriander, and 1½ pt/8½ dl water in a pot. Bring to the boil. Cover, turn heat to low and simmer for 1½ hours.

In the *dal* pot, a thin broth will have risen to the top. Take out a cup of this and add it to the pot with the tomatoes. Now take out 2 fl oz/½ dl of the thick *dal*, mash it slightly and add it to the tomato pot as well. Strain this mixture through a sieve, extracting as much liquid as you can. (Any remaining thick *dal* may be refrigerated and added to other soups.)

Put the strained liquid in a pot and bring to the boil. Cover, and turn off the heat.

Put the oil in a small frying pan and heat over a medium flame. When hot, put in the remaining 2 garlic cloves, the mustard seeds, whole cumin seeds, *urad dal*, and the remaining ½ tbs curry leaves. As soon as the mustard seeds begin to pop and the garlic darkens — this just takes a few seconds — pour the contents of the frying pan into the hot soup and cover it again immediately. Let the pot sit, covered, for 5 minutes or longer. Now strain the soup and ladle it into cups. Sprinkle the chopped fresh coriander over the top. If the soup has cooled off, you may reheat it before serving.

MASOOR DAL SOUP
INDIA   (serves 4)

10 whole cloves	½ tsp ground turmeric
2 bay leaves	1¼–1½ tsp salt
1 tsp whole black peppercorns	1 tbs lime juice
6½ oz/185 g masoor dal*, picked over, washed, and drained	⅛ tsp cayenne pepper (use as desired)

* These are often called red split lentils or Egyptian lentils in supermarkets and health-food stores.

Tie the cloves, bay leaves, and peppercorns in a piece of cheesecloth.

Put the *dal* and 1 qt/11½ dl water into a heavy 2½–3-qt/2¾-3½-l pot and bring to the boil. Remove the scum that rises to the top and

For information about ingredients and basic techniques that may be unfamiliar, see General Information, pages 481-506.

discard it. Add the spice bundle and the turmeric to the pot. Turn heat to low, cover so the lid is very slightly ajar, and simmer very gently for 1½ hours. Remove the spice bundle and discard it. Put the soup in a blender or food processor (you may have to do this in two batches) and blend until it is smooth. Add the salt, lime juice, and cayenne. Stir to mix.

This soup may easily be made ahead of time and reheated. I like to serve mine with homemade croûtons.

TO MAKE CROÛTONS: cut 2 slices of bread into ½-in/1½-cm cubes. Heat enough oil in a frying pan to have about ½ in/1½ cm at the bottom. Do this over medium heat. Put in as many croûtons as the frying pan will hold in a single layer. Stir and fry them until they turn a golden-brown colour. Remove with a slotted spoon and drain on paper towels. (Make all croûtons this way.)

RED BEAN SOUP
INDIAN STYLE   *(serves 4)*

Here I have converted a Punjabi method of cooking beans into a puréed soup.

6 oz/170 g small red azuki beans, picked over, washed, and drained

1 medium-sized onion, peeled and chopped

2 cloves garlic, peeled

2 five-pence-piece sized slices of fresh ginger

1 whole dried hot red pepper

1¼ tsp salt, or to taste

Freshly ground black pepper

4 tbs plain yogurt

6 fl oz/1¾ dl single cream

2 tbs ghee or vegetable oil

½ tsp whole cumin seeds

Put the beans and 1½ pt/8½ dl water in a pot and bring to the boil. Cover, turn heat to low, and simmer for 2 minutes. Turn off the heat and let the pot sit, covered, for 1 hour. Bring to the boil again. Cover, turn heat to low and simmer for 30 minutes. Add the onion, garlic, ginger, and red pepper and simmer, covered, for another 30 minutes. Remove the slices of ginger and the red pepper. Add the salt and black pepper and mix.

Put the beans into the container of a food processor or blender and blend until you have a smooth soup. If you like, you may push the soup through a sieve to remove the bean skins but this is not essential.

Put the yogurt into a bowl and beat with a fork or whisk until smooth and creamy. Slowly add a ladleful of soup, mixing it in as you do so. Add another ladle of soup and mix that in as well. Pour in all the soup, mix, then return soup to a clean pot. Add the cream, mix, and heat over a low flame.

Put the *ghee* in a small frying pan or small pot and heat over a medium flame. When hot, put in the cumin seeds. Let the seeds sizzle for a few seconds. Now pour the contents of the frying pan into the soup. Stir to mix.

Serve the soup nice and hot.

CREAM OF LENTIL SOUP
INDIAN STYLE   *(serves 4)*

Here is a simple, soothing soup that I often serve to my family. With it, I offer thin slices of French bread which I crisp up in a slow oven and — would you believe it — radishes! They are a wonderful accompaniment and, with their inner leaves left on, they add a nice splash of colour as well. I put the soup in individual bowls, set the bowls on small plates, and then arrange a crisped slice of bread and a radish on each plate.

6½ oz/185 g whole green lentils, picked over, washed, and drained
1 medium-sized onion, peeled and chopped

1 tsp salt, or to taste
Freshly ground black pepper
8 fl oz/¼ l single cream
¼ tsp ground, roasted cumin seeds
2 tsp lemon juice, or to taste

Put the lentils, onion, and 1¼ pt/¾ l water in a pot and bring to the boil. Cover, turn heat to low and simmer gently for 1 hour. Purée the lentil mixture in a food processor or blender. Add 6 fl oz/1¾ dl water and blend again to mix. Push this mixture through a sieve into a clean pot. Make sure you push all the pulp through and leave only a small quantity of skins behind. Add the salt, pepper, cream, cumin, and lemon juice. Mix and bring to a simmer. Taste for seasonings.

For information about ingredients and basic techniques that may be unfamiliar, see General Information, pages 481-506.

HARICOT BEAN AND CELERIAC SOUP
MIDDLE EAST (serves 4)

This is a hearty soup, ideal for cold winter days, that may be served as a meal in itself. Some crusty French or pitta bread, a yogurt cheese, and some olives would be all that would be required as accompaniments. You may sour this soup with either vinegar or lemon juice. Each gives its own taste and both are traditional.

6 oz/170 g haricot beans, picked over, washed, and drained
About ½ lb/225 g celeriac, peeled, and cut into ¼-in/¾-cm dice
4 medium-sized tomatoes, peeled, and finely chopped
1 medium-sized onion, peeled, and cut into ¼-in/¾-cm dice
3 cloves garlic, peeled, and finely chopped

1 oz/30 g finely chopped fresh parsley
¼ tsp dried rosemary
¼ tsp dried thyme
2 tsp salt, or to taste
Freshly ground black pepper
4 tsp white, distilled vinegar or lemon juice, or to taste
2 tbs olive oil

Put the beans and 1½ pt/8½ dl water in a pot and bring to the boil. Cover, turn heat to low and simmer for 2 minutes. Turn off the heat and let the pot sit, covered, for 1 hour. Bring the contents of the pot to the boil again. Cover, turn heat to low and simmer for 45 minutes. Add the celeriac, tomatoes, onion, garlic, and parsley. Crush the rosemary and thyme together and add along with 8 fl oz/¼ l water. Bring to the boil. Cover, turn heat to low and simmer for 20 minutes. Uncover, and add the salt, some black pepper, the vinegar or lemon juice, as well as the oil. Cook, uncovered, on low heat, for another 15 minutes, stirring the soup every now and then and also mashing some of it against the sides of the pot with the back of a large spoon. If the soup seems too thick, you may thin it out with some water.

CHICK PEA SOUP
MIDDLE EAST (*serves 6*)

This thick, stew-like soup is eaten in many countries of the Middle East, often forming the centrepiece of simple peasant meals. Salads, olives, bread, and yogurt dishes are served with it. Although soaked chick peas are generally tender enough to eat after an hour of cooking, it is important here that they cook longer. This way the chick peas themselves get somewhat softer, the liquid thickens considerably, and the soup develops a cohesion that it would otherwise lack.

It might be a good idea to taste the soup before putting in the lemon juice. Chick pea broth has a natural sweetness that you may prefer to leave untouched.

12 oz/340 g dried chick peas,
　picked over, washed, and
　drained
2 medium-sized onions, peeled,
　and chopped
2 medium-sized potatoes, peeled,
　and cut into ½-in/1½-cm dice

1 tbs salt, or to taste
½ tsp ground turmeric
1 tsp ground cumin seeds
1 tsp ground coriander seeds
⅛ tsp cayenne pepper, or to taste
Freshly ground black pepper
2 tbs lemon juice

Soak the chick peas in 3 pt/1¾ l of water for 12 hours. Drain and rinse thoroughly. Put the chick peas, onions, and 3 pt/1¾ l water into a large pot and bring to the boil. Cover partially, turn heat to low, and simmer gently for 1 hour. Add the potatoes, salt, turmeric, cumin, coriander, cayenne, and another 12 fl oz/3½ dl water. Bring to the boil. Cover and simmer on very low heat for another 1½ hours. Stir a few times during this period. Check seasonings. Add the black pepper and lemon juice. Stir to mix.

CHICK PEA, CABBAGE, AND DILL SOUP

MIDDLE EAST   (serves 4–6)

6 oz/180 g dried chick peas, picked
　over, washed, and drained
1 medium-sized onion, peeled and
　chopped
1 medium-sized potato, peeled and
　cut into ½-in/1½-cm dice
1 good-sized tomato, peeled and
　cut into ½-in/1½-cm dice

½ lb/225 g cabbage, cut into
　½-in/1½-cm squares
2 oz/55 g chopped fresh dill
2 tsp tomato paste
2 tsp salt, or to taste
Freshly ground black pepper

Soak the chick peas in 1½ pt/8½ dl water for 12 hours. Drain and rinse thoroughly. Put the chick peas, onion, and 1½ pt/8½ dl water into a 3½-qt/4-l pot and bring to the boil. Cover partially, turn heat to low, and simmer gently for 1 hour. Add the potato, tomato, cabbage, dill, tomato paste, salt, and 4 fl oz/1 dl water. Bring to the boil. Cover, turn heat to very low and simmer for 1½ hours. Add the black pepper and mix.

For information about ingredients and basic techniques that may be unfamiliar, see General Information, pages 481-506.

9 Little Salads, Appetizers, Snacks, and Drinks

Spicy nibbling food that could be taken along on car trips, split-pea wafers that may be served with drinks, the cold aubergine dip that is fun to eat with pitta bread, the cold yogurt or strawberry drink that is so refreshing in summer — well, they are all here. This is the catch-all chapter for the good things that do not quite fit anywhere else in this book.

I would not dream of travelling, even from London to Brighton, without some *cheewra* (or, for that matter, writing without it — I'm eating some now). Before the Western world discovered muesli, India had *cheewra*, one of the most satisfying hot, sweet, salty, and sour mixtures of seeds, nuts, dried fruit, beans, and grains that you can ever hope to encounter. It is not eaten with milk as a breakfast food but devoured, plain and unadulterated, as a snack between meals. I grew up with it in India and my children seem to be thriving on it in America.

Then there are the Middle Eastern *dolmades*, vine-leaf rolls stuffed with a mixture of rice, pine nuts, and herbs. The rolls are cooked slowly in a garlicky oil and lemon dressing. By the time they are done, it is really hard to keep one's hands off them. They make a very pleasant first course and are also perfect picnic food. An equally pleasant first course from Armenia is Artichoke Hearts and Potatoes Cooked in Oil and Lemon. Rather like *dolmades*, this may be made ahead of time and refrigerated.

My mother's Fresh Peach Salad, on the other hand, cannot be prepared ahead of time as it wilts in the most pathetic manner. If you want to eat this salad in the true bazaar style, serve it on large leaves and eat it with toothpicks.

I have included a recipe for the classical, flaky *samosas*, deep-fried pastry cones filled with spicy potatoes and peas. They should be fried slowly so that they turn nice and crisp — and then they should be eaten with dollops of the sweet-and-sour Tamarind-Mint Chutney. Among the drinks, you will find quite a few made with yogurt and buttermilk. My mother always kept big jugs of these in the refrigerator during the summer months, all nicely seasoned with salt, pepper, and roasted cumin. We would come home from school, peel off our shoes and socks, and run to the refrigerator. One healthy swig and the whole hot, bothersome school day would be left far behind us.

CARROT AND WHITE RADISH SALAD
KOREA

(serves 4–6)

1 medium-sized carrot
½ lb/225 g white radish
1 tsp salt
1 tbs sesame oil

1 tbs rice vinegar
¼ tsp Japanese soy sauce
¼ tsp sugar
Dash of cayenne pepper

Peel the carrot and cut it into thin, diagonal slices. Cut these slices into slim julienne strips.

Peel the radish and cut it into julienne strips that are about the same size as the carrot strips.

Put the carrot and radish in a bowl. Add the salt, mix well, and set aside for an hour. Drain thoroughly, pressing out as much liquid as possible. Put the vegetables in a serving bowl. Add the sesame oil, vinegar, soy sauce, sugar, and cayenne. Mix.

SAWSAWANG KAMATIS
(Filipino Tomato Salad)
PHILIPPINES

(serves 4–6)

In this simple salad, the souring agent is green mango, the kind that is dark green on the outside, quite hard, and has not given a single thought to ripening. If you cannot find such a fruit, use lime juice as a substitute.

¾ lb/340 g ripe tomatoes
1 tsp coarsely grated fresh ginger
2 tbs peeled, chopped green mango
  or 1 tbs lime juice

1 spring onion, finely sliced
¼–⅓ tsp salt
Freshly ground black pepper

Cut the tomatoes into ⅛-in/½-cm-thick rounds and arrange them in a single layer in a platter. Sprinkle the ginger, green mango, and spring onion evenly over the tomatoes. Now sprinkle the salt and pepper over the top.

JAPANESE CUCUMBER SALAD
JAPAN

(serves 6)

6 pickling cucumbers* (about
  1½ lb/675 g)

1 tsp salt
1 tbs soy sauce

*Ordinary cucumbers may be substituted; peel them if they have been waxed.

1½ tbs rice vinegar   1 tbs lightly crushed, roasted
                                       sesame seeds

Wash cucumbers well, scrubbing them if necessary. Slice, unpeeled, into very, very fine rounds either by hand or with the
slicing blade of a food processor. Put cucumber slices in a bowl,
sprinkle with salt, mix well, and set aside for an hour.

Squeeze cucumber slices and discard all accumulated liquid.
Now add the soy sauce, vinegar, and sesame seeds. Mix well and
check seasonings.

This dish may be refrigerated for a few hours prior to eating or it
may be served at room temperature.

WATERCRESS SALAD
WITH SESAME SEEDS
JAPAN   (serves 4)

2 bunches fresh watercress   ½ tsp sugar
1½ tbs rice vinegar   1 tbs crushed, roasted sesame seeds
2 tbs soy sauce

Trim away about 1½ in/4 cm of the coarser watercress stems. Wash
watercress.

Bring 1½ pt/8½ dl of water to the boil. Add the watercress. Boil
on medium heat for about 5 minutes or until watercress is just
tender. Drain in a colander and run cold water over the watercress
to fix the bright-green colour. Drain, squeezing out as much water
as possible.

Separate watercress sprigs so they are not in a tight wad and
place in a bowl. Mix the vinegar, soy sauce, sugar, and sesame
seeds in a small cup. Pour this dressing over the watercress and
mix well.

Make four mounds of the watercress salad and place a mound
each in the centre of four small Oriental bowls or small plates.
Serve cold or at room temperature.

CELERY, CARROT AND
CUCUMBER SALAD
HONG KONG   (serves 4)

You could add peeled and julienned broccoli stems or kohlrabi to
this salad as well.

2½ celery sticks
1 carrot
A 6-in/15-cm length of cucumber
1 tbs Chinese light soy sauce

2 tsp distilled white vinegar
1 tsp sesame oil
½ clove garlic, peeled and mashed
  to a pulp

Cut the celery into thin, 2½-in/6½ cm-long matchsticks.

Peel the carrot and cut into ⅟16-in/¼ cm-thick diagonal slices. Cut the slices into thin matchsticks.

Peel the cucumber and cut in half, lengthwise. Scoop out the seeds and discard them. Cut the cucumber shells into matchsticks.

If you are not eating immediately, put the vegetables into a plastic bag and refrigerate.

Meanwhile, mix the soy sauce, vinegar, sesame oil, and garlic.

Just before eating, put the salad into a bowl, pour the dressing over it, and mix.

KOREAN-STYLE CUCUMBER SALAD
KOREA
(serves 6)

I use pickling cucumbers for this salad. You may substitute ordinary cucumbers.

3 lb/1350 g pickling cucumbers,
  peeled
1 medium-sized onion, peeled
1 tbs salt

3½ tbs lemon juice
About ¼–½ tsp cayenne pepper
2 tbs crushed, roasted sesame seeds
1½ tbs sesame oil

For information about ingredients and basic techniques that may be unfamiliar, see General Information, pages 481-506.

Cut the cucumbers and onion into very fine slices (a food processor may be used for this). Sprinkle with salt, mix well, and set aside in a bowl for an hour.

Drain all the accumulated liquid and discard. Add the lemon juice, cayenne pepper (Koreans like this dish very hot), sesame seeds, and sesame oil. Mix well, cover, and refrigerate. Serve cold or at room temperature.

CUCUMBER AND DRIED SHIITAKE MUSHROOM SALAD
JAPAN   (serves 2)

1 ridge cucumber* (about 6½ oz/ 200 g)
1 tsp salt
5 medium-sized dried shiitake mushrooms
2 tsp sesame seeds, roasted and crushed coarsely

2 tsp Japanese rice vinegar
1 tsp mirin
½ tsp sugar
2–3 drops Japanese soy sauce

*If a ridge cucumber isn't available, use part of an ordinary cucumber.

Peel the cucumber and cut it in half, lengthwise. Then cut it into very thin, half-moon-shaped slices. Sprinkle with salt and mix well. Set aside for an hour. Rinse under cold water to wash off salt. Squeeze out as much liquid as possible.

Soak the mushrooms in 4 fl oz/1 dl boiling water for half an hour. Remove coarse stems and cut mushroom caps into ⅛-in/½-cm-wide slices.

Combine cucumber, mushrooms, sesame seeds, vinegar, *mirin*, sugar, and soy sauce. Mix well.

GUJARATI CARROT SALAD

INDIA *(serves 4)*

3 carrots (about ¾ lb/340 g),   2 tbs vegetable oil
    peeled, and grated   1½ tsp whole black mustard seeds
¼ tsp salt

In a bowl, toss the grated carrots with the salt. Heat the oil in a small frying pan or small pot over a medium flame. When hot, put in the mustard seeds. As soon as the mustard seeds begin to pop (this will take just a few seconds), pour the contents of the frying pan – oil and mustard seeds – over the carrots. Stir to mix.

GUJARATI CUCUMBER AND PEANUT SALAD

INDIA *(serves 4)*

For this recipe, either raw or boiled peanuts may be used. (For more on cooking with peanuts, see pages 124–6.) I happen to like the chestnut-like flavour of boiled peanuts.

4 oz/115 g raw, shelled, skinned   ½–1 fresh hot green chilli, finely
    peanuts   chopped (or use ⅛ tsp cayenne
¾ lb/340 g cucumbers (small   pepper)
    pickling preferred), peeled and   2 tbs finely chopped fresh green
    cut into ⅓-in/1-cm dice   coriander
2 tbs roasted sesame seeds   2 tbs vegetable oil
1 oz/30 g freshly grated coconut   1½ tsp whole black mustard seeds
    ½ tsp salt
    1 tbs lemon juice

If you are using the peanuts raw, crush them lightly. This may be done in a mortar, a food processor, or you can place the peanuts between two sheets of waxed paper and hit them lightly with a rolling pin. Each whole peanut should break up into 8 to 10 pieces. If you wish to boil the peanuts, soak them in 16 fl oz/½ l of water for 3 to 4 hours and then boil them, covered, in the same water for about 15 minutes. Drain and let cool. Do not crush the boiled peanuts.

In a serving dish, combine the peanuts (raw or boiled), the diced cucumbers, sesame seeds, coconut, green chilli, and fresh coriander. Mix.

For information about ingredients and basic techniques that may be unfamiliar, see General Information, pages 481–506.

Heat the oil in a small frying pan or a small pot over a medium flame. When hot, put in the mustard seeds. As soon as the seeds begin to pop (this takes just a few seconds), pour the contents of the frying-pan − oil and seeds − over the salad. Stir again. Just before serving, add the salt and lemon juice. Mix well.

FRESH PEACH SALAD

INDIA   *(serves 6)*

This is a wonderful salad to make when the fresh fruit is in season. As peaches discolour and turn very limp and watery if left in spices for too long, the salad should be made just before you sit down to eat. In India, such savoury fruit salads are served with meals or as snacks and may be made with a variety of fruit. Peeled and sliced bananas, peeled and sliced guavas, even peeled orange segments may be used − singly or in any preferred combination. Of course the salt, sugar, and lemon juice have to be balanced with the natural qualities of the fruit that is being used.

My mother often made savoury fruit salads to go with our lunches. Lunch could consist of a simple rice dish − perhaps Rice with Sautéed Onions and Mushrooms; a *dal* − perhaps Chana Dal with Cucumber; a vegetable − perhaps Cauliflower and Potatoes cooked with Fenugreek and Fennel Seeds; a glass of ice-cold buttermilk, and a fruit salad to perk up the meal. We did not always leave it to our mother to make the salad. In the late afternoon, with tea-time still far way and hunger pangs distracting us from our homework, we took to concocting these salads ourselves. Perhaps as a result of this, I often offer such salads to my children when they come in from school.

I might add that I have frequently served this salad as a first course at a Western-style meal.

2½ lb/1125 g fresh peaches, peeled
  and sliced
3 tbs sugar
¾ tsp salt
Freshly ground black pepper, to
  taste

1½ tsp ground, roasted cumin
  seeds
1½ tbs lemon juice
⅛–¼ tsp cayenne pepper

Combine all ingredients in a glass, ceramic, or stainless steel serving dish. Serve at room temperature.

FRIED, MUNCHABLE MUNG DAL

INDIA   *(makes ¾ lb/340 g)*

As a child, this was one of my favourite snack foods. I would buy it in a little paper cone from the bazaar, empty it into my pockets, and then munch it quietly as I accompanied my mother on her shopping sprees. While my mother searched for the perfect gold brocade Benarasi border to match her latest chiffon sari from France, I kept myself busy with the mung *dal*. When I grew up and had my own children in America, I took them to India as little tots. Imagine my sense of *déjà vu* as I watched them fall upon the crunchy fried mung *dal* with the same mindless pleasure that I had exhibited decades earlier. I found myself complaining, just as my mother had done, of finding mung *dal* in little coat pockets, all mixed up with unidentifiable fluff.

This is not a spicy snack. It is generally seasoned with just salt and, if one likes, some black pepper. Cayenne may be sprinkled over it, if one so wishes. And there is no particular time of the day when it is meant to be eaten. Like peanuts, fried mung *dal* is eaten whenever one feels like eating it, as a snack or with drinks.

NOTE: Although this *dal* is deep-fried and appears oily when first removed from the fire, it does not remain oily if handled properly.

6½ oz/185 g mung dal	*Freshly ground black pepper to*
Vegetable oil for deep frying	*taste*
½ tsp salt	

Pick over the *dal* and wash it in several changes of water. Drain. Soak the *dal* in 1 qt/11½ dl of water for 5 to 8 hours. Drain thoroughly. Dry off *dal* by rubbing gently in a towel.

Heat oil for deep frying in a wok over a medium flame. You should have a good 2½ in/6½ cm of oil in the centre of the wok. Line two plates with kitchen paper and keep them beside you. Have a fine, medium-sized sieve handy that you can lower into the oil.

When the oil has heated, lower the sieve into it. Put two modest handfuls of *dal* into the oil in the sieve. The *dal* will begin to sizzle and the oil will bubble. When the sizzling and bubbling subside (about 1½ minutes), the *dal* should be a golden colour (not brown), crunchy, and done. Lift up the sieve, shake it gently to drain off the oil, and then empty the *dal* on to one of the two plates. Keep doing this until all the *dal* is cooked, dividing it up between the two plates.

Change the kitchen paper on the plates again and again until it

---

For information about ingredients and basic techniques that may be unfamiliar, see General Information, pages 481-506.

no longer appears oily. You may also rub the top of the *dal* with kitchen paper. (But do this fairly quickly, as you should salt the *dal* while it is still hot.) Consolidate the *dal* on one plate, lined with fresh kitchen paper. Sprinkle with salt and pepper. Mix and allow to cool completely.

Put the *dal* in a jar and cover with a tight lid. If kept in a tightly lidded jar, the *dal* will stay fresh for several weeks.

FRIED,
MUNCHABLE SOY BEANS
CHINA   *(makes 14 oz/400 g)*

You may salt these beans or not, just as you like. I actually prefer them unsalted.

*6 oz/170 g yellow soy beans, picked   Vegetable oil for deep frying
   over, washed, and drained   Salt (optional)*

Soak the beans in 1½ pt/8½ dl water for 5 to 6 hours. Drain, removing any skins that may have come loose. Pat the beans dry. There should be no external moisture clinging to them. If it is a dry, sunny day, spread out the beans on a tray and leave them in the sun for a couple of hours. If you have no access to the sun, spread the beans out on a tray and leave them in a dry, airy place for a couple of hours.

Put the oil in a wok and heat over a flame that is slightly lower than medium. When the oil is hot, put in all the soy beans. Stir and fry for 6 to 7 minutes or until the beans turn a shade darker and turn crisp on the outside. Remove with a mesh strainer or a small-holed slotted spoon and spread out on kitchen paper to drain. Change the kitchen paper a few times. Rub the beans gently with kitchen paper as well to remove as much oil as possible.

If you like, sprinkle a little salt over the top and mix.

PEANUTS, FRIED
AND ROASTED
                                                  (8 oz/225 g)

Fried and roasted peanuts are used in many parts of South, Southeast, and East Asia in main dishes as well as in sauces, and as toppings for both sweet and savoury dishes. While it is perfectly all right to use shelled but unskinned raw peanuts for snack foods, it is best to use the shelled, skinned raw peanuts for all other recipes. Such peanuts are available in varying sizes at health-food, Oriental, and Indian grocery stores.

8 oz/225 g shelled, skinned raw   *Vegetable oil, as and if needed*
  peanuts   *¾–1 tsp salt, if desired*

DEEP FRYING: this is by far the best method for frying peanuts as there is no chance of burning or browning them unevenly. I like to use my deeper Indian wok for this but you could use a Chinese wok as well. Heat enough oil over a medium flame so you have about 2½–3 in/6½–8 cm of it in the middle of the wok. Now put 4 oz/115 g of peanuts into a sieve that is about 8 in/20 cm in diameter at the top and has a handle. When the oil has heated, lower the sieve into the oil. As soon as the peanuts have turned a golden colour, lift the sieve out of the oil. Let it drain over the oil for a few seconds. Now put the peanuts on kitchen paper (my mother used brown-paper bags for this) and sprinkle them with half the salt. Do a second batch the same way.

SHALLOW FRYING: even though less oil is used in this method, the advantage is somewhat nullified by the uneven colour of the end product. This unevenness may well have to do with one not being able to remove all the peanuts from the oil at the same time. However, there is a way around it. Heat enough oil in a frying pan over a medium flame so you have ¼ in/¾ cm at the bottom of the pan. While it heats, place a sieve over a bowl. Put as many peanuts into the hot oil as the frying pan will hold in a single layer. Stir and fry until the peanuts turn a golden colour. Now empty the contents of the frying pan into the sieve. Let the peanuts drain briefly and then empty them onto kitchen paper and sprinkle some salt on them if you want to. Put the oil in the bowl back into the frying pan and do a second batch and, if necessary, a third batch the same way.

ROASTING: raw, shelled, or unshelled peanuts are generally not roasted in ovens in Asia. The most common method is to put them into a heavy wok and then to stir and cook them over a lowish flame until they give off a roasted aroma. A cast-iron frying pan may be used instead of a wok. Put all the peanuts into the wok or frying pan. Stir constantly and cook over a lowish flame until the peanuts look and smell roasted. Put into a bowl and sprinkle with salt, if desired.

For information about ingredients and basic techniques that may be unfamiliar, see General Information, pages 481-506.

When the fried and roasted peanuts have cooled, they may be stored in airtight bottles or tins for several weeks.

PAPADUM
(Dal Wafers)
INDIA   (serves 6)

Called *papadum* in South India and *papar* in the North, these thin wafers (generally made out of *dal* but occasionally out of potatoes and sago as well) are served at most vegetarian meals. Southerners often crush them towards the end of their meals and then mix them with rice, yogurt, and pickles for a simple finale. North Indians prefer to nibble them along with their meal, dipping them now and then into the yogurt for a variation. Both Northerners and Southerners have developed the habit of serving *papadum* as a convenient cocktail snack.

Although members of my grandmother's generation did, now and then, make their own *papadum* — I remember thousands of yellow discs drying on cots set out on a sunny courtyard — very few people make them at home any more. Almost all grocery stores sell them, nicely rolled out and dried. All that then remains to be done is to cook them.

The quickest — and most traditional — way of cooking *papadum* is to deep fry them. This takes just a few seconds and allows the *papadum* to expand to their maximum size and turn quite light and airy. *Papadum* may also be toasted, either under the grill or over a direct flame. They are less calorific this way but they do not expand quite as much.

Papadum may be bought plain, flavoured with garlic, dotted with black pepper or dotted with red pepper.

6 papadum   *Vegetable oil for deep frying*
                                    (optional)

FRYING METHOD: break each *papadum* into two pieces.

Set the oil to heat in a wok or frying pan over a medium flame. When hot, drop in a *papadum* half. Within seconds, it will expand. (If it browns at all, the oil is too hot. It should remain a pale yellow colour.) Turn the *papadum* over and cook the second side for a few seconds. Remove with a slotted spoon and drain on kitchen paper. Do all the *papadum* this way.

THE TOASTING METHOD: lay a *papadum* on the griddle of the grill and set the grill at 'medium'. Now watch carefully. The *papadum* will begin to bubble, expand slightly, and turn lighter in colour. As soon as all of it is this lighter colour, remove it from the grill. Do not let it brown. Do all the *papadum* this way.

If you wish to toast directly over a flame, do not break the *papadum* in half. Turn the flame on to low. Hold a *papadum* with a pair of tongs about ½ in/1½ cm above the flame. As one part of the *papadum* bubbles and turns lighter in colour, put another part of the *papadum* above the flame. Keep doing this until the entire *papadum* is toasted.

GREEN PLANTAIN WAFERS
INDIA   *(serves 4 as a snack)*

Plantain wafers, in some form or other, are eaten in most tropical countries. The unusual quality of the Indian wafer comes from the use of turmeric. Like potato crisps, they may be eaten at almost any time of the day or night. They are excellent to take on long car rides and on picnics.

2 green plantains	*1¼ tsp salt*
¼ tsp ground turmeric	*Vegetable oil for deep frying**

* South Indians would use coconut oil for this recipe.

Peel the plantains with a knife, removing all the green skin. Using a food processor with the slicing blade, a mandolin, or a potato-slicing gadget, slice the plantains into very, very thin rounds (rather like potato crisps) and soak in iced water for 30 minutes. Drain and pat dry.

In a small bowl or cup, combine the turmeric and salt with 2 tbs of warm water.

Heat the oil in a wok or deep-frying utensil over a medium

For information about ingredients and basic techniques that may be unfamiliar, see General Information, pages 481-506.

flame. You should have about 1½ in/4 cm of oil. When the oil is hot, put in as many plantain wafers as will fit in a slightly overlapping single layer. Dip your fingertips into the turmeric–salt solution and sprinkle whatever liquid you pick up over the wafers. This has to be done in a fast motion, as soon as the wafers are put into the oil. Fry wafers 1½ to 2 minutes, turning them over midway during this cooking time. Wafers should be crisp but retain their yellow colour. Remove with a slotted spoon and drain on a platter lined with kitchen paper. Do all the wafers this way. Cool the wafers and then store them in airtight jars. They should stay fresh for 3 to 4 days.

ROASTED LAVER
KOREA

For this recipe you need sheets of the dark-green, paper-like dried laver that the Japanese call *nori* and the Koreans call *kim*. The sheets come in different sizes and in different qualities. For each sheet that is roughly 6 × 7 in/15 × 18 cm, brush both sides lightly with sesame oil − 1 tsp should be enough for both sides − and then sprinkle very lightly with salt. Now hold the *nori* with a pair of tongs and wave over a lowish fire, keeping it about 3 in/8 cm away from the flame. Roast for about 5 seconds on each side. Offer each person one sheet of *nori*, cut into halves or quarters.

ROASTED MONUKKA RAISINS
INDIA

It was so strange to find something called monukka raisins in my local health-food store. As a child, one of my favourite treats was to ask the cook to prepare what *we*, in India, called monukka. This was a large, dark raisin that the cook would thread on a slim wooden skewer − he would actually thread a whole garland of them − and then wave them over the charcoal fire in our stove. The outside edges of the raisins would get slightly blackened. He would hand me the skewer and I would wander off into the vegetable garden, stingily pulling off one raisin at a time and gobbling it up. By the time I had inspected the tomatoes and the beans and the peas, all the raisins would be gone and it would be time to return to the kitchen for another freshly roasted, hot batch of skewered monukka.

If you want to roast some monukka, thread about 3 in/8 cm of them, all tightly packed, on to a long metal skewer. Now wave this skewer over a low flame, holding it about 1½ in/4 cm away from the source of heat. Every 1 second, turn the skewer a bit. It takes no time at all to roast a batch. The raisins burn quickly, so watch what you are doing. Roast more as you need them. If you have a camp fire, roast monukka instead of marshmallows!

KHARI POORI
(Savoury Biscuits with Peppercorns)
INDIA   (makes about 50)

These savoury, deep-fried 'biscuits' are made with a combination of whole-wheat and white flour. In Gujarat, khari pooris or 'salty pooris' are often studded with crushed black peppercorns.

These pooris are generally eaten as a snack, accompanied by lassi, buttermilk, or tea. They can be eaten plain, or they may be smeared with hot pickles or sweet chutneys (like the Apricot Chutney). Khari pooris have been a standard 'journey food' in India for centuries. Packed into tins and bags, the pooris are still carried on long bullock-cart, car, rail and aeroplane trips. You could take them on picnics or hiking trips. You could also serve them with drinks.

3½ oz/100 g wheatmeal flour
4 oz/115 g plain white flour
1 tsp salt
1 tbs coarsely crushed black pepper

3½ tbs vegetable oil or softened unsalted butter plus oil for deep-frying

Sift the wheatmeal flour, white flour, and salt into a bowl. Add the black pepper as well as the 3½ tbs oil or butter. Rub the oil or butter into the flour with your fingers until the flour resembles coarse oatmeal. Now slowly add very hot water — about 4 fl oz/1 dl plus 3 tbs — and begin to gather the flour together. Squeeze the dough into a ball. It should just about hold. Do *not* knead.

Break the dough into about 50 balls. Keep them covered with cling film or a lightly dampened towel.

Heat about 1½–2 in/4–5 cm of oil in any utensil for deep frying (an Indian karhai or Chinese wok is an ideal utensil for this) over a medium flame. While the oil is heating, begin to roll out the pooris. Take each dough ball, flatten it, and roll it into a very rough round, about 2 in/5 cm in diameter. (Don't worry about the cracked edges.) Roll and fry as many pooris as your frying utensil will hold in a single layer. Fry 2 to 3 minutes on each side or until pooris are lightly browned on both sides and crisp. Adjust heat, if necessary.

For information about ingredients and basic techniques that may be unfamiliar, see General Information, pages 481-506.

Remove *pooris* with a slotted spoon and drain on kitchen paper. Make all *pooris* this way. Allow them to cool and then store them in an airtight container. *Khari pooris* do not need refrigeration and will stay fresh for several weeks.

MUTTHRIES
(Savoury Biscuits with Ajwain Seeds)
INDIA   *(makes about 28)*

While the preceding recipe for savoury biscuits (*khari poori*) is from the western state of Gujarat, this recipe is from my home town, Delhi. The traditional method for making both styles of biscuit is very similar, except that the Delhi version uses white flour as its base and the delicate *ajwain* seeds as a flavouring. You could, if you want the more traditional *mutthrie*, follow the preceding recipe and just substitute 2 tsp of *ajwain* seeds for the crushed black pepper. Or you could follow this new recipe that I have worked out in which, instead of deep frying the biscuits, I bake them. The result is quite excellent. I love to eat these *mutthries* at tea-time with lots of Sweet Tomato Chutney smeared on them. You could also have them with butter and jam.

7 oz/210 g plain white flour (plus a   ¼ lb/115 g unsalted, ice-cold
    little more for dusting)   butter, cut into 8 pats
¾ tsp salt   2 fl oz/½ dl iced water
1 tsp ajwain seeds

Stir the flour and the salt and put into the container of a food processor with its metal blade fitted into place. Add the *ajwain* seeds and the butter. Turn the machine on and off quickly a few times until the flour resembles coarse bread crumbs. Turn the machine on and slowly pour in the cold water. Let the machine run for a few seconds more but stop it *before* the dough forms a ball. Empty the contents of the food processor on to a sheet of waxed paper. Form a very loose ball out of the dough.

(If you do not have a processor, put the sifted flour and salt into a chilled bowl. Add the *ajwain* seeds and the butter. Rub the butter in with your fingertips until the mixture resembles coarse bread crumbs. Slowly pour in the cold water as you begin to gather the dough into a loose ball.)

With the heel of your hand, press down on the dough and stretch it along the waxed paper in a few quick strokes to blend the flour and butter. Do not overdo this. Gather the dough into a loose ball again, cover with the waxed paper, and refrigerate for an hour.

Spread out a clean sheet of waxed paper on a slightly dampened counter or board. (This prevents the waxed paper from sliding.) Dust lightly with flour. Put the ball of dough on the paper. Dust the top of the ball with a little flour. Put another sheet of waxed paper on top of the ball. Now begin to roll the dough. Every now and then lift up the top waxed paper and dust with a little flour, then flip the dough over so the bottom waxed paper is on top. Remove it and dust this side of the dough, too. Put the waxed paper back and continue rolling out. Keep doing this until you have a round of dough that is about ¼ in/¾ cm thick. Use a round pastry cutter (it could be scalloped at the edges) that is 2½ in/6½ cm in diameter, and cut out as many biscuits as you can. Put the biscuits on a cold baking sheet, prod each of them several times with a fork, and refrigerate.

Gather the remaining dough and quickly form a loose ball. Wrap in a sheet of waxed paper and refrigerate for about half an hour or until cold enough to roll out again easily.

Repeat the process of rolling out the dough and making more biscuits. Use up all the dough. Keep all the biscuits refrigerated on the baking sheet.

Preheat oven to 425° F/220° C/Mark 7.

Put the baking sheet on to the oven and bake biscuits for about 20 minutes or until done. Let biscuits cool. Store in an airtight container.

SAMOSAS
(Stuffed Savoury Deep-Fried Pastry Cones)
INDIA   (makes 24 medium-sized samosas)

Like most Indian snack foods, samosas may be eaten at any time of the day or night, preferably with healthy swigs of tea, coffee, or fruit juice. On the streets in India, itinerant vendors serve them on leaves, with a little Tamarind-Mint Chutney (see page 422) on the side. 'Take-away' samosas are invariably wrapped in two leaf bowls, one inverted over the other, while the chutney is handed over in a terra-cotta pot. At formal lunches and dinners, samosas are placed on the centre of the thali — the individual food platter — along with rice and the bread, while all other foods — dals, numerous vegetables, relishes — surround it in small bowls.

For information about ingredients and basic techniques that may be unfamiliar, see General Information, pages 481-506.

Even though many homes like ours made fine *samosas*, experts like my mother and grandmother were of the secret belief (secret because the men in our family were firm, and often loquacious believers in clinical cleanliness) that the *best samosas* came from the open-to-the-elements, hygienically questionable stalls of the local bazaar. The best thing that I can say about my *samosas* is that they do happen to have a bazaar taste!

I have a *samosa* recipe in my first cookery book, *An Invitation to Indian Cooking*. That recipe makes a simplified *samosa* with a soft, whole-wheat wrapping — a kind of *samosa* that I made quite often for my children when they were little and dinner seemed more amusing to them if it came in a triangular wrapping. The recipe here is for the classical *samosa* with a crisp, flaky white-flour crust. For best results, the *samosas* should be fried quite slowly.

FOR THE PASTRY
6 oz/180 g plain white flour
¼ tsp salt
4 tbs soft, unsalted butter

FOR THE STUFFING
4 medium-sized potatoes, boiled unpeeled and cooled
4 tbs vegetable oil
1 medium-sized onion, peeled and finely chopped
6 oz/170 g shelled fresh or defrosted frozen peas
1 tbs peeled and grated fresh ginger
1 fresh hot green chilli, finely chopped

3 tbs finely chopped fresh green coriander
1½ tsp salt
1 tsp ground coriander
1 tsp garam masala
1 tsp ground roasted cumin seeds
¼ tsp cayenne pepper
2 tbs lemon juice or 1 tbs lemon juice and 1 tbs amchoor
1 tsp anardana (dried pomegranate seeds)

Oil for deep frying
Extra flour for dusting

Sift the flour and salt into a bowl. Add the softened butter and rub it in with your hands so that the flour resembles fine bread crumbs. Add water, a tablespoon at a time, and begin to gather the flour into a ball. You will need about 5 tbs of water. Form a ball and begin to knead it. Knead well for about 10 to 15 minutes or until dough is pliable. (If you have a food processor, put the steel blade in place and empty the sifted flour and salt into the container. Add the softened butter and turn on the machine. When you have a breadcrumb consistency, begin to add about 5 tbs of water slowly through the funnel. Stop when the dough forms a ball. Take out the ball and knead it for 5 to 10 minutes or until it is pliable.) Wrap the dough in cling film and let it sit for an hour in the refrigerator. The dough can be made a day in advance and refrigerated.

Make the stuffing. Peel the potatoes and dice them into roughly ¼-in/¾-cm pieces. Heat the 4 tbs oil in a 10–12-in/25–30-cm frying pan over a medium flame. Put in the onion, stirring and frying until it turns a light-brown colour. Add the peas, the ginger, green chilli, fresh coriander, and 3 tbs of water. Cover, lower heat and simmer very gently until peas are cooked. Stir every now and then and add additional water, a tablespoon at a time, if the frying pan seems to dry out. Now put in the diced potatoes, salt, ground coriander, *garam masala*, roasted ground cumin, cayenne pepper, lemon juice (or lemon juice and *amchoor*), and *anardana*. Keep heat on low and mix the spices with the potatoes. Continue cooking gently, stirring frequently, for 3 to 4 minutes. Check salt and lemon juice. Turn off heat and leave potato mixture to cool.

Take the dough out of the refrigerator and knead again. Divide dough into twelve equal balls. Keep balls covered with cling film.

Place a small bowl of water on your work surface. Lightly flour a pastry board. 1. Flatten one of the dough balls on it and then roll it out into a round about 6 in/15 cm in diameter. 2. Now cut the round in half with a sharp knife. 3. Pick up one half and form a cone, making a ¼-in/¾-cm overlapping 'seam', 4. and using a little water from the nearby bowl to seal the 'seam' (see illustration). 5. Fill the cone with a heaped tablespoon of the stuffing. Close the top of the cone by sticking the open edges of the triangle together, again with the help of a little water. This seam should also be ¼ in/¾ cm wide. 6. Press the top seam again and, if possible, 'flute' it with your fingers. Put the *samosa* on a platter in a cool spot. Make all 24 samosas this way.

Heat oil for deep frying (about 2½ in/6½ cm deep) in a wok or other wide utensil over a medium-low flame. When the oil is hot, drop in the *samosas*, as many as will lie in a single layer. Fry them

1

2 3

4 5

slowly until they are a golden brown, turning them over when one side seems done. When the second side of the *samosas* has turned a golden colour, remove them from the oil with a slotted spoon and place them on a kitchen paper-lined plate. Do all *samosas* this way.

Samosas may be served at room temperature or they may be served warm. *Samosas* may be made ahead of time (up to a day), refrigerated neatly layered in flat plastic containers, and then reheated in a 350° F/180° C/Mark 4 oven. If you wish to freeze *samosas*, fry them partially, drain them, and freeze them in a single layer in flat plastic containers. When you wish to eat them, defrost and fry them a second time. Generally, *samosas* are served with a tart, spicy chutney, like Tamarind-Mint Chutney.

6

CHEEWRA
(A Mélange of Nuts, Grains, Dried Fruit, and Spices)
INDIA   *(enough to fill a 1½-qt/1¾-l jar)*

For those people who cannot stop at one peanut, this irresistible snack or 'munch' food from Western India might well prove to be their undoing. I have to confess to you here and now that this cookery book might never have been finished without the necessary 'breaks' for hot cups of Darjeeling tea and small bowls full of *cheewra*. A glorious, spicy, complex ancestor of muesli, *cheewra* combines cashews, peanuts, split peas, puffed rice, sesame seeds, and sultanas with spices like cloves and cinnamon. The roasted split peas (*chana dal*) and small variety of puffing rice (*poha*) used are available only in Indian shops, but you could substitute roasted chick peas, available in nut shops and Middle Eastern stores, and commercial Rice Krispies (in this case the puffed rice wouldn't have to be fried). It is full of protein, extremely nourishing, and, with its delicate blending of sweet, sour, salty, and hot flavourings, so very satisfying. *Cheewra* can be eaten between meals, it can replace biscuits and cake at tea-time, and it can also be served with drinks before dinner. It keeps very well for a couple of months if stored in airtight jars or plastic bags. Because many of the ingredients in this recipe need to be fried briefly, you might conclude that this snack would turn out to be greasy. It does not. *Cheewra* ends up with a very dry appearance, not unlike that of muesli.

For information about ingredients and basic techniques that may be unfamiliar, see General Information, pages 481-506.

3 whole cloves
A ¾-in/2-cm-long stick of
 cinnamon, broken into small
 pieces
½ tsp whole black peppercorns
Vegetable oil for deep frying
3 oz/85 g raw cashews, split in half
 lengthwise
3 oz/85 g raw peanuts, preferably
 without the brown inner skin
1½ oz/45 g roasted chana dal or
 roasted chick peas (see page 384)
3 tbs sultanas
6 oz/170 g poha or Rice Krispies
 (see page 384)

1½ tbs vegetable oil
A generous pinch of ground
 asafetida (optional)
½ tbs whole black mustard seeds
2½ tbs sliced fresh hot green
 chillies or 1–1½ tsp cayenne
 pepper (optional)
3 tbs sesame seeds
¼ tsp ground turmeric
1¼ tsp salt
2½ tsp sugar
1½ tsp ground amchoor

Place cloves, cinnamon, and black peppercorns in a mortar and pound with a pestle until they are powdery. Set aside.

Line two large plates with kitchen paper.

Put 2½ in/6½ cm of oil in a wok or other wide utensil for deep frying and heat over a medium flame. You will need a sieve or other fine mesh gadget that you can lower into the oil to fry the different batches of nuts, grain, and dried fruit. Once the oil is hot (a nut dropped into it should begin to sizzle immediately), put the cashews in the sieve and lower the sieve into the oil. When the cashews are a golden brown, lift up the sieve and empty them on to one of the plates lined with kitchen paper.

Now put the peanuts in the sieve and lower into the oil. Fry until the peanuts turn a golden brown. Spread out the peanuts near the cashews.

Put the *chana dal* (or roasted chick peas) in the sieve and lower sieve into the hot oil. Fry until *dal* turns a shade darker. Spread *dal* out near the peanuts.

Put the sultanas in the sieve. Lower sieve into the oil and fry until sultanas puff up. Spread the sultanas out near the *dal*.

To fry the *poha*, put the empty sieve into the hot oil. Sprinkle a small fistful of *poha* into the sieve. It will begin to froth immediately. As soon as the froth dies down, the *poha* is cooked (it takes just a few seconds). Empty the *poha* on to the second plate. Do all the *poha* this way in small batches. Turn the heat off under your deep-frying utensil. Remove the oily kitchen paper on the two plates and replace with fresh kitchen paper.

Heat 1½ tbs fresh oil in a very small pot (like a butter-warmer) or in a small frying pan over a medium flame. When hot, put in the asafetida and the mustard seeds. As soon as the mustard seeds begin to pop (this just takes a few seconds), put in the sliced green chillies and fry them, stirring, until all the moisture in them disappears and they turn crisp. (If you are using the cayenne pepper, hold on to it.) Add the sesame seeds and fry, stirring, until they turn a shade darker. Now add the turmeric (and cayenne, if you are using it) and stir for another second. Remove from heat.

In a large bowl, combine all the ingredients from the two plates: (the Rice Krispies, if you are using them), the freshly fried spices from the small pot with their oil, the pounded spices from the mortar, as well as the salt, sugar, and *amchoor*. Toss gently until well mixed. Allow to cool. Toss again and store in airtight jar.

POTATO SEV
(Snack Noodle)
INDIA   *(will serve 20 to*
                                           accompany drinks)

Sev is a kind of squiggly, crisp, vermicelli-like snack food made out of gram flour. Indians, both in the north and the south, approach it with the same mindless devotion as Westerners shower on potato crisps — munching it in cinemas, on trains, while listening to the radio, at college beer parties, at tea-parties, and even at formal cocktail parties.

Just as there are noodle machines for those who want to make fresh noodles in their own kitchens, there are *sev* machines for those who frown on the bazaar variety and wish to produce their own. These gadgets are fairly cheap and may be bought in Britain from Indian grocery stores. The most handsome *sev*-maker available at the moment is made out of brass and comes equipped with changeable discs. You attach the disc with the small holes, fill the container with the prepared dough, turn a handle around, and tiny worm-like *sev* come squiggling out, only to fall into hot oil to be deep fried instantly. If you do not have a *sev*-maker, a potato-ricer or sieve may be substituted.

2½ lb/1125 g boiling potatoes	*About 1½ tsp cayenne pepper*
(about 8–9 medium-sized)	*2 tbs lemon juice*
10 oz/285 g gram flour, sifted	*1 tbs sugar*
1 tbs and 1 tsp salt	*Vegetable oil for deep frying*

For information about ingredients and basic techniques that may be unfamiliar, see General Information, pages 481-506.

Boil potatoes. Peel them while they are still hot (hold them, one at a time, with a fork, and peel) and then put them through a potato-ricer or mash them well.

Since you need half as much gram flour as mashed potatoes, measure your mashed potatoes in tea cups. You should have 5 cups of potato to 2½ cups of gram flour. If you have a little more or less, adjust the amount of your flour. Put the mashed potatoes in a large bowl. Add the gram flour, salt, cayenne pepper (1½ tsp will make the *sev* mildly hot; use more or less as desired), lemon juice, and sugar. Mix well and knead with the heel of your palm to make a dough. If the dough is sticky, add more gram flour.

Heat the oil in a wok or other deep-frying utensil over a medium flame. You will need about 2 in/5 cm of oil. Put a tangerine-sized ball of dough into a *sev* machine fitted with the disc that has the smallest holes. (If you do not have a *sev* machine, put the same amount of dough into a potato-ricer or sieve.) When the oil is hot, hold your *sev*-making gadget over it and push the dough through (by turning a handle or by pressing, depending upon the machine). Squiggly *sev* will begin to drop into the hot oil. Move your machine around a bit so the entire surface of the oil is covered, up to ¼ in/¾ cm in depth, with the *sev*. Let the *sev* fry for 1 to 1½ minutes or until they are golden brown on the underside. Using a slotted spoon, turn the entire batch over and fry another 1 to 2 minutes. The *sev* should be a golden, honey colour and crisp (they turn even crisper as they cool). Remove the *sev* with a slotted spoon and place on a plate lined with kitchen paper. Use a fork to separate the *sev* if they have bunched up. Now fry another batch. Continue this way in batches until the dough is used up.

When all the *sev* batches have cooled, store them in airtight jars. The *sev* will keep for several weeks.

COLD CHINESE-STYLE AUBERGINE
HONG KONG *(serves 4)*

In the Hong Kong restaurant where I was served this dish as an appetizer, the aubergine had been steamed in one of the many enormous aluminium steamers that seem to have become standard kitchen equipment in this part of the world, replacing the more charming bamboo steamers of the past. You may use any steaming contraption that is convenient. I just balance a colander on top of a pot of boiling water and then put a lid on top of the colander.

1 large or 2 smaller aubergines (about 1 lb 6 oz/630 g)
4 tsp Chinese thin soy sauce
1 tbs distilled white vinegar
2 tsp sesame oil
1 clove garlic, peeled and mashed to a pulp

¼ tsp Hot Oil (see page 418), optional
⅛ tsp salt, or to taste
1 tbs very finely sliced spring onions
1 tbs finely chopped fresh green coriander (optional)

Set up your steaming equipment. Remember that the water in the lower container should not touch the bottom of the perforated steamer. There should be a lid to hold in the steam.

Peel the aubergine and cut it into large, 1-in/2½-cm chunks.

Bring the steaming water to the boil. Put the aubergine in the perforated steamer, cover, and steam for 20 minutes or until aubergine is tender.

Put the aubergine in a bowl and mash lightly with a fork. You do *not* want a purée. Mix the soy sauce, vinegar, sesame oil, garlic, hot oil, and salt in a small bowl and pour over the aubergine. Mix. Cover and chill until ready to serve. Garnish with spring onions and fresh coriander before serving.

COLD AUBERGINE DRESSED WITH YOGURT
MIDDLE EAST *(serves 6)*

Here is a very easy-to-make appetizer that is quite refreshing in its simple flavours. Serve it nicely chilled, with pitta bread or crispbread.

For information about ingredients and basic techniques that may be unfamiliar, see General Information, pages 481-506.

1 large or 2 smaller aubergines
   (about 1½ lb/675 g)
8 fl oz/2¼ dl plain yogurt
¾ tsp salt, or to taste

Freshly ground black pepper
¼ tsp paprika
1 tbs olive oil

Follow the preceding recipe for directions on setting up steaming equipment, peeling, cutting, and steaming aubergine.

Remove the aubergine from the steamer. Put in a bowl and mash coarsely. Allow to cool. Beat the yogurt with a fork or whisk until smooth and creamy. Pour this over the aubergine. Add the salt and pepper. Mix and adjust seasonings. Sprinkle paprika over the top and then dribble some oil over the paprika.

BABA GHANOUSH
(Creamed Aubergine with Tahini)
MIDDLE EAST   (makes 8 oz/225 g)

This dish makes a good appetizer and may be used as a 'dip'.

1 medium-sized aubergine (about
   1 lb/450 g)
1–2 cloves garlic, peeled
3 tbs tahini

3–4 tbs lemon juice
½ tsp salt, or to taste
1 tbs finely chopped fresh parsley

Preheat the grill.

Prick the aubergine with a fork (about 3 or 4 jabs to a side) and place on a foil-lined baking tray. Set under the grill. When the skin gets charred on one side, give the aubergine a quarter turn. When this side gets charred, turn a little bit again. Continue until the entire skin is charred and the pulp is soft and mushy.

Peel away the charred skin. Quickly rinse the peeled aubergine to remove little bits of charred skin and pat dry. In a blender or food processor combine the garlic, aubergine, tahini, lemon juice, and salt and blend until smooth. Or mash the garlic by hand; then chop the aubergine very fine on a chopping board and mash it with a fork; combine the garlic, aubergine, and tahini in a bowl and beat with a fork, adding the lemon juice and salt until well blended.

This dish may be prepared ahead of time and refrigerated for at least a day. Put the baba ghanoush in a bowl. Smooth over the top and garnish with the finely chopped parsley. Serve at room temperature or cold with pieces of pitta bread.

HUMMUS

MIDDLE EAST   *(serves 6–8 as a dip)*

This dish is usually served as a dip for pitta bread and may be eaten at breakfast, along with goat's cheese, olives, and coffee, or it may be served as an appetizer with drinks.

1–2 cloves garlic, peeled	½ tsp salt
11 oz/310 g cooked, drained chick	3 tbs tahini
peas, homemade (see page 103)	2 tbs cold water
or tinned	¼ tsp paprika
4 tbs lemon juice	2 tbs olive oil

(This dish is best made in a blender or food processor, though you could pound the garlic, salt, and chick peas in a mortar and then add the lemon juice, *tahini*, and cold water.)

Start your food processor and then put in the garlic. As soon as the garlic is chopped, put in the chick peas, lemon juice, salt, *tahini*, and cold water. Blend until quite smooth. Add a little more cold water if you want it thinner.

Empty the contents of the food processor into a shallow, 6-in/15-cm-wide (approximately) bowl. Smooth over the top of the paste with a flattened knife. Sprinkle the paprika over the paste and then dribble the oil over it.

HARICOT BEAN PURÉE WITH POMEGRANATE JUICE

MIDDLE EAST/CASPIAN SEA AREA   *(makes about 8 oz/225 g)*

Purées made with dried beans and peas are generally seasoned with lemon juice and olive oil in this part of the world. What sometimes replaces the lemon juice is pomegranate juice, either bottled or fresh, which lends its own sweet-and-sour flavour to the purée.

This purée is eaten as a dip and served at breakfast or as a snack. Bread or crispbreads would be suitable accompaniments.

3 oz/85 g haricot beans, picked	5 tbs olive oil
over, washed, and drained	¾ tsp salt
5½ tsp bottled pomegranate juice	Freshly ground black pepper

For information about ingredients and basic techniques that may be unfamiliar, see General Information, pages 481-506.

Put the beans and 1½ pt/8½ dl water in a pot and bring to the boil. Cover, turn heat to low and simmer for 2 minutes. Turn the heat off and let the pot sit, covered, for 1 hour. Bring the contents of the pot to the boil again. Cover, turn heat to low, and simmer for about 40 minutes or until the beans are tender. Drain. (The liquid may be used for a soup.)

Purée the beans, either by hand or in a food processor. Fold in the pomegranate juice and 4 tbs of the oil. Season with salt and pepper and mix. Put the purée in a serving bowl. Dribble the remaining 1 tbs oil over it.

ARTICHOKE HEARTS AND POTATOES COOKED IN OIL AND LEMON
ARMENIA   *(serves 4–6)*

This delightful dish used to be served in New York's Sayat Nova restaurant as a first course. The restaurant, alas, is no more, but here is my version of their recipe.

1 tsp whole fennel seeds	*4 fl oz/1 dl olive oil*
1 tsp whole black peppercorns	*1½ tsp salt, to taste*
2 tsp whole coriander seeds	*¼ tsp sugar*
2 whole bay leaves	*4 fresh medium or large artichokes*
4 cloves garlic, peeled and lightly mashed	*1 good-sized (about 8 oz/225 g) potato*
3 tbs lemon juice plus 1 whole lemon	*1 smallish onion*

Tie up the fennel, peppercorns, coriander seeds, bay leaves, and garlic in a cheesecloth bundle and drop into a 2½-qt/2¾-l pot. Add 16 fl oz/½ l water and bring to the boil. Cover, turn heat to low and simmer 20 minutes. Turn off the heat and remove the cheesecloth bundle, squeezing out as much liquid as possible. Add the lemon juice, olive oil, salt, and sugar. Mix and set aside.

Halve the lemon. Cut off the long artichoke stems, if there are any. Starting near the stem end, press back the artichoke leaves, one by one, and then snap them off. Keep doing this until you have gone past the bowl part of the artichoke that harbours the heart and have reached the paler inner leaves. Using a sharp knife (a serrated one is particularly good), cut off the remaining leafy area and discard it. Immediately rub all cut sections with a lemon half. Scoop away the 'choke' in the centre of the artichoke with a grapefruit spoon. Squeeze a little lemon juice into this area and rub it in.

Using a sharp paring knife, trim the outside of the artichoke bowl so there are no more dark green sections left and the bowl gets a smooth appearance. Rub these newly cut sections with lemon. Cut each artichoke heart into four, again rubbing cut sections with lemon. Cut and prepare the remaining artichokes the same way.

Peel the potato and cut into sections that seem roughly the same size as the pieces of artichoke heart.

Peel the onion and cut it into eight sections.

Put the artichoke hearts, potatoes, and onion into the prepared liquid and bring to the boil. Cover, lower heat and simmer for about 12 minutes. Remove a piece of potato and a piece of artichoke. Cut off sections of each and taste for doneness and balance of salt and lemon. You may add more of either seasoning at this time if you wish. Cover and simmer another 3 to 7 minutes or until vegetables are tender. Uncover and cool the vegetables in the liquid. You may refrigerate the contents of the pot if you wish.

When serving, remove the cool (or cold) vegetables with a slotted spoon. Do not serve the liquid.

For information about ingredients and basic techniques that may be unfamiliar, see General Information, pages 481-506.

POTATO PATTIES STUFFED WITH SPICY PEAS

INDIA   *(makes about 10 patties)*

These patties, often referred to as 'potato cutlets' and 'potato chops', may well be one of North India's favourite restaurant snacks. People on short breaks rush in for a quick coffee and patty just as the British might for a coffee and sandwich. The most common shape for these patties is the flattened teardrop. I prefer my patties smaller than normal and quite round.

You may serve these patties with Tamarind-Mint Chutney (see page 422) or Fresh Coriander and Mint Chutney (see page 422) or with plain old tomato ketchup.

FOR THE POTATOES
*4 medium-sized potatoes (a little
   over 1 lb/450 g)*
¾ tsp salt
Freshly ground black pepper
⅛ tsp cayenne pepper

FOR THE STUFFING
3 oz/85 g frozen peas
*1 heaped tbs finely chopped fresh
   green coriander*
¼ tsp salt
⅛ tsp cayenne pepper
¼ tsp ground cumin seeds
¼ tsp ground coriander seeds
Freshly ground black pepper
1 tsp lemon juice

FOR THE CRUST
2 large eggs
*6 oz/180 g unflavoured bread
   crumbs*
½ tsp salt
Freshly ground black pepper
½ tsp ground turmeric
⅛–¼ tsp cayenne pepper
½ tsp ground cumin seeds

Vegetable oil for frying

Boil the potatoes in their jackets. Peel while still hot (you can hold one at a time with a fork to do this) and mash with a fork. Add the seasonings for the potatoes, mix, and divide roughly into 10 patties.

Drop the peas into 16 fl oz/½ l of boiling water and boil rapidly for 2 minutes. Drain, rinse under cold water, and drain again. Mix the peas with all the ingredients for the stuffing. Mash lightly and divide into 10 parts.

Beat the eggs in a shallow, bowl-like dish. Put the crumbs in a separate dish. Put all the seasonings listed for the crust into the dish of crumbs and mix.

Put one part of the stuffing in the centre of one of the patties. Now fold the potato mixture over it to form a rough ball. Flatten the ball gently and form a neat patty, about 2½ in/6½ cm in diameter.

Dip the patty first in the beaten egg and then in the crumbs. Pat down and set aside. Prepare all the patties this way.

In a frying pan over a lowish flame, heat enough oil to cover the bottom by ⅛ in/½ cm. Put in as many patties as the frying pan will hold in a single layer and fry until the bottoms turn a nice reddish colour. Turn the patties over and cook the second side the same way. Remove with a slotted spatula. Fry all the patties this way, adding a little more oil for the second batch if you need to. Serve hot.

POTATO AND TEMPEH PATTIES
INDONESIA   *(makes 5 patties)*

This is a tasty and nourishing snack which may be served with Spicy Peanut Sambal (see page 421), Sambal Tomat (see page 420), or with ordinary tomato ketchup. You might even try thin slices of raw onion on top of it.

FOR THE POTATOES
10–12 oz/285–340 g potatoes
½ tsp salt
Freshly ground black pepper
¼ tsp ground cumin seeds
¼ tsp ground coriander seeds
⅛ tsp cayenne pepper
1 clove garlic, peeled and mashed
  to a pulp

FOR THE TEMPEH
2 oz/60 g tempeh
⅛ tsp salt
Freshly ground black pepper
⅛ tsp ground cumin seeds
⅛ tsp ground coriander seeds
⅛ tsp cayenne pepper

Vegetable oil for frying

FOR THE CRUST
1 large egg
3 oz/85 g unseasoned bread crumbs

Boil the potatoes in their jackets. Peel while still hot (you could hold one at a time with a fork) and then mash with a fork. Add the seasoning for the potatoes and mix.

Chop the *tempeh* finely and mash with a fork. Add the seasonings for the *tempeh* and mix.

Mix the mashed potato and mashed *tempeh*. Form 5 firm patties.

Beat the egg in a shallow, bowl-like dish and spread the bread crumbs in another similar dish. Dip the patties first in the egg and then in the crumbs. Pat the crumbs so they adhere.

For information about ingredients and basic techniques that may be unfamiliar, see General Information, pages 481-506.

In a frying pan over a lowish flame, heat enough oil to cover the bottom by ⅛ in/½ cm. Put in the patties and fry until the bottom turns a nice, reddish colour. Turn them over carefully and cook the second side in the same way. Remove with a slotted spatula and serve hot.

FILO PASTRIES
MIDDLE EAST   *(makes 24 small pastries)*

These small, buttery pastries make impressive appetizers. You could fill them with almost anything you fancy. My stuffing, containing feta cheese, herbs, and hard-boiled eggs, is a very traditional one.

Filo pastry, also called phyllo and fila, consists of large, paper-thin rectangles of dough. It is now so easily available in the freezers of speciality stores and Middle Eastern stores that there is no need to go through the cumbersome process of making it at home.

Filo pastry must be handled with care as it dries out very quickly. Every single sheet and part of a sheet not being used should be folded and covered. A Greek friend of mine uses heavy plastic sheets for this. You could also use greaseproof paper topped with a damp towel.

6 sheets filo pastry (less than
  ½ lb/225 g)
¼ lb/115 g feta cheese
2 large hard-boiled eggs, peeled
4 tbs finely chopped fresh parsley
2 tbs finely chopped spring onion,
  including some green

2 heaped tbs finely chopped fresh
  dill
Freshly ground black pepper
⅛ tsp salt, or to taste
4 oz/115 g unsalted butter, melted

If the pastry is frozen, defrost it slowly according to packet instructions.

Mash the feta cheese with the back of a fork. Chop the eggs finely. Mix together the cheese, eggs, parsley, spring onion, dill, and a generous amount of black pepper. Taste for salt (the cheese is fairly salty) and add as much as you need. Mix and mash gently.

Generously butter a baking tray. Preheat the oven to 350°F/180°C/Mark 4. Remove one sheet of the pastry and cover up the rest. Cut this sheet lengthwise into four strips, each 3 in/8 cm wide. Fold up three of the strips and put them under the covers. Work fast now. Spread the remaining strip in front of you on a dry surface. Brush it generously with butter. Put 1 heaped tsp of the stuffing down on the place marked in the diagram. Fold a corner over the stuffing, forming a triangle. Continue to fold, forming triangles as you go, until the entire length of pastry has been used up. You will end up with a many-layered triangle. Place it, seam side down, on the tray. Brush the top with butter. Make all the pastries this way. Bake for 35 minutes or until pastry is golden brown.

DOLMADES
(Stuffed Vine Leaves)
CAUCASUS/MIDDLE EAST   (serves 8)

Almost every nation in the Middle East and Caucasus region makes a version of *dolmades*. Along with rice, some people wrap bits of dried fruit inside the vine leaves, some add tomatoes, others dried peas and nuts, and the inclusion of herbs such as dill, mint, and parsley is not at all uncommon. Of all the *dolmades* that I have eaten, the ones I like best are also the simplest. These are stuffed with rice, parsley, spring onions, and pine nuts and then cooked in a garlicky oil and lemon dressing. I just cannot stop eating them.

Either fresh or preserved vine leaves may be used for the outer shells. If you use fresh leaves, pick tender ones that are about 4 in/ 10 cm across their widest section. Snip off their stems and then plunge them in boiling water for 2 to 3 minutes. You should start off with about 50 leaves. The preserved leaves come in tins and jars, in brine. The brine needs to be washed off before the leaves can be used.

For information about ingredients and basic techniques that may be unfamiliar, see General Information, pages 481-506.

1-lb/450-g jar of preserved vine
  leaves
6 oz/170 g long-grain rice
2 oz/55 g finely chopped fresh
  parsley
4 spring onions, sliced fine,
  including green
1 oz/30 g pine nuts, chopped

1½ tsp salt
Freshly ground black pepper
4 fl oz/1 dl olive oil
2 fl oz/½ dl lemon juice
2 tsp sugar
3 cloves garlic, peeled and mashed
  to a pulp

Drain the vine leaves. Rinse them, separating them as you do so.
Put the leaves in a bowl and pour boiling water over them. Drain
and rinse them off again.

Bring 2 qt/2¼ l of water to a rolling boil. Pour in the rice in a
steady stream. Stir and bring to the boil again. Boil rapidly for 5
minutes. Drain immediately and rinse under cold water. Drain
again.

In a bowl, mix together the rice, parsley, spring onions, pine
nuts, 1 tsp salt, and a generous amount of black pepper.

Line a wide, 3-qt/3½-l-sized pot with some of the coarser or
broken vine leaves.

Begin stuffing the leaves: lay a leaf in front of you with the shiny
side down and its stem end nearest you. Put a good heaped tsp
(more for larger leaves) of the stuffing in a mound not too far from

the stem. Fold the stem end of the leaf over the stuffing and hold it down. Next, fold the two ends of the leaf to the left and right of the stuffing over it as well. Tightly roll the leaf away from you. Lay this roll neatly in the pot, seam side down. As you do each leaf, put it in the pot, forming tightly fitting rows. When the bottom of the pot is covered with one layer, do a second and, if necessary, a third layer.

Put the olive oil, lemon juice, sugar, ½ tsp salt, garlic, and some more black pepper in a bowl. Beat to mix. Add 8 fl oz/¼ l water and mix again. Pour this mixture over the *dolmades*. Lay a plate, turned upside down, over the *dolmades* to prevent them from opening up. Bring to the boil. Cover the pot, turn heat to low and simmer for 1 hour. Every 10 minutes or so, lift up the plate and baste the upper leaves with the liquid. (A bulb baster is useful for this.) If all the liquid seems to evaporate, add some more water. At the end of the cooking time, just a little oil should be left at the bottom of the pot.

Let the *dolmades* cool completely before serving them. They may be made 24 to 48 hours in advance, covered, and refrigerated.

SALABAT
(Ginger Tea)
MOST OF ASIA   (serves 4)

Salabat is the Filipino name for it, but ginger tea is drunk from Syria to Korea. Syrians add cloves, cinnamon, and anise to it and serve it on festive occasions. My own grandmother served it to us in India when we had colds, saying that it would make us feel all better. It did. In the Philippines, *salabat* is often sweetened with honey or caramelized sugar and served just as tea might be, at breakfast and with all manner of sweet cakes and snacks. In Korea, whole dried fruit — such as persimmons — are sometimes dropped into the hot tea. As it cools, it picks up the subtle flavour of the fruit. This Korean tea is drunk cold, dotted with a few pine nuts — and, of course, you get to eat the fruit as well.

2 1-in/2½-cm cubes of fresh ginger   3 heaped tbs honey, or to taste

Peel the ginger and chop it coarsely. Put it into a pot along with 1½ pt/8½ dl water and the honey. Bring to the boil. Cover, turn heat to low and simmer for 25 minutes. Uncover, turn up heat to medium-low, and cook another 15 minutes. You now should have 1¼ pt/¾ l of liquid. Strain and serve.

FRESH GINGER-FLAVOURED LIMEADE
INDIA   *(makes 1 tall glass)*

On summer days, limeade is often served in India flavoured with fresh ginger. Here is a recipe to make one tall glassful. The recipe can easily be doubled or quadrupled. You can, if you like, substitute soda water for the plain water.

5 tbs freshly squeezed lime juice   *¼–½ tsp finely grated fresh ginger*
4 tbs sugar   *Ice cubes*

Mix the lime juice and sugar in a small bowl. Put the grated ginger in a small strainer. Lower the bottom of the strainer into the sweetened lime juice. Stir the ginger around with a spoon. (The ginger will still be in the strainer.) Lift up the strainer and discard any remaining ginger pulp (there may not be much). Pour the ginger-flavoured lime concentrate into a tall glass. Add 6 fl oz/1¾ dl water and a few ice cubes. Stir.

INDIAN-STYLE HOT TEA
WITH FRESH MINT
INDIA   *(serves 4–6)*

Cold tea with mint sprigs is very popular in America but hot tea with mint tastes equally good. To make it, put 2 tbs of black tea leaves into a tea pot that you have just heated by rinsing it with boiling water. Also put in 3 sprigs of fresh mint. Now pour in 1 qt/11½ dl of water that you have just brought to a rolling boil (put in 1¼ qt/1½ l if you like your tea on the weaker side). Cover the tea pot and let the tea steep for 4 minutes. Stir the tea.

Serve this tea with milk and sugar, with honey and lemon, or just plain.

HOT TEA WITH CARDAMOM
AND CINNAMON
MIDDLE EAST/INDIA   *(serves 4–6)*

Put 2 tbs of black tea leaves into a tea pot that you have just heated by rinsing it with boiling water. Add 6 cardamom pods and a 2-in/5-cm piece of stick cinnamon. Now pour in 1 qt/11½ dl of water that you have just brought to a rolling boil (put in 1¼ qt/1½ l if you like your tea on the weaker side). Cover the tea pot and let the tea steep for 4 minutes. Stir the tea.

Serve this tea with milk and sugar (in India, it would be hot milk), honey and lemon, or just plain.

ANISE TEA
MIDDLE EAST   (*serves 4*)

Bring 1½ pt/8½ dl of water to the boil. Throw in 4 tsp anise seeds, cover and steep for 10 minutes. Strain and bring to the boil again. Meanwhile, rinse out a tea pot with hot water to warm it. Put in 4 tsp black tea leaves. Now pour the boiling anise water over the tea leaves. Cover and steep for 3 to 4 minutes. If the tea is too strong for you, you may add more boiling water.

Serve plain or with honey and lemon or, if you prefer, with milk and sugar.

OCHA
(*Japanese Green Tea*)
JAPAN   (*serves 4–6*)

I have used *bancha*, the cheapest type of Japanese leaf tea, to make this *ocha*.

Bring 1½ pt/8½ dl of water to a rolling boil. Meanwhile, put 2 tbs green *bancha* tea leaves in a tea pot or divide them up among individual cups. Now pour the water over the leaves and let them steep for 2 minutes. If you have put your tea directly into tea cups, which the Japanese often do, the leaves will sink to the bottom by the time the steeping period is over.

You may, if you like, make your tea with roasted *bancha*. Just put the tea leaves in a heavy frying pan over a lowish flame and stir them for a few minutes or until they smell roasted. Roasted *bancha* tastes excellent if it is strained, refrigerated, and served cold.

For information about ingredients and basic techniques that may be unfamiliar, see General Information, pages 481-506.

GINSENG TEA
KOREA

In Korea, this slow-growing root is prized for curing everything from insomnia to impotence. On the other hand, it is not supposed to be good for patients with high-blood pressure. Whether any of these claims have benefited from careful scientific scrutiny, I cannot tell. At any rate, ginseng tea is very popular in Korea and is becoming so here as well. I prefer the taste of the brew made from fresh roots, but as only instant tea, tea bags, and the dried root are available here, it is best to follow instructions on the packet.

RICE TEA
EAST ASIA   *(serves 4)*

There are just so many versions of this tea that it would be impossible to enumerate them all. It probably all started with the East Asian love of rice and the resultant desire to see that no precious grain be wasted. When rice was cooked the traditional way in large heavy pots, some grains invariably stuck to the bottom of the pot and got slightly burnt. After all the non-burnt rice had been served, hot water was poured over the burnt section, brought to the boil, and served as rice tea. Some rice grains invariably accompanied the liquid. Needless to say, this tea was served at the end of a meal. It was considered to be a digestive.

It was not just poor peasants who drank such a tea. In Japan, for example, it was and is still served very formally at the end of the *kaiseki* meal that accompanies a tea ceremony. As electric rice-cookers replace the iron kettles of Japan, rice tea made with genuinely burnt rice is fast becoming a part of Japanese nostalgia. At one very formal Japanese vegetarian lunch I attended, the meal ended with a rice tea made, like barley tea, from roasted rice kernels.

In Hong Kong, I noticed something else. After a lunch was over, my Chinese companion poured the ordinary tea from his tea cup into his empty rice bowl. I asked if he was trying to cool off his tea. No, he answered, tea tasted much better when drunk from the rice bowl. It picked up the rice flavour, and a few odd remaining rice grains as well.

TO MAKE RICE TEA: put 2 tbs rice in a small, cast-iron frying pan and set over a medium-low flame. Stir the grains until they turn dark in spots and give out a nice roasted aroma. Put the rice kernels into a small pot. Add 1½ pt/8½ dl boiling water. Simmer for 1 minute. Cover, and turn off the heat. Let the tea steep for 3 minutes. Strain and serve. (The Japanese do not strain the tea. They just leave a few grains sitting quietly at the bottom of each bowl.)

BORI CHA
(Barley Tea)
KOREA/JAPAN   (serves 4)

Korea is surrounded by mighty tea-drinking nations but its own people rarely touch the stuff, relying more on a drink made with roasted barley. In summer this brownish 'tea' is served cold and in the winter it is served hot. It comes as automatically to tables as water does in Britain and tea in China and Japan. It is a most pleasant, smoky drink – quite free of caffeine.

Roasted barley is available in Japanese stores where it is known as *mugi cha*.

TO MAKE BARLEY TEA: put 2 tbs roasted barley and 1½ pt/8½ dl water in a pot and bring to the boil. Turn heat down and simmer fairly aggressively for 5 minutes. Strain. Serve hot or chilled.

For information about ingredients and basic techniques that may be unfamiliar, see General Information, pages 481-506.

TAMARIND SHARBAT
(Tamarind Syrup)
MIDDLE EAST/SOUTH ASIA   *(makes 10 fl oz/3 dl and serves 5)*

Tamarind drinks, known variously as tamarind tea and tamarind water, are basically infusions made with the peeled pulp of the sweet-and-sour tamarind pods. They are meant to be particularly beneficial in hot weather and are supposed to bring down raging fevers as well. (Sleeping under the tamarind *tree*, however, is supposed to bring *on* fever.) As a child, I was given a cold infusion of tamarind and cumin seeds at least once every two weeks during the burning summer months. This would, I was told, cool my body and cleanse my system.

The recipe here is for the most common of all tamarind drinks found through much of Asia, the sweetened tamarind juice. I have seen it being sold in places as far from each other as the *souks* of Old Jerusalem and the bazaars of Old Delhi.

It consists of a thick, concentrated syrup that is then diluted with cold water and ice.

4 fl oz/1 dl tamarind paste
7 oz/200 g sugar

Combine the tamarind paste, sugar, and 4 fl oz/1 dl water in a small pot and bring to a simmer on a medium-low flame. Turn the heat to low and simmer, stirring frequently, until the sugar is completely melted. You should now have a syrup with the consistency of golden syrup. If it is thicker, add a bit more water and cook another minute. As the syrup cools, it will thicken. Remember that the syrup should end up being slightly thicker than golden syrup but still quite pourable. You will probably end up with about 10 fl oz/ 3 dl syrup. This syrup may be bottled and kept for several days; it's not necessary to refrigerate it.

To make a drink, combine 2 fl oz/½ dl Tamarind Sharbat, 4 fl oz/ 1 dl water, and about 4 ice cubes. Stir to mix.

STRAWBERRY AND LEMON SHARBAT
(Strawberry and Lemon Syrup)
WEST AND SOUTH ASIA   *(makes 1 pt/½ l and serves 9)*

Sharbats, concentrated syrups, may be made out of many fruits, vegetables, and aromatic seasonings. Raspberries, mangoes, sour cherries, oranges, limes, pomegranates, rhubarb, and mint may all be used. Once you understand the basic technique of making syrups, you can easily concoct your own recipes.

I have used frozen strawberries here. If you can get cheap summer strawberries, substitute 1½ lb/675 g of the fresh ones. Chop them up and increase the sugar by 3½ oz/100 g and the water by 4 fl oz/1 dl.

2 10-oz/285-g packets of frozen　　　　*1 lb/455 g sugar*
　strawberries, sliced　　　　　　　　*4 fl oz/1 dl lemon juice*

Combine the strawberries, their liquid, sugar, lemon juice, and 8 fl oz/¼ l water in an enamelled or stainless steel saucepan. Stir and bring to a simmer. Simmer on low heat, stirring gently, for 30 to 40 minutes. The liquid in the pan should resemble a thin syrup.

Line a sieve with two layers of cheesecloth and place the sieve over a bowl. Pour the contents of the pan into the sieve. The syrup will flow through into the bowl. Gently press the strawberry pulp with the back of a wooden spoon, pushing out as much liquid as possible. (The very thick strawberry pulp may be discarded or eaten as jam.) You should end up with about 1 pt/½ l of syrup.

Pour the syrup into a jar. Allow to cool and cover.

To make a drink, combine 2 fl oz/½ dl of the syrup, 4 fl oz/1 dl water, and 4 ice cubes in a glass. Stir to mix.

QAHWAH
(Turkish Coffee)
MIDDLE EAST　　　　　　　　　　　　　　　　　　　　　　(*serves 4*)

What we call 'Turkish' coffee is served all through the Middle East, by wandering Bedouins and more stationary city dwellers alike. Business is conducted over cups of this thick, sweet brew and no host lets a guest depart without at least a cup of it.

Turkish coffee is made from very finely ground — but not powdered — coffee beans. Sometimes a few cardamom seeds are ground with the coffee. As the coffee is thick and strong, it is generally drunk quite sweet. Heavy coffee grounds sink to the bottom of each cup and are not meant to be consumed. (Instead, the coffee cups are turned upside down and the grounds used for fortune-telling.) The froth at the top of each cup, on the other hand, *is* meant to be consumed.

For information about ingredients and basic techniques that may be unfamiliar, see General Information, pages 481-506.

In order to make this coffee properly and get an adequate amount of froth, it is best to buy a *tanaka*, the narrow-necked and long-handled pot available in Middle Eastern stores. The pots come in different sizes. There is even a ½ pt/3 dl size. Turkish coffee is drunk from demi-tasse cups.

2–4 tsp sugar, to taste
2 whole cardamom pods (optional)
4 heaped tsp Turkish coffee

Put 4 demi-tasse cups of water into the *tanaka*. Add sugar and cardamom and bring to the boil. Add the coffee, stirring as you do so. The froth will begin rising to the top. As soon as it reaches the top, remove the pot from the fire. Let the froth subside. Put the *tanaka* back on the fire. As soon as the froth reaches the top, remove the pot again. Do this a third time. Now spoon the froth into 4 demi-tasse cups. Pour the coffee over the froth. (Discard the cardamom pods.) The froth will rise to the top of the cups.

BUTTERMILK
INDIA   *(serves 2)*

Of all the dairy products, buttermilk is easily my favourite. By buttermilk I mean *real* buttermilk, the slightly tart, liquid residue which is left when cream is churned to make butter. Real buttermilk is much thinner than the cultured supermarket variety and was, until the turn of the century, used in America mainly to feed pigs. Known as *chha* or *chhaas* in northern India, it is a popular breakfast and lunchtime drink.

My problem with cultured, supermarket buttermilk is that while I know it to be nutritious, I find it hard to adjust to its thick texture. I have found a way around that. I just thin it down to the texture of real buttermilk with cold water!

½ tsp whole cumin seeds, roasted   *½ pt/3 dl cold buttermilk*
   and ground   *¼ pt/1½ dl ice-cold water*

½ tsp salt

A pinch of cayenne pepper

Freshly ground pepper to taste

(optional)

Combine all ingredients in the container of an electric blender and blend for 3 seconds. You could, if you like, mix all the ingredients with a wire whisk instead. Pour into two glasses and serve.

You may make this drink several hours ahead of time and store it, covered, in the refrigerator. Serve very cold and stir before serving.

SWEET LASSI
(Sweet Yogurt Drink)
INDIA
(serves 2)

In this drink plain yogurt is thinned out with iced water and sweetened. *Lassi* may be drunk with meals or, as was generally done in my family, it can be served between lunch and dinner. In India, both the *lassi* and the preceding buttermilk drink are often served after vigorous games of tennis, badminton, or hockey.

4 fl oz/1 dl plain yogurt

1½ tbs sugar, or to taste

12 fl oz/3½ dl ice-cold water

¼ tsp rose essence (optional)

Combine all ingredients in the container of an electric blender and blend for 3 seconds. Pour into two glasses and serve.

This drink may be made several hours ahead of time and stored, covered, in the refrigerator. It should be served very cold. Stir before serving.

SALTY LASSI
(Salty Yogurt Drink)
INDIA
(serves 2)

This is very similar to the preceding Sweet *Lassi*, only it is salty.

4 fl oz/1 dl plain yogurt
12 fl oz/3½ dl ice-cold water
¼ tsp salt, or to taste

Combine all ingredients in the container of an electric blender and blend for 3 seconds. Pour into 2 glasses and serve.

For information about ingredients and basic techniques that may be unfamiliar, see General Information, pages 481-506.

DOOGH
(Persian-Style Yogurt Drink, Flavoured with Mint)
IRAN   *(serves 2)*

Rather like salty Indian *lassi*, *doogh* is made out of thinned yogurt. It may be served plain or flavoured with mint. I often freeze sprigs of fresh mint in ice cubes to serve with my *doogh*. To make these cubes, half fill your ice-cube trays with water. Let the ice form. Now lay a sprig of fresh mint (or a leaf) on top of each cube and pour a tbs of iced water over each sprig of mint and freeze again. Take the tray out once more and fill to the top with water. Let the cubes freeze.

Instead of thinning out the yogurt with water, you could use soda water.

4 fl oz/1 dl plain yogurt   *4 ice cubes with mint in them (see*
12 fl oz/3½ dl ice-cold water   *above)*
¼ tsp salt, or to taste   *2 sprigs fresh mint*

Put the yogurt in a bowl. Slowly add the iced water, beating with a fork or whisk as you do so. Season with salt to taste.

Pour *doogh* into 2 glasses. Put 2 ice cubes into each glass and garnish with a sprig of mint.

CALPIS

Japan, which has almost no tradition of consuming milk products, has come up with a new drink that is likely to prove very popular. It is called Calpis and is sold in this country under the name 'Calpico'. It is based on nonfat dried milk that has been treated with lactic acid. The drink is milky white, with a slightly tart, slightly sweet, fruity flavour. It is most pleasant. What you buy in the bottle is a concentrate that can be diluted with cold water, hot water, or soda water. The directions for mixing the drink are on the bottle.

THANDAI
(A Milk and Almond Drink)
INDIA   (serves 2)

This is a very refreshing, cool, summer drink made out of milk and almonds and sold from terra-cotta pots throughout the plains of North India. Normally, whole milk is used in the recipe but since very few people in India own refrigerators, the milk is always diluted with small chunks of block ice. I substitute cold skimmed milk for the whole milk and do without the ice. The end result tastes very much like the *thandai* in India. The second major ingredient is almonds. Almonds, besides providing extra nourishment, are very popular in India as they are supposed to sharpen the brain! The flavouring in this drink comes from the aromatic cardamom. If you wish to vary the flavour, you might substitute fresh mint or fresh holy basil leaves for the cardamom seeds. Holy basil (*Ocymun sanctum*), also of the mint family, is used frequently in Thai cooking. It is not easily available so you would probably have to grow it in your own garden or on your windowsill. In India, holy basil or *tulsi* is considered sacred to Vishnu, the Preserver. My grandmother grew plants of it just outside our family Prayer Room and used the leaves to make a 'holy drink', not unlike *thandai*.

The recipe here would serve two people but it can easily be doubled or tripled. I tend to under-sweeten most of my drinks, but *thandai* is generally drunk quite sweet. You can increase or decrease the suggested amount of sugar.

Seeds from 1 cardamom pod (or 4–5 fresh mint leaves or fresh holy basil leaves)
16 fl oz/½ l very cold skimmed milk

12 blanched almonds, soaked in ½ pt/3 dl water overnight or for at least 5 hours and then drained
1 tbs sugar

Crush the cardamom seeds finely in a small mortar or place seeds between two sheets of waxed paper and pound gently with the wide section of a hammer until you have a powder. (If you are using mint or holy basil leaves, throw them into the blender.)

For information about ingredients and basic techniques that may be unfamiliar, see General Information, pages 481-506.

Pour 4 fl oz/1 dl of the milk into the container of an electric blender. Add cardamom powder, almonds, and sugar. Blend well. Stop the blender and pour in the rest of the milk. Blend for just 1 second. Pour into two glasses and serve.

This drink can be made several hours ahead of time and stored, covered, in the refrigerator. It should be served *very* cold. Stand it in crushed ice, if necessary. Stir before serving. (If you have flavoured your drink with fresh mint or holy basil, you might want to garnish your glasses with sprigs of the herbs.)

MILK WITH SAFFRON AND NUTS
INDIA   *(makes 16 fl oz/½ l)*

Many Indians begin their day with a glass of hot milk. Those who can afford it add saffron and nuts to it as well. It is not an uncommon sight, even today, to see turbaned, liveried servants in the palaces of those who were once maharajas, moving about gracefully in the early morning hours, bearing silver trays that hold glasses of frothy saffron-coloured milk. The froth is considered important in India and is made by pouring the milk from one glass to another several times. The distance between glasses sometimes reaches an impressive three feet! The same froth can, however, be created in a blender with much less fear of mishaps.

16 fl oz/½ l milk
3 cardamom pods, lightly crushed
A generous pinch of leaf saffron
2 tsp sugar, or to taste
1 tsp unsalted, peeled pistachios,
  cut into slivers

Combine the milk, cardamom pods, saffron, and sugar in a heavy pot and bring to a simmer. Turn heat to low and simmer the milk for 2 minutes.

Meanwhile, rinse out a blender container in very hot water. Strain the milk into it. Blend at high speed to make a froth. Pour into two glasses. Sprinkle the pistachios over the froth and serve immediately.

10 Condiments, Dips, Chutneys, and Relishes

'Nice flowers,' my daughter said a few days ago as she glanced offhandedly at the dinner table on the way from the front door to her room. They weren't flowers at all but spring onions that I had arranged, green side up, in a cut-glass, water-filled tumbler set in the centre of our dining table. And the spring onions were not decorative, but meant for eating. My mother used to arrange spring onions that way. Somehow, I had forgotten about them until just the other day.

Table condiments in Asia can be very simple – spring onions, onion slices, green chillies, roasted sesame seeds mixed with salt, salt mixed with Szechuan peppercorns, salt mixed with pepper and roasted cumin seeds, hot oil, red chillies pounded with garlic and salt and then soured with lemon juice, and crushed peanuts. Or they can get very elaborate – you might be served a rare pickle that was ten months in the making. Among the nicest part of Asian meals is just this – the number of condiments, pickles, sauces, dips, chutneys, relishes, and *sambals* that appear miraculously at the table, giving it variety and zest. Vegetarian food in particular gets such a boost from this approach. Each bite of the same food can be made to taste quite different, depending on what you eat it with or what you dip it in.

In Japan, for example, the simplest of bean-curd dishes, Udofu, is served with a heated sauce containing soy sauce, stock, and wine. But there are other condiments at the table as well, such as grated radish, grated ginger, shredded *nori* (laver), and sliced spring onions. Each cube of bean curd can be eaten with a new combination of seasonings. Eating becomes quite an adventure.

Simple relishes and everyday chutneys in India may be made out of chopped-up tomatoes and puréed herbs such as fresh green coriander and mint. They are not only supposed to provide the much-needed contrasts of tastes but some very necessary vitamins as well.

Pickles in Asia enjoy an even higher status. Much time and effort goes into preparing them as whole families trim, peel, and cut vegetables. Koreans spend the late autumn months making mountains of cabbage *kimchee*, generously flavoured with garlic, ginger, spring onions, and red pepper. They eat it in generous portions, too, at every single meal. Japanese pickles tend to be much more

410

sedate, and served always in tiny portions. Many meals, all over Japan, end with the felicitous combination of plain rice, pickles, and tea. Indian pickles tend to be very hot and spicy. They sharpen appetites and give lethargic systems a fresh charge. In the Middle East, a great deal of pickling is done in vinegar. The addition of fresh herbs such as mint and dill gives the pickled vegetables an aromatic freshness.

All pickles and chutneys are palate-teasers and flavour-enhancers. They give colour to the simplest of meals.

SALT AND PEPPER, INDIAN-STYLE
INDIA   (makes about 1⅔ tbs)

On our dining table in India, we always had a spice mixture that we referred to as 'Bauwa's salt'. ('Bauwa' is what we called our mother.) It consisted of freshly ground coarse salt, freshly ground black pepper, and ground, roasted cumin seeds, all mixed together and put inside a cut-glass salt cellar. We used this mixture to season radishes, cucumber, tomato slices, guava wedges, tart apple slices, tangerine sections, and sometimes we even put it on buttered toast.

1 tbs salt
1 tsp freshly ground black pepper

1 tsp freshly ground, roasted cumin seeds

Mix all the ingredients together.

It is best to keep this in a tightly closed jar and take it out as needed. Although this mixture is most aromatic and pungent when the spices have just been ground, you can store it for a few weeks.

SALT AND PEPPER, CHINESE-STYLE
CHINA   (makes about 4 tbs)

Here is a combination of salt and pepper with a slight difference. Instead of ordinary peppercorns, the highly fragrant Szechuan peppercorns are used. This salt makes an excellent dip for raw vegetables, for batter-fried vegetables, and even for some sour fruit such as green apples. You might also use it in place of salt when boiling vegetables. It gives them a special aroma.

4 tbs coarse salt

1½ tsp Szechuan peppercorns

4 tbs coarse salt   *1½ tsp Szechuan peppercorns*

Put the salt and peppercorns in a small, heavy, cast-iron frying pan and set it over a medium-low flame. Stir and cook for 4 to 5 minutes or until the salt turns slightly darker and the peppercorns not only darken but give off a wonderful aroma. Put the contents of the frying pan into the container of a clean coffee grinder and grind.

GOMA SHIO
(Black Sesame Seeds and Salt)
JAPAN   *(makes about 2½ tbs)*

This is a combination of roasted black sesame seeds and coarse salt that may be sprinkled over soups, vegetables, egg dishes, and rice dishes. Although sesame seeds do taste best when freshly roasted, you could store this mixture in a tightly lidded jar for a couple of weeks. I love it on lightly boiled vegetables like green beans and broccoli. It is also good on eggs, cucumber slices, tomatoes, white radish slices, light soups, and plain rice. It makes an excellent dip for raw vegetables.

2 tbs roasted black sesame seeds
1 tbs coarse salt

Mix together.

DRY NORTH INDIAN DIP
INDIA   *(makes about a teacup)*

Here is a wonderful dip for raw vegetables. Arrange them all around the bowl of spices and serve as a snack for children or with evening drinks. It may be frozen.

2 tbs whole coriander seeds   *3 tbs sesame seeds*
1 tbs whole cumin seeds   *1½ tbs salt*

For information about ingredients and basic techniques that may be unfamiliar, see General Information, pages 481-506.

¼ tsp cayenne pepper, or more to   ¼ tsp freshly ground black pepper
taste

Put the coriander seeds, cumin seeds, and sesame seeds into a small, heavy frying pan over a medium-low flame. Stir and dry-roast the seeds gently until the seeds are a few shades darker and emit a deliciously nutty odour. Empty the spices on to a plate and let them cool slightly. Now put them into the container of a clean coffee grinder and grind as finely as possible.

Put the spice mixture into a serving bowl. Add the salt, cayenne, and black pepper. Mix.

Neela's
MAULKA PORI
(Dry South Indian Chutney)
INDIA   *(makes about 4 tbs)*

This is a South Indian fried spice combination that is used as a kind of relish with Indian pancakes, rice, and vegetable dishes. It is stored in jars (I know one South Indian vegetarian photographer who travels through Europe and America with a jar lovingly prepared by his wife) and can be sprinkled over foods as it is or – and this is how it is commonly used – it can be mixed with oil or *ghee* before being served. Rather like Chinese hot oil, it can be used to season all kinds of foods, from soups to salads, or it can be placed on the edge of a dinner plate and eaten, in small amounts, like prepared English mustard. It should be eaten with discretion as it is *very* hot. In this recipe you will notice the South Indian habit of using *dals* like spices.

2 tsp vegetable oil   *¾ oz/20 g toovar (arhar) dal*
A generous pinch of ground   *2 tsp salt*
  asafetida   *10 whole dried hot red peppers*
1 tsp whole cumin seeds   *Extra vegetable oil or* ghee *to be*
1½ oz/45 g urad dal   *used when serving*
1½ oz/45 g chana dal

Heat the 2 tsp of oil in a small, heavy frying pan over a medium flame. When hot, put in the asafetida and, a few seconds later, the cumin seeds. Stir and fry for 8 to 10 seconds. Now add the *urad dal*, *chana dal*, and *toovar dal*. Fry, stirring, until the *dals* turn reddish in colour. Empty the contents of the frying pan into a blender container. (If your blender will not grind *dals* well, you could empty contents of the frying pan on to a paper towel. Let the spices drain for a minute and then put them into a coffee grinder reserved for spices. You can then proceed with the recipe.) Add the salt and red peppers. Pulverize the spices so they are coarsely powdered. Let the spices cool completely and then store in a tightly closed jar. This spice mixture should be good for 3 to 4 weeks.

To serve as a relish to be eaten with dinner, put as many tea-spoons of the mixture into a small serving bowl as there are people eating. Add just as many teaspoons of vegetable oil or melted *ghee* and mix well. After that, people can serve themselves with as much as they want.

TEMPURA DIPPING SAUCE
JAPAN   (makes 6 portions)

This is an excellent sauce for Japanese batter-fried foods. Pour it into individual bowls and serve with a dish like Tempura.

8 fl oz/¼ l Japanese Stock (see page 339)
4 tbs Japanese soy sauce
4 tbs mirin

1 tsp sugar
4 tbs peeled white radish, or 2 tbs peeled fresh ginger, grated to a pulp

Combine all ingredients in a bowl.

CHINESE DIPPING SAUCE
CHINA   (serves about 4)

This sauce may be dribbled over congee or eggs or it could be used as a dipping sauce for batter-fried vegetables and breads. It could also be used as a dressing for cold noodles.

2 tbs Chinese thin soy sauce
1 tsp sesame oil
2½ tsp distilled white vinegar

1 tsp sugar
A few drops Hot Oil (see page 418)

Mix all the ingredients together.

For information about ingredients and basic techniques that may be unfamiliar, see General Information, pages 481-506.

JAPANESE DIPPING SAUCE
JAPAN   *(serves 6)*

This recipe makes a very concentrated sauce. For dishes such as Japanese Omelette with Bean Curd (see page 230), you should thin it out with 2–4 tbs of *dashi*.

4 tbs Japanese soy sauce	*1½ tsp sugar*
2 tbs mirin	*2–4 tbs* dashi *(see page 339),*
1 tbs sesame oil	*optional*

Mix all ingredients together. If you are serving a Japanese-style meal, you might want to pour the sauce into small, individual bowls.

FILIPINO DIPPING SAUCE
PHILIPPINES   *(serves 4)*

This sauce may be served with Ukoy or with any other batter-fried vegetables.

4 tbs distilled white vinegar
½ tsp garlic, peeled and mashed
¼ tsp salt, or to taste

Mix all ingredients together and divide among four very small bowls.

KOREAN DIPPING SAUCE
NUMBER 1
KOREA   *(serves 4)*

Serve this with *bindaetuk* or with batter-fried vegetables.

4 tbs Japanese soy sauce
4 tsp Japanese rice vinegar
1 tsp sesame oil

Mix all ingredients.
  To serve, divide sauce among four small saucers.

KOREAN DIPPING SAUCE
NUMBER 2
KOREA   *(makes about 7 tbs)*

This sauce may be served with Sautéed Bean Curd, used as a dressing for noodles, and used as a dip for sliced vegetables.

4 tbs Japanese soy sauce
2½ tbs Japanese rice vinegar
1 tsp sugar
1 tbs very finely sliced spring
  onion

1 clove garlic, peeled and mashed
1 tsp roasted and lightly crushed
  sesame seeds

Mix all ingredients together.

KOREAN DIPPING SAUCE NUMBER 3

KOREA   (makes about 7 tbs)

This sauce may be used to season the cold noodle soup, Naeng Myon; it may be used as a dip for vegetables or for cubes of hot or ice-cold bean curd; and it may be used to season Plain Japanese Rice for Korean-style rice dishes.

4 tbs Japanese soy sauce
2½ tbs Japanese rice vinegar
1 tsp sugar

1 tbs very finely sliced spring
  onion
1 clove garlic, peeled and mashed

Mix all ingredients together.

SIMPLE KOREAN SAUCE

KOREA   (serves 4–6)

This sauce may be used as a dip for vegetables, cooked and raw, or it may be used to season Korean rice dishes.

3 tbs Japanese soy sauce
3 tbs sesame oil
¾ tsp sugar

1 tsp roasted and lightly crushed
  sesame seeds

Combine all ingredients. Mix again before serving, as the oil tends to rise to the top.

The sauce may be served in small individual saucers or in a somewhat larger single bowl.

For information about ingredients and basic techniques that may be unfamiliar, see General Information, pages 481–506.

SPICY KOREAN SAUCE
KOREA   *(makes about 4 fl oz/1 dl)*

This sauce may be used as a dipping sauce for Korean pancakes, raw vegetables, vegetable fritters, and bean curd. It may also be eaten with Korean rice dishes.

6 tbs Japanese soy sauce
1 tbs sesame oil
½ tsp kochu chang; *or more, as desired*
½ tsp very finely chopped garlic

1 tbs roasted and lightly crushed sesame seeds
1 tsp sugar
½ spring onion sliced into very fine rounds (bottom half only)

Combine all ingredients and mix well.

TAHINI DIPPING SAUCE
MIDDLE EAST   *(makes about ¼ pt/1½ dl)*

This simple sauce, with ground sesame paste, or *tahini*, as its base, is found all over the Middle East. It may be used as a dip for raw vegetables, pitta bread, or, when thinned and mixed with chopped parsley, it can be used as a sauce for *falafel* (see variation below), the chick-pea 'hamburgers' that are stuffed into pitta-bread pockets along with shredded lettuce and sliced tomatoes.

2–3 cloves garlic, peeled
2 fl oz/½ dl tahini
4 tbs lemon juice

¼–½ tsp salt
3 tbs cold water

Crush the cloves of garlic to a paste. Put this paste in a stainless steel or non-metallic bowl. Add the *tahini* and beat it in with a fork. Add the lemon juice, beating it in as you do so. Now add the salt and mix it in. Add the cold water, a little bit at a time, beating in as well. (You could do all this in a food processor or blender, too.) Check the balance of sour and salt. Adjust, if necessary.

VARIATION: FALAFEL SAUCE—Add 1 tbs very finely chopped parsley and 1 tbs more cold water.

WASABI
(Horseradish)
JAPAN

Wasabi is a green, pungent and nose-tingling Japanese horseradish paste that is best when made from the peeled and finely grated fresh vegetable. As this is not always available in Britain, the next best alternative is to use the dry, powdered variety which needs to be reconstituted (about ¾ tsp water to every tsp of the powder) or to use a processed paste.

CRISPLY FRIED ONIONS

(makes enough to fill a ½-pt/2¾-dl jar)

These onions are more than a garnish. They are sprinkled over many Asian dishes for extra flavour. You might try them over rice dishes, egg dishes, noodle dishes, and even in salads.

2 medium-sized onions, peeled
Vegetable oil for shallow frying

Cut the onions in half lengthwise, and then crosswise into very, very thin half rings. Press the half rings between layers of kitchen paper for half an hour.

Heat ½ in/1½ cm of oil in an 8–9-in/20–23-cm frying pan over a medium flame. When hot, put in the onions. Fry, stirring gently, until the onions are a reddish-brown colour and no longer limp-looking. Some onion will become dark brown and that is quite all right. Remove the onions with a slotted spoon and spread out on kitchen paper. Once the onions have drained and cooled, they should turn very crisp. You may now use them the same day or else store them in a tightly closed container for a few days.

HOT OIL

CHINA

(makes about 4 fl oz/1 dl)

This is the orange-coloured oil that seems to sit permanently on tables in Chinese restaurants, along with soy sauce and vinegar. It is a hot seasoning that may be dribbled into soups and sauces, in the minutest quantities, of course.

For your oil to get a nice colour, you need a cayenne pepper – or ground hot red chilli pepper (same thing) – that is really bright red and not faded with time and exposure. I find that among the best places to buy this are Indian and Chinese stores. Once the oil has been seasoned with the hot pepper, it needs to be strained properly. The best way seems to be to use a clean but discardable piece of cloth, such as a 10-in/25-cm square torn out from an old sheet or pillow case.

For information about ingredients and basic techniques that may be unfamiliar, see General Information, pages 481-506.

4 fl oz/1 dl vegetable oil
1½ tsp ground hot red pepper
  (cayenne pepper or chilli pepper)

Heat the oil in a small cast-iron frying pan over a medium flame. As soon as the oil is hot — you will be able to tell as it will start swirling and moving — put in the red pepper. Stir once and turn off the heat. Let the oil cool off just slightly. Then strain it through a clean cloth and store it in a bottle with a well-fitting top.

If you wish to bring oil to the table to offer as a seasoning, you could transfer it to a bottle with a narrow neck such as the old-fashioned bottles for table vinegar. Drops of Hot Oil may be put into congees, soups, and dipping sauces.

TOMATO SAUCE

(makes about 16 fl oz/½ l)

This plain, simple sauce may be used for cooking all manner of bean, *paneer*, and vegetable dishes. Make it when good, ripe tomatoes are in season. You could easily double or quadruple this recipe. What you do not use immediately may be refrigerated or frozen.

2 lb/900 g ripe tomatoes or peeled   *½ tsp salt*
  tinned tomatoes   *½ tsp sugar*

Chop up the tomatoes and put them into a heavy stainless steel pot or a pot lined with a non-metallic substance. Add the salt and the sugar and bring to the boil. Cook on medium heat, stirring frequently, until you reduce the contents of the pot by half. Push the tomatoes through a sieve in order to get rid of the skins. You could leave the tomato sauce this way, but if you want it any smoother, put it into an electric blender or food processor and blend for a minute.

CHILLI SAMBAL
INDONESIA   *(makes about 3 tbs)*

In Indonesia, this *sambal* is made by pounding lots of fresh hot red peppers in a mortar and then adding tamarind paste and salt. It is quite fiery. I have calmed the fire somewhat in this recipe by adding some peanuts. It still remains very hot and should be approached with caution. This is a relish that should be spooned in a very small quantity on to one's plate. It can then be eaten with almost any food that needs pepping up. I love to put small amounts in soups and in dressings for green vegetables and beans.

4 tbs whole dried hot red peppers   2 tbs tamarind paste
2 tbs fried or roasted unsalted   ⅓ tsp salt
  peanuts

Put the red pepper in a coffee grinder reserved for spices and grind to a powder. Add the peanuts and grind them as well. Empty into a small bowl. Add 2 tsp of water as well as all the other ingredients. Mix well.

SAMBAL TOMAT
(Hot Tomato Sambal)
INDONESIA   *(makes about 2 tbs)*

You need ripe tomatoes for this *sambal* but they can be fresh or tinned. If fresh, peel them (see glossary); if tinned, lift them out of their liquid. This is another hot relish that could be smeared on a cheese sandwich, eaten with Fried Pre-seasoned Tempeh, or served as a condiment at all South Asian, South-east Asian, and even Mexican meals.

2 tbs vegetable oil   ½ tsp cayenne pepper
½ lb/225 g peeled tomatoes,   ¼ tsp salt
  chopped   2 tsp lime or lemon juice

Heat the oil in a heavy 6-in/15-cm saucepan over a medium flame. When hot, put in the tomatoes. Stir and cook for 10 to 12 minutes, turning the heat down as the oil separates and the tomatoes begin to fry. Stir continuously through this cooking period. The tomatoes should turn a nice darkish colour. Lift the tomato mixture out of the oil and put it in a small bowl. Add all the other ingredients and mix.

For information about ingredients and basic techniques that may be unfamiliar, see General Information, pages 481-506.

SPICY PEANUT SAMBAL
INDONESIA   *(makes about 4 fl oz/1 dl)*

This hot, nutty sauce is generally served with the salad-like dish, Pecel (see page 87), about 2 tbs per person — or else it may be used as a dip for potato crisps, fried *tempeh* sticks, or for raw, cut vegetables. In Indonesia, I have always seen it made in a mortar but you could use a blender instead.

*3–4 fresh hot green chillies, sliced
  into thin rounds
4 cloves garlic, peeled
1 oz/30 g fried or roasted unsalted
  peanuts*

*5 tsp Japanese soy sauce
4 tsp lime juice
4 tsp tamarind paste
4 tsp dark brown sugar*

If you are using a mortar, pound the chillies and garlic first. When they are well mashed, add the peanuts. Pound them too. I like to leave the peanuts a little grainy, but you could pound them until they are quite smooth. Now add the soy sauce, lime juice, tamarind paste, and sugar. Pound gently to mix. Add about 2 tbs plus 2 tsp water to get a thickish sauce with about the consistency of prepared English mustard. If you are using a blender, put all ingredients, as well as 2 tbs plus 2 tsp water into the blender container. Blend until smooth. If the sauce seems too thick, add another tsp of water.

Usha's
HOT AND SPICY HYDERABADI TOMATO CHUTNEY
INDIA   *(makes 6 fl oz/1¾ dl)*

This is a perky relish to have around in the refrigerator. A dollop of it could brighten up almost any meal. It is garlicky and it *is* hot. It is *not* sweet. Instead, it has the natural tartness of fresh tomatoes.

*1 lb/450 g ripe tomatoes, peeled,
  and finely chopped
1 tsp finely grated fresh ginger
1 tsp well-mashed garlic pulp
½ tsp ground turmeric
¼ tsp cayenne pepper
4 tbs vegetable oil*

*4 cloves garlic, peeled
1 tsp whole cumin seeds
½ tsp whole black mustard seeds
¼ tsp whole fenugreek seeds
2 whole dried hot red peppers
½ tsp salt, or to taste*

Put the chopped tomatoes, ginger, garlic pulp (*not* the whole cloves), turmeric, and cayenne in a bowl and mix.

Heat the oil in a 7–8-in/18–20-cm frying pan over a medium

flame. When hot, put in the cloves of garlic. Stir and fry until they are brown. Add the cumin seeds, mustard seeds, and fenugreek seeds. Let the seeds sizzle for 2 seconds. Put in the red peppers. Stir them once; they should swell up and turn dark red. Now put in the tomato mixture (keep face averted). Stir and cook on medium heat for 10 to 12 minutes or until tomatoes are fairly dry. You should have about 6 fl oz/1¾ dl chutney, but this could vary with the water content of the tomatoes. Add the salt and mix it in.

Serve hot, cold, or at room temperature. Store in a jar in a refrigerator. The chutney should last at least a week.

FRESH CORIANDER AND MINT CHUTNEY
INDIA   *(serves 6)*

This chutney may be served with almost any Indian meal. It makes an excellent — and nutritious — dip for Vegetable Pakoris.

2 oz/55 g chopped fresh green   *1 tbs lemon juice*
  coriander   *6 fl oz/1¾ dl plain yogurt*
1 oz/30 g chopped fresh mint   *¼–½ tsp salt*
1 fresh hot green chilli (optional)

Put the fresh coriander, mint, green chilli, lemon juice, and 3 tbs water into the container of a blender or food processor. Blend until smooth, pushing down, if necessary, with a rubber spatula.

Beat the yogurt in a small bowl until it is creamy. Add the mixture from the blender and fold in. Add ¼ tsp of the salt, mix, and taste. Add more salt if you need it.

TAMARIND-MINT CHUTNEY FOR SNACK FOODS
INDIA   *(makes about 8 fl oz/2¼ dl)*

Throughout North India, there are certain chutneys that are associated just with snack foods, foods like *samosas* or potato patties, or lentil patties. These chutneys tend to be sour or sweet and sour and frequently they are poured over savoury foods in order to provide a contrast of flavour. Here is a fairly typical sweet-and-sour chutney in which tamarind is combined with mint and fresh green coriander. It is quite wonderful when swirled over lightly beaten and seasoned yogurt.

For information about ingredients and basic techniques that may be unfamiliar, see General Information, pages 481-506.

1 heaped tbs chopped fresh green
   coriander
1 heaped tbs chopped mint
3–4 tbs chopped gur (jaggery) or
   dark brown sugar
A ¾-in/2-cm cube of fresh ginger,
   peeled and chopped

¼ tsp pounded or ground kala
   namak (black salt)
5½ fl oz/1½ dl tamarind paste
⅛ tsp freshly ground black pepper
⅛–¼ tsp cayenne pepper
1 tsp ground, roasted cumin seeds
½ tsp salt

Put the fresh coriander, mint, *gur*, ginger, *kala namak* and 4 tbs water into the container of an electric blender or food processor. Blend until you have a smooth paste. Mix contents of the blender with the tamarind paste (use a non-metallic or stainless steel bowl). Add all the remaining ingredients. Mix well and keep covered in the refrigerator until ready to use.

SOUTH INDIAN COCONUT CHUTNEY
INDIA   (makes about 8 fl oz/2¼ dl)

In South India, *chana dal*, small yellow split peas, are often used as a flavouring. They are fried in oil first and then either mixed with other roasted spices and ground or, as in this fresh coconut chutney, they are mixed with chutney ingredients and pulverized. The frying makes the *chana dal* very red and gives it an interesting nutty taste. This chutney may be eaten with Indian *dosas* and Mung Dal na Poora, with any batter-fried vegetables, or served as a dip for raw vegetables.

1½ tbs chana dal
4 tbs vegetable oil
1 fresh hot green chilli, sliced
8 tbs chopped fresh green coriander

½ medium-sized coconut, split,
   peeled and grated
¼–½ tsp salt
4 tbs lime or lemon juice

Pick over the *dal*.

Heat the oil in a small frying pan over a medium flame. Fry the *dal* in this oil until it is a rich reddish colour. Remove *dal* with a slotted spoon (leave the oil behind — you do not need it) and put it into the container of an electric blender. Add the green chilli, fresh coriander, and 4 fl oz/1 dl water. Blend until smooth. Now add the grated coconut, salt, and lime or lemon juice. Blend again, using a rubber spatula to push down the coconut, if necessary.

Pour the chutney into a stainless steel or non-metallic bowl. It should have the consistency of thick batter. Add more water, if necessary. Check the salt and lemon juice. Cover and refrigerate.

Kamal's
SWEET TOMATO CHUTNEY
INDIA   *(makes 16 fl oz/4½ dl)*

This chutney may be served with almost all Indian meals. I love to eat it at tea-time, spread over freshly made *mutthries*. You could also eat it with toast!

2 lb/900 g ripe tomatoes	½ tsp dried powdered ginger
¼ tsp whole fennel seeds	2 bay leaves
¼ tsp whole fenugreek seeds	¼ tsp ground mace
16 fl oz/½ l distilled white vinegar	¼ tsp garam masala
14 oz/395 g sugar	¼ tsp cayenne pepper
10 cloves garlic, peeled and very	About 1¼ tsp salt
finely chopped	1 oz/30 g raisins

Wash the tomatoes and dry them thoroughly.

Grind the fennel and fenugreek seeds in a coffee grinder, spice grinder, or mortar.

Heat the vinegar in a 7½–8in/19–20-cm-wide, heavy stainless steel or porcelain-lined pot over a medium flame. When it begins to boil, put in as many of the tomatoes as the pot will hold in a single layer. Turn the tomatoes around for 15 to 20 seconds, then remove with a non-metallic slotted spoon and place on a plate. Do all tomatoes this way. Turn the heat under the vinegar to medium-low.

While the tomatoes cool, put the sugar into the vinegar and let it melt slowly. Peel the tomatoes and cut them into 1-in/2½-cm cubes. Put the tomatoes and any accumulated liquid into the pot with the vinegar and the sugar. Add the ground fennel and fenugreek, the garlic, ginger, bay leaves, mace, *garam masala*, cayenne, and 1¼ tsp of the salt. Mix and bring to the boil. Now arrange the heat so that the chutney keeps boiling fairly rapidly – a medium-low temperature is usually about right – and let it cook this way for about 40 minutes. Stir every now and then during this period.

Add the raisins to the chutney and stir.

From now on the chutney needs to be watched more closely as it can stick on the bottom. Stir more frequently and continue to cook another 25 to 35 minutes or until chutney has thickened and is no longer watery. It should have a nice sheen to it. Remember that it will thicken some more as it cools. You should have about 16 fl oz/4½ dl. Taste for salt and add a bit more if you think you need it. Mix.

For information about ingredients and basic techniques that may be unfamiliar, see General Information, pages 481-506.

Allow the chutney to cool completely, put it in clean jars, and cover tightly. I keep my chutney in the refrigerator and it stays in perfect condition for months.

APRICOT CHUTNEY WITH SULTANAS AND CURRANTS
INDIA   *(makes about 1½ pt/8½ dl)*

In North India, we often make a chutney out of the flesh of a sour, dried plum known as *aloo bokhara* (the plum of Bokhara). I have changed that recipe somewhat and used the more available dried apricots instead. I find that this sweet-and-sour, pectin-rich fruit makes a superb chutney.

1 lb/450 g dried apricots	*½ pt/3 dl red wine vinegar*
10 large cloves garlic, peeled and coarsely chopped	*14 oz/395 g sugar*
	¼ tsp salt
A 1×3-in/2½×8-cm piece of fresh ginger, peeled and coarsely chopped	*⅛–¾ tsp cayenne pepper*
	3 oz/85 g sultanas
	2 oz/60 g currants

Put the apricots in a bowl. Pour 1½ pt/8½ dl of hot water over them and let them soak for an hour.

Put the garlic and ginger into the container of an electric blender or a food processor along with 2 fl oz/½ dl of the vinegar. Blend until smooth.

Empty the apricots and their soaking liquid into a heavy stainless steel or porcelain-lined pot. Add the garlic–ginger mixture, the remaining vinegar, sugar, salt, and cayenne. Bring to the boil. Simmer on a medium flame, stirring frequently, for 45 minutes. Do not let the chutney catch at the bottom of the pot. Lower heat if necessary. Add the sultanas and currants and cook, stirring, another half hour or until chutney takes on a thick, glazed look. (Remember that the chutney will thicken slightly as it cools.) Let the chutney cool and store, refrigerated, in lidded glass or ceramic jars.

GOAN CABBAGE SALAD
INDIA   *(serves 4–6)*

The Goan peasants on the west coast of India eat this salad with many of their simple meals. Though carrots are not normally added to the salad, I find that they provide a nice contrast of colours. This salad gets sharper in taste as the hours and days go on. It can be kept for several weeks. You could serve it with almost any bean dish in this book.

12 oz/340 g finely shredded
cabbage
1 carrot, trimmed, peeled, and cut
into 1½-in/4-cm-long julienne
strips

1–3 fresh hot green chillies, cut
into fine, 1½-in/4-cm-long
shreds
1 pt/5¾ dl distilled, white vinegar
1½ tbs salt

Put the shredded cabbage, carrot, and green chillies into a clean, wide-mouthed 1 qt/11½ dl jar. Mix the vinegar with the salt and pour that into the jar. Mix with a clean spoon. Cover, and leave for an hour.

PICKLED GREEN CHILLIES
INDIA   (makes enough to fill a ¾-pt/4¼-dl jar)

Here is my family's recipe for a fiery pickle that combines three of God's most potent creations — hot green chillies, cayenne, and mustard. It is astoundingly good but only recommended for the stout of heart. There is no getting away from it — it is hot. Just as the English use droplets of their made mustard on their foods, so do we in India add the minutest portions of this pickle to whatever else we may be eating. It works wonders with all kinds of foods, perking up anything from cheese sandwiches to tomato salads.

½ lb/225 g fresh hot green chillies
4 tbs whole black mustard seeds
4 tsp salt
1 tsp cayenne or other hot ground
red pepper

A 1-in/2½-cm cube of fresh ginger,
peeled and finely chopped
2 tbs mustard oil
3 tbs lemon juice

Wipe each green chilli with a damp cloth. Spread out on a tray and leave to dry in a sunny or airy place.

Grind the mustard seeds to a powder in a coffee grinder or other spice grinder.

Trim away the stems of the green chillies and then slice them crosswise into ⅙-in/½-cm-thick rounds. (You may want to wear fine rubber gloves while doing this. If not, refrain from touching any part of your face before washing your hands thoroughly with soap and water.)

Combine the green chillies, ground mustard, salt, cayenne, and ginger in a bowl. Mix well.

Heat the oil in a small frying pan or a very small pot over a medium flame. As soon as the oil begins to smoke, turn off the

---

For information about ingredients and basic techniques that may be unfamiliar, see General Information, pages 481-506.

flame and let the oil cool completely. Pour the oil over the seasoned green chillies and mix well. Put the chilli mixture into a ¾-pt/4½-dl-jar or crock and cover with a non-metallic lid. Put the jar in a warm sunny spot and let it get as many hours of sunlight as you can manage in the next 24 hours. Shake the jar a few times during this period.

On the following day, add the lemon juice. Put the lid back on and shake the jar thoroughly. For the next few days, put the jar out in a warm, sunny spot in the daytime and, if that spot is outdoors, bring the jar in at night. The pickle should take 3 to 4 days to mature in the summer and up to 7 days in the winter. The pickle is ready when it has turned slightly sour and the green chillies have lost their bright-green colour. It may now be refrigerated.

My Grandmother's
SOUR LIME PICKLE
INDIA   *(fills a 1 qt/11½ dl jar)*

This is a simple version of my grandmother's black lime pickle, the one I wrote about but did not give a recipe for in my book, *An Invitation to Indian Cooking*. It is salty and sour. The only 'heat' it has comes from black pepper. I grew up on this pickle and can recall almost no picnic, banquet, or, for that matter, car journey, that wasn't associated with it. Apart from its excellent taste, my grandmother insisted that the pickle had a very 'settling' effect on the stomach. As children, we often sucked on it the way British kids do on lollipops, while we watched an itinerant puppet show or giggled our way through a mock monkey wedding, another travelling show that still goes from house to house in India. My grandmother's pickle, which turned darker − and better − as the months rolled on, was quite unlike the yellowish or greenish sweet or hot lime pickles that we ate in other Indian homes. Ours was definitely considered superior.

6 *unblemished limes*
1 *tsp whole black peppercorns*
4 *large black cardamom pods*
2 *tsp whole cumin seeds*

A 2-in/5-cm *stick of cinnamon,*
   broken up a bit
12 *whole cloves*
6 *tsp salt*
6 *tbs lime juice*

Wipe the 6 limes with a damp cloth and leave to dry off in the sun or in an airy place.

Put the black peppercorns, black cardamoms (skin and all),

cumin seeds, cinnamon, and cloves into the container of a coffee grinder or other spice grinder. Grind as fine as possible. Empty the spices into a cup. Add the salt and mix.

Find a wide-mouthed jar or crock that will hold the 6 limes easily with enough room to shake them around. I use a jar with a 1-qt/11½-dl capacity.

Quarter the limes lengthwise in such a way that the four sections remain attached at the bottom. Remove seeds, if any.

Divide the spice mixture into six parts. 'Stuff' one portion into each of the limes, rubbing the spices well into the cut section. Close up the limes and put them, cut side up, into the jar. Cover the jar with a non-metallic lid and place it in a warm, sunny spot for as many hours of sunlight as you can manage to get in the next 24 hours.

On the following day, add the 6 tbs of lime juice to the pickle jar. Cover and shake well. For the next month, put the jar in a warm, sunny spot in the daytime and then, if that spot is outdoors, bring the pickle in at night. Shake the jar three or four times a day. The pickle is still not ready. You may cease putting it out in the sun, but continue to shake the jar for another month. You may now begin to remove wedges of the pickle for eating. Do not refrigerate the pickle and remember that it will keep improving with age.

To serve four people, remove two wedges and then cut each wedge into halves. Arrange these halves in a small, shallow bowl and set the bowl in the centre of the table along with other chutneys and relishes.

For information about ingredients and basic techniques that may be unfamiliar, see General Information, pages 481-506.

CAULIFLOWER AND WHITE RADISH PICKLED IN WATER

INDIA   *(makes enough to fill a 1¾-pt/1-l jar)*

You may substitute turnip slices for the radish in this recipe. Peeled and sliced carrots, peeled and sliced kohlrabi, as well as scraped and sliced lotus roots, may also be added.

½ lb/225 g cauliflower (½ smallish head)	½ tsp ground turmeric
½ lb/225 g white radish	½ tsp cayenne or other ground hot red pepper
1 tbs whole black mustard seeds	1½ tsp salt

Cut the cauliflower into slim flowerets that are about 1–1½ in/2½–4 cm across at the head, ⅓–½ in/1–1½ cm wide, and 1½–2 in/4–5 cm in length.

Peel the radish and cut it crosswise into ⅓-in/1-cm-thick rounds. Radish slices that are 1 in/2½ cm in diameter or less may be left in rounds; radish slices that are 1½ in/4 cm in diameter should be cut into halves; radish slices that are bigger should be quartered.

Bring 3 qt/3½ l of water to the boil in a big pot. Throw in all the cut vegetables and bring to the boil again. Boil rapidly for 15 seconds and drain immediately, making sure that you save 4 fl oz/1 dl of the boiling liquid. Spread the drained vegetables out on a platter and allow to cool off.

Grind the mustard seeds coarsely in a coffee grinder or other spice grinder.

Combine the vegetables, ground mustard seeds, turmeric, cayenne, and salt in a bowl. Mix well. Empty the contents of the bowl into a 1¾-pt/1-l-sized jar or crock. Add the 4 fl oz/1 dl warm reserved liquid. Cover with a non-metallic lid and shake the jar well. For the next few days, put the jar in a warm, sunny spot in the daytime and if that spot is outdoors, bring the jar in at night. This pickle may take 4 days to mature in the summer and up to 8 days in the winter. Make sure to shake the jar at least 3 or 4 times a day. When the pickle is sour enough for your liking, it is ready. It may now be refrigerated.

Asha's
CARROT AND TURNIP PICKLE

INDIA   *(makes enough to fill a 1¾-pt/1-l jar)*

Traditionally, this sweet-and-sour pickle is sweetened with jaggery, a raw, lump sugar. Even though jaggery is available in most Indian grocery stores, it is generally rock-hard and not crumbly enough to use easily in this pickle. If you can manage to find soft, crumbly jaggery, do use it; if not, brown sugar makes an adequate substitute.

8 oz/225 g carrots (about 2½ carrots)

8 oz/225 g young turnips (about 2 turnips)

5 tbs whole black mustard seeds

¾–1 tsp cayenne or other ground hot red pepper

2 tsp salt

8 fl oz/¼ l mustard oil

About 3 tbs brown sugar or jaggery

Peel the carrots and cut into ¼-in/¾-cm-thick rounds.

Peel the turnips and quarter, lengthwise. Cut the quarters crosswise into ¼-in/¾-cm-thick slices.

Put the mustard seeds into the container of a coffee grinder or other spice grinder. Grind coarsely.

Bring 1¼ pt/7 dl of water to the boil in a 3-qt/3½-l pot. Throw in the cut vegetables and bring to the boil again. Boil rapidly for 5 seconds. Drain thoroughly.

The vegetables need to be dried off a bit. Pat them with kitchen paper and then either leave in the sun for a couple of hours or place them in a 200° F/93° C (lowest gas setting) oven for 45 minutes, all nicely spread out on a tray.

Make a paste of the ground mustard seeds, cayenne, salt, and 4 fl oz/1 dl of the mustard oil in a bowl. Add the vegetables and mix. Spoon all the contents of the bowl into a 1¾-pt/1-l jar or crock. Cover with a non-metallic top and place the jar in a warm, sunny spot. For the next 4 to 5 days, make sure that the jar spends as many of the daylight hours as possible in a warm, sunny spot, indoors or outdoors. If it is put outdoors, it should be brought in at night. Shake the jar 2 or 3 times a day to ensure even pickling. After 4 to 5 days, the pickle will start to turn sour. Add the remaining 4 fl oz/1 dl mustard oil and mix well. Continue to place the jar in the sun for another 3 to 6 days or until the pickle has soured to your taste. (This process will take longer in the winter.) Now empty the contents of the jar into a bowl. Add 2 tbs of the sugar and mix. Taste for sweetness. Add more sugar, if you like. Put the pickle back in the jar. Cover. The pickle may now be refrigerated.

For information about ingredients and basic techniques that may be unfamiliar, see General Information, pages 481-506.

Sharad Nanavati's
SWEET-AND-SOUR LIME PICKLE
INDIA   *(makes enough to fill a 1-qt/11½-dl jar)*

I love to eat this pickle with Lentils with Spinach, rice, and yogurt. I also enjoy eating it with a cheese sandwich.

6 limes	20 cloves of garlic, peeled
6 fresh hot green chillies	6 tsp salt
3 1-in/2½-cm cubes of ginger, peeled	14 oz/395 g sugar
	16 fl oz/½ l distilled white vinegar

Wipe the limes and green chillies with a damp cloth. Leave to dry in an airy or sunny spot. Cut each lime, lengthwise, into six wedges. Cut the stems off the green chillies.

Cut the ginger into very thin slices and then cut the slices into very thin strips.

Quarter the cloves of garlic lengthwise.

Find a wide-mouthed jar or crock with a 1 qt/11½ dl capacity. Put in a layer of lime wedges at the bottom, with their cut sides facing upwards. Sprinkle some of the garlic and ginger over the lime wedges. Lay a green chilli over the garlic and ginger. Now sprinkle some salt over this first layer. (Make a guess about the number of layers your jar will hold. Mine takes six layers so I sprinkle 1 tsp of salt over each layer. You do not have to be too exact about all this.) Keep making such layers until the jar is full. Push down a bit, if necessary.

Heat the sugar and vinegar in a 7–8-in/18–20-cm-wide porcelain-lined or stainless steel saucepan. When the syrup begins to boil, turn down the heat to keep up a fairly active simmer. Cook for 12 minutes or until you have a light syrup. Let this syrup turn lukewarm, then pour it over the layered limes in the jar. Cover with a non-metallic lid.

This pickle must be put in a sunny area every day for at least a month. If it is taken outdoors, then it should be brought in in the evenings. If the top layer seems to float above the liquid, push it down every few days with a clean, stainless steel spoon. After a month of sun, the pickle will still need another 2 to 4 weeks to mature. Taste it after 6 weeks and, if you like it, begin to eat it. Remember that this pickle, if any is left, will still be good enough to eat a year or more after you have made it. Long pickling makes the lime wedges turn almost gelatinous, and wonderfully tasty. It does not need refrigeration.

ATJAR KUNING
(Yellow Mixed Pickle)
INDONESIA   *(serves 4–6)*

There are versions of this tasty pickle all through Indonesia. Basically, chopped-up or julienned vegetables are either blanched or quickly stir-fried in a little oil. They are then allowed to cook briefly in a 'dressing' that contains, among other things, vinegar, lemon grass, ground candle nuts, garlic, ginger, and, of course, turmeric, which makes them all yellow. The result is a salad-like 'pickle' that can be eaten as soon as it is made. It can also be refrigerated and eaten up to 5 to 6 days later. My pickle is only mildly hot. You can make it as hot as you like. As well as serving it with any kind of meal, I toss a little of it in with a green salad sometimes — it's very good. In this recipe I have substituted the more easily available almonds for candle nuts.

½ tsp sliced, dried lemon grass
1 tsp whole cumin seeds
1 oz/30 g slivered, blanched
  almonds
½ tsp ground turmeric
½ tsp ground coriander seeds
¼ tsp cayenne pepper
2 cloves garlic, peeled and mashed
½ tsp peeled and very finely grated
  ginger
4 fl oz/1 dl distilled white vinegar
3 tbs vegetable oil
2 oz/60 g very finely slivered
  peeled shallots

3 oz/85 g peeled carrot cut into
  strips about 2 in/5 cm long and
  ¼ in/¾ cm thick
2 oz/60 g green beans cut
  diagonally into 2-in/5-cm long
  strips
1 small green pepper, cut into
  strips 2 in/5 cm long and
  ¼ in/¾ cm wide
4½ oz/125 g cauliflower flowerets,
  2 in/5 cm long, ¾ in/2 cm wide,
  and ⅓ in/1 cm thick
1¼ tsp salt, or to taste
¼ tsp sugar

Put the lemon grass and cumin seeds into the container of an electric coffee grinder reserved for spices. Grind to a powder. Add the almonds. Grind them as well. Empty these ingredients into a small cup. Add the turmeric, coriander, and cayenne and keep the cup near the cooker.

Mix the garlic and ginger and keep near the cooker as well.

Mix the vinegar with 4 fl oz/1 dl of water. Keep that near by, too.

Put all your cut vegetables near the cooker.

Heat the oil in a wok or heavy sauté pan over a medium flame. When hot, put in the shallots. Stir and fry for ½ minute. Put in the carrots, beans, green pepper, and cauliflower. Stir and fry for

For information about ingredients and basic techniques that may be unfamiliar, see General Information, pages 481-506.

about ½ minute. Add all the spices in the cup as well as the garlic–ginger mixture. Stir for ½ minute. Add the vinegar–water mixture and stir once. Add the salt and sugar. Stir and bring to a simmer. Turn heat to low and simmer, stirring gently, for 2 to 3 minutes. The vegetables should stay crunchy.

ONIONS PICKLED IN VINEGAR

IRAN   *(makes about 1 qt/11½ dl)*

1 lb/450 g small, even-sized white
  boiling onions
15 cloves garlic, peeled

3–4 sprigs fresh mint
16 fl oz/½ l distilled white vinegar
3½ tsp salt

Peel the onions. Cut a deep cross into them, lengthwise, so that each onion is almost quartered but still stays attached at the bottom. Put the onions into the 1-qt/11½-dl jar (you may have a couple left over).

Put the garlic cloves and mint into the container of a blender or food processor. Add 2 fl oz/½ dl of the vinegar (or a bit more, if you need it) and blend until you have a smooth paste. Pour in the remaining vinegar and salt and blend quickly to mix.

Pour this seasoned vinegar over the onions. Cover with a non-metallic lid and set aside for 24 hours. The pickle is now ready. It may be refrigerated.

CAULIFLOWER PICKLED WITH DILL

IRAN   *(makes enough to fill a ¾-pt/4¼-dl jar)*

6 oz/180 g cauliflower
8 fl oz/¼ l distilled white vinegar
1¾ tsp salt
12 whole black peppercorns

1–2 whole dried hot red peppers
4 tbs finely chopped fresh dill, or
  1 tbs dried
2 cloves garlic, peeled and slivered

Cut the cauliflower into flowerets about 1½–2 in/4–5 cm long, ¾ in/2 cm wide, and ⅓ in/1 cm thick.

Mix the vinegar, salt, peppercorns, red pepper, dill, and garlic in a cup.

Bring 2½ pt/1½ l of water to a rolling boil. Put in the cauliflower and bring to the boil again. Immediately empty the pot into a colander set in the sink.

Put the flowerets in a jar that holds ¾ pt/4¼ dl easily. Pour the seasoned vinegar over them. Cover with a non-metallic top and set aside for 12 hours. The pickle is now ready. It may be refrigerated.

CABBAGE TSUKEMONO
(Salted Cabbage Pickle)

JAPAN   *(makes enough to fill a ¾-pt/4¼-dl jar)*

If you are using part of a Chinese cabbage, as I did here, cut it in half lengthwise, and core it before proceeding with the recipe. If half of the cabbage does not add up to 1¼ lb/560 g, take some from the second half.

1¼ lb/560 g Chinese cabbage, cut
  in half lengthwise and cored
1 tbs plus 1 tsp salt

Wash the cabbage and cut it crosswise into 2-in/5-cm-wide sections. Put in a glass or plastic bowl. Add the salt and rub it well into the leaves. Find a ceramic or glass plate that will not only sit on top of the cabbage leaves inside the bowl, but will also sink down with them as they reduce in bulk. Put this plate on top of the cabbage and then put a heavy jar, filled with water, on top of the plate.

The cabbage will soon begin to sweat profusely and water will begin to accumulate. You may have to adjust your jar as it might decide to tilt this way or that. In about 3 to 4 days the pickle will probably have soured enough. If it has not, leave it longer.

Put the pickle and its liquid into a jar and refrigerate.

To serve, remove as much pickle as you need. Wash it to rid it of extra saltiness, make a wad of it, and then cut it crosswise into ½-in/1½-cm-wide sections. Each person should be served no more than 1 cubic in/2½ cubic cm of pickle. Put this tiny portion in the centre of small individual plates or very small individual bowls. It is traditional to dot one's pickles with soy sauce before eating them.

For information about ingredients and basic techniques that may be unfamiliar, see General Information, pages 481-506.

KOMBU RELISH

JAPAN   *(makes enough to fill a small, 6-fl oz/1¾-dl bowl)*

Like most Japanese relishes, very little of this is served with each meal, perhaps 4 to 5 slices on a small plate that also holds other salty vegetable preserves and pickles. The Japanese love to end meals with plain rice, pickles, and tea.

A piece of kombu	*3 tbs sugar*
3 tbs rice vinegar	*1 tbs mirin*
5 tbs soy sauce	*1 tbs roasted sesame seeds*

Use *kombu* that has previously been used to make broth. Its original size when dry would have been about 7 × 4 in/18 × 10 cm. Cut it into ½-in/1½-cm squares. If you wish to start out with a fresh piece of *kombu*, just wipe a 7 × 4-in/18 × 10-cm section with a damp cloth, drop it in boiling water for a minute, cut it into ½-in/1½-cm squares, and proceed.

Combine the cut *kombu*, 1½ pt/8½ dl water (you may re-use some of the boiling water), and 1 tbs of the vinegar in a small pot and bring to the boil. Cover, lower heat, and simmer 2 hours or until *kombu* is quite tender.

Add the other 2 tbs vinegar, the soy sauce, sugar, and *mirin*. Boil, uncovered, until liquid is reduced to 1–2 tbs. Turn off heat. Mix in the roasted sesame seeds. Put into a small jar and let the relish cool. When it is cool, it can be covered and refrigerated. It should last at least a month.

QUICK-SALTED WHITE RADISH PICKLE

JAPAN   *(serves 6)*

¾ lb/340 g white radish
2 tsp salt
2 tsp Japanese soy sauce
2 tsp rice vinegar
¼ tsp sugar
A dash of 7-spice seasoning

Peel the white radish and cut it into ¼-in/¾-cm-thick slices. Depending upon the diameter of the radish, cut each slice crosswise into halves or quarters. A radish that is 2½ in/6½ cm in diameter should be cut in quarters. A radish that is 1½ in/4 cm in diameter should be cut into halves. Smaller radishes should just be left in rounds. Put the radish slices in a bowl. Sprinkle the salt over the slices and mix well. Find a plate that will not only sit on top of the radish slices inside the bowl, but will also sink down with them as they wilt. Put this plate on top of the radish slices and then put a heavy jar, filled with water, on top of the plate. Set aside for 4 hours.

Drain the radish well. Add the soy sauce, vinegar, and sugar and mix well.

To serve, arrange 6 to 7 pieces for each person in small, individual saucers. Sprinkle with a little 7-spice seasoning.

SHOYU DAIKON
(White Radish Pickled in Soy Sauce)
JAPAN   (serves 6–9)

¾ lb/340 g white radish
4 fl oz/1 dl Japanese soy sauce

Peel the radish and cut into ¼-in/¾-cm-thick rounds. Depending upon the diameter of the radish, cut each slice crosswise into halves or quarters. A radish that is 2½ in/6½ cm in diameter should be cut into quarters. A radish that is 1½ in/4 cm in diameter should be cut into halves. A radish that is smaller should be left in rounds.

Put the radish slices in a bowl. Pour the soy sauce over them. Mix well. Cover and refrigerate for 24 to 36 hours. Stir and mix every 4 hours during your waking periods in order to ensure even pickling and a uniformity in colour.

To serve, lift the pickle out of the soy sauce and place 6 to 7 pieces each in small, individual saucers. The pickle should, if kept refrigerated, last 5 to 6 days. It goes well with most Japanese, Korean, and Chinese dishes.

GINGER QUICK-PICKLED IN SOY SAUCE
CHINA   *(makes enough to fill a small, 4-fl oz/1-dl bowl)*

It is best to make this dish with young ginger, the kind that has a pale golden, almost translucent skin which seems to turn to pink at the extremities. If you cannot find young ginger, use any fresh ginger.

2 oz/60 g young ginger (about 2   ½ tsp sugar
*   1-in/2½-cm cubes)   6 tbs Chinese thin soy sauce*
¼ tsp salt

For information about ingredients and basic techniques that may be unfamiliar, see General Information, pages 481-506.

Peel the ginger (if the ginger is young, you should be able just to scrape off the skin) and then cut it into paper-thin slices. Add the salt and sugar, toss well, and set aside for 1 hour. Pour the soy sauce over the ginger and cover. Set aside for 24 hours. You may refrigerate the ginger, if you like.

QUICK-SALTED CUCUMBER PICKLE
JAPAN   (serves 4–6)

4 small pickling cucumbers (about   1 tsp salt
¾ lb/340 g) or ¾ lb/340 g of an   Japanese soy sauce
ordinary cucumber

Wash the cucumbers well but do not peel them. Trim the ends. Cut the cucumbers crosswise into ⅓-in/1-cm-thick rounds and put them in a bowl. Add the salt and mix well. Set aside for an hour. Drain thoroughly.

To serve, put about 6 slices each in the centre of small individual saucers or tiny individual bowls. Pass around some soy sauce. I have a very small 'tea pot' for soy sauce that I bought in Japan that is just perfect for this purpose. It is customary to dot the cucumber pieces with soy sauce before eating them. The Japanese often end their meals with rice, pickles, and green tea.

TOMATO, CUCUMBER, AND ONION RELISH
INDIA   (serves 4)

1 medium-sized, ripe tomato,   2 oz/60 g finely chopped onion
peeled   ¼ tsp salt
1 smallish cucumber (pickling   ¼ tsp ground roasted cumin
cucumber, if possible) or a 4-in/   ⅛ tsp cayenne pepper
10-cm section of an ordinary   1 tbs lemon juice
cucumber

Cut the tomato in half, crosswise. Cup the halves, one at a time, in your hands — cut side down — and gently squeeze out and discard all the seeds. Now core the tomato shell and cut it into ¼-in/¾-cm dice.

Peel the cucumber, cut it in half, lengthwise, and then into ¼-in/ ¾-cm dice.

In a small bowl, combine the tomato, cucumber, onion, salt, roasted cumin, cayenne, and lemon juice. Mix.

The Tawaraya Inn's
AOMIDAIKON
(Quick-Pickled Small White Radishes)
JAPAN   *(serves 4–6)*

I had this pickle for the first time at the 300-year-old Tawaraya Inn in Kyoto. The radishes were small, about 2 in/5 cm long and ½ in/ 1½ cm wide. While most of the larger leaves had been pulled off, the tender shoots had been left attached. *Aomidaikon* is a very popular accompaniment to *sake* and, indeed, complements it very well, cutting through its silky potency with its own mellowed pungency.

If you cannot find white radishes of the required size, use slightly larger ones, halving or quartering them (lengthwise and crosswise, if necessary) to achieve the approximate size needed.

For this recipe, I bought 1 lb/450 g of white radishes — 1 lb/450 g with all the leaves. Once I had trimmed the radishes, they weighed somewhat less than ¾ lb/340 g.

1 lb/450 g small white radishes (see note above)	*Slightly sweet yellow* miso, *measured to the 4-fl oz/1-dl level in a glass measuring jug*
¾ tsp salt	

Trim the radishes by pulling off all the large outer leaves — the tender inner leaves should be left attached — and by cutting off the tail-like bottoms. Peel or scrape the radishes. If they are too long or too thick, cut them up into pieces that are about 2 in/5 cm long, ½–¾ in/1½–2 cm wide, and ½ in/1½ cm thick. Put the radishes in a bowl and sprinkle the salt over them. Toss to distribute the salt and set aside for 4 hours.

Find a dish that will hold the radishes in a single layer. (You can do this in several layers, if you prefer.) Line it with a single layer of cheesecloth. Spread half the *miso* over the cheesecloth as if you were putting on a thin layer of peanut butter. Now cover the *miso* with another single layer of cheesecloth. Spread out the radishes on top of the cheesecloth. Do not let them overlap. Now cover the radishes with another layer of cheesecloth. Spread the remaining *miso* on this piece of cheesecloth and then cover the *miso* with a fresh layer of cheesecloth. Pat down the contents of the dish and then refrigerate for 1 to 4 days. If you like, you may cover the dish with another one, upturned.

For information about ingredients and basic techniques that may be unfamiliar, see General Information, pages 481-506.

To serve, remove the cheesecloth. Rinse the radishes lightly. Arrange them prettily in the centre of a ceramic plate and serve with *sake* that has been warmed to just under the simmering point. (To warm *sake*, put it into a ceramic *sake* bottle and put the bottle into a pan of water. Heat the water. When the *sake* is hot, remove the ceramic bottle. *Sake* is served in small *sake* cups or small shallow *sake* bowls.) Or slice the radishes crosswise and serve with plain Japanese rice and tea at the conclusion of a Japanese meal.

WHITE RADISH PRESERVE
JAPAN   *(makes enough to fill a 1¼-pt/7-dl jar)*

This is the very yellow-looking Japanese preserve that you might have seen in Japanese restaurants and grocery stores. The yellowness, unfortunately, comes from food colouring which I have eliminated in my recipe. As a result, the vegetable looks less appetizing, perhaps, but it is quite wonderful to eat. Like all Japanese pickles and preserves, this should be eaten in small quantities, either with a meal or at its conclusion with rice and tea.

About 1½lb/675 g white radish   *3 tbs salt*
 (1 large or 2 smaller)   *4 tbs Japanese rice vinegar*
7 oz/200 g sugar

Trim the ends of the white radish and peel it. Cut it in half lengthwise, and then slice crosswise into fine, ¹⁄₁₆-in/¹⁄₆-cm-thick pieces (a food processor can speed this up). Put white radish slices in a bowl.

Combine the sugar, salt, vinegar, and a cup of water in an enamelled or stainless steel pan. Bring to the boil. Stir the sugar so it dissolves. Pour the hot liquid over the radish slices and mix gently, pushing the radish into the liquid. Let cool. Put the radish slices and the liquid into a jar, cover, and refrigerate for 3 to 4 days. If kept in the refrigerator, this preserve will last indefinitely.

KIMCHEES

Just as a meal without wine is inconceivable for a Frenchman, a meal without *kimchee* is inconceivable for a Korean. *Kimchee* is not a liquor but a pickle − a hot, tart, often garlicky pickle that has an honoured place at all Korean meals, from breakfast to dinner. *Kimchees* may be made out of several vegetables, like cucumbers and radishes, but the most popular *kimchee* − perhaps because it is the cheapest − is made with Chinese cabbage.

In the late autumn trucks piled high with the pale-green vegetable drive into towns and villages and the entire female population of the country succumbs to feverish bouts of pickle-making.

First the cabbage is washed and soaked in wooden tubs filled with salted water. It turns wan and pale under this initial treatment. Then the cabbage is smothered − or stuffed − with a mixture of ginger, garlic, spring onions, salt, a little sugar, and lots of fiery red pepper freshly made from the new autumn crop. Now the cabbage is ready for a period of not-so-peaceful hibernation. It is packed into large, dark-brown clay vats − some waist high − loosely covered, and left to ferment. The fermenting takes its own time. It cannot be urged to hurry. The vats seethe and bubble. The cabbage eventually turns deliciously sour and is ready to be removed from the vats to be devoured.

In the severest winter months, *kimchee* vats are buried up to their necks in the earth and covered − first with a lid and then with hay. This keeps the pickle from freezing and helps provide necessary supplies until the coming of the spring.

Kimchees, full of vitamins and minerals, are not only eaten as a side dish, but also put into rice dishes, soups, and stews as a flavouring. A watery summer *kimchee* is an ingredient of Naeng Myon, one of Korea's spectacular noodle soups, while the usual cabbage *kimchee* is used to flavour everything from pancakes to country-style stews.

CABBAGE KIMCHEE
(Cabbage Pickle)
KOREA   (makes 3¼ pt/1¾ l)

1 lb/450 g Chinese cabbage (about ½ a large head)
1 lb/450 g white radish
3 tbs salt
2 tbs finely chopped fresh ginger
1½ tbs finely chopped garlic
5 spring onions, cut into fine rounds, including green
1 tbs cayenne or hot Korean red pepper
1 tsp sugar

If you are using a small, whole cabbage cut it in half lengthwise, and then cut it across at 2-in/5-cm intervals. If you are using half of a large cabbage, cut it in half again lengthwise, and then crosswise at 2-in/5-cm intervals.

For information about ingredients and basic techniques that may be unfamiliar, see General Information, pages 481-506.

Peel the white radish, cut it in half lengthwise, and then cut it crosswise into ⅛-in/½-cm thick slices. In a large bowl put 2½ pt/1½ l water and 2 tbs plus 2 tsp of the salt. Mix. Add the cabbage and radish to this water and dunk them in a few times, as they have a tendency to float. Leave the vegetables in the salty water. Cover loosely and set aside for 12 hours. Turn the vegetables over a few times.

Put the ginger, garlic, spring onions, cayenne, sugar, and 1 tsp salt in another large bowl. Mix well.

Take the cabbage out of its soaking liquid with a slotted spoon (save the liquid) and put it in the bowl with the seasonings. Mix well.

Put this cabbage mixture into a 2-qt/2¼-l jar or crock. Pour enough of the salt water over it to cover the vegetables (about 16 fl oz/½ l). Leave 1 in/2½ cm of empty space at the top of the jar. Cover loosely with a clean cloth and set aside for about 3 to 7 days. In the summer, *kimchees* mature with much greater speed; in the winter, the process slows down unless the central heating is ferocious. Taste the pickle after 3 days to check on the sourness. When it is done to your liking, cover the jar with a non-metallic lid and refrigerate.

To serve, remove just as much of the *kimchee* solids as you think you will need for a meal − a cupful is enough for 4 people − and put it in the centre of a bowl. The *kimchee* liquid in this pickle is left behind in the jar and may be used to flavour stews and soups. Serve this cabbage *kimchee* with any Korean meal.

KAKDOOKI
(Pickle Made with Cubes of White Radish)
KOREA   *(makes 2½ pt/1½ l)*

1½ lb/675 g white radish, peeled
*   and cut into ¾-in/2-cm cubes*
4 spring onions, cut into fine
*   rounds, including green*
2 tbs finely chopped peeled garlic

2 tsp salt
2 tsp sugar
2 tsp cayenne or hot Korean red
*   pepper*

Put all the ingredients in a bowl and mix well. Cover and set aside for 6 to 8 hours.

Liquid will have accumulated at the bottom of the bowl. Pour this liquid and the seasonings in it into a 2½-pt/1½-l jar. Now put in the cubes of radish, pushing them down so the liquid rises all the way to the top. Cover the jar loosely with a piece of cloth and set aside for 3 to 7 days. In the summer, *kimchees* mature with much greater speed; in the winter, the process slows down unless the central heating is ferocious. Taste the pickle after 3 days to check on the sourness. When it is done to your liking, cover the jar and refrigerate.

When serving, remove about 5 to 6 cubes for every person who is eating and put them in a glass or ceramic bowl. The liquid which is left behind in the jar may be used to flavour soups and stews when all the pickles have been consumed.

STUFFED CUCUMBER KIMCHEE
KOREA   *(makes about 2½ pt/1½ l)*

*1½ lb/675 g small pickling
  cucumbers (about 16)*
3 tbs plus 2 tsp salt
¾ lb/340 g white radish
*A 1-in/2½-cm cube fresh ginger,
  peeled*

*2 tbs peeled and very finely
  chopped garlic*
*6 spring onions, cut into very fine
  rounds*
1½ tsp sugar
*2½ tsp cayenne or other ground
  hot red pepper*

Scrub the cucumbers but do not peel them. Cut them across, slightly diagonally, at ½-in/1½-cm intervals, letting the knife go only three-quarters of the way down. The cucumber 'slices' should all remain attached at the bottom.

Make a solution of 1 qt/11½ dl water and 3 tbs salt in a bowl. Put in the cucumbers. As they will float, invert a plate, somewhat smaller in circumference than the top of the bowl, over them to keep them submerged. Set aside for 3 to 4 hours.

When the soaking period is almost over, prepare the stuffing. Peel the radish and cut it into very, very fine slices. You could use a potato slicer to do this. Now cut these slices crosswise into very, very fine julienne strips. The radish strips should not be longer than 1 in/2½ cm. If necessary, cut them in half. Cut the ginger into paper-thin slices and then cut the slices across into very fine strips. Mix the radish, ginger, garlic, spring onions, sugar, cayenne, and 2 tsp salt in a bowl.

Remove the cucumbers from their soaking liquid and pat dry. (Save the liquid.) Put as much stuffing into the cucumber slits as they will hold easily, and put finished cucumbers in a bowl. Empty any remaining stuffing and stuffing juices over the cucumbers. Cover loosely and set aside for 8 hours.

For information about ingredients and basic techniques that may be unfamiliar, see General Information, pages 481-506.

Pack the cucumbers fairly tightly, but carefully, in a wide-mouthed, 1½-qt/1¾-l jar. Extra stuffing may be pushed in the spaces between cucumbers. All accumulated juices should be poured over the cucumbers. Push the cucumbers down slightly. Liquid should rise to the top. There should be ½ in/1½ cm of liquid over the cucumbers. If you do not have enough liquid, pour in some of the salted water left over from soaking the cucumbers. Cover jar loosely with a plastic or ceramic top and set aside for 3 to 6 days or until the pickle has soured to your taste.

When you serve, separate the cucumber 'slices' with a knife and arrange on a small plate.

DONG CHIMI
(White Radish Water Kimchee)
KOREA   (makes enough to fill a 2½-pt/1½-l jar)

Koreans serve water *kimchees* with nearly all their meals. Because of its cooling liquid, this pickle is particularly popular in the summer months. It is also used in the making of that delicious cold noodle soup, Naeng Myon (see page 342).

½ lb/225 g white radish (without
  leaves)
½ lb/225 g turnips
2 spring onions
1 clove garlic, peeled
A ¾-in/2-cm cube of ginger,
  peeled

½–1 fresh hot green chilli
¼ tsp cayenne or other ground hot
  red pepper
4 tsp salt
½ tsp plain white flour
½ tsp sugar

Peel the white radish and then cut it into rectangles that are roughly 1½ in/4 cm long, ½ in/1½ cm wide, and ½ in/1½ cm thick. Peel the turnips and cut them into similar rectangles.

Cut the spring onions into 1½-in/4-cm sections and then cut the sections lengthwise into very thin strips.

Cut the garlic into very thin matchstick strips that are the length of the clove.

Cut the ginger into very fine slices and then cut the slices lengthwise into very thin strips.

Cut the green chilli in half lengthwise and remove the seeds. Cut the halves into thin, 1½-in/4-cm-long strips.

Combine the radish, turnips, spring onions, garlic, ginger, green chilli, cayenne, and 2 tsp of the salt in a stainless steel or a non-metallic bowl. Mix well. Cover loosely and set aside for 8 to 10 hours.

Put the flour in a small bowl. Slowly add 1 tbs of water to make a smooth paste. Add another 3 tbs of water and mix well. In a 1½-qt/1¾-l pot, combine 1½ pt/8½ dl water, 2 tsp salt, and the sugar. Stir the flour mixture once and pour it into the pot. Stir again and bring to the boil. Turn heat to low and simmer very gently for 10 minutes. Turn off the heat and let the mixture cool completely.

Pour this cooled mixture into the radish bowl and mix. The *kimchee* may now be left in the bowl to sour or may be emptied into a wide-mouthed 1½-qt/1¾-l jar. Cover loosely with anything non-metallic. The pickle should be ready in 1½ to 3 days in summer and 3 to 6 days in winter. Remove just a little bit of the liquid each day and taste it. When the liquid has soured to your satisfaction, the pickle is ready. It may now be covered more securely, again with something non-metallic, and refrigerated.

SPICY TURNIP PICKLE
KOREA *(Serves 6–8)*

2 small turnips (about 5 oz/140 g
  without leaves)
1½ tsp salt
1 whole dried hot red pepper,
  coarsely crushed in a mortar

1 tbs finely chopped spring onions
3 cloves garlic, peeled and finely
  chopped
¼ tsp sugar

Peel the turnips and cut them in half, lengthwise. Now cut them crosswise into ⅟₁₆-in/¼-cm-thick, half-moon-shaped slices. Put turnip slices in a small bowl and sprinkle 1 tsp salt over them. Rub the salt in with your fingers. Set the bowl aside for 2½ to 3 hours, turning the slices over every half hour.

For information about ingredients and basic techniques that may be unfamiliar, see General Information, pages 481-506.

Drain the turnip slices and rinse under water. Drain again. Add the remaining ½ tsp salt as well as the red pepper, spring onions, garlic, and sugar to the turnips and mix well.

Put the turnips in a small (12-fl oz/3½-dl) glass jar. Pour in enough water to cover the turnip slices. Cover the jar loosely with a small saucer and set aside, unrefrigerated, for 6 to 8 days. Once the pickle is sour enough for your taste, it can be covered and refrigerated. Metal lids tend to corrode so it is a better idea to use plastic ones.

PICKLED GARLIC
KOREA   *(makes about 1 cupful)*

Most Asians believe that raw garlic is very good for all blood-circulation ailments. Pickled raw garlic exists in many versions and may be eaten with meals or cut up and put into salads. This Korean pickle is generally made with whole heads of green garlic. When served, the drained head is sliced crosswise into 3 rounds, exposing a very pretty cross-section of the cloves. All of the green garlic, including the skin, is edible. Since I could not find green garlic, I have used whole peeled cloves instead.

2 heads large-cloved garlic, peeled
4 fl oz/1 dl Japanese soy sauce
4 fl oz/1 dl Japanese rice vinegar
2 tbs sugar
½ tsp salt

Combine all ingredients in a glass jar or non-metallic bowl. Cover, and set aside for 3 days.

Remove the cloves of garlic from the liquid and put them in a 12-fl oz/3½-dl jar. Bring the liquid to the boil in a small pot. Turn heat to low and simmer, uncovered, until liquid has reduced to a little more than 4 fl oz/1 dl (4 fl oz/1 dl plus 1 tbs seems the right amount). Pour the liquid over the garlic cloves. Allow to cool. Cover and set aside for 3 to 4 weeks.

11   Desserts and Sweetmeats

Imagine a mound of crushed ice overflowing with a green-tea syrup and dotted with sweetened red beans. This ethereal summer dessert is served in one of Japan's most prestigious restaurants.

Asians are, on the whole, fairly familiar with European cakes, tarts, and jellies and serve them with the same easy familiarity that they show their own, more traditional desserts and sweetmeats. These traditional sweets are made with grains, such as rice, with beans, fruit, coconut, nuts, vegetables, and milk.

Halwas, of Middle Eastern origin, are now made in many parts of Asia. An enriching whole-wheat *halwa*, filled with nuts and raisins, is often made for new mothers, whereas carrot and gourd *halwas* are frequently made for banquets and feasts. If the idea of a vegetable *halwa* seems strange, you need think no further than a pumpkin pie or a carrot cake. The vegetables are grated and cooked slowly with milk until all the liquid evaporates. They are then sautéed in oil or butter, sweetened, and loaded with nuts. I have discovered that the humble courgette makes a really delicious *halwa*.

In Japan, Korea, and China, the small red *azuki* bean is used to make a sweet paste that is very much like chocolate. Sweet 'soups' are made with it, as well as stuffings for pastries and jellies. Rice creams and puddings are also very well liked, though as one travels farther east, the use of glutinous rice becomes far more extensive. I like the sticky texture of glutinous rice. One of my favourite ways of eating it is with peeled slices of ripe mango, the way the Thais do it. In Thailand, glutinous rice is flavoured with coconut milk, sugar, and salt and then served with some of the sweetest mangoes I have ever eaten. Extra coconut cream is offered with the dish. The tastes and textures blend together most harmoniously.

The cassava root, also known as fresh tapioca or yucca, is a vegetable that resembles glutinous rice in its texture, especially when it is grated and cooked. The Filipinos add egg and coconut milk to this grated cassava and make a wonderfully sticky, chewy cake. Cassava can be found in Indian and West Indian grocery stores. It is a shame that it is not better known.

You will find a recipe for the Middle Eastern baklava here, paper-thin pastry sheets layered with pistachios, walnuts, almonds, and sesame seeds; there is a Caucasian stew of dried fruit flavoured with slices of fresh lemon; and you will also find a

446

scrumptious sweet Chinese walnut soup that can be made fairly quickly in a blender. I have kept a whole section for Indian milk sweets because so many people have written to me and asked for them.

Indian milk sweets are really a world unto themselves. The sweets that I have been asked about — such as *chumchum*, *rasgulla*, and *rasmalai* — are made with milk that is curdled, hung up briefly in a cheesecloth, and then kneaded until it is smooth. The resulting cheese is called *chhena* in Bengal, where these sweets originated. This *chhena* is then formed into different shapes — diamonds, hearts or balls — and boiled in syrup. The shapes, whatever they happen to be, puff up as they drink in the syrup, and become spongy. The sweets are then finished off as tradition dictates: *chumchums* are taken out of the syrup and 'frosted' with freshly condensed milk; *rasgullas* are removed from the boiling syrup and put in a cleaner, lighter syrup where they bounce around until they are served; for *rasmalais*, the *chhena* balls are removed from the syrup and put into a large pot of thickened, cardamom-flavoured milk to cook some more, after which time they are cooled in their milky sauce.

It might be said here that many of Asia's sweetmeats are eaten as snacks and that dinners and lunches often end with fresh fruit.

BANANA FRITTERS IN TEMPURA BATTER
JAPAN   *(serves 4–6)*

4 to 5 bananas
About 4 oz/115 g flour for
  dredging
Vegetable oil for deep frying

FOR THE BATTER
Freshly made Tempura Batter
  Number II (see page 91), using
  ½ pt/3 dl ice-cold water instead
  of 8 fl oz/¼ l

Icing sugar

Cut the bananas crosswise into 1-in/2½-cm chunks. Dredge lightly in flour.

Heat the oil in a wok or frying pan over a medium flame to about 375° F/190° C.

Dip the banana pieces a few at a time in the batter and then fry in the oil until golden. Remove with slotted spoon and drain on kitchen paper. Do all bananas this way. This much can be done ahead of time.

Just before you eat this sweet, heat the oil again over a medium flame. When hot, fry the bananas again. This will make them crisp.

Shake icing sugar on the fritters and serve immediately.

MANGOES WITH GLUTINOUS RICE
SOUTH-EAST ASIA   *(serves 4)*

For those who have a passion for sweet, ripe mangoes, glutinous rice, and coconut cream, this dish is an ambrosial delight. Slices of peeled, ice-cold mango are served with glutinous rice steeped in sweetened coconut milk. Once you start eating it, it is almost impossible to stop.

Freshly cooked glutinous rice (see page 142), filled to the 15-fl oz/4¼-dl level in a glass measuring jug

4 fl oz/1 dl coconut cream
½ tsp salt
2 oz/60 g sugar
2 chilled mangoes*

*Mangoes are almost never fully ripe when bought in this country. Ripen at home by wrapping each mango in several layers of newspaper. Then lay the mangoes in a basket or box, covering with another few layers of newspapers. Leave in a warm place until ripe. Chill mangoes as you would champagne − drop into a bucket of ice and water for a couple of hours.

Combine the hot, freshly cooked rice with the coconut cream, salt, and sugar. Set aside until cool.

Peel the mangoes and cut two wide slices off the sides of each.

In each of four dessert plates, arrange a slice of mango and a mound of rice.

STEWED DRIED FRUIT
CAUCASUS   *(serves 4)*

I love to sip the liquid − the broth − that dried fruits produce. Which explains the abundance of it in this recipe. If you prefer, you could remove the fruits with a slotted spoon after they have been sweetened and reduce the liquid somewhat.

This stew may be served plain or with cream or yogurt.

4 large dried prunes
4 oz/115 g small dried figs
8 oz/225 g dried apricots

4 slices lemon
8 oz/225 g sugar

Wash and drain the fruit. Put in a pot with 1½ pt/8½ dl water. Add the lemon slices and bring to the boil. Cover, lower heat and simmer gently for ½ hour or until fruit is tender. Add the sugar and simmer another 5 minutes or until sugar has dissolved.

Serve warm or cold.

For information about ingredients and basic techniques that may be unfamiliar, see General Information, pages 481-506.

LECHE FLAN
(Coconut Custard)
PHILIPPINES   (serves 4)

8 fl oz/¼ l tinned, unsweetened   3 large eggs
   coconut milk (stir before   7 oz/200 g sugar
   removing from tin)

Preheat oven to 350° F/180° C/Mark 4.

Heat the coconut milk on a lowish flame. When it starts bubbling, turn off the heat.

Beat the eggs. Add 4 oz/115 g of the sugar and beat again until the eggs are light and creamy. Add the hot coconut milk slowly, beating as you do so.

Put the remaining sugar in a small heavy pot over a low flame. Stir and let the sugar caramelize. As soon as it melts and turns a brownish colour (do not let it burn) pour it out equally into four 8-oz/¼-l custard cups. Now strain the custard over the caramelized sugar, dividing it equally among the four cups.

Put the custard cups in a baking pan. Pour enough hot water around them so it comes halfway up the cups. Bake for 40 minutes.

When the custards have cooled slightly, run a knife around the edges of the bowls and invert on to plates. Chill.

FIRNEE
MIDDLE EAST/SOUTH ASIA   (serves 4)

This is one of those light, aromatic creams that both children and adults find very soothing.

5 tsp rice flour (also called rice   ⅛ tsp cardamom seeds
   powder)   2 oz/60 g sugar, or to taste
3 tbs plus 16 fl oz/½ l milk   1 tbs chopped pistachios

Put the rice flour in a bowl. Slowly add the 3 tbs milk and mix to a smooth paste.

Set the 16 fl oz/½ l milk to boil over a medium-low flame. Crush the cardamom seeds in a mortar and add them, as well as the sugar, to the milk. As soon as the milk begins to boil and rise, remove it from the fire. Stir the rice paste in the bowl once again. Slowly pour the hot milk into the bowl, mixing with a whisk as you do so. Now pour the contents of the bowl back into the pot and place over a low flame and bring to a simmer. Stir frequently with a whisk and simmer very gently for about 15 minutes. Pour into four shallow bowls and allow to cool and set slightly. Sprinkle the pistachios on top and refrigerate. *Firnee* is always served cold.

PEANUT TOFFEE
MOST OF ASIA   *(makes a 7-in/18-cm disc that can then be cut up)*

Almost every nation in Asia makes toffees and brittles. What varies is not so much the nuts and seeds that they contain, but the type of sugar that is used. For this recipe, I have used one of the oldest forms of raw cane sugar in the world — jaggery. Jaggery is available in Indian stores but you could use brown sugar.

When my mother made this toffee for us, she always used freshly roasted peanuts — the kind that one has to shell. I remember all of us girls would sit around shelling the peanuts and then blowing their inner skins away. If you do not have access to such peanuts, you may use fried, unsalted peanuts instead.

I use a pie plate which is 7 in/18 cm in diameter at the bottom to set the toffee.

4 oz/115 g roasted, shelled, and   2 tsp vegetable oil
*   skinned, unsalted peanuts   6 oz/180 g jaggery*

Break the peanuts into halves. Brush the pie plate with 1 tsp oil.

Put the jaggery, 4 fl oz/1 dl water, and the remaining 1 tsp of oil in a small pot. Bring to the boil. Cover, turn heat to low, and simmer until the jaggery has melted completely. Remove the lid. Continue to cook the syrup on low heat, stirring now and then as you do so. The syrup should reduce considerably and get very thick. A sugar thermometer should register 250° F/120° C. Now take the pot off the flame. Mix the peanuts in and quickly pour the mixture into a 7-in/18-cm pie plate. Spread evenly and let it cool.

Cut into squares.

SESAME SEED TOFFEE
MOST OF ASIA   *(makes a 7-in/18-cm disc that can then be cut up)*

Follow the directions for the preceding recipe, Peanut Toffee. Substitute 4 oz/115 g roasted sesame seeds (see General Information) for the peanuts. The seeds, of course, can be left whole.

SHAKKAR-PAARA
(Deep-Fried Biscuits)
INDIA   *(enough to fill a 1-qt/11½-dl jar)*

Shakkar-paaras are sweet, diamond-shaped biscuits that are deep-fried and flavoured with cardamom, as many Indian sweetmeats are. You could substitute cinnamon as a flavouring, if you prefer.

Shakkar-paaras, in some form or other, are found all over the India–Pakistan subcontinent.

3½ oz/100 g sugar
2 tsp cardamom seeds
6 oz/180 g plain white flour
2 tsp ghee *or softened unsalted butter*
2 tbs vegetable shortening
Vegetable oil for deep frying

In a small pot, combine the sugar with 4 fl oz/1 dl water. Turn heat to medium-low and melt the sugar completely to form a syrup.

Meanwhile, crush the cardamom seeds fairly finely, either in a mortar or by placing the seeds between two sheets of waxed paper and pounding gently with the blunt end of a hammer. Add the crushed cardamom seeds to the syrup. Turn off heat under syrup.

Sift the flour in a wide bowl. Add the *ghee* (or butter) and the shortening. Rub the *ghee* and shortening into the flour with your fingers until the mixture resembles coarse oatmeal. Now pour in the hot syrup (heat it if it has gone cold), mix, and gather the flour together so it holds and forms a ball. Knead lightly with the heel of your hand for a minute or two. Break dough into balls about 2 in/5 cm in diameter (4 balls).

Put oil to heat in a *karhai*, wok, or other utensil for deep frying over a medium flame. (You should have about 2 in/5 cm of oil.)

As the oil heats, roll out your biscuits. You may roll and cut one batch at a time; while it fries you can roll and cut the next batch. Or, if you have the space, you can roll and cut out all the *shakkar-paaras* and fry them in several batches later. Dust your rolling pin and rolling surface *very lightly* with flour. Roll out a dough ball into a 6-in/15-cm round. Using a sharp knife, cut the round into 1¼-in/2¼-cm-wide strips going from north to south (as it were). Now cut diagonal strips, also 1¼ in/2¼ cm wide, going from north-west to south-east. You should thus end up with diamond shapes (see diagram). Scraps that are not perfect diamonds can be collected to make another ball of dough. Make all *shakkar-paaras* this way.

The oil should be hot by now (about 350° F/180° C). Put as many *shakkar-paaras* into the oil as will fit in a single layer (a good-sized wok should hold all the biscuits) and fry them about 2 to 3 minutes on each side or until they turn a golden honey colour. Adjust your heat, if necessary. Remove with a slotted spoon, drain on kitchen paper, and allow to cool and harden. Fry all the *shakkar-paaras* this way, a batch at a time. Let each batch drain and cool.

Store the *shakkar-paaras* in an airtight tin or a wide-mouthed jar; they should stay fresh for about a week.

COURGETTE HALWA
MIDDLE EAST/INDIA   *(serves 4)*

Halwa is an Arabic word but the art of making it has spread all the way from the Mediterranean Sea to the Bay of Bengal. Among the most delicate of *halwas* are those made from vegetables. Here is one that I have adapted from the green bottle gourd. For all of you with overproductive courgette patches, this is one more thing that you can do with that vegetable in the summer.

NOTE: Use a heavy pot with an even distribution of heat. I find cast-aluminium pots excellent.

4 smallish courgettes (slightly over
  1 lb/450 g)
16 fl oz/½ l milk
5 cardamom pods

2 tbs vegetable oil
6 tbs sugar, or to taste
1 tbs sultanas
1 tbs pistachios, coarsely chopped

Scrub the courgettes and trim the ends. Grate coarsely by hand or in a food processor.

Combine the grated courgette, milk, and cardamom pods in a wide heavy pot. Bring to a simmer over a medium flame. Turn the heat slightly lower and cook, stirring now and then, until almost all the milk has evaporated. Stir more frequently now and keep cooking until you cannot see any more liquid. Add the oil and sugar. Turn the heat down, if necessary, and keep frying for 10 minutes or until the *halwa* resembles mashed potatoes. Add the sultanas and pistachios. Stir for another minute.

Serve at room temperature or cold.

WHOLE-WHEAT HALWA
MIDDLE EAST/INDIA   *(serves 6)*

This simple, quick-cooking *halwa* is often prepared for mothers who have recently given birth. It contains one of the most nourishing food combinations — whole grains (whole-wheat flour), nuts (pistachios, cashews, and almonds), dried fruit (sultanas), and dairy products (butter and milk). It is also an excellent snack or dessert for growing children and active adults.

4 oz/115 g unsalted butter
1 tbs blanched, slivered almonds
1 tbs pistachios, slivered
1 tbs coarsely chopped raw cashews

1 tbs sultanas
4½ oz/125 g whole-wheat flour
6½ tbs sugar, or to taste
1¼ pt/¾ l scalding hot milk

For information about ingredients and basic techniques that may be unfamiliar, see General Information, pages 481-506.

Take a square cake tin, about $8 \times 8 \times 1\frac{1}{2}$ in/$20 \times 20 \times 4$ cm, and grease the inside lightly with butter. Set the tin aside.

Put the remaining butter into an 8–10-in/20–25-cm, heavy-bottomed frying pan and melt on medium-low heat. As soon as the butter melts, put in the almonds, pistachios, cashews, and sultanas. Stir until the nuts turn a shade darker and the sultanas swell. Do not let the butter burn. Add the whole-wheat flour and stir gently for about three minutes or until the flour is no longer raw and is lightly roasted. It will give off a wonderful smell of roasted wheat. Add the sugar and mix well. Add the scalding hot milk. Stir and mix. Cook, stirring, another minute or so.

Empty the contents of the frying pan into the buttered cake tin. Spread the *halwa* and pat down evenly. Allow to cool. Cover with cling film until ready to eat.

Remove cling film and cut *halwa* into $1\frac{1}{2}$-in/4-cm cubes or diamond shapes. Serve at room temperature. This *halwa* may also be served warm, shortly after it is made.

BAKLAVA
(Filo Pastry Stuffed with Nuts)
MIDDLE EAST   *(fills an 8-in/20-cm square cake tin)*

Baklava is one of those sweets that looks as if it is very hard to make and is actually quite easy. The filo pastry itself may be bought from speciality, Middle Eastern, and Greek stores. Then, once you learn how to handle the sheets and keep them from drying out (for more details on filo pastry, see page 395), making baklava is really a breeze.

Just remember to be very generous with your butter and make sure that there is a layer of butter between every single sheet. And don't worry too much if you have a cake tin of a different size. (The cake tin I used was about 7 in/18 cm at the bottom and increased to about 7¾ in/19½ cm at the top. *Officially*, it was $8 \times 8 \times 2/20 \times 20 \times 5$.) Each pastry sheet is about 12×18 in/30×45 cm. How much of the sheet you will need to fold over to fit the cake tin can be easily adjusted.

FOR THE STUFFING
2 oz/60 g walnuts
2 oz/60 g pistachios
2 oz/60 g blanched almonds
1 oz/30 g roasted sesame seeds
2 tbs sugar

FOR THE PASTRY
½ lb/225 g unsalted butter, melted
11 sheets filo pastry (about
½ lb/225 g)

FOR THE SYRUP
14 oz/395 g sugar
3 tbs honey
1 stick cinnamon
5 whole cardamom pods (optional)

Chop the walnuts, pistachios, and almonds. (If each pistachio were chopped into 4 to 6 pieces, that would be a good indication of size.) In a bowl, combine the nuts, sesame seeds, and sugar.

Preheat the oven to 300° F/150° C/Mark 2.

Brush an 8-in/20-cm square cake tin generously with butter.

Keep all filo sheets that are not being used properly covered, first with a piece of kitchen parchment (or plastic sheet) and then with a damp towel. Remove one sheet at a time and work quickly.

Spread the first sheet in front of you on a clean, dry surface and brush generously with butter. Lay this sheet inside the cake tin. The sheet will overflow on two sides. Fold the short side over first. Brush with butter. Then fold the long side over. Brush butter on the top. Repeat with two more sheets. After you have buttered the third sheet, sprinkle about 2½ tbs of the nut–seed mixture evenly over the top. Lay another buttered sheet over the nuts and seeds. Fold it as before and butter it. Put another layer of nuts and seeds. Alternate a sheet of pastry and a layer of nuts three more times. Top the final layer of nuts with 3 more buttered sheets. Butter the top generously. If there is any butter left, it may be poured over the top. (But do *not* pour the milky residue.) Using a sharp knife, cut the baklava to form five even rows. Cut again at a diagonal to form diamonds.

Bake at 300° F/150° C/Mark 2 for ½ hour and at 350° F/180° C/Mark 4 for another ½ hour.

Let the baklava cool.

Combine all the ingredients for the syrup with 12 fl oz/3½ dl water. Bring to a simmer over a medium flame. Turn heat to very low and simmer, uncovered, for 8 to 10 minutes. Pour the hot syrup over the cool baklava, making sure it seeps through to the bottom of the tin.

For information about ingredients and basic techniques that may be unfamiliar, see General Information, pages 481-506.

BESAN BARFEE
(Gram-Flour Fudge)
INDIA/IRAN   *(makes 144 little cubes)*

6 oz/180 g gram flour
8 fl oz/¼ l vegetable oil
14 oz/395 g sugar
½ tsp ground cardamom seeds

2–3 tbs unsalted pistachios, lightly
  crushed
1–2 tbs coarsely chopped blanched
  almonds

Sift the gram flour. Heat the oil in a heavy, 10–12-in/25–30-cm frying pan, wok, or sauté pan over a medium flame. Put in the sifted gram flour. Stir and fry 2 to 3 minutes or until flour turns a shade darker and is cooked (it should taste fried, not raw). Put the flour into a large bowl, stir once, and allow to cool.

Make a syrup with 8 fl oz/¼ l water and the 14 oz/395 g sugar by bringing the water–sugar combination to the boil and then simmering very gently for about 20 minutes or until the syrup reaches a one-thread consistency. (To test this, dip in a wooden spoon and let coat slightly. Pinch some syrup off the back of the spoon with two fingers and then try separating the fingers. One sticky thread should form. This is the Indian method. If you have a better one, use it.)

Pour the hot syrup into the cooled gram-flour mixture. Add the ground cardamom seeds, and the nuts, and mix well. Keep stirring until mixture begins to harden slightly. (It should still be pourable.) Pour into a 9-in/23-cm square cake tin, tilt tin so *barfee* mixture flows to the edges, and allow to cool. Cut into ¾-in/2-cm cubes.

Besan Barfee, if tightly wrapped in aluminium foil and then placed in plastic containers, freezes very well.

RAVA NA GHUGRA
(Sweet, Stuffed Pastry)
INDIA   *(makes about 40 pastries)*

Ghugras are small Gujarati turnovers that are stuffed with a sweetened, cardamom-flavoured mixture of almonds, pistachios, sultanas, and semolina. They are not baked, but deep fried. If packed in a tightly closed biscuit tin, *ghugras* will last for several days.

6 oz/180 g plain white flour
8 tbs ghee or vegetable oil
3 oz/85 g blanched almonds

2 oz/60 g shelled unsalted
  pistachios
1 oz/30 g sultanas

3 oz/85 g semolina
1 tbs white poppy seeds
½ tsp ground cardamom seeds

5 oz/140 g caster sugar
Oil for deep frying

Make dough as for *samosa* pastry (see page 381), using the 6 oz/ 180 g flour, 4 tbs of the *ghee*, and 5 tbs of water. Cover with cling film and refrigerate.

Chop the almonds and pistachios very fine. Keep them separate. Set aside.

Heat the remaining 4 tbs of *ghee* or oil in a small, heavy-bottomed pot or in an 8-in/20-cm frying pan over a medium flame. When hot, put in the sultanas. Fry them for a few seconds, or until they swell. Remove them with a slotted spoon and put them with the finely chopped pistachios. Add the semolina, finely chopped almonds, and poppy seeds to the *ghee* or oil in the pot. Fry, stirring gently, until the semolina, almonds, and poppy seeds turn a shade darker. Turn off heat. Add the pistachios, sultanas, and crushed cardamom seeds to the pot. Mix well and allow to cool slightly. Mix in the sugar.

Take out the dough from the refrigerator and let it soften a bit. Break it into 40 balls. Keep balls covered with cling film.

Flatten one ball at a time and roll it out into a 3½-in/9-cm round. Place about 1½ tsp of the nut mixture slightly off-centre on the round of dough. Wet the edge of half the round and fold it over to make a stuffed semicircle or a turnover. Press the seam so it closes and then flute it with a fork or with your fingers. Make all the pastry and keep in a single layer. Heat 1½–2 in/4–5 cm of oil in a utensil for deep frying over a medium flame. When the oil is hot (350° F/180° C) drop in as many turnovers as will fit easily and fry them until they are golden brown on both sides. Drain on kitchen paper. Do all *ghugras* this way. Allow to cool and then store in an airtight tin or jar. This pastry will stay fresh for several days.

For information about ingredients and basic techniques that may be unfamiliar, see General Information, pages 481-506.

CARROT CAKE WITH AN INDIAN FLAVOUR
INDIAN STYLE   *(serves 6–8)*

Over the years, as I ate American carrot cake, it occurred to me that it was very similar in taste to Indian carrot *halwa*. If one took away the cinnamon flavour and the walnuts, then added cardamom flavour and pistachios... After experimenting for a while, I have come up with a carrot cake that tastes as if it came from the shop of an Indian *halvai* (sweetmaker).

1½ tsp vegetable oil	*2 oz/60 g softened* **ghee**
4 oz/115 g plain white flour plus extra for dusting	*Grated carrots measured to the 12-fl oz/3½-dl level in a glass measuring jug*
1 tsp bicarbonate of soda	
¼ tsp salt	*2 tbs chopped pistachios*
2 large eggs	*2 tbs chopped blanched almonds*
¼ tsp ground cardamom seeds	*2 tbs raisins*
8 oz/225 g granulated sugar	

I use a round, nonstick cake tin that is 9 in/23 cm in diameter and 1½ in/4 cm in height to make this cake. Rub it with the vegetable oil and then dust it very lightly with flour.

Preheat oven to 350° F/180° C/Mark 4.

Sift 4 oz/115 g flour with the bicarbonate of soda and salt.

Beat the eggs well in a large bowl. Add the cardamom powder, sugar, and *ghee*. Keep beating until all ingredients are thoroughly mixed.

Add the sifted flour mixture to the ingredients in the large bowl and fold it in gently with a spatula. Add the carrots, pistachios, almonds, and raisins. Fold them in gently as well.

Empty the cake batter into the oiled and floured cake tin and bake in the preheated oven for 35 to 40 minutes or until a toothpick inserted inside comes out clean and the top is a golden-red colour.

BIBINGKA KAMOTENG KAHOY
(Filipino-style Cassava Cake with Sultanas)
PHILIPPINES   *(serves 6)*

This coconut-flavoured, sultana-studded cake has a delightfully glutinous texture. In the Philippines, thick individual pancakes are baked in earthen baking dishes lined with banana leaves to prevent sticking. I find that a nonstick cake tin makes a good substitute. Of course, I do end up with a larger cake, which I then cut into wedges. Cassava is also sold as fresh tapioca.

6 oz/170 g freshly grated coconut   8 oz/225 g sugar
About 1½ lb/675 g fresh cassava   ¼ tsp salt
   (yucca)   1 oz/30 g sultanas
2 eggs

Put the grated coconut into the container of an electric blender or food processor and turn the machine on. Slowly add 8 fl oz/225 g hot water and let the machine run for a couple of minutes. Line a sieve with a triple thickness of cheesecloth and then balance the sieve in a bowl. Empty the contents of the blender or food processor into the sieve. Draw up the ends of the cheesecloth and squeeze out as much coconut milk as you can. Put this milk in a clear glass cup and set aside in a fairly warm place for 2 hours.

Preheat oven to 350° F/180° C/Mark 4.

Hold the cassava root under running water and peel it with a potato peeler. Grate the cassava coarsely, using a food processor if you have one.

Beat the eggs until they turn a pale yellow colour. Add the sugar and salt. Keep beating until the mixture is smooth.

Thick coconut cream will have risen to the top of your coconut milk. You should be able to see it clearly through the glass. Remove 2 tbs of this cream and set it aside.

Combine the grated cassava, the egg mixture, sultanas, and the remaining coconut milk in a bowl. Mix well.

Pour this batter into a round, nonstick, 9-in/23-cm cake tin and bake for 1 hour. Brush the top of the cake with the coconut cream and bake another 10 minutes. The top of the bibingka should be a nice golden-brown colour. If it is not, place the cake tin under the grill for a minute or so.

Let the cake cool and serve at room temperature.

CASSAVA SUMAN
(Small, Filipino-style Cassava Cakes)
PHILIPPINES   (makes 4 cakes)

In the Philippines, these small cakes, containing grated cassava, coconut, and sugar, are wrapped in banana leaves and then steamed. They taste a bit like glutinous rice cakes, though they have a firmer texture. This suman is generally eaten at merienda – or afternoon snack-time, with some coconut sprinkled over it. What I

For information about ingredients and basic techniques that may be unfamiliar, see General Information, pages 481-506.

do frequently is to offer it as an after-dinner dessert, along with neatly cut tropical fruit.

About 1¼ lb/560 g fresh cassava   *4½ oz/125 g freshly grated coconut*
(yucca)   *6 oz/180 g sugar*

Hold the cassava root under running water and peel it with a potato peeler. Grate the cassava coarsely, using a food processor if you have one.

In a bowl, mix the grated cassava, 4 oz/115 g coconut, and the sugar.

Spread out four pieces of aluminium foil, each about 12 in/30 cm square. Divide the cassava mixture into four parts and lay a portion in the centre of each of the pieces of foil. Pat each portion into a cake that measures 3½ in/9 cm in length, 2 in/5 cm in width, and ¾ in/2 cm in height. Now wrap the foil neatly and tightly around each cake, making watertight bundles.

Arrange a utensil for steaming. If you are using a trivet that will be placed inside the water, make sure that the water level stays just below the top of the trivet. Bring the water to the boil. Put in the four bundles, cover, and steam on a medium-low flame for an hour.

The cakes are eaten at room temperature. Unwrap them when you are ready to serve them and sprinkle their tops with some freshly grated coconut. If you like, you could arrange individual dessert plates this way: put half a cassava cake in the centre, sprinkling it with some fresh coconut; around the cake, in a pretty ring, arrange a half slice of fresh pineapple, a slice of peeled, ripe mango, and 3 banana slices.

SWEET WALNUT SOUP – A CONTEMPORARY HONG KONG VERSION
HONG KONG   *(serves 4)*

Served hot in the winter and cold in the summer, this delicious soup is really a dessert which is served at the end of meals. (I might add that my daughters like to eat it for breakfast and as a late-night snack.) Although it is made out of walnuts, it tastes, strangely enough, as if it had some grain in it as well.

The soup can be made easily and quickly, especially if you know what you are aiming for in each step. First the walnuts have to be blanched quickly in boiling salted water to remove a certain amount of scum. Then they have to be fried quickly in oil. The temperature of the oil is important as the walnuts must not burn or they will turn bitter. A good idea is to take the wok off the flame as soon as you have put the walnuts in. After that the walnuts are puréed in a blender. The purée, some water, sugar, and cornflour for thickening are combined in a wok and the mixture cooked briefly. You could serve the soup just this way, but the addition of cream — and I suspect that the cream is British Hong Kong's contribution to this Chinese recipe — makes it exceedingly smooth and comforting.

It may be made ahead of time and reheated.

2 tsp cornflour	4 fl oz/1 dl vegetable oil
½ tsp salt	3½ tbs sugar, or to taste
3½ oz/100 g shelled walnut halves	4 fl oz/1 dl single cream

Mix the cornflour with 2 tbs of water in a small cup and set aside.

Add salt to 1 qt/11½ dl of water and bring to a rolling boil. Drop in the walnuts and bring to the boil again. Boil for 10 seconds. The scum should rise to the top. Pour off half the water so the scum floats away and drain the walnuts in a strainer. Leave the walnuts in the strainer.

Heat the oil in a wok over a medium flame. When the oil is around 325° F/170° C (a medium heat — nowhere near smoking), put in the walnuts and take the wok off the fire. Stir and fry the walnuts for 5 seconds. Remove the walnuts with a slotted spoon and put them in a strainer placed over a bowl. Let them drain for a minute or two. Meanwhile wash and dry the wok.

Put the walnuts in the container of a blender and turn it on. Add 8 fl oz/225 g water, a little bit at a time. Blend until you have a fairly smooth mixture.

Empty the contents of the blender into the wok and set it to heat over a medium flame. Pour 8 fl oz/225 g water into the blender. Swish the water around so it picks up all remaining walnut paste and then pour this water into the wok. Add the sugar and mix. When the soup begins to simmer, stir the cornflour mixture and add it to the contents of the wok. Stir and cook for 30 seconds. Put in the cream and bring to a simmer.

Ladle the soup into small Chinese soup bowls and serve as dessert or as a snack.

For information about ingredients and basic techniques that may be unfamiliar, see General Information, pages 481-506.

SWEET RED BEAN SOUP
CHINA   *(serves 6)*

Like the preceding Walnut Soup, this is a dessert. In the winters, it is served hot. In the summers, it is served chilled, with the addition of cream in more Westernized centres like Hong Kong. While this soup is generally eaten at the end of a meal, it may also be eaten as a snack.

4 oz/115 g azuki *beans, picked*   *6–8 tbs sugar*
   over, washed, and drained   *4 fl oz/1 dl single cream (optional)*
2 tbs long-grain or short-grain
   rice, washed and drained

Put the beans, rice, and 2½ pt/1¼ l water in a heavy pot and bring to the boil. Lower heat and simmer, uncovered, for 2 minutes. Turn off the heat and let the pot sit, uncovered, for 1 hour. Bring the beans and rice to the boil again. Cover so that the lid is very slightly ajar. Turn heat to low and simmer very gently for 1 hour.

   Pour the contents of the pot into an electric blender and blend until smooth.

   Reheat the soup. Add the sugar and taste for sweetness. You may serve the soup this way. If you wish to serve the soup cold, add the cream and stir it in. Let the soup come to room temperature. Cover and refrigerate until chilled. Stir again before serving.

   Pour into small soup bowls and serve at the end of a meal.

GREEN SNOW
(Green Tea Syrup and Sweet Beans on Crushed Ice)
JAPAN   *(serves 4)*

I had this dish for the first time at the Kitcho restaurant on the outskirts of Kyoto. I was entranced by it. It was so light — and such a perfect way to finish off a summer meal. It consisted of a mound of crushed ice, overflowing with a green tea syrup and topped with sweet *azuki* beans. You may use one of two different types of powdered green tea for this dish. There is an instant green tea which is cheaper, and then there is the more expensive *matcha*, a fine powdered tea used in the elegant Japanese tea ceremony.

FOR THE BEANS
1½ oz/45 g azuki *beans*   *5 tbs sugar*

FOR THE GREEN TEA SYRUP
4 oz/115 g sugar
4 tsp instant green tea or 1½–2 tsp
matcha
4 cups crushed ice

Put the beans and 1¼ pt/¾ l water in a small pot. Bring to the boil. Cover, turn heat to low and cook for 2 minutes. Turn off the flame. Let the pot sit, covered, for 1 hour. Bring to the boil again. Cover, turn heat to low and simmer 30 minutes. Add the 5 tbs sugar and simmer vigorously, uncovered, for another 10 to 12 minutes. Cool the beans in their liquid and then drain.

Combine the 4 oz/115 g sugar with 4 fl oz/1 dl water in a small pot and bring to the boil. Turn heat to *very* low and simmer 3 to 4 minutes. Cool. Mix in the tea. (Taste as you go; add more or less tea, as you like.)

Pile a cupful of crushed ice in the centre of each of four ice-cream bowls. Pour the syrup over the ice. Divide the beans into four portions and scatter them over the top.

Audrey Chan's
CHINESE-STYLE JELLIED BEAN-CURD SWEETMEAT WITH A PEANUT TOPPING
SINGAPORE   *(makes 16 2-in/5-cm squares)*

The Chinese use agar-agar, a clear vegetable gelatine in the form of flat, noodle-like strips. As the packed wads generally weigh 1 oz/30 g or less, it is a little difficult to tell you just how much you need in a recipe. The method that I have used for this book is to squeeze the ends of the strips together very tightly in my hand and to measure the diameter or thickness of the bundle just where I am squeezing it. Then I measure the length of the strips. This method is not too exact, but it does seem to work.

You need very soft bean curd for this dish. It needs to be mashed thoroughly. This can be done either by pushing it through a fine sieve and then beating it, or by whirring it in a food-processor or blender for a few seconds.

The main body of this sweetmeat is almond-flavoured. For this, Audrey uses the bottled almond powder that is available in Chinese grocery stores.

For information about ingredients and basic techniques that may be unfamiliar, see General Information, pages 481-506.

Agar-agar strips, measuring
  1½ in/4 cm in diameter when
  squeezed tightly, and 9 in/23 cm
  in length
4 oz/225 g sugar, or to taste

4 tbs almond powder
1 lb/450 g soft bean curd, mashed
2 oz/60 g roasted peanuts, crushed
  lightly

Bring 1 qt/11½ dl of water to the boil in a 2½–3-qt/2¾–3½-l pot. Add the agar-agar and turn the heat to medium-low. Let the agar-agar melt completely. Add the sugar and let it dissolve. Blend the almond powder and mashed bean curd together with 3 fl oz/¾ dl water and stir into the agar-agar, mixing well.

Pour the contents of the pot into an 8-in/20-cm square cake tin. Allow it to cool slightly. When it has just begun to set, sprinkle the crushed peanuts over the surface. Let the sweetmeat set completely. Cut into 2-in/5-cm squares, cover, and refrigerate until ready to eat.

Chill for several hours before serving.

There is another way of serving this cooling dish as a dessert. Do *not* put the peanut topping on it. When it has cooled, cut it into rectangles that are 1 in/2½ cm long and ½-in/1½ cm wide. Put about 6 rectangles each into individual serving bowls. Add about 6 tinned litchis and 6 tinned loquats to each bowl, as well as a little of their syrup. Make sure that you have chilled the fruit thoroughly first.

Audrey Chan's
CHINESE-STYLE JELLIED WHOLE MUNG-BEAN SWEETMEAT

SINGAPORE   *(makes 36 1½-in/4-cm squares)*

This is a simple and tasty sweetmeat, made with just whole mung beans, sugar, and agar-agar, the vegetable gelatine. See the note at the beginning of the recipe for Chinese-Style Jellied Bean-Curd Sweetmeat with a Peanut Topping, page 462, for directions on how to measure agar-agar.

6 oz/180 g whole mung beans,
  picked over, washed, and
  drained
4 oz/115 g sugar

Agar-agar strips, 1½ in/4 cm in
  diameter when squeezed and
  7 in/18 cm long

Combine the beans and 1 qt/11½ dl water in a heavy, 2½-qt/2¾-l pot and bring to the boil. Cover, turn heat to low and simmer very gently for 1 to 1½ hours or until beans are tender. Add the sugar. Mix. Put in the agar-agar. Cook, stirring occasionally, until the agar-agar has melted completely. Pour the contents of the pot into a 9-in/23-cm square cake tin. Allow to cool and set. Cut into 1½-in/4-cm squares.

JELLIED SWEET AZUKI-BEAN SQUARES

JAPAN   *(makes about 64 squares)*

These small red beans (they are slightly larger than whole mung beans and are often labelled 'red beans' in Oriental stores) are used in Japan and China to make sweetmeats of various sorts. A puréed and sweetened red bean paste looks very much like melted chocolate and is, in fact, used to make bars and cakes and sweet stuffings. Here is one of the simplest of these red bean sweetmeats — one that I was offered, along with green tea, in almost every Japanese home that I visited.

3 oz/85 g whole red azuki *beans,*   *Agar-agar strips, 1½ in/4 cm in*
    picked over, washed and drained   *diameter when squeezed and*
8 oz/225 g sugar   *4 in/10 cm in length (see page*
                                               462)

Put the beans and 1 pt/5¾ dl water in a heavy, 1¾-qt/2-l pot and bring to the boil. Lower heat and simmer, uncovered, for 2 minutes. Turn off the heat and let the beans sit, uncovered, for 1 hour. Bring the beans to the boil again. Cover in such a way as to leave the lid very slightly ajar. Turn heat to low and simmer very gently (but the liquid should always have a few bubbles coming up) for 1 hour.

As the beans cook, cut up the agar-agar strips into ½-in/1½-cm lengths with a pair of scissors and put them into a 1¾-qt/2-l pot. Add 16 fl oz/½ l cold water and soak for 30 minutes. Now bring the contents of this pot to a simmer over a medium flame. Cover, turn heat to low and simmer very gently for 5 to 8 minutes or until all the agar-agar has melted. Turn off the heat. Leave the agar-agar covered in a warm spot.

When the beans have finished cooking, measure the amount you have. The beans and their liquid should add up to 16 fl oz/½ l. If there is less water, add some hot water to make up the difference. Put the beans and their liquid into the container of an electric blender and blend until you have a smooth paste. Add the sugar.

For information about ingredients and basic techniques that may be unfamiliar, see General Information, pages 481-506.

Blend again to mix. Pour this bean paste back into the pot in which you have been cooking the beans and bring to a simmer over a medium-low flame. Once it is bubbling, turn heat to low (there should still be some bubbles coming up) and cook, stirring all the time with a wooden spoon, for about 10 minutes. The mixture should now look like a very thick, chocolaty paste.

The agar-agar solution should still be hot and liquid. If not, put a low flame under it for a minute or two. Do not neglect the stirring of the bean paste, though, or it might burn. Pour the hot agar-agar solution into the bean paste. Stir and mix. Bring to a simmer over a medium-low flame. Now turn heat to low and cook, stirring all the time with a wooden spoon, for another 15 minutes or until the mixture resembles a thick chocolate sauce.

Pour this mixture through a strainer into an 8-in/20-cm square cake tin and allow to cool completely. It will set. Now cut the jellied paste with a knife into 1-in/2½-cm squares.

HOW TO MAKE CHHENA

INDIA *(makes enough to fill a 10-fl oz/2¾-dl cup)*

Chhena is a fine-grained cheese that is used for making many Indian milk sweets. Its freshness is essential to the final quality of sweets. It does not keep well. Most sweets made with *chhena* should be eaten within 48 hours.

3¼ pt/18½ dl milk

2 fl oz/½ dl (approximately) lemon juice

Heat the milk in a large heavy pot. As soon as it comes to the boil, turn off the heat and slowly pour in the lemon juice, stirring constantly with a plastic or wooden spoon. *All* the milk should curdle, blobs of *chhena* separating from the thin, watery whey. (On rare occasions, all the milk will not curdle. You will see a few blobs of *chhena*, but most of the liquid will remain milky. Bring to the boil again, add another tbs of lemon juice and repeat the process.) Leave the pot, covered, on a work surface for 10 minutes.

Line a sieve or colander with a man's handkerchief or a triple layer of cheesecloth.

(Put the sieve in a bowl if you wish to save the whey for cooking — use it instead of water.) Pour the curds and whey into the sieve. A lot of the whey will drain away. Lift the handkerchief by its four corners. Tie the curd inside into a loose bundle using a piece of twine. Suspend this bundle somewhere where it can drip for half an hour. (I hang the bundle on the tap of my kitchen sink.) After about half an hour, the *chhena* should have dripped some more and be cool enough to handle. Squeeze out as much liquid with your hands as you can manage easily and empty the *chhena* on to a clean, smooth surface like a Formica work surface. Now knead the *chhena* by pressing it and spreading it out at the same time with the palm and heel of a flattened hand, gathering it up, and then repeating the process again and again. This technique is not unlike the *fraisage* used to incorporate butter into pastry dough, though it is much more thorough. Knead for 10 to 15 minutes or until the *chhena* is of a *very* fine, slightly grainy, spongy consistency, not unlike whipped cream cheese.

Snigdha Mukerji's
CHUMCHUM AND DILBAHAR
(Chhena Diamonds and Hearts)
INDIA   *(makes about 16 pieces)*

Made out of *chhena*, *chumchums* are diamond-shaped and often yellow in colour whereas *dilbahars*, as their name indicates (*dil* means 'heart', *bahar* means 'spring'), are heart-shaped and may be white or yellow. Once the desired shapes have been formed out of the *chhena*, they are boiled in sugar syrup and then garnished with an 'icing' of boiled-down milk and cream, as well as with cardamom-flavoured crushed pistachios.

To make *chumchums* yellow, I use vegetable food colouring. You may omit the colouring, if you like. If you decide to make the sweets in two separate colours, boil the white batch in syrup first. Then do the yellow batch. If you do them together, the yellow colour will bleed into the syrup and discolour the white sweets.

For information about ingredients and basic techniques that may be unfamiliar, see General Information, pages 481–506.

3¼ pt/18½ dl milk

2 fl oz/½ dl (approximately) fresh
   lemon juice

8 fl oz/¼ l single cream

8 fl oz/¼ l milk

14 oz/395 g sugar

4 whole cardamom pods

2 tsp fine-grained semolina

1 tsp yellow food colouring
   (optional) — use ½ tsp if
   colouring half the chhena

1 tbs shelled, unsalted pistachios,
   finely chopped and mixed with
   ⅛ tsp ground cardamom powder

Make the *chhena* with the 3¼ pt/18½ dl of milk and the lemon juice according to the recipe on page 465, kneading it very thoroughly. Make a ball and set it aside.

Put the 8 fl oz/¼ l each of milk and cream into a heavy frying pan or saucepan and bring to the boil. Turn heat to medium and cook, stirring frequently to prevent sticking, until it reduces to 2–3 fl oz /½–1 dl. Pour reduced milk and cream into a small cup and leave to cool.

In a large, 12–14-in/30–35-cm frying or sauté pan (with lid, to be used later), combine the sugar, the cardamom pods, and 1½ pt/ 8½ dl of water. Bring to the boil over medium heat. Once the sugar has dissolved completely, turn heat to low and let the syrup simmer for 2 minutes. Turn off the heat.

Flatten the ball of *chhena* and add the semolina to it. Knead again for 5 minutes, making sure that the semolina is well mixed in. If you are going to add the yellow food colouring to half or all of the *chhena*, do it now. Mix well and knead some more. Now make 16 firm, crack-free balls. Flatten the balls and make diamond and heart shapes. The diamonds should be no longer than 1½ in/4 cm, no wider than ¾ in/2 cm and no thicker than ¼ in/¾ cm. The heart shapes may be 1¼ in/3¼ cm in length and width. If you have biscuit cutters in these shapes, flatten all the *chhena* so it is ¼ in/¾ cm in thickness and then cut out the diamond and heart forms. You will need to work the forms in your hands some more to make sure that they are tightly packed and crack-free. In order to make the sweets look more traditionally Bengali, round off all edges and points slightly.

Bring the syrup to the boil. Put in as many sweets as the frying pan will hold easily in one layer, remembering that they will expand to 1½ times their size. Cover and boil on medium heat for 15 minutes. Every 4 minutes, lift the cover and pour 2 tbs of water into the syrup. Cover again and keep boiling. Remove the sweets with a slotted spoon and place on a dish. (If you need to do a second batch, add 4 fl oz/½ dl water to the syrup and repeat the process.) The syrup may now be discarded.

Put about ½ tsp of the reduced milk and cream mixture on the centre of each sweet. It will spread out a bit but should not cover the entire sweet. Nor should it dribble off it. Sprinkle the pistachio and cardamom mixture on top of the 'icing'.

Like many Indian sweetmeats, *chumchums* and *dilbahars* are generally served at room temperature, either at tea-time — with tea or coffee — or after festive meals. But they may also be served cold. Arrange them in a single layer in a flat plastic container, cover, and refrigerate. You may keep them this way for 24 hours.

RASGULLAS
(Chhena Balls in Syrup)
INDIA   *(makes 20 rasgullas)*

This is the sweet that you have probably seen in many Indian restaurants — white balls floating in syrup. When they were little, my children used to call them 'squeaky balls' because the *rasgullas* squeaked a little as they bit into them. In India, *rasgullas*, perhaps Bengal's most popular sweet, are almost never made at home. They are made by professional *halvais* — sweetmakers — and sold in small, 'take-away', terracotta pots. They are generally offered at tea-time, though they are sometimes served as dessert after a meal. But for me, *rasgullas* taste best if eaten just after someone near and dear has passed a final exam.

For information about ingredients and basic techniques that may be unfamiliar, see General Information, pages 481–506.

Let me explain. When I was growing up in Delhi, all final examinations for high school and college took place in the intense heat of April and May. That, of course, was bad enough. What was worse than sweating through the exams though was sweating for the results, which never came privately in a sealed envelope as they do here. No, ours were boldly printed in a Delhi newspaper. If one managed to graduate at all from one's high school or college, all Delhi knew one's grades. So during the waiting period, students sweated and parents sweated as well.

When the results were finally announced, and if they were favourable, families did several things simultaneously – they hugged and kissed, made telephone calls to relatives who might have missed the news, and sent out for *rasgullas*. To pass an exam and *not* have *rasgullas* was quite unthinkable in our family. There would be a 'tea-party' later with chilled mangoes and ice cream – and more *rasgullas* – but some *rasgullas* had to be bought immediately to 'sweeten the mouths' of family members and friends who dropped by to offer their congratulations.

3¼ pt/18½ dl milk
2 fl oz/½ dl (approximately) lemon juice
2 lb 6 oz/1080 g sugar
10 whole cardamom pods
1 tsp fine-grained semolina
3–4 drops rose essence

Make *chhena* with the milk and lemon juice according to directions on page 465, but *with this difference*. Hang up the milk curds for 2 hours instead of ½ hour. Knead the *chhena* thoroughly. Make a ball and set it aside.

You now need two batches of syrup – a thinner syrup for boiling the *chhena* balls and a slightly thicker one in which the balls can be immersed after they have cooked.

Put 1 lb 5 oz/600 g of sugar, 2½ pt/1½ l of water, and 5 cardamom pods in a deep, 9½–10-in/24–25-cm frying pan or sauté pan. Bring to a fast simmer over medium heat. Once the sugar has dissolved completely, turn heat to low and let the syrup simmer gently for 2 minutes. Turn off the heat. For purposes of clarity, I shall call this the first syrup.

Make the second syrup by combining the remaining 1 lb 1 oz/480 g sugar, 1½ pt/8½ dl water, and 5 cardamom pods in a medium-sized saucepan. Bring to a fast simmer over medium heat. Once the sugar has dissolved completely, turn heat to low and let the syrup simmer gently for 2 minutes. Turn off the heat. Put this syrup in a bowl (leave the cardamom pods in).

Flatten the ball of *chhena* and add the semolina as well as the rose essence to it. Knead again for 5 minutes, making sure that the semolina and the rose essence are well mixed in. Now make 20 crack-free balls, rolling each with just a little pressure between the palms of your two hands.

Bring the first syrup to a simmer over a medium flame. Drop the balls into the syrup. Bring to a simmer again. Adjust the heat so that the syrup simmers gently for 5 minutes. During this period, move the balls around and turn them over occasionally, using a *very* gentle touch. Make sure you do not damage the balls.

Turn the heat up and bring the syrup to what might be called a furious simmer. The syrup should look like a mass of tiny moving bubbles, but it should never boil over. Sprinkle the balls with 2 tbs of water, cover and cook for 10 minutes. During this period, the *rasgullas* should swell up.

Uncover, sprinkle another 2 tbs of water over the balls, cover and cook, simmering furiously for another 10 minutes. Turn off the heat. Using a slotted spoon, transfer the *rasgullas* to the second syrup in the bowl. (The first syrup can now be discarded.) Let the *rasgullas* cool. Cover and refrigerate for at least 4 hours or overnight. Serve at room temperature or cold.

Even though the syrup is essential for keeping the *rasgullas* moist, it is not eaten. If you put some *rasgullas* in a serving dish, offer a slotted serving spoon. This way, guests may take just the *rasgullas* and leave the syrup behind.

RASMALAI
(Chhena Balls in a Sweet Creamy Sauce)
INDIA   (makes 20 balls)

Rasmalai, a very close cousin of the *rasgulla*, is almost the same sweet, taken a step further. After the *rasgulla* is made, it is taken out of the syrup and soaked in a mixture of milk and cream (rich milk is used in India). This is then boiled down until it is creamier and it is further enriched with crushed pistachios and ground cardamom. *Rasmalai* may be made in a round patty form or in balls.

3¼ pt/18½ dl milk	1 tsp fine-grained semolina
2 fl oz/½ dl (approximately) lemon juice	3–4 drops rose essence
	15 fl oz/4¼ dl single cream
1 lb 5 oz/600 g plus 1 tbs sugar	15 fl oz/4¼ dl milk
5 whole cardamom pods	⅛ tsp cardamom seeds

For information about ingredients and basic techniques that may be unfamiliar, see General Information, pages 481-506.

1 tbs shelled, unsalted pistachios

Make the *chhena* with the 3¼ pt/18½ dl of the milk and the lemon juice according to directions on page 465 *with this difference*. Hang up the milk curds for 2 hours instead of ½ hour. Knead thoroughly. Make a ball and set it aside.

Put the 1 lb 5 oz/600 g of sugar, 2½ pt/1½ l of water, and the cardamom pods in a deep 9–10-in/24–25-cm frying pan or sauté pan. Bring to a fast simmer over a medium flame. Once the sugar has dissolved completely, turn the heat to low and let the syrup simmer gently for 2 minutes. Turn off the heat.

Flatten the ball of *chhena* and add the semolina as well as the rose essence to it. Knead for 5 minutes, making sure that the semolina and rose essence are well mixed in. Now make 20 crack-free balls, rolling each with just a little pressure between the palms of your two hands.

Bring the syrup to a simmer over a medium flame. Drop the balls into the syrup. Bring to a simmer again. Adjust the heat so the syrup simmers gently for 5 minutes. During this period, move the balls around and turn them over occasionally, using a very gentle touch. Make sure you do not damage the balls.

Turn the heat up and bring the syrup to what might be described as a furious simmer. The syrup should look like a mass of tiny moving bubbles, but it should never boil over. Sprinkle the balls with 2 tbs of water, cover and cook for 10 minutes. During this period, the balls should swell up.

Uncover, sprinkle another 2 tbs of water over the balls, cover and cook, simmering furiously for another 10 minutes. Turn off the heat. Using a slotted spoon, transfer the balls to an empty bowl. (The syrup can now be discarded.) Combine the 15 fl oz/4¼ dl each of milk and cream and pour over the balls. Let them soak in the mixture for 3 hours.

Take balls gently out of the milk and cream mixture with a slotted spoon and put them in another bowl. Pour the milk and cream into a frying pan or saucepan and boil it down until you have about 16 fl oz/½ l left. Turn off the heat. Crush the cardamom seeds in a mortar and chop the pistachios finely. Add the crushed cardamom, the finely chopped pistachios, and the 1 tbs sugar to the reduced milk and cream mixture. Pour this over the *chhena* balls. Allow to cool. Cover and refrigerate for at least 2 hours, and serve cold, as a dessert together with the creamy sauce.

Ismail's
SHEER KORMA
(An Indian Vermicelli Milk Dessert)
INDIA   *(serves 6–8)*

My friend Ismail is a very good cook. He is more than that. He is a fast, relaxed cook. While other cooks labour and agonize in the kitchen, Ismail whips up exquisite meals with casual flicks of his hands. He never takes long over anything. This *sheer korma* was cooked in under 15 minutes, while he talked nonstop about the Cannes Film Festival where he had just shown a film, about a holiday in Corfu, and about the latest Indian miniature painting he had bought in London! Ismail takes the seriousness out of cooking. This *sheer korma* is simplicity itself to make and it tastes wonderful.

Sheer korma is made with very, very fine *sev* (also called *seviyan*) — a kind of thin wheat vermicelli that is available only in Indian grocery stores. Buy vermicelli marked 'thinnest'. (Indian stores also sell a vermicelli that has been browned. That is not what you want. You need the white vermicelli for this dish.) To make *sheer korma*, you first brown the vermicelli in butter and then add milk, sugar, nuts, and saffron. You cook the *korma* until it thickens, which happens fairly quickly. That is all there is to the dish. You could, if you like, describe *sheer korma* as a glorious vermicelli pudding, which may be served hot, warm, or cold. If you want the pudding to be somewhat 'flowing', use less of the *seviyan*, for a thicker dessert, use the entire quantity.

4 oz/115 g unsalted butter
Indian vermicelli (seviyan),
*   broken up into 2-in/5-cm pieces,*
*   and just enough to fill a glass*
*   measuring jug to the 10-fl oz/*
*   2¾-dl level*
1¾ pt/1 l milk

4 oz/115 g sugar
2 oz/60 g shelled, unsalted
*   pistachios, finely chopped*
2 oz/60 g blanched, sliced almonds
1 oz/30 g charoli nuts
10 threads saffron

Heat the butter in a 7–8-in/18–20-cm-wide, 2½–3-qt/l pot over a medium-low flame. Put in the vermicelli. Stir and sauté it until it turns an even golden colour. Now add the milk. Turn the heat to medium and bring the milk to the boil. Lower heat again to let the milk simmer and add the sugar, nuts, and saffron. Cook, stirring frequently, for 3 to 5 minutes or until the *korma* has thickened.
   Serve hot, warm or cold.

For information about ingredients and basic techniques that may be unfamiliar, see General Information, pages 481-506.

Sample Menus

The menus here should only serve as a guide to help you put together dishes of your choice. Even though I have indicated how different Asians eat their traditional foods, such information should only be used if it seems like fun.

TRADITIONAL KOREAN MENUS

In Korea, there is no great difference between breakfast, lunch, and dinner other than the number of dishes, which seem to increase as the day wears on. Most of the food, with the exception of the fruit, comes to the table at the same time. All food is communal; only bowls of rice and glasses of barley tea are served individually. Each person is given a pair of thin, knitting needle-like, metal chopsticks, long-handled spoons, and small, saucer-like plates. The chopsticks are for picking up solids, the spoon for liquids, and the plate for disposing of bones or for mixing individual combinations of foods. The fruit at the end of the meal always comes peeled and sliced, with tiny forks, one for each person, embedded in the slices.

(THIS MENU IS IDEAL FOR THE SUMMER)
Soy-Bean and Mung-Bean Sprouts Seasoned with Sesame Oil
Naeng Myon (Cold Noodle Soup)
Cabbage Kimchee
Cold Bori Cha (Cold Barley Tea)
Fruit

Oshitashi (Spinach with Roasted Sesame Seeds)
White Radish Soup
Carrots in Batter
Korean-Style Bean Curd in a Hot-Water Bath
Cabbage Kimchee
Honsik Bab (Rice with Barley)
Bori Cha (Barley Tea)
Fruit

Bibimbab (Korean Rice with Egg and Vegetable Topping)
Cabbage Kimchee or Spicy Turnip Pickle
Bori Cha (Barley Tea)
Fruit

473

Korean-Style Cucumber Salad
Roasted Laver
Mushrooms Cooked in Aluminium Foil with Korean
  Dipping Sauce Number 1
Noodles with Spinach and Mung-Bean Sprouts
Cabbage Kimchee
Bori Cha (Barley Tea)
Fruit

Carrot and White Radish Salad
Bindaetuk (Mung-Bean Pancakes) with Korean
  Dipping Sauce Number 1
Chapchae ('Cellophane' Noodles with Vegetables)
Kakdooki (Pickle Made with Cubes of White Radish)
Bori Cha (Barley Tea)
Fruit

Sautéed Bean Curd with Korean Dipping Sauce Number 2
Rice with Bean Sprouts, Spinach, and Laver
Cabbage Kimchee
Bori Cha (Barley Tea)
Fruit

TRADITIONAL JAPANESE MENUS

Japanese food is eaten with chopsticks. Chinese-style soup spoons are used for custards such as *chawanmushi*. At formal meals, each person is served individually. Course follows course, with the foods prearranged in attractive bowls and plates, not necessarily from matching sets. Meals generally end with rice, pickles, and tea.

Carrots and Beans with a Bean-Curd Dressing
Chawanmushi with Spring Onions, Dried Shiitake Mushrooms,
  Water Chestnuts, and Mangetouts
Aubergine Slices with White Miso
Green Beans with Soy Sauce
Plain Japanese Rice with Cabbage Tsukemono (Salted Pickled
  Cabbage)
Ocha (Japanese Green Tea)

Japanese Cucumber Salad
Miso Soup with Bean Curd
Tempura (Vegetables in Batter)
Plain Japanese Rice
Kombu Relish and Cabbage Tsukemono (Salted Cabbage Pickle)
Ocha (Japanese Green Tea)

Oshitashi (Spinach with Roasted Sesame Seeds)
Miso Soup with Carrots and Mushrooms
Cabbage Cooked with Bean Curd
Plain Japanese Rice
Quick-Salted Cucumber Pickle
Ocha (Japanese Green Tea)

Cucumber and Dried Shiitake Mushroom Salad
Stew of Baked Wheat Gluten, Potato, Turnip, Carrot, and
    Cabbage Rolls
Plain Japanese Rice
Quick-Salted White Radish Pickle
Ocha (Green Japanese Tea)

Watercress Salad with Sesame Seeds
Mixed plate of Datémaki (Japanese Rolled Omelette), Hijiki
    with Shiitake Mushrooms, and Peas with Ginger
Udofu (Simmering Bean Curd with Seasonings)
Japanese Rice
Shoyu Daikon (White Radish Pickled in Soy Sauce)
Ocha (Japanese Green Tea)

Datémaki (Japanese Rolled Omelette) with Japanese Dipping
    Sauce
Thick Noodles in a Winter Stew
Cabbage Tsukemono (Salted Cabbage Pickle)
Ocha (Japanese Green Tea)

TRADITIONAL CHINESE MENUS

Formal Chinese meals start with cold dishes, go on to stir-fried
foods, soups, simmered dishes, and spicy dishes to be eaten with
rice. Tea comes at the end. All dishes are placed in the centre of the
table and are communal. Each person has a plate, chopsticks, and a
soup spoon. They take from the centre whatever they want.

Stir-Fried Asparagus, Flavoured with Sesame Oil
Sweet Corn and Egg Soup
Bean Curd with a Deliciously Spicy Sauce
Green Beans with Garlic and Red Pepper
Plain Boiled Rice
Any Chinese tea

Chinese-Style Salad of Celery, Carrot, and Cucumber
Cold Noodles with Sesame Sauce
Bean Curd with Fresh Coriander
Courgettes Stir-Fried with Garlic
Plain Boiled Rice
Any Chinese tea

Cold Chinese-Style Aubergine
Salad of Mung-Bean Sprouts and Egg Strands
Fried Wheat Gluten with Broccoli, Carrot and Mushrooms
Plain Boiled Rice
Any Chinese tea

Hot-and-Sour Soup
Crisp-Soft Noodles with a Broccoli, Mushroom, and Courgette
    Topping
Peanuts with Long Green Beans
Plain Boiled Rice (if desired)
Any Chinese tea
Fruit

Salad of Pressed Bean Curd, Mung-Bean Sprouts, and Agar-Agar
Cauliflower with Almonds and Beans
Spicy Aubergine with Onion
Plain Boiled Rice
Any Chinese tea

Clear Soup with Soft Bean Curd and Chinese Leaves
Three Aunties and Three Grandmothers (Three Kinds of
    Mushrooms and Three Kinds of Vegetables)
Plain Boiled Rice
Any Chinese tea
Fruit

TRADITIONAL INDIAN MENUS

Most Indians eat with their hands, though the more Westernized
ones do resort to knives, forks, and spoons. Generally speaking,
all the food is placed in the centre of the table. People help themselves to whatever they want, putting it on to their own plates
before they eat it. In some parts of India, the food comes all
prearranged in large, individual metal platters (*thalis*), with the
more 'wet' dishes ensconced in small bowls (*katoris*). These platters

have everything from salty snacks, such as *samosas* (stuffed pastry cones) to sweets.

Chana Dal with Cucumber
Spiced Rice with Nuts and Sultanas
Green Beans with Sesame Paste and Garlic
Cauliflower with Courgette
Spiced, Heated Yogurt
Tomato, Cucumber, and Onion Relish

Very Spicy, Delicious Chick Peas
Sweet-and-Sour Aubergine
Potatoes with Whole Spices and Sesame Seeds
Yogurt with Cucumber and Mint
Bhaturas (Deep-Fried Leavened Breads)

Oily Toovar Dal with Green Beans and Tomatoes
Rice with Sautéed Onions and Mushrooms
Peas with Parsley and Coconut
Yogurt with Banana in the Gujarati Style

'Dry' Mung Dal
Khatte Baigan (Sour Aubergines)
Sauced Mushrooms with Sesame Seeds
Potatoes and Tomatoes Cooked with Fresh Coconut
Rotis or Pooris (Breads)
Sweet or Salty Lassi (Yogurt Drink)

South Indian Dosas (Rice and Urad Dal Pancakes)
Potatoes and Onions
Green Beans Cooked with Mustard Seeds and Red Pepper
Cabbage with Yogurt
Any Indian pickle

Sprouted Mung Beans with Spinach
Cabbage and Tomatoes Cooked in Mustard Oil
Vangi Bhat (Rice and Aubergine, Cooked in the Maharashtrian Style)
Yogurt with Chick Peas and Tomatoes
Any Indian pickle

MIDDLE EASTERN MENUS

The Middle East is, of course, a large region made up of many countries. As this area does not really have a history of vegetarianism but many fine vegetarian dishes, I have taken the liberty of putting these dishes together in a way that makes them quite compatible. (I might point out here that there are many religious figures in the Middle East who live on grains and yogurt.)

Pitta Bread stuffed with Falafel (Chick Pea Patties)
Tahini Dipping Sauce (as well as some tomato and lettuce)
Yogurt with Garlic (as an accompaniment)

Persian-Style Cold Yogurt Soup
Rice with Fresh Herbs and Baby Broad Beans
Aubergine with Tomatoes
Fresh Melon
Tea

Pilaf of Bulgar Wheat and Red Lentils
Yogurt with Spinach and Parsley
Okra with Tomatoes
Qahwah (Turkish Coffee)
Baklava

Stuffed Courgettes in a Hot Yogurt Sauce
Fresh Broad Beans with Thyme
Plain Baked Rice
Qahwah (Turkish Coffee)
Besan Barfee (Gram-Flour Fudge)

Lentils with Spinach
Plain Baked Rice II
Carrots with Raisins and Dates
Doogh (Yogurt Drink)
Fruit

(THIS MENU IS IDEAL FOR THE SUMMER)
Patlican (Fried Aubergine with a Yogurt Sauce`
Lentil Salad
Tabouleh (Bulgar Wheat and Parsley Salad)
Pitta Bread
Stewed Dried Fruit

SUGGESTIONS FOR MIXED MENUS

LUNCH

Uppama (Semolina Pilaf)
Green Salad
Salty Lassi (Salty Yogurt Drink)

Kookoo with Courgette, Dill, and Sultanas (Egg Pie)
Green Salad
French bread, or Italian bread, or Naan (Leavened Flat Bread)
Tea or Coffee

Bulgar Wheat with Chick Peas and Tomatoes
Green Beans Cooked with Mustard Seeds and Red Pepper
Fruit
Tea, Coffee, or a yogurt drink

Carrot and White Radish Salad
Cold Noodles with Sesame Sauce
Omelette with Bean Curd and Japanese Dipping Sauce
Ocha (Japanese Green Tea)

Mongo (Mung Beans with Spinach and Tomatoes)
Rice with Garlic
Yogurt with Cucumber and Mint
Anise Tea

Soy-Bean Sprouts Sautéed with Fried Bean Curd
Kohlrabi with Chinese Black Mushrooms
Rice with Millet

Chick Pea, Cabbage, and Dill Soup
Green Salad
French bread or Naan
Fruit

A COLD BUFFET

Cold Chinese-Style Aubergine
Hummus
Artichoke Hearts and Potatoes, Cooked in Oil and Lemon
Tabouleh
Yogurt with Courgettes
Dolmades
Korean-Style Cucumber Salad
Chick Pea and Green Bean Salad
Pitta bread, French bread or packaged Scandinavian crispbreads

DINNER

Butter Beans with Sultanas
Baghara Baigan (Stuffed Aubergine)
Zarda Pullao (Sweet Saffron Rice)
Yogurt with Dill

Frozen Broad Beans Braised with Swiss Chard and Dill
Stuffed Courgettes in a Hot Yogurt Sauce
Gucchi Pullao (Morel Pilaf)
Fruit

Stir-Fried Asparagus Flavoured with Sesame Oil
Chawanmushi with Shiitake Mushrooms, Water Chestnuts, and
   Mangetouts
Crisp-Soft Noodles with a Broccoli, Mushroom, and Courgette
   Topping
Fruit
Ocha (Japanese Green Tea)

Persian-Style Cold Yogurt Soup
Courgette 'Meatballs'
Tomatoes Cooked in the Bengali Style
Fried Potatoes
Spiced Rice with Cashews

Chinese-Style Salad of Celery, Carrot, and Cucumber
Three Aunties and Three Grandmothers (Three Kinds of
   Mushrooms and Three Kinds of Vegetables)
Bean Curd with a Deliciously Spicy Sauce
Plain Boiled Rice
Any Chinese tea

Salad of Pressed Bean Curd, Mung-Bean Sprouts, and Agar-Agar
Inari-Zushi (Bags of Fried Bean Curd Stuffed with Sushi Rice)
Chapchae ('Cellophane' Noodles with Vegetables)
Green Beans with Garlic and Red Pepper
Bori Cha (Barley Tea)

Haak (Spring Greens)
Chick Pea and Tomato Stew
Sweet-and-Sour Aubergine
Plain Basmati Rice
Doogh (yogurt drink)

GENERAL INFORMATION

Aburage *See* Bean Curd, Fried.

Agar-Agar Unlike most other gelatines that are made from animal products, this vegetarian gelatine is made from a kind of red seaweed, available in Japanese, Chinese, and other East Asian grocery stores as powder, flakes, and sticks. Only the sticks, resembling clear, long, uneven noodles, are called for in this book. Cut off the required amount with a pair of scissors and store the rest in a tin or a plastic bag.

When soaked in cold water, agar-agar sticks turn pliable and bouncy but retain a nice crunch. They are excellent as they are in salads and cold dishes, adding a new texture and picking up the flavours of the dressing. However, when agar-agar is cooked in hot water, it melts and may be used as gelatine for desserts and sweetmeats; it sets much faster than gelatine and does not require refrigeration. Desserts made with it may easily be cut into squares and diamonds without coming apart.

Age *See* Bean Curd, Fried.

Ajwain This celery-seed-sized spice has a flavour that seems to combine anise and oregano with just a hint of black pepper. Used in Indian cooking and may be purchased from Indian stores.

Almond Powder Very finely ground almonds, used in Chinese desserts, available in Chinese grocery stores.

Aloo Bokhara Sour, dried plums (or prunes), available in Middle Eastern and Indian grocery stores.

Amazu Shoga Pink, pickled ginger, usually eaten with *sushi* dishes, available in Japanese grocery stores, packed in its briny pickling solution. Buy the paper-thin slices, otherwise you'll have to cut the chunks of pickled ginger into paper-thin slices yourself. Store unused portion in its brine in the refrigerator. An average serving with *sushi* is about a packed tablespoon of the slices, piled in a heap.

Amchoor Dried slices and powder, made from sour, unripe mangoes. *Amchoor* gives foods a slightly sweet sourness. My recipes call for only ground (i.e., powdered) *amchoor*, available in Indian grocery stores.

Anardana Dried seeds from sour pomegranates. Used in Indian cooking and available in Indian grocery stores.

Asafetida A brown, somewhat smelly resin used in small quantities in Indian cooking partly for its flavour and mostly for its digestive properties. Indian stores sell it both in its lump form and

481

as a grainy powder. The lump is supposed to be purer. Break off a small chip with a hammer and then crush it between two sheets of paper to make your own powder.

Asakusa Nori *See* Nori.

Ata *See* Chapati Flour.

Azuki Beans *See* Beans, Dried.

Baby Corn Tiny, delicate ears found only tinned in Chinese grocery stores. Store unused portion covered with its own liquid in a jar in the refrigerator.

Bamboo Shoots Only tinned bamboo shoots are, alas, available to us, sold whole, sliced, and diced. Once the tin has been opened, store excess in a jar, well covered with fresh water, to be changed every day (they should last a week or more). If bamboo shoots taste very tinny, blanch them in rapidly boiling water for a minute and then drain them before using.

Basmati Rice *See* Rice.

Bean Curd White, milky, custard-like squares made out of soaked, mashed, and strained soy beans. It may be made at home (see page 191), or bought from health-food, Chinese, and Japanese grocery stores, either fresh or in tins. Fresh bean curd is generally available in three textures — soft, medium (or regular), and hard. It is best eaten the day it is made or bought, though the cakes may be put in a container with water to cover, changed daily, and refrigerated for 2 to 3 days. While there is a difference between Chinese and Japanese bean curds, for the purposes of this book just use whatever good, fresh bean curd you can get.

    Fried bean curd Some types of fried bean curd may be made at home (see page 205). All fried bean curds may be bought from Chinese and Japanese grocery stores, either fresh or sometimes tinned and frozen. Chinese fried bean curd, is usually sold in 1½ -in/4-cm cubes, which may be kept, well covered, in the refrigerator for 4 to 5 days or else frozen. There are two major types of Japanese fried bean curd — **Age** and **Aburage** (or **Abura Age**). *Age* consists of thick, rectangular slabs of bean curd that have been fried so the outside is brown and crisp but the inside is still soft. *Aburage* consists of much thinner slabs of fried bean curd that can be opened up into pouches, with a brown and crisp outside; the inside, what there is of it, is spongy. Both *age* and *aburage* are sold in the refrigerated sections of Japanese stores. *Aburage* may also be bought tinned and frozen. Most fried bean curd should be doused in boiling water to soften the exterior somewhat and to get rid of extra oil.

    Fermented bean curd Sold as '*Fu-ju*' or '*Nam-yee*' in Chinese stores and as '*Tao-hoo-yee*' in Thai stores, it consists of ¾–1-in/2–2½ -cm cubes of bean curd sitting in a briny liquid in bottles and tins.

The cubes taste like a soft, very salty and very strong cheese, which can be mashed and added as a flavouring to vegetables such as spinach or to sauces. I find some Thai sauces that cut the salty cheese with lime juice, ginger juice, and green chillies to be particularly delicious. There are many types of fermented bean curd. You can usually see them quite clearly when they are in bottles. Some look rather plain, others seem quite spicy, and yet another kind is packed in a red, winy broth (the latter, called 'red bean curd', is my favourite).

If stored in tightly closed bottles in the refrigerator, fermented bean curd can last indefinitely.

Pressed bean curd Sold as 'doufu kan' in Chinese grocery stores, this bean curd has had much of the water pressed out of it. It is sold in about ½-in/1½-cm-thick cakes. As the bean curd becomes quite hard, it may be cubed and julienned and then added to salads, almost as if it were, well, Swiss cheese. It may also be julienned and put into soups and stir-fried dishes. It should be stored in the refrigerator, covered with a salty solution − about 1 tbs salt to 1½ pt/8½ dl of water. It could last for a couple of weeks this way.

Pressed seasoned bean curd Sold in Chinese grocery stores as 'pai doufu kan' and very similar to the preceding bean curd, except that it has been cooked in star-anise-flavoured soy sauce and therefore has a brownish colour and a mild anise-like taste. It, too, may be julienned and added to salads, soups, and stir-fried dishes. Stored in the refrigerator covered with a solution that has about 1 tsp salt and 2 fl oz/½ dl Chinese dark soy sauce to 1½ pt/8½ dl of water, it could last a couple of weeks.

Dried bean-curd skin This is really the skin that forms over soy milk when it is heated. It is sold by many different names according to size and shapes (sticks, small rectangular pieces, etc.) in Chinese stores. When I call for sheets of dried bean-curd skin, I mean the rectangular sheets 5×1½×1/32 in/13×4×1/8 cm labelled 'Dried Bean Curd Skin, Sliced Type' to be found in small packets in Chinese grocery stores. The Japanese sell it as **yuba** in rolls, sheets, and rectangles. All kinds need to be soaked in water, the time varying according to the thickness of the skin − anywhere from 10 minutes to 1 hour. When reconstituted, bean-curd skin has a very rich, creamy taste. The dried skin does not need refrigeration, but should be used up quickly, as it can turn rancid in time.

Beans, Dried Legumes − dried beans and split peas − are rich sources of protein for Asians and are consumed, one way or another, at almost every single meal. All beans should be picked over and washed in several changes of water before cooking. Store in a dry, cool place in airtight containers. Remember that old beans will take much longer to cook than fresh ones.

Indian split peas, of which there are many varieties, are called *dals*. Some *dals*, fried in small quantities, are also used as a flavouring, almost as if they were a spice.

Here are some of the more unusual Asian beans and split peas I have used:

Azuki bean Also called *aduki* bean. Small red beans sometimes cooked with rice, sometimes by themselves, and sometimes mashed into sweet pastes for desserts, available in Oriental, Indian, and health-food stores. Sometimes they are unlabelled, so you just have to learn to recognize them.

Broad beans *See* Fava beans.

Chana dal The Indian version of yellow split peas, though somewhat smaller in size. *Chana dal* comes hulled and split and may be cooked by itself or with rice and vegetables. It has quite a nutty taste and is sometimes used as a spice in South India. Available both raw and roasted in Indian grocery stores. Roasted are used in Indian snack foods.

Fava beans Large beans sold with or without their seed coats in Middle Eastern and Chinese grocery stores. I have substituted braod beans. For more information, see page 97.

Masoor dal A hulled, salmon-coloured split pea that is used both in Indian and Middle Eastern cooking. Available in some supermarkets, health-food stores and in all Indian and Middle Eastern stores. Called red split lentils, *masoor dal*, and lentils respectively. This split pea loses its salmon colour when cooked and turns yellowish.

Mung beans Small, green-skinned, slightly cylindrical beans sold in all Oriental, Indian, and health-food grocery stores. They may be cooked as beans or used for making the Oriental and Indian types of bean sprouts (see pages 113–16).

Mung dal Split mung beans, available in Indian stores hulled and unhulled. My recipes use only the hulled, all-yellow kind.

Soy beans Round, dull-yellow beans which may be boiled, fried, and also used to make soy milk, bean curd, and soy-bean sprouts. Available in all Oriental and health-food stores, sometimes in supermarkets. For soy-bean sprouts, see page 119.

Toovar dal Also called *'arhar dal'*, this hulled, dull-yellow split pea is somewhat larger than the yellow split pea and has an earthy taste. Available in Indian grocery stores both plain and in its 'oily' Western Indian form — rubbed with castor oil which acts as a preservative and also keeps off the bugs. The oil needs to be washed away in several changes of water. 'Oily' *toovar* has a slightly different taste from the untreated, though they may be used interchangeably.

Urad dal The kind I've used is hulled and split and has a pale yellow colour and a somewhat viscous texture. It is used by South Indians for savoury cakes and pancakes, and sometimes as a spice. Available in Indian grocery stores.

Bean Sauce Available in tins in Chinese and other Oriental grocery stores, sometimes as a fine and other times as a coarse purée of fermented soy beans. It is salty, brown in colour, and thickened with flour. After opening, it should be transferred to a glass jar and refrigerated. It lasts indefinitely.

Bitter Gourd Courgette-shaped and of the marrow family, this green, crocodile-skinned vegetable can, indeed, be quite bitter. Asians decrease this bitterness somewhat by parboiling, salting, or soaking in salted water, but never eliminate it completely, as it is prized for cleansing the blood and for adding a new taste.

Bitter gourds come in various sizes; I have only seen the larger variety in Chinese and Indian stores here. When cooking them, use only the skin. The pulp and the large seeds embedded in it should be scraped away.

Black Cumin Seeds *See* Cumin Seeds, Black.

Black Mustard Seeds *See* Mustard Seeds, Black.

Black Salt or **Kala Namak** is a dark, smelly salt that is used in some Indian foods for its digestive properties. It is available either ground or in a lump at Indian grocery stores. If you get the lump, store it in a tightly closed tin in a very dry place. Break off what you need and crush it in a mortar.

Bok Choy This Chinese vegetable of the cabbage family has thick, whitish stalks that turn into dark-green leaves. The entire vegetable may be cooked. Available in Chinese grocery stores and some supermarkets, where it is apt to be called Chinese cabbage.

Bori Cha *See* Mugi Cha.

Bulgar Wheat The cracked kernels of boiled and dried wheat available in small, medium, and large sizes at Middle Eastern and health-food stores, as well as some supermarkets. For more information, see page 179.

Calpis A new, milky Japanese concentrate made out of non-fat dry milk and lactic acid, to be diluted with water to make hot and cold drinks. Available in Japanese and speciality stores under the name Calpico.

Cardamom An aromatic spice, generally sold in its pod. The green-coloured pods sold in Indian stores are more aromatic than the plump, bleached, whitish ones sold more generally in grocery stores. Some Indian stores sell the seeds separately, a great convenience when grinding spice combinations such as **garam masala**. If a recipe calls for ground or powdered cardamom seeds, just use a mortar and pestle as the quantities are usually quite small. Cardamom pods are often sucked in India as mouth fresheners.

Cardamom Pods, Large Black They look like black beetles and have an earthier, deeper flavour than green cardamoms. Sold in Indian grocery stores.

Cassava Also called yucca, manioc, and tapioca, this root of Brazilian origin resembles a large, brown, elongated sweet potato. It can be almost 12 in/30 cm long. It was introduced to tropical Asia by the Portuguese in the seventeenth century and has been used since in stews and desserts. In the southern Philippines it is grated and steamed and eaten as a staple instead of rice.

Cassava needs to be peeled under running water. It has a hard, white flesh which turns slightly glutinous when cooked. It is sold in West Indian and in Indian stores, where it is called tapioca.

Cayenne Pepper Use any powdered, hot red pepper. Indian supplies are usually fresher and brighter in colour.

'Cellophane' Mung-Bean Noodles *See* Noodles.

Chana Dal *See* Beans.

Chapati Flour. Very finely ground whole-wheat flour generally made from a wheat that is low in gluten. It is also called *'ata'* and is used in making many kinds of Indian breads. Available in Indian grocery stores.

Charoli A small nut available shelled in Indian grocery stores. It is generally used in sweets and stuffings.

Chhena A very fine, fresh cheese made from curdled milk (see recipe, page 465). Used for making Indian milk sweets such as *rasgullas*.

Chillies, Fresh Hot Green and Red Very rich sources of iron and vitamins A and C, chillies − or peppers − were introduced into Asia by the Portuguese in the sixteenth century. They were adopted with a vengeance. The chillies used for the recipes in this book are anywhere from 2 to 4 in/5 to 10 cm long and usually not more than ⅓ in/1 cm thick. They are available in Chinese and Indian grocery stores, as well as in greengrocers' in cosmopolitan areas. As chillies vary in strength according to variety and strain, care should be exercised in using them. Sometimes tasting a minute segment of a chilli is quite a good idea as they can vary so much, even within the same batch. The top seeded section is usually much hotter than the tapering bottom. Handle cut chillies as little as possible. When you do, refrain from touching any part of your face, and wash your hands with soap and warm water immediately afterwards. If fresh green chillies are unavailable, tinned ones (usually not as hot) may be substituted.

To store fresh green chillies, wrap them first in newspaper, then in plastic, and store in the refrigerator. They should last several weeks. Any that begin to rot should be discarded, as they tend to affect the whole batch.

Chilli Paste with Soy Bean Also sold as **Chilli Paste with Soy Bean and Garlic,** this paste has ground hot red chillies, fermented soy beans, and garlic in it. It is hot and quite delicious. Small amounts may be added to sauces that need perking up. Sold in jars in Chinese grocery stores. If kept well sealed and refrigerated, it should last indefinitely. If it starts to dry up, add a little sesame oil.

Chinese Black Mushrooms, Dried *See* Mushrooms.

Chinese Cabbage and Chinese Leaves. Since there are many notions of what Chinese cabbage is, let me offer my own definition for the purposes of this book. Chinese cabbage is a slightly elongated but chunky, somewhat curly version of our cabbage, with fairly white and quite wide ribs. It is called *'hakusai'* in Japanese stores and is used to make *kimchee*, cabbage rolls, and assorted vegetable dishes. When a recipe calls for Chinese cabbage, substitute Chinese leaves only if the cabbage is unavailable.

Chinese leaves are a slimmer, much longer version of Chinese cabbage and may be used in some of my soups and vegetable dishes.

Look at the illustrations of Chinese leaves on page 301 and Chinese cabbage on page 434.

Chinese cabbage is available in some Chinese and Japanese grocery stores. Chinese leaves are sold more widely, even in some supermarkets.

Chinese Chives In Chinese markets where they are sold, Chinese chives resemble bunches of long grass with a mild onion-garlic flavour. Ordinary chives may be substituted. To store, refrigerate unwashed chives wrapped in newspaper and then in plastic.

Chinese Parsley *See* Fresh Green Coriander.

Choy Sum This is yet another type of Chinese cabbage. It looks rather like **bok choy** except that it has slenderer, bright-green stems and leaves of almost the same colour. Occasionally, there are some small, bright-yellow flowers as well. It is quite delicious. Stems and leaves are all eaten. Sold only in Chinese grocery stores. Look at the illustration on page 35.

Coconuts From the Philippines to Pakistan coconuts are used in making dishes that include vegetables, beans, snacks, and desserts.

How to buy a coconut Look for a coconut that shows no sign of cracks and is free of mould. Pick it up and shake it. It should be heavy with water, which, in turn, ensures a moist interior. Always buy an extra coconut or two just in case one is rancid. Extra coconuts can always be grated and frozen.

How to break a coconut Take a heavy cleaver and, using the *un*sharpened side, hit the coconut all around its equator. You may rest the coconut on any hard, unbreakable surface or you may hold the coconut in one hand while hitting with the other. At the first sign of a crack, hold the coconut over a bowl to collect its water, which is not generally used in cooking, though in India it is highly recommended for 'women's problems', whatever they be! The coconut should break into two halves. Most Asian coconut graters are designed to scrape meat off these two halves, but if you do not have such a gadget, break the coconut into smaller pieces with a hammer. Remove the tough outer shell by slipping a knife between it and the meat and then prising the meat off. Use a sharp paring knife or potato peeler to pare away the brown skin on the pieces of meat. Rinse the coconut pieces.

There is yet another method of breaking open coconuts that has found much favour in the West. Preheat an oven to 400°F/200°C/Mark 6. Make two holes in the coconut, using an ice pick or a screwdriver. Drain the water and put the coconut in the oven for 15 minutes. Its shell should contract. Now hit the coconut with a hammer. The shell should come off. Even if it does not, you should be able to prise off the meat with greater ease. Peel the meat in the same way with a paring knife or with a potato peeler and then rinse the coconut pieces.

Always taste a small piece of coconut just after you have broken it open. If it has turned rancid in the slightest, do not use it. Coconut should be sweet and moist.

How to grate a coconut Excellent frozen grated coconut is available in some Asian stores. It is frozen in flat rectangles and defrosts very fast. It may be used in all my recipes that call for grated fresh coconut. (It may also be used to make coconut milk.)

If you cannot find the frozen variety, grind the coconut yourself. Once you have opened and peeled the coconut the grinding is simplicity itself, especially if you have a blender or food processor. The blender and food processor method: cut the coconut into ¾–1-in/2–7½-cm pieces. Throw them into a blender or a food processor *fitted with its metal blade*. Blend 3 to 5 minutes or until you have very fine particles. You may also grate coconut pieces by hand, using the finest holes in your grater.

Many stores sell dried coconut, both sweetened and unsweetened. The sweetened variety is rarely used in Asia and I do not call for it in any of my recipes. The unsweetened variety, however, is used but should not be substituted for the fresh kind unless that is indicated in the recipe.

How to make coconut milk and coconut cream To make 8 fl oz/¼ l of coconut milk, put 3 oz/85 g (or 6 oz/170 g if you want a richer milk) of grated coconut into the container of a food processor or blender. Add 8 fl oz/¼ l hot water and blend for 5 minutes. Let the mixture cool for about half an hour. Strain the mixture through a triple thickness of cheesecloth, making sure you get out as much liquid as possible. (This is sometimes called the first coconut milk. You can put the coconut grounds back into your food processor or blender, add another 8 fl oz/¼ l of hot water and repeat the process to get a second coconut milk.)

Put the strained coconut milk into a glass container and let it rest for half an hour or longer. The coconut cream will rise to the top. You should be able to see it through the glass and spoon it off with ease for recipes that require it. Otherwise just stir it into the milk and use it all as coconut milk.

Many Asian stores sell tinned coconut milk as well as an unsweetened coconut cream packaged like butter. Use the tinned milk whenever my recipes suggest it. It is much richer than what we can make with the coconuts available to us. Stir the contents of the tin before removing the amount you need. If you wish to use the packaged coconut cream, you might want to thin it out with a little single cream. This combination is excellent as a topping for fruit and South-east Asian desserts.

How to store coconuts, whole and grated Use coconuts as soon as possible. Store them in the refrigerator until that time. Grated coconuts freeze very well and defrost quite fast. It is a good idea to keep your freezer stocked with some freshly grated coconut.

Coriander, Fresh *See* Fresh Green Coriander.

Coriander Seeds These are used throughout much of the Middle East, South Asia, and East Asia, both whole and ground. If you wish to roast and grind coriander seeds, follow the general method given below for roasting and grinding cumin seeds. It is a good idea to sift the roasted and ground seeds with a fine sifter to get rid of some of the coarse shells. Indian stores sell both whole and ground seeds.

Cumin Seeds This spice is used a great deal in Middle Eastern and Indian cooking. Sometimes it is used whole, sometimes ground, and sometimes roasted and ground. It is fairly easy to find. Indian and Middle Eastern stores sell both the whole and the ground seeds.

To roast and grind cumin seeds, put about 4 tbs of the seeds into a small, heavy (preferably cast-iron) frying pan and set it over a medium flame. Stir and roast the seeds until they turn a few shades darker and give out a wonderful 'roasted' aroma. The seeds may now be ground in an electric coffee grinder or in a mortar. Store in a tightly closed jar in a cool, dark place. The flavour will lessen with time but the seeds should still be good for a month or so. Ground roasted cumin seeds may be sprinkled into soups, salads, bean, and yogurt dishes.

Cumin Seeds, Black Also called 'siyah zeera' and 'shah zeera'. The seeds are darker, finer, and more complex in flavour than ordinary cumin. They are also more expensive. Indian stores sell them in small packets.

Curry Leaves The highly aromatic fresh curry leaves, shaped rather like small bay leaves, are used a great deal in Indian cooking and have a wonderful aroma. The dried leaves have minimal aroma and flavour but may be used as a desperate measure.

Daikon *See* White Radish.

Dals *See* Beans, Dried.

Daun Salaam An aromatic leaf used fresh in Indonesian cooking. Only dried leaves with minimum flavour are available in Southeast Asian grocery stores.

Day-Lily Buds, Dried Also called 'golden needles', these are, indeed, the dried buds of day lilies. Follow directions in recipes for soaking, draining, and cutting off the hard knots. Available in Chinese grocery stores.

Domsiah Rice *See* Rice.

Dried-Hair Seaweed Always used when cooking Buddha's Delight for Chinese New Year celebrations, this seaweed looks like a tangled mass of curly black hair. It needs to be soaked and pulled apart before cooking.

Dried Hot Red Peppers *See* Red Peppers.

Fennel Seeds These taste and look like anise seeds, only they are milder and plumper. Fennel seeds are used a great deal in Indian cooking and may be purchased from Indian grocery stores.

Roasted fennel seeds are often offered in India as an after-dinner mouth freshener and digestive. For roasting, follow general direction for cumin seeds. You can prepare a whole jarful, let them cool, and then put a tight lid on.

Fenugreek Seeds Yellow, square, and flattish, these seeds are supposed to soothe the intestinal tract, even relax inflamed innards. Fenugreek seeds are sold in Indian grocery stores.

Feta Cheese A crumbly goat's cheese found in many Greek and Middle Eastern grocery stores.

Filo Pastry Also called 'phyllo' and 'fila'. Paper-thin sheets of pastry dough found in the refrigerators and freezers of most Middle Eastern and speciality grocery stores. The pastry has to be handled with care as it dries when left exposed. For more information, see page 395.

Fresh Green Coriander Also known sometimes as Chinese parsley or 'cilantro'. This herb is used all the way from the Caucasus to Korea. Most countries use just the leaves. In India, the stalks are used to add flavour to beans and stocks. In Thailand, the roots are used in the making of various curry pastes.

Fresh coriander may be grown from the coriander seed available in spice racks.

The best way to store fresh coriander is to put the whole bunch, unwashed roots and all, in a container of water, as if it were a bunch of cut flowers. Cover the leaves and container with a plastic bag and refrigerate. Every other day, pick off the dead or rotted leaves. Your coriander should last several weeks this way.

Galanga Root Also called '*laos*'. A root of the ginger family, though somewhat larger in size. It is used in the cooking of much of Southeast Asia and is available in stores that sell Thai, Indonesian, and Malayan groceries. Unfortunately, it is only possible to get the dry root here. Both dried slices and powder are sold, though not always in the same places.

Garam Masala Every home in India and Pakistan probably has its own handed-down-from-grandmother recipe for **garam masala**, an aromatic mixture of spices such as cardamom, cloves, and cinnamon which are supposed to 'heat' the body. My current favourite **garam masala** recipe goes as follows: put 1 tbs cardamom seeds, a 1-in/2½-cm stick of cinnamon, 1 tsp whole black cumin seeds (use ordinary whole cumin as a substitute), 1 tsp whole cloves, 1 tsp black peppercorns, and about ⅓ of an average-sized nutmeg into the container of an electric coffee grinder. Grind until the spices are powdery. Yield: 3 tbs. There is another slightly tarter **garam masala**, called '*multani garam masala*', used in an area that is now north-western Pakistan, that has sour pomegranate seeds in it. Here is that recipe: put 1½ tsp whole black cumin seeds, 1½ tsp cardamom seeds, 1½ tsp black peppercorns, 2 tsp **anardana** (dried pomegranate seeds), a 1½-in/4-cm stick of cinnamon, and ½ tsp whole cloves into the container of an electric coffee grinder. Grind until the spices are powdery. Yield: 3½ tbs.

Any **garam masala** should be stored in a tightly lidded jar, away from heat and sunlight. As time goes on, the spice mixtures will inevitably lessen in aroma and potency. That is why they are made in small quantities. But do use them up.

Ghee This is butter that has been so well clarified that you can even deep-fry in it. Because it is totally free of all milk solids, it does not need refrigeration. **Ghee** has a very special, nutty taste. If you have access to Indian stores, my own advice would be that you buy ready-made **ghee**. If you cannot buy ready-made **ghee**, here is how you go about making your own: take 1 lb/450 g of the best quality unsalted butter that you can find. Put it in a heavy, smallish pot and let it melt over a low flame. Soon it will begin to simmer. Let it simmer on low heat for 10–45 minutes (timing really depends upon the amount of water in the butter), or until the milky solids turn brownish and either cling to the sides of the pot or else fall to the bottom. Because you have to boil all the water away without letting the butter brown, you must watch it, especially towards the end of the cooking time. Now strain the **ghee** through a quadrupled layer of cheesecloth. Homemade *ghee* is best stored covered in the refrigerator. Unlike butter, it will not spoil.

Ginger, Dry Powdered The ground ginger available in most supermarkets and grocery stores.

Ginger, Fresh This is a knobby rhizome, known for its sharp, pungent, cleansing taste and its digestive properties. Its tan potato-like skin is usually peeled away, after which it is grated, sliced, or chopped. To make ginger paste in the food processor, it is best to start the machine first, with its metal blade in place. Then throw in coarsely chopped chunks of ginger through the feed tube. Add water last. If a recipe calls for 'very finely grated ginger' or 'ginger grated to a pulp', use one of the very efficient, fine-toothed ginger/horseradish graters sold in most Japanese grocery stores. The teeth in these graters catch the tough ginger fibres and all that you are left with is the pulp. If unavailable, use the finest part of a hand grater.

Always look for ginger with a smooth, unwrinkled skin. Wrinkles mean that the ginger has begun to dry out and will be quite hard and woody inside.

A five-pence-piece sized slice of ginger just means a rough cross-section, about the size of a five-pence piece.

Sometimes a very pale, pinkish, young ginger is available in Oriental and Indian markets. Because it is very tender, it is prized. It is therefore more expensive. Young ginger is ideal for pickling. If you find any, you could just scrape it, slice it, and then season it with lemon juice and salt. It will turn very pink − and make an excellent relish.

To store ginger, either wrap it up in newspaper and keep it in the vegetable bin of your refrigerator or else plant it in dryish soil and water it infrequently. If you plant it, the ginger might even sprout new shoots. If you use ginger quite a lot, as I do, just keep it in an airy basket, along with your onion and garlic.

Do not substitute dry ginger powder in any recipe that calls for fresh ginger.

Gingko Nuts Buy fresh gingko nuts, if you can get them. They can usually be found in the autumn and winter in Oriental grocery stores. They must first be cracked open with a hammer to remove the hard shell. The inner skin can be removed by dropping them into boiling water for a couple of minutes and then peeling. Fresh gingko nuts turn a wonderful jade-green colour when they are cooked. They can be stir-fried, skewered and grilled, and dipped in tempura batter and deep fried. If you cannot get fresh nuts, use the tinned variety, though their taste and texture hardly matches that of the fresh ones.

Fresh nuts may be stored in the refrigerator for a couple of months. Tinned nuts should be kept in the refrigerator, covered with water that is changed every other day.

Ginseng The very prized Korean root considered to be a cure-all. The fresh root is used in Korea for salads and to flavour soups and stews. Only the dry kind is available here and may be used to make ginseng tea. For more information, see page 401.

Glutinous Rice *See* Rice.

Gram Flour Flour made out of chick peas. Used in India and the Middle East both as a thickener for sauces and stews and for making pancakes, dumplings, and sweetmeats. I store mine in the refrigerator to discourage bugs.

Green Mango Now that ripe mangoes have begun to make their way into British markets, perhaps unripe green mangoes will be next. It is these pectin-rich, sour green mangoes that are the basis for most Indian chutneys and pickles. They are also eaten raw in countries like the Philippines and Thailand. If you cannot find them, use the suggested substitutes.

Green Plantain Large green unripe plantains are used throughout South and South-east Asia to make everything from chips to sweets. They can be found in most Indian and West Indian grocery stores.

Gur *See* Jaggery.

Hijiki A calcium-rich sea vegetable that resembles strands of black twine in its dried form. Sold in Japanese and health-food stores.

Hoisin Sauce A slightly sweet, thick, smooth Chinese bean sauce with a light garlic flavour. It may be used in cooking or as a dip. Available widely in Chinese and speciality grocery stores. If tinned, unused contents should be transferred to a lidded bottle and refrigerated. It lasts indefinitely.

Holy Basil Known as '*tulsi*' in India and '*bai ka-prow*' in Thailand, the fresh leaves are excellent for making a soothing tea and for flavouring soups, drinks, and vegetables. Available only in South-east Asian grocery stores.

Jaggery A form of raw lump sugar, generally honey-brown in colour. Available in Indian grocery stores. The best kind looks clean and is easily breakable, not brick hard. It should be stored in a tightly closed plastic container in the refrigerator.

Jujubes (Chinese Dates) They look like small, hard, red crinkly prunes and are available only in Chinese grocery stores. Jujubes need a good soaking before they can be used in cooking.

Kaffir Lime A dark-green knobby lime. Its peel, juice, and leaves are all used in Thai cooking. Only the dried leaves and dried peel are available in Thai and South-east Asian grocery stores. The Thais call the fruit *magrut*.

Kala Namak *See* Black Salt.

Kalonji (Nigella) Little tear-shaped black seeds used in Iran and India when cooking breads and vegetables as well as for pickling. *Kalonji* is the name by which this spice is sold in Indian stores. Middle Eastern stores sell it as '*siyah-daneh*' or 'black seeds'. Sometimes it is also called 'onion seeds'. This spice has a wonderful flavour and, once you know it, you might want to sprinkle some on your breads before you bake them.

Kampyo Ribbon of dried gourd, available in Japanese stores. It has to be cooked (or soaked) in water or seasoned stock before it can be eaten.

Karhai *See* Wok.

Katori Small metal bowls made out of anything from gold and silver to the more common stainless steel, used for serving individual portions of food at Indian meals. Generally, several **katoris** are arranged just inside the rim of a matching **thali,** a large metal plate. There are usually as many **katoris** as there are dishes, though rice, bread, and pickles are frequently placed directly on the **thali.**

Kim *See* Nori.

Kimchee Hot Korean pickle, generally made out of Chinese cabbage, white radish, or cucumber and sold in some Chinese and Japanese grocery stores. If you wish to make your own, see recipes on pages 439–43.

Ki-Soba *See* Noodles.

Kohlrabi A greatly neglected vegetable of the cabbage family. It consists of a solid green ball with stemmed leaves growing upwards from its surface. It is the ball that is generally peeled and eaten, both raw and cooked. In India, we always cooked the tenderer leaves as well.

Kombu (or Konbu) Green, calcium-rich dried kelp, used in making stock (*dashi*) and preserves, available in Japanese and health-food stores. It resembles a large, long leaf and is sold either folded up or cut into smaller pieces. There is a light dusting of powdery stuff on *kombu* which should be wiped off with a damp cloth *very lightly* so as not to remove the flavour, which is very near the surface. Store leftover portions in an airtight container.

Laos *See* Galanga Root.

Laver *See* Nori.

Lemon Grass A tall, hard, greyish-green grass used for its aroma and flavour in much South-east Asian cooking. Usually the lower 5 in/13 cm or so of the stalk is bruised and thrown into foods to release a lemon-peel-like taste. Fresh lemon grass is available in some Chinese grocery stores. If you cannot find it, use the sliced dried kind. A stalk of lemon grass is equivalent to about 2 to 3 tbs of sliced, dried.

Litchi A delicious fruit, about the size of a small egg, grown in much of East and South Asia. The outside skin ranges in colour from brown to red. Once peeled, the inside flesh is white and translucent, with an oval brown stone at its centre. Increasingly available fresh at greengrocers' and supermarkets. Always available tinned in syrup.

Lo Mein *See* Noodles.

Long Beans Also known as 'asparagus beans', these fresh green beans can be about a foot long. Their flavour is somewhat stronger than ordinary green beans, though the latter may always be substituted. Available in Chinese and Indian stores.

Loquat An egg-shaped, orange-coloured, sweet-and-sour fruit from East and South Asia. Available fresh on rare occasions in Chinese and speciality stores. Always available tinned in syrup in Chinese groceries.

Lotus Root Fresh lotus roots look a bit like plump sugar cane or a string of sausages from the outside. Inside, they are crisp, white, and filled with the most prettily arranged holes. The roots need to be peeled and cut into slices. Young roots may be eaten raw, perked up with a dressing of some sort. Maturer roots need to be cooked like potatoes. Even when the roots are cooked, they retain a nice crispness. They taste a bit like artichoke hearts, though there is an edge in there somewhere. Try throwing them into any stew that you are making. In India, they are invariably added to mixed pickles.

Lotus Seeds (Dried) Yellowish in colour and about the size and shape of peanuts. Used in Chinese stews and desserts. In India, they are roasted to make a kind of popcorn. Available in Chinese grocery stores.

Mangetouts The flat, edible pods used in Oriental cooking. Snap off the stalk and pull backwards to remove the coarse thread. They cook very fast.

Mangoes My favourite fruit. The best way to buy good mangoes is to taste one right in the shop. (I carry a penknife for the purpose.) If it is sweet and not too fibrous, buy as many as you need. They are probably hard and not fully ripe at this stage. Wrap each mango separately in newspaper and layer them close together in a cardboard carton or a bowl. Cover with more newspaper and leave in a warm place several days, if necessary, until ripe. The mangoes should begin to smell like mangoes and be very slightly soft to the touch. They should not have black spots, though. You may now either refrigerate them or chill them, like champagne, in a bucket of ice and water.

Masoor Dal *See* Beans, Dried.

Matcha An excellent-quality powdered green tea generally whipped with hot water to make the ritual tea in a Japanese tea ceremony. Not cheap.

Mee *See* Noodles.

Millet Tiny, hulled grains that look like birdseed. Available in health-food stores. May be cooked with rice or in place of rice.

Mirin A sweet, syrupy wine available in Japanese grocery stores. Used mainly for cooking. If not obtainable, a combination of *sake* and sugar may be substituted.

Miso This term includes many pastes of different hues and textures that are made in Japan from fermented soy beans and grains. *Misos* are used to make soups, stews, sauces, and marinades. They are fairly salty and are sometimes used in Japan to pickle vegetables.

As there are just so many *misos* sold under different names, I have identified them by colour. 'Red' *miso* is really reddish-brown; what is sold as 'white' *miso* is sometimes yellow, and so on. You may use whichever *miso* you like for the soups. I think it is best to start with the 'red'. Each *miso* has a slightly different taste and a different proportion of salt and sugar. Lighter *misos* tend to be sweeter. You might want to mix two different *misos* in the same soup.

Misos are sold in Japanese and health-food stores. You should store them in a tightly closed container in the refrigerator. They last for several months and are wonderful for quick, nourishing soups.

Monukka Raisins Very large, brown raisins, available in health-food stores.

Morel Mushrooms *See* Mushrooms.

Mugi Cha Roasted barley kernels used for making barley tea. Available in Japanese stores. (Called *'bori cha'* in Korea.)

Multani Garam Masala *See* Garam Masala.

Mung Beans *See* Beans, Dried.

Mung-Bean Sprouts *See* Beans, Dried.

Mung-Bean Vermicelli *See* Noodles.

Mung Dal *See* Beans, Dried.

Mushrooms

Chinese dried black mushrooms are available in Chinese grocery stores. Soak in hot water for half an hour, then snip off their hard inedible stems.

Japanese Shiitake mushrooms are fairly similar to the Chinese black mushrooms, always available dried in Japanese and speciality stores. Some even sell them fresh. Dried need to be soaked for half an hour or longer until soft. Stems are coarse and must be cut off.

Morel mushrooms are the very expensive mushrooms that have elongated, black, spongy heads. They are sometimes available fresh. They can always be had dried from speciality stores. They should be washed well.

Straw mushrooms, when they are fresh, are among the world's tastiest mushrooms. They have very fleshy caps that seem to enclose the stems. I have only seen them tinned in Britain. Chinese grocery stores as well as some speciality stores stock them.

Summer oyster mushrooms are large and meaty. They are available tinned in Chinese grocery stores. You may, if you are lucky, find fresh ones occasionally.

Mustard Oil Rather like mustard seeds, mustard oil has a split personality. Raw, it smells hot and pungent. When it is heated, the pungency evaporates and the oil turns slightly sweet. Used a great deal in Bengali and Kashmiri cooking and throughout India for pickling. Experiment with it making salad dressings and sautéing vegetables. Mustard oil is sold in Indian grocery stores. It can go rancid, so store in a cool place.

Mustard Seeds, Black These tiny, round, blackish-reddish-brown seeds are used throughout India for pickling and for seasoning everything from yogurt to beans. 'Seasoning' is a peculiar Indian-English translation of the word *'baghar'*, which means the quick popping of whole spices in very hot oil. Raw foods are then cooked in already seasoned oil or seasoned oil is poured over cooked foods just before they are served. When mustard seeds are used as seasoning, they impart an earthy sweetness to all foods.

Quite another aspect of mustard seeds becomes evident when the seeds are ground or crushed for pickling and sauces. They turn nose-tinglingly pungent. I do my grinding in a coffee grinder. When a recipe calls for lightly ground mustard seeds, see that the seeds break up into halves or quarters and do not become powder.

Old mustard seeds tend to become bitter. This does not seem to matter much if you are using the seeds as seasoning. However, if you are going to grind or crush them, it is best to have a fresh batch. Available in Indian grocery stores.

Nam Yee *See* Bean Curd, Fermented.

Nigari I use natural *nigari* flakes, distilled from clean sea water, as a coagulant to curdle soy milk and make bean curd. These white flakes are sold in Japanese and health-food stores.

Noodles There must be hundreds of different types of noodle that are eaten in Asia, made from ingredients such as mung beans, buckwheat, wheat flour, gram flour, and rice. Here are the ones I have used in my recipes:

'Cellophane' mung-bean noodles, also called Bean threads and Mung-bean vermicelli: very thin, brittle, opaque noodles made from mung beans and sold in all Oriental stores. When cooked, they are quite slippery.

Fresh Chinese egg noodles Ask for fresh 'lo mein' noodles in Chinese grocery stores and for fresh 'larmen' or 'ramen' in Japanese grocery stores. Usually sold in 1-lb or 500-g bags and found in the refrigerated sections. What you don't use, cover and either refrigerate for 3 to 4 days or freeze. Dry vermicelli may be used as a substitute in most dishes.

Ki-soba Thin, dried Japanese buckwheat noodles, available in Japanese stores. Vermicelli may be used as a substitute.

Korean buckwheat noodles Very thin dried noodles. Use Japanese somen or the very thin capellini as a substitute.

Mee Very thin, dried rice vermicelli sold in Thai grocery stores. If you cannot see what you want, ask for noodles to make Mee Krob. Use the thinnest possible Chinese rice sticks as a substitute.

Rice sticks A very thin, dried, crisp Chinese rice vermicelli, sold in Chinese grocery stores.

Sev Generally, this Indian word means crisp gram-flour noodles eaten as snack food. For recipe, see page 386.

Seviyan, sometimes also called 'sev'. Very, very thin wheat vermicelli from India, used mainly for desserts. Sold in Indian grocery stores.

Soba Japanese buckwheat noodles. I have used the dried kind, sold in Japanese and some health-food stores. Spaghetti may be used as a substitute.

Somen Very thin, dried wheat noodles, sold in Japanese grocery stores. Vermicelli or capellini may be used as a substitute.

Udon Thick, starchy Japanese wheat noodles, sold in Japanese stores. Spaghetti or linguini may be substituted.

Nori Although often called seaweed, even on the packets, this is really laver. There are many varieties and qualities, from dark green to purplish-black and from medium-priced to expensive. All nori is crisp and paper thin. I have used the sheets of nori — asakusa nori — for all the recipes in this book. In Korea, the same laver is called 'kim'.

All nori needs to be toasted lightly before it is eaten (see page 377). It is rich in vitamin A and calcium and may be just nibbled as a toasted sheet or else it may be used to make sushi rolls. It may also be crumbled over rice and noodle dishes. Sold in Japanese and health-food stores, it should be stored in an airtight container or frozen.

Ocha Japanese green leaf tea. Different qualities available at Japanese grocery stores and some speciality stores. The cheapest, *bancha*, generally has coarse leaves and even stems in it. It is brewed with boiling water in tea pots or in tall, handleless tea cups. *Sencha*, a higher grade of tea, is brewed in tea pots with very hot, not boiling water and then served, strained, in smaller cups than those used for *bancha*. *Gyokuru*, the best type of leaf tea, is brewed in small tea pots with water that is merely hot and then is sipped from tiny tea cups. The first time I was served this, I found the taste very strong; it does grow on one.

Oily Toovar Dal *See* Beans, Dried.

Oshi-Mugi *See* Pressed Barley.

Panchphoran (5-Spice Mixture) This very Bengali spice combination contains whole cumin seeds, whole black mustard seeds, whole fennel seeds, whole *kalonji*, and whole fenugreek seeds, mixed in equal proportions. You may put the mixture together yourself or else buy it already mixed from an Indian grocery store.

Paneer Indian-style fresh cheese. It has very little flavour of its own and is always cooked with other foods. Very rich in protein. For recipe, see page 277.

Papadum Also called *'papar'*. Indian wafers, generally made out of legumes, sold plain, with red pepper, with black pepper, and with garlic. The best varieties are, unfortunately, not sold in well-sealed tins but plastic packets, often clumsily stapled shut. The better quality speciality food stores generally carry the better packed but poorer quality *papadums*. It is best to buy them from an Indian grocery store. Keep what you do not use in a tightly sealed tin.

Peppers, Hot Green and Red *See* Chillies.

Poha Indian puffing rice. What you buy are flattened rice grains that puff up when they are fried. There are usually two types of *poha* in Indian grocery stores: a small, dense kind and a flatter, flakier version. Buy the latter. If you have any doubt, ask for the *poha* used to make *cheewra*.

Pomegranate Juice A sour concentrate, available in Middle Eastern grocery stores.

Poppy Seeds, White Used in both Indian and Japanese cooking. Available in Indian grocery stores. As they can become rancid, keep in a tightly lidded bottle and store in a cool place. You may even freeze poppy seeds.

Preserved Snow Cabbage Available tinned in Chinese grocery stores. It is fairly salty and is used as a flavouring.

Pressed Barley I've had this only in Korea, though I am told that the Japanese eat it as well. It has the virtue of cooking faster than barley. Once it has been soaked for half an hour, it cooks in the same amount of time as rice, a grain with which it is often combined. Its Japanese name is *oshi-mugi*.

Pressed Bean Curd *See* Bean Curd.

Pressed Seasoned Bean Curd *See* Bean Curd.

Quails' Eggs Hard to find fresh in this country. Some specialist grocers may sell them. Tinned, boiled quails' eggs are sold in most Chinese grocery stores but I can't say I like their taste or texture too much.

Red Bean Curd *See* Bean Curd, Fermented.

Red Peppers, Dried Hot Also called dried hot red chillies. There are many varieties. The kind I have used are about 1½ in/4 cm long and ⅓ in/1 cm thick. They are quite commonly available. When used whole in a dish, it's a good idea to remove them before serving.

Rice Almost every region of Asia has its own favourite type of rice – very often a local rice, on which the inhabitants of the region have been nurtured since childhood. It could be smooth and firm, soft and fluffy, sticky and chewy, partially milled, long-grain, short-grain or whatever. Not every type of Asian rice is available in Britain and, even if it were, you could not be expected to stock everything. Of the rices that one can get easily, I have chosen a few that seem to complement the major Asian cuisines. Of course, you are free to eat whichever rice you like best.

American long-grain rice is an excellent-quality rice and is quite suitable for most Asian meals. This is the long-grain rice I have used throughout this book, unless otherwise stated, and because it is labelled 'long grain' on the packet, I have used that terminology.

Basmati rice A fine-grained, aromatic rice from North India and Pakistan. It needs to be picked over and washed in several changes of water before it is used. Available in Indian and some speciality stores.

Brown rices, which are available both long-grain and short-grain in health-food stores, are unmilled – their hulls still on. I prefer the texture of the long-grain.

Domsiah rice A fine-grained, expensive, Persian rice, sold in some Middle Eastern grocery stores. Needs to be picked over, washed, and soaked before cooking.

Japanese rice refers to the fat-grained rice sold in Japanese and Korean grocery stores. It has a somewhat sticky texture and needs to be washed before cooking. The most common brand in Britain seems to be Japan Rose.

Glutinous rice, sometimes called 'sweet rice', has fat, opaque white grains. It is very sticky and is used in much of East Asia for desserts and snacks. This is sold in Chinese and Japanese grocery stores.

Rice Flour Also called 'rice powder', not to be confused with ground rice. It is similar to cornflour in texture. Sold in all Indian and Oriental grocery stores.

Rice Vinegar *See* Vinegars.

Rose Essence Used for flavouring sweets in the Middle East and India. The best kind is made from real roses, not chemicals. Read the label.

Saffron I have used only 'leaf' saffron here — the whole, dried stigmas of the crocus. Find a good, reliable source for your saffron, as there is a great deal of adulteration. To bring out the flavour and colour of saffron to its fullest, it is best to *dry-roast* it first. Put the required amount in a small, heavy frying pan over a lowish flame. Stir it about until the threads turn a very dark reddish-brown colour. Now crumble the threads into a small amount of hot milk (your recipe will say how much). Let the saffron soak for a few hours and then use this milk to tint and flavour rice or whatever else you want.

Sake A Japanese rice wine widely sold in many wine stores. It is generally warmed in ceramic bottles and then served in tiny cups. It may be drunk before, during, and after meals. It is also used in Japanese cooking. Once a bottle has been opened, it should be used up fairly soon.

Salted Ducks' Eggs These are raw eggs that have been kept in brine and are eaten almost as a condiment with congees and noodle dishes. The saltiness gets absorbed, all the way to the yolk. Chinese stores sell them raw so you have to boil them for about an hour. I like to change the water a few times to get rid of some of the saltiness.

Sambal This term is used in much of South-east Asia and implies a chilli-hot relish or else any dish that has been cooked with a paste of red hot chillies.

Sansho Pepper A fragrant Japanese pepper, available in Japanese grocery stores.

Sesame Oil Do *not* use the refined, colourless sesame oil for any of the recipes in this book. Buy the thick, brownish sesame oil available in Oriental grocery stores. It is very aromatic and smells gloriously of sesame seeds. It is used more as a flavouring than as a cooking oil. Store in a cool, dark place.

Sesame Seeds Extremely nutty and flavoursome as well as a high source of protein and calcium, sesame seeds are used throughout Asia in dishes from main courses to salads and desserts. Three types of sesame seeds are available on the market: polished, hulled whitish seeds; unhulled buff-coloured seeds; and unhulled black seeds. Here, sesame seeds refer to the unhulled buff-coloured variety unless I specify otherwise.

Ideally, sesame seeds should be picked over before being used, especially if they don't look too clean. They should then be stored in a cool place, well enclosed in a tightly lidded jar.

To roast sesame seeds Heat a small, preferably cast-iron, frying pan over a medium flame and put the required amount of sesame seeds into it. Stir and roast until they turn a few shades darker and begin to give out a slightly 'roasted' smell. Sesame seeds have a tendency to fly out of the frying pan as they are roasting; covering the pan with a mesh spatter-shield or a strainer helps. If you roast sesame seeds a great deal, as I do, it is worth trying to find a Japanese *goma-iri* or sesame-seed roaster. The kind I have is quite cheap and looks like a very fine-meshed wire box with a handle. The box has a 'door' at the top into which you feed the seeds. Then all you have to do is to hold the box over a flame and shake it.

(Many Indian recipes call for dropping sesame seeds into hot oil. This *quick-frying* brings out the nutty taste of the seeds the same way that roasting does. Again, the seeds tend to fly as they hit the hot oil. If this bothers you too much, use a spatter-shield.)

Roasted and ground roasted sesame seeds Roast the seeds as suggested above and then pulverize the seeds in one of the following ways: 1. use an electric coffee grinder – stop the machine whenever it begins to slow down, dislodge the paste-like collection at the bottom of the machine, and start again; 2. use a Japanese *suribachi*; 3. use a mortar and pestle. Many recipes call for lightly ground or crushed seeds, which do not need to be totally pulverized. The Japanese now have a gadget that resembles a pepper grinder. It is kept permanently filled with roasted sesame seeds and can be adjusted to a coarse or a fine grind. You may also crush sesame seeds the way I have seen some Koreans do it – between two flat-bottomed ceramic plates.

Sesame paste Here is a simple paste that can enhance the taste of the simplest boiled or steamed vegetable: roast and grind 3 tbs of sesame seeds. Slowly add 1 tbs of sesame oil, mixing it in as you do so. Yield: about 2 tbs. (Also see Tahini, page 417.)

Sev *See* Noodles.

7-Spice Seasoning (Shichimi) Also sold as 7-Spice Red Pepper (Shichimi Togarashi). A hot Japanese spice mixture that can contain finely crushed red pepper flakes, coarsely ground **sansho** pepper, roasted sesame seeds, roasted white poppy or hemp seeds, tiny bits of orange peel, tiny bits of toasted **nori**, and white pepper, mixed in different proportions. It is available, already mixed, in Japanese grocery stores. You could also mix your own, if you like. It may be sprinkled on soups, salads, and noodle dishes.

Seviyan *See* Noodles.

Shaohsing Wine A Chinese cooking wine, available in some Chinese stores. Dry sherry may be substituted

Shichimi *See* 7-Spice Seasoning.

Shiitake Mushrooms *See* Mushrooms.

Silver Ear Fungus Also called 'white fungus' or *'pai mo-er'* in Chinese grocery stores. Resembles small pieces of whitish sponge or coral. Considered to be both medicinal and a delicacy. This fungus needs to be soaked in hot water for half an hour before being used. It expands considerably.

Soba *See* Noodles.

Somen *See* Noodles.

Soy Beans, Fresh Small, hairy pods, available occasionally in Chinese greengrocers. After boiling or steaming and peeling they make a nice snack.

Soy-Bean Sprouts *See* Beans, Dried.

Soy Milk The thick, milky liquid that is formed when dried soy beans are soaked, ground, and then strained. The recipe is on page 191.

Soy Sauce Every region of East and South-east Asia has local soy sauce, going from light to dark to syrupy-sweet. To simplify matters, I have used just three soy sauces: **Japanese soy sauce**, which is the dark **Kikkoman**; **Chinese dark** (also called **'thick'**) **soy sauce** and **Chinese thin** (also called **'light'**) **soy sauce**. 'Thin' soy sauces are lighter in colour but also saltier.

Soy sauces are made from fermented soy beans and each type has its own flavour. You might want to experiment with many others that are on the market, including the **Japanese usukuchi shoyu**, a light soy sauce, and the **Indonesian ketjap manis**, which is sweet and syrupy.

Star Anise A star-shaped, anise-flavoured spice used in Oriental cooking. Available in all Chinese grocery stores.

Sudare Mat A small bamboo mat that is very helpful in making Norimake-Zushi. Sold in Japanese stores.

Suribachi A bowl-like ceramic Japanese mortar with a wooden pestle to crush foods against its ridged interior. Sold in Japanese stores.

Szechuan Peppercorns Reddish-brown, highly aromatic pods, about the size of peppercorns. Store in a tightly closed jar. Available in Chinese grocery stores.

Tahini This is the ground paste made from hulled sesame seeds that is used in making a variety of Middle Eastern sauces and dips. Most Middle Eastern and health-food stores sell it.

If you wish to make your own *tahini*, heat a 7-in/18-cm cast-iron frying pan over a medium flame. When hot, put in 4 oz/115 g of hulled sesame seeds. Keep shaking the frying pan until the seeds are roasted. Empty the seeds into a blender. Begin blending and adding cold water at the same time. Stop adding the water when you have a paste that is slightly thinner than peanut butter. You will probably need about 6 tbs of water. Excess *tahini* may be refrigerated for a week or frozen.

Tamarind These sour brown pods, rich in vitamins, get their name from the Arabic *'tamar-i-hind'* or 'the dates of India'. They are used in much of Asia as a souring agent, just as we use lemon. The pods may be sold whole, but generally they are peeled, seeded, and then packed into mounds or bricks − the cellophane-wrapped 1-lb/450-g bricks are what are usually available in Indian stores. Make sure that the brick you buy is slightly pliable. The harder it is, the longer it will take to release its pulp. To get the pulp − and this is the only part of the tamarind that is edible − break off as much tamarind as you need and soak it in water.

To make thick tamarind paste Break off ½ lb/225 g from a brick of tamarind and tear into smaller pieces, if you can. Put in a stainless steel or a non-metallic bowl covered with 16 fl oz/½ l of very hot water, and set aside overnight or at least 5 hours. (In an emergency, you may simmer the tamarind for 10 minutes.) Set a sieve over a stainless steel or non-metallic bowl. Empty the soaked tamarind and its liquid into the sieve and push as much pulp through with your fingers or with the back of a wooden spoon as you can. Put whatever tamarind remains in the sieve back into the soaking bowl. Add 4 fl oz/1 dl hot water to it and mash it a bit. Return it to the sieve and try to extract some more pulp. Do not forget to collect all the thick, strained paste clinging to the bottom of your sieve. Yield: about 12 fl oz/3½ dl. (Whatever tamarind remains in your sieve may be used for polishing brass!) Tamarind paste freezes well and will also last a good 2 to 3 weeks in the refrigerator. As long as it has no mould on it, you may use it.

Tanaka A spouted, narrow-necked, long-handled pot for making Turkish coffee. Available in many sizes, including a 1-cup size, at Middle Eastern and speciality stores.

Tao-Hoo-Yee *See* Bean Curd, Fermented.

Tempeh Flat 'cakes' made with soy beans (as well as some other grains and seeds) that are allowed to develop a kind of edible mould. They are extremely rich in protein and the B-12 vitamin. For more on *tempeh*, see page 127. Available in the refrigerators of macrobiotic stores.

Thali A very large, round metal plate used in India for formal and informal dining. Although gold *thalis* are not entirely unknown, those made out of silver, stainless steel, and bell metal are more common. A *thali* set includes 3 to 6 matching *katoris* (bowls) and usually a metal tumbler for water as well. Each person is served a full, individual *thali*.

Tomatoes We can usually count on getting ripe tomatoes in the summer, and even during the winter months fairly good tomatoes appear from Southern Europe. You can improve the colour and texture of even second-grade tomatoes by leaving them unrefrigerated until they turn a deep red colour. When all else fails, use tinned tomatoes.

To peel a tomato Drop the tomato into boiling water for 15 seconds. Remove with a slotted spoon and peel.

To seed a tomato Cut a peeled tomato in half. Cup one half in your hand, cut side down, and gently squeeze out the seeds into a bowl − or the sink. Repeat with the second half.

Toovar Dal *See* Beans, Dried.

Tree Ear Fungus Also called 'cloud ears' and 'mo-er mushrooms', looks like rounded pieces of charred paper. Sold in Chinese stores in two sizes, a larger, thicker kind and a smaller, thinner one. Buy the latter. Soak in hot water for about half an hour or less. It expands considerably.

Turmeric A rhizome of the ginger family. Fresh, it resembles fine, ginger-like fingers, bright yellow inside. Only the dried, ground turmeric is available here − also bright yellow. In India, it is considered a digestive. When used externally, it is an antiseptic. It is available widely but is probably freshest at Indian grocery stores.

Udon Noodles *See* Noodles.

Umeboshi Preserved, very salty, very sour, pink plums that come in various sizes and are sold in Japanese and health-food stores. The Japanese eat them at breakfast because they believe they aid digestion and cleanse the system. They certainly wake one up! Can also be stoned, mashed, and used as a seasoning. Keep them refrigerated in a tightly closed jar.

Urad Dal *See* Beans, Dried.

Vine Leaves Available already cleaned and packed in brine at all speciality as well as Greek and Middle Eastern stores. If you wish to use fresh leaves, see directions on page 396.

Vinegars Each region in Asia produces its own vinegar − palm vinegars, cane vinegars, rice vinegars, and so on. The only two Asian vinegars I have used here are **Japanese rice vinegar**, which is clear and light and sold quite widely, and **Chinese black vinegar**, also made from rice but very dark in colour. The latter is sold only in Chinese grocery stores.

Wakame A dark, dried seaweed, rich in calcium and vitamins. It is sold in health-food and Japanese grocery stores. It needs a soaking, after which it turns green and fairly slippery.

Wasabi A strong, green Japanese horseradish, available here only prepared (powdered or paste). For more information see page 417. Sold in Japanese grocery stores.

Water Chestnuts Dark-skinned and chestnut-sized, they grow in the water and are sold fresh only in Chinese grocery stores. For more information, see page 84. Tinned water chestnuts do not compare with the fresh but may be used in an emergency.

Wheat Gluten Protein-rich gluten removed from whole-wheat flour by washing away all the starch. Recipe for making wheat gluten and wheat-gluten balls is on page 213.

White Fungus *See* Silver Ear Fungus

White Poppy Seeds *See* Poppy Seeds, White.

White Radish These radishes vary in size from finger length to giants 12 in/30 cm long and 3 in/8 cm thick. It is the smaller, finger-sized ones that are used for Aomidaikon, the pickle on page 438. For all the other dishes, use whatever size you can find, and cut off what you need. White radishes are sold in Japanese grocery stores as *daikon*. Also available in Chinese grocery stores. The radishes that are about 1 in/2½ cm in diameter are usually more tender and juicy than the very large ones.

Wok Also called 'karhai' (in India). The wok is now very well known in Britain. It is excellent for stir-frying and very economical for deep frying. My only reason for mentioning it at all is that new woks have recently been designed that are not rounded off at the bottom so they sit firmly on electric cookers. If you have not bought a wok because you have an electric cooker, you might now wish to get one. Cast-iron and stainless steel woks are the best.

Yuba *See* Bean Curd.

Sources

The foods of many Asian nations overlap — hence Middle Eastern stores may have some Indian foods, Japanese stores may have Thai ingredients, and Chinese stores may have Japanese goods. Health-food stores sell many of the basics — sesame oil, sesame seeds, soy sauce, nuts, bean curd, mung beans, azuki beans, and bulgar wheat.

Here is a list of stores that specialize in Asian groceries. The foods that each shop stocks are listed after the address, abbreviated as follows: *ME* — Middle Eastern; *I* — Indian; *C* — Chinese; *J* — Japanese; *T* — Thai; *In* — Indonesian.

OUTSIDE LONDON

Birmingham

Wing Yip Supermarket
96–8 Coventry Street
Birmingham
I C J T In

Bournemouth

The Delicatessen
164 Old Christchurch Road
Bournemouth
ME C J T In

Taj Mahal Oriental Store
44 Charminster Road
Bournemouth
ME I C J T In
Mail order: minimum order £5

Bradford

Quality Foods
Edder Thorpe Street
off Leeds Road
Bradford
ME I C J T In

Cardiff

Far East Emporium
Lockwith Industrial Estate
Hadfield Road
Cardiff
I C

Nam-Kiu Supermarket
32–4 Tudor Street
Cardiff
C J

Colchester

Golden Crown Oriental Supplies
37 Crouch Street
Colchester
ME I C J T In

Coventry

Alma Coventry Ltd
89 Lower Precinct
Coventry
ME I C J T In

Dover

John Mann Supermarket
45 High Street
Dover
I C

Edinburgh

Edinburgh Chinese Company
26 Dublin Street
Edinburgh
I C J T In

Glasgow

Chung Ying Supermarket
63 Cambridge Street
Glasgow
I C J T In

Grantham

Chong Kee
2–6 Manthorpe Road
Grantham
I C

Leeds

Friendship Supermarket
27–9 Lady Lane
Leeds
C T

Leicester

Sabat Bros
1 Portsmouth Road
Leicester
I

Manchester

J A Centre
Unit 3
Heron House
46 Brazenose Street
Manchester
J

Woo Sang & Company
19–21 George Street
Manchester
I C J T In

Wing Yip Supermarket
45 Faulkner Street
Manchester

and

Addington Street
Ancoats
Manchester
I C J T In

Newcastle

Wing Hong Company (Grocer)
45–51 Stowell Street
Newcastle upon Tyne
I C J T In

Northampton

Continental Grocery Supply
166 Kettering Road
Northampton
ME I C J T In

Oxford

Palm's Delicatessen
The Market
High Street
Oxford
ME I C J T In

Plymouth

Continental Food Centre
148 Cornwall Street
Plymouth
ME I C J In

Wah Lung Supermarket
95 Mayflower Street
Plymouth
C J

Portsmouth

Eastern Stores
214–16 Kingston Road
Portsmouth
I C J T In

Southampton

Yau's Food Store
9–10 St Mary's Street
Southampton
I C In

LONDON

Indian

Shops selling Indian ingredients
are so numerous in London that
it seems unnecessary to list any
by name. It is worth mentioning, however, that in Southall,
Middlesex, there is probably the
largest concentration of Indian
stores in the whole area, and the
very widest range of ingredients
can be found there.

Middle Eastern

A1 Supermarket
567 Green Lanes
N8

T Adamou
126 Chiswick High Road
W4

Athenian Grocery
16a Moscow Road
off Queensway
W2

Fitzroy Stores
18 Charlotte Street
W1

Greek Food Centre
12 Inverness Street
NW1

Hellenic Stores
53 St John's Wood High Street
NW8

Istanbul Emporium
477 Liverpool Road
N7

Mediterranean and Continental
  Provision Stores
42 Goode Street
W1

Superstore
35 Grafton Way
W1

Chinese

G Anthony Groceries
37 Roundwood Road
Willesden
NW10

Asian Food Centre
175–7 Staines Road
Hounslow
Middlesex

Chung Ying Supermarket
6 Lisle Street
WC2

Great Wall Supermarket
31–7 Wardour Street
W1

Lee's Emporium
2f Dyne Road
off Kilburn High Road
NW6

Loon Fung Chinese
  Supermarket
39 Gerrard Street
W1

Loon Moon Supermarket
9a Gerrard Street
W1

See Woo Hong
19 Lisle Street
WC2

Japanese

Furusato
67a Camden High Street
NW1

J A Centre
70 Croydon Road
West Wickham
Kent

J A Centre
348–56 Regent's Park Road
N3
(supplies bulk mail order)

J A Centre
250 Upper Richmond Road
Putney
SW15

J A Centre
9 Wallbrook Street
EC4
(within shop, Ay Ko Ku-Kaku)

Japanese Publication Centre
5 Warwick Street
W1

Ninjin
244 Great Portland Street
W1

Nippon Food Centre
483 Finchley Road
NW3

Nippon Food Centre
61 High Street
Wimbledon
SW19

Nippon Food Centre
193 Upper Richmond Road
Putney
SW15

Tokyo-Ya
20 North End Road
Golders Green
NW11

Thai

Krung Phep Market
182 South Ealing Road
W5

The Thai Shop
3 Craven Place
W2

Indonesian

Ganesha
6 Park Walk
SW10

Macrobiotic

Sunwheel Foods Ltd
196 Old Street
EC1

An Invitation to Indian Cooking

Madhur Jaffrey

To Bauwa and Dadaji
with love

Contents

Acknowledgments

I would like to gratefully acknowledge the help given to me by the following — my grandmother, whose black lemon pickle opened my taste buds at an early age; my mother, who patiently gave me a two-year correspondence course in cooking; K and Motiboo, for unearthing old family recipes; Hussain, for inspiring me with his endless culinary experiments; V, for finding Indeera; Indeera, for her delicious chutney; Maya, for helping out in moments of panic; Zakiya and John, for willingly eating a lunch composed of five different soups; Ved, for showing such positive approval of a banana relish; Virginia, whose enthusiasm for the book in general and specific recipes in particular kept me buoyed up during the agonizing days of remeasuring and retesting; Zia, Chub (especially Chub), and Mitth, for showing a profound understanding of the chapter system and obligingly eating chicken one month, soups and appetizers the next month, vegetables the following, and so on; Sanford, for saying, 'You can do it', when I was convinced I couldn't and each batch of a certain sweet dessert was coming out tasting sour; Ismail, for keeping me striving by calling me the second-best cook; Norma and Mrs S. Matthai, for their expertise in seafood; the Blinkworths, for graciously parting with their recipe for mulligatawny soup before emigrating to Australia; and, most of all, Judith, for her gentle encouragement, unpressured advice, and her very reassuring presence.

517

Introduction

On a recent visit to London, I was astounded to see Indian restaurants flourishing in practically every neighbourhood. Mistakenly, I took this efflorescence to signify an increased supply of good quality, authentic, regional Indian foods. After all, the Indians who have settled in England—and there are over a million of them—come from some of the remotest areas of the subcontinent. It would not, I thought, be unreasonable to expect the restaurants to mirror this diversity in the foods that they served at their tables.

Upon visiting the restaurants, I found most of them to be second-class establishments that had managed to underplay their own regional uniqueness as well as to underestimate the curiosity and palate of contemporary Britons. Instead of specializing in foods from particular states or districts, they served a generalized Indian food from no area whatsoever; a restaurant calling itself 'Delhi' had no *karhi*, that thick soupy dish with its bobbing flotilla of gram flour dumplings; another, advertising food from the Punjab, was minus those delicious Punjabi mainstays, corn bread and mustard greens; at another called 'Bombay', where were the spongy, cakelike *dhhoklas* or those delicious sweet breads called *puranpoli*? And at all those new Bangalee restaurants I saw no roe fritters, or fish smothered with crushed mustard seeds and cooked gently in mustard oil or *bhapa doi*, that creamy, steamed yogurt.

The greatness of India's cuisine lies in its regional foods and its regional menus. There are several reasons why a great many of the restaurants shy away from them. One is timidity—fear that the diner's unfamiliarity with regional specialities will make certain dishes unpopular. (After all, if *tandoori* chicken and lamb *korma* are selling well, why bother with potatoes cooked with asafetida and cumin or shredded cabbage cooked with mustard seeds and freshly grated coconut?) Another reason is the calibre of the cooks. Good cooks are, in all parts of the world, a rare commodity. And those cooks going in for large-scale restaurant work need, on top of their basic talent, years of apprenticeship and training. The cooks in these proliferating Indian, Pakistani, and Bangalee restaurants are often former seamen or untrained villagers who have come to England in the hopes of making a living, somehow or other, in alien surroundings. Since cooking seems to them to require no unusual skills, a great many become restaurateurs, copying the standardized menus of other Indian restaurants and refusing to experiment with dishes from their own villages and home towns which they perhaps know much better. The result is that sauces in such eating places inevitably have the same colour, taste, and consistency; the dishes generally come 'mild, medium or hot', which is an indication that the food is not being cooked with the spices, as it should be, but that something is being ladled on; mediocre chutneys and relishes are piled on the table to fake an appearance of 'a lot for your money'; appetizers are suggested not because Indians eat them but because it is felt that the Western world cannot do without them.

This is, of course, not true of *all* Indian restaurants. There are a few *very* good ones, specializing generally in certain types of North Indian food. But even here, the menus are stubbornly limited to the tried and the true. Since the introduction of *tandoori* foods over a decade ago, nothing new has been added. The same menu repeats itself over and over again. The only difference between restaurants is that some cook the general run of *kormas* and *biryanis* well, while others do not. One restaurant owner, however, proudly presented me with a *new* dish which he alone served—*niramish* vegetables cooked with the typically Bengali five-spice combination of cumin, fennel, fenugreek, mustard, and onion seeds. Unfortunately, the vegetables he had used were from a frozen packet of 'mixed vegetables', thus completely negating all his own sincere and well-meaning efforts at authenticity.

The only way to eat superb Indian food, with a guarantee of variety, quality and freshness of ingredients, is to learn to cook it for yourself. And that is the purpose of this book — to open up the infinite possibilities offered by a cuisine that is over a thousand years old! Most of the recipes here have been adapted to the English kitchen. Some, like the fried aubergines, are very easy and quick to make. Others require a little time and patience. Just as you cannot expect to turn out a home-made apple pie in two minutes, you cannot expect the stuffed green peppers to be ready for eating with just two turns of the spatula. Good food cannot always be rushed.

I realize that many of you may be cooking Indian food for the first time. I have tried to write the recipes in great detail, describing how the food should look at the end of each major step as well as when it is fully cooked. This may make the recipes a bit long, but don't let that put you off. My intention is merely to lessen the chances for error. Also, don't be discouraged by a long list of spices. Once you have them on your shelf, it is just as easy to sprinkle in five of them as it is to add two.

It may, perhaps, encourage you to know that I myself learned to cook not from observation and practice in our family's kitchen in Delhi but from recipes written on flimsy air-letters, mailed to me by my mother. As a teenager growing up in India I was preoccupied with the usual teenage concerns — boys (whom we saw only at a distance and therefore coveted), my ambitions (why can't *I* play Hamlet?), and other such nonsense. I went into the kitchen only as a dilettante, more to taste than to help or learn.

It was when I was twenty and went to England as a student that I started to learn how to cook. I was extremely homesick, and this homesickness took the form of a longing for Indian food.

The canteen at my drama school served a see-through slice of roast beef accompanied by some watery potatoes and cabbage which no amount of H.P. sauce could improve. My limited scholarship funds did not allow me to eat out at the Indian restaurants. So I decided to learn how to cook, and I wrote to my mother in India for recipes. She would answer with long letters in Hindi which I would take with me to school. As I ate my roast and two vegetables, I would ponder her advice ... put in a pinch of asafetida — don't let it burn — now put in the cumin and stir for a second or two ... add the chopped-up tomatoes and fry ... my mouth would water and the cabbage would stick in my throat. At this point I couldn't even make tea.

But with expert long-distance help from my mother, I started learning. I began adapting her recipes to the ingredients and appliances that I found in Britain. Over the years I discovered that the electric blender could do much of what the Indian grinding stone did, and much faster; that instead of roasting aubergines in hot ashes as my mother recommended, I could do it directly over a gas burner; that English meats just couldn't be fried the Indian way because they contained too much water and that it was often better to cook with tinned tomatoes than fresh ones because they had more taste and colour. Slowly I began changing the recipes to suit the conditions. I managed to arrive at the genuine taste of traditional dishes, but often had to take quite a circuitous and unorthodox route to get there.

I'm sure by now you want to know what special ingredients are required to produce that genuine flavour, what special spices you need before you embark on this culinary adventure. Let me start negatively by saying that what you don't need is curry powder, which many of you may already realize. But for those who don't, let me explain.

To me the word 'curry' is as degrading to India's great

cuisine as the term 'chop suey' was to China's. But just as the English are learning to distinguish between the different styles of Chinese cooking and between the different dishes, I fervently hope that they will soon do the same with Indian food instead of lumping it all under the dubious catchall title of 'curry'. 'Curry' is just a vague, inaccurate word which the world has picked up from the British, who, in turn, got it mistakenly from us. It seems to mean different things to different people. Sometimes it is used synonymously with all Indian food. In America it can mean either Indian food or curry powder. To add to this confusion, Indians writing or speaking in English use the word themselves to distinguish dishes with a sauce, i.e., stew-like dishes. Of course when Indians speak in their own languages, they never use the word at all, instead identifying each dish by its own name.

The origin of this English word could be *kari*, a Tamil word meaning 'sauce', it could be a spice called the *kari* leaf, or it could be *karhi*, a North Indian dish made with buttermilk and chickpea flour. Who knows where some wandering sixteenth-century Englishman found his inspiration! Whatever its source, the word is obviously a British oversimplification for what is universally recognized as a richly varied cuisine.

If 'curry' is an oversimplified name for an ancient cuisine, then 'curry powder' attempts to oversimplify (and destroy) the cuisine itself. Curry powders are standard blends of several spices, including cumin, coriander, fenugreek, red peppers, and tumeric—standard blends which Indians themselves never use. Here again I am sure the British are responsible for its creation. This is how I imagine it happened:

A British officer in full uniform (possibly a young David Niven) is standing under a palm tree and looking fondly at his bungalow as Indian servants go back and forth carrying heavy trunks from the house into a waiting carriage. When the carriage is loaded, the servants line up on the veranda with tears in their eyes. The officer, overcome with emotion, turns to khansamah (cook).

OFFICER: How I shall miss your delicious cooking. My good man, why don't you mix me a box of those wonderful spices that you have been using. I will carry it back with me to Surrey, and there, whenever I feel nostalgic about India, I will take out this box and sprinkle some of your aromatic spice mixture into my bubbling pot.

KHANSAMAH: Yes, sa'ab, as you say, sa'ab. (*Runs off to kitchen.*)

Scene shifts to kitchen, where cook is seen hastily throwing spices into box. He runs back with it to officer.

KHANSAMAH: Here is the box, sa'ab. Sa'ab, if your friends also like, for a sum of two rupees each, I can make more boxes for them as well ...

Several years later: Former cook is now successful exporter. He is seen filling boxes marked 'Best Curry Powder'. When boxes are filled, he puts them in a large crate and stamps it in black: FOR EXPORT ONLY. Then he goes to his money box, opens it, takes out his money, and gleefully counts it. As scene fades away, former cook and present exporter is doing Dance of Joy ...

So much for my scenario. The point is that no Indian ever uses curry powder in his cooking. Nor do we mix our own, because if we did we would end up with our own blend of collective spices. Cooking again and again with the same blend of spices would make all dishes taste alike. It would be the same as taking a tablespoon each of dried thyme, basil, rosemary, tarragon, bay leaves, and allspice, putting them in a jar, shaking the jar, labelling it 'French Spices', and then using a portion of this mixture for every French dish one made, from soup to salad. Also, since 'curry powder' is a blend of *ground* spices, it tends to get stale very quickly and lose its flavour. So one ends up with something that has the negative aspects of being standardized and somewhat rancid at the same time.

And it isn't just Britons and Americans who are misguided.

The Chinese, who insist on the freshest herbs and vegetables for all their own food, use some of the stalest curry powder for the curried dumplings they serve in Hong Kong's best tea rooms. The Japanese, who are probably the world's greatest culinary aesthetes, don't hesitate to serve a greenish-yellow glutinous mess over their rice and label it 'curry', and the Frenchman, who insists on a perfect *velouté*, also eats the most ghastly 'shrimp Indienne' in a curry-tinted cream sauce.

But eating habits are changing, and today's English populace seems to have a great desire to experience the 'real' thing, an authentic taste, a different life style. Anything fake is deplored, fake foods included. It is a hopeful trend and leads me to believe that if the variety of authentic Indian food is ever going to be discovered, this is perhaps the time for it.

What is it then that gives Indian food its particular range of flavours? It may surprise you to know that a great many of the spices we use are ones that you probably have on your kitchen shelves already—cloves, cinnamon, bay leaves, black pepper, nutmeg and mace. These, along with cardamom, are what we call *garam masalas*, 'hot spices'. They are hot only inasmuch as they are supposed to provide heat for the body. The spices which you may not have would include cumin, coriander, turmeric, fenugreek, black mustard seeds, fennel, and dried hot peppers. All these, I find, are readily available on the spice racks of most large supermarkets and delicatessens.

There is a slight problem with supermarket spices which you might as well be aware of. Those spices which do not 'move'—i.e., sell fast—tend to stay on the shelves and get stale. A few lose their aroma, others fade in the light, some get oily and rancid. Therefore, try to buy only whole spices and grind them yourself in small quantities. The grinding is best done in a coffee-grinder, or, if the spices are slightly roasted first, some can be crushed between waxed paper with a rolling pin. The electric blender will grind spices, if you do them in sufficiently large quantities. If all else fails, you could use a mortar and pestle, though that tends to crush spices rather than grind them. Whole spices retain their flavours for very long periods. Make sure you store them in jars with tightly screwed lids, well away from dampness and sunlight. Ground cumin and coriander are fine if bought from Indian spice dealers in small quantities.

Even though the Indian styles of cooking require, in general, a fair number of spices, we do not, of course, use all of them for each dish we cook. Cauliflower, for example, may be cooked with just turmeric, fresh ginger, fresh green coriander, and ground cumin. A chicken dish I make requires only whole cloves, black peppercorns, cinnamon sticks, bay leaves, and cardamom pods. One potato dish needs just a pinch of asafetida, whole cumin seeds, and turmeric.

Sometimes, as you glance at a couple of recipes, the spices used might look identical, which may lead you to the conclusion that the two dishes will taste the same. But that's not necessarily true. It is not only *what* spices you use but also *how* you use them that gives dishes their special taste and appearance. Take cumin, for instance. If it is roasted whole and crushed, its coffee colour will darken the looks of any food and its strong aroma will fill not just your kitchen but your entire house. This way it has a sharp, nutty taste. Whole cumin, when it is 'popped' in very hot fat, has a mild aroma and a gentle, liquorice-like taste. Ground unroasted cumin provides a third flavour and has perhaps the mildest taste of the three.

Different spices require different treatment during cooking. Turmeric burns easily and becomes bitter, so it is generally used in conjunction with some liquid. Saffron gives off its best colour when lightly roasted, crushed, and then left to soak in warm milk. Too many fenugreek seeds can make a dish bitter, so while you can play around with the number of peppercorns or cardamom pods you put into a dish, you cannot do the same with fenugreek.

Spices, herbs, and other seasonings are always added to the cooking pot in a specific order, and this again changes the taste of the dish. For example, if a hot, dried red pepper is browned in oil and then mixed in with cooked lentils, the lentils will not be very hot but will have gained the subtle flavour of the pepper. On the other hand, if the pepper is browned in oil first and then cooked *with* the lentils, you will end up with a fairly hot dish. This applies to nearly all the spices, as each has its own peculiarities. The order in which they are put into a pot is extremely important. All this may sound confusing, but it is really easier to master than, say, a French custard. If you follow the recipes carefully, you will soon begin to understand the properties and idiosyncrasies of each spice.

Not all Indian dishes are stew-like, as some people imagine. We distinguish between 'wet' and 'dry' dishes, and of course we have every category in between. Sometimes we start cooking a meat dish like a stew, then boil down the liquid and end up by frying the meat. At other times we fry a fresh ginger paste with turmeric, sauté a vegetable in this mixture briefly, sprinkle a little water over it, and let it cook, covered, in its own steam. Potatoes can be cooked in a variety of sauces, or they can be boiled, diced, and cooked 'dry' with a little oil, fennel, and cumin seed. We deep-fry vegetables in batter and eat them with a fresh green coriander chutney, and we roast chicken and fish whole in clay ovens. Just as there is no one spice used for every single Indian dish, there is really no single technique that is common to all Indian foods.

A great many people stay away from Indian food because they assume it is hot. This 'heat', when it exists, is generally provided by the red or green pepper (or chili), spices which can easily be omitted without any loss of authenticity. In fact, in my own family, we rarely ate hot food, because it didn't 'agree' with my father. Being perverse, I naturally developed a very strong liking for it, but there is no reason why you must do the same. Some Englishmen feel that they lose face if they are confronted with very hot food and then cannot eat it. Perhaps they will relax when they know that there are also many Indians who prefer their food 'mild'. It is not the chili pepper which makes Indian food Indian. After all, the Thais,

Mexicans, Nigerians, and many others use it as well. It is the preparation and combination of whole or freshly ground spices which makes Indian foods unique.

There is another slight misconception even among knowledgeable Englishmen, which is that most Indian food is cooked in *ghee*, and that *ghee* is clarified butter. Actually, there are two kinds of *ghee*. The *usli ghee*, or 'real ghee', is indeed clarified butter, but if you consider India as a whole, it is very rarely used. In a nation where milk and butter are luxuries, cooking in *usli ghee* for the masses is unthinkable. Most people keep a small jar of *usli ghee* in their kitchen and use it occasionally on *chapatis* or *dal*, for cooking special dishes, or for religious and medicinal purposes. (I remember when at the age of twelve I had my ears pierced, for a month my mother applied hot fomentations of *usli ghee* and turmeric to my tortured earlobes!) In the western state of Punjab, however, *usli ghee*, butter, buttermilk, and milk are used much more frequently. The Punjabis, a tall, strong people, tend to believe that their enterprising spirit and immense energy come from the meat, corn bread, mustard greens, and dairy products they consume, and in some households it is quite common to give each child a daily spoonful of *usli ghee* pretty much in the same way that English parents pop vitamin pills into their children's mouths.

The other *ghee*, the one that is more commonly used, is made up of various vegetable oils. It is sold under various brand names — Dalda and Palm being the most popular — and can be purchased in large cans. In my own family we always used this vegetable *ghee* because my father insisted that *usli ghee* was too rich for a daily diet.

The cooking medium that is used almost as frequently as vegetable *ghee* is oil. It is cheap and excellent for deep frying. Also, different states show their individuality by using local oils — coconut oil in Kerala, mustard oil in Bengal, and peanut or sesame oil in various parts of North India.

In the last few years India, like most other nations, has become increasingly aware of the possible harm that can be caused by saturated fats. They are said to contain saturated oils and are therefore being rejected in favour of peanut oil, mustard oil, and other unsaturated oil mixtures. For this reason, I have used vegetable oil as the cooking medium in most of my recipes. You can use peanut oil or any other unsaturated oil mixture that you prefer. If, however, you wish to use *usli ghee*, directions for making it are on page 550.

Newborn Indian infants do not, of course, start off life on spicy foods (I have been asked this question several times.) They thrive on mother's milk, like most other infants. I do remember one particular custom in our family, however. As soon as an infant is born, whether at home or in the hospital, my grandmother would come and write the sacred syllable 'OM' (I am) on its tongue, with a finger dipped in honey. Children develop the taste and desire for spicy foods rather slowly. Our standard excuse, as six-year-olds, when we didn't want to eat was that the cook had put some red pepper in our food by mistake. If my mother was the only one presiding at the table, we would generally get away with it, but sometimes my father would arrive and insist on tasting the food and then our ruse was discovered. At the age of six, I loved to put sugar on my bread, but by nine I had graduated to a thick layer of hot mango pickle.

Children in Britain are always being told not to eat too many sweets. We were always being told not to eat too many sour things like tamarinds, raw mangoes, and *aam papar* (*aam papar* is made with sour mangoes, and the tastiest variety looks like thick, dirty brown leather). Even though our garden was full of fruit trees, the only ones that bore fruit were the mulberry and mango trees. We weren't interested in the mulberries because they were sweet; we left those to the old folks. But the raw mangoes were attacked and seldom given a chance to ripen. The best time to steal the mangoes was mid-afternoon when the temperature was 110 degrees and most of the household napped in air-cooled comfort. Often we would climb the mango tree equipped with knife, salt, and pepper. We would then picnic on the boughs, along with the twittering sparrows.

My father and mother were both born in the heart of the old city of Delhi, where the streets are so narrow that a man and a cow can barely pass each other. Most of the old town houses there are three or four floors high and are built around an inner courtyard. They have many small rooms, niches for closets, and no view, except other houses, other courtyards, other floors. On all the floors are balconies, running around the courtyard. When my paternal grandfather had become a successful barrister and had returned from his travels abroad, being an adventurous and ambitious man, he decided to move out of the area and bought himself a garden estate on the banks of the Jumna. But my mother's people stayed on in the old city. Every now and then my mother would take us to visit her family. Here I must rather shamefacedly admit that I felt, in those days, that I had very little in common with my old-city cousins. I loved to go there because of the food, which was superb—the best Kayasth (the name of my community) food one could ever hope to have. There were not many servants in this house, and all the cooking was done by the women, squatting on the kitchen floor. The odours would draw me to the kitchen door, where I would stand, first on one foot, then another, watching and sniffing. I wanted to go inside, but the kitchen was tiny and I would have had to take my shoes off— which was always difficult because of my mother's tight, well-knotted shoe-lacing techniques. So I would stand, peering from the outside, until my aunt, a gentle woman with large teeth, would tell me to go and play on the roof. I would do as she said, but eventually the odour of mushrooms cooking would draw me down again.

Sunset signalled the approach of dinner. A large cotton rug was unfolded in the courtyard. On this was spread a clean cotton sheet. Food was brought in on serving plates and placed in the centre of the sheet. I always liked to carry in my favourite dishes, so I could look at them longer. Everyone sat around the food. Unfortunately, the men ate first and the women served them. I would watch my favourite dish of mushrooms, which I *loved*, being devoured by greedy males. As I took the empty plate ro refill it for them, I would pray that at least *some* would be left for us. Finally our turn came. Fresh food was put on the serving plates and the women and girls would eat. We ate directly from the serving plate, breaking off a piece of bread from one plate and dipping it into another. My favourite mushrooms were obtainable only briefly during the rainy season. They were cooked with onions, garlic, tomatoes, cumin, coriander, turmeric, and a lot of hot red pepper. We ate them with *pooris*, an unleavened whole-wheat bread, round and puffed with hot air. We would also have potatoes, boiled first and then cooked with coriander, cumin, fenugreek, turmeric, onions, garlic, ginger, and yogurt. There would be lamb, prepared in the best Moghul tradition—with saffron, cardamoms, and nutmeg. And there were always pickles called water pickles because the pickling base in not oil or vinegar but water. To make them, green marrows (long and pale green), turnips, carrots, or watermelon rinds are blanched or put raw into a large earthenware container, together with crushed mustard seeds, salt, and, of course, water. The container is lightly covered, and the pickle is allowed to mature for one to two weeks. Even the liquid is totally irresistible.

Childhood taste habits never completely die out. They seem to leave their mark on us and often dictate the areas that we are willing to explore or not explore as adults. That is why I feel, rather strongly, that children should be exposed to not only the best foods but also foods of as many different countries as possible. Culinary insularity is really nothing more than a set of stubborn taste habits. And the best way to break these habits is through enlightened exposure at an early age. You'd be surprised at what some children are willing to try if adults are not sitting there looking apprehensive. I've had my daughters' non-Indian friends drop by and eat, with great relish, all sorts of Indian foods, including betel nuts! I keep my brass betel box in the living room. By now I am quite accustomed to seeing my daughters' friends come through the front door, say hello, walk straight to the betel box, rifle it, scattering seeds all over the floor, and then calmly walk on to the children's room, munching away like any Indian child. They seem to love the cauliflower cooked with fresh ginger and the chicken cooked with whole spices, and the marinated butterflied leg of lamb is, of course, an all-time favourite. One group of girls astonished me by eating (and enjoying) some hot mango pickle! All these children are under twelve years of age and belong to a pizza-Coke sorority that I have long despaired of.

I have tried to begin each chapter with simpler recipes which are easier to make and not too surprising to the palate.

At the end of each recipe I give serving suggestions in which I sometimes indicate if the dish is one which is likely to find popularity with children. Don't underestimate them. They'll surprise you. I remember so well one of our trips to Paris. We were seated in a restaurant slightly beyond our means, studying our menus, when my husband asked the children what appetizer they wanted. The eldest, who was supposed to be studying French, didn't want to admit that she couldn't understand a word of the menu, so she countered with, 'Well, what are *you* having?' My husband translated that section of the menu and said he was having snails and would they like to try that. Two children immediately turned up their noses and said, 'Eeeu', a favourite word in school that year. The third, whose glasses always seem to rest halfway down her nose, peered over them at my husband and asked, 'Do you *like* snails?' My husband said he liked them very much. She looked up at the ceiling for a good minute as if consulting someone in that direction and then said, 'Okay, I'll try 'em'. Well, she loved them and now orders snails at every opportunity she gets.

Try out these Indian dishes on your whole family. Take some of them with you on picnics. You'll be amazed to see how fast they are eaten up.

There is another group of people for whom this book should prove very useful. And they are vegetarians. One of the hardest things to find in this country is a good, balanced, fresh vegetarian meal. The choice seems to lie between macaroni and cheese, salads, raw or boiled vegetables, cheeses and fruit. The reason is that the English menu is planned around meat, poultry, or fish, the vegetables being just accessories. This country has not developed a vegetarian cuisine because, until now, there seemed to be no need for it. But a lot of young people are turning to vegetarianism because of a horror of all forms of killing, and many of the middle-aged are turning to it out of despair—they are wary of beef, pork, and lamb because of cholesterol, wary of fish because of mercury pollution, veal is ridiculously expensive, and just how many days a week can you eat chicken?

I happen to feel that Indian vegetarian food is perhaps the best in the world. It almost has to be. Our vegetarian population goes into the hundred millions! The Brahmins, upper-caste Hindus from both North and South India, rarely touch meat, fish, or eggs. The Buddhists and Jains abhor all killing, orthodox Jains going so far as to wear masks over their noses and mouths so as not to accidentally entrap some minute victim that strays in as they inhale. The poor in India are also generally vegetarian because meat is simply beyond their means.

The result of all this is that in the last few thousand years, Indians have developed a most balanced and varied vegetarian cuisine. The essential proteins in these meals are provided by the many *dals* (lentils, split peas, black-eyed peas, chickpeas, etc.) and by yogurt relishes and milk desserts. The variety is provided by the sheer number of vegetable dishes. Each is cooked with a different combination of spices—some with sauces, others 'dry', some vegetables cooked in combination with others, like potatoes, peas, and cauliflower, others grated and stuffed in bread, some boiled, some sautéed, some fried, some pickled and some puréed into fresh chutneys.

The longest chapter in this book is the one on vegetables. That, as well as the chapters on Rice; Breads; Chutneys, Pickles, and Other Relishes; and Desserts should provide enough material for vegetarians to make interesting and wholesome menus.

I also give, a little later, a list of sample menus both vegetarian and non-vegetarian. Use them if you feel you need initial guidance, but experiment and try any combination that strikes your fancy. Also, don't feel compelled to plunge into Indian cooking with a full-scale banquet. An Indian soup with your meal one day, a tomato chutney with your roast lamb the next, some sweet rice with your duck at the weekend—these are good beginnings. If you are in the habit of serving spaghetti and meat sauce quite often, try rice and *kheema* instead. It is a pleasant variation and equally simple.

All the dishes in this book can be made in standard English pots, saucepans, and frying-pans. It does help, however, to use good-quality heavy-bottomed pots, especially for rice. For making Indian bread a *tava*, a rounded iron plate, is very convenient, but you can use instead a cast-iron frying-pan. For deep frying we use a *karhai*, which is similar to a Chinese wok. Many kitchenware stores carry woks. If you can find one easily, do buy it. It is a worthwhile investment. If you cannot find one, don't be discouraged, as I will suggest substitutes whenever a *karhai* (or wok) is called for.

A word about the limitations of this book. If you are looking for an encyclopedic tome encompassing *all* Indian food, you certainly won't find it here. Such a task would have taken me at least twenty years, as I would have had to approach it slowly, region by region. What this book does offer you is the chance to understand and cook the food of one specific area—the region in and around Delhi, including the adjacent sections of Uttar Pradesh.

Since Delhi is a city and not a large province, you might consider knowing the food of this area alone as being rather limited. But that is not so. First of all, the best Indian food is that which is specifically regional. I would rather that you started with a thorough understanding of the cuisine and eating habits of one region than with a vague superficial understanding of the cuisines of the entire subcontinent. Second, even though Delhi is just one city, it is the capital and was, until the British threw them out in the nineteenth century, the seat of the great Moghul emperors. And it was in their royal kitchens that the Delhi cuisine was conceived. Because of the Moghuls' power and prestige, their cuisine was then aped, with interesting local variations, in the courts of the lesser maharajahs, rajahs, generals, and governors scattered across the nation.

The Moghuls were originally nomadic Tartars from the plains of Mongolia. They were so unused to living in permanent structures that the first palaces they built in India in the sixteenth and seventeenth centuries resembled gigantic tents but were made of red sandstone and marble. They were also unused to the heat, so they immediately set about building canals everywhere—they even had canals going through their bedrooms! They sent runners up to the Himalayas to bring them ice for their drinks, and in the summers the entire city— to the last courtesan—moved up to the royal gardens in the cool vale of Kashmir. The country they admired most was Persia. They had passed it on their way to India and had been awed by the glitter of courtly robes and the delicacy of the miniature paintings, and by the exquisite food they had been served. Much of it they introduced into their own courts, sending off to Persia and Afghanistan regularly for melons, pomegranates, plums, grapes, dates, and nuts.

But India has a way of influencing, if not overpowering, everything it comes in contact with. Very soon the mighty Moghuls were chewing the betel leaf, crying in ecstasy over the mango, adding more spices to their Persian meats, and relishing the vegetarian dishes prepared for them by their Hindu wives and mistresses. It was this combination of richly cooked Persian meats and rice (sometimes called Moghul food) with the local vegetarian styles that gave birth to what I call the Delhi cuisine.

Although this book basically contains the food of the Delhi region, I have, I must confess, cheated slightly to include a few recipes for foods which were cooked in our home but which originated in other states. I feel very attached to these dishes, and as this is essentially a personal book, I had no compunction about including things that have been adapted in my own kitchen.

I'm sure many readers are curious about just how different the other Indian cuisines really are. One tends to think of India as one large subcontinent almost the size of Europe (without Russia). It is divided into about twenty states and territories. (I say 'about' because the number keeps changing.) Each state has its own language, history, literature, dress, and culinary traditions. Transportation of fresh produce isn't particularly efficient, reliable, or cheap, so each area tends to eat what it produces locally. In some states like Kerala, Bengal, and Andhra Pradesh, the staple is rice, whereas in others like Punjab and Uttar Pradesh, the staple is wheat. Along the coast fish and seafood are eaten extensively and are often cooked in coconut milk. In the northern interior, where people see neither the sea nor coconut palms, they usually eat an unleavened whole-wheat bread with *dal* and vegetables.

In Bengal, I've had an entire meal consisting of five different lobster dishes served with rice, the most delicious being one in which the lobster was cooked with mustard seeds and freshly grated coconut. This was followed by Bengali sweets — tiny squares, rectangles, and balls, no bigger than a sugar lump, coloured pink, green, and yellow and made with milk, cheese, and sugar.

In Kashmir, where the people are often red-haired, green-eyed, and freckled, the staple diet is meat, fish, and rice. Meat and vegetables are dried during the summer months and stored to be used once the snow begins to fall and movement becomes restricted. The spices used are those which are thought to provide heat for the body—cardamom, cinnamon, cloves, black peppers, chilies. Even their tea is delicately spiced. Kashmiri food often has a red appearance owing to the liberal use of the Kashmiri chili, which is not very hot but provides flavour and colour. I've had meals in Srinagar in which every course was meat, including a mincemeat dessert.

Modern Bombay boasts of hundreds of instant products; the label on one reads: 'Instant Dal. SAVE time, labour, money. By adding only water, READY within three minutes'. Side by side with this evidence of 'progress', Gujarati-speaking people of Bombay still relish more traditional foods. One great favourite is a paper-thin bread, eaten with the pulp of the best seasonal mangoes. This bread is made by dipping two balls of whole-wheat dough into fat and flour, rolling them out together very thinly, and toasting them on a hot griddle. The two layers are then separated, making an even finer, lighter bread. Another favourite is *undhya* (meaning upside down). Whole, often unpeeled vegetables, coated with oil, red pepper, garlic, ginger, fenugreek, coriander, fennel, and cumin, are put into an earthenware pot and covered with moistened hay. The pot is then turned upside down over smouldering cinders.

In Madras, it is customary to eat on the floor, out of a banana leaf, which serves as a plate. A mountain of rice is piled on the leaf, and a visitor unaccustomed to the southern ways begins to wonder how he can ever find room for all that rice. The host's deft hands quickly make a crater-like hole in the mountaintop, and into this is poured the highly spiced hot *sambar* (yellow lentils, cooked with asafetida, fenugreek, coriander, cumin, turmeric, chilies, mustard seed, and tamarind, to which have been added sliced vegetables such as tomatoes, onions, and aubergine). This is eaten with great relish, the entire palm of the right hand, from fingertips to wrist, being used to transport the food from leaf to mouth. The Northerners tend to look down on the Southerners for what they consider to be rather messy eating habits. In the

North, the finicky pale when they see anyone soiling more than the top section of his fingers with food. I remember being scolded by my mother for letting the food slip from fingertip to mid-finger. Whenever that happened, she would say, 'Chhi, chhi, chhi' (dirty, dirty, dirty) and make me wash my hand. Whether we soil the digital end or the whole palm, one thing at least is generally true of all Indians: we like to eat with our hands. For this reason we have strict rules about washing hands and mouths before and after meals. This rule is followed meticulously by the poorest villager and the richest urbanite.

Some day, I hope, books will be written about all of India's cuisines—Gujarati food, Malayali food, Assamese food, Punjabi food, Maharashtrian food, Sindhi food, Bengali food, Goan food, Kashmiri food, Hyderabadi food, to name just a few. But until that happens, my book can introduce you to the smells and tastes which *I* grew up with as a child in Delhi and which I have struggled over the years to re-create in an English kitchen. These dishes, some traditional and some adapted to the produce in English supermarkets, you can now cook in your own homes instead of having to rely on second-rate eating places or the mercy of Indian acquaintances.

Two words of advice

Avoid using aluminium pans when cooking with any ingredients that have acidity.

If you aren't familiar with Indian cooking, it is wise to grind, measure, and set out *all* your ingredients before starting the cooking because so often parts of a recipe require that you work without interruption.

Sample menus

Kheema with fried onions
Green beans with onion paste
Moong dal
Rice with potatoes and cumin seeds
Yogurt with spinach
Chopped onions in vinegar
Gulab jamun · Fruit

Koftas (Indian meatballs)
Potatoes with asafetida and cumin
Rice with peas and whole spices or *Parathas*
Chana masaledar
Yogurt with tiny dumplings (boondi-ka-dahi)
Cucumber and tomato with lemon juice
Kheer · Fruit

Chicken cutlets
Sookhe aloo ('dry' potatoes)
Green beans with ginger
Rice with cauliflower and cumin seeds
Gulab jamun · Fruit

Chicken with tomato sauce and butter
Whole pea pods with cumin
Maya's potatoes
Chapati or Plain boiled rice
Cucumber *raita*
Malpua · Fruit

Prawn with dill and ginger
Crisp fried okra
Rice with spinach cooked in aromatic broth
Yogurt with potatoes
Tamarind chutney with bananas
Kheer · Fruit

'Butterflied' leg of lamb, marinated and barbecued
Green beans with onion paste
Rice with spinach
Cucumber and tomato with lemon juice
Kheer · Fruit

Pullao (rice with lamb)
Shrimp with peas and green coriander
Cauliflower with onion and tomato
Aubergine *bharta* (smoked aubergine)
Yogurt with potatoes
Chopped onions in vinegar
Kheer · Fruit

Tandoori chicken
Rice with cauliflower and cumin seeds
Naan
Whole unhulled *urad* and *rajma dal*
Onions pickled in vinegar
Cucumber and tomato with lemon juice
Kulfi · Fruit

Sea bass in green chutney
Cauliflower with ginger and green coriander
Buttered saffron rice
Sweet tomato chutney
Kulfi · Fruit

Pork chops à la Jaffrey
Green beans with onion paste
Sweet rice with carrots and raisins
Cucumber and tomato with lemon juice
Gajar-ka-halva · Fruit

Green peppers stuffed with kheema
Okra with onions
Plain boiled rice
Karhi (with *pakoris*)
Carrots pickled in oil
Gulab jamun · Fruit

Sindhi gosht (Sindhi meat)
Fried aubergines with sour green chutney
Cabbage with onions
Pooris or *Parathas*
Tomato and onion with lemon juice
Malpua · Fruit

Menu for a party

Koftas (Indian meatballs)
Pullao (rice with lamb)
Prawn with brown sauce
Cauliflower with ginger and green coriander
Whole unhulled *urad* and *rajma dal*
Yogurt with spinach
Cucumber and tomato with lemon juice
Tamarind chutney with bananas
Kheer · Fruit

Vegetarian

Green beans with onion paste
Fried aubergines with sour green chutney
Chickpeas with garlic and ginger
Rice with peas and whole spices
Cucumber and tomato with lemon juice
Kulfi · Fruit

Cabbage leaves stuffed with potatoes
Green beans with ginger
Black-eyed peas (*lobhia*)
Rice with spinach
Yogurt with tiny dumplings (*boondi-ka-dahi*)
Kheer · Fruit

Okra with onions
Cauliflower with onion and tomato
Pyazwale sookhe aloo ('dry' potatoes with onions)
Lentils
Parathas
Fresh mint chutney with fruit
Cucumber and tomato with lemon juice
Fried dates · Fruit

Cauliflower with ginger and green coriander
Aubergine *bharta* (smoked aubergine)
Mushrooms with cumin and asafetida
Sookhe aloo ('dry' potatoes)
Moong dal
Pooris
Cucumber *raita*
Gulab iamun · Fruit

Potatoes in thick sauce
Green beans with onion paste
Mushrooms with cumin and asafetida
Basmati rice with spices and saffron
Masoor dal with vegetables
Yogurt with roasted aubergine (*baigan-ka-bharta*)
Tamarind chutney with bananas
Fruit

Chickpeas with garlic and ginger
Cauliflower with onion and tomato
Bhaturas
Yogurt with potatoes
Carrot 'water' pickle or Onions pickled ⸱ in
    vinegar
Yogurt with spinach
Malpua

Karhi (with *pakoris*)
Cauliflower with ginger and green coriander
Stuffed whole okra
Plain boiled rice or Plain *basmati* rice
Tomato and onion with lemon juice
Tamarind chutney with bananas
Gajar-ka-halva · Fruit

Menu for a party

Cauliflower with ginger and green coriander
Whole pea pods with cumin
Cabbage with onions
Mushrooms with cumin and asafetida
New potatoes cooked in their jackets
Fried aubergines with sour green chutney
Rice with spinach
Whole unhulled *urad* and *rajma dal* with Fried
   onion rings for garnishing
Yogurt with tiny dumplings (*boondi-ka-dahi*)
Sweet tomato chutney
Cucumber raita
Kheer · Fruit

A note on flavourings

Most of the spices used for Indian cooking are available in English supermarkets. It is best to buy spices whole, as they tend to retain their flavour for longer periods. They can be ground at home in an electric blender or coffee-grinder in small quantities and then stored in tightly covered containers. (A mortar and pestle can be used to crush spices, but it will not grind them finely.)

There are, however, certain spices and ingredients which are unavailable in local supermarkets. These can generally be found in or obtained by mail from specialist suppliers.

There are also some special herbs which give Indian foods their characteristic flavours—like green coriander and ginger. The best places to find such ingredients are Chinese, Middle Eastern, or Indian grocery stores.

AMCHOOR Raw mango, dried and ground. It makes food tangy and sour. In North India it is used as freely as lemon is in American cooking. It also comes in dried slices.

ASAFETIDA A smelly resin which is used in very small quantities for vegetarian foods. It is available as a lump, or broken into pebbles, or powdered. The lump variety is generally the purest. Break off tiny chips (with a hammer, if necessary) and keep the rest in a tightly covered jar.

CARDAMOM   Three varieties are available in England: the greenish pod and the slightly plumper whitish pod are the most common. The seeds in the greenish pod are generally more fragrant. The cardamom pod is sometimes used whole, and at other times the skin is discarded and the seeds are ground (a clean pepper mill is excellent for this) and sprinkled over meats and desserts. There is also a large black cardomom which is used for certain rice and meat dishes. When this is unavailable, either variety of the smaller cardamom can be substituted. For cardamom as a mouth freshener, see page 843.

CAYENNE PEPPER   Same as ground red pepper. Use with discretion.

CINNAMON   Indians use both stick and ground cinnamon. Stick cinnamon is used whole in certain meat and rice dishes, whereas ground cinnamon is used in meat sauces and vegetables.

COCONUT   When you buy a coconut, make sure it is not cracked. Shake it to make sure it contains liquid. Even though this liquid is later discarded, it ensures a moist inside. To open, hit the coconut with a hammer and pry it apart. Get the meat out by sliding a sharp knife between the shell and the meat. Before grating the coconut, cut off the dark brown crust on the meat. To roast grated coconut, place it in a heavy frying-pan (iron is best) over a medium flame. Stir for 3 to 4 minutes or until it begins to turn brown.

CORIANDER   Coriander seeds can be used whole, ground, or roasted. To roast coriander, place desired amount of ground coriander in a heavy frying-pan (iron is best) over a medium flame. Stir for 2 to 3 minutes or until coriander turns a few shades darker. Be careful not to burn it. When buying ground coriander, purchase in small quantities.

CORIANDER LEAVES   Called small *cilantro* in Spanish shops, fresh coriander or fresh *dhania* in Indian food shops, and Chinese parsley in Chinese shops, it is used in our food as a herb and a garnish. If unavailable, Italian or ordinary parsley can be substituted. If you have a herb garden, you can grow your own fresh coriander by planting coriander seeds and waiting until the plants are about 10 inches high. Keep the leaves refrigerated in a plastic bag. *N.B.* Dried coriander powder cannot be substituted for fresh green coriander.

CUMIN   Indians use this spice whole, ground, or roasted. To roast cumin, place desired amount of whole seeds in heavy frying-pan (iron is best) over a medium flame. Stir 2 or 3 minutes or until seeds turn a darker brown. Remove from heat. The cumin can now be ground on an Indian grinding stone if you happen to have one, or it can be crushed just as easily with a mortar and pestle or with a rolling pin. It is best when freshly roasted, but you could keep it a few days in a tightly covered jar. In North India, ground roasted cumin is sprinkled over many yogurt relishes, snacks, and cooked vegetables. When buying ground cumin, purchase in small quantities. There is also an expensive, aromatic, black cumin seed.

DRY RED PEPPERS   Dry red peppers or dry red chilies are available in many sizes with just as many variations in their degrees of potency. The kind I have used in my recipes are about an inch long and *very* hot. I generally use them whole. Remember that red peppers are not essential to Indian food. If you don't like them you can use fewer than suggested or none at all. If whole red peppers are used in cooking, it is a good idea to remove them before serving. They are deadly if bitten into!

FENNEL   The fennel seed is really a larger, plumper sister of the anise seed. It is excellent in vegetables. It is also roasted and used as an after-dinner freshener — see page 843.

FENUGREEK   Fenugreek seeds are yellow in colour and rather flat. Since their taste borders on bitterness, very few are used at a time. They are excellent with aubergine and potatoes.

GARAM MASALA   This is a mixture of several 'hot' spices, generally prepared ahead of time in small quantities and used as needed to flavour meats and vegetables. It can be bought in delicatessens, but has a fresher taste if you grind it yourself. To make about 3 tablespoons, you will need:

- 1 tablespoon cardamom seeds
- 1 2-inch stick cinnamon
- 1 teaspoon black peppercorns
- 1 teaspoon black cumin seeds
- 1 teaspoon whole cloves
- ¼ of an average-sized nutmeg

Combine all ingredients and grind very fine, in a coffee-grinder reserved for spices. (If you want to make your *garam masala* less hot, decrease the amount of black peppercorns and increase the cumin proportionately.) Store in a tightly covered container, away from sunlight and dampness. If carefully stored, this *garam masala* can be kept for a couple of months.

GHEE   *Ghee* is the cooking medium used in many parts of India. There are two kinds of *ghee*. *Usli ghee* or clarified butter is used rarely, partly because of its expense and partly because many Indians consider it 'heavy'. The more commonly used *ghee* is a mixture of various vegetable oils. See page 528 in the Introduction. I tend to use unsaturated oils for most of my cooking. Many Indians use peanut oil or mustard oil. Use whatever you prefer. If you wish to make *usli ghee* or clarified butter, here is how you do it: Melt butter. Pour off the clear liquid, discarding the milky residue. Boil the clear liquid for a minute or two. Cool. Store, covered, in the refrigerator.

GINGER   This is a tan-skinned, knobbly rhizome with a sharp, pungent taste, available in Indian and Chinese food shops. Some delicatessens carry it as well. It is used for making meat dishes, vegetables, and chutneys. Ginger is generally peeled and then grated or ground. It is easier to grate it if you don't break off the needed section but rather grate it off the whole piece instead. To grind it, chop it coarsely and place in electric blender with a little water. To store ginger, cover it well with plastic wrap and keep in the refrigerator. It is good until it begins to mould. Another way to keep it is to plant it (bury it) in sandy soil. Water it infrequently. It not only stays fresh this way but also sprouts fresh knobs. Cut off what you need and put the rest back in the soil. Dried ginger 'root' (called so mistakenly) is bottled and put out by major spice companies. This can be used as a second-best substitute. It is preferable to powdered ginger, which in India is considered to be so different from fresh ginger that it is called by another name altogether. Follow the instructions on the bottle for presoaking, which must be done a few hours before you plan to cook.

GREEN CHILIES Fresh, hot green peppers or chilies are available in some Chinese, Indian, Spanish, and Italian shops. Since chilies vary in their strength, caution must be exercised in using them. The hottest part of the chilies is their seeds, and there are more seeds near the stem. Ideally, each chili should be sampled before being used. You can cut it in half and take the tiniest bite from its centre. If it is hot use it sparingly. Most Indians can generally gauge the hotness of a chili by breaking it in two and just smelling it. As a substitute, tinned Mexican *jalapeños* or cayenne pepper can be used. Neither has the taste of a green chili, but both are hot. (See instructions for substitutions in individual recipes.)

KALONJI These are black onion seeds which are used occasionally for meat dishes and often for vegetables. If you can't find them, leave them out of the recipe.

KARI LEAVES Fresh leaves from the *Kari* tree, used as flavouring. There are really no substitutes for this. The dried leaves, more freely available, seem to lack both aroma and flavour.

MUSTARD SEEDS We generally use black mustard seeds, but if you cannot find them, yellow mustard seeds may be substituted. For some recipes, mustard seeds need to be crushed. This is best done with a heavy mortar and pestle or an electric coffee-grinder.

NUTMEG Buy whole nutmeg and store it in a tightly closed jar. Use a nutmeg grater and grate whenever needed.

POPPY SEEDS We use the white poppy seeds. They are generally ground before being cooked. To facilitate grinding, roast them first. Place them in a heavy frying pan (iron is best) over a medium flame. Stir them around for 3 to 4 minutes. Now they can be ground with an Indian grinding stone or in a coffee-grinder. If white poppy seeds cannot be found, do without them.

SAFFRON This very expensive stigma of the crocus flower is used in Moghlai meat and rice dishes as well as in desserts. Ideally, saffron stigmas or 'leaf' saffron should be lightly roasted in a hot frying-pan, crumbled, and allowed to soak in a tablespoon or so of warm milk before being used.

TAMARIND PASTE The tamarind is a kind of bean, which grows on large trees. For commercial use it is peeled, seeded, and pressed into a lump. Indians use its paste to add a special kind of tartness to their foods. Lump tamarind is available in Indian and Middle Eastern groceries in Britain. These shops also sell a bottled tamarind paste, but this is often extremely fermented. To make your own tamarind paste, break or pull a golf-ball-sized piece from the lump tamarind and soak it in $\frac{1}{4}$ pint hot water for 3 to 4 hours or overnight. Use a small, non-metallic cup or bowl. Press pulp through a strainer and reserve. (You may need to add extra water to the strainer in order to dislodge all the pulp.) Discard whatever is left in the strainer. Covered tamarind pulp can be stored several days in the refrigerator. Lump tamarind should be wrapped in a plastic bag and stored in the refrigerator. It will last for months.

TURMERIC This spice is really a boiled-down root which is

available in small lumps in India but only in its ground form in Britain. It is this yellow spice which gives colouring to a lot of our foods. It burns easily, so care should be taken when cooking with it.

VARK These are extremely fine, delicate sheets of real silver (or gold) foil, used for garnishing. (They *are* eaten.) When you buy them, generally each sheet is between 2 layers of tissue paper. *You cannot lift a sheet by picking it up with your hands:* it will disintegrate or fly away. Remove one layer of tissue paper carefully, leaving the *vark* on the other sheet. Slide your hand under the paper and invert the *vark* on the food. Garnish thinly, as you should not really be able to taste the *vark*. The effect is prettier when the *vark* lies on the food in an unbroken sheet, but it's all right if it disintegrates slightly. *Vark* is available only at Indian stores. Since it can tarnish, like any real silver, it should be stored in a dark, airtight container.

Kitchen utensils &
other equipment

Here is a list of some utensils which are found only in Indian kitchens.

CHIMTA   These flat, smooth-edged, long tongs are used for everything from picking up live coals to turning over bread.

KARHAI   This is a utensil for deep frying. Like the Chinese wok, it is curved at the bottom and very wide at the top, resembling half-moon. It can be made of cast iron, aluminium, stainless steel, or brass.

KATORI   Small bowl made out of gold, silver, stainless steel, or aluminium, used to serve individual portions of meat, vegetables, and *dals*. Often several filled *katoris* are arranged on a *thali* and the *thali* is then placed before the diner.

MUTKA   Round pot of half-baked clay used for storing water and excellent for making 'water pickles'.

PARAAT   This is a large, wide-rimmed brass tray, used for kneading bread. It is also used as a serving tray at weddings.

SIL BATTA   The North Indian grinding stone comes in 2 sections. The *sil*, or larger stone, is about a foot long, 9 inches wide, and 2 inches high. It is pockmarked with tiny, shallow ridges. Food is placed on this larger stone for grinding. The grinding is done by the *batta*, the second, smaller, half-moon-shaped stone, which is about 6 inches long and 1½ inches thick. (*N.B.* The sizes and shapes of Indian grinding stones vary in the different states.)

TANDOOR   A large clay oven utilizing coal or wood as fuel and used for baking chicken, fish, meat, lentils, and breads. Very popular in the Punjab.

TAVA   This is a slightly curved, cast-iron plate, useful for making breads and patties.

THALI OR THAL   Gold, silver, brass, or aluminium tray used both for serving and as a plate. The Bohris of Gujarat place a large *thal* on a stool and use it as a table.

Soups & Appetizers

SOUPS

Mulligatawny soup
White soup (safed sarvo)
Dal soup
Potato soup
Cold yogurt soup

APPETIZERS

Khatte aloo (sour potatoes)
Vegetable pakoris
Pappadums, or papars
Seekh kabab flat style
Left-over ham on toast
Pacific king prawns on toothpicks
Whole-wheat samosas
Cocktail koftas
Grilled chicken strips

SEE ALSO

Vegetables stuffed with kheema (pages 588–90)

WHILE India does not, as a nation, drink soup, we have, fortunately, many communities within the subcontinent that insist on being exceptions to the rule. The Anglo-Indians (a 300-year-old community with a mixed English and Indian heritage) make a delicious mulligatawny soup (a corruption of the Tamil words *milagu-tannir*, meaning 'pepper water') with meat and chickpea flour, and the Bohris of Gujarat make a superb 'white soup' (*safed sarvo*) with goat's meat and milk.

The appetizers you will find in this chapter are those among the Indian 'snack' foods that can be most conveniently eaten with drinks—triangular *samosas*, filled with meat or potatoes, vegetable fritters, and minced meat *kababs*. *Kababs*, often sprinkled with finely sliced onion rings, are favourites among Indian Scotch drinkers. The North Indian word for alcoholic beverages is *sharab*, and it is very interesting that the North Indian label for a man who drinks and eats well is *sharabi-kababi*!

Mulligatawny soup

Serves 4

Judging from the Tamil origin of the name 'mulligatawny' (see page 559), one might deduce that it originated in the Madras region 100 to 300 years ago under the benevolent gaze of British patronage. British in concept but Indian in its ingredients, this hearty soup became very popular with the Anglo-Indians scattered all across India, and there are probably as many recipes for it as there are Anglo-Indian families. My favourite was the one made by a family who eventually decided to migrate to Australia. The day before their departure they came to our house to say goodbye. I remember that we all sat out on the lawn and I begged them to leave their recipe for mulligatawny soup with me. This is their recipe.

4 cloves garlic, peeled and chopped

a piece of fresh ginger, about ½-inch cube, peeled and chopped

½ lb boneless lamb (from shoulder or leg), with fat removed, and cut into ¾-inch cubes

2 tbs vegetable oil

1 tbs white poppy seeds, roasted and ground (see page 552)

½ tsp ground coriander

½ tsp ground cumin

¼ tsp ground turmeric

½ tsp salt (more if the broth is unsalted)

⅛ tsp cayenne pepper (optional)

⅛ tsp freshly ground black pepper

2 tbs chickpea flour (*besan*)

1 pint chicken broth (tinned or homemade)

1 tbs lemon juice

2–3 tbs cooked rice, or 1–1½ tbs uncooked rice (optional)

Put the garlic and ginger into the container of an electric blender with 3 tablespoons of water. Blend at high speed until you have a smooth paste. Set aside.

Pat dry the pieces of lamb. Heat the oil in a 2-quart pot over medium-high flame, and add the meat. Turn, and fry until the pieces are lightly browned on all sides. Remove with slotted spoon and set aside. Turn the heat off.

To the same pot, add the paste from the blender, the roasted and ground poppy seeds, the coriander, cumin, and turmeric. Turn the heat to medium, and fry, stirring constantly, for about a minute. Turn heat to low.

Now add the browned meat and any juice that may have accumulated, the salt, cayenne, and black pepper. Stir and leave on low flame.

Combine chickpea flour and 4 tablespoons water in a bowl, mixing thoroughly until you have a smooth paste. Slowly add the chicken broth, stirring as you do so. Pour this mixture over the meat in the pot. Turn heat to high and bring soup to the boil. Add uncooked rice if you are using it. Cover, lower heat, and simmer gently for half an hour or until meat is tender. Stir in the lemon juice.

If you are using cooked rice, mix it into the soup just before serving. Pour the soup into a tureen or into individual bowls. Mulligatawny soup can be served with both Indian and Western-style meals. Since it is thick and fairly filling, it can be a main course for lunch or a light supper followed by a green salad and fruit.

White soup
(safed sarvo)

Serves 4–6

This relatively unknown but delicious soup is made by the Bohris of Gujarat. It is brought to the table in a large serving bowl. The eldest lady of the house then asks how many people want their soup flavoured with lemon, and she squeezes fresh lemon over one section, leaving the rest plain. Next, she ladles the soup into small Chinese-style bowls, the lemony part of the soup going to those who asked for it. The white colour comes from the milk and almonds (or cashews, if you like).

4 cloves garlic, peeled and chopped

a piece of fresh ginger, about ½-inch cube

1½ lbs neck of lamb, with bone left in, cut into 1–1½-inch cubes

1 medium-sized onion, finely chopped

1¾ pints beef broth (tinned or fresh; do not use bouillon)

½ tsp salt (more if beef broth is unsalted)

1 bay leaf

1 tbs blanched slivered almonds (or unroasted cashews)

½ pint milk

4 tbs whole-wheat flour (use plain flour as substitute)

⅛ tsp cayenne pepper (optional)

1 tbs vegetable oil

⅛ tsp whole cumin seeds

Garnish

2 tbs fresh mint leaves, chopped (parsley may be substituted)

1 lemon cut into 6 wedges

Put the garlic and ginger into the container of an electric blender, along with 4 tablespoons water. Blend at high speed until you have a smooth paste.

In a largish pot, combine the meat, chopped onions, garlic and ginger paste, beef broth, salt, and bay leaf. Bring to the boil. Cover, and simmer gently for 1½ hours.

Meanwhile, soak the blanched almonds in the milk.

In a small, heavy-bottomed frying-pan, dry-roast the whole-wheat flour over a medium flame, stirring constantly until the flour is 2 or 3 shades darker (this should take about 3 minutes). Then turn off flame and pour flour into a medium-sized bowl.

When the soup has cooked for an hour and a half, take out a teacup of the boiling liquid and mix it well with the roasted whole-wheat flour in the bowl. When the mixture is smooth, pour it back into the pot of soup.

Put the milk and almonds into the blender and blend at high speed until you have a thin, smooth paste. Add to the simmering soup.

Taste the soup. Add cayenne if you desire.

Heat the oil in a small frying-pan over a medium flame. When hot, put in the whole cumin seeds, stirring for a few seconds until seeds begin to pop and darken, then add to the soup. Stir soup again. Turn off heat and leave soup covered.

To serve: This soup can be served with or without the pieces of meat (remove bay leaf though!). Garnish with chopped mint leaves and serve lemon wedges on the side.

Dal soup

Serves 8

My mother used to make this mild-flavoured 'split-pea' soup. The only spices in it were cloves, peppercorns, and turmeric. It was served with lemon wedges and homemade croutons.

10 oz green or yellow split peas, washed

2½ pints chicken broth (tinned or homemade)

24 black peppercorns and

15 whole cloves (tied in cheesecloth)

½ tsp ground turmeric

½–¾ tsp salt (more if broth is unsalted)

Garnish

8 lemon wedges

croutons made from 6 slices of slightly stale bread and

enough vegetable oil to cover ½–¾ inch in a 10-inch frying-pan

Combine the split peas and chicken broth in a pot and bring to the boil. Remove scum from the top.

Add the spices in the cheesecloth, the turmeric, and the salt. Cover, lower heat, and simmer gently for 1 to 1½ hours or until peas are tender. Remove cheesecloth from soup, squeeze its juices into soup, and discard. Check salt.

Press the soup through a strainer, using the back of a wooden spoon, or put it through a food mill. If the soup seems too thick, add a little water.

To serve: Heat soup. Serve in bowls, garnished with a lemon wedge. Pass around croutons on the side.

To make croutons: (These can be prepared ahead of time.)

Remove crusts and cut slices of bread into ½-inch cubes.

Heat oil in frying-pan over medium flame, and put in a third of the croutons. Fry for 3 or 4 minutes, turning them around, until they are golden brown. Lift out with slotted spoon and leave to drain on paper towels. Prepare the rest of the croutons in two more batches, and leave to drain.

Potato soup

Serves 4

1 tbs vegetable oil
a pinch of ground asafetida
  or a $\frac{1}{16}$-inch pebble broken
  from the chunk asafetida
¼ tsp whole cumin seeds
2 medium-sized potatoes,
  peeled and quartered

2 tbs tomato purée
¼ tsp ground turmeric
1¼ tsp salt
⅛ tsp cayenne pepper
  (optional)

Heat the oil in a 3-quart pot over a medium flame, put in the asafetida and the cumin, and stir once. In a few seconds, when the cumin seeds begin to sizzle, add the quartered potatoes, tomato purée, turmeric, salt, and cayenne. Stir, and continue to fry for 2 minutes.

Add 1¾ pints of water and bring to the boil. Cover and simmer gently for 45 minutes.

Turn off heat and lift cover. Mash potatoes coarsely with a potato masher or with the back of a slotted spoon.

To serve: Pour soup into small bowls or *katoris* (see page 555) and serve.

Cold yogurt soup

Serves 4

Here is a very refreshing summer soup.

½ pint plain yogurt
¼ pint double cream
⅓–½ tsp salt
a sprinkling of freshly
  ground black pepper

4 tbs peeled and grated
  cucumber
10–12 fresh mint leaves,
  finely chopped

Combine all ingredients in bowl with ¼ pint of cold water. Mix well. Cover and chill for several hours until ready to serve.

To serve: Serve on hot days in small chilled bowls or *katoris* (see page 555).

Khatte aloo
(sour potatoes)

Serves 10–12

This is an adaptation of a street-side snack to be found in different forms all over North India.

7 medium-sized potatoes,
  boiled ahead of time, and
  set aside for at least 2
  hours to cool
1½ tsp salt (or to taste)
2–3 tbs lemon juice (or to
  taste)

2 tsp ground roasted cumin
  (see page 549)
¼ tsp freshly ground pepper
¼–½ tsp cayenne pepper
2 tbs finely chopped fresh
  green coriander

Peel the cooled potatoes and dice them into ½-inch cubes. Place in large bowl. Add remaining ingredients. Mix well. Check to see if salt and lemon juice are in correct proportion.

To serve: Place potatoes on platter and stick with toothpicks. Serve with drinks.

Vegetable pakoris

Serves 6–8

These *pakoris* are vegetable fritters—similar to Japanese tempura. They are generally eaten with tea, but there is no reason why they cannot be served with drinks. I have specified potatoes in this recipe, but you could use any of the following instead:

1-inch flowerets of cauliflower (a small head), or $\frac{1}{16}$-inch-thick onion rings (4 medium-sized onions), or Italian peppers, cut in half lengthwise ($\frac{1}{2}$-$\frac{3}{4}$ lb)

You can also make a plate of mixed *pakoris*, using different vegetables. Chickpea flour is very light, so do weigh it.

The batter

4 oz chickpea flour (*besan*), sifted
$\frac{1}{4}$ tsp salt
$\frac{1}{4}$ tsp ground turmeric
$\frac{1}{4}$ tsp ground cumin
$\frac{1}{4}$ tsp baking soda
$\frac{1}{8}$ tsp freshly ground pepper
$\frac{1}{8}$ tsp cayenne pepper (optional)

The filling

3 medium-sized potatoes, peeled (or other vegetables —see above)
vegetable oil, enough for $2\frac{1}{2}$–3 inches in wok,
karhai (see page 555), or other utensil for deep frying
salt and pepper for sprinkling on cooked pakoris

Put the chickpea flour in a bowl. Gradually mix in about 7 fl. oz. water, until you have a thickish batter—thick enough to coat the vegetables. Add the other batter ingredients and mix well.

Cut the potatoes into rounds $\frac{1}{16}$ inch thick, and put into a bowl of cold water.

Heat oil over a low flame until hot but not smoking. Take a few potato slices at a time, wipe them dry, and dip them in the batter. Now drop them into the oil. Fry slowly, 7 to 10 minutes on each side, until they are cooked through and have turned a golden-brown. Remove with slotted spoon and drain on paper towels. Sprinkle with salt and pepper. Do all *pakoris* this way, never putting in more at one time than your deep-frying utensil will hold in one layer.

To serve: Serve *pakoris* while they are crisp and hot with either the Fresh Green Chutney with Coriander Leaves and Yogurt or Fresh Mint Chutney with Fruit. The chutney is used as a dip. If you're feeling lazy, tomato ketchup or Chinese duck sauce or a combination of soy sauce, white vinegar, grated fresh ginger, and a dash of Tabasco can be used as alternative dips.

Pappadums, or papars

Serves 8–10

Pappadums (as they are called in the South) or *papars* (as they are called in the North) are wafers, usually made out of a *dal* dough which is rolled out and dried. (You can also buy *sago* wafers and potato wafers, but they are less popular.) *Papars* can be bought in delicatessens in two basic varieties — spiced and unspiced. The spiced ones often have a liberal sprinkling of crushed black pepper in them. They are deep-fried in hot oil and served at cocktail parties. The frying takes just a few seconds. *Papars* cannot be fried too far in advance, as any moisture in the air tends to make them go limp and they should be crisp. *Papars* come in several sizes. The large ones can be broken in half and then fried. They expand a bit as they are cooked. Before you set out to make them, put a large platter, well lined with paper towels, beside the stove to drain the *papars*.

10 papars or pappadums
oil for deep-frying, enough
   for 2 inches in 10-inch
   frying-pan

Heat oil in frying-pan over medium flame. When hot, put in one *papar*. It should sizzle and expand immediately. (If it doesn't, your oil is not hot enough!) Turn it over, leave for a few seconds, and remove with slotted spoon. Place on platter with paper towels and drain. Do all *papars* this way, one at a time. If they begin to brown, your oil is too hot. Turn down the heat. The *papars* should retain their yellow colour.

To serve: Serve warm or at room temperature with drinks.

Seekh kabab,
flat style

Serves 8–10

This version of the ground meat *kabab* is excellent to serve with drinks and to take out on picnics. The meat and spices can be combined a night in advance and left, covered, in the refrigerator.

½ medium-sized onion,
   peeled and chopped
4 cloves garlic, peeled and
   chopped

3 tbs lemon juice
4 tbs chickpea flour (*besan*)
2½ lbs minced lamb or beef,
   minced three times

a piece of fresh ginger,
   about 1-inch cube, peeled
   and chopped
20 whole black peppercorns
10 whole cloves
seeds from 8 cardamom pods
1 fresh hot green chili,
   sliced (optional)
½ tsp ground nutmeg
½ tsp ground cinnamon

1 teacup (loosely packed)
   chopped fresh green
   coriander
1 tsp ground cumin
1 tsp ground coriander
1½ tsp salt
½ tsp cayenne pepper
   (optional – use as desired)
1 egg, beaten
5 tbs melted butter

In the container of an electric blender, combine the chopped onions, garlic, ginger, peppercorns, cloves, cardamom seeds, green chili, nutmeg, cinnamon, and lemon juice. Blend at high speed until you have a smooth paste.

Heat a small iron frying-pan over medium flame. Put in the chickpea flour and stir until it is 2 or 3 shades darker. Remove from heat.

In a large bowl, combine the meat, the chopped green coriander, the contents of the blender container, the cumin, coriander, salt, cayenne, and roasted chickpea flour. Mix well with your hands. Cover and refrigerate until ready to grill (overnight if convenient).

Take meat out of refrigerator 45 minutes before serving.

Preheat grill.

Add beaten egg to meat and mix well.

Line 10-by-15-inch baking tray with aluminium foil, and brush it with half the melted butter.

Spread the meat mixture in the tray: it should be ⅓ to ½ inch thick. Brush the top with the rest of the melted butter. Place under grill, 3 to 4 inches away from heat. Grill until golden brown, about 15 to 20 minutes. Remove with a bulb baster any liquid that may accumulate.

Cut meat into 1½–2-inch squares.

Serve hot, or cold, with Raw Onion Rings and Fresh Green Chutney with Coriander Leaves and Yogurt or Fresh Mint Chutney with Fruit.

Left-over ham on toast

Serves 8–10

This dish of my own devising can be made with any left-over roasts. I have used ham, but you could use lamb or beef or pork, in which case salt should be added.

2 teacups (well packed) diced cooked ham
1 medium-sized potato, boiled, peeled, and diced
½ medium-sized onion, peeled and chopped
1 tsp fresh ginger, peeled and grated
2 cloves garlic, peeled and chopped finely
¼ teacup washed fresh green coriander
⅛ tsp freshly ground pepper
¼ tsp cayenne pepper (optional — use as desired)

⅛ tsp ground cloves
⅛ tsp ground nutmeg
⅛ tsp ground cinnamon
3 tbs tamarind paste (see page 552) or 1½ tbs lemon juice
rounds of small cocktail rye bread, or Melba toasts, or any firm bread slices, crust removed, cut into 4 rectangles
3 tbs melted butter

Put the ham, potato, onion, ginger, garlic, and green coriander through the fine blade of a meat grinder. Add black pepper, cayenne pepper, cloves, nutmeg, cinnamon, and tamarind paste or lemon juice. Mix well with hands. You can do this much ahead of time and keep it covered in refrigerator.

Twenty-five minutes before serving time, preheat grill.

If using bread, spread out as many slices as will fit on a large baking sheet, and lightly toast one side. Remove from grill.

Spread other side with the ham paste ¼–⅓ inch thick. (Melba toasts do not need to be browned. You can just spread ham mixture on them directly.) Make sure the edges of bread or Melba toast are covered or you will burn them. Brush with melted butter. Grill 7 to 8 minutes or until golden-brown. Do as many batches as you need.

To serve: Place on platter and serve hot with drinks.

Pacific king prawns on toothpicks

Serves 4

5 cloves garlic, peeled and
  chopped
a piece of fresh ginger,
  about 1-inch cube, peeled
  and chopped
1½ lbs Pacific king prawns
  peeled and deveined (see
  page 655)

3 tbs vegetable oil
3 tbs tomato purée
½ tsp ground turmeric
1 tbs lemon juice
¾ tsp salt
⅛–¼ tsp cayenne pepper

Put the garlic and ginger in the container of an electric blender
along with 3 tablespoons water. Blend at high speed until you
have a smooth paste.

Wash prawns well and pat them dry. Cut each prawn into 3
sections. Set aside.

Heat oil in 10–12-inch frying-pan over medium flame. When
hot, pour in the paste from blender and fry, stirring constantly,
for 2 minutes. Add tomato purée and turmeric. Fry and stir
another 2 minutes. Add 4 tablespoons water, the lemon juice,
salt, and cayenne pepper. Cover, and simmer gently for 2 to 3
minutes. (This much can be done in advance.)

Five minutes before serving time, lift off cover, put in the
prawns, and turn heat to high. Stir and fry the prawns for about
5 minutes or until they just turn opaque.

To serve: Place on platter and stick toothpicks into each
prawn piece. Serve hot.

Whole-wheat samosas

Serves 8–10

Samosas are deep-fried patties, filled with potatoes or ground meat. I have a simple version of them. This is how they are made. (For stuffing use recipe for *Sookhe Aloo*, page 722, or *Kheema*, page 584).

8 oz whole-wheat flour	**½ tsp salt**
3 tbs vegetable oil (plus a little extra for brushing on dough)	**vegetable oil for deep frying, enough for 3–3½ inches in pot**

Combine oil and flour and rub together. Add salt and mix. Add about 8 fl. oz. water, a little at a time, until you have a firm dough. Knead the dough well for 7 to 10 minutes, until smooth. Form into a ball. Brush with a little oil, and cover with a damp cloth. Set aside until ready for use.

If using *Sookhe Aloo* for stuffing, cook it according to the recipe and then crush potatoes coarsely with the back of a slotted spoon.

If using *Kheema* for stuffing, cook *Kheema* until it is very dry, with no liquid left at all. If any fat has accumulated, it should be discarded.

Divide dough into 28 to 30 equal balls. (Each ball makes 2 *samosas*, so you'll end up with about 60.) Flatten each ball and roll it out on a floured surface until it is 3½ to 4 inches in diameter. Cut each round in half. Taking one semicircle at a time, moisten half the length of the cut edge with a finger dipped in water. Form a wide cone with the semicircle, using the moist section to overlap ¼ inch and hold it closed. Fill *samosa* three-fourths full with the stuffing. Moisten the inside edges of the opening and press it shut. Seal this end by pressing down on the outside with the tip of a fork, as you would a pie crust. Prepare the *samosas* this way and keep them covered with a plastic wrap.

When you are ready to fry them, heat the oil in a wok, *karhai* (see page 555), or a utensil for deep frying. Keep the heat at medium. When oil is hot, drop a *samosa* in to check the temperature. It should start sizzling immediately. Fry 2 to 3 minutes, or until it looks a warm brown. Remove with slotted spoon and drain on paper towels. Do all *samosas* this way. If they brown too fast, lower your heat.

They can be reheated in a 300°F., Mark 3 oven.

To serve: Place *samosas* on platter and serve hot or warm with either Fresh Green Chutney with Coriander Leaves and Yogurt or Fresh Mint Chutney with Fruit. The chutney is used as a dip.

Cocktail koftas

Serves 15

Follow recipe on page 590. Make the *koftas* smaller, about ¾ inch in diameter. They can be made a day in advance, and then reheated.

When serving, keep *koftas* warm in chafing dish. Place toothpicks nearby to aid self-service.

Grilled chicken strips

Serves 8–10

See recipe on page 639. Instead of cutting chicken breasts into strips 1½ to 2 inches long, cut them into strips that are 1 inch long and ½ inch wide. Follow the rest of the recipe.

To serve: Place on warm platter and stick with toothpicks. Serve with drinks.

Meat

Khare masale ka gosht (meat with whole spices)
Pyazwala khare masale ka gosht (meat with whole spices and onions)
Kheema (minced meat)
Kheema with fried onions
Kheema with fried onions and peas
Kheema used as stuffing: for green peppers and long Italian peppers,
*   for tomatoes, for aubergines*
Koftas (Indian meatballs)
Nargisi koftas (large meatballs stuffed with hard-boiled eggs)
Cubed lamb with onions and raisins
Lamb with onions and mushrooms, or lamb do pyaza
Lamb korma
Lamb (or beef) korma with almonds, pecans, and sour cream
Lamb cooked in dark almond sauce (badami roghan josh)
Lamb with vinegar and mint
Lamb with spinach
Sindhi gosht (Sindhi meat)
Lamb chops with whole spices and yogurt
Pork chops cooked with whole spices and tamarind juice
Pork chops cooked with cabbage
Pork chops à la Jaffrey
Sweetbreads with fresh green coriander

SEE ALSO

Mulligatawny soup (page 560)
White soup (page 561)
Seekh kabab, flat style (page 568)
Left-over ham on toast (page 570)
'Butterflied' leg of lamb, marinated and barbecued (page 678)
Cubed leg of lamb, barbecued (page 681)
Boti kabab (cubed meat kabab) (page 681)
Kidney kabab (page 683)
Seekh kabab (page 683)
Marinated pork chops (page 686)
Pullao (page 763)
Chana dal cooked with lamb (page 782)

WHEN an Indian sits down to eat meat, it is nearly always goat meat. The English have translated the meat as mutton, but it is not to be confused with the aged sheep meat available in England, Australia, and New Zealand. Perhaps the English in India didn't know what else to call it—or perhaps they found a dish called 'mutton chops' more palatable than if it was called plain old 'goat chops'. Who knows!

At any rate, 'mutton' in India is not old sheep meat—far from it. It is usually *very* fresh goat meat and therefore not always very tender. Because of the lack of proper refrigeration facilities in India (most butchers cannot afford any) the animals are slaughtered daily and the meat is sold within 24 hours. In the richer homes it is then washed and refrigerated or frozen. But in the poorer homes it is cooked immediately. Since the meat is fairly tough, it is cooked slowly, over a longish period of time. For quicker fried and grilled dishes, the meat has to be tenderized first. The cheapest and most common tenderizer is crushed green papaya, but marinades of vinegar and yoghurt are also used.

Not only is Indian goat meat a little on the tough side; it is also very lean. The result is that we use a great deal of cooking fat to brown our meats. We tend to like this 'browned' look. When I buy lamb in Britain (lamb is the best substitute for the Indian 'mutton'), I first trim away all signs of fat. Then, to make it taste like the food I have in India, I cook it in lots of oil. This cooking fat can, of course, be removed later, once the dish is completely cooked, by spooning it off the top just before serving.

There is another significant difference in the quality of Indian meat which influences cooking techniques. In India, meat dropped into fat can be expected to fry, slowly or quickly, as the cook desires. Here, in Britain, if a pound of meat is put into oil to fry, unless one has taken careful preliminary steps, it will start boiling. The meat here gives off a lot of water, possibly because of prior freezing or because of the water-injecting habits of some butchers. There is no really good way to avoid this extra water, but defrosting frozen meat completely and wiping it well before cooking will be somewhat helpful. You can also fry the meat over a high flame in small quantities or boil off the extra liquid towards the end of the cooking time. As I go along I will tell you, in each recipe, which step to follow. What I want you to understand here is *why* an Indian meat dish cooked in Britain will never taste quite the same as it does in India.

Contrary to what most outsiders think, beef *is* eaten in India. About 80 per cent of India is Hindu (those who, technically, do not eat beef) but the other 20 per cent includes 60 million Muslims and 12 million Christians, i.e., 72 million people who can eat beef without battling with their consciences first. Every now and then, when it seems politic, there is a rousing debate in our parliament on the subject of cow slaughter. But while cows ('The cow is your mother', they say) are being heatedly discussed, no one is saying much about the buffalo (a kind of poor relation, I suppose), so this creature is being slaughtered and sold—though not always in the open market. A very popular dish in most 'Western'-style Indian restaurants is the 'sizzling' steak (alas—buffalo), and I must say I have seen many a Hindu devour this with great relish. It does not taste as good as the best English steak, but it is served very attractively right on the platter on which it is cooked, accompanied by a lot of hissing and sizzling vegetables.

When beef is cooked in the Indian manner, it is cooked like mutton, slowly, over a period of time. In some areas, beef is dried and then fried with onions and served at breakfast. I have also eaten it cooked with spinach and with potatoes. One strange thing that I have noticed about us Indians is that although many Hindus will eat beef in restaurants, in Muslim and Christian homes, and when they are abroad, very few will cook it in their own kitchens. Each country has its own varieties of national hypocrisy. Self-righteously proclaimed rules on diet and cleanliness seem to be part of our heritage.

Besides 'mutton' and beef, pork, lamb, and venison are also eaten in the areas where they are found. *Dumba*, a fan-tailed sheep, is used for a special *pullao* (a rice and meat dish) cooked at the Muslim festival *Id*. Venison, considered rather dry, is often made into *koftas* (meatballs) or *shami kababs* (ground meat patties).

Meat is, of course, cooked very differently in the different regions of India. Most of my recipes are for dishes eaten in and around my hometown, Delhi. I will start with the easier recipes. My aim is to interest you first, and then entice you on — slowly.

Cuts of meat to use

Generally, when Indians cook a simple, everyday meat dish, they use meat with bone. This could come from the neck, shoulder, shank, ribs, or elsewhere from the goat or sheep. Often they combine these different parts, add some chunks from the leg, and throw in a few extra dark marrow bones for good measure. (These coveted marrow bones, once cooked, are fought over by the children with the winner gleefully digging out the delicious marrow with long, slim spoons!) When I buy lamb in Britain for stew-type dishes, I use all the cuts just mentioned. But I find that the English, eating with a knife and and fork, do not seem to be much attracted to cubes of meat that are often three-fourths bone and one-fourth meat. When you eat with your hands, there is a great deal of pleasure to be derived from tearing meat off a bone with your teeth, and from sucking the bones. Since this is seldom done in Britain, I have limited myself a great deal to cubed, boned meat from shoulder of lamb. Any butcher will bone and trim the meat, but if you do not have access to a butcher you can buy shoulder chops from the supermarket and cut and trim them yourself. Just cut around the bones (these can be saved for soup), trim off the big concentrations of fat, and then cut the meat into 1–1½ inch cubes. Generally, you can assume a waste of about 40 to 50 per cent – so if you buy 4 lbs of shoulder chops, you are likely to end up with about 2 lbs of meat or a bit more.

Leg of lamb can be used for a great many of the following recipes that require cubed meat, but it tends to get rather dry when cooked in a stew-like manner. It should be saved for grills and barbecues (see the chapter on summer cooking, pages 673–92). However, if you wish to use it, cook it for the same length of time as meat from the shoulder – about an hour and fifteen minutes.

Neck and shank are excellent for stews but require longer cooking time – about 1½ to 2 hours. Serve them to people who like bones. You will need to buy about 4 lbs to serve 4–6 since so much of it will be bone. You will also need to increase the salt a bit as some of it will be absorbed by the marrow.

Stewing beef may be substituted for cubed lamb. Here again, increase the cooking time, in this case to about 2½ hours, and adjust the recipes accordingly.

Khare masale ka gosht
(meat with whole spices)

Serves 4–6

Here is my first meat recipe for this book. It is very easy to make and has a delicately flavoured taste. By placing it first, I hope to lure you all towards the more complicated and the more heavily spiced meat recipes. This dish is normally made with goat meat, using either the leg or the neck and shoulders, cubed into 1-inch pieces. If the neck and shoulders are used, the bones are always left in. Since we eat with our hands, none of the meat is wasted, the fingers making their way around the oddly shaped bones more easily than a knife and fork. You can, however, use either beef or lamb. If you use beef, get cubed stewing beef. If you use lamb, and don't want bones, get the butcher to give you 2 lbs of meat from the shoulder. Trim the larger chunks of fat from the meat, and cut it into 1-inch cubes.

8 tbs vegetable oil
1 stick cinnamon, 2 inches
   long
20 whole black peppercorns
15 whole cloves
10 whole cardamom pods
2 bay leaves
1–4 whole dried hot peppers
   (or more, according to
   taste)

2 lbs boneless meat from
   shoulder of lamb, cut into
   1-inch cubes, with fat and
   tissues removed
1–1½ tsp salt (according to
   taste)
1 tsp garam masala
   (optional)

Garnish

1 tbs trimmed, chopped
   fresh green coriander

Pat the meat dry on paper towels.

Heat the oil in a heavy-bottomed pot over medium heat. When it is very hot, put the spices in quickly in this order: first the cinnamon, then black peppercorns, cloves, cardamom pods, and bay leaves, and finally the hot peppers.

When the hot peppers begin to change colour and darken, add the pieces of meat and the salt. Stir for 5 minutes or until the pot begins to make boiling noises. Cover, lower heat, and cook for approximately 1 hour and 10 minutes — or until the meat is tender.

Remove the cover and continue cooking on medium heat for a final 3 to 5 minutes, gently stirring the meat pieces. Take care not to break them. The meat is done now. It should look a nice brown, be tender, and have no sauce other than what is clinging to it and the fat it cooked in.

To serve: In India the contents of the pot are put into a serving bowl, 1 teaspoon of *garam masala* is sprinkled on the top, and the dish is served with hot *chapatis* or Rice with Spinach. I tend to think the English would be rather put off if they saw so much fat lining the serving dish, so I suggest that you lift the meat and spices out with a slotted spoon (the spices, though not to be eaten, make an attractive garnish). Place them on a serving platter and serve them sprinkled with chopped green coriander. You could serve almost any vegetable or *dal* as an accompaniment — for example, green beans and *urad dal*. Plain rice or hot *chapatis* are also good. This dish can be made a day before, cooled, covered, and refrigerated. Reheat gently and serve.

Pyazwala khare masale ka gosht
(meat with whole spices and onions)

Serves 4–6

When I was a student in London and had written home begging my mother to teach me how to cook, one of the earliest letters I received from her was dated March 9th, 1956, and said, 'I received your letter. I am glad to know you have gained weight. I miss you and cannot wait to see you in your new "plump" state. Your younger sister is supposed to be studying for her exams and your father has even given up his room for her, but she spends all her time reading novels. Here is the recipe for the *Khare Masale Ka Gosht* that you asked for. Write and tell me how it works out … ' It worked out very well!

Here it is. It's very much like the preceding recipe, with the addition of onions, ginger, and cumin seeds, and it has one extra step.

2 lbs boneless meat from shoulder of lamb, with extra fat removed, cut into 1–1½ inch cubes	6–7 bay leaves
	1 tsp whole cumin seed
	1–4 whole hot dried red peppers (optional)
4 onions	5 whole black peppercorns
9 tbs vegetable oil	1 piece fresh ginger, 1½ inches by 1½ inches, peeled and minced or grated
10 whole cardamom pods	
4 whole large black cardamom pods (if available)	1 tsp salt (according to taste)

Prepare all the ingredients first. Pat dry the meat pieces thoroughly with paper towel. Peel the onions, cut them in half, then slice in very thin half-circles.

Heat the oil in a 10–12-inch heavy-bottomed pot over medium heat. When it is very hot, put in the onions. Fry, stirring occasionally, for about 15 minutes or until the onions are a darkish brown and crisp, but not burned and black. Lift out the onions with slotted spoon, taking care that the fat drains back into the cooking pot first. Spread the onions on paper towels, and leave uncovered.

In the same pot, put in the small and large cardamoms, bay leaves, cumin, red peppers, peppercorns, and finally the ginger. Stir for a minute until bay leaves turn dark and ginger sizzles awhile. Now add the wiped meat and the salt.

Stir for about 5 minutes or until the pot begins to make boiling noises. Cover, lower heat, and simmer very gently for 1 hour and 10 minutes or until meat is tender.

Take cover off, add onions, and let the meat cook over medium heat a final 3 to 5 minutes, stirring gently. Take care not to break the meat. All extra liquid should be boiled away, and the meat should look a nice brown and have no sauce other than what is clinging to it and the fat left in the pot.

To serve: See suggestions for preceding recipe.

Kheema
(minced meat)

Serves 6

This is the first Indian dish all Indian students abroad learn to make. It can be cooked plain or with potatoes, peas, or mushrooms.

2 medium-sized onions,
  peeled and coarsely
  chopped
4 cloves garlic, peeled and
  coarsely chopped
1 piece fresh ginger, 2 inches
  long and 1 inch wide,
  peeled and coarsely
  chopped
4 tbs vegetable oil
1 stick cinnamon, about
  2 inches long
4 whole cloves
4 black peppercorns

1 bay leaf
1–2 hot red peppers to taste
  (optional)
1 tbs ground coriander
1 tsp ground cumin
$\frac{1}{2}$ tsp ground turmeric
1 large tinned tomato or 2
  small ones, coarsely
  chopped
2 lbs finely minced lamb or
  minced beef
$\frac{3}{4}$–1 tsp salt (or to taste)
1 tsp lemon juice

Place chopped onions, garlic, and ginger in blender with 3 tablespoons water and blend to smooth paste (1 minute). Set aside.

Heat oil in a 10–12-inch frying-pan over medium heat. When hot, add cinnamon stick, cloves, black peppercorns, bay leaf, and then the red peppers. In about 10 seconds, when the peppers turn dark, add paste from blender, keeping your face averted. Fry for about 10 minutes, adding a sprinkling of water if the food sticks to the bottom. Add the coriander, cumin, and turmeric, and fry another 5 minutes. Now put the chopped tomato in, fry for another 2 to 3 minutes, and add the minced meat and the salt. Fry on high heat about 5 minutes. Break up all the lumps in the meat and brown it as much as you can. Add $\frac{1}{4}$ pint water and the lemon juice. Bring to the boil and cover. Lower flame and let it simmer for 1 hour.

To serve: Spoon off any accumulated fat and discard. Serve the *kheema* with rice, or *chapatis*, or *parathas*, and any vegetables you like. If serving it with a rice dish, e.g., Rice with Potatoes and Cumin Seed, serve a *moong* or *masoor dal* with it.

Kheema with fried onions

Serves 6

This is easily my favourite *kheema* recipe. Nutmeg, mace, and yogurt are added to the meat for a slight variation.

1 medium-sized onion, peeled and cut into very thin rings
4 tbs vegetable oil
2 bay leaves
1 cinnamon stick, 3 inches long
6 whole cloves
2 medium-sized onions, finely chopped
a piece of fresh ginger, 1 inch long and 1 inch wide, finely chopped
5 cloves garlic, minced

1 tbs ground coriander
1 tbs ground cumin
1 tbs ground turmeric
2 tbs plain yogurt
1 medium-sized tomato (tinned or fresh), peeled and chopped
2 lbs minced lamb or minced beef
$\frac{1}{4}$ tsp ground mace
$\frac{1}{4}$ tsp ground nutmeg
1 tsp salt
$\frac{1}{4}-\frac{1}{2}$ tsp cayenne (optional)

Halve the onion rings and separate. Heat the oil in a heavy-bottomed 10–12-inch frying-pan over medium heat. When hot, add the halved onion rings and fry them for about 5 minutes until they are dark brown but not burned. Remove with a slotted spoon and spread on paper towels. They will not be needed until the meat is almost cooked.

Put the bay leaves, cinnamon, and cloves in the hot oil. When the bay leaves begin to darken and the cinnamon starts uncurling slightly, add the finely chopped onions, ginger, and garlic. Fry, stirring, for 10 to 12 minutes, until the onions darken to a medium brown with darkish edges. Lower flame a bit and add the coriander, cumin, and turmeric. Fry for about 2 minutes, stirring all the time. Add the yogurt and cook, stirring, another minute. Now put in the chopped tomato, and keep frying and stirring for 2 to 3 minutes.

Add the meat. Raise the flame to medium (medium high if

the meat is very watery) and fry, breaking up all the lumps with the back of a slotted spoon, for about 7 or 8 minutes. Next, put in the mace, nutmeg, salt, cayenne, and ¼ pint water, and stir. Bring to the boil, cover, turn flame down to low, and let it simmer for 1 hour. Stir every 10 minutes or so. After an hour, mix in the browned onion half-rings and remove the cinnamon.

To serve: Serve with Rice with Spinach, Potatoes with Asafetida and Cumin, Green Beans with Ginger, and Yoghurt with Tiny Dumplings. Or serve with plain boiled rice, *moong dal*, and a cauliflower dish. This *kheema* is also excellent served with *chapatis* and *pooris* instead of rice.

Kheema with fried onions and peas

Serves 6

Follow the preceding recipe. Instead of cooking the minced meat for 1 hour, cook it for 50 minutes. Add 1 cup freshly shelled (or frozen) peas to it, mix, cover, and let cook another 5 to 10 minutes or until peas are tender. Add the fried onion half-rings and serve as in the previous recipe.

Kheema used as stuffing

Minced meat, *kheema*, is used very often as stuffing for vegetables. If the *kheema* is cooked well, and the sauce used over the vegetable is flavourful, these dishes can be superb. Sometimes, when serving four people, I have bought two large aubergines, stuffed them, and bought them to the table covered with a red tomato and tarmarind chutney. They have created a sensation.

The vegetables easiest to stuff are green peppers, long Italian peppers, tomatoes, and, of course, aubergines. (The discarded inside of the aubergine can be used for an unsmoked version of Aubergine Bharta, page 714.) These vegetables come in different sizes, so it will be up to you to decide how many you need. Pick your vegetables of a uniform size.

For the stuffing I use *Kheema* with Fried Onions (page 586). You can use any *kheema* left-overs as well. The stuffing can, if necessary, be made the day before and refrigerated. You could also make the chutney a night before and store it in a closed jar in the refrigerator. It will keep well.

To stuff green peppers and long Italian peppers: Preheat oven to 350°F., Mark 4.

Wash the peppers, then with a small sharp pointed knife cut a small cap around the stem of each pepper. Pull off the cap by the stem. Scoop out and discard the seeds inside the pepper and cut off seeds attached to the cap. Be sure to keep track of which cap belongs to which pepper.

Using a teaspoon, stuff each pepper with the prepared *kheema* and stick the cap back on. Lay or stand the peppers in one layer in an ovenproof baking dish. Pour Tomato Tamarind Chutney (page 802) over them, reserving a little chutney to pour over peppers just before you serve them. Cover the baking dish with a lid or aluminium foil, making sure it is tightly covered.

Bake in the preheated oven 45 to 55 minutes, or until peppers are tender.

To serve: Transfer peppers and chutney onto warm serving platter and spoon fresh chutney over them. Serve with *Sookhe Aloo*, Cucumber *Raita*, and *parathas*. Or you could serve them with rice, a chicken or shrimp dish, a vegetable, and a salad type of relish, e.g., Cucumber and Tomato with Lemon Juice. Or serve the peppers alone as an appetizer.

To stuff tomatoes. Preheat oven to 400°F., Mark 6.

Wash the tomatoes, then with a small sharp pointed knife cut a cap off at the stem end of each tomato. Reserve the caps. Remove the seeds and pulp from each tomato. (A grapefruit knife or serrated spoon is useful for this.)

Using a teaspoon, stuff each tomato with the prepared *kheema*. Replace the caps.

Stand the tomatoes in a single layer in an ovenproof baking dish. Pour Tomato Tamarind Chutney (page 802) over them, reserving a little chutney to pour over tomatoes just before you serve them. Cover the baking dish tightly with a lid or aluminium foil.

Place in preheated oven, and bake 15 to 20 minutes or until tomatoes wrinkle slightly.

To serve: Lift the tomatoes gently with large kitchen spoon and place on serving platter. Pour extra chutney over them, and serve as an appetizer or as in the preceding recipe for stuffed peppers.

To stuff aubergines: Pick medium or large aubergines. Wash them.

Bring water to which 1 teaspoon of salt has been added to the boil in a pot large enough to hold the aubergines. Since the aubergines will float, you can half-fill the pot with water. When the water comes to the boil, put in the aubergines and boil 15 minutes. Turn them over halfway through boiling time.

Preheat oven to 350°F., Mark 4.

Pour water carefully out of the pot, so as not to bruise the aubergines, and leave them to cool. Prepare each aubergine this way: when it is cool, cut off a cap at the stem area, and reserve. Now scoop out the inside, leaving only ½ inch of flesh all around. This is not easy. Use a grapefruit knife, a long sharp knife, spoons, a spoon handle—anything that will help you gouge out the inside—holding the aubergine carefully so you don't break the skin. (If you begin to despair, cut the aubergine in half lengthwise and scoop out the inside, leaving ½ inch around the skin, then proceed with the recipe.) When the pulp is out, the aubergine will shrink into itself and look like a very sad sack. Fatten it back into shape by stuffing it with lots of *kheema*. If it is still whole, put its cap on, pour Tomato Tamarind Chutney (page 802) over it, and bake, covered, for 45 minutes to 1 hour or until the aubergine is tender. Turn over once halfway during baking time. (If you had to halve the aubergines and stuff them that way, place snugly, skin side down, covered, in a baking dish.)

Follow serving directions for stuffed peppers (page 589).

Koftas
(Indian meatballs)

Serves 6–8. Makes about 48 meatballs

Koftas take a fairly long time to make, so I suggest that you prepare them a day in advance. They can be covered and left in the refrigerator overnight (they will taste even better) and can be reheated before serving. Take care not to break them while stirring and serving.

For the meatballs

2 lbs finely minced meat from a leg of lamb, or minced beef (put meat twice through fine blade of grinder, or ask your butcher to do so)	**¾ tsp salt** **¼ tsp freshly ground pepper** **1 tbs garam masala** **1 tsp ground coriander** **½ tsp ground cumin**

For the stuffing

1–2 fresh hot green chilies (optional), finely chopped
2 cloves garlic, peeled and minced
a piece of fresh ginger, about 1 inch square, peeled and minced
6 spring onions, minced, or 1 medium-sized onion, peeled and minced
3 tbs lemon juice
a dash of salt and freshly ground pepper

For browning the meatballs

7 tbs vegetable oil
1 cinnamon stick, 2 inches long
2 dried red peppers (optional)
4 whole cardamom pods
6 whole black peppercorns
4 whole cloves

For the sauce

vegetable oil (as needed to make up 5 tbs)
4 medium-sized onions, peeled and coarsely chopped
6 cloves of garlic, peeled and coarsely chopped
a piece of ginger, 1 inch square, peeled and coarsely chopped
2 tbs ground coriander
2 tsp ground cumin
1 tsp ground turmeric
2 medium-sized tomatoes (tinned or fresh), drained and chopped
1 tbs paprika
1 tbs garam masala
1 tsp salt

Garnish

1 tbs chopped fresh green coriander
1 onion, peeled and fried in rings (see page 766)
$\frac{1}{4}$ tsp freshly ground cardamom seeds (see page 548)

Mix all the ingredients for meatballs and keep covered in a bowl.

Mix all the ingredients for the stuffing in another bowl.

Preparing the *koftas* takes a little time, so you might as well make yourself comfortable. If you have a table and chair in your kitchen, sit down there. Otherwise, spread a newspaper on any handy table and pull up a chair. Place before you the bowls of minced meat and stuffing, a platter with a cover, and a bowl of warm water.

Two lbs of meat will make about 48 *koftas* about 1 to 1½ inches in diameter. To simplify, portion the meat into 8 equal sections and then make 6 *koftas* out of each section.

Pick up enough meat for one *kofta* and form into a rough ball. Depress the ball and place a generous pinch of stuffing in its centre. Cover the stuffing by bringing around the meat from the outer edges and making it into a ball again. Smooth out the ball by moistening your palms and fingertips slightly and by working it in your hand. As each ball is made, place it on the platter and cover. Continue this way until you have used up all the meat and stuffing.

Heat the oil in a 10-12-inch frying-pan over medium heat, and put in the cinnamon, red peppers, cardamom pods, peppercorns, and cloves. Stir once. In 10 seconds or so when the cloves begin to expand and the red peppers swell and turn dark, add the meatballs, just enough of them so they don't overcrowd the frying-pan. Brown them on all sides, remove with slotted spoon, and return to platter. (Remember, you are just browning the *koftas*, not cooking them through.) When all the *koftas* are browned, cover the platter and set aside.

The last step is making the sauce: Lift out the whole spices from the oil used for browning the *koftas* and place them with the *koftas*. Pour the oil into a very large and wide heavy-bottomed pot. Add more oil, if needed, to make 5 tablespoons.

Place the chopped onions, garlic, and ginger in a blender with 4 tablespoons water and blend at high speed until you have a smooth paste.

Heat the oil, then pour in the paste from the blender. Fry over medium heat for about 15 minutes or until all the liquid has evaporated, stirring frequently. Add the coriander, cumin, and turmeric, and keep frying another 5 minutes. If the spices stick at the bottom of the pan, add 1 teaspoon of warm water at a time and keep stirring. (Never put too much water in. The idea is to fry the spices and onions, not to boil them.)

Add the chopped tomatoes, and continue to stir and fry 2 to 3 minutes. Add 1 tablespoon water, cover pan, and let the tomatoes simmer 3 to 5 minutes, lifting the cover two or three times to make sure they are not burning. Remove cover, stir again, and fry for 1 more minute.

Now add 12 fl. oz. water, the *koftas*, the spices used in frying meatballs, the paprika, the *garam masala*, and the teaspoon of salt. Mix gently, and bring to the boil. Cover, and simmer slowly for half an hour.

To serve: Gently spoon out the *koftas* into a heated serving dish, taking care not to break them. Stir the sauce and pour it over them.

Sprinkle the green coriander and onion and cardamom on top. This dish can be served with plain boiled rice, *moong dal*, and a cucumber and tomato salad, at its simplest. (As a child I used to love this combination. On Sundays, we very often substituted *Karhi* for the *dal*.) At a banquet, you could garnish it with *vark* and serve it with Chicken *Biryani*, Carrots and Peas with Ginger and Green Coriander, and Yogurt with Spinach.

At picnics, it goes well with 'stale' *pooris* or *parathas* and pickles.

Made a little smaller, the *koftas* can be served with drinks.

Warn diners not to eat the whole spices, but to leave them delicately on one side of their plate!

Nargisi koftas
(large meatballs stuffed with hard-boiled eggs)

Serves 4

Koftas, as you know by now, are meatballs. *Nargis* is the Indian word for the narcissus flower. Why these particular meatballs are considered narcissus-like, I am not too sure. I can only guess that when cut in half (they are nearly always served that way) these egg-filled *koftas* remind some people of the yellow and white spring flower.

Nargisi koftas are definitely not an everyday dish in India. It may be *my* particular experience, but I have eaten them only at weddings and banquets. You, of course, need not limit yourself this way! They are not difficult to make, look beautiful, and taste quite marvellous. They are actually meatballs stuffed with whole hard-boiled eggs and cooked in a thick sauce.

1¼ lbs minced lamb or minced beef (put through the mincer 3 times)

¼ tsp ground cloves

¼ tsp cayenne pepper (optional)

⅛ tsp ground cinnamon

⅛ tsp ground mace

⅛ tsp freshly ground pepper

1½ tsp ground cumin

1½ tsp salt (or a little more if needed)

8 tbs plain yogurt

2 tbs finely chopped fresh green coriander

2 medium-sized onions, peeled and coarsely chopped

3 cloves garlic, peeled and coarsely chopped

a piece of fresh ginger, about 1-inch cube, peeled and coarsely chopped

4 medium-sized eggs, hard-boiled and peeled

6 tbs vegetable oil

6 lightly crushed cardamom pods

2 bay leaves

2 whole dried hot red peppers (optional)

2 tsp ground coriander

½ tsp ground turmeric

1 tsp paprika (for colour)

1 medium-sized tomato (tinned or fresh), peeled and finely chopped

If your butcher has not minced the meat 3 times, do it yourself at home. It should be *very* finely minced.

In a large bowl combine the meat, cloves, cayenne pepper, cinnamon, mace, black pepper, ½ teaspoon of the cumin, 1 teaspoon of the salt, 2 tablespoons of the yogurt, and the chopped green coriander. Mix well, cover bowl, and leave aside.

Place onion, garlic, and ginger in container of an electric blender with 6 tablespoons water and blend to a smooth paste.

Divide the minced meat into 4 portions. Wrap one portion around each peeled hard-boiled egg, covering it well.

Heat the vegetable oil in a 10-12-inch frying-pan over a medium-high flame, and put in the cardamom pods and bay leaves, and the red peppers if you want them. The spices will darken in a few seconds. Now put in the four meatballs and brown them all over. Turn them carefully so as not to break them. They will brown unevenly, but don't let that worry you. When they have browned, lift them out gently with a slotted spoon and place them on a plate.

To the same oil, add the paste from the blender container, keeping face averted, and fry, stirring, for about 10 minutes.

Now turn the flame to medium and add the coriander, the remaining 1 teaspoon cumin, and the turmeric. Keep frying and stirring for a minute. Add 1 tablespoon yogurt and stir for ½ minute. Add another tablespoon yogurt and stir for ½ minute. Repeat this process until all the yogurt has been added. Now put in the remaining ½ teaspoon salt, the paprika, the chopped tomato, and 6 fl. oz. water. Bring to the boil. Cover and simmer gently for 10 minutes.

Lift up lid and add the *koftas*. Cover and simmer gently for ½ hour. Turn the *koftas* every 7 or 8 minutes and spoon sauce over them.

To serve: Cut *koftas* in half and place on a warm platter. Spoon sauce over them and serve with almost any rice dish or with hot *chapatis*. Any yogurt *raita* and a pea or green bean dish would also go well with them.

Cubed lamb with onions and raisins

Serves 6-8

This dish is an adaptation I have made from *mullah do pyaza*, a Moghul favourite in which the meat is served with a lot of fried onions. These onions are cooked separately but are added to the meat for the last 5 minutes of cooking time. I brown the lamb pieces before I cook them, because, as I explained earlier, the meat in Britain seems to have a very high water content and will not brown with the spices, as it does in India. The raisins I add are optional. You could omit them if you do not like raisins or add more if you really like them.

3 lbs boneless meat from shoulder of lamb (stewing beef may be substituted)
11 tbs vegetable oil
10 medium-sized onions
5 cloves garlic, peeled and coarsely chopped
a piece of fresh ginger, 2 inches long and 1 inch wide, peeled and coarsely chopped
1 tbs ground coriander
2 tsp ground cumin

1 tsp ground turmeric
3 heaped tbs plain yogurt
1 medium-sized tomato (tinned or fresh) peeled and finely chopped
1½ tsp salt
½ tsp ground cloves
½ tsp ground nutmeg
½ tsp ground cinnamon
⅛–¼ tsp cayenne pepper (optional)
⅛ tsp freshly ground black pepper
2 tbs golden seedless raisins

Trim fat off the cubes of lamb. Pat dry with paper towels.

Heat 5 tablespoons of oil in a wide, heavy-bottomed pot. When oil is very hot, fry 7 or 8 pieces of meat at a time, browning well on all sides, and then remove with a slotted spoon. When all the meat has browned, turn off the heat.

Peel and coarsely chop 2 of the onions and place them with the garlic, ginger, and 5 tablespoons of water in the container of an electric blender. Blend at high speed until you have a smooth paste.

Turn on the heat to medium under the pot in which you

browned the meat. Pour in the paste from the blender and fry, stirring constantly, for about 5 minutes. Add the coriander, cumin, and turmeric, and fry, stirring, for 1 minute. Add the yogurt, a tablespoon at a time, and keep stirring and frying. Then add the peeled and finely chopped tomato, and keep stirring. (In all, this should take about 10 minutes.) If after you have added th: tomato some sticks to the bottom of your pot, add warm water, a teaspoon at a time, scraping the bottom and continuing to cook. The paste should turn a rich brown colour.

Put in the browned pieces of lamb along with any liquid that has accumulated, ½ pint of water, the salt, cloves, nutmeg, cinnamon, cayenne (if desired), and black pepper. Mix well. Bring to the boil. Cover, lower heat, and allow to simmer gently for 1 hour. (The beef should cook for 2½ hours.)

Meanwhile peel the other 8 onions, cut them in half lengthwise, and slice them into half-rings ⅛ inch thick.

Heat 3 tablespoons of oil in each of two frying-pans over medium heat. (It is quicker and easier to use two frying-pans, frying half the onions in each simultaneously. You can also do them in two batches.) When the oil is hot, fry the onion slices 10 to 12 minutes, until they are browned but not crisp. If the lamb has cooked 55 minutes to an hour by this time, remove onions with a slotted spoon and add them to the meat. If not, remove with a slotted spoon to a bowl and set aside. Turn off the heat under one frying-pan. Into the other put the raisins and fry for a few seconds until they turn brown and puff up, then add to the meat pot if the meat is done or hold in the bowl with the fried onions. Once the onions and raisins have been added to the meat, simmer for 5 minutes.

To serve: Serve with *pooris* or *chapatis*, a yoghurt dish, a relish —Sweet Tomato Chutney or Cucumber and Tomato with Lemon Juice—and a vegetable: cabbage or cauliflower would be good. Almost any plain rice or vegetable and rice dish can be served with it as well. I often serve it with Rice with Whole Spices and *Karhi*.

Lamb with onions and mushrooms,
or lamb do pyaza

Serves 4–6

Any meat *do pyaza* usually means meat cooked with an equal weight of fried onions, *pyaz* being the North Indian word for onions. I have modified the traditional recipe slightly by adding mushrooms and by cooking with fenugreek, fennel, and onion seeds instead of the more commonly used cardamom, cloves, peppercorns, and cinnamon.

This is a mild-tasting dish, relatively easy to make and very popular with both children and adults.

2 lbs boned meat from shoulder of lamb, trimmed of excess fat, and cut into 1-inch cubes
5 medium-sized onions
vegetable oil (enough for ⅛ inch in bottom of frying-pan)
¼ tsp whole black onion seeds (kalonji), if available

½ tsp whole fennel seeds
¼ tsp whole cumin seeds
15 fenugreek seeds
½ cup plain yogurt
1 tsp salt (more if needed)
⅛ tsp freshly ground pepper
⅛–¼ tsp cayenne pepper (optional)
½ lb fresh mushrooms

Dry the meat thoroughly with paper towels and leave at room temperature while preparing the other ingredients.

Peel and halve the onions lengthwise. Slice them into ⅛-inch-thick half-rings. In a 12-inch frying-pan, heat the oil. Fry the onions over a high flame 8 to 10 minutes, until they turn dark brown in spots and soften. Stir as you do this.

Remove onions with a slotted spoon and set aside in a bowl or dish.

In the same frying-pan put the onion seeds, fennel seeds, cumin seeds, and fenugreek seeds. Within a few seconds the fennel seeds will begin to darken. As soon as this happens, put in the cubes of meat and fry 5 to 10 minutes until well browned on all sides. While the meat is browning, put the yogurt in a bowl. Add ¼ pint water to it very gradually, a tablespoon at a time, beating with a fork. Once the meat has browned, beat the yogurt mixture again and pour it into the frying-pan. Add salt, pepper, and cayenne, bring to the boil, cover, lower heat to medium low, and cook for 25-35 minutes. Clean the mushrooms. Cut off the hard ends of the stems. If the mushrooms are largish, quarter them whole (stem and all); if they are of medium size, halve them; if they are of button size, leave them whole. After the meat has cooked 25 minutes, add the mushrooms. Stir well. Cover again and cook another 25 minutes or until meat is tender.

Lift off the cover and add the fried onions. Raise heat to medium high and boil away most of the liquid. (The only 'sauce' should be what clings to the meat. At the bottom of the pan you should see just the fat.) This should take 5 minutes or less. Check the salt.

To serve: Here is an Indian dish that can be served as part of a traditional Indian dinner or as the main course of a Western-style meal.

At an Indian meal, you could serve it as we did very often on Sundays—with plain rice, *Karhi*, green beans, and Tomato and Onion with Lemon Juice.

I serve it often to my family with Rice and Peas and a fresh green salad.

Lamb korma

Serves 6–8

3 tbs ground coriander
1 tbs ground cumin
1 tbs desiccated unsweetened
   coconut
4 medium-sized onions,
   peeled and coarsely
   chopped
5 cloves garlic, peeled and
   coarsely chopped
a piece of ginger, about 1½
   inches long and 1 inch
   wide, peeled and coarsely
   chopped
1 large tomato (tinned or
   fresh) or 2 small ones,
   peeled and coarsely
   chopped
1 tsp ground turmeric

6 tbs vegetable oil
5 whole cardamom pods
6 whole cloves
7 whole black peppercorns
2 bay leaves
1 cinnamon stick, 2 inches
   long
2 or more dried hot red
   peppers (optional)
3 lbs boneless meat from
   lamb shoulder, cut into
   1-inch cubes (or shank,
   neck, or leg—see page 580
   for proportions),
   thoroughly dried
1 tbs plain yogurt
2 tsp salt
1 tsp garam masala

Garnish

fried onion rings (page 766)
¼ tsp freshly ground
   cardamom seeds (page 548)

sliced hot green chilies
chopped fresh green
   coriander

Heat a small heavy frying-pan over medium flame, and dry-roast the coriander, cumin, and coconut, tossing them around with a spoon. Roast for 2 to 3 minutes until the spices turn a few shades darker, and set aside. Remove frying-pan from heat. Place onions, garlic, and ginger in blender with tomato and turmeric. Blend at high speed for 1 minute or until you have a smooth paste, and set aside.

In a large, heavy-bottomed pot heat 4 tablespoons of the oil over medium flame. When hot, add the cardamom, cloves, peppercorns, bay leaves, cinnamon, and red peppers. Stir. As soon as the peppercorns begin to expand and the red peppers turn dark, put in a few pieces of meat at a time. Turn the flame higher and brown the meat on all sides. As each batch browns, remove it to a side plate. When all the lamb is browned, cover it and set it aside. Remove the whole spices from the pot with a slotted spoon and keep with lamb.

To make the sauce: Keep flame on medium high, and add 2 tablespoons of oil to what is left in the pot. While it is heating, add the paste from the blender, keeping face averted. Stir from time to time. As the water evaporates and the paste starts to stick to the bottom, lower heat and stir continuously, for about 5 minutes in all, sprinkling in a little water now and then to prevent scorching. Add the roasted spices and cook for another 5 minutes, then stir in the yogurt, a little at a time, to prevent scorching.

Now put in the meat, the salt, and enough water to barely cover the lamb. Bring to the boil, cover, and simmer about 1 hour or until done. Lift cover. Sprinkle in 1 teaspoon *garam masala*, and cook, stirring, for another 5 minutes.

To serve: Spoon out into serving dish and garnish with one or all of the items suggested. Serve with boiled rice, *pooris* or *chapatis*, and okra or cauliflower or Aubergine *Bharta*. This dish is also good served with sweet rice, a yogurt dish, and Sweet Tomato Chutney.

Lamb (or beef) korma
with almonds, pecans, and sour cream

Serves 4–6

This dish can be made with shoulder or leg of lamb or stewing beef. Stewing beef generally takes much longer to cook, so adjust your time accordingly (see page 580).

5 medium-sized onions
5 cloves garlic, peeled and
coarsely chopped
a piece of fresh ginger,
about 1-inch cube, peeled
and coarsely chopped
vegetable oil, enough to
have $\frac{1}{16}$ inch in frying-pan
2 lbs boned meat from
shoulder of lamb, trimmed
of excess fat, and cut into
1–1$\frac{1}{2}$-inch cubes
1 tbs ground coriander
2 tsp ground cumin
1 tsp ground turmeric

2 medium-sized tomatoes
(tinned or fresh), peeled
and finely chopped
$\frac{1}{4}$ tsp ground mace
$\frac{1}{4}$ tsp ground nutmeg
$\frac{1}{4}$ tsp ground cinnamon
$\frac{1}{4}$ tsp ground cloves
1 tsp salt (or as desired)
$\frac{1}{8}$ tsp freshly ground black
pepper
$\frac{1}{8}$–$\frac{1}{4}$ tsp cayenne pepper
(optional)
10 pecan halves
$\frac{1}{4}$ cup blanched almonds
2 tbs sour cream

Garnish

5 cardamom pods
2 tbs chopped fresh green
coriander

the fried onions

Peel the onions. Cut 4 of them into halves lengthwise, and then slice them into very thin half-rings.

Chop the fifth onion coarsely. Put it along with the garlic and ginger in the container of an electric blender. Add 4 tablespoons of water and blend at high speed until you have a smooth paste.

Heat oil in a 10–12-inch frying-pan (use a deep, heavy-bottomed frying-pan with lid or a wide casserole-type dish) over medium-high heat. Put in the sliced onions and fry, stirring, for 15 to 20 minutes or until they are dark brown and crisp, not black and burned. Remove them with a slotted spoon and spread on paper towels to drain. (You will not need them until serving time.)

Dry the pieces of meat thoroughly and brown them well, about 8 pieces at a time, in the onion-flavoured oil. As each batch gets done, remove with slotted spoon to a platter. When all the meat is browned, turn off the heat.

When the frying-pan has cooled a bit, pour in the paste from the electric blender. Stir it well, mixing it with the coagulated pan juices. Turn the heat on medium high and fry the paste, stirring all the time, for 8 to 10 minutes, or until it has browned. Now lower heat and add the coriander, cumin, and turmeric. Mix and fry, stirring, for a minute or two. Add the chopped tomatoes and fry another minute.

Next add the mace, nutmeg, cinnamon, and cloves. Mix and cook slowly for 5 minutes. Stir every now and then.

Now add ¼ pint water, the salt, black pepper, cayenne pepper, and browned meat, as well as the juices that have accumulated. Bring to the boil, cover, lower heat and simmer gently for 30 minutes.

If you want to remove the fat, skim it off as it rises to the top.

Put the pecans and almonds in a blender with 3 tablespoons of water, and blend at high speed until you have a smooth paste. You may need to stop and push down with a rubber spatula a few times.

Add the nut paste, then the sour cream, to the meat. Stir and check the salt. Bring to the boil, cover, lower heat, and simmer gently for 25 to 30 minutes or until meat is tender.

Peel the cardamoms, discarding the skin. Crush the seeds with a heavy mortar and pestle or put them through a clean pepper grinder.

To serve: Place the meat and gravy in a wide bowl. Garnish with ground cardamom seeds, chopped green coriander, and the fried onions. Serve with hot *chapatis* or *parathas*, or almost any rice dish. Cabbage, green beans, and carrot dishes would go well with this *korma*. For a relish, choose something with raw onions and tomato.

Lamb cooked in dark almond sauce
(badami roghan josh)

Serves 4–6

Roghan josh is a traditional North Indian Muslim dish. It has a thick, dark, nutty sauce made with almonds and roasted cumin, coriander, and coconut. Even though shoulder of lamb is used here, you could use leg, neck, or shank (see page 580 for directions). Stewing beef may also be substituted.

2 lbs boned meat from shoulder of lamb, cubed into 1-inch pieces
6 tbs vegetable oil
10 whole cloves
1–2 whole dried hot red peppers (optional)
12 peppercorns
6 whole cardamom pods
1 tbs ground cumin
2 tbs ground coriander
1 tbs desiccated unsweetened coconut
3 tbs blanched almonds, coarsely chopped
6 cloves garlic, peeled and coarsely chopped
a piece of fresh ginger, about 1-inch cube, peeled and coarsely chopped
½ tsp ground turmeric
¼ tsp ground nutmeg
¼ tsp ground mace
2 medium-sized onions, peeled and finely minced
3 tbs plain yogurt
3 medium-sized tomatoes (tinned or fresh), peeled and coarsely chopped
1½ tsp salt

Wipe the meat well with paper towels.

Heat the oil in a 10–12-inch frying-pan. When the oil is hot, add the cloves, red peppers, peppercorns, and cardamom. Stir them for a few seconds until they puff up and darken.

Now put in 7 or 8 pieces of meat at a time to brown. When each lot is brown on all sides, remove with a slotted spoon to a large flameproof covered casserole, taking care to leave the spices in the frying-pan. Continue to brown all the meat this way and set aside. Turn off flame under frying-pan.

You have to roast some spices now, so take out your heaviest iron-type frying-pan (I keep a small one just for this purpose). Put the cumin, coriander, coconut, and almonds in it. Turn heat on medium and roast, stirring, for about 5 minutes or until spices turn a coffee colour. Turn off heat and pour roasted spices and nuts into container of electric blender. Add chopped garlic and ginger.

With a slotted spoon, lift out the fried spices in the oil and put them in the blender container too. Add the turmeric, nutmeg, mace, and 8 tablespoons water. Blend at high speed until you have a smooth, thick paste. You may need to stop the blender and push down with a rubber spatula.

In the same frying-pan in which the lamb cooked, fry the onions over high heat, stirring and scraping up the juices for about 5 minutes, or until they turn dark in spots. Then lower heat to medium and add paste from blender. Stir and fry for another 5 minutes, gradually adding the yogurt, a tablespoon at a time. Put in the chopped tomatoes. Stir and fry another 2–3 minutes.

Now add ½ pint water. Bring to the boil. Cover, lower heat, and simmer gently for 15 minutes.

Put the meat into this sauce. Add the salt and stir. Bring to the boil, cover, lower heat, and simmer gently for 1 hour. Stir a few times as it cooks.

To serve: Place in a warm dish, cover, and take to the table. *Rogham josh* goes very well with *pooris* or *chapatis* and Rice with Peas or Rice with Spinach. Serve a yogurt dish with it, and cauliflower, or carrots.

Lamb with vinegar and mint

Serves 4–6

This is a very refreshing way of cooking lamb. I like to make this dish fairly hot, but you could use fewer red peppers or none at all, as you prefer. Fresh mint is available from the greengrocer, but as this dish requires a whole bunch of mint it would certainly be easier if you cooked it in the summer months. As a substitute, you could use dried mint flakes, but I find all dried herbs seem impregnated with a rather undesirable musty flavour.

There are three ways you could serve this meat. You could dish it out with all its sauce — in which case you should serve the meat either on rice, to soak up the sauce — or in a little bowl, like a stew, set on the dinner plate. Or you could use the last 5 minutes of cooking time to reduce the sauce by about half by cooking it uncovered over a high flame — you will then be left with a thick sauce which can be served directly on the plates with the meat. The third alternative is to use the last 10 minutes of the cooking time to dry up almost *all* the sauce and serve the meat as a 'dry' dish. The recipe given here is for the 'dry dish', which I happen to prefer.

2 lbs boneless meat from
  shoulder of lamb, cut into
  1-inch cubes (or shank,
  neck, or leg — see page 580
  for proportions)
6 tbs vegetable oil
1½ tbs ground cumin
½ tsp ground cloves
¼ tsp ground cinnamon
½ tsp ground turmeric
1 tsp dry English mustard
1–2 whole dried hot red
  peppers (optional)
6 cloves garlic, peeled and coarsely chopped

a piece of fresh ginger,
  about 1-inch cube,
  peeled and coarsely
  chopped
5 tbs red wine vinegar
2 medium-sized onions,
  peeled and minced
1½ tsp salt
4 tbs well-packed finely
  minced fresh mint, or
  1 tbs dried mint plus 2 tbs
  trimmed, chopped parsley

Wipe lamb cubes well.

Put oil in a 10–12-inch frying-pan and turn the flame on high. When hot, put in 7 or 8 cubes of meat at a time and brown them on all sides. As each lot gets browned, remove it with a slotted spoon to a heavy-bottomed pot and cover. Brown all the cubes of meat this way. Turn flame off under frying-pan and set aside to use later.

Put the cumin, cloves, cinnamon, turmeric, and mustard powder, as well as the 2 (or less) red peppers and the chopped garlic and ginger, into the container of an electric blender. Add the vinegar and blend at high speed, until you have a smooth paste.

Put the minced onions in the frying-pan in which you browned the meat. Turn the heat to high and fry the onions for 5 minutes, scraping up the meat juices in the frying-pan as you do so. The onions must turn brown in spots. Turn heat down to medium and pour in the thick blended paste. Stir and fry for 5 minutes, adding a teaspoon of water every minute.

Now put in ½ pint of water and bring to the boil. Cover, lower heat, and simmer gently for 10 minutes.

When the sauce has cooked, pour it over the meat. Add the salt and mint, bring to the boil, cover, lower heat, and simmer gently for about an hour.

Remove the cover and raise the flame to high. Cook, stirring frequently, for about 10 minutes until the sauce is almost dried up, leaving only a few tablespoons in the pot and what is coating the meat. You will need to lower the heat the last few minutes so that the sauce does not stick.

To serve: Serve with *pooris*, a potato dish, and a green vegetable dish. You could also serve it with a rice dish and a green vegetable. As part of a Western-style meal, serve it with wild rice and a green salad.

Lamb with spinach

Serves 6–8

This is a traditional Moghul recipe. I use lamb for the recipe, but you could use beef (chuck or round) if you like.

3 lbs fresh spinach (or three 12 oz packages of frozen spinach)

3 medium-sized onions, peeled and coarsely chopped

a piece of fresh ginger, 2 inches long and 1 inch wide, peeled and coarsely chopped

7–8 cloves garlic, peeled and coarsely chopped

1 fresh hot green chili, chopped (optional), or $\frac{1}{8}$–$\frac{1}{2}$ tsp cayenne pepper

8 tbs vegetable oil

3 lbs boneless meat from shoulder of lamb, cut into 1-inch cubes (or shank, neck, or leg – see page 580 for proportions)

1 cinnamon stick, 3 inches long

7 whole cloves

7 whole cardamom pods

2 bay leaves

2 tbs ground coriander

1 tbs ground cumin

1 tsp ground turmeric

1 medium-sized tomato (tinned or fresh), peeled and finely chopped

2 tbs plain yogurt

$1\frac{1}{2}$ tsp salt

1 tbs garam masala

In a large pot, bring about 4 quarts of water to boil.

Meanwhile, trim and wash the fresh spinach thoroughly in cold water. Make sure you get all the sand out.

Drop the spinach in the boiling water, a pound batch at a time, and let it boil until the leaves wilt. You may need to push it down occasionally. As each batch wilts, scoop it out into a colander and run cold water over it. (If you are using frozen spinach, cook according to directions and drain.) When all the spinach is done, squeeze out most of the water and mince it. Keep aside in bowl.

Place the chopped onions, chopped ginger, garlic, green

chili, and 5 tablespoons of water in the blender container and blend at high speed until you have a smooth paste (about 1 minute).

Heat the oil in a 4–5-quart heavy-bottomed pot over medium heat. Pat dry the cubes of meat thoroughly on paper towels. Put 7 or 8 pieces at a time into the hot oil and brown them on all sides. Remove with a slotted spoon and set aside.

Put the cinnamon stick, cloves, cardamom pods, and bay leaves in the same hot oil. Stir. When the bay leaves begin to darken (10 to 20 seconds), add the paste from the blender (keep face averted). Keep stirring and frying for 10 minutes until the mixture darkens (if it sticks to the bottom, sprinkle a teaspoon of water at a time, and keep frying).

Now lower the flame and, continuing to stir and fry constantly, add at intervals first the coriander, cumin, and turmeric, 2 minutes later the chopped tomato, then about 5 minutes later the yogurt, and finally 2 minutes later the browned meat cubes. When meat and spices are well mixed put in the spinach. Add salt, bring to the boil, then cover and lower the heat to allow the mixture to simmer gently for 50 minutes. (Most meat gives out enough water for it to cook in its own juice, as it were. If you find that the meat is sticking, you can add up to ¼ pint of warm water.) Stir occasionally as it cooks.

At the end of the cooking time, uncover, increase heat, and cook rapidly until most of the liquid evaporates, leaving a thick sauce. Put in the *garam masala* and stir gently, being careful not to break meat pieces.

To serve: Place in warm dish and serve with *chapatis*, Potatoes with Asafetida and Cumin and Yogurt with Roasted Aubergine. Or you could serve it with plain boiled rice, any lentils, and a cauliflower dish if you like.

Sindhi gosht
(Sindhi meat)

Serves 6

This is a marvellous dish from Sindh, a state on the western coast of India. I first encountered it at a friend's house in Bombay, and insisted on leaving with the recipe in my pocket.

The meat (lamb) is marinated for 3 to 4 hours in a paste of onions, garlic, ginger, coriander, cumin, turmeric, red pepper, salt, pepper, and vinegar. It is then cooked in this marinade, with the addition of onion and fennel seeds.

2½ lbs boneless meat from lamb shoulder, cut into 1-inch cubes (or shank, neck, or leg — see page 580 for proportions)

2 medium-sized onions, peeled and coarsely chopped

a piece of fresh ginger, 2 inches long and 1 inch wide, coarsely chopped

6 cloves garlic, peeled and coarsely chopped

1 tbs ground coriander

2 tsp ground cumin

1 tsp ground turmeric

⅛–½ tsp cayenne pepper (optional; use desired amount)

4 fl. oz red wine vinegar

1 tsp salt

2 tsp whole fennel seeds

1 tsp whole black onion seeds (kalonji), if available

5 tbs vegetable oil

Remove fat and tissue from the cubes of meat.

In the container of an electric blender, place the chopped onions, ginger, garlic, coriander, cumin, turmeric, cayenne pepper (if used), vinegar, and salt. Blend at high speed until you have a smooth paste.

Pour paste into a bowl large enough to contain the meat. Prick the meat with a fork or with the point of a sharp knife and place in marinade. Mix well, cover, and leave for 3 to 4 hours. (Refrigerate if it is a very hot day; otherwise leave at room temperature.)

After the meat has marinated, pour contents of bowl into a wide 4-quart cooking pot. Add the fennel and onion seeds. Bring to the boil. Cover, lower heat, and simmer about 1 hour.

Lift off cover. Taste to check the salt (you may want to add a little more). Raise the heat and boil rapidly until most of the liquid evaporates. You will need to stir more frequently as the liquid diminishes. Now add the oil and keep stirring and frying over a medium flame. This dish must be 'dry', i.e., a thickish sauce should cling to the meat, which browns as the liquid cooks down. Be careful not to break meat pieces as you stir.

To serve: Place in a warmed dish and serve with *chapatis*, *parathas*, or *pooris*. You could also serve it with almost any kind of rice. With it, serve peas, okra, beans, or cabbage, and some yogurt dish, perhaps Yogurt with Potatoes.

Lamb chops with whole spices and yogurt

Serves 4

In this dish, lamb chops are cooked with whole spices, garlic, ginger, green coriander and yogurt. It is simple to make and very delicious in its final blend of flavours.

8 lamb chops
4 heaped tbs plain yogurt
3 tbs vegetable oil
10 whole black peppercorns
10 whole cloves
2 bay leaves
8 cardamom pods
2 cinnamon sticks, 2 inches long
2 whole dried hot red peppers (optional)

a piece of fresh ginger, about 1-inch cube, peeled and minced
2 cloves garlic, peeled and minced
4 tbs chopped fresh green coriander, or use fresh mint, watercress, or regular parsley as a substitute
1 tsp salt

Trim lamb chops of excess fat, leaving ⅛ inch along the sides. Pat dry with paper towels.

Mix the yogurt with 8 fl. oz of water and set aside in a non-metallic bowl.

Heat the oil in a 10–12-inch heavy-bottomed pot. When oil is very hot, put in 4 chops at a time, brown well on both sides, and remove with slotted spoon. Turn heat down to medium and fry the whole spices (peppercorns, cloves, bay leaves, cardamom, cinnamon, and red peppers) for about 20 seconds or until the bay leaves turn darker. Now add minced ginger and garlic, and fry, stirring, for a minute. Add the parsley and keep stirring for another minute.

Now put lamb chops back into the pot along with any liquid that may have collected in the bowl. Stir the yogurt water once again and pour over chops. Add salt, bring to the boil, cover, and simmer one hour. Stir gently every 10 minutes.

To Serve: Serve with Rice with Peas, Cucumber *Raita*, and any of the green bean recipes. Or serve with plain boiled potatoes and a green salad.

Pork chops cooked with whole spices and tamarind juice

Serves 4

Indians sometimes use Western cuts of meat to cook local dishes. We did not eat pork very often in our home, but every now and then my father would drive down to a special butcher to buy pork chops. Here is one of the ways we ate them.
N.B. This dish should be cooked in a stainless steel pan or a pan lined with porcelain, enamel or teflon.

1 tamarind lump about the
size of a walnut
8 loin or rib pork chops
2 tbs vegetable oil
12 whole black peppercorns
10 whole cloves
2 cinnamon sticks, each
2½ inches long

8 whole cardamom pods
2 cloves of garlic, peeled
2 whole dried hot red
peppers (optional)
1½ tsp salt
1 tsp granulated sugar

Soak the tamarind lump in 6 fl. oz hot water for at least 2 hours.

Pat dry the eight pork chops with paper towels. Trim off all but ⅛ inch fat along the sides.

Heat oil in a 10–12-inch heavy-bottomed pot over medium-high heat. When oil is very hot, put in 4 pork chops at a time and brown them on both sides. This should take 3 to 4 minutes on each side.

Once the pork chops have browned, remove them to a side dish and keep covered. Lower flame to medium.

In the same oil place first the peppercorns, then the cloves, the cinnamon, the cardamom pods, the garlic, and finally the red pepper. Stir and fry these ingredients for about a minute or less until the red peppers darken and the garlic is a bit browned.

Now return the pork chops to the frying-pan and add ½ pint warm water and 1 teaspoon salt. Bring to the boil, cover, lower heat, and allow to cook very gently for ½ hour. Turn the chops over a few times as they cook.

Meanwhile, press the tamarind juice and pulp through a strainer into a non-metallic bowl. Discard tamarind fibres, skins, seeds, etc. (see page 552).

When the pork chops have cooked for 30 minutes, add 2 tablespoons tamarind juice, 1 teaspoon sugar, and ½ teaspoon salt. Mix well, turning the chops. Cover and keep cooking slowly another 20 to 30 minutes. By this time most of the liquid will have been absorbed, leaving just the fat behind.

To serve: In India, the fat and the spices would be served with the meat. Here, in Britain, I suggest you lift the chops from the pot with a slotted spoon, leaving all the oil and spices behind.

Place on a warm platter and serve with Rice with Peas or any other vegetable rice dish. You could also serve it with *Sookhe Aloo* ('Dry' Potatoes) instead. For a vegetable, the Cabbage with Onions would be a good idea. If you are not up to cooking a complicated vegetable dish (as I am sometimes not), serve just a salad, or sliced tomatoes.

Pork chops cooked with cabbage

Serves 4

This is another recipe for pork chops which is relatively simple and quite delicious. The chops and cabbage are cooked separately first and then combined to cook together for the last 10 minutes. At home we considered this a 'Western' dish and ate it with mashed or boiled potatoes. The combination of spices used is actually very Indian, even though the dish does lend itself to being served in a Western style.

1 medium-sized cabbage (2½ lbs or so)	10 whole cloves
1 medium-sized onion	12 whole black peppercorns
8 pork chops (loin or rib)	2 dried hot red peppers (optional)
5 tbs vegetable oil	1½ tsp salt
2 bay leaves	1 tsp sugar
2 cinnamon sticks, each 2½ inches long	½ tsp whole cumin seeds
8 cardamom pods	3 heaped tbs plain yogurt
	2 tbs lemon juice

Remove outer leaves of cabbage. Wash, quarter, remove core, and shred cabbage into long, fine slices.

Peel onion, cut into half lengthwise, and slice into thin half-rings.

Wipe the pork chops dry and trim away all the fat except about ⅛ inch along the sides.

Heat 2 tablespoons of the oil in a 10–12-inch heavy-bottomed pot over a medium-high flame. When oil is hot, put in 4 chops at a time and brown them well on both sides. This will take 3 to 4 minutes on each side. When all the chops have been browned, remove them to a plate or bowl.

In the same pot, over medium-high heat, fry the bay leaves, cinnamon, cardamom pods, cloves, peppercorns, and whole red peppers for about a minute or until red peppers darken. Now add ½ pint water, the pork chops, 1 teaspoon salt, and 1 teaspoon sugar. Bring to the boil, cover, turn down flame to very low, and simmer gently for about 35 minutes.

Meanwhile, heat the remaining 3 tablespoons of oil in a large wide pot over medium-high heat. When hot, put in the cumin seed. When the cumin seed darkens — in about 20 seconds — add the sliced onion and fry for about 5 minutes, stirring all the time. Turn the heat to medium and add the cabbage. Fry, stirring for a minute. Cover, lower flame, and allow cabbage to steam in its own liquid for 5 minutes.

Uncover and raise flame again to medium. Add ½ teaspoon salt. Now fry, stirring, for about 20 minutes until the cabbage is slightly browned. Turn off flame.

Put the yoghurt in a cup and add enough cold water to make 4 fl. oz. Mix well.

When the pork chops have cooked about 45 minutes, uncover and add the cabbage, the yogurt mixture, and the lemon juice. Mix well, cover, and simmer another 10 minutes.

To serve: Arrange pork chops and cabbage on a warm platter and serve with boiled or mashed potatoes. Some of my friends like to serve a spiced apple ring or other fruit relish with this dish.

Pork chops à la Jaffrey

Serves 2

I apologize for this name. The dish is really my very own concoction and unlikely to be served in any Indian home other than mine. Indians almost never use celery in their cooking. Nor do they often use soy sauce, though I must say that in the major cities the influence of an overcooked version of Chinese cuisine is certainly making itself felt. This recipe acknowledges its debt to that cuisine, but tastes, in the last analysis, rather Indian. The dish is simple to make and quite delicious. The recipe here serves 2 people (2 chops each). If you wish to serve 4, just double the ingredients.

N.B. This dish should be cooked in a stainless steel pan or a pan lined with porcelain, enamel or teflon.

4 pork chops (loin or rib)	a piece of fresh ginger, 1
2 tbs vegetable oil	inch long and ½ inch wide,
2 bay leaves	sliced into 3 rounds
1 hot dried red pepper	2 cloves garlic, peeled
(optional)	⅛ tsp ground cinnamon
8 whole cloves	⅛ tsp ground mace
1 large stick of celery, diced	3 tbs soy sauce
1 medium-sized onion,	1½ tsp granulated sugar
coarsely chopped	½ lemon

Try to get pork chops that are evenly cut, so that they may brown evenly. Pat the chops dry and trim all but ¼ inch of the fat. Place them in a large frying-pan and turn heat on high. The chops should brown in their own fat. When they are a golden colour on both sides (press down areas that refuse to touch the frying-pan), remove them from frying-pan and place in bowl or plate. Turn off the heat and pour off only the accumulated fat in the frying-pan.

Heat the vegetable oil along with the coagulated juices in the same frying-pan over a medium flame, and put in the bay leaves, red pepper, and cloves. Stir. When the bay leaves change colour (this should take a few seconds) add celery, onions, ginger, and garlic. Stirring, fry over medium flame for 4 to 5 minutes or until everything is slightly browned. Add the browned pork chops, cinnamon, mace, soy sauce, sugar, and 2 fl. oz. water. Cut the lemon into 4 round slices (skin and all — remove pips though) and place over chops. Bring to the boil. Cover, lower heat, and simmer gently 50 minutes to 1 hour or until tender. Turn and mix gently every 10 to 15 minutes.

To serve: Place contents of frying-pan on platter and serve with Plain *Basmati* Rice and a green salad. A yogurt type of relish would be a good side dish. If you like you can remove the pieces of ginger and garlic before you serve.

Sweetbreads with fresh green coriander

Serves 6

If you like sweetbreads, you will enjoy this dish. I happen to love it, but my children are nearly always reduced to remarks like 'I like it, but I don't want it' — remarks which I counteract by drawing my eyebrows close together and staring at the wall in a hurt kind of way. This induces some polite nibbling which I try to make easier by saying, 'It's good for you'. My mother did the same kind of thing to me, so I see no reason to break tradition. Here is my recipe for sweetbreads. Try it. It's good for you!

2 lbs sweetbreads
2 medium-sized onions
4 cloves garlic, peeled and coarsely chopped
a piece of fresh ginger, 2½ inches long and 1 inch wide, peeled and coarsely chopped
5 tbs vegetable oil
1 hot green chili, finely sliced (more or less as desired), or ⅛–½ tsp cayenne pepper (as desired)

4 tbs chopped fresh green coriander
2 tsp ground coriander
1 tsp ground cumin
½ tsp ground turmeric
1 medium-sized tomato (tinned or fresh), peeled and finely chopped
2 tbs plain yogurt
1¾ tsp salt
2 tbs white vinegar
1 tbs lemon juice

Soak the sweetbreads in ice water for 1 hour.

Meanwhile, peel the onions. Slice one into fine rings and halve the rings. Set aside. Chop the other onion coarsely.

Put the chopped onion, garlic, and ginger in container of electric blender, add 3 tablespoons of water, and blend at high speed until you have a smooth paste (about 1 minute). Leave in container.

Heat the oil in a 10–12-inch frying-pan over medium heat. When hot, put in the halved onion rings and fry them, stirring, for about 5 minutes until they are crisp, dark brown, but not burned. With a slotted spoon, remove them and spread on paper towels.

Pour the paste from blender into the onion-flavoured oil. Fry, stirring, for 6 to 8 minutes, or until mixture turns a medium golden-brown. Add at intervals, stirring continuously, the green chili (or cayenne) and the green coriander; then, after 1 minute, lower the flame and add the coriander, cumin, turmeric; after another minute, the chopped tomato; and then the yogurt, continuing to fry and stir, for 2 to 3 minutes; finally ¾ teaspoon salt and 4 tablespoons warm water. Bring to the boil, cover, lower heat, and allow the mixture to simmer for 15 minutes.

In a large pot, bring 3 quarts of water to boil. Add 1 teaspoon salt and the vinegar. Remove the sweetbreads from the ice water and drain. Plunge them into the boiling water, drain, and plunge again into the ice water. Remove connecting tissue carefully (you can almost peel it off) and break sweetbreads into 1–1½-inch pieces.

After the sauce has cooked about 15 minutes, add the sweetbread pieces and lemon juice; stir, cover again, and cook gently for another 15 minutes.

To serve: Place in a warm dish. Sprinkle with the browned onions, and serve with hot *chapatis* and a vegetable and a yogurt dish of your choice. You could also serve any tomato or onion relish.

Chicken,
Other Birds,
& Eggs

Chicken cooked with yogurt
Chicken in light sauce
Chicken with potatoes
Chicken with sliced lemon and fried onions
Chicken with tomato sauce and butter
Chicken cutlets
Marinated grilled chicken
Grilled chicken strips
Roast chicken stuffed with spiced rice
Murgh mussallam (whole chicken with spices)
Duck—stuffed and roasted
Khitcherie unda (scrambled eggs, Indian style)
Chicken Moghlai
Eggs Moghlai

SEE ALSO

Tandoori chicken (page 687)
Chicken biryani (page 760)

UNTIL a few years ago there were only two ways one could buy poultry in India. Either you went up to the poultry market where live birds were kept in coops and you selected one, or you would wait at home for the poultry man to come around, hawking his wares. If he was somewhat affluent, he would arrive on a bicycle, but more often than not he came at a half-run, on his own two feet. On his humped shoulders he carried a bamboo, bent by the weight of a large basket dangling at each end. The lower section of these baskets was wicker, while the top was made of a rope mesh which could be opened and closed like an old-fashioned pouch. The occupants of these swaying baskets were the indignant birds—chickens and ducks mostly—which could not be seen except for a head here, a foot there, and a tail sticking out of the rope mesh; but they could be heard from a distance, squawking, quacking, and cackling. One had to know how to pick a bird by feeling its flesh. Experts like my father could even tell the age of the bird by prodding and squeezing in the right places.

In the last few years refrigeration and freezing have increased tremendously. The result is that poultry farms have mushroomed all over the country. The birds are sent, cleaned and plucked, to speciality stores where they can be bought much as they are in Britain. Of course, this is true only of the larger cities. The small towns and villages still rely on the old system.

The chickens in India seem to me to have more flavour than chickens here, though they can frequently be fairly tough, requiring a much longer cooking time. The only chicken that can be grilled in India is the $1\frac{1}{2}$–$2\frac{1}{2}$-lb spring chicken, and even then the bird must first be tenderized in a marinade containing green papaya or yogurt.

623

The Moghul miniature painters of the seventeenth century often showed royalty at the hunt, the *shikar*. Seated on cushioned, throne-like howdahs atop elephants or camels, they hunted anything from tigers to quail. The *shikar* still goes on, and although big game is generally left to the very rich, duck, geese, partridge, and quail can still be had by the ordinary Mr Singh on the street. Many restaurants have partridges on their daily menu, and many homes, like mine, serve roast duck frequently during the winter season.

The chicken available in British markets is so tender that it begins to fall apart well before it can go through the several stages required in most Indian recipes. Very often the chicken is cooked before the spices have permeated the meat. I have tried to adjust the chicken recipes to the tenderness of the English supermarket birds.

Most Indian chicken recipes require the removal of the skin before the bird is cooked. My English butcher shakes his head in despair every time I request this. To spare his feelings, I have now taken to doing the task myself. It is really quite easy and can be accomplished with a sharp, pointed knife and a bit of tugging in certain places.

Also, Indians generally cut their chicken into small pieces but rarely remove the bones. Legs are separated into drumsticks and thighs, breasts are cut into four or six pieces, backs into two or three, and wings into two. The reason is to allow the spices to penetrate the meat and bones as much as possible. I often serve just legs and breasts. They are easier to handle with knife and fork, and no one is stuck with the back. Backs and wings necessitate digital manipulation. They are to be avoided if you have finicky eaters.

While chicken is considered rather ordinary fare in this country, in India it is still regarded as an indulgence reserved for the rich. To be served chicken in someone's house definitely means that you are getting special treatment. In restaurants it is always one of the more expensive items on the menu.

In my recipes you will notice that I often brown the chicken quickly before I leave it to cook. In India this browning is done either with the paste of onions, garlic, ginger, and spices or at the end, when the chicken is cooked and the sauce has been reduced over high heat. Since the bird cooks very quickly here, any attempt at browning during these two stages leaves my chicken a disintegrated, shattered mess. I have discovered that an initial browning of the chicken provides the right colour and the bird does not fall apart.

Chicken cooked with yogurt

Serves 4–6

Here is a simple chicken recipe using very few of the spices generally associated with Indian cuisine. Yet the dish is typically North Indian. It is easy to make and very popular with children and adults alike.

4 chicken legs
1 whole chicken breast
¼ pint plus 2 tbs plain yogurt
5 medium-sized onions
2 cloves garlic, peeled and
  coarsely chopped

a piece of fresh ginger, about
  1-inch cube, peeled and
  coarsely chopped
7 tbs vegetable oil
1 tsp salt
⅛–¼ tsp cayenne pepper (as
  and if desired)

Skin all the chicken pieces. Divide each leg into 2 pieces (drumstick and thigh). Quarter the chicken breast. Pat dry the chicken pieces and set aside.

Put ¼ pint yogurt in a bowl. Add 6 fl. oz water, a little at a time, beating with a fork as you do so.

Peel all the onions. Cut 4 in half, lengthwise, then slice them into half-rings, about ⅛ inch thick. Chop the other onion coarsely.

Put the chopped onion, garlic, and ginger in the container of an electric blender. Add 6 tablespoons of water and blend to a smooth paste.

Heat 5 tablespoons of the oil in a 10-inch pot over medium heat. Put in the sliced onions and fry them, stirring, 8 to 10 minutes or until they have turned dark brown at the edges but are still limp. Remove them with a slotted spoon to a small bowl and set aside.

Add the remaining 2 tablespoons of oil to the pot and put in about 4 pieces of chicken at a time. Fry them, at medium-high heat, 7 to 8 minutes or until they are browned on all sides. Remove chicken pieces to plate with a slotted spoon.

Turn heat to low and pour paste from the blender into the pot, keeping your face averted. Scrape the bottom of the pot for browned meat juices and mix in scrapings with the paste. Now raise the heat to medium and fry, stirring, 4 to 5 minutes. Add 1 tablespoon plain yogurt, scraping bottom of pot and continuing to fry and stir another minute. Then add 1 more tablespoon yogurt, stirring for another minute.

Now put into the pot the chicken pieces, the well-blended yogurt and water mixture, the salt, and the cayenne pepper (if you desire it). Stir and bring to the boil. Cover, lower heat, and simmer 20 minutes.

Remove lid, raise heat to medium, and cook for 5 minutes to boil down some of the liquid, turning the chicken pieces carefully. (You should be left with a thick sauce.)

Mix in reserved fried onions, and cook at same heat another 2 minutes, stirring occasionally.

To serve: Place contents of pot in warmed dish and serve with hot *pooris* or hot *chapatis* or almost any kind of rice. You might serve okra or aubergine or green beans as a vegetable. Since this dish is cooked with yogurt, serve a non-yogurt relish, such as Cucumber and Tomato with Lemon Juice. A fresh green chutney (mint or coriander) might also be refreshing.

Chicken in light sauce

Serves 4–6

Here is another relatively uncomplicated chicken dish made with whole spices (*khara masala*), ginger, and garlic. In India a whole chicken is used, skinned and cut into small serving portions. I often serve just legs and breasts since they are easier to handle with fork and knife and no one is stuck with the back.

This dish tastes particularly good if you make it a day in advance and let it sit in its sauce, covered and refrigerated, overnight. It can be reheated easily on top of the stove over a low flame.

1 tbs tomato purée	1 cinnamon stick, about 2½
3 tbs plain yogurt	inches long
4 cloves garlic, peeled and	2 bay leaves
coarsely chopped	5 whole cardamom pods
a piece of fresh ginger, about	5 whole cloves
1-inch cube, peeled and	2 hot dried red peppers
coarsely chopped	(optional)
4 chicken legs	1 tsp ground turmeric
1 whole chicken breast	1 tsp salt
6 tbs vegetable oil	⅛ tsp freshly ground pepper
	1 tbs lemon juice

In a small bowl, combine tomato purée, yogurt, and ½ pint of water. Mix well and set aside.

Put chopped garlic and ginger into the container of an electric blender, along with 2 tablespoons of water. Blend until you have a smooth paste.

Cut chicken into serving portions: divide legs into drumstick and thigh, and quarter the breast. Remove skin from pieces of chicken and pat dry.

Heat oil in heavy-bottomed 10–12-inch casserole-type pot over medium-high heat. Put in chicken pieces, a few at a time, and brown on all sides. When each batch turns a golden-brown, remove with slotted spoon and do the next batch. When all chicken pieces have been done, put the cinnamon, bay leaves, cardamom, cloves, and red pepper into the same oil. Stir once. The spices will darken immediately. Now pour in the paste from the blender (keep face averted as you do this) and add the turmeric. Stir and fry for about a minute.

Next, put in the browned chicken pieces, the mixture of tomato purée sauce, yogurt, and water, salt, pepper, and lemon juice. Bring to the boil. Cover, lower heat, and simmer gently 20 to 25 minutes, turning chicken pieces a few times.

Uncover pot, raise flame to medium, and cook 5 to 7 minutes or until sauce is reduced to half, turning the chicken pieces over gently.

To serve: Put contents of pot into a hot bowl and serve with plain boiled rice or hot *pooris*. Serve at least one vegetable — green beans, aubergine, or cauliflower might be nice. As a relish, Tamarind Chutney with Bananas or Cucumber and Tomato with Lemon Juice could be served.

Chicken with potatoes

Serves 2–3

This dish is fairly similar to the preceding one. No yogurt is used, however, and the addition of boiled potatoes gives it a rather thickish gravy. If you wish to double this recipe, double all ingredients except the oil. Instead of 5, use 6 tablespoons of oil. Your cooking time will not change much, except that of course you will have to fry the chicken in two batches. You will also need a bigger pot. (In this recipe I use a frying-pan.)

3 medium-sized potatoes
 for boiling
1 medium-sized onion,
 peeled and coarsely
 chopped
3 cloves garlic, peeled and
 coarsely chopped
a piece of fresh ginger, about
 1-inch cube, peeled and
 coarsely chopped
1½ lbs chicken sections
5 tbs vegetable oil

1 cinnamon stick, 2½–3
 inches long
1 bay leaf
4 whole cardamom pods
2 whole hot dried red
 peppers (optional)
2 whole black peppercorns
½ tsp ground turmeric
1 tbs tomato purée
1 pint chicken broth (tinned
 or homemade)
½ tsp salt

Put your potatoes to boil. When done, drain off water and leave potatoes to cool. (Do not use boiled potatoes which have been refrigerated for this recipe.)

Place onion, garlic, and ginger in container of blender with 5 tablespoons water and blend to smooth paste.

Remove skin from chicken pieces and pat them dry.

Heat oil in a 12-inch frying-pan over medium-high flame, then add the cinnamon, bay leaf, cardamom, red peppers, peppercorns, and chicken pieces. Fry chicken pieces quickly on all sides until golden-brown. Remove chicken with slotted spoon and set aside.

Pour the paste from blender into frying-pan, averting your face. Add turmeric and fry, stirring, for about 3 minutes. Now add the tomato purée and the chicken broth. Mix. Bring to the boil. Cover, lower heat, and simmer gently for 15 minutes.

Peel and quarter the potatoes. Add salt, the browned chicken pieces, and the potatoes to the sauce. Stir, bring to the boil, cover, lower heat, and simmer gently for 20 to 25 minutes or until chicken is tender. Turn chicken and potatoes a few times while they are cooking.

To serve: Put chicken pieces, potatoes, and sauce into a bowl and serve with hot *chapatis*, *parathas*, or *pooris*. Serve green beans or peas with it and at least one kind of relish (a yogurt relish might be a good idea).

Chicken with sliced lemon and fried onions

Serves 4–6

Cooked with lemon slices, sugar, and fried onions, this chicken dish is unusual and quite delicious. You could use a whole bird, cut into small sections, or you could buy just legs and breasts, dividing the legs into drumstick and thigh and quartering the breast.

N.B. This dish should be cooked in a stainless steel pot or a pot lined with porcelain, enamel or teflon.

3–3½ lbs chicken sections	½ tsp ground turmeric
3 medium-sized onions	2 tbs plain yogurt
a piece of fresh ginger, about	1 tbs tomato purée
1-inch cube, peeled and	1 tsp salt
coarsely chopped	¼ tsp ground cinnamon
4 cloves garlic, peeled and	¼ tsp ground cloves
coarsely chopped	⅛ tsp cayenne pepper
8 tbs vegetable oil	1 whole lemon
1 tbs ground coriander	1 tbs sugar
1 tsp ground cumin	⅛ tsp freshly ground pepper

Skin all the chicken pieces and pat them dry.

Peel the onions. Chop two of them coarsely and put them into the container of an electric blender. Cut the third one in half lengthwise, then slice it into thin half-rounds and set aside.

Add 6 tablespoons of water, the ginger, and the garlic to the onions in the blender and blend at high speed until you have a smooth paste.

Heat 6 tablespoons of the oil in a 10–12-inch pot over medium-high flame. When hot, put in the sliced onions and fry them, stirring, until they are darkish brown and crisp, though not burned. Remove onions with a slotted spoon and leave them to drain on paper towels.

In the same oil, brown the chicken pieces on all sides until they are golden. (Do this speedily over high flame so chicken browns but does not cook through. You will need to do it in at least two batches.) Remove chicken with slotted spoon to a bowl or plate.

Add the remaining 2 tablespoons of oil to the pot. Pour in the paste from the blender. (Keep face averted.) Stirring, fry on medium-high heat for about 10 minutes or until paste turns a nice golden-brown. Now put in the coriander, cumin, and turmeric and fry, stirring continuously; after another 2 minutes add yogurt, a teaspoon at a time; after 2 or 3 minutes, the tomato purée, a little at a time, continuing to stir and fry. Finally, add salt, cinnamon, cloves, cayenne pepper, and ¾ pint of water. Bring to the boil, cover, lower heat, and simmer gently for 10 minutes.

Cut the lemon into 4 or 5 slices, discarding the end pieces, and remove the seeds. Add lemon slices along with the chicken pieces, fried onions, sugar, and freshly ground pepper to the sauce, stir, and bring to the boil. Cover, lower heat, and simmer gently for 20 to 25 minutes or until chicken is tender, turning the pieces every now and then. If chicken sticks to bottom of pot, add a little more water. You should end up with a very thick sauce.

To serve: Empty contents of pot into shallow serving bowl. Arrange the cooked lemon slices on top of the chicken pieces. Serve with any rice dish or with *pooris* or *chapatis*. Yogurt with Tiny Dumplings goes well with it. For vegetables you could serve Carrots and Peas with Ginger and green coriander or cauliflower or any other vegetable you like. Almost any kind of *dal* would also complement the dish.

Chicken with tomato sauce and butter

Serves 6

The original version of this dish is to be had at the Moti Mahal restaurant in Delhi. There, the *Tandoori* Chicken (page 687) is cut into small serving sections and put into a rich sauce of creamed tomatoes, butter, and spices.

My very inventive sister, Kamal, has worked out her own version, slightly different, but equally good. The Indian chicken being as tough as it is, what she does is to combine all ingredients — tomatoes, onions, ginger, garlic, butter, whole spices, and chicken sections — in a covered pot and cook them until the chicken is three-quarters done. By this time the meat has absorbed all the necessary flavours. Then she lifts off the cover and over a high flame stirs and fries the chicken and sauce until almost all the water evaporates and the chicken and paste-like sauce are a dark reddish-brown.

This is very hard to do in Britain, because, as I mentioned earlier, the chicken is very tender and cooks too fast to allow all the flavours to be absorbed and the final frying to be accomplished without disintegration. So I have worked out a third version! Here it is.

4 chicken legs

2 chicken breasts

2 medium-sized onions, peeled and coarsely chopped

5 cloves garlic, peeled and coarsely chopped

a piece of fresh ginger, about 2 inches long and 1 inch wide, peeled and coarsely chopped

1 stick of cinnamon, 2½–3 inches, broken up

seeds from 6 cardamom pods

8 whole cloves

1 tsp whole black peppercorns

2 bay leaves, crumbled

1 hot dried red pepper (or more, as and if desired), crumbled

6 tbs vegetable oil

8 medium-sized tomatoes (tinned or fresh), peeled and finely chopped

1 tsp salt

4 tbs lightly salted butter

Remove skin from all chicken pieces. Divide legs into drumstick and thigh, and quarter the breasts. Pat dry and put aside.

In the container of an electric blender, combine the onions, garlic, ginger, cinnamon, cardamom seeds, cloves, peppercorns, bay leaves, red pepper, and 3 tablespoons water. Blend until you have a smooth paste.

Heat the oil in a 10–12-inch casserole-type pot over a high flame. When hot, put in the chicken pieces, 4 or 5 at a time, and brown them quickly (about a minute on each side). Remove with a slotted spoon. You will need to brown the chicken in several batches.

Turn heat to medium and pour in the paste from the blender. (Keep face averted.) Stir and fry the paste for 5 minutes, scraping the bottom of the pot well as you do so. Now add the chopped tomatoes, ¼ pint water, and the salt. Bring to the boil and cover. Turn heat to very low and simmer gently for 30 minutes, stirring every 6 or 7 minutes.

Add the chicken pieces to the pot, as well as any juices that may have collected. Bring to the boil, cover, and simmer over low heat for 25 to 30 minutes. Stir gently every 5 or 6 minutes to avoid sticking and burning. Be careful not to break the chicken pieces as you stir. Lift cover, turn up heat and burn off most of the liquid.

Cut the butter into 4 pats. Take the chicken off the heat. Drop in the pats of butter and stir them in gently. Serve immediately.

To serve: Place contents of pot in a warm dish and serve with Rice with Black-eyed Peas or *naan*. For vegetables, you could have Aubergine *Bharta* or Fresh Peas with Ginger and Green Coriander. You could, if you like, also serve Onions Pickled in Vinegar as they do at the Moti Mahal Restaurant in Delhi.

Chicken cutlets

Serves 2

Breaded chops and cutlets were brought to India by its last conquerors, the French and the British. They passed along the delicacy to the Indian upper classes, who were only too eager to ape and copy. But while these upper classes ate chops and cutlets as a status symbol, they were secretly very bored by the blandness of these foods. So they began to spice them up. Soon a whole new class of cooks developed. Under the distinguished titles of *khansama* ('lord of the pot') and *babarchi*, they cooked for the rich and specialized in Westernized foods adapted to the Indian palate, or, very often, Indian foods adapted to the Western palate. They could cook a treacle pudding just as easily as they could a roast duck stuffed with Indian herbs and spices, and a jam tart just as easily as a delicate *pullao*.

It is from this line of cooks that we get the recipe for chicken cutlets. Our family cook had not only inherited the recipe for an Indianized version of the cutlet, but he had also been taught a different name for it. As he said it, it sounded more like 'cutliss' than anything else. So every Friday, which was the day off for all Muslim butchers (and most butchers were Muslim), we had either fish or chicken. And when it was chicken, it was frequently 'chicken cutliss'. The 'cutliss' were very often served with boiled beans and potatoes as a first course for dinner. Then, as a second course, we had *chapatis* with the usual Indian lentils and vegetables. For dessert, we switched again to a sponge roll or lemon tarts, both of which were very popular. These sudden changes of cuisine at the same meal struck no one as peculiar.

I use chicken breasts for the cutlets. One breast (two cutlets) serves one person generously, two people skimpily. If you are having cutlets as a first course, you could serve four people easily with two breasts. The chicken breasts are boned and skinned (your butcher will do this on request, but it is easy to do yourself), and marinated overnight in a paste of onions, garlic, ginger, green coriander, lemon juice, salt, and pepper. They are then dipped in a beaten egg, breaded, and fried. Very simple, and very mild.

2 whole chicken breasts, boned, skin removed, and each breast split into 2 sections (about 1 lb of meat)

3 cloves garlic, peeled and coarsely chopped

a piece of ginger, 1 inch long and 1 inch wide, peeled and coarsely chopped

½ medium-sized onion, peeled and coarsely chopped

1 fresh hot green chili, finely sliced (this will make your chicken only very mildly hot; use 2 or 3 if you want it hotter)

2 tbs chopped fresh green coriander or Italian parsley, as a second-best substitute

3 tbs lemon juice

¾ tsp salt

⅛ tsp freshly ground pepper

1 egg

bread crumbs (homemade bread crumbs are best: leave 6 slices of white bread exposed for 24 hours, or until they harden; then crush with rolling pin or spin in the blender)

vegetable oil, enough for at least ¼ inch in frying-pan

Garnish

lemon juice and wedges
salt and freshly ground pepper

a few sprigs fresh green coriander

Four to 24 hours before cooking, marinate chicken. Place the garlic, ginger, onion, green chili, fresh green coriander, lemon juice, salt, and pepper in the container of an electric blender. Add a tablespoon of water and blend at high speed until you have a smooth paste. (You may need to stop the blender and scrape down the paste a few times.)

Place the 4 boned and skinned chicken pieces in a bowl. Prick all over with a fork. Pour the marinade paste over chicken and rub into the pieces. Cover, and leave refrigerated 4 to 24 hours.

(It will taste better if you can marinate it 24 hours.)

30 minutes before serving: Beat the egg in a bowl.

Spread out the bread crumbs on a flat plate.

Lift out chicken pieces, one at a time, leaving marinade sticking to them. Dip first in beaten egg and then in bread crumbs. Coat both sides generously with bread crumbs and set aside. Prepare all chicken pieces this way, and let them sit, breaded, for 10 minutes.

15 minutes before serving: Heat oil in a 10–12-inch frying pan over medium-low flame. When the oil is hot, place chicken cutlets in the frying-pan and fry 6 to 7 minutes on each side. (Adjust heat carefully so chicken pieces turn a rich golden-brown in the given time.) Remove gently with a spatula.

To serve: Place cutlets on a warm platter. Sprinkle with salt, freshly ground pepper, and lemon juice. Serve garnished with lemon wedges and fresh green coriander. With cutlets serve Rice with Peas or Rice with Potatoes and Cumin Seed and a green salad. If you like, you could serve boiled potatoes and peas. Almost all vegetables go with this dish.

Marinated grilled chicken

Serves 4–6

This is a simple recipe in which the marinade, a mixture of onions, ginger, garlic, cumin, coriander, vinegar, and oil, is made in the electric blender. The chicken is marinated, then grilled. It could also be barbecued over charcoal.

3–3½ lbs chicken, preferably legs, thighs, and breasts, or a whole chicken, cut into serving pieces

Marinade

2 medium-sized onions, peeled and coarsely chopped	2–3 fresh hot green chilies, or $\frac{1}{4}$–$\frac{1}{2}$ tsp cayenne pepper (optional)
4 cloves garlic, peeled and coarsely chopped	1 tsp whole cumin seeds
a piece of fresh ginger, about 1 inch long and 1 inch wide, peeled and coarsely chopped	1 tbs ground coriander
	$\frac{1}{4}$ pint wine vinegar
	$\frac{1}{4}$ pint olive or vegetable oil
	2 tsp salt
	$\frac{1}{8}$ tsp freshly ground pepper

Garnish

**fresh green coriander,
chopped**

Combine all the ingredients for the marinade in the container of an electric blender. Blend at high speed until you have a smooth paste.

Pull off and discard the skin from chicken pieces. Prick chicken all over with a fork and place in a bowl. Pour marinade over chicken. Cover and refrigerate 2 to 3 hours (24 hours would be best).

Fifty minutes before serving, heat your grill. Remove chicken pieces from bowl and, with as much marinade clinging to them as possible, place on baking sheet lined with aluminium foil. Grill 15 minutes on each side or until chicken gets well browned. (Adjust distance from grill so it does not brown too fast.)

To serve: Place chicken on a warm platter and sprinkle green coriander over it. Serve with a rice dish, a green vegetable, and a *dal*.

Grilled chicken strips

Serves 6–8

Chicken breasts are boned, cut into narrow strips, and then mixed with a paste consisting of oil, vinegar, onion, ginger, garlic, and fennel seed, and the 'hot' (*garam*) spices: cardamom, cloves, cinnamon, black peppercorns, etc. The chicken sits in the marinade 4 to 5 hours. It is then grilled and served. This dish is very easy to prepare, since most of the work is done by the electric blender. Its taste is heavenly, lightly but definitely spiced. It is very versatile—I have successfully served it as an hors d'œuvre with toothpicks, at lunches with salad, at big dinners along with a meat dish, and at picnics, having made it the night before. It tastes as good cold as it does hot.

Get your butcher to bone and skin the chicken breasts for you. Many supermarkets sell already boned and skinned chicken breast 'cutlets' which could be used, or you could do the skinning and boning yourself without undue exertion.

**3 lbs chicken breasts, boned
and skinned (weight after
boning and skinning)**

Marinade

5 tbs olive or vegetable oil
4 tbs red wine vinegar
**1 medium-sized onion,
peeled and chopped**
**1 whole head of garlic (each
clove peeled and chopped)**
**a piece of fresh ginger, about
1-inch cube, peeled and
chopped**
2 tbs whole fennel seeds
2 tbs ground cumin

2 tsp ground coriander
seeds from 8 cardamom pods
1 tsp ground cinnamon
8 whole cloves
20 black peppercorns
**½–¾ tsp cayenne pepper (use
as desired; these measures
are for a mildly hot dish)**
2 tsp salt
1 tbs tomato purée

Combine all ingredients needed for the marinade in the container of an electric blender. Blend at high speed until you have a smooth paste.

Wipe all the chicken pieces thoroughly dry. Divide breasts in 2 sections and then cut each section into strips that are 1½ or 2 inches long and about ½ inch wide.

In a bowl combine the chicken and the marinade, and mix well. I use my hands to rub the marinade into the chicken pieces. Cover and refrigerate 4 to 5 hours.

Preheat the grill (45 minutes before serving if you are going to eat it hot). Line a baking tray with aluminium foil. Spread the chicken (most of the marinade will cling to it) thinly on the tray. (You will need to do two batches unless you have an extra large grill.)

When the grill is well heated, put in the tray with the chicken. Grill for 10 minutes, turn the pieces over, and grill another 10 minutes, or until the chicken is lightly browned. Remove chicken pieces with a spatula and place in warm serving dish. Cover and keep in warm place. Do the second batch the same way. (I usually put the second batch in to grill and serve the first batch. As soon as people are ready for seconds, the next batch is almost ready.) Remember, this chicken will *not* have a uniformly dark-brown colour; it should be dark only in spots.

To serve: Place on warm platter and serve with a rice dish, a lamb dish if you are entertaining, a yogurt dish, and at least one vegetable. Serve as an appetizer with toothpicks. Eat it cold at picnics, also with the aid of toothpicks.

Roast chicken stuffed with spiced rice

Serves 4

If you are tired of your usual chicken roast, try this one. With the expenditure of just a wee bit more time and energy, you can create a sensational dish — spicy without being hot, simple without being dull!

I use precooked (usually left-over!) rice for the stuffing. Adjust the salt for the stuffing according to the saltiness of the precooked rice.

1 roasting chicken, 4 lbs (at
   room temperature)

Marinade

2 tbs olive oil (or vegetable
   oil
1 tbs lemon juice
$\frac{1}{4}$ tsp salt

$\frac{1}{8}$ tsp freshly ground pepper
$\frac{1}{2}$ tsp ground cumin
$\frac{1}{4}$ tsp ground garam masala

Stuffing

1 medium-sized onion,
   peeled and coarsely
   chopped
2 cloves garlic, peeled and
   coarsely chopped
a piece of fresh ginger, about
   1-inch cube, peeled and
   coarsely chopped
3 tomatoes (tinned or fresh),
   peeled and chopped

1 tsp ground coriander
1 tsp ground cumin
4 tbs vegetable oil
$\frac{1}{4}$ tsp whole black mustard
   seeds
$\frac{1}{4}$ tsp whole cumin seeds
2 teacups (well-packed)
   cooked rice
$\frac{1}{2}$ tsp salt (or as needed)

Mix all the ingredients for the marinade. Wipe chicken well with a cloth or paper towel so it is as dry as possible. Brush three-fourths of the marinade all over the chicken, inside and out. Let the chicken sit, unrefrigerated, for about 2 hours. Save rest of marinade.

Preheat oven to 450°F., Mark 8.

Place the onions, garlic, ginger, tomatoes, coriander, and cumin in the container of an electric blender. Blend at high speed until you have a smooth paste.

Heat the 4 tablespoons of oil in a 10–12-inch frying-pan over medium-high flame. When very hot, drop in the mustard and cumin seeds. When the mustard seeds begin to rise and pop (15 to 30 seconds), add the paste from the blender, keeping face averted, as the mixture will bubble rapidly and splatter. Stirring, fry the paste on medium-high heat until it is browned. The oil should separate from the paste (this will take about 10 minutes). You will need to stir more frequently as the moisture evaporates.

Add the cooked rice, and the salt as and if you need it. Turn heat to low and mix the browned paste with the rice. Loosely stuff the chicken with the rice and truss it. Place it in an oven-proof baking dish, breast up, and put it in the preheated oven.

Let the chicken brown for about 20 minutes, basting it with the remaining marinade mixture every 5 minutes. Turn down the heat to 350°F., Mark 4. Cook another hour or until the leg moves easily when pushed up and down at its socket. Baste every 10 minutes with the juices that will come out of the chicken.

To serve: Lift chicken gently and put on a warm platter. Let it sit for 15 minutes so juices will not flow out when carved. Serve simply with a green salad or, if you like, with any green beans, peas, or cauliflower dish. Sweet Tomato Chutney also tastes good with this roast.

Murgh mussallam
(whole chicken with spices)

Serves 4

In this royal dish, a whole chicken is first marinated in a paste consisting of garlic, ginger, turmeric, hot green chilies, *garam masala*, yogurt, and salt for about 2 hours. It is then browned and simmered with a second paste made up of fried onions and garlic, ginger, almonds, lemon juice, and an array of spices like cardamom, cinnamon, nutmeg, mace, etc. Hard-boiled eggs are put into the sauce about 10 minutes before the chicken is done and then arranged around the chicken.

1 whole chicken, about 3½ lbs
1 tsp loosely packed leaf
   saffron

4 hard-boiled eggs

Marinade

6 cloves of garlic, peeled and
   coarsely chopped
a piece of fresh ginger, about
   2 inches long and 1 inch
   wide, peeled and coarsely
   chopped
1½ tsp salt

½ tsp garam masala
½ tsp ground turmeric
4 tbs plain yogurt
2 fresh hot green chilies,
   sliced, or ¼–½ tsp cayenne
   pepper (optional)

Cooking paste

8 tbs vegetable oil

4 medium-sized onions, peeled and coarsely chopped

4 cloves garlic, peeled and coarsely chopped

a piece of fresh ginger, about 1 inch long and 1 inch wide, peeled and coarsely chopped

1 tbs blanched almonds, slivered

1 tbs ground coriander

1 tsp ground cumin

seeds from 4 large black or 8 small green cardamom pods

¼ tsp ground cloves

½ tsp ground cinnamon

¼ tsp ground nutmeg

¼ tsp ground mace

1½ tsp salt

¼ tsp freshly ground black pepper

½ tsp cayenne pepper (optional)

3 tbs lemon juice

Garnish

2 tbs finely chopped fresh green coriander

First make your marinade.

Put the ingredients for the marinade into the electric blender. Blend at high speed until you have a smooth paste.

Peel the skin off the whole chicken. Where it is hard to peel, as on the wing tips, you can leave it on. Prick the chicken all over with a fork, place in a bowl, and pour marinade over it. Rub the chicken well with the marinade, both inside and out, and leave, unrefrigerated, for about 2 hours.

Rinse out your blender container. You will need it again.

Soak the saffron in 2 tablespoons of hot water.

Now make the paste to cook the chicken in. Heat 6 tablespoons of the vegetable oil in a 10–12-inch heavy-bottomed pot over a medium-high flame. When hot, put in the chopped onions, garlic, and ginger. Stir and fry for 8 to 10 minutes or until the onions are brown at the edges but still soft. With a slotted spoon, remove onions, garlic, and ginger and place them in the blender container. Reserve the cooking oil.

Place a small iron or aluminium frying-pan over a medium flame. When it is hot, put the blanched almonds in it. Stir them around until they turn golden, then add them to the blender container. In the same small frying-pan put the ground coriander and cumin. Stir, watching, until the spices turn a few shades darker (do *not* let them burn). They will smoke quite a bit, but don't worry—it is to be expected. Then put them in the blender along with the cardamom seeds, cloves, cinnamon, nutmeg, mace, salt, black pepper, cayenne, lemon juice, and ¼ pint of water. Blend all to a smooth paste, pausing, if necessary, to push the mixture down with a rubber spatula a few times.

When the chicken has marinated for 2 hours, heat the reserved oil and add 2 more tablespoons of oil to it. Do this over medium-high flame. Lift the chicken out of the bowl along with any clinging marinade and place in the oil. Brown it as well as you can on all sides. You will not be able to do this too evenly, but it does not matter.

When the chicken has browned, turn heat down to low. Take the paste from the blender and, using a rubber spatula, spread it all over the chicken. Add ½ pint of water to the pot and bring to the boil. Cover tightly. Turn heat to low and simmer gently for about 40 minutes or until chicken is tender. Turn chicken 2 or 3 times during the first 15 minutes of this cooking time. After that, leave it breast up and baste it every 5 to 7 minutes with the sauce.

Peel the hard-boiled eggs, and 10 minutes before the chicken is fully cooked put them in the pot, spooning some sauce over them as well. Pour saffron and saffron water over chicken. Cover and continue simmering until chicken is tender.

To serve: Lift chicken carefully out of pot and place it on warmed platter. Arrange eggs around it. If you like, skim the oil off the sauce before pouring it over chicken and eggs. Sprinkle with chopped green coriander. Serve with a fish *pullao* or Rice with Peas. You could also serve any vegetable you like: Fried Aubergines with Sour Green Chutney, or a cauliflower or bean dish might be nice. A yogurt relish is almost a must with *Murgh Mussallam*. I often serve Yogurt with Spinach.

Duck — stuffed and roasted

Serves 2

The duck here is stuffed with rice, spices, raisins, and nuts to make a superbly festive meal. I find that a 4–4½-lb duck really serves only two people well. It has a large cavity inside and rather small legs. Most of the meat is around the breast area, and that is not too much.

1 duck, 4–4½ lbs, at room temperature — liver, gizzard, and heart included

2 tbs vegetable oil

½ tsp whole cumin seeds

½ tsp whole fennel seeds

15 fenugreek seeds

1 medium-sized onion, finely chopped

a piece of fresh ginger, 1 inch long and ½ inch wide, grated or minced

1 hot green chili, cut into thin rounds, or ⅛–¼ tsp cayenne pepper (optional)

1 tbs tomato purée mixed with 2 tbs water

3 tbs minced fresh green coriander

2 teacups cooked rice

2 tbs golden raisins

1 tbs dried apricots, chopped to the size of raisins

3 tbs pine nuts or slivered blanched almonds

½ tsp salt (more if the rice is unsalted)

⅛ tsp freshly ground black pepper

1½ tsp lemon juice

1½ tsp sugar

additional salt, pepper

If the duck was frozen, defrost completely well ahead of time. It must be at room temperature before you cook it. Pat it dry (otherwise it will not brown well). Prick the skin with a fork to allow the lining of fat to ooze out as it melts. Mince the liver, gizzard, and heart.

Preheat oven to 450°F., Mark 8.

Heat the oil in a 10–12-inch frying-pan over medium-high flame, and add the cumin, fennel, and fenugreek seeds. Stir. When the cumin seeds begin to darken (this will take 10 to 20 seconds) add the onions, ginger, and green chili if you wish to use it. Fry, stirring, for about 2 minutes or until onions turn a little brown. Now add at intervals, continuing to stir and fry, the minced liver, gizzard, and heart; after a minute or two, the tomato purée and minced green coriander; in another 2 minutes, the cooked rice, turning heat to low; and finally, the raisins, apricots, and pine nuts or almonds, mixing everything well. Stir and fry another 5 minutes.

Season with salt, cayenne pepper (if you wish to use it instead of the green chili), black pepper, lemon juice, and sugar.

Stuff the duck loosely with the mixture in the frying-pan, truss, place it in roasting pan breast up, and set in the preheated oven.

Let duck brown for 20 to 25 minutes. There is no need to baste. Remove fat with a bulb baster as it accumulates in roasting pan.

Turn heat to 350°F., Mark 4, and let duck cook another 1½ hours, or until the juices of the bird run a clear yellow when it is pricked

To serve: Place duck on a warm serving platter. Sprinkle skin with a little salt and freshly ground pepper. Serve with green beans or peas, or with a simple green salad if you like.

Khitcherie unda
(scrambled eggs, Indian style)

Serves 2–3

3 tbs butter
½ medium-sized onion,
   finely chopped
1 small tomato, chopped
1 tbs chopped fresh green
   coriander

½–1 hot green chili, finely
   sliced
4 medium–large eggs, well
   beaten
salt and pepper to taste

Melt the butter in a 10-inch frying-pan over medium heat. Add onions and sauté them for a minute or until they begin to turn translucent.

Add diced tomato, green coriander, and sliced green chili. Stir and cook for 3 to 4 minutes or until tomatoes soften a bit.

Pour in the beaten eggs. Sprinkle on salt and pepper lightly. Stir and move eggs around with a fork. Indians like their scrambled eggs rather hard (cooked about 3 minutes), but you can stop whenever the desired consistency has been achieved.

To serve: While some Indians eat their scrambled eggs with toast, others eat them with hot *parathas*, *chapatis*, or *pooris*.

Chicken Moghlai

Serves 6

This rich, elaborate, saffron-flavoured dish justifies the time taken in preparing it by its exquisite taste and appearance. It has a burnt-red colour and smells of cardamom, cloves, and cinnamon. It tastes even better if you cook it a night before serving it, thus allowing the sauce to act as a marinade for the chicken.

I use legs, thighs, and breasts of chicken for this recipe, but you could buy a whole 2½–3-lb chicken and have it cut into smallish serving portions. It may, then, feed only 4 people. You could also use 6 whole quail, skinned, or 6 whole partridges, skinned.

2½–3 lbs chicken legs, thighs, and breasts

4 medium-sized onions, 2 peeled and chopped and 2 cut into half lengthwise, then sliced into thin half-rings

a piece of fresh ginger, about 1½ inches long and 1 inch wide, peeled and chopped

8 cloves garlic, peeled and chopped

10 tbs vegetable oil

2 cinnamon sticks, 2½–3 inches long

2 bay leaves

10 cardamom pods, slightly crushed

10 whole cloves

1 tsp whole cumin seed

1½ tbs ground coriander
½ tbs ground cumin
Dry-roasted together, following instructions for roasting ground coriander, page 548.

½ tsp ground turmeric

¼–½ tsp cayenne pepper

3 tbs yogurt

1 medium-sized tomato (tinned or fresh), peeled and finely chopped

1–1½ tsp salt

1 well-packed tsp leaf saffron, roasted and crumbled (see page 552)

1 tbs warm milk

Skin the chicken pieces. Quarter the breasts and divide the legs into drumstick and thigh. Pat chicken dry and set aside.

Put the chopped onions, ginger, and garlic in the container of an electric blender along with 4 tablespoons of water. Blend at high speed until you have a smooth paste.

In a 10-inch, heavy-bottomed pot, heat 8 tablespoons of the oil. Put in the sliced onions and fry, stirring, over a medium-high flame for 10 to 12 minutes or until onions are dark brown and crisp but not black and burned. Remove them with a slotted spoon and set aside in bowl or plate.

Raise heat to high and put the chicken pieces in the same oil a few at a time. Without letting chicken cook too much, brown to as dark a colour as possible. Remove each batch to a platter.

Turn heat down to medium high. Add remaining 2 table-spoons of oil to the pot, and put in the cinnamon sticks, the bay leaves, the cardamom pods, the cloves, and the cumin seed. Stir and turn the spices once. Now put in the paste from the blender, and fry, stirring, for 10 minutes. Turn heat down to medium and add the dry-roasted coriander and cumin powder, the turmeric, and the cayenne pepper. Stir and mix for 1 minute.

Add at intervals, constantly stirring and frying, the yogurt, a little bit at a time, the chopped tomato, and after another minute, the chicken pieces and salt, and finally, after another 2 minutes, $\frac{1}{4}$ pint water. Mix well, bring to the boil, cover, lower heat, and simmer gently for 30 minutes, turning chicken pieces gently every 8 to 10 minutes.

While the chicken is cooking, soak saffron in warm milk for 20 to 30 minutes.

When chicken is cooked, add the browned onions and the saffron-milk. Mix, cover, and simmer gently another 5 minutes.

To serve: This royal dish can be served very simply with *pooris* and a relish, or it can be a part of a banquet along with a *pullao*, a baked stuffed fish, and *Kheer* for dessert.

Eggs Moghlai

Serves 6

Follow preceding recipe for Chicken *Moghlai*, but substitute 12 hard-boiled eggs for the chicken.

Omit the step in which chicken is browned, and cook hard-boiled eggs in the sauce for only about 20 minutes. Put browned onions and saffron-milk over eggs and cook gently another 5 minutes.

To serve: See preceding recipe.

Fish &
Shellfish

Marinated prawns with whole spices
Prawns with crushed mustard seeds
Prawns with peas and green coriander
Prawns with sweet Italian peppers
Prawns in bread crumbs, Indian style
Prawns with brown sauce
Prawns with dill and ginger
Prawn, crab, or lobster, Kerala style
Baked sea bass with yellow rice
Sea bass in green chutney
Codfish steaks in yogurt
Stuffed flounder
Mackerel with onions

SEE ALSO

ROUND the age of seven, while I was still fishing with a bent pin for a hook and a piece of cane for a float, my greatest heroes were my brothers. A decade separated us in age — but it was more than the age difference that elicited my respect. They were 'proper' fishermen. When *they* went fishing it was not just to the Jumna River. The Jumna was, after all, just across the street from us, and therefore quite ordinary. With their tapering fishing rods and their complex array of reels, hooks, bait, jars, and nets, they set out to catch *rahu* at the Okhla dam and trout in the cold streams of Kashmir.

They were always accompanied, on these trips, by *their* hero, a mysterious, magnificent man called Munnia. I never knew his second name. I never really understood exactly who he was. Munnia was then about forty, tall and silent with shining dark brown skin and thick black wavy hair. He knew *everything* about fish. He knew where the fish were biting, and when. He knew which bait was most effective on which day. I once saw him clad in a white loincloth, leaping on the slippery rocks that formed stepping stones across a shallow stream of water at the Okhla dam. Suddenly he stopped and jerked his head to one side. Silently he bent over. He held that pose patiently for fifteen minutes. Then he straightened up, triumphantly holding a *singhara* that he had 'tickled' and caught. Once the fish for the day had been caught, Munnia would open his knapsack, pull out a pot and some spices, light a fire with twigs, and produce an instant feast for his entire party. Often he would rub the fish with salt, turmeric, and hot red pepper and then fry it. Munnia's world was, of course, limited to fresh-water fish. I doubt if he ever saw an ocean or a fish from the sea.

With improved refrigeration some seafood is now available

653

in all the major cities of India. While availability of molluscs remains limited to the coast, prawns of varying sizes, lobster, and pomfret can be found even in Delhi. And pomfret is, in my family, easily the most popular fish. It is a flat salt-water fish, on an average about 8 to 9 inches long, with its skeletal structure so obligingly designed as to make filleting a pleasure and eating a bone-free ecstasy. Its flesh is tender but firm, flaking delicately when cooked. The pomfret can be fried, baked, grilled, or cooked in banana leaves or green chutney. It is served at lunches, dinners, and official banquets.

Unfortunately, neither the pomfret nor the *rahu* and *singhara* mentioned earlier are available in Britain. What I will do in this chapter is to give you Indian recipes adapted for fish normally found in British fish markets. The recipes for prawns and lobsters remain basically unchanged, but I have modified some of the pomfret recipes and used them for the sea bass, mackerel, and the flounder. Instead of *rahu*, I have used cod. You could also use carp.

Coconut palms fringe most of the India's coast from Bombay down to Cape Comorin and up again to Calcutta. Quite naturally, therefore, the fish caught along there are often cooked with grated coconut or with the 'milk' obtained from soaking freshly grated coconut in water. In Bengal, where the populace has rioted when fish was temporarily unavailable, a paste made out of ground black mustard seeds is often added to fish to give it a very special nose-tingling pungency. Moghul recipes from North India call for neither mustard seeds nor coconuts, but often for northern spices like saffron.

I need hardly stress that fish must be bought fresh – the eyes must look bright and the gills very red. It must also smell fresh. Cook it until just done. Overcooking will make it disintegrate or – in the case of prawns and lobster – become hard and leathery.

How to peel and devein prawns

This is really not as tiresome as it sounds. The secret is to make yourself entirely comfortable as you go about the task. Spread a double layer of newspaper at a table. Bring a clean plate, a sharp pointed knife, and a bag of prawns to the table.

Cut off the head of each prawn. Then pull off the legs that dangle on the belly side. Next, peel the shell from the body. It will come off in wide rings. Pull off the tail separately. To devein, make a shallow incision along the length of the prawn, right where the backbone would be if the prawn had one—all the way from head to tail. Here you will see a threadlike tube, often filled with black or green or yellow substance. Pull this out. If you don't find it, do not discard the prawn. It is still quite edible. Place all peeled and deveined prawns on a clean plate. Next, wash prawns thoroughly in cold running water and pat dry.

Marinated prawns with whole spices

Serves 6–8

Prawns are marinated in a paste of garlic, ginger, hot green chilies (or use cayenne pepper as a substitute), lemon juice, salt, and pepper. They are then fried with a bay leaf, cinnamon, cardamom, cloves, and peppercorns. The actual cooking time is less than 10 minutes. The prawns should be fried *just* before serving.

3 lbs prawns (large prawns are particularly good for this recipe)

10 cloves of garlic, peeled and coarsely chopped

a piece of fresh ginger, 2 inches long and 1½ inches wide, peeled and coarsely chopped

2 fresh hot green chilies, sliced (or use ¼–½ tsp cayenne pepper as substitute)

3 tbs lemon juice

1 tsp salt (more for sprinkling later if necessary)

⅛ tsp freshly ground black pepper

6 tbs olive oil (or vegetable oil)

1 cinnamon stick, 2½–3 inches long

5 cardamom pods

6 whole cloves

10 whole peppercorns

1 bay leaf

¼ tsp ground turmeric

Garnish

2 spring onions

Peel and devein prawns (see page 655). Wash under cold running water. Drain and pat dry as thoroughly as you can.

In the container of an electric blender, combine the garlic, ginger, green chilies, lemon juice, salt, and freshly ground pepper. Blend at high speed until you have a smooth paste.

In a bowl, combine the prawns and the paste from the blender. Mix well. Cover. Leave, unrefrigerated, for an hour. If you wish to leave it longer (2 to 4 hours is fine), put bowl in the refrigerator.

Ten minutes before serving, heat the oil in a 10–12-inch frying-pan over a high flame. Add the cinnamon, cardamom, cloves, peppercorns, and bay leaf. Stir for 10 seconds or until bay leaf darkens. Then put in the prawns and marinade and let this mixture bubble and cook, stirring constantly, only until the prawns turn pink and opaque all over. Remove them (and any whole spices that cling to them) with a slotted spoon and place them in a bowl. Add turmeric to contents of frying-pan. Keep cooking the marinade mixture over high flame, stirring all the time, until it becomes thick and paste-like. This will take just a few minutes. Now put the prawns back into the frying-pan. Stir around until the prawns are well coated; there should be no sauce left in the frying-pan. Check the salt. You may need to sprinkle on a bit more. Turn off heat.

To serve: Place the prawns on a warm platter. Wash the spring onions and slice into fine rounds, including at least an inch of the green part as well, and sprinkle them over the prawns. Serve with a rice dish, some kind of lentils, a vegetable, and a yogurt dish. Warn people not to bite into the whole spices.

Prawns with crushed mustard seeds

Serves 3–4

1 lb prawns
1 tsp black mustard seeds, crushed (use heavy mortar and pestle, coffee-grinder or grinding stone)
$\frac{1}{8}$ tsp ground turmeric
2 tsp tomato purée
4 tsp mustard oil (or any other vegetable oil)

2 cloves of garlic, peeled
2 slices of fresh ginger, 1 inch long, 1 inch wide, and $\frac{1}{16}$ inch thick, peeled
1 hot dried red pepper
$\frac{3}{4}$ tsp salt
$\frac{1}{8}$ tsp freshly ground pepper
1 tbs lemon juice

Peel and devein the prawns (see page 655). Wash under cold running water. Pat dry as thoroughly as you can.

In a cup, combine the crushed mustard seeds, turmeric, tomato purée, and 3 tablespoons of water. Set aside.

Heat the oil in a 10–12-inch frying-pan over a medium-high flame. When hot, put in the cloves of garlic, the ginger slices, and the hot red pepper. Stir and turn around. In a few seconds, as soon as contents begin to darken, add the prawns. Keep stirring until the prawns turn pink and opaque. Now put in the mustard seed paste. Turn heat to a moderate low. Keep stirring. Add the salt, pepper, and lemon juice. Stir and fry another 2 minutes. Turn off heat.

To serve: Place on heated platter and serve with a rice dish or with hot *pooris*. Serve one or two vegetables with it, perhaps cabbage and peas, as well as a yogurt relish.

Prawns with peas and green coriander

Serves 3–4

1 lb prawns
1 tbs lemon juice
salt
freshly ground pepper
5 cloves garlic, peeled and coarsely chopped
a piece of fresh ginger, 1 inch long and 1 inch wide, peeled and coarsely chopped
4 tbs olive oil (or vegetable oil)

¼ tsp ground turmeric
3 tbs tomato purée
5 tbs minced fresh green coriander
1 small (or ½ large) sweet green pepper, cut in ¼-inch squares
½ teacup freshly shelled peas
⅛–¼ tsp cayenne pepper (optional)

Peel and devein the prawns (see page 655). Wash under cold running water. Pat dry. Sprinkle lightly with salt and pepper.

Place the garlic and ginger in the container of an electric blender, along with 3 tablespoons of water. Blend at high speed until you have a smooth paste.

Heat the oil in a 10–12-inch frying-pan over a medium-high flame. When hot, put in the prawns. Fry and stir the prawns until they barely turn pink and opaque all over. Remove them to a bowl with a slotted spoon.

Into the same frying-pan pour the paste from the blender. Add the turmeric and fry, stirring, over medium heat for about 2 minutes.

Lower the heat and add tomato purée, coriander, green pepper, peas, lemon juice, salt and pepper to taste, cayenne pepper, and 3 tablespoons of water. Bring to the boil, cover, and simmer gently for about 5 minutes or until peas are just cooked.

Remove the cover from the frying-pan, raise heat, and boil away most of the liquid. When a thick paste-like sauce remains, put the prawns back in. Stir and cook until the prawns are well coated (there should be almost no sauce left in the pan). Taste, and add more salt if necessary. Turn off heat.

To serve: Place in a warm dish and serve with hot *pooris*, *chapatis*, or *parathas*, or with any kind of rice dish. You could also have a sauced potato dish, e.g., Potatoes with Asafetida and Cumin or, if you like, Mushrooms with Cumin and Asafetida.

Prawns with sweet Italian peppers

Serves 3-4

Even though green peppers are normally used for this dish, I often substitute the Italian peppers because of their sweeter taste. Try to pick them so they are about the same length — about 3 inches long. This dish has a wonderful sauce made up of onions, garlic, coriander, cinnamon, cardamom, bay leaf, tomato purée, and lemon juice.

1 lb prawns
¾ tsp salt
¼ tsp ground turmeric
6 medium-sized Italian
    peppers
5-6 tbs olive or vegetable oil
1 medium-sized onion,
    peeled and very finely
    minced
4 cloves garlic, peeled and
    very finely minced

5 whole cardamom pods
1 bay leaf
1 cinnamon stick, 2½-3
    inches long
2 tbs tomato purée
1 tsp ground coriander
¼ tsp cayenne pepper
    (optional)
1 tbs lemon juice
1 tsp brown sugar

Peel and devein the prawns (see page 655). Wash thoroughly under cold running water, drain, and then pat dry.

Place the prawns in a bowl. Sprinkle them with ¼ teaspoon of the salt and the turmeric. Mix well with your hands, rubbing the salt and turmeric into the flesh.

Cut the caps off the green peppers. Slice each in half lengthwise, then each half into 3 or 4 long strips. Remove seeds.

Heat 4 tablespoons of the oil in a 10-12-inch frying-pan over a medium-high flame, and fry the slices of pepper, stirring, for about 5 minutes or until they brown a bit and turn slightly limp. Remove them with a slotted spoon to a plate.

In the same frying-pan, adding a little more oil if necessary, stir and fry the prawns for 2 to 3 minutes or until they become pink and opaque on the outside. Remove with a slotted spoon to a bowl.

Turn heat to low. Add a tablespoon of oil to the frying-pan, and put in the minced onions and garlic, cardamom, bay leaf, and cinnamon. Sauté for 4 to 5 minutes or until onions get a bit soft. Now add the tomato purée, coriander, cayenne pepper, lemon juice, brown sugar, the remaining ½ teaspoon of salt, the fried green pepper slices, and ¼ pint of water. Bring to the boil. Cover and simmer very gently for 10 minutes.

Remove the cover and add the prawns along with any juice that may have accumulated in bowl. Turn heat to medium high. Stir the prawns to coat them with the sauce, and continue cooking and stirring 4 to 5 minutes while the sauce thickens. You should be left with only a little sauce at the bottom of the frying-pan.

To serve: Place in a shallow bowl and serve with rice and some kind of *dal*. Plain boiled rice and *karhi* together with Cucumber and Tomato with Lemon Juice would make a very nice meal.

Prawns in bread crumbs, Indian style

Serves 3–4

Follow recipe for Chicken Cutlets, page 635. Substitute 1 lb of large prawns for the chicken breasts. To prepare prawns, peel and devein them first, leaving the tails on. As you slit their backs for deveining, cut almost all the way through the prawns but not quite—leave a bit of flesh intact so the prawn can open up like a butterfly. Flatten each prawn by hitting it with the broad side of a cleaver so it lies open (otherwise it will curl up).

You do not need to prick prawns with a fork or to marinate them for 4 hours—2 hours in the refrigerator will do.

Directions for breading and frying prawns are the same as for the chicken. You will, of course, be able to fry more prawns in the frying-pan at one time.

Prawns with brown sauce

Serves 6–8

3 lbs prawns (medium or
large size)

2 medium-sized onions,
peeled and coarsely
chopped

8 cloves garlic, peeled and
coarsely chopped

a piece of fresh ginger, about
1-inch cube, peeled and
coarsely chopped

3 tbs vinegar (white or red)

5 tbs vegetable oil

¼ tsp whole fennel seeds

¼ tsp whole cumin seeds

12 whole fenugreek seeds

1 tsp ground coriander

1 tsp ground cumin

½ tsp ground turmeric

2 medium-sized tomatoes
(tinned or fresh), peeled
and finely chopped

5 tbs tamarind paste (see
page 552)

2 tsp salt

⅛ tsp freshly ground pepper

½ tsp cayenne pepper
(optional—use as desired)

1 tbs brown sugar

¼ tsp ground cinnamon

¼ tsp ground cloves

¼ tsp ground mace

3 tbs finely chopped fresh
green coriander

Peel and devein prawns (see page 655). Wash, drain, and dry
thoroughly. Cover and set aside.

Place the onions, garlic, ginger, and vinegar in the container
of an electric blender. Blend at high speed until you have a
smooth paste.

Heat the oil in a wide, heavy-bottomed, 3-quart pot over a
medium-high flame. Drop in the whole fennel, cumin, and
fenugreek seeds, and as soon as they begin to darken pour in
the blender paste, using a rubber spatula to get it out quickly.
Stir and fry the paste for 10 to 12 minutes or until it is a golden
brown.

Add the coriander, cumin, and turmeric to the fried paste,
lower the heat, and continue to stir and fry for 2 minutes.
Pour in the chopped tomatoes, raise the heat to medium, and
stir and fry another 5 minutes. Finally, add the tamarind paste,
salt, pepper, cayenne, brown sugar, cinnamon, cloves, mace,

green coriander, and ½ pint of water. Mix well, bring to the boil, cover, lower heat, and simmer gently for 30 minutes. (This much of the recipe can be made ahead of time if necessary.)

Ten minutes before serving, wipe the prawns again. Bring the brown sauce to the boil and drop in the prawns. Stir and mix well; continue cooking and stirring at high temperature from 5 to 10 minutes, until the prawns turn opaque.

To serve: Spoon into warm serving bowl and serve with a rich dish. Rice with Peas might be nice, as well as a vegetable, a *dal*, and a few relishes.

Prawns with dill and ginger

Serves 4–6

a piece of fresh ginger, about 1-inch cube, peeled and coarsely chopped
4 tbs vegetable oil
½ tsp whole black mustard seeds
1 fresh hot green chili, finely sliced (use more or less as desired)
1 tsp ground coriander

1 tsp ground cumin
1 tsp garam masala
1 tsp salt
1 tsp lemon juice
2 teacups fresh dill, washed and trimmed
2 lbs medium-sized prawns, peeled and deveined (see page 655)

Place the ginger in the container of electric blender along with 3 tablespoons water. Blend until smooth.

Heat the oil in a 10–12-inch frying-pan over medium flame. When hot, put in mustard seeds. As soon as they begin to pop (10 to 15 seconds), add the following at intervals, continuing to stir and fry over medium heat: first, the paste from blender; after a minute, the green chili, adding a teaspoon of water if the mixture sticks; then the coriander, cumin, *garam masala*, salt, lemon juice; and after another 2 minutes, the dill and ¼ pint of water. Bring to the boil. Cover, lower heat, and simmer 10 minutes.

Pat the prawns dry and add to frying-pan. Turn heat to high, stir well and cook until prawns turn opaque, about 5 minutes.

To serve: Serve with Buttered Saffron Rice and a salad. A relish with tomato or onion in it would also go well with it.

Prawns, crab, or lobster, Kerala style

Serves 4–6

This dish comes from Kerala, a state along India's southwestern coast. Roasted coconut is added to the seafood to give it a thick, dark sauce. It is quite delicious.

3 tbs vegetable oil
2 medium-sized onions, peeled and finely chopped
a piece of fresh ginger, about $\frac{1}{4}$-inch cube, peeled
4 cloves garlic, peeled and chopped
$\frac{1}{2}$ teacup grated and roasted fresh coconut (see page 548)
$\frac{1}{2}$ tsp ground turmeric
1 tbs ground coriander, roasted (see page 548)
$\frac{1}{4}$ tsp cayenne pepper

3 tbs tamarind paste (see page 552)
3 medium-sized tomatoes (tinned or fresh), peeled and chopped
$\frac{1}{2}$–$\frac{3}{4}$ tsp salt
2 lbs medium-sized prawns, peeled and deveined (see page 655), or 2 lbs uncooked lobstermeat, cut into 1-inch pieces, or 2 lbs uncooked crabmeat, cut into bite-sized sections

Heat oil either in deep 10-inch frying-pan or in 10-inch heavy-bottomed pot over a medium-high flame. Put in the chopped onions and fry, stirring, for 7 to 8 minutes or until the onions are slightly browned, but soft. Turn off heat.

In a blender container combine the ginger, garlic, tomatoes, and grated roasted coconut. Blend at high speed until you have a paste. Add contents of blender container to frying-pan or pot. Also add the turmeric, coriander, cayenne, tamarind paste, salt, and $\frac{1}{4}$ pint water. Bring to the boil. Cover, lower heat, and simmer gently for 5 minutes.

(This much of the recipe can be made up to a day in advance. Keep covered and refrigerated until ready for use.)

Seven to 8 minutes before serving, bring the sauce to the boil. Add the prawns or lobstermeat or crabmeat, fold in, and cook at high temperature, stirring continuously, until the meat turns opaque (about 5 minutes). The sauce should be very thick and cling to the meat, but if you desire a thinner sauce, add a bit more water.

To serve: Place in warm bowl and serve with a rice dish and some kind of *dal. Masoor Dal* with Vegetables would be good on this menu.

Baked sea bass with yellow rice

Serves 4–6

Pomfret is normally used in this recipe. It also seems to work very well with sea bass. A paste of onion, ginger, garlic, and turmeric is first browned in oil. The fish is covered with it and then baked. The yellow rice is served on the side.

1 sea bass, 3½–4 lbs, cleaned thoroughly, with head and tail still on

1 medium-sized onion, peeled and coarsely chopped

a piece of fresh ginger, 2 inches long and 1 inch wide, peeled and coarsely chopped

6 cloves garlic, peeled and coarsely chopped

½ tsp ground turmeric

4 tbs olive or vegetable oil

¼ tsp whole cumin seeds

¼ pint tomato sauce (see page 733)

3 tbs chopped fresh green coriander; reserve a bit for garnishing (as substitute, use regular parsley or fresh dill)

¾ tsp salt

⅛ tsp freshly ground pepper

⅛–½ tsp cayenne pepper (optional)

¼ tsp ground cloves

2 tbs lemon juice

Preheat oven to 400°F., Mark 6.

Wash the fish thoroughly in cold running water and pat dry, inside and out.

Place the onion, ginger, garlic, turmeric, and 4 tablespoons of water in the container of an electric blender. Blend at high speed until you have a smooth paste.

Heat oil in 8–10-inch frying-pan over medium flame, put in the whole cumin seeds, and as soon as they darken add the paste from the blender. Fry, stirring, for 5 or 6 minutes. Now add the tomato sauce and green coriander. Cook, stirring, another 2 to 3 minutes. Remove frying-pan from heat. Add salt, pepper, cayenne, cloves, and lemon juice, stir, and leave to cool slightly. (Check the salt in the paste. Remember it has to be enough to season *all* of the fish.)

Cut 4 diagonal slits, at the same angle as the gills, on each side of the fish. Distribute paste inside fish, over fish, and inside the slits. Place fish on baking platter or on baking tray covered with aluminium foil, and bake 40 to 50 minutes, basting every 8 to 10 minutes. Meanwhile, prepare the Yellow Rice.

1 tbs vegetable oil	**½ tsp ground turmeric**
½ tsp whole cumin seeds	**1 tsp salt**
12 oz long-grain rice	

Heat oil in a 2-quart heavy-bottomed pot over medium heat. When hot, add cumin seeds. Stir a few seconds or until cumin seeds begin to darken. Add rice and turmeric. Mix and stir, fry for a minute, lower heat a bit if necessary. Add 1¼ pint water and salt. Bring to the boil, cover, turn heat down very low, and cook, without lifting lid, for 30 minutes.

To serve: It is much easier if your baking dish is also your serving platter. This way there is less danger of breaking the fish. If you do need to move it, however, be very, very careful during the transfer. You can arrange the rice around the fish if the platter is large enough. If not, serve the rice separately and garnish your fish with freshly chopped green coriander. Serve with a green salad and sweet tomato chutney.

Sea bass in green chutney

Serves 2

Here is my version of a very popular dish in which the pomfret is smothered in green chutney and then cooked in banana leaves. Having no banana leaves handy, I use the prosaic but serviceable kitchen-aid — aluminium foil. It seems to work.

1 sea bass, 1½–2 lbs (with head and tail on, but otherwise cleaned)

a piece of fresh ginger, 1 inch long and 1 inch wide, peeled and coarsely chopped

5 cloves garlic, peeled and coarsely chopped

2 tbs olive or vegetable oil

½ tsp whole black mustard seeds

2 whole hot dried red peppers (optional)

½ tsp ground turmeric

1 teacup chopped fresh green coriander

2 tbs lemon juice

½ tsp salt

Clean and wash fish thoroughly under cold running water. Pat dry, inside and out.

Preheat oven to 400°F., Mark 6.

Place the ginger and garlic in the container of an electric blender, along with 3 tablespoons of water. Blend at a high speed until you have a smooth paste.

Heat oil in 8–10-inch frying-pan over medium-high flame, and add the mustard seeds. Within a few seconds, they will begin to expand and pop. Add the red peppers, and stir them once. Pour in the paste from the blender, add the turmeric, and fry, stirring, for about 2 minutes.

Pour contents of frying-pan into the blender. Add the green coriander, lemon juice, and salt. Blend at high speed until you again have a smooth paste, adding up to 2 tablespoons of water if necessary.

Line a large baking dish with a sheet of aluminium foil, large enough to fold over the fish. Cover the fish with the green paste, inside and out. Fold the foil over so the fish is completely enclosed in it. Place in the oven and bake 30 minutes.

To serve: Remove fish carefully, place on warm platter, and serve with Plain *Basmati* Rice. A tomato or onion relish would also go well with it.

Codfish steaks in yogurt

Serves 2

This easy-to-make dish is absolutely scrumptious. My Bengali sister-in-law, Maya, makes it with cut-up chunks of *rahu*, a very popular fresh-water fish. Not finding any *rahu* around, I've turned to cod. (You could also use fresh-water carp.) Cod flakes rather easily, so handle it very gently as it cooks. I leave the codfish in steaks (instead of cutting it into smaller sections) to avoid disintegration. In India, sliced hot green chilies are added to the fish 2 or 3 minutes before the cooking time ends. I have used cayenne pepper instead.

2 codfish steaks, $\frac{3}{4}$ inch thick (about 1 lb of fish)
$\frac{1}{4}$ tsp ground turmeric
$\frac{3}{4}$ tsp salt
3 medium-sized onions
6–8 cloves garlic
$\frac{1}{4}$ pint plain yogurt
freshly ground black pepper

$\frac{1}{4}$ tsp cayenne pepper (optional)
$\frac{1}{8}$ tsp sugar
6–8 tbs vegetable oil
6 whole cardamom pods
2 cinnamon sticks, 2–2$\frac{1}{2}$ inches long

Wash the codfish steaks. See that no scales adhere to skin. Pat them as dry as possible. Sprinkle steaks on both sides with the turmeric and ¼ teaspoon of the salt, rubbing the seasonings gently in.

Peel the 3 onions. Chop 2 of them very finely and set aside. Chop the third one coarsely and place in the container of an electric blender.

Peel and chop the cloves of garlic. Put them in the blender container along with the yogurt, remaining ½ teaspoon salt, black pepper, cayenne, and sugar. Blend at high speed until you have a smooth, thin paste.

Heat 5 tablespoons of the oil in a 12-inch frying-pan over a medium flame. Put in the 2 steaks and sauté them lightly, about 3 minutes on each side, turning them over gently and carefully. (They should not get brown or crisp.) Remove with a spatula to a plate. Pour the oil from the frying-pan into a small bowl, leaving behind any sediment or pieces of fish.

Wash and dry the frying-pan. Measure the oil in the bowl and put it back in the clean frying-pan. Add more oil to make up 5 tablespoons. Turn heat to medium, and when the oil is hot, put in the 2 finely chopped onions, the cardamom, and the cinnamon. Fry the onions lightly, stirring, until they turn a light, golden-brown, about 5 minutes. Turn the heat down to low and pour in liquid from blender. Simmer (do not boil) on low heat for 10 minutes, stirring now and then.

Remove half of the sauce to a small bowl. Spread out the sauce in the frying-pan evenly, place codfish steaks on top, then pour the reserved sauce over them, spreading it evenly on top of the steaks. Cover and keep simmering at low temperature for about 10 minutes or until fish is cooked through.

To serve: I like to serve these steaks with plain boiled rice and a green salad with an oil and vinegar dressing, but you could choose any other rice dish and green beans, cauliflower, peas, or okra.

Stuffed flounder

Serves 2

Get your fishmonger to slit the whole flounder from its stomach down to its tail on the underside, and to remove its backbone. (You could do this yourself with a little patience and a very sharp knife, taking care not to destroy the outside appearance of the fish.) Make sure all the scales are removed and that the fish is washed out thoroughly. In this recipe, again borrowed from one for pomfret, the whole fish is stuffed with a mixture of potatoes, fried onions, ginger, and fennel, and then grilled. It is quite delicious. You can easily double or triple the recipe if you are feeding more people.

3½ tbs oil, preferably olive or mustard oil
1 tbs whole fennel seeds
4 medium-sized onions, finely minced
a piece of fresh ginger, 1 inch long and 1 inch wide, grated
1 large potato, boiled and roughly mashed
salt

freshly ground black pepper
⅛–¼ tsp cayenne pepper (optional)
½ tsp garam masala
1½ tbs lemon juice
1 flounder, about 2 lbs, with head and tail on, cleaned, with scales and backbone removed
2 tbs butter

Garnish

fresh green coriander

Preheat the grill.

Heat 3 tablespoons of oil in an 8–10-inch frying-pan over a medium flame, put in the fennel seeds, and fry, stirring, for about 5 seconds. Add onions and ginger, and continue to cook, stirring, for 5 to 8 minutes, or until onions are a darkish golden-brown. Turn off heat. Add the mashed potato, ½ teaspoon salt, ⅛ teaspoon black pepper, cayenne, *garam masala*, and 1 tablespoon of lemon juice. Mix well.

Line a baking tray with aluminium foil. Rub a little oil on it. Stuff fish with the potato stuffing and either close opening with skewers or sew it with a needle and thread. Place fish on aluminium foil. Sprinkle the upper side with salt, pepper, half the remaining lemon juice. Cut the butter into 6 pats and lay 3 of them over the fish. Place under grill. Grill slowly, basting with the butter. When one side is a golden-brown, turn the fish over carefully, sprinkle this side with salt, pepper, and remaining lemon juice, lay the remaining pats of butter on it, and grill it also to a golden-brown, basting with the butter. Remove carefully.

To serve: Place on warm platter, decorate with coriander, and serve with either a green salad with an oil and vinegar dressing or some Indian vegetable dishes, such as green beans or carrots or peas.

Mackerel with onions

Serves 2

5 tbs vegetable oil

4 medium-sized onions, peeled and chopped

5 cloves garlic, peeled and minced

3 tbs (loosely packed) grated fresh ginger

½ tsp ground cinnamon

¼ tsp freshly ground black pepper

½ tsp ground fennel or crushed fennel seeds

5 cardamom seeds, crushed

½ tsp ground cloves

½ tsp cayenne pepper (optional—use more or less as desired)

1 tsp salt

4 tbs tamarind paste (see page 552)

2 mackerels, 1–1½ lbs each, cleaned, with head and tail removed if desired

Garnish

4 tbs chopped fresh green   **extra salt and pepper**
  coriander

**(To double the recipe, use 6–7 tbs cooking oil and double all
  other ingredients.)**

Preheat oven to 350°F., Mark 4.

In 10–12-inch frying-pan, heat oil over medium-high heat.
When hot, put in the chopped onions, the minced garlic, and
the grated ginger. Fry, stirring, for 7 to 8 minutes or until the
onions are lightly browned and translucent. Turn heat to low
and add cinnamon, black pepper, fennel, cardamom, cloves,
cayenne, salt, and tamarind paste. Stir and mix. Cook on low
heat for 2 to 3 minutes until well mixed. Turn off heat.

Wash fish well and pat dry. Sprinkle inside and out lightly
with salt and pepper. Make 3 or 4 diagonal slashes on either
side of each fish. Place fish in oval baking dish. Put onion
mixture inside, under, and over fish, stuffing some in the slashes.
Pour any oil or juice left in frying-pan over fish. Cover fish
with waxed paper cut about the same size as the oval dish.
Place dish in oven and bake about 30 minutes or until fish is
cooked through.

To serve: Place fish on a large warm platter and sprinkle with
green coriander, salt, and pepper. Serve with a rice dish and a
simple green salad. I also like to serve it with grilled tomato
halves, sprinkled with salt, pepper, cayenne, and lemon juice.

Summer Cooking &
Barbecued Foods

'Butterflied' leg of lamb, marinated and barbecued
Cubed leg of lamb, barbecued
Boti kabab (cubed lamb kabab)
Kidney kabab
Seekh kabab
Marinated pork chops
Tandoori chicken — my version
Barbecued Pacific king prawns
Barbecued salmon steaks

SEE ALSO

Cold yogurt soup (page 565)
Seekh kebab, flat style (page 568)

HERE are several kinds of Indian cooking that are done out of doors over a charcoal grill. Many of these dishes can make welcome additions to English summer menus.

Chicken, fish, beef, lamb, and pork are rubbed with a well-spiced marinade (slits are often made in the meat to absorb the spices) and then grilled over hot coals. An indoor grill could of course be used for all the recipes in this chapter, but the taste will never equal that achieved by the outdoor grill. I find these recipes are particularly good for the summer months. If you wish to spend a day at the beach, you can marinate the meat in the morning, leave it refrigerated, and then come back just in time to light the grill and barbecue it.

Tandoori cooking

The most popular school of outdoor cooking in India is the one from the former north-west frontier. (This was the north-west frontier of India until 1947, and is now the north-west frontier of Pakistan.) In Delhi, this style of cooking was totally unknown before the partition of the Indian subcontinent. Shortly after 1947, as waves of refugees crossed the border from both sides, a tiny restaurant opened in a lower-middle-class section of town. A family of refugees, with little more than a determination to start again, owned it. Called Moti Mahal (Pearl Palace), it was right on the main thoroughfare; it didn't look exactly hygienic; and it specialized in chicken, meats, fish, and bread cooked in a *tandoor* (a clay oven with a charcoal

675

or wood fire). Within a few months, the cars of the rich began rolling up to its rather humble front doors to buy the very red-looking *tandoori* chicken and the long, flat bread, *naan*. Now, almost two decades later, it is considered a Delhi landmark which no tourist is allowed to miss, frequented by ambassadors, princes, and movie stars (as well as the lower middle class for whom it was intended!). It now offers a choice of air-conditioned indoor seating or canopied outdoor seating accompanied by recitals of *qavvalis*, poems set to a specific style of music. The tables, chairs, cutlery, plates, and waiters all have a very rough and ready look, but that is part of the attraction. *Tandoori* chicken (chicken being a great delicacy in India) is now famous throughout the country and is served in all major restaurants. The chicken (or meat, fish, or bread) is placed in a clay oven, open at the top, with a blazing fire inside. The foods get deliciously roasted and are served with small onions pickled in vinegar. All the meats are marinated in yogurt and spices before being cooked. In India, they are also tenderized with crushed green papaya and given a bright orange appearance with a vegetable colouring, rather like the Spanish *bijol*.

Muslim cooking

Another style of outdoor cooking which, for want of a better word, I'll call the 'Muslim' school, includes the *seekh kabab* and *boti kabab*. It consists of putting minced or cubed meat (kidney, liver, and udders can be used as well) on skewers and grilling it over live coals. The meats are either marinated first or, as in the case of chopped meat, ground to a paste with yogurt and then patted around a thick skewer. As they are turned and roasted, they are basted with *ghee*.

In Delhi, the best sampling of this Muslim school can be had around Jama Masjid, one of the largest and most beautiful mosques in Asia, built in the seventeenth century by the emperor who built the Taj Mahal, Shah Jahan. Under the shadows of its massive walls, surrounding it on all sides, are hundreds of tiny stalls. They sell everything—pots, pans, bedcovers, saris, lungis (a kind of male 'sarong'), and of course all the different *kababs*. On hot days, huge buckets of *thandai*—a cool drink made with milk, almonds, and cardamom—are prepared and sold to thirsty passers-by.

The recipes in this chapter are not Moti Mahal's, nor are they acquired directly from a Jama Masjid cook. They are mine— and are adaptations of the *tandoori* and Muslim styles to the kinds of meat available here. When marinating meats, I tend to use olive or peanut oil in the marinade. Indians never use olive oil, but I like its taste and use it frequently.

Vegetables for outdoor meals

In the introduction to the chapter on vegetables I discuss corn on the cob, grilled outdoors and served with lemon juice, salt, and pepper. In India this kind of corn usually is not served *with* a meal, but only as a snack or with tea; still, you may like to try it with some of the meat dishes in this chapter. Traditionally, the vegetables, rice, and potatoes are cooked indoors and then served with the barbecued foods, but when the days are too hot or I am at the beach too long, I serve lots of salads and raw vegetables, all good accompaniments to Indian barbecued food.

I also serve at least one kind of *raita* or yogurt dish; this is very easy to make and very refreshing. For good cold dishes, yogurt can be combined with boiled potatoes, with cucumber, with tomatoes and onion, with dumplings, with cooked or raw spinach, and best of all, with a combination of roasted auber- gine (which you can do on the charcoal grill), raw onions, and finely minced fresh mint (see Aubergine *Bharta*, page 714).

For dessert I generally serve just fruit, but when confronted with guests who have a sweet tooth, I often prepare *Kulfi*, a rich Indian ice cream made with nuts and milk, or *Kheer*, a kind of cold custard made with milk and rice.

'Butterflied' leg of lamb, marinated and barbecued

Serves 10–12

This is, quite easily, one of my favourite meat dishes. I ask the butcher to 'butterfly' a 8–9 lb. leg of lamb for me. The 'butterflying' process involves boning the leg in such a manner that the whole piece of meat lies flat, rather like a large, uneven steak. I then marinate it for 24 hours in olive oil, lemon juice, and a paste of onions, garlic, ginger, coriander, cumin, turmeric, mace, nutmeg, cloves, cinnamon, black pepper, cayenne pepper, *garam masala*, salt, and an orange food colouring which gives it the orange look that traditional *tandoori* meats have. After it is well marinated, it is best grilled outdoors on charcoal, though you could do it in your indoor grill—with less spectacular results! It is excellent to take along on cook-out picnics (pack the meat in a couple of plastic bags and the marinade in a tight jar—take along a pastry brush for brushing on the thick marinade paste), and refrigerated left-overs taste superb the next day. It is difficult to describe what 'style' this meat is cooked in. It is perhaps a combination of the *tandoori* school, my sister Kamal's lamb chops, and our Indian cook's roast mutton.

Note: You can always freeze half a butterflied leg of lamb and cook the rest. Halve all the ingredients in the marinade and cook the same way.

1 leg of lamb, 8–9 lbs,
  butterflied
2 medium-sized onions (1
  coarsely chopped, 1 for
  garnishing)
a piece of fresh ginger, 3
  inches long and 1 inch
  wide, peeled and coarsely
  chopped
5–7 cloves garlic (depending
  on preference—I use 7),
  peeled and coarsely
  chopped
6 fl. oz lemon juice
1 tbs ground coriander
1 tsp ground cumin
1 tsp garam masala

1 tsp ground turmeric
$\frac{1}{4}$ tsp ground mace
$\frac{1}{4}$ tsp ground nutmeg
$\frac{1}{4}$ tsp ground cinnamon
$\frac{1}{4}$ tsp ground cloves
8 fl. oz olive oil
$2\frac{1}{2}$ tsp salt
$\frac{1}{4}$ tsp freshly ground pepper
$\frac{1}{2}$–1 tsp cayenne pepper
  (optional—use less if you
  like, or none)
2 tsp orange food colouring
  (Spanish bijol, or Indian
  food colouring obtainable
  in powdered form, or
  Bush's orange-red powder)

Garnish

12 radishes

Put the chopped onion, ginger, garlic, and 4 tablespoons of the
lemon juice in the container of the electric blender, and blend
at high speed to get a smooth paste (about 1 minute).

In a bowl or a pot with non-metallic lining large enough to
hold the meat, put the paste from the blender and all the other
ingredients except the meat and the onion and radishes to be
used for garnishing later. Mix well.

Carefully cut off all fat and tissue from the meat, and with the
point of a knife make lots of jabs in it on both sides. Put the
meat in the marinade paste. Fold the meat over, or cut it into
2 pieces, if there is not room. Make a few more jabs with the
knife, and be sure the paste gets rubbed into the meat and goes
way inside the gashes. Cover the container and leave refrigerated for 24 hours. Turn the meat over at least 3 or 4 times during
this period.

The meat is now ready for grilling. But before you start, get
your garnishes ready.

Peel the second onion and slice it into *very* fine rounds (paper-thin if possible). Separate the rounds into rings and put them into a bowl of ice water, cover, and refrigerate.

Cut off the stems, leaves, and tips from the radishes and then cut them into flowers. (Starting from the tip end, start cutting into halves, but stop short as you reach the stem end. Next, cut into quarters and eighths the same way.) Put into a small bowl of ice water, cover, and refrigerate. It will look prettier if you use unblemished radishes of approximately the same size for this.

Now light your fire. If it takes 20 to 30 minutes to get red hot, start about 1 hour and 15 minutes before you intend to eat. When hot, place the metal grill at the lowest notch.

Lift meat from bowl (leaving marinade) and place on grill. Sear 5 to 8 minutes (depending on your stove) on either side. Now raise the grill to its topmost notch and cook about 20 minutes on each side. Brush frequently with the marinade until it is all used up. If you don't have a grill that moves up and down, just remember that the meat needs to cook about 50 minutes and it should be very dark on the outside and pinkish inside. Most Indians like their meat well done; you may prefer it a bit rare, but don't cook it too rare, as the spices inside won't get a chance to cook through.

To serve: Warm a large platter. Meanwhile place the meat on a carving board and cut it into thin slices. Use a very sharp knife, and do this as fast as you can, as you don't want the meat to cool off too much. Now slide the meat pieces onto the warm platter, leaving the slices in roughly the same shape as the piece of meat. Drain off the water from the radishes and onion rings. Arrange radishes around meat and lay raw onion rings on top of meat. Serve immediately.

This meat can be served with many kinds of foods. At a picnic, you could have it with a green salad and roasted corn. If you are cooking it at home, you could serve it with *Sookhe Aloo* ('Dry' Potatoes) and Green Beans with Onion Paste.

Cubed leg of lamb, barbecued

Serves 10–12

Here the leg of lamb is cut into 1-inch cubes, marinated as above, skewered, cooked, and served pretty much the same way as the butterflied leg of lamb.

Read the preceding recipe.

Just remember to remove all the fat and tissue from the meat cubes. After they have marinated overnight, push 6 or 7 cubes on each skewer and first sear on all four sides (5 to 8 minutes on each side). Now raise grill and cook on each side for about 10 minutes, basting frequently.

Garnish and serve as above.

Boti kabab
(cubed lamb kabab)

Serves 6

In this recipe, cubed lamb pieces are marinated overnight in a blend of yogurt, tomato purée, dry mustard, oil, lemon juice, garlic, ginger, turmeric, and a host of other spices. The next day, they are skewered and grilled over charcoal. The meat must cook slowly, as it needs to cook through. Also, nothing tastes worse than uncooked turmeric! (You could make this same recipe in a gas or electric grill.) Keep the meat about 4 inches from heat and cook 7 to 10 minutes on each side or until each side is well browned, depending on the heat of the grill. It should not be too rare inside or the spices will taste uncooked.

3 level tbs tomato purée
6 level tbs plain yogurt
2 tsp dry English mustard
2 tsp salt
¼ pint olive oil (or vegetable oil)
4 tbs lemon juice
1 tbs ground coriander
1 tbs ground cumin
1 tbs ground turmeric
1 tbs garam masala
½ tsp ground cloves

½ tsp ground mace
½ tsp ground nutmeg
½ tsp ground cinnamon
10 cloves garlic, peeled and coarsely chopped
a piece of ginger, 1 inch square, peeled and coarsely chopped
¼–1 tsp cayenne pepper (optional, or use as desired)
2½ lbs meat from leg of lamb, cut into 1-inch cubes

Garnish

1 medium-sized onion

In the container of an electric blender, place the tomato purée, yogurt, mustard, salt, 2 fl. oz. of the olive oil, lemon juice, coriander, cumin, turmeric, *garam masala*, cloves, mace, nutmeg, cinnamon, garlic, ginger, and cayenne. Blend marinade paste at high speed until all the spices are well mixed and the ginger and garlic have puréed (about 1 minute).

Remove all the fat from the meat pieces. Stab pieces with the point of a sharp knife, then place them in a glass or ceramic bowl. Pour the marinade over the meat. Mix well, cover, and refrigerate at least 4 hours but preferably overnight.

The meat will take 30 to 40 minutes to cook, so light your charcoal fire or preheat your grill accordingly. String the meat cubes loosely on several skewers. If you crowd them too tightly, adjacent sides of the cubes will not brown. Arrange the grill so that it is not too close to the flame (4–5-inches away). Place skewers on grill and cook each side 7 to 10 minutes or until it is nicely browned. Baste frequently with remaining olive oil. When all sides are browned, remove meat from skewers and place on warm platter.

To serve: Peel the onion and slice into *very* fine rings, paper-thin if possible. Separate the rings and place them on top of meat. Serve simply with green salad and boiled potatoes. (A good idea is to boil the potatoes ahead of time and then, when you begin your grilling, peel the potatoes, rub them with oil and some of the marinade paste, and grill them along with the meat for about 20 minutes, turning them as they brown.) This meat could also be served with Rice with Spinach or Rice with Peas. At a banquet, if you wish to serve a 'sauced' meat and a 'dry' meat, serve *Koftas* and *Boti Kabab*.

Kidney kabab

Serves 6

Follow the preceding recipe. Substitute $2\frac{1}{2}$ lbs of lamb kidney for the cubed leg of lamb.

Seekh kabab

Serves 6

This delicious recipe involves grinding the meat to a paste before wrapping it around the skewers. This fine paste is a little difficult to handle, but patience and perseverance will take care of *that* problem.

2 slices white bread

2 lbs minced lamb meat or
   minced beef (put twice
   through the mincer)

5 cloves garlic, peeled and
   coarsely chopped

a piece of fresh ginger, 1
   inch square, peeled and
   coarsely chopped

½ teacup chopped fresh
   green coriander, or fresh
   mint, or ¼ teacup each
   green coriander and fresh
   mint

1 tsp ground cloves

1 tsp ground cinnamon

1 tsp ground cumin

1 tsp ground nutmeg

1 tbs ground coriander

¼ tsp freshly ground pepper

2 tsp salt

1 tbs garam masala

½–1 tsp cayenne pepper
   (optional), or 1–2 hot
   green chilies, finely
   chopped (optional)

1 egg

8 tbs melted butter

Garnish

1 medium-sized onion
2 lemons

extra lemon juice

Soak the bread in just enough water to dampen it; squeeze out any excess. Set aside.

If your butcher has not put the meat twice through the mincer, do it yourself.

In a large non-metallic bowl, combine the meat, bread, chopped garlic, ginger, green coriander and/or mint, cloves, cinnamon, cumin, nutmeg, coriander, pepper, salt, *garam masala*, and cayenne or green chili. Mix well. Put this mixture through the fine blade of a mincer once. Taste (if you are up to it), and add more salt if needed.

(This much can be done the night before. The meat can then be tightly covered and refrigerated. The *seekhs* can be grilled in the afternoon, covered in aluminium foil, and set aside. In the evening they can be reheated, covered, in a 300°F., Mark 2 oven, and served.)

The meat should be covered and refrigerated for at least 2 hours.

Light the charcoal fire. (This dish can also be made in an

indoor grill.) While the grill is heating, peel the onion for the garnish and slice it paper-thin. Separate the rings and set them in a bowl of ice water, cover, and refrigerate.

When the fire is almost ready, begin to prepare your first batch of *seekhs* for grilling. (The number of batches will depend on the size of your stove and the number of skewers you possess.) Break the egg into the bowl with the meat mixture. Mix well. Using your palm and fingers, wrap meat around the skewers, making sausage shapes about 6 inches long and 1 inch in diameter. You have to work fast, as the meat is very fine and tends to fall off; if it is too difficult to handle, add more dampened bread. As each skewer is done, place it on the grill, which should be about 5 inches away from the fire. You may need to put your palm under the meat as you carry each skewer to the fire.

In a small bowl, mix melted butter with 4 tablespoons warm water, and baste meat frequently with this combination. When one side is browned, slide a long spatula or cleaver under the meat and gently turn it over. Cook slowly until all sides are lightly browned and cooked through. Each batch of *seekhs* will take you 15 to 20 minutes. As they are done, lift the skewers gently, putting a plate underneath in case of accidents, slide *seekhs* off skewer, and place on warmed platter. Keep platter covered with aluminium foil and in a warm place. Prepare the remaining *seekhs* in the same way.

To serve: Cut the lemons into wedges. Drain the onion rings and pat them dry on paper towels. Arrange the lemon wedges around the platter and lay the onion rings on top of the *seekh kababs*. Squeeze lemon juice over *seekhs* before eating. Serve with *naans* or *parathas* or *pooris* and a vegetable—perhaps Cauliflower with Ginger and Green Coriander—or if you like, with Rice with Spinach and Yogurt with Tiny Dumplings.

Marinated pork chops

Serves 4

In this recipe the pork chops should marinate for at least 6 hours.

1 medium-sized onion, peeled and coarsely chopped	½ tsp ground turmeric
	¼ tsp ground mace
	¼ tsp ground cloves
a piece of fresh ginger, 1 inch square, peeled and coarsely chopped	1 tsp salt
	⅛ tsp freshly ground pepper
4 cloves garlic, peeled and coarsely chopped	2 tbs olive or peanut oil
	2 tbs lemon juice
2 tbs tomato purée	¼–½ tsp cayenne pepper (optional) or to taste
3 tsp ground coriander	8 rib or loin pork chops
½ tsp ground cumin	

Put the chopped onions, ginger, and garlic in blender along with 4 tablespoons of water and blend to a smooth paste about 1 minute at high speed).

Combine paste with remaining ingredients except the pork chops and mix well.

With a fork, prod holes in the chops and put them in the marinade. Rub them well with the marinade, cover, and leave refrigerated for at least 6 hours.

Light the charcoal. When the fire is really hot, put the grill on its lowest notch. Lift the pork chops out and place them on the grill. Reserve any marinade. Sear for about 8 minutes on each side. Now put the grill in its highest notch and cook for about 20 minutes on each side. Brush with the marinade before you turn chops over each time.

To serve: If you want a very simple meal, these chops could be served with plain boiled potatoes and a salad of spinach, radishes and onion rings. Or if you like, you could serve it with Sweet Rice with Carrots and Raisins.

Tandoori chicken—my version

Serves 6–8

I have already discussed *tandoori* chicken at the beginning of
this chapter. There are, however, two things that I need to
point out here. The chickens used for the *tandoor* in India are
usually spring chickens, weighing 2–2½ lbs each. They are
cooked whole, with only wings and neck removed, on all
sides at once. I find it more convenient to marinate and cook
the chicken cut in pieces (it is also easier to serve and to eat this
way). I buy the legs and breasts of grilling or frying chickens.
(You may have an odd member of the family who just loves
wings, and who will need to be placated some other way at
some other time.) Also, I should point out again that Indians
seem to dislike the chicken skin and always remove it before
cooking.

The chicken in this recipe should be marinated for about
24 hours. Assuming that most people like both dark and light
meat, I am allocating one whole leg and half a breast for each
of 6 people.

1 medium-sized onion, peeled and coarsely chopped
6 whole cloves garlic, peeled and coarsely chopped
a piece of fresh ginger, about 2 inches long and 1 inch wide, peeled and coarsely chopped
3 tbs lemon juice
8 oz plain yogurt
1 tbs ground coriander
1 tsp ground cumin
1 tsp ground turmeric
1 tsp garam masala
¼ tsp ground mace
¼ tsp ground nutmeg
¼ tsp ground cloves
¼ tsp ground cinnamon
4 tbs olive oil (or vegetable oil)
2 tsp salt
¼ tsp freshly ground black pepper
¼–½ tsp cayenne pepper (optional, or use as desired)
½–1 tsp orange food colouring (use the Spanish bijol, or Indian powdered food colouring, or Bush's orange-red powder; its use is optional)
6 chicken legs
3 chicken breasts, halved

Garnish

1 medium-sized onion
2 lemons

extra lemon juice (optional)

Make the marinade first. Put the chopped onions, garlic, ginger, and lemon juice in an electric blender, and blend to a smooth paste, about 1 minute at high speed. Place this in a bowl large enough to accommodate the chicken. Add the yogurt, coriander, cumin, turmeric, *garam masala*, mace, nutmeg, cloves, cinnamon, olive oil, salt, black pepper, cayenne, and food colouring. Mix thoroughly.

Skin the chicken legs and breasts. With a sharp knife make 3 diagonal slashes on each breast section, going halfway down to the bone. Make 2 diagonal slashes on each thigh, also going halfway down to the bone. With the point of a sharp knife, make 4 or 5 jabs on each drumstick.

Put the chicken in the marinade and rub the marinade into the slashes with your finger. Cover and leave refrigerated for 24 hours. Turn 4 or 5 times while the chicken is marinating.

About $1\frac{1}{2}$ hours before serving, light your charcoal. It should take 20 to 30 minutes to get red hot. Place the grill on its lowest notch.

Peel the onion for garnishing and slice it paper-thin. Separate the rings and set in a small bowl of ice water, cover, and refrigerate.

When the fire is hot, lift out the chicken pieces and place on the grill. Cook about 7 or 8 minutes on each side, then raise the grill a few notches to cook more slowly for another 15 to 20 minutes on each side. Baste with marinade as you cook.

To serve: Warm a large platter. Place the chicken pieces on it. Drain the water from the onion rings and lay them on top of the chicken. Quarter the lemons lengthwise and place them around the chicken. The chicken tastes very good with extra lemon juice squeezed on it.

This chicken is considered a delicacy and can be served at a banquet with *Pullao, naans,* a few vegetable dishes, and onions pickled in vinegar.

Try it also with Rice with Spinach and Yogurt with Potatoes.

Barbecued Pacific king prawns

Serves 6

This dish tastes best when the prawns are fresh. If, however, you wish to use the peeled frozen prawns available in most supermarkets, allow them to thaw completely first. Then squeeze out all the water by pressing between your palms, and marinate after that.

3 lbs fresh Pacific king prawns	a piece of fresh ginger, about 1 inch square, peeled and coarsely chopped
¼ pint olive oil (or vegetable oil)	1–3 fresh hot green chilies (if desired), sliced, or
3 tbs lemon juice	¼–1 tsp cayenne pepper (if desired)
1 medium-sized onion, peeled and coarsely chopped	salt
1 whole head of garlic, peeled and coarsely chopped	freshly ground pepper

Garnish

2 lemons cut into wedges	fresh green coriander sprigs or fresh dill

Peel the prawns and devein them. As you devein them, slit their backs three-quarters of the way through and then spread the prawns out, butterfly fashion. When all the prawns are done, wash them and leave aside to drain.

In the container of an electric blender, put 2 tablespoons of the olive oil, lemon juice, chopped onion, garlic, ginger, chilies or cayenne, 1½ teaspoons salt, and ½ teaspoon pepper, and blend at high speed until you have a smooth paste (20 seconds).

(*Note:* If you are unsure of your ability to gauge how 'hot' it will turn out to be, first blend in half a green chili, then the other half, then a whole, and so on. Taste a drop each time. Remember, though, that once the mixture is spread over the prawns, it will taste only about half as hot.)

Place the marinade in a non-metallic bowl. Pat the prawns dry and marinate. Mix well, cover, and refrigerate for an hour.

Light your charcoal, keeping grill at a medium distance from the fire, about 5 inches. Next to the stove place salt, pepper, the remaining olive oil, and a pastry brush for basting.

When the fire is ready, brush the underside of prawns with oil and place them on the grill, leaving as much marinade on them as clings naturally. Sprinkle salt and pepper on the upper side and baste with oil. Let the prawns cook until they brown slightly, 5 to 10 minutes, depending on your stove. Then turn over with a pair of tongs, season again, and baste with oil. Cook another 5 to 10 minutes.

To serve: Place prawns on warmed platter. Garnish with lemon wedges and sprigs of parsley or dill. For a simple meal, serve with Rice with Peas and a green salad. At a more elaborate dinner, serve with meat and chicken dishes.

Barbecued salmon steaks

Serves 6

I barbecue salmon steaks very much the way I do prawns, and it tastes delicious. The marinade is almost the same as for prawns, except for the addition of a teaspoon of ground turmeric. It is, of course, best to use fresh salmon steaks.

6 salmon steaks, ¾–1 inch thick
4 fl. oz olive oil (or vegetable oil)
3 fl. oz lemon juice
1 medium-sized onion, peeled and coarsely chopped
1 whole head of garlic, peeled and coarsely chopped

a piece of fresh ginger, about 1 inch square, peeled and coarsely chopped
1–3 fresh hot green chilies (if desired), sliced, or ¼–1 tsp cayenne pepper (if desired)
salt
1 tsp ground turmeric
freshly ground pepper

Garnish

2 lemons cut into wedges

6 sprigs fresh green coriander

In the container of an electric blender, place 2 tablespoons of the olive oil, the lemon juice, and the chopped onion, garlic, ginger, green chilies or cayenne, $1\frac{1}{2}$ teaspoons salt, turmeric, and $\frac{1}{2}$ teaspoon pepper, and blend at high speed until you have a smooth paste (20 seconds).

(*Note:* If you are unsure of your ability to gauge how 'hot' it will turn out to be, first blend in half a green chili, then the other half, then a whole, and so on. Taste a drop each time. Remember, though, that once the mixture is spread over the fish, it will taste only about half as hot.)

Place the marinade in a non-metallic bowl. Wash and pat dry the pieces of fish and place in marinade. Mix well, cover, and refrigerate at least 2 hours. (Longer won't hurt.)

Heat the charcoal, keeping grill about 2–3 inches from fire. Next to stove place salt, pepper, the remaining olive oil, and a pastry brush for basting.

When the fire is ready, brush the salmon steaks with oil and place on grill. Sprinkle the top with a little salt and pepper. Baste with oil. Let them grill until one side gets little brown patches (about 5 to 6 minutes). Turn over with a spatula and grill on the other side. Sprinkle top with salt and pepper. Baste again with oil. Cook another 6 minutes or until this side is also lightly browned. Remove.

To serve: Place on warmed platter and garnish with lemon wedges and green coriander. Serve with Rice with Spinach, Carrots and Peas with Ginger and Green Coriander, and Tomato and Cucumber with Lemon Juice. You could also serve it very simply with boiled parslied potatoes and a green salad.

Vegetables

Green beans with onion paste
Green beans with ginger
Green beans with mustard
Cabbage with onions
Cabbage leaves stuffed with potatoes
Carrots and peas with ginger and green coriander
Cauliflower with ginger and green coriander
Cauliflower with onion and tomato
Fried aubergines with sour green chutney
Fried aubergines
Fried aubergines with tomato chutney
Aubergine bharta (smoked aubergine)
Mushrooms with cumin and asafetida
Crisp fried okra
Okra with onions
Stuffed whole okra
Whole pea pods with cumin
Fresh peas with ginger and green coriander
Sookhe aloo ('dry' potatoes)
Pyazwale sookhe aloo ('dry' potatoes with onions)
Potatoes with asafetida and cumin
New potatoes cooked in their jackets
Maya's potatoes
Maya's potatoes with yogurt
Potatoes in thick sauce
Potato patties (aloo-ki-tikiya)
Tomato sauce

SEE ALSO

Kheema used as stuffing (for peppers, tomatoes, and aubergines) (pages 588–9)
Recipes in the Rice chapter for rice cooked with various vegetables
    (pages 746–58)
Recipes in the Dals chapter for dals cooked with various vegetables
    (pages 778–9, 789)
Recipes in the Chutneys, pickles, and other relishes chapter (pages 798–814)

INDIAN vegetable markets are an absolute delight to the eye and a source of great anticipatory glee to the palate. The wily shopkeepers have been tutored by centuries of salesmanship and by fierce competition. They call to you as you walk by, offering you samples to handle. What better enticement can you have than a couple of small, firm, shiny aubergines placed on the palm of your hand, or a ripe Alphonso mango waved under your nose? Or they will entice you with: 'These fresh fenugreek greens just came in from the fields — at least take a look!' Another of their tricks is to begin peeling a fruit just as you think you have succeeded in resisting them. A bunch of fresh red leechees is hard enough to pass up, but when they start peeling them and the fragrant fruit juice drips to the ground, you need no further urging to pull out your wallet.

India produces most of the kinds of fruit and vegetables found in Britain and many, many more. But, of course, everything is seasonal. You can expect corn only in August, September, and October, mangoes only in the summer, cauliflower only in the winter, and fresh mushrooms only during the humid monsoons. So a change of seasons for us is more than just a change of weather. Our menu changes considerably, and for most Indians who are vegetarians it changes drastically. If you eat carrot 'water pickles' in the winter, you eat watermelon-rind pickles in the summer, and if you eat tangerines, guavas, and apples in the winter, you can have melons, loquats and *cheekoos* (a kind of round, all-brown persimmon) in the summer. There are no frozen vegetables or fruit to be had all year round, and no large-scale hot-houses raising out-of-season vegetables. India does, now, produce varieties of dried vegetables, but they are used rather rarely. Winter is our good vegetable season, and summer brings the most luscious varieties of fruit.

When an Indian housewife goes shopping and buys about 50 pence worth of vegetables, the shopkeeper, if he is friendly, will throw in a handful of green chilies and a bunch of fresh green coriander free. These two items are, as you may have already noted in many recipes, essential to a lot of our cooking, and there is a detailed note on them at the beginning of the book (pages 548 and 551). The Indian housewife will also stock up on ginger (the rhizome or 'root', see page 550), considering herself very lucky indeed if she manages to find the young, tender ginger. This has many advantages. Its skin can be lightly scraped instead of peeled; the tough fibres have not yet developed so it can be used for an instant relish which combines ginger slices, lime juice, and salt; it can also be cut, chopped, grated, or minced with much greater ease. This young ginger looks slightly pink, and if you ever happen to see it in some store, do buy it.

Onions are another important vegetable. Raw, they are used for relishes and garnishing. Ground, they are used to make the paste in which some vegetables and meats are cooked. They can be sautéed or fried and then cooked along with cauliflower or aubergine or used as stuffing for okra pods.

India grows many varieties of mushrooms, the most delicious (and expensive) of which is one that grows in Kashmir and resembles a heart-shaped black sponge! Since I have been unable to find the small, slim mushroom commonly seen in North India, my recipes are adapted to the commercial variety found in most English grocery stores.

Indians eat a lot of greens—fenugreek greens, mustard greens, white radish greens, gram (or chickpea) greens, and, of course, spinach. Each is seasonal, and each area has traditional ways of cooking its greens. In northern India, where I come from, fenugreek greens, being very strong-flavoured, are nearly always cooked with tiny new potatoes in their jackets, or with carrots. The Punjab, in north-western India, is famous for its creamed mustard greens, which both the poorest and the richest

Punjabi serves with flat corn bread and a glass of butter-milk. A very popular dish in Bengal is *chorchuri* in which various greens are first sautéed and then allowed to simmer gently with fried fish-heads. When cooking white radishes, we tend to use both the radish and its leaves. Chickpea, or gram, greens, which I used to eat raw with salt and pepper, are not to be found in this country. Spinach, which is popular throughout India, is often creamed, or dipped in batter and fried, or cooked with meat.

Corn, in India, is available only during the late summer months. The fresh cobs, peeled and roasted, are sold on street corners, rather like chestnuts. The corn seller carries a light, portable charcoal stove on which he roasts his corn, and he sells it sprinkled with salt, red pepper, black pepper, and lime juice. I have tried roasting the hybrid 'sweet corn' available in most English shops, but it is too tender, and very often it just shrivels up. The only times I have been successful have been with what the English would call the 'tougher' ears of corn. If you ever do manage to find some 'tougher' ears which won't 'melt in your mouth', peel them and roast them over charcoal. They can be superb. And don't, for heaven's sake, put butter on them. Eat them either plain or sprinkled with salt, freshly ground pepper, and a little lime or lemon juice.

Fresh okra is not always easy to find, and when it is available be sure to buy it as you would green beans. Pick a pod up and snap it, and if it is young and crisp, you buy. Otherwise, walk on. If you are lucky enough to find good fresh okra, you can slit and stuff the pods with fried onions and spices (page 719); you can slice them very fine, deep-fry them until they are crunchy (page 717) and serve them with an omelet; you can also slice them and cook them with onions, garlic, ginger, and tomatoes.

Potatoes are a popular staple throughout North India. Not only are they cooked in combination with meats, other vegetables, rice, and *dals*, but they are also cooked with every imaginable permutation of spices. A young child may want his potatoes boiled and then fried with cumin seeds; at a picnic one might have 'dry' potatoes cooked with red peppers, fenugreek, fennel, cumin, and mustard seeds; at a banquet one might be served potatoes cooked with yogurt and the *garam masalas*, cinnamon, cloves, cardamom, bay leaves, etc.; and of course, there is my favourite, potatoes cooked with asafetida and cumin, a 'wet' dish best enjoyed with *pooris*.

A vegetable that was once basically ignored in Britain and that is now evoking the first stirrings of interest, is the aubergine. Still, it seems confined to the occasional parmigiana, moussaka, or ratatouille. It deserves better. Stuffed, baked, and covered with sauce, it makes a glorious main course. Its roasted pulp, when mixed with yogurt and fresh mint, makes a refreshing summer 'salad'. Deep-fried in slices and smothered in one of many sour chutneys, it can serve as an appetizer or an accompanying vegetable dish.

I can't really begin to list all the Indian vegetables and fruit. We have a 'pickling' carrot that is dark red, like a beetroot; during late winter, Indians buy green chickpeas, or *chholas*, which can be cooked or eaten raw; our sweet potato has the consistency of a crumbly baking potato; we eat lotus stems and water chestnuts; we have *jamuns* and *falsas* and *bair* and *kaseru* and *parval*—fruits and vegetables which don't even have any English names. And this list could go on and on.

The recipes in this chapter are mostly for vegetables that can be found in supermarkets—beans, carrots, cauliflower, cabbage, aubergines, peas, potatoes, etc. I do have some recipes for okra which should be cooked only when fresh pods are available.

Green beans with onion paste

Serves 4–6

Green beans can be cooked in many ways. In India we tend to overcook them—at least according to the best Chinese and French standards. But as I have explained earlier, it is mainly to kill germs and because we love spices. We like our spices to permeate a vegetable, and this cannot happen unless a vegetable is allowed to become fairly tender. When you finish preparing this recipe, your beans will not look bright green, nor will they be very crisp. They will be a brownish dark-green, smothered in spices, and utterly delicious.

1½ lbs fresh green beans	2 tsp ground coriander
1 medium-sized onion, peeled and coarsely chopped	1 tsp ground cumin
	½ tsp whole cumin seeds
3 cloves garlic, peeled and coarsely chopped	½ tsp whole black mustard seeds
a piece of fresh ginger, about 1 inch square, coarsely chopped	1 or 2 whole dried red peppers (optional), or ½ hot fresh green chili, sliced in half (optional), or ¼ tsp cayenne pepper (optional)
1 medium-sized tinned or fresh tomato, peeled and coarsely chopped	
½ tsp ground turmeric	1 tsp salt (or to taste)
10 tbs vegetable oil	2 tsp lemon juice (or to taste)

Garnish

1 tbs finely chopped fresh green coriander

Wash the beans. Trim the ends. Slice them into fine rounds about ⅛ to ¼ inch thick. (This takes a while, so it is best to sit down somewhere with chopping board and sharp knife and do about 8 beans at a time.)

Put the onion, garlic, ginger, tomato, and turmeric in a blender and blend to a smooth paste.

Put 6 tablespoons of the vegetable oil in an 8-inch frying-pan or heavy-bottomed pan, and heat it on medium. Pour in mixture from blender and fry for about 5 minutes, stirring all the time, adding a teaspoon of warm water if and when it starts to stick at the bottom. Now put in the coriander and cumin and continue frying another 5 minutes, again adding a teaspoon of warm water if necessary to prevent sticking. Turn off heat.

In a 10-inch frying-pan, heat the remaining tablespoons of oil over medium flame. When very hot, put in the whole cumin and mustard seeds. After 10 seconds, add the whole red peppers if you are using them. Stir once, and as the peppers darken and the mustard seeds begin to pop, put in the sliced green beans and the sliced green chili if you are using it. Now scrape up all the mixture from the first frying-pan and add it to the beans. Fry the beans on medium flame for 5 minutes, stirring all the time. Turn heat to low, add the salt and lemon juice, and let the beans cook covered, stirring now and then, until they are tender (about 35 minutes). If you are using cayenne pepper, stir it in 5 minutes before end of cooking time. If the beans stick to the frying-pan, add 1 tablespoon of water, stir, and keep cooking.

To serve: These beans can be cooked in advance and reheated over a low flame. Serve them in a warm dish and, if you like, sprinkle finely chopped green coriander over them. They are good with *Koftas* and plain rice, go well with nearly all meats, and especially well with *parathas*, *pooris*, and *chapatis*.

Green beans with ginger

Serves 4–6

This dish is simple to make and has a very fresh, gingery taste.

1½ lbs fresh green beans
a piece of fresh ginger, about
   2 inches long and 1 inch
   wide, peeled and coarsely
   chopped
6 tbs vegetable oil
¼ tsp ground turmeric
½ fresh hot green chili
   (optional), washed and
   sliced very fine

3 tbs chopped fresh green
   coriander
1 tsp ground cumin
2 tsp ground coriander
1¼ tsp garam masala
2 tsp lemon juice (or to
   taste)
1 tsp salt (or to taste)

Wash the green beans and trim the ends. Slice into fine rounds, ⅛ to ¼ inch thick. When all the beans are chopped. set aside in a bowl.

Put the ginger in the blender with 3 tablespoons of water and blend at high speed until it is a smooth paste.

Heat the oil in a 10-inch frying-pan over medium heat. While it is heating, pour in paste from blender and add turmeric. Fry, stirring constantly, for 2 minutes, then add the sliced green chilies and the green coriander, and after another minute, put in the green beans and continue cooking and stirring for about a minute. Add the cumin, coriander, 1 teaspoon of the *garam masala*, lemon juice, salt, and 3 tablespoons of warm water. Cover frying-pan, turn flame very low, and let beans cook slowly for about 40 minutes, stirring every 10 minutes or so.

To serve: These beans can easily be cooked in advance and reheated. Serve them in a warm dish, with ¼ teaspoon *garam masala* sprinkled on top.

They go well with nearly all meat and chicken dishes. They can be eaten with plain boiled rice and *Moong Dal*, or served with hot *pooris* or *parathas* or *chapatis*.

Green beans with mustard

Serves 4–6

Here is another easy recipe for beans, in which they are slightly sweet.

1½ lbs fresh green beans	1 tsp sugar
3 level tbs plain yogurt	¾ tsp dry English mustard
½ hot fresh green chili, sliced very thinly, or ¼ tsp cayenne pepper (optional)	¾ tsp ground cumin
	2 tsp lemon juice
	5 tbs vegetable oil
3 tbs finely chopped fresh green coriander	5 whole fenugreek seeds
	¼ tsp whole cumin seeds
1 tsp salt	¼ tsp garam masala

Wash green beans and trim ends. Slice finely into rounds of about ¼ inch.

In a cup or small bowl, mix the yogurt with the green chili or cayenne, parsley, salt, sugar, dry mustard, cumin, and lemon juice. Add 3 tablespoons water and mix well.

Heat the oil in a frying-pan over medium heat. When hot, add the whole fenugreek and cumin seeds. When the fenugreek seeds begin to change colour (about 20 seconds) put in the beans. Fry, stirring, for about 5 minutes.

Beat the yogurt mixture once again and stir into the beans. When the frying-pan begins to make bubbling noises, cover, reduce heat to very low, and allow to cook slowly for 40 minutes. Stir every 10 minutes or so.

To serve: Place in warm serving dish and sprinkle with with *garam masala*. Serve with Rice with Cauliflower and Cumin Seed, *Masoor Dal*, and Chicken with Tomatoes and Butter. Or serve with *Kheema*, plain boiled rice, and *Moong Dal*. Or serve with *parathas*. If you are having many vegetables, then serve these beans with Cauliflower with Ginger and Green Coriander, *Sookhe Aloo, Khare Masale Ka Gosht*, and hot *chapatis* or *pooris* — an excellent meal.

Cabbage with onions

Serves 4–6

There are many ways of cooking cabbage in India. It can be cooked by itself or with peas or potatoes. It can be cooked with prawns and with meat. Here are some of these recipes. Just remember that when you start cooking the cabbage, it looks like a lot. But it reduces. So make sure you cook enough to feed all the people you are planning for. I find that one medium-sized head of cabbage will feed 4 people easily. It can be stretched to 6 if there are many other dishes. As with most of our vegetables, we tend to overcook cabbage, but the end result tastes very good, so who cares!

1 medium-sized head of cabbage

2½ medium-sized onions

9 tbs vegetable oil

6 whole fenugreek seeds

½ tsp whole cumin seeds

½ tsp whole black mustard seeds

¼ tsp whole fennel seeds

2 cloves garlic, peeled and coarsely chopped

a piece of fresh ginger, 1 inch by 1½ inches, peeled and coarsely chopped

1 medium-sized tomato (tinned or fresh), peeled

½ tsp ground turmeric

½–1 hot green chili, thinly sliced (optional)

¾–1 tsp salt

1 tsp garam masala

1 tbs lemon juice

Trim away the outer damaged leaves of the cabbage, wash it, and cut it in quarters. Remove the stem and hard core and shred cabbage lengthwise as finely as you can.

Peel 2 of the onions and cut them each into half, lengthwise. Now slice finely into half-circles.

Heat 6 tablespoons of the oil in a 10-inch heavy-bottomed pot over medium heat, and add the fenugreek, cumin, mustard, and fennel seeds. As the seeds start sizzling and changing colour (about 10 seconds), put in the sliced onions. Fry them over medium heat for about 3 minutes. Add the shredded cabbage, stir a few times, put the lid on, lower flame, and cook for 15 minutes.

Uncover and cook over fairly low heat for 30 minutes, stirring occasionally to prevent burning.

Meanwhile, peel and coarsely chop the remaining ½ onion and put it with the garlic, ginger, and peeled tomato in electric blender. Blend to a paste.

In a frying-pan heat the 3 remaining tablespoons of oil. Add the paste from the blender, the turmeric, and the green chili. Fry, stirring all the time, for 8 to 10 minutes (adding, if necessary, 1 teaspoon of warm water at a time to prevent sticking). When the cabbage has cooked for 30 minutes, add this fried paste mixture, along with the salt, *garam masala*, and lemon juice. Stir and let it cook for another 5 minutes.

To serve: Serve with *parathas*, *pooris*, or *chapatis*. If serving with rice, serve *karhi* or *dal* and a chicken or meat dish like Chicken Cooked with Yogurt or Lamb *Korma* or *Koftas*. Plain yogurt or Yogurt with Potatoes would also go well with it.

Cabbage leaves stuffed with potatoes

Serves 6–8

Cabbage leaves can be stuffed with meat or potatoes. Here is my mother's recipe for the latter.

5 medium-sized potatoes	3½ tsp salt
7 medium-sized onions	¼ tsp cayenne pepper
10 tbs vegetable oil	(optional)
2 tsp whole fennel seeds	1 tbs lemon juice
1 tsp whole cumin seeds	1 medium-sized head of
1 tsp garam masala	cabbage

The stuffing: Boil the potatoes, then peel and dice them into ¼-inch pieces.

Peel the onions, cut them in half lengthwise, and slice them into fine half-circles.

In a frying-pan, heat 6 tablespoons of the oil over medium heat. Add the onions, frying, stirring, and separating the rings until the onions are brownish, about 7 or 8 minutes; they should not get crisp.

Add the fennel and cumin seeds and fry another 7 or 8 minutes on lower flame. The onions should look a rich reddish-brown now.

Add the diced boiled potatoes to the onion mixture and continue frying. As you fry, mash the potatoes with the back of a slotted spoon or potato masher.

To the potato and onion mixture add the *garam masala*, $2\frac{1}{2}$ teaspoons salt, cayenne pepper if desired, and lemon juice. Mix it all up and set aside, uncovered, to cool slightly.

The cabbage: Cut off the hard stem of the cabbage, remove the hard, damaged outer leaves, and wash it. In a pot large enough to hold the whole cabbage, bring to the boil water to which 1 teaspoon salt has been added. Drop the cabbage in (the water should cover at least three-quarters of it), cover, and allow to boil for 5 minutes. Lift cabbage out of boiling water, run under cold water, and carefully remove each leaf, taking care not to break it. Dry. If the inner leaves are still crisp, drop them again in the boiling water until they go limp. Remove and cool under cold water.

Spread out one leaf at a time. Snip out the hard core of the outer leaves with a sharp knife or a pair of kitchen shears. You can snip to about an inch into the leaf, removing a kind of narrow V. Now place a tablespoon of the stuffing in the centre of the leaf and fold the edges over. Put the stuffed leaf on your left palm and with your right palm gently squeeze out any extra moisture. This also helps to keep the stuffed cabbage leaves tightly closed.

In a 10-inch frying-pan, heat the remaining 4 tablespoons of oil over medium heat. Squeeze each stuffed cabbage leaf again between paper towels and put in frying-pan. Fry, a few pieces at a time, until each piece is browned on all sides. Take care not to let the leaves open. Remove them to a plate. When all the pieces are done, lower the heat, arrange the stuffed cabbage pieces in the frying-pan in tight layers, add 2 tablespoons water, cover, and cook on very low flame for 10 to 15 minutes.

To serve: Remove very carefully and serve on large, warm platter. Serve with Cubed Lamb with Onions and Raisins and Rice with Peas or with *Karhi, Koftas,* and plain boiled rice. This dish is also very good served with hot *parathas.*

Carrots and peas with ginger and green coriander

Serves 4–6

a piece of fresh ginger, 2 inches by 1 inch, peeled and coarsely chopped
1½ lbs young, slim carrots
6 tbs vegetable oil
¼ tsp whole black mustard seeds
5 whole fenugreek seeds
¼ tsp ground turmeric
1 packed teacup coarsely chopped fresh green coriander

1 fresh hot green chili, washed and finely sliced (optional, or substitute ¼ tsp cayenne pepper)
1 lb fresh peas, shelled
1 tsp ground coriander
1 tsp ground cumin
1 tsp garam masala
1 tsp salt

Put the ginger in blender with 3 tablespoons of water and blend until smooth (about one minute).

Peel the carrots and slice them into rounds about ⅛ inch thick.

Heat the oil in a 10–12-inch frying-pan over medium heat. When very hot, add the mustard and fenugreek seeds. When mustard seeds begin to pop (10 to 20 seconds), put in the ginger paste and turmeric, keeping your face averted. Fry for about 2 minutes, stirring frequently. Add chopped green coriander and green chili or cayenne, and cook, stirring, another 2 minutes. Add carrots and peas and cook 5 minutes more, stirring frequently.

Now put in the coriander, cumin, *garam masala*, salt, and 3 tablespoons of warm water. Stir for a minute, cover, lower heat, and cook slowly 30 minutes. Stir gently every 10 minutes or so.

To serve: Lift gently out of frying-pan and place on serving dish. Serve with hot *pooris* or *parathas*. This dish goes well with any sauced meat dish—Lamb with Onions and Mushrooms, etc. It is also good with Shrimp with Dill and Ginger, plain *Moong Dal*, and Rice with Potatoes and Cumin Seed.

Cauliflower with ginger and green coriander

Serves 6–8

a piece of fresh ginger, about 2½ inches by 1 inch, peeled and coarsely chopped

1 large head fresh cauliflower, or 2 small ones

8 tbs vegetable oil

½ tsp ground turmeric

1 fresh hot green chili, finely sliced, or ¼ tsp cayenne pepper (optional)

1 packed teacup coarsely chopped fresh green coriander (coriander greens or cilantro)

1 tsp ground cumin

2 tsp ground coriander

1 tsp garam masala

1 tbs lemon juice

2 tsp salt

Put the ginger into a blender jar with 4 tablespoons of water, and blend until it becomes smooth (about 1 minute).

Cut off the thick, coarse stem of the cauliflower and remove all leaves. First break the cauliflower into large flowerets, using your hands if it is a loosely packed head and a sharp knife if it is too tightly packed. Since you want to end up with *small* flowerets, not longer than 1 to 1½ inches and not wider at the head than ½ to 1 inch, I find that the best way is to take each large floweret and begin by slicing the stems crosswise into fairly thin rounds. Keep these, as they are quite edible. When you reach the upper end of the stem, start breaking off the small flowerets. Slice the stem into rounds whenever it seems too long, and keep the rounds. Wash the flowerets and the stem rounds in a colander and leave to drain.

Heat oil in 10–12-inch frying-pan over medium heat. Add the ginger paste and turmeric. Fry, stirring constantly; after about 2 minutes, add green chili or cayenne and green coriander; after another 2 minutes, put in the cauliflower, continuing to cook and stir for 5 minutes. (If necessary, add 1 teaspoon warm water at a time to prevent sticking.) Now add the cumin, coriander, *garam masala*, lemon juice, salt, and 3 tablespoons warm water, cook and stir for about 5 minutes, then cover, lower flame, and let cook slowly for 35 to 45 minutes (the tightly packed cauliflower takes longer to cook), stirring gently every 10 minutes. The cauliflower is done when it is tender with just a faint trace of crispness along its inner spine.

To serve: Lift out gently and place in serving dish—a low, wide bowl would be best. Serve with hot *chapatis*, *pooris*, or *parathas*, or serve with any kind of lentils and plain boiled rice. It is particularly good with Lamb *Pullao* and Cucumber *Raita*.

Cauliflower with onion and tomato

Serves 6–8

1 medium-sized onion, peeled and coarsely chopped	1 medium-sized fresh or tinned tomato, peeled and chopped
4 cloves garlic, peeled and coarsely chopped	1 tbs chopped fresh green coriander
a piece of fresh ginger, 2 inches long and 1 inch wide, peeled and coarsely chopped	1 fresh hot green chili, washed and finely sliced, or ¼ tsp cayenne pepper (optional)
1 large head fresh cauliflower, or 2 small ones	2 tsp ground coriander
8 tbs vegetable oil	1 tsp ground cumin
½ tsp ground turmeric	1 tsp garam masala
	2 tsp salt
	1 tbs lemon juice

Put chopped onion, garlic, and ginger in blender with 4 tablespoons of water and blend to a paste.

Break off cauliflower into small flowerets (see preceding recipe), not longer than 1 to 1½ inches, and not wider at the head than ½ to 1 inch. Wash in colander and leave to drain.

Heat the oil in a heavy-bottomed 10–12-inch pot over medium flame, pour in the paste from the blender, and add the turmeric. Fry, stirring, for 5 minutes.

Add the chopped tomato, green coriander, and green chili or cayenne, and fry 5 minutes. If necessary, add 1 teaspoon of warm water at a time and stir to prevent sticking. Now put in the cauliflower, coriander, cumin, *garam masala*, salt, and lemon juice. Stir for a minute. Add 4 tablespoons warm water, stir, cover, lower flame, and allow to cook slowly 35 to 45 minutes (the tightly packed cauliflower heads take longer to cook). Stir gently every 10 minutes or so. The cauliflower is done when each floweret is tender with just a faint trace of crispness along its inner spine.

To serve: Follow suggestions of previous recipe.

Fried aubergines with sour green chutney

Serves 6

1 packed teacup chopped
  fresh green coriander
1 fresh hot green chili,
  washed and finely sliced,
  or ¼ tsp cayenne pepper
  (optional)
8 oz plain yogurt
½ tsp salt (a little more if you
  need it; sometimes yogurt
  is more sour than at other
  times)
½ tsp roasted, ground cumin
  seeds (see page 549)
1 tbs lemon juice
vegetable oil for deep frying

6 small, oval aubergines or
  1 large one (aubergines
  come in so many sizes
  that after reading this
  recipe, I'm afraid you have
  to be your own judge
  about how many you need)
8 fenugreek seeds
½ tsp fennel seeds
½ tsp black onion seeds
  (kalonji), if available
¼ tsp cumin seeds
salt
freshly ground black pepper

For the chutney: Put green coriander and chili in blender with 3 tablespoons water and blend until smooth paste (about 1 minute). You may need to push coriander down a couple of times.

In a bowl, combine yogurt, salt, roasted ground cumin seeds, lemon juice, and the paste from blender. Cover and refrigerate green chutney until ready for use.

Cooking the aubergines: Ten minutes before eating time, heat oil at a depth of 1½ to 2 inches in frying-pan, wok, or *karhai* over medium heat. While heating, wash and dry aubergines. If you have the small, oval ones, quarter them lengthwise, preserving the stem and the sepals. If you have a very large one, quarter it lengthwise and slice each quarter into ½-inch thick pieces.

When oil is very hot, add the fenugreek, fennel, onion, and cumin seeds. After 10 or 20 seconds, drop in as many aubergine pieces as the container will hold in one layer. Deep-fry each batch until golden-brown. Drain on paper towels, sprinkle each batch with salt and freshly ground pepper, and place in a warm dish. When the aubergines have fried, spoon one-quarter of the cold chutney over them and serve immediately. Serve the rest of the chutney on the side.

To serve: While the aubergine fries, I usually put all the rest of my dinner into serving dishes and bring them to the table. I bring the aubergine dish out last. This dish is usually served at meals along with other vegetables. It is very rarely the only vegetable at the table. Try it at a Sunday lunch along with Prawn with Dill and Ginger, Rice with Black-eyed Peas, and green beans.

You can also cut the aubergine fairly small, insert toothpicks, and serve it with drinks.

Fried aubergines

Serves 4

This dish is made best with the small young aubergines that are only 3 or 4 inches long. It is very simple, but *cannot* be prepared in advance. Ten minutes before you are to eat, excuse yourself and go and cook the aubergines. Serve them crisp and piping hot. (You can take the rest of the food to the table while the aubergines fry.)

vegetable oil for deep frying
8 whole fenugreek seeds
½ tsp whole fennel seeds
¼ tsp whole cumin seeds
½ tsp black onion seeds (kalonji), if available

4 small oval aubergines, 3–4 inches long
salt and freshly ground black pepper
dash of cayenne pepper, if desired
1 tbs lemon juice

Put $1\frac{1}{2}$ to 2 inches of oil in a wok, *karhai*, or frying-pan and heat on medium heat.

Measure out fenugreek, fennel, cumin, and onion seeds and keep handy. Wash and wipe the aubergines (leave them unpeeled), and slice lengthwise into flat, $\frac{1}{8}$–$\frac{1}{6}$-inch slices.

When the oil is heated, put in all the seeds. When they change colour or begin to pop (5 to 10 seconds), put in the sliced aubergine pieces – only as many as your utensil will hold in one layer. Fry to a golden-brown on both sides. Drain on paper towels and sprinkle with salt, black pepper, cayenne, and lemon juice.

To serve: Serve each batch hot, as soon as it is seasoned. The aubergine should be slightly crunchy. This is really a side dish which should never be the only vegetable at a meal. Serve it along with Carrots and Peas with Ginger and Green Coriander or cauliflower as an accompaniment to any meat, chicken, or fish. You can also use it as a garnish for baked fish or a chicken roast by arranging the slices, petal-like, around a platter.

Fried aubergines with tomato chutney

Serves 6

To make this recipe, first prepare the tomato chutney, and 10 minutes before serving, fry the aubergines according to directions in preceding recipe. They will be served with the hot chutney spooned over them.

Tomato chutney

lump of tamarind size of large walnut	**$\frac{1}{2}$ tsp whole cumin seeds**
	$\frac{1}{2}$ pint tomato sauce (page 733)

1 medium-sized onion, peeled and coarsely chopped

4 cloves garlic, peeled and coarsely chopped

4 tbs vegetable oil

⅛ tsp ground asafetida, or ⅛-inch lump asafetida

4 whole cardamoms

4 whole cloves

1 tsp whole mustard seeds

1 tsp salt (or more to taste)

⅛–¼ tsp cayenne pepper (optional)

1 tsp garam masala

⅛ tsp ground cinnamon

1 tsp sugar

⅛ tsp freshly ground black pepper

4 tbs finely chopped fresh green coriander

Soak the lump of tamarind in 6 fl. oz. hot water. Leave at least 4 hours or overnight. Make paste (about 4 fl. oz.), following directions on page 552).

Put onion and garlic in electric blender with 3 tablespoons of water. Blend at high speed to a smooth paste (1 minute).

Heat olive oil in 2-quart pot, preferably with non-metallic lining, over medium heat. Put in the asafetida, then add the cardamoms and cloves, and finally the mustard and cumin seeds. When the seeds pop, expand, and change colour (10 to 20 seconds), add the paste from the blender, keeping face averted. Fry paste, stirring, for 4 to 5 minutes, sprinkling a teaspoon of warm water in it if it sticks.

Now add the tamarind paste, tomato sauce, salt, cayenne (if desired), *garam masala*, cinnamon, sugar, and black pepper. Bring to the boil. Cover and allow to simmer gently for 15 minutes.

While chutney is simmering, prepare aubergines according to preceding recipe.

Taste the chutney, and check the salt and sugar. You may want to put in more of one or the other. At this stage, I pick out the cardamoms and the cloves from the chutney and discard them. Mix the green coriander with the chutney.

To serve: Arrange the fried aubergines on a platter. Pour some of the hot chutney over them and serve the rest on the side. See preceding recipe for suggested accompaniments.

Aubergine bharta (smoked aubergine)

Serves 4–6

Until the advent of gas, most cooking in India was done on wood or coal, and one of the waste products of wood and coal is, of course, ash. Not wishing to waste even a waste product, we geared our cuisine so that while some foods were cooking on top of the flame, others were being roasted in the ashes. (Later, the ash was used like Brillo pads to scour the pots and pans.) As a child, I remember begging the cook to put some onions in the ashes, just for me. He would pick out a tiny onion from the vegetable basket and bury it deep in the ashes with his iron tongs. Then, about an hour later, he would whisper to me that it was ready. I would pick off the burned outside, scorching my hands as I did so, and gobble up the succulent inside.

Another vegetable that was roasted was the aubergine. Once roasted, it was peeled and the inside was either mixed with chopped raw onion, fresh mint, and yogurt (page 811) or cooked further with onions and tomatoes — which is the recipe I'm going to give you now.

Lacking ashes in my 'modern' kitchen, I roast the aubergine right on top of the stove over an open flame. This is a bit messy, so I would advise you to insert an aluminium burner liner before you start.

1 large aubergine, preferably with a stem

1 medium-sized onion, peeled and coarsely chopped

a piece of fresh ginger, about 1 inch square, peeled and coarsely chopped

½ fresh hot green chili, finely sliced (optional)

1 tbs chopped fresh green coriander; reserve a little for garnishing

2 medium-sized tomatoes (tinned or fresh), peeled and coarsely chopped

2 cloves garlic, peeled and
   coarsely chopped
5 tbs vegetable oil
½ tsp ground turmeric

¾–1 tsp salt (according to
   size of aubergine)
1 tsp lemon juice
1 tsp garam masala

Line your gas burner with aluminium foil. (If you have an electric stove, place the aubergine under a preheated grill, and turn it around until it is blackened on all sides, although it will never taste quite as smoky as when done over a flame.) Stand your aubergine, stalk up, directly over a medium-low flame. Leave it there until the bottom has burned black and looks completely scorched. Now lay it on its side. As soon as the area nearest the flame darkens and turns soft, turn the aubergine slightly. Use the stem of the aubergine to turn with. Keep turning until the whole aubergine is done. (You could use tongs, but take care not to burst the aubergine or you will have a big mess.) As more and more of the aubergine is 'scorched' it will turn softer and be more difficult to handle. Don't give up. This whole process will take 20 to 25 minutes.

Once the aubergine is 'smoked', put it on a plate and carry it to the sink. Put it under cold running water and peel the blackened outer skin under the running water. Drain, shaking off as much water as you can.

Put the peeled inside of the aubergine on a chopping board and chop it coarsely. Set aside in a plate or bowl.

Put the onion, ginger, and garlic in a blender with 3 tablespoons of water and blend to a paste at high speed.

Heat the oil in a frying-pan over medium heat. While heating, pour in the paste from the blender and add the turmeric. Fry this mixture, stirring frequently; after about 5 minutes, when it begins to turn brown, add the green chili and the green coriander; then after about 1 minute, the chopped tomatoes. Lower the flame and cook for 10 minutes, stirring occasionally. Finally, add the chopped aubergine, raise the flame to medium low, and fry, stirring, for 10 to 15 minutes, seasoning with the salt, lemon juice, and *garam masala*.

To serve: Remove the *bharta* to a warm dish and serve sprinkled with green coriander. It is best when eaten with *pooris* or hot *chapatis*. Serve *Khare Masale Ka Gosht* with it and *Sookhe Aloo* ('Dry' Potatoes).

Mushrooms with cumin and asafetida

Serves 4–6

1½ lbs fresh mushrooms
2 tbs vegetable oil
a generous pinch ground
    asafetida, or ⅛-inch lump
    asafetida
½ tsp whole cumin seeds

2 whole hot dried red peppers
¼ tsp ground turmeric
½ pint tomato sauce (see
    page 733)
1 tsp salt

Clean mushrooms. Chop off the coarse stem ends.

Heat oil in 2–3-quart pot over medium heat, and put in the asafetida. It will sizzle and expand within 5 seconds. Now add the cumin seeds, and as soon as they darken (5 to 10 seconds), the red peppers. Stir once and add the turmeric and the mushrooms. Stir mushrooms for ½ minute and add the tomato sauce, 1 pint of water, and the salt. Cover, lower heat, and simmer gently 15 to 20 minutes.

Remove from heat. The mushrooms can be eaten now, but it is better to let them sit 1 to 2 hours to absorb the taste of the broth-like sauce and then reheat.

To serve: Serve in little individual bowls. The thin, delicious sauce can be eaten with a spoon or with hot *chapatis* or *pooris*. You can easily build a meal around the mushrooms. *Sindhi Gosht*, Yogurt with Tiny Dumplings, and a *dal* would complete the meal nicely.

Crisp fried okra

Serves 4

I have discussed okra earlier (see page 697). Buy it only when it is young, fresh, and crisp. Serve this crisp-fried okra to people who think they dislike okra—they will hardly recognize it. Another advantage of this dish is that it cooks easily and quickly. It can take less than 15 minutes from the time you begin washing the okra until you serve it.

1 lb fresh young okra	$\frac{1}{8}$ tsp cayenne pepper
oil for deep frying	(optional)
salt	$\frac{1}{2}$ tsp garam masala
freshly ground black pepper	(optional)

Wash the okra. Wipe it with paper towels. Remove head and tail and slice the pods in rounds of $\frac{1}{8}$-inch thickness. You can slice 2 or 3 at the same time.

Heat 1 inch of oil in a 10-inch frying-pan over medium-low flame. Check heat by dropping in one slice of okra; if it sizzles immediately, the fat is ready. Put in as much okra as will fit in one layer. You will need to do at least three batches. Fry each batch 4 to 5 minutes, until the okra turns crisp and a bit brown.

Remove from frying-pan with a slotted spoon and place on paper towels to drain. Sprinkle each batch with salt, pepper, cayenne, and *garam masala*. Serve immediately.

To serve: Fried okra is delicious with a mushroom omelet for lunch or with a variety of other vegetables at dinner. Okra goes particularly well with *Urad Dal* and with *Koftas*. Or you could use it as an unusual garnish for a lamb roast, frying about 2 lbs of okra and surrounding the leg of lamb with it.

Okra with onions

Serves 4–6

This is the way okra is generally cooked in most parts of Delhi. The success of this dish depends upon the onion paste's being cooked to the right consistency before the okra is added.

4 medium-sized onions, peeled and coarsely chopped

5 cloves of garlic, peeled and coarsely chopped

a piece of fresh ginger, about 2 inches long, 1 inch thick, and 1 inch wide, peeled and coarsely chopped

6 tbs vegetable oil

1 tsp whole cumin seeds

2 tsp whole fennel seeds

1 tsp ground turmeric

1 tbs ground coriander

1 tbs tomato purée

1 lb fresh young okra

1 tsp salt

2 tsp garam masala

2 tbs lemon juice

¼ tsp cayenne pepper (optional)

Put onion, garlic, and ginger in electric blender, add ¼ cup warm water, and blend to a paste.

Heat oil in a 10–12-inch frying-pan over medium heat. Add the cumin and fennel seeds. When the fennel begins to change colour (20 seconds or so), add the paste from the blender and the turmeric.

Cook this paste over medium heat for about 20 minutes, stirring frequently and scraping the bottom. The paste will reduce and turn a lovely brown colour.

Add the coriander and fry, stirring; after a minute, add the tomato purée and cook, stirring, for about 1 minute. Turn off the heat under the frying-pan.

Wash the okra and wipe it with a paper towel. Slice a few pods at a time into ¼-inch rounds.

Turn the heat to medium again under the frying-pan with the onion paste. Add the okra, salt, *garam masala*, lemon juice, and 4 fl. oz. of warm water. When the onion paste starts bubbling, cover, turn heat very low, and allow to cook slowly for 35 minutes, or until tender. Stir every 10 minutes or so to prevent sticking.

To serve: Serve like stuffed okra, the next recipe.

Stuffed whole okra

Serves 4–6

This recipe, which comes from my maternal grandmother, is perhaps *the* most delicious way to cook okra. Fresh young okra pods are slit and stuffed with a mixture of fried onions, fennel, cumin, and fenugreek. Then they are lightly fried and allowed to simmer until cooked. Stuffing the slim okra requires a little patience, but don't let that stop you. The most confirmed okra hater will be converted and the ooooh's and aaaah's of your guests will be ample reward for your trouble.

8 medium-sized onions, peeled and finely chopped
8 cloves garlic, peeled and. minced
a piece of fresh ginger, about 2 inches by 1½ inches by 1 inch, peeled and grated
2 tsp whole cumin seeds
4 tsp whole fennel seeds
20 whole fenugreek seeds
10 tbs vegetable oil
1 tsp ground turmeric
salt
4 tsp garam masala
2 tbs lemon juice
1 lb fresh young okra

The stuffing: Since this dish is to be cooked in two 10-inch frying-pans to accommodate all the okra, divide the onions, garlic, and ginger into two equal piles. Make two separate equal piles of the cumin, fennel, and fenugreek seeds.

Heat 5 tablespoons of oil in each frying-pan over medium heat, and when hot, put in the cumin, fennel, and fenugreek seeds. As they begin to pop and change colour (5 to 10 seconds), put half the onion, garlic, and ginger and ½ teaspoon turmeric into each frying-pan. Stir and fry over medium heat for about 10–12 minutes until the onions look a rich brown. Stir frequently.

Add ½ teaspoon salt and 1 teaspoon *garam masala* to each frying-pan and stir. Turn off heat under both frying-pans. Using a slotted spoon, remove onion mixture from frying-pans, leaving as much of the cooking fat behind as possible. You will need it later. Collect the onion mixture from both frying-pans in a bowl, add 2 more teaspoons *garam masala* and the lemon juice, mix, and set aside to cool.

The okra: Wash the okra and pat it dry with paper towels. Trim off the head and the lower tip.

Since the stuffing of the okra takes a little time, place the okra, the bowl of stuffing, a clean platter, and a small sharp knife on a table, and settle yourself on a chair. Pick up one okra pod at a time. Make a slit along its length, being sure that you do *not* go through the opposite side and that you leave about ⅛ inch at the top and bottom unslit.

Assuming you are right-handed, slip your left thumb into the pod to keep the slit open. With your right thumb and fingers, pick up a little stuffing at a time and push it into the slit. You will need from ¼ to 1 teaspoon of stuffing for each pod, depending on its size. As each pod is stuffed, set it aside on the platter.

Turn on the flame under both frying-pans and keep on medium-low heat. Divide the okra between the two frying-pans and lay them slit side up in the pans in a single layer if possible (a few overlapping won't matter). Cook for 5 minutes, shake salt (about ¼ teaspoon to each pan) over okra, add 2 tablespoons warm water to each pan, cover, lower flames to very, very low, and cook gently for 30 minutes or until the okra is tender.

To serve: Lift out gently and arrange on warm platter. Serve with Lamb *Pullao* or Rice with Peas, Pork Chops à la Jaffrey, and Potatoes with Asafetida and Cumin. It also goes very well with all Indian breads.

Whole pea pods with cumin

Serves 4

This is an unusual dish which I have eaten only in my own family. The peas are not shelled, but cooked whole, and are eaten rather like artichokes. Each pea pod is picked up by its stem, placed in the mouth between the teeth, and then pulled; you are eating not just the peas but the fleshy part of the pod as well. All that you leave is the stem and the inner tough lining of the pea pod. Needless to say, the peas that you buy must be very fresh and tender and not too long or you might just gag! The peas must also look very green and undamaged.

1½ lbs fresh peas	1 tbs lemon juice
2 tbs vegetable oil	½–1 tsp garam masala
⅛-inch lump asafetida, or	1 tsp salt
⅛ tsp ground asafetida	⅛ tsp freshly ground pepper
½ tsp whole cumin seeds	

Wash the pea pods, discarding any old ones.

Heat the oil in a wide 10–12-inch casserole-type pot over medium heat. When hot, add the asafetida and cumin seeds. In 10 or 20 seconds the cumin seeds will begin to change colour. Put in the pea pods immediately and stir for a minute. Now add the lemon juice, ½ teaspoon *garam masala*, salt, and pepper. Stir, put in 2 tablespoons of warm water, cover, turn heat to very low, and allow to cook gently for 20 to 30 minutes, until tender. Stir once or twice while cooking, but do it gently.

To serve: Lift pea pods out very carefully (some may have split, but that is quite normal). Serve in a warm dish, sprinkled with ½ teaspoon *garam masala*, if desired.

This dish may be served at a lunch, with an Indian 'tea', or as an appetizer at dinner.

Fresh peas with ginger and green coriander

Serves 4–6

Follow the recipe for Carrots and Peas with Ginger and Green Coriander on page 706. Substitute for the carrots and peas 3 pounds of fresh peas. Shell them and then proceed according to the recipe. Cook till peas are tender, about 10 minutes.

Serve with fresh *parathas*, Potatoes with Asafetida and Cumin, and *Koftas*. Instead of *parathas*, you could substitute Rice with Potatoes and Cumin Seed, *Moong Dal*, and Cucumber *Raita*.

For a Western meal, try serving it with a loin of pork or roast leg of lamb.

Sookhe aloo
('dry' potatoes)

Serves 6–8

Here is a very simple potato dish which can even be made with left-over boiled potatoes. In fact, it is best if the potatoes are boiled at least 4 hours in advance of the final cooking.

7 medium-sized potatoes, boiled in their jackets and cooled

10 tbs vegetable oil

⅛ tsp ground asafetida, or ⅛-inch lump asafetida

1 tsp whole fennel seeds

1 tsp whole cumin seeds

1 tsp whole black mustard seeds

12 whole fenugreek seeds

3 whole dried hot red peppers

½ tsp ground turmeric

1½ tsp salt (or to taste)

1 tbs lemon juice

Peel the boiled potatoes and dice them into pieces about 1 inch by ½ inch.

In a wok, *karhai*, or 10–12-inch pot, heat the oil over medium flame. When very hot, put in first the asafetida, 5 seconds later the fennel and cumin seeds, then the mustard seeds and fenugreek seeds in quick succession. As they begin to change colour and pop (about 10 seconds), add the red peppers. As soon as the red peppers swell and darken, add the diced potatoes, turmeric, and salt. Keep on medium heat and fry, turning gently so as not to break the potatoes. Fry for 15 to 20 minutes, until the potatoes are browned unevenly. Squeeze lemon juice over potatoes, and check the salt.

To serve: Lift out carefully with a slotted spoon and serve in a shallow dish. Warn guests not to bite on red peppers unless they mean to. This dish goes very well with most Indian meals. (I used to take *sookhe aloo*, *parathas*, and mango pickles to school as my lunch.) It can be taken on picnics, where it can be heated in aluminium foil and served with *parathas* or *pooris*, or it can be served with a lamb or pork roast as a 'different' kind of starch. Try it also with my marinated charcoal-grilled 'Butterflied' Leg of Lamb.

Pyazwale sookhe aloo
('dry' potatoes with onions)

Serves 6–8

Here is another simple potato dish that can be served as a vegetable with *pooris* or as an appetizer, on top of savoury biscuits.

6 medium-sized potatoes	1 medium-sized onion,
5 tbs vegetable oil	peeled and coarsely
$\frac{1}{8}$ tsp ground asafetida, or	chopped
$\frac{1}{8}$-inch lump asafetida	$\frac{1}{2}$ tsp ground turmeric
$\frac{1}{2}$ tsp whole cumin seeds	$1\frac{1}{4}$ tsp salt
$2\frac{1}{2}$ tsp whole black mustard	1 tsp garam masala
seeds	2 tbs lemon juice
1–3 whole dried red peppers	
(optional—1 red pepper	
will make it mildly hot;	
3 very hot)	

Boil the potatoes in their jackets. Peel them and mash them coarsely with a fork or hand masher.

Heat the oil in a 10–12-inch frying-pan over medium heat. When hot, first put in it the asafetida; after it has sizzled for a few seconds, add the cumin and mustard seeds; then in 10 seconds or so, the red pepper (or peppers). When pepper changes colour (1 to 5 seconds), put in the chopped onions and turmeric. After the onions have cooked 3 to 5 minutes and turned brown at the edges, put in the mashed potatoes, salt, *garam masala*, and lemon juice. Fry, stirring and mixing, for 5 to 7 minutes.

To serve: Place in a warmed dish and serve with *chapatis*, *pooris*, or *parathas*. This is a good dish to take on picnics, too. Serve as an appetizer on top of Melba toast or savoury biscuits. (Remove whole red peppers before placing on any kind of toast.)

Potatoes with asafetida and cumin

Serves 4–5

This was one of the most popular potato dishes in our family. It is a 'wet' dish and needs to be served in small individual bowls. It is very good—and easy to make.

4–5 medium-sized potatoes
2 tbs vegetable oil
⅛ tsp ground asafetida, or
   ⅛-inch lump asafetida
½ tsp whole cumin seeds
1–2 dried hot red peppers
   (optional)

½ tsp turmeric
12 fl. oz tomato sauce
   (see page 733)
1 tsp salt

Wash, peel, and quarter potatoes. Put them in bowl with cold water to cover.

In 2–3-quart pot, heat oil over medium heat. As it heats, put potatoes in colander to drain. When the fat is hot, put in the asafetida; after it sizzles (5 seconds), add the cumin seeds; when they sizzle and change colour (5 to 10 seconds), add the red peppers, which will begin to change colour in a couple of seconds. Now put in the drained potatoes and the turmeric. Fry the potatoes for about 2 minutes, stirring them now and then.

Now put in ¾ pint water, tomato sauce, and salt. Bring to the boil. Cover and allow to simmer very gently for about 1½ hours.

To serve: Take to the table in a deep dish. Give each person a little bowl to serve himself the potatoes as well as the sauce. These potatoes are best served with *pooris*, *chapatis*, or *parathas*, but they are also good with plain boiled rice and Lamb with Onions and Mushrooms. Left-overs can be put in the blender or mashed to make an excellent soup.

New potatoes cooked in their jackets

Serves 4–6

In India we get tiny new potatoes which are about ¾ inch in diameter. They have soft skins and are satiny inside. We cook them in many ways, one of my favourites being a dish in which they are cooked whole with fenugreek greens. Use fenugreek greens if available. If not, I have worked out a substitute dish with green coriander. Also, if you cannot find the very tiny potato I just use the regular 'new potato' and dice it.

6–8 medium-sized new potatoes (depending on size) or 1 lb tiny new potatoes	**½ fresh hot green chili, finely sliced (optional), or ¼ tsp cayenne pepper**
a piece of fresh ginger, about 1½ inches square, peeled and coarsely chopped	**2 teacups chopped fresh green coriander or fresh fenugreek greens**
½ tsp ground turmeric	**1¼ tsp salt**
5 tbs vegetable oil	**1 tsp garam masala**
¼ tsp whole cumin seeds	**1 tbs ground coriander**
	2 tbs lemon juice

Wash the potatoes well, but do not peel. Leave whole if small. If not, quarter them lengthwise, then dice them. Set aside in a bowl of cold water.

Put the ginger in the electric blender with the turmeric and 3 tablespoons water. Blend at high speed until smooth.

Heat the oil in a 10–12-inch heavy-bottomed pot over medium heat. Add the whole cumin seeds, and after about 10 or 20 seconds, when they change colour, add the paste from the blender and cook for about 1 minute. Put in the sliced green chili if you are using it, and cook another 30 seconds.

Drain the potatoes and add them to the pot. Fry them, stirring, for about 5 minutes. Scrape the bottom of the pan as you stir. Put in the green coriander or fenugreek greens, lower heat a bit, and fry another 5 minutes, stirring gently. Add the salt, *garam masala*, coriander, lemon juice, cayenne pepper if you are using it, and 3 tablespoons warm water. Stir, scrape bottom gently, and cover. Reduce flame to very low and let the potatoes cook about 25 minutes, until done. Stir very gently every 10 minutes or so.

To serve: Lift out carefully and serve in warm shallow dish or platter. Try these potatoes with roast pork or lamb. They are very versatile in an Indian meal and can be served in an all vegetarian lunch with cabbage, Whole Pea Pods with Cumin, *Pappadum*, *Karhi*, and rice—or they can be served with almost any meat or poultry dish. They are very good with hot *chapatis* and Tomato and Onion with Lemon Juice.

Maya's potatoes

Serves 6–8

My sister-in-law makes this dish, so I've named it after her. In India, we take it with us on picnics, heat it on a portable charcoal stove, and eat it with 'stale' *pooris* and hot mango pickle.

8 medium-sized potatoes
oil for deep frying
1 onion, peeled and coarsely chopped
4 garlic cloves, peeled and coarsely chopped
6 tbs oil (or re-use 6 tbs strained deep-frying fat)
asafetida (optional), ⅛-inch-square piece or 1 large pinch ground
7 fenugreek seeds
½ tsp fennel seeds
¼ tsp black onion seeds (kalonji), if available
¼ tsp black mustard seeds
1 bay leaf
3 dried hot red peppers (optional, or use less)
½ tsp ground turmeric
2 medium-sized tomatoes (tinned or fresh), peeled and chopped
1 pinch sugar
1½ tsp salt

Boil potatoes, preferably 2 hours ahead, and leave to cool. Just before you begin cooking, peel the potatoes and halve them; quarter them if they are large.

Heat over medium flame 1 to 2 inches of oil in 10–12-inch frying-pan, wok, or *karhai*, and fry the potatoes in two or three batches until golden-brown on all sides. (If you prefer, you can fry the potatoes in much shallower fat. Just make sure you get them lightly browned on all sides.) Drain and set aside.

Put the chopped onion and garlic into blender with 3 tablespoons water and blend to a paste.

Heat 6 tablespoons of oil in a heavy-bottomed 10–12-inch pot. Keep heat on medium. When very hot, add asafetida, fenugreek seeds, fennel seeds, onion seeds, mustard seeds, bay leaf, and red peppers in this order and in quick succession. Fry 10 to 20 seconds, until bay leaf and peppers begin to turn dark. Add paste from blender and turmeric, and fry, stirring, for 5 minutes; then add chopped tomatoes and sugar and cook another 5 minutes. Stir in gently 1 pint water, salt, and fried potatoes, and bring to boil. Cover, lower flame, and simmer 10 minutes. Raise cover, gently lift each potato and turn it over, cover, and simmer another 10 minutes.

To serve: Place potatoes gently in a shallow serving dish. Pour the sauce over them and serve with *pooris* or *parathas*. For a simple meal try *Kheema* with Fried Onions, *chapatis*, and this potato dish. It would also go well with a lamb roast and Aubergine *Bharta*, or you could serve it with Prawn *Pullao* and plain yogurt.

Maya's potatoes with yogurt

Serves 6–8

This is a mild variation on the preceding recipe and is quite delicious.

5 oz plain yogurt   **½ tsp salt**

Prepare preceding recipe. While it cooks, empty yogurt into a small bowl, add ¼ pint cold water and salt, and stir to a smooth paste. Strain it and set aside. When potatoes are done, take them off heat and leave 10 minutes to cool a bit.

Five minutes before serving, pour the yogurt over the potatoes, making sure to distribute it evenly. Stir and mix it in very gently. (The potatoes tend to break a little as you do this, but don't worry!) Now heat the dish. Don't let it boil, or the yogurt will curdle. When heated through, turn flame off.

To serve: Place potatoes gently in serving bowl and pour sauce over them. Serve with *pooris* or *parathas*, a 'dry' meat like *Khare Masale Ka Gosht*, or grilled chicken pieces. You could also have it with *Pullao* and a cauliflower dish.

Potatoes in thick sauce

Serves 6

My mother's family in Delhi still lives a stone's throw from Parathe-wali-gulley, the 'gulley' or lane where *parathas* (special Indian breads) are cooked. This narrow lane is flanked on right and left by stalls which have been famous for their *parathas* for more than a century. Each *paratha* costs less than 5 pence. And with it you can have as many vegetables and pickles as you like—free! This potato recipe is one of the dishes served there.

5 medium-sized boiling
  potatoes
1 piece of fresh ginger, 2
  inches long, 1 inch thick,
  and 1 inch wide, peeled
  and coarsely chopped
1 tbs ground coriander
1 tsp ground cumin
2 medium-sized tomatoes
  (tinned or fresh), peeled
  and chopped

6 tbs vegetable oil
1 tsp whole fennel seed
10 fenugreek seeds, whole
½ tsp black onion seeds
  (kalonji), if available
½ tsp black mustard seeds
1–3 whole dried hot red
  peppers (optional)
1½ tsp salt
1½ tsp lemon juice
1 tsp garam masala

Boil the potatoes in their jackets at least 2 hours ahead. Leave to cool.

Put ginger in electric blender along with the coriander, cumin, tomatoes and 3 tablespoons warm water. Blend to a paste at high speed.

Peel the cooled potatoes. The charm of this dish is that the potatoes are not cut with a knife; they are broken by hand. Break each potato in half, then in half again, and the larger pieces once again. Each potato should be broken up into about 6 to 8 pieces, depending on its size.

Heat the oil in a 10-inch heavy-bottomed frying-pan over medium heat. When hot, add the fennel, fenugreek, onion, and mustard seeds. When the mustard seeds begin to pop (20 seconds or so), put in the red peppers. As they darken, put in the paste from the blender. Fry for about 5 minutes, stirring frequently. Now put in the pieces of potato and fry another 3 to 5 minutes, stirring constantly. Add ¾ pint hot water, salt, and lemon juice. Bring to the boil. Cover, lower flame, and allow to simmer gently for 15 to 20 minutes. The sauce should now be fairly thick.

To serve: Sprinkle with the *garam masala*, stir, and serve in a warm bowl or dish. This tastes best eaten with most Indian breads—*pooris* and *parathas* in particular—but it is also good with plain boiled rice, *Moong Dal*, and *Kheema*.

Potato patties
(aloo-ki-tikiya)

12 patties

These delicious patties are sold on street corners in India pretty much the way chestnuts are sold here. Eaten as snacks or with meals, they consist of mashed potatoes stuffed with lentils and spices.

6 medium-sized potatoes	**2 tbs vegetable oil plus oil**
3 tbs yellow split peas (the	**for frying patties**
kind available in super-	**5 fenugreek seeds**
markets), soaked overnight	**2 tbs chopped onion**
in ½ pint cold water and	**3 tbs trimmed, chopped**
½ tsp salt	**fresh green coriander**
3 tsp salt	**½–1 fresh hot green chili,**
	finely sliced (optional)

Two hours before dinner, boil the potatoes in their jackets.

While potatoes are boiling, drain split peas. Then boil them in a 1–2-quart pot with 1 pint cold water and ½ teaspoon salt for 15 minutes. Remove from heat and drain in a colander or strainer, shaking it to get out as much water as you can, and invert peas in bowl. Cover the bowl.

In a frying-pan heat 2 tablespoons oil over a medium flame. When very hot, add the fenugreek seeds, and when they begin to change colour (5 to 10 seconds), put in the onions, continuing to fry about 2 minutes until the onions begin to turn brown at the edges. Add the green coriander and green chili, and stir another 2 to 3 minutes. Next, put in the drained split peas and ½ teaspoon salt. Keep stirring and cook for about 5 minutes, until all the water has evaporated and the mixture in the frying-pan seems to become one lump. Cover and set aside.

Peel and mash potatoes with a fork or hand masher. (Do not use a whipping gadget or an electric mixer. Don't add butter.)

A few lumps will remain, but don't worry—just get the potatoes as smooth as you can. Add 2 teaspoons salt and mix thoroughly.

To form patties: Divide the mashed potatoes into 12 balls. Divide the split pea mixture into 12 portions. Flatten each potato ball on the palm of your hand, put a portion of the split pea stuffing in the centre of it, and cover the stuffing with the mashed potato by bringing the outer circumference to the centre. Make a ball again. Flatten it gently to have a patty about 3 inches in diameter. Make all the patties this way, keeping them covered on a platter if you are not going to be eating soon. (You can prepare this much of the recipe from a few hours to a day ahead.)

Cooking these patties is an art in itself. In India they are cooked on a *tava*, a large, slightly curved iron plate. If you have a *tava*, it is really the ideal utensil to use. If you don't, use a heavy-bottomed frying-pan, but remember to cook only two or three patties at a time. If you crowd them it becomes difficult to lift and turn them.

Since these patties are cooked like pancakes with very little oil, use only enough to coat the bottom of your frying-pan or *tava*, and heat over medium-low flame. Put in a few potato patties and cook them slowly—about 8 to 10 minutes on each side. When one side turns a golden-red, carefully work your spatula under it without breaking the hard crust and drop it over on its unfried side. Add another teaspoon of oil, swirling it around. Fry this side for 8 to 10 minutes also, until it has formed a red-brown crust. If the patties brown too quickly, lower the heat.

Note: Since these have to be served hot, and since you may not be able to make many at a time in a frying-pan, you could use two frying-pans.

To serve: Place on a heated platter and serve hot. These patties are marvellous for snacks. They are usually served with Tomato Tamarind Chutney, or Fresh Green Chutney with Coriander Leaves and Yogurt.

Or you could serve them as part of any meal. I once cooked a rather pleasant lunch of chicken breasts grilled with just butter, salt, pepper, and lemon. I also made a simple green salad and we had these potato patties. It was wonderful!

Tomato sauce

Tomato sauce is used in some of my recipes. This is how you can make it:

Take 1 lb tin of tomatoes and pour the contents into a stainless steel pot or a pot lined with a non-metallic substance. Add ¼ teaspoon salt and ¼ teaspoon sugar. Bring to the boil. Cook on medium heat, stirring frequently and breaking up the tomatoes, until you reduce contents of pot by half. Pour these contents into an electric blender and blend until you have a smooth paste. A 1 lb tin of tomatoes should yield 8 to 10 fl. oz of sauce. The sauce can be frozen or kept covered in the refrigerator for at least a week.

Rice

Plain boiled rice
Plain baked rice
Plain basmati rice
Buttered saffron rice
Basmati rice with spices and saffron
Sweet rice
Sweet rice with carrots and raisins
Sweet rice with carrots and raisins cooked in aromatic broth
Rice with whole spices
Rice with peas
Rice with peas and whole spices
Rice with potatoes and cumin seed
Rice with cauliflower and cumin seed
Rice with spinach
Rice with spinach cooked in aromatic broth
Rice with black-eyed peas
Rice with yellow split peas
Left-over rice with mushrooms
Prawn pullao
Halibut or cod pullao
Chicken biryani
Pullao (rice with lamb)
Fried onion rings for garnishing

SEE ALSO

Roast chicken stuffed with spiced rice (page 641)
Duck — stuffed and roasted (page 646)
Baked sea bass with yellow rice (page 665)

THE statistics astonish me. They say an average Indian eats one-half to two-thirds of a pound of rice per day whereas the Englishman eats, on an average, about four pounds of rice per year! You may think that the poor Indians eat so much rice because they have nothing better to fill themselves up with. Recently, there was a great shortage of rice in an area of South India, and famine conditions were beginning to prevail. The government offered the people a flour rich with soybean and fish protein as a substitute. The people refused it. They wanted rice. They *liked* rice. The English, on the whole, have really not discovered rice. They dismiss rice as a 'starch' and as a poor relative of the more popular 'starches'—potatoes and pasta. Potatoes can be baked, fried, mashed, boiled, 'duchessed', varied ad infinitum, and there are so many different kinds of pasta ... But rice? What can you do with rice? So even when it *is* served here, more often than not it is cooked unimaginatively and amateurishly. I have seen the English eat mushy rice without any complaints. I have watched some of the better cooks using precooked and partially cooked rices in recipes. While most of the English are aware of what good roast beef should taste like, few indeed are even conscious of what good rice *is*.

Let us start at the very beginning. What kind of rice should you buy? Looking at the varieties available in the average supermarket, I can more easily tell you what not to buy. Don't buy quick-cooking or 'instant' rice. Don't buy parboiled or partially cooked rice. Neither of them really tastes like rice. Also, don't buy prepackaged mixes with herbs and spices. There is no 'mix' that you cannot manage better on your own. Once you understand and master the different methods of cooking rice, there is no limit to the number of recipes you can invent.

Buy a long-grain uncooked rice. Patna rice is good and easily available. If you are lucky enough to be near a delicatessen carrying *basmati* rice do buy it. This rice is grown in the foot-hills of the Himalayas. It has a narrow, long grain and a very special flavour and smell. The best *basmati* is aged before it is cooked—and it is cooked only by the rich because it is also very expensive. In the last few years, India, being short of foreign exchange, has been exporting so much of its *basmati* rice that it is often easier to buy it in London than it is in New Delhi! But keep the *basmati* for special occasions.

For most of the recipes in this book, I have used long-grain rice. If you use some other variety, you may have to experiment with the amount of water needed and the cooking time. All uncooked rices are not the same. Where I have used Indian *basmati* rice, I have indicated how it should be cooked.

Even though India consumes a lot of rice, not all Indians are rice eaters. In fact, the Indians can be divided into the rice eaters and the wheat eaters. While most of South India and Bengal are considered rice-eating areas, Delhi, Punjab, Uttar Pradesh, and Madhya Pradesh are generally conceded to be the wheat-eating areas. During times of grain rationing, each Indian has to declare himself a wheat eater *or* a rice eater and have a big 'W' or 'R' stamped on his ration card. This entitles him to get the major portion of his weekly ration in the grain of his choice.

To confuse matters further, there are those Indians, too, who eat both rice *and* wheat. Even though I come from a wheat-eating area, our family in India ate both rice and wheat bread for lunch, and wheat bread (*chapatis*) for dinner. With the rice and the *chapatis*, we ate our meat, vegetables, and lentils (*dals*). When rice and wheat breads (*chapatis*, *pooris*, *parathas*, etc.) are served at the same meal, one is usually served before the other. In our family rice was always served first, but I have eaten in homes where the *chapatis* were served first.

Most Indians eat rice with their hands. It is mixed with the lentils or meat and vegetables and eaten with the tips of the fingers. Not all the rice is mixed with the rest of the food at once. You serve yourself each dish on a separate part of your plate. The only things you may put on top of your rice are the lentils and other soup-like and semi-liquid dishes.

Rice can be cooked with almost any meat, vegetable, or fish and served as a main dish. It can be cooked with whole or powdered spices; it can be boiled, steamed, or baked; it can be cooked in water or in aromatic broths. It can be the side dish as in plain boiled rice, or it can be the main course as in *pullao* and *biryani*. It can be pounded or ground to make desserts like *kheer* and *phirni*. The visiting physician prescribes it when he leaves with the injunction, 'Give her *khitcherie* and chicken soup'. (*Khitcherie*, which means 'hodge-podge', consists, in this case, of a porridge made of rice and lentils.) The wary tourist with stomach tremors is advised, 'Eat nothing but boiled rice and yogurt for a few days!' Every festival, the rice-growing villagers get drunk on their local variety of rice wine — 'wine' being a polite word for the rotgut they generally produce.

For important occasions, rice is tinted a bright yellow with turmeric or vegetable colouring or, best of all, with saffron, which gives it not just a yellowish-orange saffron colour but a delicious fragrance as well. I'll never forget my first introduction to saffron. I was in my early teens and on my first visit to Kashmir. We were riding past a hill and valley that were completely purple from all the crocuses growing there. I remarked on their beauty to my Kashmiri companions, who in turn told me that the flowers meant something more than just beauty to them. 'This is *zaafraan*,' they said. *Zaafraan*? I thought. I wondered vaguely why, if this was the saffron flower, it was not saffron-coloured. One of the young Kashmiri boys got off his horse, plucked a flower, and brought it to me. He pulled its petals apart, showing me the stigma, which is dried and called saffron, and he told me that thousands of stigmas were needed to get a tablespoon of saffron.

Rice is not used merely for eating, though. It has its place in all the Hindu religious ceremonies; it is thrown into the fire at weddings because it is the great symbol of fertility. My family priest explained it to me this way: 'A young girl is like a rice plant. The rice is planted in one field, but it cannot bear fruit until it is transplanted into another field. So it is with the girl. She is born in her father's house, but she cannot bear children until she is transplanted into her husband's house.'

There are several methods of cooking rice so that each grain comes out firm and separate, as you will see in the recipes that follow. Rice will always stay warm, left covered, for about 20 minutes after the burner has been turned off.

Plain boiled rice

Serves 4–6

12 oz long-grain rice   **1 tbs butter**
1¼ pints water   **1 tsp salt**

Combine all the ingredients in a 2–3-quart heavy-bottomed pot with tight-fitting lid. Bring to the boil, cover, and turn flame as low as it will go. Leave for 25 to 30 minutes. Lift cover and quickly check to see if rice is cooked through. Turn off heat, and leave lid on until ready to serve.

(When cooking plain boiled rice, I always cook more than I need because there are such wonderful ways of dressing up cooked rice. I cover and refrigerate the left-overs, and cook them for breakfast, lunch, or dinner.)

Plain baked rice

Serves 6

12 oz long-grain rice   **4 tbs butter**
1 tbs salt

Preheat oven to 300°F., Mark 2.

Fill a 3-quart pot with about 5 pints of water, add the salt, and set over a high flame.

Meanwhile, wash and drain the rice in a colander.

When the water is boiling, put the rice in it. Bring to a second boil, and boil rapidly for exactly 5 minutes.

Drain the rice by pouring it through a colander.

Put the rice in an ovenproof dish. Cut the butter into 4 patties and place over the rice. Now cut a piece of aluminium foil 2 inches larger than the rim of the dish, cover the dish, and then put the lid on top of the foil. Crinkle foil around the edges to seal as thoroughly as possible. The rice has to cook in its own steam, so that steam must not be allowed to escape.

Place dish in oven for 45 to 50 minutes (check after 45 minutes to see whether rice is done).

Plain basmati rice

Serves 6

I love the taste of a plain *basmati* rice eaten with *moong dal.* When I was a child, these two items were always on our luncheon menu—but today, with most of the *basmati* supply controlled by exporters or black marketeers, even the thought seems extravagant! *Basmati* is, however, available in English delicatessens, so do buy it and cook it when you can. This method of cooking rice can also be used for any long-grain fine-quality rice.

12 oz basmati rice	**1 tbs butter**
1¼ tsp salt	

Wash the rice well in cold water. Soak it in a bowl with 2 pints of water and ½ teaspoon salt for 30 minutes. Then drain.

Melt the butter in a heavy-bottomed pot over medium flame. Pour in the drained rice and stir for a minute. Add 18 fl. oz water and ¾ teaspoon salt. Bring to the boil, cover, lower heat to *very* low, and cook for 20 minutes.

Lift lid. Mix rice gently with fork. Cover again and cook another 10 minutes, or until rice is tender.

Serve with almost any dish you like. I love it with *Moong Dal, Pyazwala Khare Masale Ka Gosht*, lime wedges, and a cucumber relish of some kind.

Buttered Saffron rice

Serves 6

2 tsp leaf saffron, loosely packed, roasted and crumbled according to directions on page 552	**2 tbs warm milk** **1 tbs salt** **12 oz long-grain rice** **4 tbs butter**

Preheat oven to 300°F., Mark 2.

Soak saffron in warm milk. (I just leave the milk to heat on top of the pilot light area of my stove. You could heat it slightly in a small pot if you like.)

Fill a 3-quart pot with about 5 pints water. Add the salt and bring to the boil.

Meanwhile, wash and drain the rice in a colander.

When the water is boiling, put the rice in it and bring to a second boil. Boil rapidly for exactly 5 minutes.

Drain the rice in a colander.

Put the rice in an ovenproof dish. Pour the saffron milk over it in streaks. Cut the butter into 4 patties and place over the rice. Now cut a piece of aluminium foil 2 inches larger than the rim of the dish. Place foil on top of the dish and put the lid on top of the foil. Crinkle foil around edges to seal.

Place dish in oven for 45 to 50 minutes, checking after 45 minutes to see if the rice is done.

To serve: The rice, when ready to serve, will have saffron-coloured streaks in it. Spoon it out onto a large warm platter and serve with any Indian meal. It goes particularly well with Lamb with Spinach, Lamb *Korma*, and Chicken with Tomato sauce and Butter. Try it also with 'Butterflied' Leg of Lamb and with Codfish Steaks in Yogurt.

Basmati rice with spices and saffron

Serves 6

Even though this recipe is for Indian *basmati* rice, any long-grain, fine-quality rice can be used instead.

1 tsp leaf saffron, loosely
  packed, roasted and
  crumbled according to
  directions on page 552
2 tbs warm milk
12 oz basmati or long-grain
  rice

1¼ tsp salt
2 tbs vegetable oil
5 cardamom pods
2 cinnamon sticks, 2½–3
  inches long

In a small container, soak saffron in warm milk.

Wash the rice well in cold water. Soak it in a bowl with 2 pints water and ½ teaspoon salt for 30 minutes, then drain.

Heat the oil over medium flame in 2–3-quart heavy-bottomed pot (with a tight-fitting lid—to be used later), put in the cardamom pods and cinnamon sticks, and stir a few times. Add the rice, frying and stirring about a minute.

Add 18 fl. oz water and ¾ teaspoon salt. Bring to the boil, cover, reduce heat to *very* low, and cook for 20 minutes.

Lift off cover. Gently but quickly mix rice with a fork, turning it around a bit. Pour the saffron milk in 2 or 3 streaks over the rice. Cover and keep cooking another 10 minutes or until rice is quite done.

To serve: Turn the rice onto a platter with a fork (this keeps the grains whole). Serve with Chicken *Moghlai* and Yogurt with Spinach.

Sweet rice

Serves 6

This is a very simple recipe for sweet rice. It goes rather well with many English dishes, like baked ham, pork chops, roast loin of pork, lamb chops, etc. It is mild flavoured and not too sweet. If you like, you could elaborate on the recipe by adding nuts and raisins.

2½ tbs vegetable oil	1 tbs ground coriander
4 whole cloves	½ tsp ground cinnamon
3–4 whole cardamom pods	¼ tsp ground nutmeg
4 black peppercorns	1¼ pints homemade beef or
1 bay leaf	lamb stock or tinned
1 medium-sized onion,	beef broth (not bouillon)
peeled and sliced into fine	½ tsp salt (more if broth is
rings	unsalted)
12 oz long-grain rice	1 tbs granulated brown sugar

Over a medium flame, heat the oil in a 2-quart heavy-bottomed pot (with a tight-fitting lid—to be used later). When very hot, add the cloves and cardamom pods, peppercorns, and bay leaf. Fry for about 5 seconds, until the spices begin to expand and change colour. Now add the onion rings and fry for about 3 to 5 minutes, until the onions turn light brown with darkish edges. Put in the rice, coriander, cinnamon, and nutmeg, and stir for 5 minutes.

Next, pour in the broth and salt, stir, cover, and turn the flame very low. Let cook about 15 minutes.

Lift the lid, put in the brown sugar, and stir quickly with a fork. Cover again and cook another 15 to 20 minutes.

To serve: Serve plain, or garnished with slivered almonds, with *Koftas*, or Lamb *Korma*, or with English dishes as suggested above.

Sweet rice with carrots and raisins

Serves 6

In this recipe carrot strips and raisins are fried in butter and then cooked with the rice. I sweeten the rice with 2 tablespoons of sugar, but you could make it sweeter if you like.

12 oz long-grain rice	½ tsp salt
½ lb (2 large) carrots	¼ tsp ground nutmeg
3 tbs butter or usli ghee	¼ tsp ground mace
(see page 550)	¼ tsp ground cinnamon
2 tbs golden raisins	¼ tsp ground cardamom
2 tbs granulated sugar	seeds (if you keep a
1¼ pints chicken broth	pepper-grinder for carda-
(homemade or tinned)	mom seeds, use that)

Wash the rice in a colander and leave to soak in 2 pints water for 30 minutes.

Cut carrots into julienne strips. I find the easiest way to do this is to cut the carrots diagonally into long, flat slices—the kind that are used in Chinese cooking. Then I cut the slices into strips, doing two or three at a time.

Melt the butter in a heavy-bottomed frying-pan over medium heat. Put in the carrot strips and the raisins, and fry, stirring, for 10 to 12 minutes, until the carrots wilt and turn brownish at the edges. Turn off flame.

Preheat oven to 300°F., Mark 3.

Put the sugar in a 2–3-quart flameproof and ovenproof dish and heat over medium flame. The sugar will melt and then begin to turn brown. As soon as it becomes a golden-brown, pour in the chicken broth, keeping face averted. Add the rice, salt, nutmeg, mace, cinnamon, and cardamom, and bring to the boil. Keep boiling gently on medium flame for 8 to 10 minutes, until the liquid is almost absorbed. Stir frequently towards the latter half of cooking time to prevent sticking. Once the liquid is almost absorbed, turn off the heat. Cover the dish with a piece of aluminium foil 2 inches wider than the rim of the dish. Place the cover on the foil, and crinkle and arrange ends of aluminium foil so that no steam can escape. If you have a very heavy and tight-fitting lid, you can do without the foil.

Place rice dish in the oven and bake for 25 to 30 minutes. Check after 25 minutes to see if rice is done. If not, leave longer.

To serve: Spoon out onto warm platter and serve with Lamb *Korma* or *Sindhi Gosht*. Any yogurt dish would go well with it.

If you are cooking a Western meal, try eating this rice with roast duck, roast turkey, roast chicken, or baked ham.

Sweet rice with carrots and raisins
cooked in aromatic broth

Serves 6

Follow preceding recipe. Instead of chicken broth, use aromatic broth or *yakhni* (see directions on page 755). This *yakhni* gives the rice the added flavours of whole cumin and whole fennel seeds. It can be made weeks in advance and stored in the freezer.

Rice with whole spices

Serves 6

Rice is cooked with whole cinnamon sticks, bay leaves, cloves, black peppers, and cardamom pods. It is a very light and fragrant dish—and easy to make.

1 medium-sized onion	2 cinnamon sticks, about
2 tbs vegetable oil	3 inches long
6 whole cloves	3 bay leaves
10 black peppercorns	12 oz long-grain rice
5 cardamom pods	1 tsp salt

Peel onion and slice into fine rounds. Halve the rounds.

Heat the oil in a 3-quart heavy-bottomed pot (with tight-fitting lid—to be used later) over medium heat, put in the onions, and fry, stirring, until they are brown and crisp (but *not* burned)—about 8 to 10 minutes. With a slotted spoon, remove the onions and leave them on a paper towel to drain.

In the same fat, fry the cloves, peppercorns, cardamom pods, cinnamon sticks, and bay leaves for 10 to 20 seconds or until spices begin to expand and change colour. Add the rice, and fry, stirring, another minute or two. Now put in 1¼ pints water and the salt. Bring to the boil, cover, and reduce heat to very low. Cook 25 to 35 minutes, until done. Halfway through the cooking, stir once gently with a fork.

To serve: Spoon out the rice onto a warm platter, breaking any lumps with the back of a slotted spoon. The whole spices serve as a garnish—just warn your family or guests not to bite into them. Sprinkle fried onions over rice.

Serve with baked fish and almost any meat or chicken dish.

Rice with peas

Serves 6

Rice can be cooked with either fresh or frozen peas. In India, of course, it is always cooked with the fresh, hard, shelled variety, but I find that frozen peas work just as well for this dish.

2 tbs vegetable oil
½ tsp whole black mustard seeds
12 oz long-grain rice
1¼ pints chicken broth (fresh or tinned)

1 tsp salt
1 teacup shelled peas, fresh or frozen

Over medium flame, heat the oil in a 3-quart heavy-bottomed pot (with tight-fitting lid — to be used later). When hot, add the mustard seeds and wait until they begin to darken (10 to 20 seconds). Put in the rice, and the peas if you are using fresh ones. Stir for a minute. Add broth and salt. Bring to the boil. Cover and reduce flame to very, very low. Leave to cook for 25 to 30 minutes.

If you are using frozen peas, defrost them by placing a cupful in colander and running under warm water. Leave to drain. When rice has cooked 25 minutes, lift cover off and quickly put defrosted peas on top of rice. Replace cover and cook about 5 minutes longer or until done.

To serve: Mix the rice and peas gently and serve on large platter.

This is a relatively bland dish. It goes well with Indian lentils and meats, and equally well with almost any English meat dish.

Rice with peas and whole spices

Serves 6

2½ tbs vegetable oil
5 whole cloves
5 black peppercorns
1 cinnamon stick, 2 inches
   long
4 cardamom pods
12 oz long-grain rice

1 teacup shelled peas, fresh
   or frozen
1 tbs ground coriander
1 tsp ground cumin
½ tsp ground turmeric
1 tsp salt

Heat oil in a 3-quart heavy-bottomed pot (with tight-fitting lid —to be used later) over medium heat. Add cloves, peppercorns, cinnamon, and cardamom. Stir for about 10 to 20 seconds, until spices begin to expand and change colour. Add the rice, peas if using fresh ones, coriander, cumin, and turmeric. Stir for 3 minutes. Add 1¼ pints water and salt, stir again, and bring to the boil. Cover, and turn flame very low. Cook for about 25 to 30 minutes.

If you are using frozen peas, defrost them by placing a cupful in colander and running under warm water. Leave to drain. When rice has cooked 25 minutes, lift cover off and quickly put defrosted peas on top of rice. Replace cover and cook about 5 minutes longer or until done.

To serve: Gently mix the rice and peas and serve on large platter. Warn diners not to bite into the whole spices. This dish tastes good with *Koftas*, or with Chicken with Sliced Lemon and Fried Onions. Also serve yogurt, plain or with cut-up tomatoes, salt, and pepper.

Rice with potatoes and cumin seed

Serves 6

Rice *and* potatoes? A double starch? It's not really all *that* frightening. After all, if you were going to serve yourself a spoonful of rice, you could just as easily serve yourself a spoonful of rice *and* potatoes. The starch content is about the same, whether you're eating one starch or two, and in Britain at least the combination has the virtue of novelty.

2 medium-sized or 1 large potato	½ tbs whole cumin seeds
4 tbs vegetable oil	12 oz long-grain rice
	1 tsp salt

Peel potato, dice into ¾-inch cubes.

Heat oil in a heavy-bottomed pot (with tight-fitting lid — to be used later) over medium heat. When very hot, add the cumin seeds, and after they have begun to change colour and 'pop' (about 10 to 20 seconds), put in the potatoes. Let the potatoes brown to a nice golden colour on all sides. Then add the rice and stir for about 2 minutes. Add 1¼ pints water and salt, stir, and bring to the boil. Cover, turn the flame very low, and cook for 25 to 30 minutes. See if rice is done; if not, stir and cook for another 5 minutes.

To serve: Serve with marinated pork chops — or with *Kheema* and green beans. This is a simple yet very versatile dish that could be served with plain yogurt to an invalid or with *Korma* at a banquet.

Rice with cauliflower and cumin seed

Serves 6

This dish is very much like the preceding one, only cauliflower is substituted for the potatoes.

1 small head cauliflower	2½ tbs vegetable oil
vegetable oil (enough to have about 1½ inches in cauliflower frying-pan)	½ tsp whole cumin seeds
	12 oz long-grain rice
freshly ground pepper	salt

Break cauliflower into flowerets not bigger than 1½ inches in length and 1 inch in width at the head. Wash and drain flowerets thoroughly on paper towels.

Heat enough oil in frying-pan, wok, or *karhai* to have about 1½ inches. Keep on medium flame, much as you would for potato-chips. When hot, put in the flowerets a batch at a time and deep-fry until they are light brown on all sides and almost cooked through. Leave the insides a bit crunchy. As each batch is done, drain on paper towels, put into a dish, sprinkle with a dash of salt and a crunch of the pepper-grinder, and cover.

Heat 2½ tablespoons oil in 3-quart heavy-bottomed pot over medium flame. When very hot, stir in the cumin seeds. As soon as they change colour (about 10 seconds), add the rice and stir 2 to 3 minutes. Pour in 1¼ pints water. Add 1 teaspoon salt. Stir and bring to the boil. Cover and turn heat very low. Cook about 25 minutes.

Lift cover off rice pot and quickly (also carefully) lay the flowerets on top of the rice. Cover pot again, and cook about 10 minutes, until cauliflower is heated through.

To serve: Very carefully move all the cauliflower to one side of the pot. Spoon the rice onto a large platter first, then lay the cauliflower on top of the rice.

Serve with any combination of meats, vegetables, and lentils.

This again is a very useful and versatile dish that goes well with most English roasts and chops.

Rice with spinach

Serves 6

12 oz long-grain rice	6 tbs vegetable oil
3 tsp salt	2 medium-sized onions,
1½ lbs fresh spinach or 2	peeled and finely chopped
12 oz packages chopped	1 tsp garam masala
frozen spinach	

Wash rice thoroughly in colander. Invert into large bowl, and cover with cold water and 1 teaspoon of the salt. Leave for 2 hours.

Fill a 4–5-quart pot with water. Add 1 teaspoon salt and bring to the boil.

If you are using fresh spinach, trim and wash thoroughly, making sure all the sand is out. Wilt the spinach by dropping it, a little at a time, in the boiling water. As the spinach wilts, remove it to a colander and rinse with cold water. Squeeze the moisture out by pressing between palms of hands, and put on chopping board. When all the spinach is done, chop very finely. (*Or:* following package directions, cook frozen spinach until it is just defrosted. Drain, then squeeze out moisture.)

In a 3–4-quart flameproof and ovenproof casserole, heat the oil, add the onions, and sauté on medium flame about 5 minutes. They should just turn golden. Now put in the chopped spinach and *garam masala*. Sauté for about 30 minutes. (This much can be done in advance and the dish left covered for a few hours.)

Preheat oven to 300°F., Mark 2.

Drain rice and add to spinach with 1 pint water and 1 teaspoon salt; bring to the boil. Lower heat and simmer for 15 minutes, stirring occasionally.

Cut aluminium foil to cover top of pot snugly. Cut a hole about ½ inch in diameter in the centre of the foil to let the steam escape and the rice dry out. Place foil-covered dish in the middle of the oven for 30 minutes. Check to see if rice is done. If not, leave 5 minutes longer.

To serve: The rice is now ready to serve. If dinner is delayed, turn the oven off and leave rice in it for another 10 minutes.

Even though this dish is best served straight out of the oven, you can, if necessary, cook it 3 or 4 hours earlier. When cooked, leave it out for 5 minutes with foil on. Then cover it with a tight lid, but do not refrigerate. Fifteen minutes before serving reheat it in a preheated 300°F, Mark 2 oven for 15 minutes.

To serve: Spinach rice can be served plain or garnished with Fried Onion Rings.

For an Indian meal, serve with *Koftas*, *Seekh Kababs*, Lamb *Korma*, Chicken Cutlets, or Eggs *Moghlai*. Serve a yogurt dish with it and a vegetable, cauliflower or carrots. As for an English meal, we tried it recently with liver, bacon, and grilled tomatoes, and it was wonderful. It is also good with lamb chops or a lamb or beef roast. This is an excellent dish to impress guests with because it tastes very good and looks spectacular.

Rice with spinach
cooked in aromatic broth

Serves 6

This dish is very much like the preceding recipe, Rice with Spinach, except that instead of cooking the rice in water, it is cooked in *yakhni*, a deliciously flavoured lamb or beef broth. (Another *yakhni* recipe, using pieces of lamb, is given as part of the *pullao* recipe, on page 764.)

Follow the preceding recipe, adding 2½ cups of the following flavoured beef or lamb broth instead of water:

Yakhni

1 pint tinned or homemade lamb or beef broth (not bouillon)	2 tsp whole fennel seeds
	1 tsp whole cumin seeds
	1 tsp whole coriander seeds
1 medium-sized onion, peeled	1 cinnamon stick, $2\frac{1}{2}$–3 inches long
4 cloves garlic, peeled	6 black peppercorns
7 whole cloves	1 bay leaf
4 whole cardamom pods	

Put the broth into a pot with a lid. Tie onion, garlic, cloves, cardamom, fennel, cumin, coriander, cinnamon, peppercorns, and bay leaf in cheesecloth and drop in pot. Bring to the boil. Cover, turn heat low, and allow to simmer for half an hour. Remove the cheesecloth, squeezing out most of the liquid it holds.

When using the broth, measure to make sure you have 1 pint. If a little less, add water to make 1 pint.

If broth is already salted, use only $\frac{1}{2}$ teaspoon salt when adding spinach to rice and broth.

Serve as in preceding recipe.

Rice with black-eyed peas

Serves 6

4 oz black-eyed peas (lobhia) soaked overnight in 1 pint water with ½ tsp baking soda	7 whole cloves
	7 black peppercorns
	12 oz long-grain rice
2 tbs vegetable oil	1 tsp garam masala
	1½ tsp salt

Empty black-eyed peas and liquid into a pot. Add ½ pint water and ½ teaspoon salt. Bring to the boil. Skim off all the froth. Cover and simmer gently 4 to 5 minutes. Drain and discard liquid.

In a 4-quart heavy-bottomed pot, heat oil over medium heat. When hot, add cloves and peppercorns and fry until they expand (10 to 20 seconds). Put in the rice and black-eyed peas and fry for 5 minutes. Add the *garam masala*, 1 teaspoon salt, and 1¼ pints water. Bring to the boil, cover, lower flame to very low, and leave for 30 minutes. Lift cover to see if rice is done. If not, cover and cook another 5 minutes. Turn flame off. Covered rice will stay warm 15 to 20 minutes.

To serve: Place on a warm platter, gently breaking lumps with back of large spoon. Garnish with Fried Onion Rings (see page 766) if desired, or serve plain.

For Western meals try serving this with pork or lamb roasts and chops. It is also good with roast duck. Or try it with a German or Polish sausage accompanied with grilled tomatoes and mustard or beetroot greens!

For an Indian meal, have it with Pork Chops Cooked with Whole Spices and Tamarind Juice. Serve some kind of yogurt dish with it.

Rice with yellow split peas

Serves 4

4 oz yellow split peas	½ tsp whole cumin seeds
4 tsp salt	2–4 small white boiling
6 oz long-grain rice	onions, peeled
2 tbs vegetable oil	3 tbs butter

Soak split peas in ¾ pint cold water and leave for an hour.

Preheat oven to 300°F., Mark 2.

Bring 2 pints of water and 1 teaspoon salt to the boil. When the water is boiling rapidly, drain the split peas and put them in. Boil rapidly for 6 to 7 minutes, and drain.

In a large pot bring 5 pints of water and 3 teaspoons salt to a rolling boil, put in the rice, and boil rapidly for 5 minutes. Drain.

In a 3–4-quart flameproof and ovenproof dish, heat the oil over medium heat. When hot, put in the cumin seeds and fry for 10 to 20 seconds, until they begin to change colour. Add the onions, rolling them around once, then add the drained rice and the drained split peas and fry for 2 to 3 minutes, stirring frequently.

Cut the butter into 3 patties and place on top of rice. Cut a sheet of aluminium foil 2 inches wider than the rim of the dish. Cover dish with it. Place the lid on top. Now crinkle the protruding aluminium around the edges to seal them. Place dish in oven for 45 to 60 minutes. Check after 45 minutes and leave longer only if not yet done.

To serve: Spoon out onto warm platter and serve with *Kheema* and Yogurt with Tiny Dumplings, or with any other meat and vegetable combination you like.

Left-over rice with mushrooms

Serves 4

4 tbs vegetable oil	1 tsp ground coriander
1 medium-sized onion, peeled and finely chopped	1 tsp ground cumin
	2 teacups plain left-over cooked rice (with salt)
6–8 medium-sized mushrooms, cleaned and chopped (approximately ¼-inch squares)	3–4 tbs tinned beef broth, chicken broth, or water
	¼ tsp salt (more as needed)
½–1 fresh hot green chili, finely sliced (optional)	

Heat oil in 10–12-inch frying pan on medium flame. Add first the onions and mushrooms, frying and stirring continuously, then after 3 to 4 minutes the sliced green chili, after another minute the coriander and cumin, and finally the rice, breaking any lumps there may be with the back of a slotted spoon.

Cook for 5 minutes, then put in 3 tablespoons of broth or water and the salt. Stir again, cover, lower heat, and cook for 5 minutes. Lift cover, and if rice seems to be sticking at the bottom of the frying-pan, add another tablespoon of broth or water. Allow the rice to heat through, covered, for another 5 minutes or so.

To serve: If serving this with a Western meal, you could omit the coriander and green chili. The dish goes very well with ham, pork roasts, and roast beef. Try it with bacon and eggs for breakfast or brunch. It is unusual and very good. If you are cooking this as part of an Indian meal, serve it with a simple meat like *Khare Masale Ka Gosht*. You could also serve it with Sweetbreads with Green Coriander. Serve some yogurt dish as well.

Prawn pullao

Serves 6

This pullao can be cooked with prawns or with any firm-fleshed fish like cod or halibut (see following recipe).

¾ lb fresh prawns	1 tbs lemon juice
3 tbs finely chopped fresh green coriander	½–1 fresh hot green chili, finely sliced (optional)
1 tsp ground turmeric	4 tbs vegetable oil
1 tsp garam masala	1 medium-sized onion
1½ tsp salt	12 oz long-grain rice

Peel and devein prawns (see page 655).

In a teacup, mix 1 tablespoon warm water, the chopped green coriander, turmeric, *garam masala*, ½ teaspoon salt, the lemon juice, and green chili.

Heat 2 tablespoons of oil in a 10-inch frying-pan over medium-low heat. Pour in the contents of the cup and fry, stirring, for 2 to 3 minutes. Add the prawns, and on a medium flame fry them with the spices for about 4 minutes.

With a slotted spoon, remove the prawns to a covered dish, leaving the sauce behind. Pour 9 fl. oz warm water into the frying-pan and scrape up all the spices stuck to the bottom and sides, turning up the heat if necessary.

Peel the onion, cut into fine rounds and cut rounds in half.

In a heavy-bottomed 3–4-quart pot, heat remaining 2 tablespoons oil over medium heat. Put in the sliced onions, and fry them 3 to 4 minutes until the edges begin to turn brown. Now add the rice, ¾ pint water, 1 teaspoon salt, and the liquid from the frying-pan. Stir and bring to the boil, then cover and reduce heat to very low. Cook for 25 minutes.

Lift the cover off the saucepan and add the prawns. Mix quickly with a fork and cover again. Cook another 5 minutes.

To serve: Serve with Cabbage with Onions and any yogurt side dish—Yogurt with Roasted Aubergine would be especially good.

Halibut or cod pullao

Serves 6

Follow the preceding recipe, only substitute halibut or cod for the prawns. Buy ¾ lb cod or halibut steaks or fillets. Make sure they are at least ½ to ¾ inch thick. Cut the steaks or fillets into strips, each at least 1½ to 2 inches long and about 1 inch wide.

To serve: Lift rice and fish gently out of pan and place on warm platter. You could serve it with *Moong Dal*, yogurt, and Chicken with Tomato Sauce and Butter.

Chicken biryani

Serves 6–8

Biryani is perhaps one of our most elaborate rice dishes. Of Moghul origin, it is cooked with lamb or chicken, streaked with saffron, and garnished with raisins and nuts. The chicken is first marinated for at least 2 hours in a delicious paste of ginger, garlic, onions, yogurt, lemon juice, and spices. It is then cooked briefly. Partially cooked rice is placed over it, and the chicken and rice are allowed to steam for about an hour.

6 medium-sized onions	¼ tsp ground mace
4 cloves garlic, peeled and coarsely chopped	4½ tsp salt
	3 tbs lemon juice
a piece of fresh ginger, about 2 inches long and 1 inch wide, peeled and coarsely chopped	10 oz plain yogurt
	8 tbs vegetable oil
	2 bay leaves
10 whole cloves	4 large black cardamoms, if available
20 whole black peppercorns	2 lbs chicken legs and breasts
seeds from 8 whole cardamom pods	¼ tsp ground cinnamon
	1 tsp ground coriander

2 tsp leaf saffron, loosely
   packed, roasted and
   crumbled according to
   directions on page 552)

1 tsp ground cumin
1 tsp whole poppy seeds
2 tbs milk
12 oz long-grain rice

Garnishes (optional)

2 tbs golden raisins, fried
2 tbs blanched almonds

2 hard-boiled eggs, sliced
   or quartered lengthwise

First you have to make the marinade for the chicken.

Peel and coarsely chop 3 of the onions.

Place chopped onion, garlic, and ginger in an electric blender, along with the cloves, peppercorns, the seeds only from the 8 cardamoms, cinnamon, coriander, cumin, poppy seeds, mace, 1½ teaspoons salt, and the lemon juice. Blend all of these at high speed until you have a smooth paste. Place this paste in a large bowl. Add the yogurt and mix well.

Now peel the 3 remaining onions. Slice them into very fine rings, and halve all the rings.

In a 10-inch heavy-bottomed frying-pan, heat the oil over medium flame. When hot, add the bay leaves and 4 black cardamoms. Fry for about 10 to 15 seconds. Now put in the onions and fry them, stirring, for about 10 minutes or until they get brown and crisp (but *not* burned). Remove them carefully with a slotted spoon, squeezing out as much of the oil as possible. Reserve all the onion-flavoured oil, the black cardamoms, and the bay leaves. You will need them later. Mix in two-thirds of the fried onions with the marinade paste. Place the rest on a paper towel to drain. Set aside for garnishing.

Remove skin from the chicken legs and breasts. Cut the legs into two pieces each (drumstick and thigh), and quarter all the breasts. Pierce the chicken pieces with a fork and place in the bowl with the marinade paste. Mix well. Cover the bowl and refrigerate for at least 2 hours. Turn occasionally.

After 2 hours (or more), remove the bowl from the refrigerator and place all its contents in a 3–4-quart heavy-bottomed pot. Bring slowly to the boil, cover, lower heat, and simmer for 15 minutes. Remove only the chicken pieces, place them in a 5-quart casserole dish, and cover. Set aside. On a medium flame, boil down the marinade paste, stirring, until you have about 9 to 10 tablespoons left. Spoon the paste over the chicken. Cover again.

Preheat oven to 300°F., Mark 2.

Soak the saffron in 2 tablespoons hot (not boiling) milk.

Bring about 5 pints of water with 3 teaspoons of salt to the boil in a 3-quart pot, then add the rice. After it has come to the boil again, cook 5 minutes, timing very carefully (the rice must not cook through). Drain the rice in a colander, then place it on top of the chicken in the casserole. Pour the saffron milk over the rice, streaking it with orange lines. Spoon out the onion-flavoured oil from the pan, reserving a level tablespoon to fry the raisins if you like. Sprinkle the oil, cardamom, and bay leaves over the rice. Cover the casserole dish with aluminium foil, cut 2 inches wider than the rim of the dish. Now put the lid on and use the protruding foil edges to seal the dish as best you can by crinkling it and pushing it against the sides. Bake 1 hour.

Garnishes: There are several garnishes that can be used for *biryani*; you can use them all, or only what you like, but the fried onions are a must. If you wish to use raisins, you can fry them in a tablespoon of the onion-flavoured oil just after you have fried the onions.

To serve: As you lift the cover off your casserole dish, you will see beautiful saffron streaks on the white rice. Spoon the rice and chicken out onto a large platter. Sprinkle fried onions and other garnishes of your choice over, and serve hot. With *biryani*, serve *Koftas* and some yogurt dish — Yogurt with Tiny Dumplings, or Yogurt with Potatoes. If you wish to serve a vegetable, Cauliflower with Ginger and Green Coriander would be very good.

Biryani is quite definitely not an everyday dish. It is served at weddings and important dinners. Try serving it at a late supper party. It was, and is, a dish worthy of a king.

Pullao
(rice with lamb)

Serves 6

In my father's household, Sunday lunches were always rather special, as this was the only lunch we all ate together. Our family was divided into two camps: there was the group headed by my father that liked *pullao* for Sunday lunch, and there was the second group (to which I belonged), headed rather timidly by my mother, which preferred *karhi* and plain boiled rice. My mother, being very diplomatic, alternated these dishes. But also, being as awed by my father as the rest of us, she alternated the dishes in my father's favour, so we ended up by eating more *pullao* than *karhi*. And if I complained and said, 'But it was our turn to have *karhi* this Sunday,' my mother would say, 'Oh, dear, I completely forgot. You can have it next week!' 'Hmmm,' I would think, 'cheated again!' But, strange as it may seem, as I have grown older, I have begun to love *pullao*. I don't know why. The pleasures of one's palate do change — or perhaps it's the memory of my father, sitting at the head of the table, the *pullao* in front of him, surveying his wife and six children and feeling good and at peace.

Here is my mother's recipe for *pullao*, a dish of rice and meat cooked in flavoured broth. In India, the meat that is traditionally used for the dish is goat ribs, cut up in pieces about 1½ to 2 inches in length. The meat is a little fatty, more bone and less meat. Rib meat in Britain tends to be very fatty. So I would suggest you use one of two kinds of meat: if you like meat pieces with bone, ask the butcher to chop up 2½ lbs of shoulder or neck of lamb into 1½-inch cubes. If you are trying this recipe for the first time and don't want to be bothered with bones, get 1½ lbs of meat off a leg of lamb and ask the butcher to cut it into 1-inch cubes. (I usually buy a whole leg of lamb and get some cut off into chops and some boned and cut into cubes. You can freeze what you don't need.) I find that the

English prefer the boned, cubed meat. However, remember that traditionally *pullao* uses meat with bone and that *some* day, if not *today*, you should try making it that way.

1½ pints tinned or homemade lamb or beef broth (not bouillon)

1½ lbs of meat from leg of lamb cut into 1-inch cubes, or 2½ lbs of meat and bone from neck and shoulder of lamb, cut into 1½-inch cubes

2 medium-sized onions, peeled

4 cloves garlic, peeled

a piece of fresh ginger, about 1-inch cube, peeled

20 black peppercorns

6 large black cardamom pods (if available), or 14 small or greenish-yellow pods

2 tsp whole cumin seeds

1 cinnamon stick, 2½–3 inches long

2 tsp whole coriander seeds

2 tsp whole fennel seeds

4 bay leaves

2 tsp salt

5 tbs vegetable oil

12 oz long-grain rice

To make the *yakhni*, or flavoured broth: In a 3-quart pot, put the broth and the pieces of lamb. Tie up in a piece of cheesecloth 1 peeled onion, the garlic cloves, the piece of ginger, the peppercorns, 4 of the black cardamoms or 10 of the small cardamom pods, 1 teaspoon cumin seeds, the cinnamon stick, the coriander seeds, fennel seeds, and bay leaves. Drop the cheesecloth into the pot with the broth. Add 1 teaspoon salt. Bring to the boil. Skim off the surface scum. Cover, reduce heat to low, and allow to simmer slowly for 35 minutes.

While the broth is simmering, cut the other peeled onion in half lengthwise. Now slice it finely into half-circles.

In a 10-inch frying-pan heat the oil over a medium flame. Add the onion slices and fry until they are a crisp dark brown (about 10 minutes). Don't burn them—adjust flame if necessary. Remove with a slotted spoon, draining the fat back into the frying-pan. Spread onions on paper towels and set aside for later use. Turn flame under frying-pan off, leaving its residue of fat.

When the broth is made, fish out the cheesecloth, squeeze it slightly so as not to lose any flavours, and discard. Strain the broth and set aside. Reserve the meat in the strainer.

Heat the onion frying-pan again over a medium-high flame. When hot, add remaining 1 teaspoon whole cumin seeds and either 2 large black cardamom pods or 4 small green ones. Fry for about 20 seconds or until the spices begin to expand and change colour. Now add the drained meat and fry for 3 to 5 minutes or until the meat is lightly browned on all sides.

In a 6-quart pot put 6 oz of the uncooked rice, half the meat, then the second 6 oz of rice, and the rest of the meat. Measure the flavoured broth; pour 28 fl. oz of it over the rice. If you have less (you shouldn't), add a little water. Put in 1 teaspoon salt and bring to the boil. Cover, turn flame very, very low, and leave for 20 minutes. Lift cover and stir gently with a fork; cover again and cook another 20 minutes until rice is done. (If upper layer is still uncooked, stir gently with a fork, cover again, and cook 10 minutes longer.) Turn heat off and leave covered on stove until ready to serve.

To serve: Arrange the *pullao* on a large platter. Crumble the browned onions and sprinkle all over rice. Serve with plain yogurt or Yogurt with Potatoes. Also serve a vegetable — perhaps a cauliflower dish — and a salad (tomato, onion, and cucumber salad).

Remember that this rice dish will stay hot for 20 to 25 minutes after it is cooked if you leave it covered on the stove. Also, after the rice is cooked, it is best to give the steam 5 to 10 minutes to settle before you serve.

Fried onion rings for garnishing

**vegetable oil, enough to have
at least 1 inch in pan**

1 medium-sized onion

Heat oil in small frying-pan over medium heat. Peel onion and slice very finely. Wipe onion rings with paper towels and drop into heated fat. As they fry, separate rings with slotted spoon. Fry until rich brown (they should be a rich dark brown without being burned!). Remove with slotted spoon and drain on paper towel. (This can be done ahead of time and the garnish left uncovered in a saucer.) Arrange onion rings over rice or meats.

Dals

Lentils
Black-eyed peas (lobhia)
Chana masaledar
Chickpeas with garlic and ginger
Moong dal
Kala chana aur aloo (black chickpeas with potatoes)
Masoor or arhar dal with vegetables
Cold chana dal with potatoes
Hot chana dal with potatoes
Chana dal cooked with lamb
Karhi
Tomato karhi
Whole unhulled urad and rajma dal
Baris (or vadees) with aubergine and potatoes

SEE ALSO

Dal soup (page 553)

Dals—lentils or pulses—are varieties of dried beans and peas. In some form or other they are eaten daily in almost every Indian home, frequently providing the poor with their only source of protein. While people in England and America speak of making their living as earning their 'bread and butter', Indians who earn a bare wage complain that they make just enough for their 'dal roti' (roti is bread).

Both the rice eaters and the wheat eaters of India consume dal with equal enthusiasm. Each state, however, cooks its dals in a completely different way. Punjab excels in whole, unhulled dals—whole urad and rajma cooked slowly in the clay oven (tandoor), as well as in chana bhatura, a spicy dish of chickpeas eaten with puffy deep-fried bread. The fussy Delhi-wallahs like the hulled and split moong dal, delicately spiced with cumin and sprinkled with lime juice and browned onions. In Bombay, a hot, sweet and sour toovar dal is made by the addition of tamarind paste and jaggery (a dry, lump variety of molasses) to the cooked dal. In Madras, the scorchingly spicy dal often contains vegetables—aubergines, okra, or tomatoes.

In America and England, where a very thin watery dal is often served in Indian and Pakistani restaurants, people have come to the conclusion that dal is a soup. Well, it isn't; one of North India's favourite expressions, 'Dey dal may pani' (put water in the dal), refers to foods that are diluted in order to stretch them out among more people, a practice which is, naturally, deplored. A well-cooked dal is generally quite thick. It is hard to describe the exact consistency: it is thinner than porridge, but not quite as thin as pea soup. Having made that generalization, let me add that in some dal recipes the grains stay dry and almost whole, while in others, particularly some cooked in southern India, the *dal* is indeed quite soupy.

Dal is always eaten with rice or Indian breads. It can be poured over rice, especially when it is thin, or placed beside the rice, or half can be poured over the rice and the rest beside it on the plate. This way it can be eaten with the rice or with other vegetables. It leaves more options open, and is the way I prefer to do it. *Dals* can also be served in *katoris* (see page 555), which can be placed on the plates. This is the best method if you are serving *dal* with breads (see pages 815–26).

What gives *dal* dishes their final flavour or pep is the *tarka*, or *baghar* or *chhownk*. This does to the *dal* what a *rouille* does to a fish soup in the south of France. It makes it come alive! You can 'give a *tarka*' of whole mustard seeds or cumin seeds or fenugreek seeds, or of asafetida *and* cumin seeds, or of browned onions and ginger, and so on. Basically what happens is that oil or shortening (in India it is *ghee* – see page 550) is heated in a small pot or frying-pan. Whole spices are added, and the *ghee* and spices are then poured over the cooked *dal*.

Here is a list of the commonly used *dals*; you should learn to recognize them by their shape and colour.

MOONG DAL Hulled and split: small, yellow, rectangular grains; unhulled and whole: small, green, cylindrical grain, called mung beans in health food stores.

URAD DAL Hulled and split: small, off-white rectangular grains; unhulled and whole: small, black, cylindrical grain.

CHANA DAL Hulled and split: round, yellow grain, larger than *moong dal*. This *dal* is of the chickpea family.

ARHAR OR TOOVAR DAL Hulled and split: round, dull yellow grain, slightly larger than *chana dal* and often with irregular edges.

RAJMA Whole and unhulled: red kidney bean, which comes in a medium and small size.

MASOOR DAL Hulled and split: very tiny, round, shiny salmon-coloured grains that turn yellow when cooked.

KALA CHANA Whole and unhulled: small black chickpeas.

CHHOLA OR KABLI CHANA Whole: chickpeas or garbanzos.

LOBHIA Whole: black-eyed peas.

In this chapter, I have also included recipes for the *dals* available in your supermarket (lentils, black-eyed peas, chickpeas) and for dishes made with ground chickpea flour (*Karhi*, page 784) and ground *urad dal* (*Baris*, page 789).

WASHING AND CLEANING DALS: All *dals*, with the exception of those packaged especially for supermarkets, are usually very dirty. First, they have to be *picked* clean. Dishonest wholesalers and retailers have long made it a thriving practice to add tiny stones, often the same colour as the *dal*, to boost the weight. Also, occasionally, you will find a few discoloured or deformed grains that need to be removed, or there may be stalks, twigs, and what-have-you's lurking around. The best way to remove this is to put the amount of *dal* you wish to cook at one end of a large platter. Now slide 10 or 15 grains at a time to the other end of the same platter, spotting and removing all unwanted objects as you do so. Keep your hawk's eyes open because there is nothing worse than crunching a stone as you eat your dinner! Next, the *dal* must be washed several times in cold water to remove any dust that may be clinging to the grains. After draining it is ready to be cooked.

Lentils

Serves 6–8

This is a recipe for the dry lentils as bought in an English supermarket.

1 lb lentils
1 cinnamon stick, 2–3 inches long
1 bay leaf
5 cloves garlic, peeled
2 slices fresh, peeled ginger, $\frac{1}{8}$ inch thick, and about 1 inch in diameter
1 tsp ground turmeric
$\frac{3}{4}$ lemon

$1\frac{1}{2}$ tsp salt
$\frac{1}{8}$ tsp freshly ground black pepper
$\frac{1}{4}$–$\frac{1}{2}$ tsp cayenne pepper (optional)
3 tbs vegetable oil or usli ghee (see page 550)
a pinch ground asafetida or tiny lump asafetida
$\frac{1}{2}$ tsp whole cumin seeds

Wash the lentils. Drain.

In a 3-quart heavy-bottomed pot, combine the lentils, $2\frac{1}{2}$ pints water, cinnamon stick, bay leaf, garlic cloves, ginger slices, and turmeric. Bring to the boil. Cover, lower heat, and simmer gently until tender, about 30 to 45 minutes.

Slice lemon into 5 or 6 rounds. Remove seeds. Lift cover of pot and put in the lemon slices, salt, black pepper, and cayenne. Stir, cover and simmer another 5 minutes.

Just before serving, heat the vegetable oil in a 4–6-inch frying-pan over medium-high heat. When very hot, put in the asafetida and the cumin seeds. As soon as the asafetida begins to sizzle and expand, and the cumin seeds darken, pour the contents of frying-pan over the lentils and stir.

To serve: Serve the lentils with rice or any of the breads. A meat, chicken, or fish dish and a vegetable would complete the meal.

Black-eyed peas
(lobhia)

Serves 6

8 oz black-eyed peas soaked overnight in 2 pints water with ¼ tsp baking soda
2 tsp salt
3 tbs vegetable oil
a generous pinch ground asafetida or tiny lump asafetida
½ tsp whole cumin seeds
1½ medium-sized onions, peeled and chopped

¼ tsp ground turmeric
1 tsp ground coriander
1 tsp ground cumin
1 teacup tomato sauce (see page 733)
¼–½ tsp cayenne pepper (optional)
3 tbs tamarind paste (see page 552), or 2 tbs lemon juice

Empty black-eyed peas and liquid into a pot. Add ¾ pint water and 1 teaspoon salt. Bring to the boil. Skim off all the froth. Cover and simmer gently 4 to 5 minutes. Drain and discard the liquid.

In another 3-quart, heavy-bottomed pot, heat the oil over a medium-high flame. When hot, put in the asafetida and the cumin seeds. As soon as the asafetida expands and sizzles and the cumin seeds darken (this will take a few seconds), put in the chopped onions. Fry onions, stirring, for 7 or 8 minutes, or until they are lightly browned. Add the turmeric, coriander, and cumin, and cook, stirring, 1 minute. Put in the tomato sauce, lower heat, and simmer 5 minutes, stirring now and then.

Add the black-eyed peas, ¼ pint water, the rest of the salt (1–1½ teaspoons), the cayenne, and the tamarind paste. Bring to the boil. Cover, lower heat, and simmer gently for 25 to 35 minutes. Lift off cover, and if there is any extra sauce, turn up heat and boil it down, stirring. All the sauce must adhere to the peas.

To serve: This versatile dish can be served with pork or lamb roasts as well as with almost any Indian meal.

Chana masaledar

Serves 6

Chickpeas (large *chanas*) are cooked with onion, garlic, ginger, and the *garam* (hot) spices. This is a traditional 'snack' dish from the state of Punjab.

6 oz chickpeas (large chanas) soaked overnight in 1½ pints water with ¼ tsp baking soda

4–5 tbs vegetable oil

¼ tsp whole cumin seeds

1 medium-sized onion, peeled and chopped

1–1½ tsp garam masala

1 tsp ground coriander

2 cloves garlic, peeled and minced

a piece of fresh ginger, about ½ inch square, peeled and grated

1 tbs tomato purée

1½–2 tsp salt

⅛–¼ tsp cayenne pepper

1 tsp ground amchoor or 1 tbs lemon juice

Garnish

1 firm tomato, washed and quartered

1 medium-sized onion, peeled, halved and cut into coarse slivers

4 fresh hot green chilies (only if someone is going to eat them; otherwise use 4 long slices of a green pepper)

Empty chickpeas and liquid into a large pot. Add 1 pint water, 1 teaspoon salt and bring to the boil. Remove froth. Cover, lower heat and simmer gently for about 1 hour or until chickpeas are tender. Turn off heat, remove cover and leave chickpeas in liquid.

Heat the oil in a heavy-bottomed 10-inch frying-pan over a medium-high flame. When hot, put in the whole cumin seeds. As soon as they begin to darken, after a few seconds, add the chopped onion. Stir and fry 7 to 8 minutes or until onion begins to turn a golden brown.

Turn heat to low and add the *garam masala* and coriander.

Mix, add the garlic and ginger, and fry, stirring for 2–3 minutes. Add the tomato purée and stir again.

Drain the chickpeas, reserving about ¼ pint of the liquid. Pour this into the frying-pan. Add the chickpeas, ½ teaspoon salt, cayenne and *amchoor* or lemon juice. Mix well, cover, and let the chickpeas cook with the spices for about 30 minutes. Check the salt, adding more if necessary. Stir gently every now and then, taking care not to break the chickpeas.

To serve: Traditionally, the *chanas* (chickpeas) are placed in a bowl lined around the edge with quartered tomatoes, raw onion slivers, and green chilies, and then eaten with *bhaturas*. I have served them with *pooris* as well as with rice. A meal with Chicken Moghlai, Prawn Kerala Style, and these chickpeas as well as Cucumber *Raita* served with plain rice is very nice. This dish can be prepared a day in advance, covered, and refrigerated. Reheat gently over a low flame.

Chick peas with garlic and ginger

Serves 6

6 oz chickpeas (large chanas) soaked overnight in 1½ pints water with ¼ tsp baking soda

10 cloves garlic, peeled and chopped

a piece of fresh ginger, 2 inches long and 1 inch wide, peeled and chopped

5 tbs vegetable oil

a pinch of ground asafetida or a tiny lump asafetida

½ tsp ground turmeric

3 medium-sized tomatoes (tinned or fresh), peeled and finely chopped

4 medium-sized potatoes, freshly boiled and peeled

2 tsp salt

⅛ tsp freshly ground black pepper

½ tsp cayenne pepper (less if desired)

2 tbs lemon juice

Empty chickpeas and liquid into a large pot. Add 1 pint water, 1 teaspoon salt and bring to the boil. Remove froth. Cover, lower heat and simmer gently for 1 hour or until chickpeas are tender. Turn off heat. Drain the chickpeas, reserving ½ pint of the liquid.

Put the garlic, ginger and tomatoes into the container of an electric blender. Add 2 tablespoons water and blend until you have a smooth paste.

Heat oil in a large frying-pan or a 10-inch heavy-bottomed pot over a medium flame. When hot, put in the asafetida. After a few seconds, as soon as it sizzles and expands, pour in the paste from the blender, keeping face averted, and add the turmeric. Stir and fry this for 1 to 2 minutes. Now pour in the ½ pint liquid and add the chickpeas. Quarter the potatoes and add them as well. Put in 1 teaspoon salt, black pepper, cayenne, and lemon juice. Bring to the boil, cover, lower heat and simmer gently for 30 minutes.

These chickpeas taste best with some kind of Indian bread — *pooris*, *parathas*, or *bhaturas*. Serve yogurt or cucumber relishes as an accompaniment. Any meat or chicken dish would go with this too.

Moong dal

Serves 6

This is North India's most popular *dal*, and it is eaten with equal relish by toothless toddlers, husky farmers, and effete urban snobs. The simple recipe given below can be used for the white *urad dal*, the salmon-coloured *masoor dal*, and the large *arhar* or *toovar dal* as well.

10 oz moong dal (hulled
and split)

2 cloves garlic, peeled

2 slices peeled fresh ginger,
1 inch square and $\frac{1}{8}$ inch
thick

1 tsp chopped fresh green
coriander

1 tbs ground turmeric

$\frac{1}{4}$–$\frac{1}{2}$ tsp cayenne pepper
(optional)

1$\frac{1}{2}$ tsp salt

1$\frac{1}{2}$ tbs lemon juice

3 tbs vegetable oil or usli
ghee (see page 550)

a pinch ground asafetida or
tiny lump asafetida

1 tsp whole cumin seeds
lemon or lime wedges

Clean and wash *dal* thoroughly (see page 771.) Put *dal* in
heavy-bottomed 3-quart pot, add 2 pints water, and bring to
the boil. Remove the froth and scum that collects at the top.
Now add the garlic, ginger, parsley, turmeric, and cayenne
pepper. Cover, leaving the lid very slightly ajar, lower heat,
and simmer gently for about 1$\frac{1}{2}$ hours. Stir occasionally. When
dal is cooked, add the salt and lemon juice (it should be thicker
than pea soup, but thinner than porridge).

In a 4–6-inch frying-pan or small pot, heat the vegetable oil
or *ghee* over a medium-high flame. When hot, add the asafetida
and cumin seeds. As soon as the asafetida sizzles and expands
and the cumin seeds turn dark (this will take only a few
seconds), pour the oil and spices over the *dal* and serve. (Some
people put the *dal* in a serving dish and then pour the oil and
spices over it.)

To serve: Serve with plain rice, *Kheema*, and a vegetable for a
simple meal. Most meat and chicken dishes go well with this
dal. Since some people like to squeeze extra lemon or lime
juice on their *dal*, serve some wedges separately. Note: Finely
sliced onion rings, fried until brown and crisp (see page 766),
are often spread over the *dal* as a garnish before it is served.

Kala chana aur aloo
(black chickpeas with potatoes)

Serves 4

This is one of my favourite lunch dishes. India produces several varieties of chickpeas. *Kala chana* are small and black. They need to be cleaned and soaked in water for 24 hours before cooking. I use tamarind paste to give this dish a tart taste, but you could use lemon juice instead.

6 oz black chickpeas (kala chana)
1½ tsp salt
½ tsp baking soda
1 medium-sized onion, peeled and chopped
3 cloves garlic, peeled and chopped
a piece of fresh ginger about 1 inch square, peeled and chopped
3 tbs vegetable oil

a generous pinch ground asafetida or tiny lump asafetida
¼ tsp whole cumin seeds
4 medium-sized potatoes, peeled and quartered
1 tsp ground coriander
¼ tsp ground turmeric
1 tsp garam masala
¼–½ tsp cayenne pepper
3–4 tbs tamarind paste (see page 552), or 2 tbs lemon juice

Sort and clean the chickpeas and wash them under cold water. Drain. Soak for 24 hours in a bowl containing ½ teaspoon of the salt, the baking soda, and 1¾ pints of water.

Place chopped onion, garlic, and ginger in the container of an electric blender with 3 tablespoons of water. Blend at high speed until you have a smooth paste.

In a 3-quart heavy-bottomed pot, heat the oil over a medium-high flame. When very hot, put in the asafetida and the cumin seeds. After a few seconds, when the asafetida expands and the cumin darkens, put in the paste from the blender, keeping face averted. Fry, stirring, for about 5 minutes.

Now drain the chickpeas and add them to the pot. Also put in the potatoes, coriander, turmeric, *garam masala*, 1 teaspoon salt, the cayenne pepper, and ¾ pint of water. Bring to the boil. Cover, and allow to simmer gently for 1 hour.

Add 3 to 4 tablespoons of tamarind paste or lemon juice (you could use more or less) to chickpeas according to tartness desired. Stir. Check salt. Cook for another 10 minutes, stirring occasionally.

To serve: This dish tastes very good with hot *pooris* or *parathas*. Some kind of relish—perhaps Cucumber and Tomato with Lemon Juice—should be served with it. For a more complete meal add meat and a green vegetable dish.

Masoor or arhar dal
with vegetables

Serves 6–8

12 oz masoor or arhar (toovar) dal (hulled and split)

½ tsp ground turmeric powder

3 tbs chopped fresh green coriander

2 tsp salt

any one of the following vegetables: 2 medium-sized yellow marrows, washed and sliced in rounds or ½ lb mushrooms, cleaned and sliced or 1 medium-sized aubergine, washed and cut in ¾-inch cubes or 1 medium-sized onion, cut in half, sliced and sautéed for 5 minutes in 3 tbs vegetable oil

4 tbs tamarind paste (see page 552),

½ tsp sugar

3 tbs vegetable oil or usli ghee (see page 550)

10 whole black peppercorns

½ tsp whole cumin seeds

½ teaspoon whole black mustard seeds

10 whole fenugreek seeds

10 white urad dal grains (optional)

1–3 whole dried hot red peppers

Clean and wash *dal* (see page 771).

Put *dal* in 3-quart heavy-bottomed pot with 2½ pints water and bring to boil. If there is any scum, remove it with a spoon. Add the turmeric and green coriander and cover. Lower heat and simmer gently until tender, about 1½ hours, stirring every 15 minutes or so. Add the salt, the vegetables you are using, tamarind paste, and sugar. Cook another 15 minutes or until vegetable is tender.

In a 4–6-inch frying-pan, heat the 3 tablespoons of oil or *ghee* over medium-high heat. When hot, put in the peppercorns, cumin seeds, mustard seeds, fenugreek seeds, *urad dal*, and lastly the red peppers. When the mustard seeds begin to pop and the fenugreek and red pepper darken (this should take just a few seconds), pour the contents of frying-pan into the pot containing *dal* and vegetables. Stir, cover again and turn off heat.

To serve: Serve with plain rice and any meat, chicken, or fish dish of your choice.

Cold chana dal
with potatoes

Serves 4

In this dish the *chana dal* is first boiled and then mixed with diced boiled potatoes, salt, pepper, cayenne pepper, roasted cumin, and lemon juice. If you like, you can slice spring onions and add them as well. It is served at room temperature or, if you wish, just very slightly chilled.

3 oz chana dal, cleaned and
washed (see page 771)
1 tsp salt
3 peeled slices fresh ginger,
about 1 inch in diameter
and ⅛ inch thick
4 new potatoes, boiled and
diced into ½-inch cubes

⅛ tsp freshly ground pepper
1 tsp roasted, ground cumin
seeds (see page 549)
2 tbs lemon juice, or 3
tbs tamarind paste (see
page 552)
⅛-¼ tsp cayenne pepper
(optional)

Put the *dal* to boil with 1¼ pints of water, ½ teaspoon salt, and
the ginger slices. Cover, simmer gently for 1 hour. Drain.
Discard ginger slices.

In a serving bowl, combine the *dal*, ½ teaspoon salt, and the
remaining ingredients. Mix well.

To serve: Serve with lamb roast or pork chops. Indians often
eat this as a snack, at tea-time.

Hot chana dal
with potatoes

Serves 4

This is a hot (i.e., not cold) version of the preceding recipe.

3 oz chana dal, cleaned and
washed (see page 771)
1 tsp salt
4 tbs vegetable oil
¼ tsp black mustard seeds
¼ tsp whole cumin seeds
10 fenugreek seeds
2 fresh green chilies (as an
alternative, use ⅛-¼ tsp
cayenne pepper)

1 medium-sized onion,
peeled and chopped
a piece of fresh ginger, about
¾ inch square, peeled and
grated
4 new potatoes, boiled and
diced into ½-inch cubes
⅛ tsp freshly ground pepper
2 tbs lemon juice, or 3 tbs
tamarind paste (see page
552)

Put the *dal* to boil with 1¼ pints of water and ½ teaspoon of the salt. Cover, lower heat, and simmer gently for 1 hour. Drain and set aside.

In a 10-inch frying-pan, heat the oil over a medium-high flame. When hot, put in the mustard, cumin, and fenugreek seeds. In a few seconds, as soon as the cumin and fenugreek seeds darken and the mustard seeds begin to pop, add the green chilies. Turn them over once (this will take another second), then put in the chopped onion and grated ginger. Stir and fry the onions for 4 to 5 minutes. Now put in all the remaining ingredients, i.e., the boiled *dal* and diced potatoes, ½ teaspoon salt, the pepper, cayenne, if you are using it, and lemon juice or tamarind paste. Mix well and cook over medium flame for 5 minutes, stirring frequently but gently.

To serve: Serve with *chapatis*, *bhaturas*, or *parathas* and a yogurt relish. Any meat, chicken, or fish dish can be served with it as well.

Chana dal cooked with lamb

Serves 6

I use meat from shoulder of lamb for this recipe, but you could use leg of lamb or stewing beef. The *chana dal* cooks in an hour, or a bit less, so you will have to adjust the time when you put it in. If you use stewing lamb or beef, cook the meat for 1½ hours and *then* add the *dal*.

2–2½ lbs boned meat from shoulder of lamb, cut into 1–1½-inch cubes	**1 tsp ground turmeric**
	1 tbs tomato purée
5 medium-sized onions (1 peeled and chopped, 4 halved and sliced into fine half-rings)	**¼ tsp ground mace**
	¼ tsp ground nutmeg
	¼ tsp ground cinnamon
	¼ tsp ground cloves
	1½ tsp salt (or as desired)

5 cloves garlic, peeled and
 chopped
a piece of fresh ginger, about
 1 inch cube, peeled and
 chopped
10 tbs vegetable oil
1 tbs ground coriander
2 tsp ground cumin

⅛ tsp freshly ground black
 pepper
¼–½ tsp cayenne pepper
 (optional)
4 oz chana dal, cleaned and
 washed (see page 771)
2 tbs lemon juice

Garnish

3 tbs chopped fresh green coriander

Pat the meat pieces dry with a paper towel. Set aside.

Put the 1 chopped onion, garlic, and ginger into container of an electric blender. Add 4 tablespoons water and blend at high speed until you have a smooth paste.

Heat the oil in a 10-inch heavy-bottomed casserole-type pot, over medium-high flame. Put in the 4 sliced onions and fry them, stirring, for 15 to 20 minutes, or until they are a darkish brown and crisp. Remove them with a slotted spoon and spread on a paper towel.

Drop 7 or 8 pieces of meat at a time in the onion-flavoured oil and brown them well over high heat on all sides. Remove each batch as it gets done. When all the meat has browned, turn off the heat under the pot.

When the remaining oil has cooled a bit, pour in the paste from the electric blender. Stir it well, mixing it with the juices in the pot. Turn up the heat and fry the paste, stirring all the time, 8 to 10 minutes or until it has browned. Now lower heat and add, at intervals, frying and stirring, the coriander, cumin, and turmeric; after a minute or two, the tomato purée; and after another minute, the mace, nutmeg, cinnamon, and cloves. Finally, after 5 minutes, add ½ pint water, salt, black pepper, cayenne, the browned meat, and the cleaned and washed *chana dal*. Bring to the boil. Cover, lower heat, and simmer for 1 hour, stirring gently every 10 minutes or so. Do not let the grains of *dal* break.

When done, add the lemon juice and stir gently.

To serve: Place in a warm bowl. Sprinkle the browned onions and chopped green coriander over the *dal* and meat and serve with plain rice or *chapatis*. Serve a green vegetable (green beans or peas) and at least one relish (a yogurt relish would be good).

Karhi

Serves 6–8

This dish looks like a very thick soup with dumplings. It is usually eaten with plain rice, and it was a great Sunday favourite with my family. It is made with chickpea flour (*besan*) and buttermilk (the more sour the buttermilk, the better), flavoured with fennel, cumin, fenugreek, and mustard seeds.

N.B. Chickpea flour is very light so do weigh it.

For the Karhi

3 oz chickpea flour (besan)
¾ pint buttermilk
2 tbs vegetable oil
1 generous pinch ground asafetida or tiny lump asafetida
¼ tsp whole fennel seeds
¼ tsp whole cumin seeds

¼ tsp whole black mustard seeds
⅛ tsp whole fenugreek seeds
¼ tsp black onion seeds (kalonji), if available
2–3 whole dried hot peppers
1 tsp ground turmeric
1½–2 tsp salt
2–3 tbs lemon juice

For the pakoris, or dumplings

4 oz chickpea flour (besan)
½ tsp baking powder
½ tsp salt

½ tsp ground cumin
vegetable oil for deep frying

To make the karhi: Sift the 3 oz chickpea flour into a bowl. Add ¼ pint of the buttermilk, a little at a time, and mix well until you have a thick, smooth paste. Now add the remaining ½ pint buttermilk, mixing as you pour it in. Add 2 pints of water to the bowl, mix again, and set aside.

* In a heavy-bottomed 3–4-quart pot, heat the oil over medium-high flame. When hot, put in the asafetida. In a few seconds, as soon as the asafetida expands, add the fennel, cumin, mustard, fenugreek, and onion seeds. When the seeds darken, put in the dry peppers. When they start to darken, add the turmeric, and a second later, the liquid from the bowl. Bring to the boil, cover, lower heat, and simmer gently for 1 hour.

Add salt and lemon juice. Cook another 10 minutes covered. Turn off heat.*

To make pakoris, or dumplings (these can be made while *karhi* is cooking): Sift the 4 oz of chickpea flour and the baking powder into a bowl. Add salt and cumin. Add water slowly, mixing as you go, until you have a very thick, doughy paste — thick enough to stand in peaks. You will need about 4 fl. oz of water, perhaps a little less.

The ideal utensil for deep-frying *pakoris* is a *karhai* or Chinese wok. If you do not have one, use any other utensil you find convenient. Put at least 2½ inches of oil in and heat over a medium-low flame. Give it 10 minutes to heat. Meanwhile, fill a large bowl halfway with warm water and set it somewhere near you.

When the oil is heated, drop the doughy paste, a teaspoonful at a time, into the oil, using a second teaspoon to help release the paste. Make sure you do not drop one dumpling right on top of another. Put in enough to cover the surface and no more. The dumplings will sink first and then rise and float. Fry each batch slowly, for 6 to 7 minutes, turning them at least once; they must not brown. If they begin to darken, lower your flame. They should retain their yellowish colour, but cook through. As soon as each batch is done, lift them out with a slotted spoon and drop into the warm water. Let them soak 2 minutes, then remove from the water and squeeze them *very* gently, taking care not to break them. Set them aside, covered.

When the *karhi* is done and the heat turned off, lift the cover and put all the dumplings in. Stir gently. Do not cook the *karhi* and the dumplings together until 10 minutes before you are ready to eat. Otherwise the dumplings will disintegrate. Now you can bring the *karhi* to the boil, covered. Lower the heat and simmer gently for 10 minutes.

To serve: Take *karhi* and *pakoris* carefully out of the pot so as not to break the *pakoris*. Place in serving bowl. Serve with plain rice, *Khare Masale Ka Gosht*, a vegetable, and a relish.

Tomato karhi

Serves 6–8

This is a variation of the North Indian *karhi*. It is served in Hyderabad and is cooked with tomatoes. It can be served with or without the *pakoris*, or dumplings.

N.B. Chickpea flour is very light so do weigh it.

2 oz chickpea flour (besan)
1½ pints tomato sauce (see page 733)
2 tbs vegetable oil
a generous pinch ground asafetida or tiny lump asafetida
¼ tsp whole fennel seeds
¼ tsp whole cumin seeds
¼ tsp whole black mustard seeds

⅛ tsp whole fenugreek seeds
¼ tsp black onion seeds (kalonji), if available
2–3 whole dried hot peppers
1 tsp ground turmeric powder
1½–2 tbs salt
4 tbs lemon juice
8–10 fresh kari leaves, if available

Sift the flour into a bowl. Slowly add 3 fl. oz water, mixing as you go, until you have a thick, smooth paste. Add another 1 pint water, slowly, stirring all the time. Pour in the tomato sauce. Mix well. Set aside.

Now follow the rest of the recipe for *karhi* on page 785, the section marked between the two asterisks. Add the *kari* leaves when you put in the salt.

If you wish to make the *pakoris*, follow preceding recipe.

Instead of *pakoris*, sliced vegetables (green peppers, onions, mushrooms, marrows or aubergines) can be lightly sautéed in oil, sprinkled with salt and pepper, and dropped into the tomato *karhi* 10 minutes before the cooking time is over.

To serve: See serving suggestions for preceding recipe.

Whole unhulled urad and rajma dal

Serves 6

The whole unhulled *dals*, particularly *urad* and *rajma*, take a very long time to cook. This recipe takes 5 hours. You can, however, take comfort from the fact that they are 5 effortless hours. Once you put the *dal* on, apart from an occasional stir, not much else is required of you. In the Punjab, where the whole *urad* and *rajma dal* are specialities, they are left to cook in a slow earthen oven (*tandoor*) for 24 hours. Both *dals* can be cooked individually, using this same recipe, or they can be mixed, in whatever proportion you desire. I have mixed them half and half.

3 oz whole unhulled moong dal, cleaned and washed

3 oz whole unhulled rajma dal, cleaned and washed

a piece of fresh ginger, about ½-inch cube, peeled and sliced

2 cloves of garlic, peeled

5 tbs plain yogurt

⅛ tsp cayenne pepper (optional)

1¾ tsp salt

⅛ tsp freshly ground pepper

3 tbs vegetable oil or usli ghee (see page 550)

1 medium-sized onion, cut in half lengthwise, then finely sliced

a piece of fresh ginger, about ½-inch cube, peeled and grated (see page 550)

a pinch of ground asatetida or a small lump about ⅛ inch square

½ tsp whole cumin seeds

2 dried hot red peppers

In a very heavy-bottomed pot, combine the two *dals*, 2 pints water, the sliced ginger, and the peeled garlic cloves. Bring to the boil, cover, lower heat, and simmer gently 4½ hours, stirring every hour or so.

Put the yogurt in a small bowl. Beat well with a fork. When the *dal* has cooked for 4½ hours, lift off cover and mash it well against the sides of the pot with the back of a kitchen spoon. Pour in the yogurt, stirring as you do so. Also add the cayenne, salt, and pepper. Stir, bring to the boil, cover, lower heat, and simmer another 30 minutes.

Heat the oil or *ghee* in an 8–10-inch frying-pan. When hot, put in the sliced onion. Fry, stirring, over medium-high flame for about 4 minutes, then put in the grated ginger and fry it along with the onions for 1 more minute, or until onions are brown and crisp. Remove onions and ginger with slotted spoon and set aside.

In the same oil put the asafetida, cumin, and red peppers. If the oil is very hot, the cumin and peppers will darken immediately. Turn off heat and pour contents of frying-pan into the pot with the *dal*. Cover pot again and leave until you are ready to serve.

To serve: Mix the *dal* and ladle it into warm serving bowl. Sprinkle browned onions and ginger over it. At Delhi's famous Moti Mahal restaurant, a common order with this *dal* is *Tandoori* Chicken, *naan*, and Onions Pickled in Vinegar.

Baris
(or vadees) with aubergine and potatoes

Serves 6

To make *baris*, *dals* are ground, mixed with spices, made into a hard dough, and then broken off into lumps and dried in the sun. My grandmother made her own *baris*: I can still see them drying on white sheets spread over rope charpoys. These were laid out in the sunniest section of our large brick courtyard and watched over by a one-eyed hawk always perched on the telephone pole. But most people nowadays just go down to a grocery shop and buy them. Usually, two kinds are available. One is *very* hot, spiced with red and black pepper, and the other is very mild. Some groceries in America and England carry both varieties.

Since *baris* come in different sizes, the large ones need to be broken into pieces roughly an inch in diameter. Use any heavy object to break them. A hammer will do. Any smaller pieces splintering off need not be thrown away. Just add them to the pot.

Baris should be browned before they are cooked. Here is my mother's recipe for them.

4 tbs vegetable oil

1 teacup baris, broken into pieces no larger than 1 inch in diameter

2 medium-sized onions, peeled and chopped

4 cloves garlic, peeled and minced

a piece of fresh ginger, about ½ inch cube, peeled and grated

1 tsp ground coriander

1 tsp ground cumin

½ tsp ground turmeric

2 tbs tomato purée

2 medium-sized potatoes, peeled and quartered

1½ tsp salt

2 small, long aubergines (if unavailable substitute 3 teacups of the larger aubergine, diced into 1-inch cubes)

Heat the oil in a 10-inch frying-pan or 10-inch heavy-bottomed pot over a medium-high flame. When hot, put in *baris* and fry them, turning frequently, for about 2 minutes or until they turn a few shades darker. (Do *not* let them get a very dark brown.) Remove them with a slotted spoon and set aside.

To the same oil, add first the chopped onions, stirring and frying continuously, for about 4 minutes, until the onions have turned dark at the edges. Lower the heat to medium low and add the garlic and ginger; keep stirring; after 2 minutes, add the coriander, cumin, and turmeric; stir again; and after 2 more minutes, put in the tomato purée and stir; finally, after another 2 minutes, add the fried *baris*, 1¼ pint water, the potatoes, and the salt. Stir and bring to the boil. Cover, lower heat, and simmer gently for 30 minutes.

Wash the aubergines. Do not break off the stem and the green part. Quarter the aubergines, lengthwise, all the way from the stem down, and drop the quarters into the pot. Add another ¼ pint water. Stir, bring to the boil again, cover, lower heat, and simmer for 20 minutes.

To serve: Bring the *baris* to the table in a warm serving bowl. Let each person serve himself in small individual *katoris* (see page 555) or bowls. Eat with *chapatis, pooris,* or *parathas.* You could serve a meat dish (Lamb *Korma* would be good) and a yogurt relish with it.

Chutneys,
Pickles, &
Other Relishes

Sweet tomato chutney
Fresh green chutney with coriander leaves and yogurt
Fresh mint chutney with fruit
Tamarind chutney with bananas
Tomato tamarind chutney
Fresh coconut chutney
Carrot 'water' pickle
Turnip 'water' pickle
Carrots pickled in oil
Onions pickled in vinegar
Cucumber raita
Yogurt with tiny dumplings (boondi-ka-dahi)
Yogurt with potatoes
Yogurt with roasted aubergine (baigan-ka-bharta)
Yogurt with spinach
Cucumber and tomato with lemon juice
Tomato and onion with lemon juice
Chopped onions in vinegar
Raw onion rings

SEE ALSO

No Indian meal is complete without at least one kind of relish. At its simplest, this can be a small, fresh, fiery green chili, or it can be a hastily peeled and quartered onion. In lower-middle-class families, when the wife packs her husband's lunch in the early hours of the morning, she may not have any meat or vegetable to offer him with his *roti* (bread). What she will tuck in, though, with great love, ensconced between two *rotis*, will be a tiny portion of a sour spicy raw mango pickle! It may well be the climate that causes appetites to wilt and turn apathetic, especially during the blazing summer months. Relishes are, perhaps, just ways of prodding sluggish bodies into perking up and eating. At any rate, Indians seem to find them both desirable and necessary.

My grandmother used to make a lime pickle which, if I remember correctly, took years to mature. We carried it with us on the long car rides to the summer resorts Simla and Mussoori. When tossing and turning at the never-ending and ever-climbing hairpin bends made our taste buds turn green, my grandmother, like a familiar magician with his equally familiar trick, would say 'aha' and produce a small brown crock filled with her lime pickles. They were sour and pungent and black with age. One tiny bite would make the mouth pucker at first, but ultimately leave it completely refreshed.

I saw my grandmother make this pickle just once. It took five servants, the ten women of the house, and my grandmother two whole days to do all the grinding, cutting, and stuffing. Then, as the pickle matured, my grandmother would walk the length of the storeroom every day, shaking the large crocks stored in several neat rows. Every month the limes needed to be stirred by hand. Not every hand, antiseptically clean though it might be, was allowed inside the crocks. According to my grandmother, the chemistry of most hands would cause the pickle to rot. It needed a very 'special' hand, and in our household she had decided that this hand belonged to Ishri, my grandfather's personal servant. So this small wizened gentleman, and he alone, was allowed to push his gnarled hand into each crock and give the pickles a 'swish'. My grandmother must have been doing something right because she was the only lady in the neighbourhood who made this pickle successfully. All others who tried it and who, unfortunately, did not have the valuable services of Ishri, ended up with various varieties of fungi! And when my grandmother died and her valuables were being parcelled out, her famous lime pickle was also carefully distributed among selected relatives. Those lucky enough to get a jar treated it with great reverence because, by now, it was supposed to have not just taste but medicinal and even magical qualities!

The recipes for most chutneys and pickles are usually handed down from mother to daughter, each family group specializing in its own particular varieties and styles. The result is that different families will serve you completely different sets of relishes. There are now a few companies that produce and bottle relishes, but at the moment they have not quite succeeded in tearing the Indian housewife away from her own home efforts. Some of these bottled relishes are available in delicatessens. You will have to taste and check them for yourself. If you like *very* hot pickles, I will recommend one particular brand to you. The firm of Har Narain Gopi Nath has been in the pickling business for decades. (Even my grandmother bought their red chili pickle, though she bought no other.) They now sell their pickles in this country. I would recommend only their stuffed red chili pickle. It is, as I said, *very* hot, so just eat a pinhead with each morsel!

I have, very arbitrarily, I confess, divided relishes into three categories—chutneys, pickles, and 'others'. 'Others' does not seem very dignified or very exotic, but you will begin to see my problem once I get to 'others'. Meanwhile, let me start with chutneys.

There are so many different kinds of chutneys — sweet chutneys, sour chutneys, sweet-and-sour chutneys, salty chutneys, hot chutneys, cold chutneys — the list could go on and on. The ingredients used in these chutneys can include tomatoes, ginger, onions, garlic, tamarind, bananas, mangoes, raisins, coconut, fresh coriander, fresh mint, lime juice, yogurt, vinegar, sugar, etc. Chutneys can be preserves — that is, they can be bottled and kept indefinitely, like Sweet Tomato Chutney, or they can be made fresh daily, like Tamarind Chutney with Bananas or Fresh Mint Chutney with Fruit (see the following recipes). In our home we had a special woman who came in daily to grind the spices. When the spices were done, her second daily task was to grind the fresh green coriander chutney which we had at every meal.

Chutneys are generally served in small non-metallic bowls if they are to accompany a meal. Sometimes, however, they are used as a sauce to go over hot or cold foods, such as in Fried Aubergines with Tomato Chutney (page 712). Food can also be cooked in a chutney or with a chutney, as in *Kheema* Used as a Stuffing (page 588). Some chutneys are eaten not as a relish but as a vegetable. In our family we eat a chutney made with the pulp of boiled green mangoes this way.

Pickles in India are a world in themselves. A whole book could be written about them. Pickles preserve, and in a land of warm climate and little refrigeration, almost everything gets pickled in order to prolong its life — hard berries, onions, raw mangoes, green chilies, cauliflower, carrots, turnips, limes, lemons, marrows, aubergines, mutton, prawns, lobsters, quail, partridge, bamboos, and what-have-you. My very dear brother-in-law once spotted a mound of rose petals on their way out to the dustbin. Appalled by the waste, he immediately retrieved and pickled them. A week later the rose-petal pickle jar was opened for tasting. Well! Not wanting my brother-in-law's morale and pickling initiative to fade away, we all kept saying,

'Not bad, not bad at all, very interesting taste.' I decided then that pickled rose petals were one thing I intended to stay away from!

Pickling is generally done in oil, vinegar, water, or lemon juice. Oil pickles can last for years, whereas water pickles have a limited life of 2 to 3 weeks, during which there are waxing, peak, and waning periods. Oil pickles can be hot and sour or hot and sweet (jaggery—or Indian molasses—often providing the sweetness). While ceramic or glass jars are used for oil pickles, the traditional water pickles are made in *mutkas*, round pots of half-baked clay. As the water pickle matures, it picks up an earthen flavour that is very refreshing. These pickles are sour (a bit like the gherkin and cucumber delicatessen pickles) and hot if you want them to be. Before each meal, a large bowl of the pickles, both water and vegetable, is removed from the earthenware pot and put to cool—in a refrigerator if there is one. This bowl is then brought to the table at mealtime. Each place setting has a cup or non-metallic bowl into which people serve themselves both the vegetable and the water.

Fresh ginger or green chilies can be pickled in lime juice. The juice is boiled first and then added to the ginger or the chilies.

Small boiling onions are often pickled in red vinegar. These are then lifted out of the vinegar and served with dishes like *Tandoori* Chicken.

There are, of course, many other relishes as well. And here we come to my category 'others'. Chopped or sliced onions, tomatoes, and cucumbers are sprinkled with lime juice (or vinegar), salt, pepper, and cayenne, and served in varying forms all over North India. Numerous dishes made with yogurt are also very popular. I feel Britain has still to discover the versatility of plain yogurt. At the moment, yogurt seems to provide nothing more than a quick lunch for the girl on a diet. Indians use yogurt as East Europeans use sour cream. Apart from cooking with it and using it as a marinade, we use it for hundreds of relishes. *Raitas* are one of them. Here cooked or raw vegetables are added to well-mixed yogurt, seasonings are sprinkled in, and the dish is cooled before being served.

Various 'dumplings' can also be made and put into yogurt. Since they never comprise a main dish, 'relish' is a very good word for them.

Most Westerners seem to think that the usual relishes served with Indian food are Major Grey's chutney and little bowls filled with nuts, grated coconut, and sliced bananas and apples. If you have developed a taste for these items, eat them, by all means. But do experiment with some of these much more interesting local relishes.

Sweet tomato chutney

Makes enough to fill 1 pint jar

I make this chutney with tinned tomatoes. You could, if you like, use fresh tomatoes when they are in season and really tasty. To peel them, you will need to drop them in boiling vinegar. When the skin crinkles, lift them out and peel. Then proceed with the recipe. When cooked, this chutney is sweet and sour, thick and garlicky.

1 whole head of garlic, peeled and coarsely chopped

a piece of fresh ginger, about 2 inches long, 1 inch thick, and 1 inch wide, peeled and coarsely chopped

12 fl. oz wine vinegar

2, 14 oz tins whole tomatoes (or 2 lbs fresh tomatoes prepared as suggested above)

$\frac{3}{4}$ lb granulated sugar

$1\frac{1}{2}$ tsp salt

$\frac{1}{8}$–$\frac{1}{2}$ tsp cayenne pepper

2 tbs golden raisins

2 tbs blanched slivered almonds

Put the chopped garlic, ginger, and 4 fl. oz of the vinegar into the container of an electric blender and blend at high speed until smooth. In a 3-quart heavy-bottomed pot with non-metallic finish, place the tomatoes and juice from the tin, the rest of the vinegar, the sugar, salt, and cayenne pepper (or, if you prefer, add the cayenne at the end, a little at a time, stirring and tasting as you do so). Bring to the boil. Add purée from the blender. Lower heat and simmer gently, uncovered, for about $1\frac{1}{2}$ to 2 hours or until chutney becomes thick. (A film should cling to a spoon dipped in it.) Stir occasionally at first, and more frequently later as it thickens. You may need to lower the heat as the liquid diminishes. You should end up with about 1 pint of chutney, and it should be at least as thick as honey after it cools. If the tinned tomatoes you use have a lot of liquid in them, a longer cooking time may be required, resulting in a little less chutney.

Add the almonds and raisins. Simmer, stirring, another 5 minutes. Turn heat off and allow to cool. Bottle. Keep refrigerated.

To serve: Since this is one of my favourite sweet chutneys, I always spoon out a small bowl of it for all my dinner parties. It goes with almost all foods and is *very* popular. Store, bottled, in the refrigerator. It keeps for months.

Fresh green chutney with coriander leaves and yogurt

Serves 6

This chutney needs to be made the day it is eaten. It can be served in a small bowl as a relish, or it can be served over meat, cooked fish, or vegetables. If pressed to classify it, I would call this a 'sour' chutney.

1 packed teacup chopped fresh green coriander
1 fresh hot green chili, sliced, or ¼ tsp ground cayenne pepper (optional)
10 oz plain yogurt
1 tbs lemon juice
½ tsp salt (add more if you need it; the sourness of yogurt can vary with its age)
⅛ tsp freshly ground pepper
½ tsp roasted, ground cumin seeds (see page 549)

Put the green-coriander and chili in the container of an electric blender with 3 tablespoons of water and blend until you have a smooth paste (you may need to push the coriander down a couple of times).

In a non-metallic bowl, combine the yogurt, salt, pepper, cumin, lemon juice, and paste from the blender. Cover and refrigerate until ready to use.

To serve: Bring the cooled bowl to the table. You could serve it with almost any Indian meal. People should take just a tablespoon at a time.

Fresh mint chutney with fruit

Serves 6

⅓–½ well-packed teacup
washed fresh mint leaves

4 tbs lemon juice

2 fresh hot green chilies (use
less or more as desired;
as substitute, use ½ green
pepper plus ½ tsp cayenne
pepper)

1 medium-sized tart apple,
peeled, cored, and diced
just before blending

1 orange, peeled, seeded,
and cubed

1 tsp salt

Combine all ingredients in the container of an electric blender. Blend at high speed until you have a smooth paste.

This chutney goes with most Indian foods. It is especially good with grilled *Seekh Kabab*, *Tandoori* Chicken, and Vegetable *Pakoris*.

Tamarind chutney with bananas

Serves 4–6

This is another sweet and sour chutney made with tamarind pulp. The addition of roasted cumin and slices of ripe bananas is, I think, very particular to Delhi dwellers. My mother's family often added raisins as well. I have not included them in my recipe, but if you wish to do so, soak a tablespoon of golden raisins in hot water for 2 hours. Then remove them from the water and add them to the tamarind pulp at the same time that you add the bananas.

Even though this chutney can be made a day in advance, it is best to add the banana slices just before serving. Banana slices that have spent a night in the refrigerator look very unhappy!

a piece of tamarind, the size of a tangerine	1 tsp roasted, ground cumin seeds (see page 549)
1–1½ tbs sugar	⅛–¼ tsp cayenne pepper (optional)
1¼ tsp salt	1 ripe but firm banana

Since the tamarind generally comes in a large block, tear off a lump about the size of a tangerine. Soak it overnight in 6 fl. oz hot water in a small non-metallic bowl or cup. (The water should cover the tamarind, so don't use a very wide bowl.) If you forget to do it overnight, do it first thing in the morning. All will not be lost! Soak it for a minimum of 4 hours.

Once it has soaked, mash down and break the lump in the water, making a thick, uneven pulp. I use my hands for this, but you could use the back of a wooden spoon.

Place a strainer over a non-metallic bowl, put the tamarind pulp in the strainer, and press down with the back of a spoon. Keep pressing until nothing but fibrous tissues and seeds are left in the strainer. Discard fibrous tissues and seeds. Make sure you scrape all the strained pulp on the outside of the strainer — it doesn't always drip down. Use extra water, if necessary, to separate all the pulp from the fibres.

Mix the strained pulp with the sugar, salt, cumin seeds, and cayenne.

Slice a peeled banana into ¼–⅓-inch slices and mix with the tamarind pulp.

To serve: Put into small ceramic or glass serving bowl and place on the table along with other chutneys and pickles.

Tomato tamarind chutney

Makes 16 fl. oz

This is, basically, a sour chutney used as a sauce for fish and stuffed vegetables. It can be made in advance, put in a jar, and refrigerated for 3 or 4 days.

4 tbs olive or vegetable oil

a generous pinch ground asafetida or ⅛-inch lump asafetida

½ tsp whole cumin seeds

½ tsp whole black mustard seeds

1 medium-sized onion, peeled and finely chopped

4 cloves garlic, peeled and minced

12 fl. oz tomato sauce (see page 733)

¼ pint tamarind pulp (see recipe for Tamarind Chutney with Bananas, page 801)

1¼–1½ tsp salt

½ tsp garam masala

⅛ tsp ground cinnamon

⅛ tsp freshly ground black pepper

⅛–¼ tsp cayenne pepper (optional)

1 tsp granulated sugar (add a bit more if you want to)

Heat the oil in a 2-quart pot over medium-high heat. When hot, put in the asafetida, and a few seconds later, add the cumin and mustard seeds. The cumin seeds will begin to darken in the hot oil within a few seconds. Put in the chopped onions and minced garlic, and fry, stirring, for about 2 minutes, or until the onions darken at the edges.

Now pour in the tomato sauce and tamarind pulp. Also add the salt, *garam masala*, cinnamon, black pepper, cayenne, and sugar. Bring to the boil. Cover, lower heat, and simmer gently for 15 minutes.

To serve: Use as a sauce with fried vegetables or with *Kheema* Used as Stuffing (for peppers, tomatoes, and aubergines).

Fresh coconut chutney

Serves 6–8

1 teacup fairly well-packed, grated fresh coconut (see page 548)

½ teacup fairly well-packed, chopped fresh green coriander

1–2 fresh hot green chilies (use as desired)

a piece of fresh ginger, about ½-inch cube, peeled and chopped

1 clove garlic, peeled and chopped

6 tbs plain yogurt

½ tsp salt

1 tsp lemon juice

1 tbs vegetable oil

⅛ tsp urad dal (the hulled, split variety) grains

¼ tsp whole black mustard seeds

Put the coconut, green coriander, green chilies, ginger, and garlic, along with 5 tablespoons of water, into the container of an electric blender. Blend at high speed until you have a smooth paste, stopping occasionally to push down the ingredients.

Pour contents of blender into a bowl. Add yogurt, salt, and lemon juice. Mix well.

In a 4–6-inch frying-pan, heat the oil. When very hot, put in the *dal* grains and mustard seeds. As soon as the *dal* darkens and the mustard seeds pop, pour contents of frying-pan into bowl with chutney. Mix well. Cover and chill until ready for use.

To serve: This South Indian chutney goes well with Vegetable *Pakoris*. It is also very good as a relish with most meals.

Carrot 'water' pickle

About 4 quarts

This is one of Delhi's most popular winter pickles. Like chestnuts, it is often sold at street corners, in large glass jars. The 'water' in the pickle turns a glorious beetroot colour because the carrot used is a special 'black' carrot which 'bleeds' like a beetroot. Enthusiasm for this pickle has now become so refined that the real gourmets do not eat the carrot at all. They just drink the juice.

Unable to find the bleeding 'black' carrot, I have substituted the ordinary orange carrot. However, I have thrown in some beetroots to supply the necessary colour. I eat both the carrot and the beetroot. The juice, of course, is the best part of all.

This pickle is good for 10 days to 2 weeks. It will get more sour as time passes. You may need to add more salt as that happens. One way to slow its deterioration is to refrigerate it.

1⅓ tbs salt	2 medium-sized beetroots
4 tbs black mustard seeds	2 hot dried red peppers
1½ lbs carrots	

Bring 7 pints water and the salt to the boil in a large pot.

Meanwhile, crush, pound, or grind the mustard seeds coarsely, so that they split at least in half, using either a heavy mortar and pestle or an Indian grinding stone or a few quick spins of an electric coffee-grinder.

Peel the carrots, removing the green top portion, and quarter them lengthwise. Halve each piece lengthwise once again.

Peel the beetroots and cut each into 3 rounds.

Place the beetroots and carrots in a clean 4–5-quart wide-mouthed jar. Pour boiling salted water over them. Add the mustard seeds and the red peppers. Allow to cool. Stir and cover.

Put a small label with the date on it so you will not forget exactly when you started the pickle. Stir once a day for 7 days with a clean wooden spoon. Keep covered. It should be ready on the seventh day.

To serve: Place in a bowl a slice or two of carrot plus half a ladleful of juice for each person eating. Cool in the refrigerator. Serve in small, individual non-metallic bowls.

Turnip 'water' pickle

About 4 quarts

Water pickles are a speciality of my family. I love them and find them very similar to the pickled gherkins and cucumbers found in good delicatessens.

This pickle takes a week to mature and then can be eaten for the next 2 weeks. It gets very sour as time passes, and you may need to add more salt to it. One way to slow its deterioration is to refrigerate it once it has matured. Both the vegetable and the juice are consumed.

5 tbs black mustard seeds
3 lbs medium-sized white turnips
1⅓ tbs salt
2 whole dried hot red chilies (optional)

Crush, pound, or grind the mustard seeds coarsely, so that they split at least in half, using either a heavy mortar and pestle or an Indian grinding stone or a few quick spins of an electric coffee-grinder.

In a large pot, bring 6½ pints of water to the boil. Add salt to the water.

Peel the turnips. Slice them into ⅓ inch rounds and place in a clean 4–5-quart wide-mouthed jar. Pour boiling salted water over them. Add crushed mustard seeds and red chilies. Allow to cool.

Stir and put lid on. Stick a label with the date on the jar.

Stir it every day with a clean wooden spoon. On the seventh day it will be ready to eat.

To serve: Place in a bowl a piece of pickle and half a ladleful of juice for each person eating. Cool in refrigerator and serve in small individual non-metallic bowls.

Carrots pickled in oil

About 1½ pints

This is perhaps the simplest oil pickle you could make. It takes about a week to mature. It can then be refrigerated and kept for months.

2 tsp black mustard seeds	1 tsp cayenne pepper
1 lb carrots of medium thickness	1 tsp ground turmeric
1 tsp salt	16 fl. oz vegetable oil

Crush, pound, or grind mustard seeds coarsely, so that they split at least in half, using either a heavy mortar and pestle or an Indian grinding stone, or a few quick spins of the electric coffee-grinder.

Peel the carrots. Cut off the coarse top and the bottom. Cut each carrot in 3 pieces. Halve or quarter these pieces lengthwise according to the thickness of the carrots.

Place carrots in clean, dry 1½ pint jar. Add salt, cayenne pepper, turmeric, and crushed mustard seeds.

Warm the oil and pour over the carrots. Put lid on tightly and shake the jar well. Leave in a warm place for 7 days. Shake the jar once or twice daily.

To serve: Shake the jar. Remove one or two carrot pieces per person, and arrange in a small bowl or on relish tray. Do not serve the oil.

Onions pickled in vinegar

About 1½ pints

This relish is served in Delhi's famous Moti Mahal restaurant. It is extremely simple to make. The onions need to marinate in the vinegar for at least 24 hours, so allow yourself sufficient time. In this recipe, I have made enough pickle to fill a 1½ pint jar. It should keep a month.

1 lb white boiling onions (pick small, clean, even-sized onions)
16 fl. oz red wine vinegar
2 cloves garlic, peeled and sliced
2 whole dried red peppers
1 tbs salt

Peel onions. Slicing only three-quarters of the way down, quarter them lengthwise. Each onion should stay whole, with the four sections attached at the bottom. Place the onions in a clean, wide-mouthed quart jar. You may have a few left over.

In a non-metallic bowl, combine the vinegar, garlic, red peppers, and salt. Mix well. Pour this mixture over the onions to cover them. Put on a tight lid and set the jar aside for 24 hours.

The pickle is now ready. Refrigerate the jar. The onions can be taken out and eaten as and when desired.

To serve: Take as many of the onions out of the vinegar as you need and place them in a glass or other non-metallic bowl. They go well with *Tandoori* Chicken and Whole Unhulled *Urad* and *Rajma Dal.*

Cucumber raita

Serves 4–6

This is a refreshing, cool yogurt and cucumber relish. In the hot summer months, it really takes the place of a salad.

1 cucumber	½ tsp roasted, ground cumin
15 oz plain yogurt	seeds (see page 549)
1 tsp salt	⅛ tsp cayenne pepper
⅛ tsp freshly ground black	(optional)
pepper	⅛ tsp paprika (for garnishing)

Peel and grate the cucumber.

Empty the yogurt into serving bowl and beat it well with a fork until it is smooth and paste-like.

Add the cucumber, salt, black pepper, roasted cumin (reserve a pinch for garnish), and cayenne to the bowl with the yogurt.

Sprinkle with paprika and the pinch of roasted cumin. Cover and refrigerate until ready to serve.

To serve: Bring bowl of cold yogurt to the table. This relish goes well with nearly all Indian meals.

Yogurt with tiny dumplings
(boondi-ka-dahi)

Serves 6–8

The only yogurt relish served at all our family wedding banquets was this one. Tiny little droplets of a chickpea flour paste are dropped into deep fat and fried. They are then softened in warm water. Finally they are combined with yogurt and spices, freshly roasted cumin being perhaps the most important ingredient used. You can make this relish as hot as you like. When I make it in Britain, I put in just a touch of cayenne pepper. But at those wedding banquets in India, it was a cool scorcher!

In India the dumplings are made by pushing the batter through the holes of a slotted spoon into the hot oil. The Indian slotted spoons have round holes about ⅛ inch wide. If you can find a spoon like that, use it. If you have a colander with holes this size, it could work as well.

For the dumplings

4 heaped tbs chickpea flour (besan)
¼ tsp baking powder
¼ tsp salt

¼ tsp ground cumin seeds
vegetable oil for deep frying, enough to have 1 inch in the frying-pan

For the yogurt

25 oz plain yogurt
1½ tsp salt
⅛–¼ tsp freshly ground black pepper

1 tsp freshly roasted, ground cumin seeds (see page 549)
⅛–¼ tsp cayenne pepper (optional)
⅛ tsp paprika

Place the chickpea flour and the baking powder in a bowl. Add a little water at a time (about 2½ fl. oz altogether) and mix to a thick, smooth paste, stiff enough to stand in tiny peaks. Use a wooden spoon or your fingers to do this. Add ¼ teaspoon salt and ¼ teaspoon cumin and mix well. Set aside.

In an 8–10-inch frying-pan, heat the vegetable oil over medium heat. Get your slotted spoon or colander, whichever you are going to use. When the oil is hot, place a tablespoon of batter on the slotted spoon or the colander and push it through with the back of a clean wooden spoon. Little droplets will fall into the oil. They should cook slowly — turning crisp, but staying a golden-yellow; they should not turn brown. This will take about 5 minutes. Adjust flame if necessary. As each batch gets done, remove it with a slotted spoon and dump it in a bowl filled with warm water. Continue until all the paste is used up. Let dumplings soak in water for 30 minutes.

Now get the yogurt ready. In a bowl, mix the yogurt well. Then add the salt, black pepper, roasted cumin, and cayenne, reserving a pinch of the cumin for garnishing later. Cover and refrigerate the yogurt until almost ready to serve.

Just before serving, take out the dumplings, a handful at a time. Lay your other palm over them and gently squeeze out excess water. Do not break them. Put them in serving bowl. Pour yogurt over them and mix well.

Garnish by sprinkling paprika and the pinch of roasted ground cumin over the top.

To serve: This yogurt dish goes very well with nearly all the lamb and pork dishes in this book. Do not serve it with other dishes containing dumplings, e.g., *Karhi.*

Yogurt with potatoes

Serves 4–6

This is perhaps the Indian version of potato salad. It is a little moister, and if I may allow myself to be prejudiced, a little tastier.

2 medium-sized boiling potatoes	1 tsp freshly roasted, ground cumin seeds (see page 549)
15 oz plain yogurt	⅛–¼ tsp cayenne pepper
1–1½ tsp salt	(optional)
⅛–¼ tsp freshly ground black pepper	

Garnish

⅛ tsp paprika

Boil the potatoes and allow them to cool thoroughly.

Put the yogurt in a bowl and mix well with a fork. Add the salt, black pepper, roasted cumin, and cayenne. Mix well.

Peel the potatoes and dice them into ½-inch cubes. Mix with the yogurt.

To serve: Pour yogurt and potatoes into serving bowl. Sprinkle with paprika and serve. This dish may be made several hours in advance, covered tightly and refrigerated.

Yogurt with roasted aubergine (*baigan-ka-bharta*)

Serves 4–6

When I was a child and all food was cooked over coals, an aubergine was often put to bake in the ashes that fell below the grates in our stove. The aubergine would cook and soften and acquire a sumptuous smoked flavour. It was then peeled, mashed, and added to yogurt, along with minced onions and fresh mint. Here is that recipe. Instead of ashes, I use the direct flame of a gas burner!

1 medium-sized aubergine
15 oz plain yogurt
1 small onion, peeled and finely minced
2 tbs finely minced fresh mint
1 tsp salt
⅛–¼ tsp freshly ground black pepper
⅛–¼ tsp cayenne pepper (optional)
1 tsp freshly roasted, ground cumin seeds (see page 549)

Wash and wipe the aubergine. Line a burner with an aluminium protector if possible. Stand the aubergine directly on the gas burner and turn the flame on medium or medium low. Roast the aubergine on all sides, turning it over carefully. (For more detailed instructions, see Aubergine *Bharta*, page 714.) It should look fairly charred on the outside, and the inside should get soft and pulpy. This may take 20 to 25 minutes.

Peel the aubergine under cold running water, making sure all the blackened skin and the stem are removed. Now mince the pulp very finely and place in a bowl.

Empty yogurt into a serving bowl and mix well with fork. Add onion, mint, aubergine, salt, black pepper, cayenne, and roasted cumin. Mix. Cover and refrigerate until ready to serve.

To serve: Serve cold as an hors d'œuvre or as salad-type relish.

Yogurt with spinach

Serves 4–6

10–16 oz fresh spinach	$\frac{1}{8}$–$\frac{1}{4}$ tsp cayenne pepper
2 tsp salt	(optional)
15 oz plain yogurt	1 tsp freshly roasted, ground
$\frac{1}{8}$–$\frac{1}{4}$ tsp freshly ground black	cumin seeds (see page 549)
pepper	

Wash and trim the spinach. Make sure no sand is left.

Bring 6 pints of water to boil in large pot. Add 1 teaspoon salt. When boiling, drop spinach in it and cover. As soon as the spinach wilts, remove it and put it in a colander. Run cold water over it until it cools. Drain. Squeeze out the water by pressing spinach between your palms and then mince.

Place the yogurt in a bowl and mix well with a fork. Add the minced spinach, 1 teaspoon salt, black pepper, cayenne, and cumin. Mix well. Cover and refrigerate until ready to serve.

To serve: Serve cold with Lamb Cooked in Dark Almond Sauce or *Koftas*. Serve also with cauliflower or carrots or potatoes.

Cucumber and tomato with lemon juice

Serves 4

1 medium-sized cucumber
1 medium-sized tomato
1 tsp salt
$\frac{1}{8}$–$\frac{1}{4}$ tsp freshly ground black
  pepper
1 tsp roasted, ground cumin
  seeds (see page 549)

1–1$\frac{1}{2}$ tbs lemon juice
2 tbs minced fresh green
  coriander
$\frac{1}{8}$ tsp cayenne pepper
  (optional)

Peel cucumber and dice it finely (about $\frac{1}{4}$-inch cubes). Dice tomato as finely as cucumber. Combine all ingredients in serving bowl. Mix well. Cover and refrigerate for 30 minutes.

To serve: Bring cold serving bowl to table. This relish can be eaten with nearly all Indian meals.

Tomato and onion with lemon juice

Serves 4

1 medium-sized tomato
1 medium-sized onion
1 tsp salt
$\frac{1}{8}$–$\frac{1}{4}$ tsp freshly ground black
  pepper

1 tsp roasted, ground cumin
  seeds (see page 549)
1–1$\frac{1}{2}$ tbs lemon juice
$\frac{1}{8}$–$\frac{1}{4}$ tsp cayenne pepper

Dice tomato in $\frac{1}{4}$-inch cubes. Peel and chop the onion. Combine all ingredients in serving bowl. Cover and refrigerate for 30 minutes.

To serve: Bring cold serving bowl to table. This relish can be eaten with nearly all Indian meals.

Chopped onions in vinegar

Serves 4–6

2 medium-sized onions,
  peeled and chopped
1 tsp salt

$\frac{1}{8}$–$\frac{1}{4}$ tsp freshly ground black
  pepper
$\frac{1}{4}$ tsp cayenne pepper
4 tbs red wine vinegar

Combine all ingredients in small serving bowl. Mix well. Cover and refrigerate for 30 minutes.

To serve: Bring cold serving bowl to table. This relish can be eaten with nearly all Indian meals.

Raw onion rings

These are very good served with barbecued meats, chicken, and fish.

Peel onions and slice them into paper-thin rounds. Place in bowl containing cold water. Add a few cubes of ice, cover, and refrigerate. Leave an hour or two.

Drain, and scatter over meat, chicken, or fish.

Breads

Chapati
Poori
Paratha
Bhatura
Naan

I N India, we call our Indian bread *roti* and we call the Western-type loaf a *dubbul* (double) *roti*, probably because of the expansion caused by the yeast. Most of our everyday breads are unleavened — somewhat like the Mexican tortilla, but much more varied in shape, taste, and texture. They are generally made out of whole-wheat flour, though barley, maize, millet, chickpea, and plain white flour are also used. We do make leavened breads like the *naan*, but they tend to be flat, rising only $\frac{1}{2}$ to $\frac{3}{4}$ inch in height.

Throughout most of North India *ata*, or finely ground whole-wheat flour, is measured out onto a very large brass platter, or *paraat*, for kneading. This *paraat* is essential because Indian kitchens do not have Formica countertops and because Indians prefer to do most of their kitchen work — chopping, cutting, grinding, and kneading — in a squatting position. Once the dough has been kneaded (this is done with clenched fists — the knuckles pressing into the dough), it is formed into a lump, covered with a damp cloth, and left on one side of the *paraat*. Just before cooking, it is kneaded again and made into little patties. These are then rolled out on a round board into *chapatis*, *parathas*, or *pooris*. Even though I do have a *paraat* in my kitchen, I find it just as easy to use my kitchen counter for both the kneading and the rolling. If you happen to have a marble slab, you could use that instead.

Breads are cooked on the *tava*, a heavy, cast-iron, slightly curved plate, or in a *karhai*, a wok-like utensil for deep frying, or they are baked in the clay oven known as the *tandoor*. For a *tava* you can substitute an 8–10-inch cast-iron frying-pan; for a *karhai* you can use any wide, heavy casserole-type pot (cast-iron would be excellent); and for the *tandoor*, one just has to use the oven or a charcoal grill.

While Indian rice can be eaten with a fork, Indian bread *must* be eaten with the hands—or rather, with one hand. A small piece of the bread is broken off, wrapped around a morsel of food, and eaten. Only one hand is used—and just the fingertips at that. The other hand has to be kept clean to pass food or pick up a glass of water.

A word of encouragement about these breads. If they do not turn out perfectly the first time, do not lose heart. There are many Indians who have not mastered them either! So much depends on how well they are rolled out, and perfection in this area comes only with long practice. If you are persistent, you will surely master them.

Here are some of the basic breads.

Chapati

Serves 4

This simple bread requires only whole-wheat flour and water. It needs to be rolled out very evenly on a floured surface. Indians keep a quantity of plain whole-wheat flour on the side and keep dusting the *chapati* with it as they roll. Next, the *chapati* needs to be cooked on a *tava*. Give the *tava* time to heat before you put the first *chapati* on. When both sides of the *chapati* are roasted, it is taken off the *tava* and placed on an open fire. This makes it puff up with hot air. A *chimta* or some flat unserrated tongs are essential for the making of the bread (see page 555). Note: Some whole-wheat flour is very coarse. Many Indians prefer to mix it half and half with all-purpose white flour.

4 oz finely ground whole-wheat flour for dough	about 2 oz finely ground whole-wheat flour to keep on the side for dusting

Place the flour in a bowl. Slowly add up to 4 fl. oz water and mix until all the flour adheres and you can knead it. (You will probably need a little less than the 4 fl. oz water.) Now knead it for 7 to 8 minutes. Roll into a ball. Cover with a damp cloth and leave for ½ to 3 hours. (If you wish to leave it longer, cover it with a plastic wrap and refrigerate. It will easily stay 24 hours.)

Dampen hands and knead the dough again. Put the *tava* or cast-iron frying-pan on a *medium* flame to heat. Knead dough while the *tava* is heating. Divide the dough into 8 balls. Keep balls covered with damp cloth. Flour the rolling surface and keep some dry flour on the side for dusting. Take out one ball. Flatten it. Dip it in the dry flour. Now roll it out evenly into a *chapati* about 5 inches in diameter. You can get it even bigger and thinner if you like. It will stick to the surface as you roll it unless you keep dipping it in the dry flour. Always keep your surface well floured.

The *tava* or frying-pan should be smoking hot by now. Place the uncooked *chapati* on it. Within half a minute or so bubbles will start rising. Now turn the *chapati* over with the *chimta* or tongs. Let the other side cook for half a minute. Both sides should have light brown spots on them. Lift off *chapati* with the tongs and lay it directly over the medium flame of another burner. (You could use the same burner, but you would have to lift off the *tava* or frying-pan every time. As a matter of fact, this *is* what most Indians do!) Keep it there a few seconds. It will puff up immediately. Now turn it over and keep the other side over the flame for a few seconds.

Either serve hot immediately, or butter on one side very lightly and place *chapati* on a large sheet of aluminium foil. Fold over the aluminium foil and shut edges firmly. Do all *chapatis* this way. They will stay warm for 20 to 30 minutes if stacked tightly and kept well covered in foil in a warm place.

To serve: Chapatis are eaten with nearly all Indian main dishes.

Poori

Serves 4–6

The dough here is rather like that of the *chapati*, only a little oil is added. Some people like to add a bit of salt as well to the dough. It is then kneaded and rolled out. Deep fat is heated in a wok, *karhai* (see page 555), or deep frying-pan, and the *pooris* are fried quickly in it. They puff up like the *chapati*. It is important that the fat be smoking hot. *Pooris* can be made ahead of time and wrapped lightly in aluminium foil. They do not stay puffed this way, but they still taste good. They can be reheated (in the foil) in a 300°F., Mark 2 oven for 10 minutes. Instead of using only whole-wheat flour for the dough you can use a combination of whole-wheat flour and all-purpose flour. I tend to use the latter, and it seems to make the *pooris* more pliable.

2 oz finely ground whole-
   wheat flour
2 oz all-purpose white flour
1½ tbs vegetable oil

oil for deep frying, enough
   to have 2-3 inches in
   frying-pan
about 2 oz finely ground
   whole-wheat flour to keep
   on the side for dusting

Place whole-wheat and white flour in a bowl. Pour the oil over it. Slowly add up to 4 fl. oz water and mix until all the flour adheres and you can knead it. (You will probably need a little less than ½ cup water.) Knead it well for 7 to 8 minutes. Form into a ball, cover with a damp cloth, and leave for 1½ to 3 hours. (If you wish to leave it longer, cover with plastic wrap or aluminium foil and refrigerate. It will keep up to 24 hours.)

Heat the oil in the *karhai*, wok, or frying-pan over a medium flame. Give it time to get smoking hot. I wait 10 minutes before I put the first *poori* in.

While the oil is heating, knead the dough again. Divide the dough into 14 balls, keeping those you are not rolling covered with damp cloth. Flatten the balls one at a time and roll them out this way: first dip the flattened ball in the whole-wheat flour that you have on the side. Now roll it evenly, sprinkling the surface and the *poori* with flour when you need to, until it is about 3½ to 4 inches in diameter. Do not allow it to stick to the surface. Whenever it does, dip it in the dry flour.

Test the hot oil by dropping a *poori* in it. It will first sink to the bottom. Then, within a few seconds, it will rise and sizzle. Now you can do one of two things. Either keep pushing the *poori* down gently — with swift but soft pushes, using the back of a slotted spoon — or, with swift strokes, baste the *poori* with the hot oil. In basting, what you actually do is push the hot oil towards and over the *poori*. Or you can do both of these things. But do it fast: Within half a minute, the *poori* should puff up. Turn it over with a slotted spoon, and cook another 30 seconds. Remove with slotted spoon, drain on paper towel, and serve immediately. If the first *poori* comes out hard, you are cooking it too long, or the oil is not hot enough, or both.

If you do not wish to serve the puffed-up *pooris* right away, deflate them as they come out of the *karhai* (watch out for that steam!) by pressing down on them; wrap tightly in a large sheet of aluminium foil. (Do not crush them, though.) As the *pooris* get done, lay them one over the other, and keep wrapping the lot with foil. This will keep them soft. If they are served this way, at room temperature, they are known as *baasi*, or 'stale', *pooris*. If you wish to reheat them, place the foil bundle in a 300°F., Mark 2 preheated oven for 10 minutes.

To serve: Pooris go well with *Kheema*, with Lamb Cooked in Dark Almond Sauce, with Chicken *Moghlai*, and nearly all the vegetable dishes.

Paratha

Serves 4–8

A *paratha* is cooked on the *tava* with butter or *ghee* rather like a pancake. In Delhi and Uttar Pradesh it is often triangular in shape, flaky, and very delicate. It can be made with whole-wheat flour or with an equal combination of whole-wheat and all-purpose white flour.

6 oz finely ground whole-wheat flour	about 4 tbs melted butter or usli ghee (see page 550)
1 tbs vegetable oil	2 oz whole-wheat flour to keep on the side for dusting
½ tsp salt	

Place the 6 oz flour in a bowl. Pour the oil over it. Add the salt. Slowly add about 4 fl. oz water (you may need a bit more), and mix until all the flour adheres and you can knead. Knead the dough well for 8 to 10 minutes. Form into a ball. Cover with a damp cloth and set aside for 30 minutes. (If you wish to leave it longer, cover with plastic wrap and refrigerate. It will keep up to 24 hours.)

Put a *tava* (page 556) or cast-iron frying-pan to heat over a medium flame. Knead dough once again for a minute. Divide dough into 8 balls. Keep balls covered with damp cloth. Take one ball out at a time and flatten it slightly. Dip it in the extra flour and roll it out evenly on a floured surface until it is about 5 inches in diameter. (You may need to sprinkle more flour on it and on the surface as you go along.) Now brush the surface of the *paratha* lightly with butter. Fold in half. Brush the surface with butter again. Fold in half a second time. You now have a triangular shape.

Roll out this triangle, with the aid of the dry flour, so that its sides are about 5 inches long (it does not have to be too even).

Brush the *tava* or frying-pan with melted butter. Place the triangular *paratha* on it. As soon as one side is a golden-brown, turn it over. Add a little more butter to the *tava* or frying-pan and cook the second side until it is also a golden-brown. A few dark spots are perfectly all right. It should not get too dark or too crisp. Adjust flame to avoid this.

As each *paratha* is done, place on a large sheet of aluminium foil and cover tightly. Put all *parathas* in the foil this way. When ready to eat, preheat oven to 300°F., Mark 2 and heat covered *parathas* for 10 minutes.

To serve: Parathas go very well with nearly all vegetable dishes, particularly peas, potatoes, and cauliflower.

Bhatura

Serves 4

The *bhatura* is a bit like a deep-fried version of the *naan*. It is very popular in the Punjab as a 'snack' bread, eaten with spiced chickpeas.

5 oz all-purpose white flour, plus a little extra flour for dusting
¼ tsp baking powder
1 egg, beaten
1–1½ tbs plain yogurt

a little vegetable oil for brushing on dough
vegetable oil for deep frying, enough to have 2½ inches in pot

Sift the 5 oz flour and the baking powder into a bowl. Add the egg and begin to mix. Slowly add the yogurt and gather together the flour. Begin kneading. Add as much yogurt as will give you a soft dough. Knead dough for 10 minutes until it is smooth. Form into a ball, brush with oil, cover with damp cloth, and keep in a warm place for 3 hours.

With moistened hands, knead dough again.

Put oil in *karhai* (see page 555), wok, or other wide utensil for deep frying. Heat over medium flame. Allow oil time to get smoking hot.

Divide dough into 8 balls and cover with damp cloth. Take one ball at a time and flatten it. Flour the rolling surface. Roll out the ball into a 4½-inch round, and drop it in when the oil is smoking. As it begins to sizzle, press down on it gently with the back of a slotted spoon. It will puff up. Turn it over and let other side brown lightly. The whole process should take about a minute. Do all *bhaturas* this way.

To serve: Serve hot with *Chana Masaledar* or any meat or vegetable dish.

Naan

Serves 6

Naan is a leavened flat bread shaped like a teardrop. It is best when cooked in the clay oven called the *tandoor*. While meats, chicken, and fish grill on large skewers inside the *tandoor*, moistened *naans* are stuck to its walls to bake.

1 lb all-purpose white flour	2 tbs vegetable oil, plus a
about 7 fl. oz milk	little more for brushing on
1 egg, beaten	dough later
$\frac{3}{4}$ tsp salt	4 tbs plain yogurt
2 tsp sugar	$\frac{1}{4}$ tsp black onion seeds
1 tsp baking powder	(kalonji), or poppy seeds
$\frac{1}{2}$ packet dry yeast (1$\frac{1}{2}$ tsp)	as substitute

Sift the flour into a bowl. Place the milk in a small pot and warm slightly. Remove from heat. In another bowl combine the egg, salt, sugar, baking powder, yeast, 2 tablespoons oil, yogurt, and 5 tablespoons of the warm milk.

Mix well. Pour mixture over flour and rub it in with the hands.

Add 1 tablespoon of warm milk at a time to the flour, and begin kneading. Add enough so that all the flour adheres and kneading is easy. You should have a soft dough. Knead well for about 10 minutes or until dough is elastic. Form into a ball, brush with oil, cover with damp cloth, and leave in a warm place to rise. If the temperature is above 80°F. or 27°C. it should take only 2 hours. Otherwise it may take about 3 hours.

Preheat grill.

Brush 3 baking trays lightly with oil.

Knead the dough again for a minute or two and divide into 6 balls. Flatten the balls one at a time, keeping the rest covered, and stretch them and pat them with your hands until you have a teardrop shape about 11 inches long and 4 inches wide. Do all balls this way, placing 2 *naans* on each baking tray as you do so.

Cover with moistened cloths and leave for 15 minutes in a warm place.

Remove moistened cloths. Brush the centre portion of each *naan* with water, leaving a ½-inch margin. Sprinkle the centre portion with the onion or poppy seeds.

Place trays, one at a time, under the grill, about 2½–3 inches away from the heat and grill *naans* for about 2½ minutes on each side or until lightly browned.

To serve: Serve *naans* hot with *Tandoori* Chicken, *Seekh Kabab*, Lamb Cooked in Dark Almond Sauce, or Chicken *Moghlai*.

Desserts
with a note on tea

Kulfi
Gajar-ka-halva
Grilled bananas
Fried dates
Shahi tukra
Malpua
Kheer
Gulab jamun

I N Europe and America, most meals end with dessert and coffee. In India most meals end with fruit — leeches, loquats, melons, watermelons, *cheekoos*, and mangoes in the summer, and apples, oranges, bananas, guavas, and pomegranates in the winter. These are often peeled at the table by the eldest woman of the house, and then passed around, always starting with the children. Desserts or 'sweets' are served mainly at very special luncheons and dinners, at snack time and tea time, and at religious festivals (which come extremely frequently!).

'Snack time' seems to have an unusually elevated place in Indian life. I remember when I was working in television shows in Delhi. We would be deep in rehearsal when, almost every hour, there would come a desperate cry from some corner of the studio: *'Quon bhai, chai hojai?'* ('Well now, brother, how about tea?'). Every actor and technician would stop (happily) in his tracks, and the whole group would saunter off to the nearest snack shop to have sweet and savoury snacks — and tea. The very spicy hot *samosas* and the sugary-sweet *gulab jamuns* were eaten simultaneously — a bite of one balancing a bite of the other and each swallowed with a soothing sip of scalding tea.

Tea has not always been drunk in India. Until the end of the last century it was more or less unknown in the subcontinent. With their sweet and sour snacks, Indians generally drank *shurbut* — fruit juice concentrates diluted with cold water — or hot, frothy milk. This milk was, and still is, sold by the snack vendor whose status often hinges upon how much froth he can raise. Since he has no frothing machine at his disposal, he achieves his bubbly result by briskly pouring the hot milk back and forth from one tumbler to another. These tumblers are first held close to each other. Slowly they are moved to a distance of several feet. The fast-flying milk never misses its mark and the stream of milk looks like white elastic being pulled between the tumblers. This sight is responsible for one of Delhi's oldest jokes, about the visitor from the old North-west Frontier who asked if he might have 'two yards of that white thing' along with his other sweets!

Tea, which is easily North India's favourite snack beverage, has now replaced both *shurbut* and milk. It was introduced to India by the British in the early 1900's. By this time the English had already been drinking Chinese teas for over two centuries. They decided to try planting Chinese tea seeds in the hilly regions of Assam. There they discovered, much to their surprise, fully grown tea trees that turned out to be not solitary accidents of nature, but parts of whole forests of tea trees. So the English went in with their Chinese seeds, their Chinese labour, and their pruning shears to tame this 'wild' area. Soon they realized that neither the Chinese seeds nor the Chinese labour was necessary and that the native Indian tea was not only good but also proving very popular with the customers in England.

The next market they looked to was India herself. This turned out to be no problem at all. The Indians took to tea like fish to water. They learned to drink it like the English—strong, with a little milk and sugar. The milk was added to the strong tea to 'fix' the tannin content and rid it of most of its astringency.

The Indian teas come from various regions of both North and South India and are generally of the dark fermented varieties. My own favourite is the Orange Pekoe from Darjeeling, with its smoky, nutty flavour. Indians almost never use teabags. They generally brew their loose tea leaves in a warm teapot. Here is how you can make a good pot of tea: 1. Use freshly boiled water. Do not let it overboil, since water that is kept boiling tends to become de-aerated. 2. Heat the teapot by rinsing it with boiling water. 3. Put into the teapot one teaspoon of tea leaves per cup of water to be used plus one teaspoon more for the pot. (If you like your tea weak add more hot water once the tea has brewed.) 4. Pour the boiling water over the tea leaves, cover and set aside for three minutes. If you are lucky enough to have a tea-cosy, cover your teapot with it. 5. Lift cover, stir, and strain into teacups. 6. Serve plain or with lemon and sugar or with hot milk and sugar or, if you like, with just sugar or just milk.

Many of the packaged teas available in Britain are blends of teas from several regions — often from several countries. Teabags also contain blends — some being slightly better than others. Pure Darjeeling teas, labelled as such, are available in some supermarkets and most delicatessens. If you buy a pound of loose tea, store it in a tightly covered, light-proof container, away from the scent of strong spices and herbs.

Indian sweets tend to be *very* sweet. They tend also to be made of ingredients like vegetables (carrots, pumpkin), nuts (pistachios, almonds, coconut), flours (plain flour, rice flour, chickpea flour), and sweeteners (sugar, jaggery). But the most important ingredient is milk. Milk forms the base of more than half our sweets, and it is often milk in a form entirely unused in the West. Milk is boiled for hours until it forms a semi-solid dough called *khoya*. Most people do not make *khoya* at home. They go out and buy it. It is simpler. Since *khoya* is unavailable here, I have used several substitutes, powdered milk being one of them. For other desserts, milk is boiled down until it is half or a third of its original quantity. Since I do this in a few of the recipes, let me give you a few tips that may help you.

How to boil milk down

1. Use a very heavy-bottomed pot. Cast-iron or aluminium covered with porcelain is particularly good for this.

2. Since the process is slow and tedious (it may take 1 to 1½ hours), bring a chair and a book to your stove.

3. Bring the milk to an 'almost' boil. Watch it. If you let it boil over, you will have a big mess to clean. As soon as it seems that the milk will start to boil and rise, turn heat down to a medium low.

4. Adjust heat so that milk is always bubbling, but will not bubble over.

5. Once the milk has begun its slow boil, settle down with your book. Stir the milk every few minutes.

6. If a creamy crust forms on top, just stir it into the milk. It will taste fine when cold.

Kulfi

Serves 6

This is Indian ice cream at its best. Milk is boiled down to a third of its original quantity. Sugar, cardamom, and nuts are added, and the thickened milk is then poured into special conical containers and frozen. Traditionally, *kulfi* is served with *falooda*, a transparent vermicelli rather like the Japanese noodles in a sukiyaki. Since I do not expect you to have the conical containers, you could use empty tins of frozen fruit juice, or individual custard cups or paper cups or even a single bowl.

2½ pints milk
4 whole cardamom pods
3 tbs sugar

1 tbs slivered unsalted pistachios

In a very heavy-bottomed pot, boil milk down to 16 fl. oz (see note on page 832). This may take up to 1½ hours. After the first hour, lightly crush 2 of the cardamom pods and add them to the milk.

When the milk has boiled down to 16 fl. oz turn off heat. Remove and discard cardamom pods. Add sugar and nuts. Stir well.

Grind the seeds from the other 2 cardamom pods (see page 548) and add them to the milk. Leave milk to cool.

When cool, stir once and pour milk equally into six 3-fl. oz or 4-fl. oz paper cups, or similar containers, or a bowl. Cover with aluminium foil and freeze. Stir the *kulfi* every 20 to 30 minutes to help break up the crystals. It will get harder to stir as it thickens. When it becomes too thick to stir, leave to freeze solid. Keep covered.

To serve: Run a warm knife along the inside of each cup or container to remove the *kulfi*. (You may need to pour warm water on the outside to loosen it.) Serve individual portions on small chilled plates.

Gajar-ka-halva

Serves 8

In this carrot halva, the carrots are completely unrecognizable. Milk and grated carrots are cooked until they become a dryish homogeneous mass. Sugar (and, if you like, lightly fried raisins and nuts) are then added, and the dish is served warm or at room temperature.

1½ pints milk
2 lbs carrots, peeled and grated
2 cardamom pods
10 tbs vegetable oil or usli ghee (see page 550)

3 tbs sugar
1 tbs each lightly fried raisins and almonds (optional)
½ pint clotted or heavy cream (optional)

Put the milk, grated carrots, and cardamom pods in a 10-inch heavy-bottomed pot. Bring to the boil. Lower heat to medium and cook, stirring occasionally, until no liquid is left. This may take about 30 minutes.

Add the oil, turn the heat down slightly, and start frying the carrot-milk mixture, stirring *all the time*. Continue until the carrots turn a reddish-brown. This may take 30 to 40 minutes.

Add sugar and, if you like, raisins and almonds. Cook, stirring, another 2 minutes. Turn off heat. Allow halva to cool. Cover and refrigerate until ready to eat.

To serve: This halva can be warmed or served at room temperature. In India, it is often served with clotted cream — the cream that forms when unhomogenized milk is boiled. You could, if you like, serve it with heavy cream just lightly whipped so it doubles in bulk.

Grilled bananas

Serves 4

1 tbs melted butter
2 very firm large bananas
1 tsp lemon juice
3 tbs orange juice

2 tbs brown sugar
1 tbs blanched slivered
   almonds

Preheat the grill.

Brush a small, flameproof baking dish (a small baking tray will do) with half the butter. Split the bananas in half, lengthwise, and lay them in the dish. Mix the lemon and orange juice and pour it over the bananas. Brush the bananas with the remaining butter, and sprinkle with brown sugar.

Place under grill for about 4 minutes or until bananas are lightly browned. Sprinkle almond slivers over bananas and put them under the grill for another minute or two, or until almonds are browned. Remove from grill.

To serve: Serve the bananas hot. This dish should be prepared just before eating.

Fried dates

Serves 4–6

This simple dessert is popular among the Bohris of Gujarat. If you like dates and chewy, sticky caramely things, you will love this. It takes just a few minutes to make and should be cooked just before serving.

3 tbs vegetable oil or usli ghee (see page 550)	1 tbs slivered unsalted pistachios
8 oz pitted good-quality dates	½ pint clotted or heavy cream

Heat the oil in a 10-inch frying-pan over a medium flame. When hot, put in the dates. Stir them around for 10 to 20 seconds. Remove with slotted spoon and place in serving dish.

Add pistachios to cream and put in serving pitcher.

To serve: Pass around the dates as well as the pitcher with the cream and nuts. The cream should be poured over the hot dates.

Shahi tukra

Serves 4

This popular dessert is made out of white bread rectangles, milk, and saffron.

3 whole cardamom pods, slightly crushed	4 tbs vegetable oil or usli ghee (see page 550)
1½ pints milk	3 slices of stale homemade-type white bread, ¾ inch thick, crusts removed, and each slice cut into 4 rectangles
2 tsp sugar plus 1 tbs sugar	
¼ tsp leaf saffron, roasted and crumbled according to instructions on page 552	

Garnish

vark, if available (see page page 553)	1 tbs slivered unsalted pistachios
1 tbs sliced blanched almonds	

Put the cardamom pods and 8 fl. oz of the milk into a small pot and bring to the boil. Turn off heat. Add 2 teaspoons of sugar and the saffron. Mix. Set aside.

In another pot (heavy-bottomed) bring the remaining milk to the boil. Turn heat down and reduce milk by half to a little more than a ½ pint (see note on page 832). This may take 35 to 45 minutes.

In a 10-inch frying-pan, heat the oil over medium temperature. When hot, put in the rectangles of bread. Fry until both sides turn golden-brown. This should take about a minute on each side. You may need to add a bit more oil. Pour out oil if any is left.

Pour the saffron milk over the bread and let it sit for 5 minutes. Turn the rectangles over once during this period.

Add the remaining 1 tablespoon sugar to the boiled-down milk and pour this over the bread as well. Bring the contents of the frying-pan to the boil. Lower heat and simmer 10 minutes. Turn bread gently once or twice with a long spatula.

Lift bread gently and place on a rimmed platter for serving. Any flat dish with a shallow rim will do.

Allow to cool. Garnish with vark, almonds, and pistachios. Cover and refrigerate until ready to serve.

Serve cold.

Malpua

Serves 6

This is a pancake immersed in a sugar syrup.

6 oz sifted all-purpose white
 flour
4 fl. oz milk
6 fl. oz heavy cream
1¼ lbs sugar

2 cardamom pods, slightly
 crushed
3 tbs vegetable oil (more
 may be needed)

Mix the flour, milk, and cream with a whisk. Cover and refrigerate overnight.

Make the syrup by combining the sugar, 16 fl. oz of water, and the cardamom pods in a pot. Bring to the boil without stirring. Lower heat and simmer 2 to 3 minutes, or until all the sugar dissolves. Put syrup into serving bowl large enough to hold pancakes as well.

Heat the oil in a 10–12-inch frying-pan over a medium flame. Pour in enough batter to make two 4–5-inch pancakes at a time. Cook pancakes slowly on both sides so they get golden-brown and crisp. As pancakes are done, lift them out and put them into the syrup. Finish all the batter this way. Adjust heat so as not to burn pancakes, and add more oil as you require it. There should be about 3 tablespoons of oil in the frying-pan constantly.

Malpua can be served either at room temperature or slightly warm. Bring bowl of pancakes and syrup to table. Each person should serve himself — only the pancakes, not any of the syrup.

Kheer

Serves 4

This is my mother's recipe for *kheer*, a dessert made with milk and rice. *Please* do not call it a 'rice pudding'. This sweet has been served to kings at banquets and to brides at wedding ceremonies — in no way does it resemble the stodgy rice pudding seen around in the Western Hemisphere!

When my mother made the *kheer* she set it in shallow half-baked earthenware bowls called *shakoras*. As a result, it picked up the delicious fragrance of freshly moistened earth. You could serve your *kheer* in individual custard bowls, or, if you prefer, you could put it all in one shallow bowl from which each person would serve himself.

2 pints milk	10 pistachios, unsalted and
1 tbs long-grain rice	slivered, plus a few more
4 whole cardamom pods,	for garnishing
slightly crushed	vark, if available (see page
2 tbs sugar	553)

Combine the milk, rice, and cardamom pods in a heavy-bottomed pot. Bring to the boil. Lower heat and reduce milk until you have 1 pint (see page 832). This may take about $1\frac{1}{4}$ hours. Turn off heat.

Remove cardamom pods and discard. Add sugar and nuts. Mix well. Leave to cool.

Mix again. Pour into serving bowl. Decorate with *vark* (see page 553). Sprinkle a few more slivered pistachios on top of the *vark*. Cover bowl with light plastic wrap. Refrigerate.

Serve cold.

Gulab jamun

Serves 6–8

This is a simple, very sweet dessert which can be served warm or at room temperature. It is made with dried milk. You could call it 'fried milk balls in syrup'.

2 lbs granulated sugar	4 fl. oz vegetable oil or
3 cardamom pods, slightly	melted usli ghee (see page
crushed	550)
6 oz powdered milk	4 fl. oz milk
3 oz all-purpose white flour	vegetable oil for deep frying,
	enough to have 3 inches in
	cooking pot

First make the syrup. In a 3-quart pot, combine 1¾ pints water, the sugar, and the cardamom. Lower heat. Simmer 2 to 3 minutes, or until all the sugar has been dissolved. Do not stir.

Pour half the syrup into a serving bowl (about a 2-quart size). Leave the other half in the pot, with the cardamom pods.

Combine the powdered milk, flour, oil, and milk in a bowl. Make a soft dough. Make small, smooth balls out of the dough, each about 1 inch in diameter. You should be able to make more than 2 dozen *jamuns*.

Heat oil for deep frying in wok, *karhai*, or any heavy-bottomed wide pot. You should have at least 3 inches of oil. Keep on *low* flame. The *jamuns* need to be fried *slowly*.

Put a *jamun* into the oil as a test. If it begins to brown immediately, your heat is too high. Each *jamun* should take 4 to 5 minutes to get a reddish-brown colour on all sides. If the first *jamun* does not turn out right, correct the heat. It is better to take this precaution than have a whole batch burn outside and stay raw inside.

Now put in 6 *jamuns* at a time. Turn them over as they turn reddish-brown on one side. As they get fried, put them into the syrup in the pot. Bring this syrup to the boil. Let each batch simmer in the syrup for 5 minutes. When the *jamuns* are 'syruped', lift them out with a slotted spoon and place them in the fresh syrup in the serving bowl. Keep frying and 'syruping' a batch at a time — as one batch fries, another can 'syrup' — until they are all done. When cool, cover serving bowl with plastic wrap and refrigerate. The syrup in the pot can now be discarded.

To serve: *Gulab jamuns* can be served cold, at room temperature, or slightly warmed. Remember, you serve yourself only the *gulab jamun*, not the syrup in the bowl!

And, to end, would you care for a paan?

The guest has eaten well. Reluctantly, he heaves himself off a low divan and makes his way to the front door. Goodbyes and see-you-soons are buzzing about his ears. Then the hostess descends upon him with yet another large silver tray. It is the final offering—one he just *cannot* refuse. It is the *paan*, or the betel leaf. He picks one up delicately with the tips of his right thumb and forefinger, opens his mouth wide, arches his body forward so it will not catch the staining spill, if any, and then stuffs the large *paan* into his mouth. He goes out into the moonlight licking his lips and chewing contentedly.

The *paan* has rounded off his meal as nothing else could and has left him with a feeling of immense and unique well-being. He is not alone in this. After a good meal, most Indians go hunting for a good *paan*. *Paan* and cigarette stalls dot all neighbourhoods just as sweet and cigarette shops do in Britain. Indians abroad ache for it and dream of the day when they will be back on home soil, where they can buy it around the corner. I recall once, while doing an Urdu radio programme at the United Nations headquarters in New York, a group of us Indians and Pakistanis were interrupted in our rehearsal by a Pakistani gentleman who had (hush) smuggled a solitary *paan* past the X-ray eyes of a New York customs inspector. (The betel leaf, being a green living thing, is not allowed into the United States before thorough examination and, I suspect, quarantine! By that time the living thing is quite dead!) This gentleman came into the studio, waving the *paan* with a look of smug achievement. There was quiet for a second. Then, like wild demons, we all leaped upon him, snatched the *paan*, tore it into equal shreds, and devoured the scraps that fell to our lot. We were very ashamed and embarrassed afterwards as we handed the Pakistani gentleman his share, watched him eat it, straighten his tie, cough, and leave the studio without a word exchanged. There was no excuse except that it was unpremeditated! This is what a *paan* can do to Indians and Pakistanis! While *paans* are now available in parts of England, they are still a rare—and illegal—sight in America.

What exactly *is* a *paan*, and is there a substitute that can be eaten? The *paan* leaf is heart-shaped, 4 to 5 inches in length, and varies in taste from sweet to slightly bitter. The two commonest types are the *Benaresi* leaf (small, tender, sweet, and yellowish-green) and the *desi* leaf (large, crisp, slightly bitter, and dark green). A *paan* costs from a few pence up to £10 or £20, depending on what is wrapped inside it. At its simplest, this could be white lime paste, or *choona*; katechu paste, or *kattha*, a red paste made from the bark of a tree, which stains the mouth red; and chopped betel nuts. Or the *paan* can contain combinations of fennel, cardamom, clove, perfumed nuts and spices, expensive tobaccos, drugs, and aphrodisiacs. An aphrodisiac like crushed pearls naturally pushes up the price a bit! The stuffing is placed on the centre of the leaf, and the leaf is then folded over in the shape of a flat triangle or a cone. Either shape is held in place by a clove, acting as a straight pin.

In private homes, *paans* are kept in *paandaans*—brass or silver boxes with compartments and trays to hold all the spices, nuts, and leaves. (A lot of the 'Indian brass boxes' sold in English shops are really the outside shells of *paandaans*.) While the *paan* leaf is unavailable in most markets in Britain, a great many of the spices are obtainable, and can easily be served after meals to departing guests. Here are some of them. Put them into silver or glass bowls or place them in tiny mounds on a silver tray.

BETEL NUT OR SUPARI This is a round, hard nut, requiring a special cutter (*sarota*) to cut it into sections. You can, however, get it already cut up. To the uninitiated, it seems hard, unyielding, and fairly tasteless. It does soften if sucked for long. It has a unique mild taste, which needs, perhaps, to be acquired.

Much easier on the palate are the scented and powdered *suparis* available in packages at the Indian shops. They are often mixed with other seeds, nuts, and spices. If you ever travel Air India, along with the sweets offered at takeoff and landing they will also offer you tiny packets of scented *supari*.

CARDAMOM OR ELAICHI Indians eat whole pods as well as the separated seeds. There are two eating varieties of pods available in Britain: one slightly greenish and the other off-white. The green one is much better for eating. The seeds are sucked and chewed slowly, allowing the flavour to linger in the mouth. In India the cardamom seeds can also be bought scented and covered with *vark* (see page 553).

FENNEL SEEDS OR SONF These are easy to buy and very refreshing to taste. Their slightly nutty, slightly liquorice-like flavour is very popular with all my English friends. Though you can eat them raw, they taste better if they are dry-roasted first. Dry-roast about a cupful at a time by placing the seeds in a heavy-bottomed frying-pan over a medium flame and stirring them until the seeds get very lightly browned. Cool and store in a lidded jar. In the Punjab, fennel is served with *misri*, grains of old-fashioned sugar candy.

CLOVES OR LONG Indians actually suck cloves. They break off and discard the small, peppercorn-like ball on the top of the clove, which is too sharp (not all cloves have it), and pop the rest into their mouths like sweets. It is very refreshing—and not as harmful to the teeth! You will often see fashionable young Indian misses take out little silver boxes from their little silver purses, remove cloves and cardamom seeds from them, and delicately place these spices on their tongues when mouth fresheners seem suddenly called for!

Glossary

AAM PAPAR sour mango pulp, dried in sheets

ALOO-KI-TIKIYA potato patties

ALPHONSO MANGO an expensive sweet variety found in the Bombay region

AMCHOOR dried, raw mango, powdered or in slices

ARHAR DAL a yellow, split pulse

ATA whole-wheat flour

BAASI stale

BABARCHI a cook

BADAMI ROGHAN JOSH a rich meat dish with almond sauce

BAGHAR different combinations of spices and flavourings dropped in hot oil, *ghee*, or *usli ghee*, used for flavouring certain meats, vegetables, dals, and relishes

BAIGAN-KA-BHARTA smoked, mashed aubergines, plain or with yogurt

BAIR a small fruit, shaped like a plum with the texture of an apple, tasting somewhat like a combination of the two

BARIS dried lumps of pounded pulse

BASMATI an expensive, fine-grained, fragrant rice grown in the Dehradun region

BENARESI from Benares

BESAN chickpea flour

BHAPA DOI sweetened, steamed yogurt (Bengali)

BHARTA *see* baigan-ka-bharta

BHATURA   a deep-fried bread made with white flour, using eggs or baking powder or both

BIRYANI   a festive dish combining rice with spiced meat or chicken

BOHRIS   a Muslim, Gujarati-speaking community

BOONDI-KA-DAHI   a yogurt dish containing tiny dumplings made of chickpea flour

BOTI KABAB   cubes of marinated meat, skewered and grilled

BRAHMIN   an Indian belonging to the highest caste and traditionally vegetarian

CHANA   chickpea

CHANA BHATURA   a spicy chickpea dish served with *bhaturas*

CHANA DAL   a split chickpea pulse

CHANA MASALEDAR   a spicy chickpea dish

CHAPATI   a flat bread made of whole-wheat flour

CHEEKOO   a round, sweet, grainy dark-brown fruit, somewhat like a persimmon

'CHHI, CHHI, CHHI' 'dirty, dirty, dirty'

CHHOLA   chickpea, green, dried or cooked

CHHOWNK   same as *baghar*

CHIMTA   Indian tongs

CHOONA   lime (white, alkaline earth) paste

CHORCHURI   a Bengali dish made with vegetables and fish-heads

DAL   pulse

DALDA   brand name of an Indian vegetable shortening

DELHI-WALLAH   a resident of Delhi

'DEY DAL MAY PANI' 'put water in the dal'

DHANIA (FRESH)   fresh green coriander

DHOKLA   a savoury snack from Gujarat with a spongy cake-like texture

DO PYAZA   dish, generally meat, cooked with lots of fried, sliced onions

DUBBUL ROTI Western-style, leavened loaf bread

DUMBA fan-tailed sheep, generally cooked at festive occasions

ELAICHI cardamom

FALOODA a transparent vermicelli

FALSA a tart, red berry

GAJAR-KA-HALVA a dessert made with grated carrots and milk

GARAM hot

GARAM MASALA a spice mixture containing black pepper, cardamom, cinnamon, cloves, nutmeg, and black cumin

GHEE vegetable shortening

GULAB JAMUN fried milk balls in syrup; a dessert

HALVA certain desserts made with vegetables or flours

ID Bakra-Id, a Muslim religious festival honouring Abraham's offer to sacrifice his son, Ishmael (according to the Koran), celebrated by animal sacrifices and feasting

JAIN member of the Jain religion, which abhors all killing

JAMUN a tart, purple, juicy plum-like fruit

KABAB skewered, grilled meat, cubed or minced. Also minced-meat patties

KABLI CHANA chickpea

KALONJI black onion seeds

KARHAI wide bowl-shaped utensil, used for deep frying

KARHI a soup-like dish, made with chickpea flour and buttermilk

KARI Tamil word meaning sauce; possible origin of the word 'curry'

KARI LEAF   small green leaf used to flavour certain dishes

KATORI   small metal bowl used for serving individual portions of food

KATTHA   red katechu paste, used in preparing betel leaves

KHANSAMA   a chef, generally of the Anglo-Muslim tradition

KHARA MASALA   a combination of whole spices, generally bay leaves, black peppercorns, cardamom pods, cinnamon sticks, cloves, and red peppers

KHARE MASALE KA GOSHT   meat cooked with *khara masala* (see above)

KHATTE ALOO   sour potatoes

KHEEMA   minced meat, raw as well as cooked

KHEER   a cold dessert made with thickened milk and rice

KHITCHERIE   a word meaning 'hodgepodge', it could be used for scrambled eggs or various combinations of rice and *dals*

KHITCHERIE UNDA   scrambled eggs

KHOYA   a substance formed by boiling milk down until all the liquid evaporates, used as a base for many Indian desserts

KOFTA   meatball

KORMA   a rich meat dish

KULFI   an Indian ice cream made with thickened milk and nuts

LOBHIA   black-eyed peas

LONG   cloves

MALPUA   Indian pancakes in syrup; a dessert

MASOOR DAL   a salmon-coloured split pulse

MILAGUTANNIR   Tamil word for 'pepper water' and origin of the name 'mulligatawny' soup

MISRI   old-fashioned sugar candy

MOGHLAI   of Moghul tradition

MOGHULS   Muslim Mongols or Tartars who ruled India in fact or in name from the sixteenth to the nineteenth century and who introduced to it Persian-style foods, jewellery, furnishings, etc.

MOONG DAL   a small yellow split pulse

MULLAH DO PYAZA   a dish made with meat and often an equal quantity of onions

MURGH MUSSALLAM   a whole chicken cooked in a thick sauce

MUTKA   a round pot of red clay used for storing and cooling water as well as foods pickled in water

NAAN   a large, tear-shaped leavened bread, generally baked on the walls of a clay oven, or *tandoor*

NARGISI KOFTA   meatball stuffed with a hard-boiled egg

NIRAMISH VEGETABLES   'vegetarian' vegetables, cooked without onions and garlic (Bengali)

OM   'I am' (Sanskrit)

PAAN   betel leaf; betel leaf stuffed with quicklime paste, katechu paste, betel nuts and other spices, nuts or tobaccos, according to desire

PAANDAAN   a metal box with trays and compartments, designed to hold the green betel leaves as well as the various nuts and spices needed in their preparation

PAKORI   dumpling or fritter

PAPAR   pulse wafer

PAPPADUM   a South Indian word for *papar*

PARAAT   a large, round, wide-rimmed tray used for kneading bread

PARATHA   a flat bread made with whole-wheat flour and cooked on a griddle with a little shortening, *usli ghee*, or butter

PARVAL   a small marrow-like green vegetable, with crisp egg-like seeds

PHIRNI   a cold dessert made with thickened milk and crushed rice

POORI   a puffy, deep-fried bread made of whole-wheat flour

PULLAO   a rice and meat dish

PURAN POLI a sweet Maharashtrian bread

PYAZ onion

PYAZWALA KHARE MASALE KA GOSHT meat with whole spices and onions

PYAZWALE SOOKHE ALOO dry potatoes with onions

QAVVALI poem sung in a particular style by a group of people

'QUON BHAI CHAI HOJAI?' 'Well now, brother, how about tea?'

RAHU a large fresh-water fish

RAITA a dish made with yogurt and a vegetable

RAJMA DAL red kidney beans

ROGHAN JOSH meat cooked in a Muslim style to look dark red and rich

ROTI bread

SA'AB short spoken form of the word 'sahib', or master

SAFED SARVO white soup (Gujarati)

SAMBAR a South Indian *dal* dish

SAMOSA triangular cones of dough, stuffed with meat or vegetables and deep fried

SAROTA betel nut cutter

SEEKH same as *seekh kabab*

SEEKH KABAB minced meat, mixed with spices, stuck around a thick skewer and grilled

SHAHI TUKRA a cold bread dessert

SHAKORA disposable bowls of red clay used for holding individual portions of food

SHAMI KABAB minced-meat patties, generally stuffed with minced onions, green chilies, and mint

SHARAB liquor

SHARABI KABABI one who likes to eat and drink

SHURBUT fruit juice or other flavouring syrups, diluted with ice-cold water and drunk throughout India

SIL BATTA the two parts to the North Indian grinding stone
SINDHI GOSHT meat cooked in the style of Sindh
SINGHARA a fresh-water fish
SONF fennel seed
SOOKHE ALOO dry potatoes
SUPARI betel nut

TANDOOR clay oven used for baking and broiling
TANDOORI cooked in a *tandoor*
TARKA same as *baghar*
TAVA a slightly curved, cast-iron plate used for cooking breads
THAL a metal tray
THALI a metal plate
THANDAI a cold drink made with milk, almonds, and cardamom
TOOVAR DAL same as *arhar dal*

UNDA egg
UNDHYA a vegetable dish from Gujarat cooked in an earthenware pot placed upside down over live coals and damp hay
URAD DAL a yellow split pulse that turns slightly viscous when cooked
USLI GHEE clarified butter

VADEES same as *baris*
VARK gossamer-thin edible silver or gold foil, used for garnishing foods, particularly desserts and festive rice

YAKHNI flavoured meat broth used for cooking rice

ZAAFRAAN saffron

Index